The Geography of War and Peace

The Geography of War and Peace

From Death Camps to Diplomats

EDITED BY
Colin Flint

2005

OXFORD
UNIVERSITY PRESS

Oxford New York
Auckland Bangkok Buenos Aires Cape Town Chennai
Dar es Salaam Delhi Hong Kong Istanbul Karachi Kolkata
Kuala Lumpur Madrid Melbourne Mexico City Mumbai Nairobi
São Paulo Shanghai Taipei Tokyo Toronto

Published by Oxford University Press, Inc.
198 Madison Avenue, New York, New York 10016

www.oup.com

Library of Congress Cataloging-in-Publication Data

The geography of war and peace : from death camps to diplomats /
edited by Colin Flint.
p. cm.
Includes bibliographical references and index.
ISBN 0-19-516208-0; 0-19-516209-9 (pbk.)
1. Political geography. 2. Military geography. 3. War. 4. Peace.
I. Flint, Colin (Colin Robert)
JC319.G445 2004
303.6'6—dc22 2003019427

9 8 7 6 5 4 3 2 1

Printed in the United States of America
on acid-free paper

TO DOUG, JACK, AND
"WILLY McBRIDE"

Acknowledgments

I thank Clifford Mills of Oxford University Press for his faith and enthusiasm for this book, and John Rauschenberg and Lewis Parker for their help in the production process. Thanks also to Peter Taylor and John O'Loughlin for their guidance. The volume can only exist because of the great efforts of the contributors—thank you. And thanks to Courtney, of course.

Contents

Contributors xiii

1. Introduction: Geography of War and Peace
   Colin Flint 3

I. FOUNDATIONS FOR UNDERSTANDING GEOGRAPHIES OF WAR AND PEACE

2. Geographies of War: The Recent Historical Background
   Jeremy Black 19

3. Geography and War, Geographers and Peace
   Virginie Mamadouh 26

4. Violence, Development, and Political Order
   Herman van der Wusten 61

5. The Political Geography of Conflict: Civil Wars in the Hegemonic Shadow
   John O'Loughlin 85

II. GEOGRAPHIES OF WAR

6. Soldiers and Nationalism: The Glory and Transience of a Hard-Won Territorial Identity
   Gertjan Dijkink 113

7. Amazonian Landscapes: Gender, War, and Historical Repetition
Lorraine Dowler 133

8. Religion and the Geographies of War
Roger W. Stump 149

9. Geographies of Genocide and Ethnic Cleansing: The Lessons of Bosnia-Herzegovina
Carl Dahlman 174

10. Dynamic Metageographies of Terrorism: The Spatial Challenges of Religious Terrorism and the "War on Terrorism"
Colin Flint 198

11. The Geography of "Resource Wars"
Philippe Le Billon 217

12. Landscapes of Drugs and War: Intersections of Political Ecology and Global Conflict
Michael K. Steinberg and Kent Mathewson 242

13. Navigating Uncertain Waters: Geographies of Water and Conflict, Shifting Terms and Debates
Leila M. Harris 259

14. Territorial Ideology and Interstate Conflict: Comparative Considerations
Alexander B. Murphy 280

15. Peace, Deception, and Justification for Territorial Claims: The Case of Israel
Ghazi-Walid Falah 297

16. Conflict at the Interface: The Impact of Boundaries and Borders on Contemporary Ethnonational Conflict
David Newman 321

III. GEOGRAPHIES OF PEACE

17. The Geography of Peace Movements
Guntram H. Herb 347

18. The Geography of Diplomacy
Alan K. Henrikson 369

19. Shifting the Iron Curtain of Kantian Peace: NATO Expansion and the Modern Magyars
Ian Oas 395

20. The Geopolitics of Postwar Recovery
Brendan Soennecken 415

Index 437

Contributors

Jeremy Black, MBE, is professor of history at the University of Exeter and one of the world's leading military historians. He is editor of the journal *Archives* and a member of the Councils of the Royal Historical Society and the British Records Association. His recent publications include *European Warfare, 1660–1815*; *The Cambridge Illustrated Atlas of Warfare, 1492–1792*; and *War and the World, 1450–2000*.

Carl Dahlman is assistant professor in the Department of Geography at the University of South Carolina. His recent research has focused primarily on the issues of forced migration and conflict, especially related to Kurdish refugees and northern Iraq. Currently, he is examining the issue of governance, refugee returns, and reconstruction in Bosnia, where he and Dr. Gearóid Ó Tuathail are conducting field research. Other interests include the governance of elections, campaign finance, and the geography of Europe and the Middle East.

Gertjan Dijkink is associate professor of political geography at the University of Amsterdam. During the last two decades his research and publications have covered the relationship between space, power, and representation on various levels: the local police organization (Ph.D. thesis, 1987), national discourses on spatial planning (1990), and national geopolitical visions (*National Identity and Geopolitical Visions*, 1996).

Lorraine Dowler is associate professor of geography at Pennsylvania State University. Her interests focus on the intersection of gender with heightened nationalisms. Her previous research has focused on issues of identity politics in Northern Ireland. She recently went to Cuba to investigate the gendering of the representations of the revolution for political tourism in Cuba. She is also examining the gendering of society's notion of heroism as a result of the September 11, 2001 attacks. She has published articles in *Urban Geography*, *Journal of Geography*, *Geopolitics*, and *Polity and Space*.

Ghazi-Walid Falah is associate professor in the Department of Geography and Planning at the University of Akron. His research interests include social, political, and urban geography, with a special focus on Israel/Palestine. Falah is the author of four books and monographs and more than thirty articles in major journals of the discipline. His publications have appeared in the *Annals of the Association of American Geographers, Transactions of the Institute of British Geographers, Canadian Geographer, Political Geography, Professional Geographer, TESG, Urban Geography*, and *Urban Studies*. Since 1998, he has been editor in chief of an international journal, *Arab World Geographer*. He teaches courses on Middle Eastern geography, global political geography, cultural diversity, and the history of geographic thought.

Colin Flint is associate professor of geography at Pennsylvania State University. His research interests include political geography and world-systems theory. He has published in the fields of electoral geography, hate crimes and hate groups, and geopolitics in journals that include *Political Geography, Geopolitics, Geojournal, Arab World Geographer*, and *American Behavioral Scientist*. He is coauthor (with Peter Taylor) of *Political Geography: World-Economy, Nation-State, and Locality*, fourth edition (2000), and editor of *Spaces of Hate* (2004).

Leila M. Harris is assistant professor of geography and a member of the Institute of Environmental Studies at the University of Wisconsin at Madison. She focuses on sociopolitical and institutional aspects of environmental and developmental change. Her recent research considers gender, ethnicity, and agroecological changes in relation to the state-led GAP (Southeastern Anatolia Project) water project in Turkey. Other topics of interest include theorizations of the state and nation, participatory resource management institutions, and conservation cartographies.

Alan K. Henrikson is professor and director of the Fletcher Roundtable on a New World Order at the Fletcher School of Law and Diplomacy, Tufts University, where he teaches American diplomatic history and also current U.S.-European relations and political geography. He has published writings related to political geography in *International Political Science Review/Revue internationale de science politique, Political Geography, Global Century: Globalization and National Security* (edited by Richard L. Kugler and Ellen L. Frost [2001]), and *Geopolitics*.

Guntram H. Herb is associate professor of geography at Middlebury College, where he teaches courses on the geography of peace and war. He received a master's-level degree from the University of Tübingen, Germany, and a Ph.D. from the University of Wisconsin at Madison. His publications include *Under the Map of Germany: Nationalism and Propaganda, 1918–1945* (1997) and *Nested Identities: Nationalism, Territory, and Scale* (co-edited with David Kaplan, 1999).

Philippe Le Billon is assistant professor at the University of British Columbia. His research focuses on relations between natural resources, conflict, and development. He holds a Ph.D. in human geography and has worked in several conflict-affected countries as a humanitarian and consultant. He has published articles in

African Affairs, Development and Change, Journal of International Development, and *Political Geography.*

Virginie Mamadouh is lecturer in political and cultural geography at the University of Amsterdam, the Netherlands. Her fields of interest include geopolitics, European integration, and globalization processes.

Kent Mathewson is associate professor of geography and anthropology at Louisiana State University, where he teaches courses in cultural geography, the history of geography, and Latin America. His books and edited volumes include *Irrigation Horticulture in Highland Guatemala* (1984); *Culture, Form, and Place: Essays in Cultural and Historical Geography* (1993); *Re-Reading Cultural Geography* (1994); *Concepts in Human Geography* (1996); (with Martin S. Kenzer) *Culture, Land, and Legacy* (2003); and (with Michael K. Steinberg and Joseph J. Hobbs) *Dangerous Harvests* (2004).

Alexander B. Murphy is professor of geography at the University of Oregon, where he also holds the James F. and Shirley K. Rippey Chair in Liberal Arts and Sciences. He specializes in cultural and political geography. He is a vice president of the American Geographical Society and North American editor of *Progress in Human Geography.* In the late 1990s he also chaired the national committee that oversaw the addition of geography to the College Board's Advanced Placement Program. He is the author of more than fifty articles and several books, including *The Regional Dynamics of Language Differentiation in Belgium* (1988), and (with Harm de Blij) *Human Geography: Culture, Society, and Space,* sixth edition (1999).

David Newman is professor of political geography in the Department of Politics and Government at Ben-Gurion University in Israel. He is editor of the journal *Geopolitics.* He has published widely on the territorial dimensions of ethnic conflict, with a particular focus on the Israel-Palestine area.

Ian Oas is a doctoral student in geography at the University of Minnesota; he received his M.S. from Pennsylvania State University. He studied in Hungary for several years during the 1990s. His research interests include nationalism in the Carpathian and trans-Danubian region, U.S. hegemonic decline, the geopolitics of cyberspace, and modernities.

John O'Loughlin is professor of geography and director of the National Science Foundation–funded graduate training program on "Globalization and Democracy" in the Institute of Behavioral Science at the University of Colorado at Boulder. He is the editor of *Political Geography.* His research interests are the geography of international relations, the post–Cold War transitions in the former Soviet Union, and Russian geopolitics.

Brendan Soennecken completed an M.A. in postwar recovery studies through the Post-war Reconstruction and Development Unit of the Politics Department of the University of York in England. Since graduate school he has worked or volunteered with various governmental and nongovernmental organizations in the Balkans, central Asia, Europe, and the Caribbean.

Michael K. Steinberg is adjunct professor of geography at Louisiana State University and geography acquistions editor for LSU Press. His research focuses on issues of contestation between local indigenous communities, national governments, and global agencies concerning the use of natural resources, paths of development, and the environmental outcomes of these conflicts. One current research theme that is related to this book examines indigenous people's participation in drug plant production, the impacts of interdiction policies on these groups, and the political and cultural conflicts that often result.

Roger W. Stump is professor of geography and religious studies at the State University of New York at Albany and chair-elect of the Department of Geography and Planning. He is the author of *Boundaries of Faith: Geographical Perspectives on Religious Fundamentalism* (2000).

Herman van der Wusten was professor of political geography at the University of Amsterdam (1984–2001). He received his Ph.D. in 1977 for work on violent and nonviolent Irish resistance to British domination during the period 1800–1921. During the last twenty years he has written various contributions on geopolitics and violence and on ethnic movements in Europe. He is now working on a book about capital cities and other political centers in Europe.

The Geography of War and Peace

COLIN FLINT

Introduction

Geography of War and Peace

According to many, we live in a time of war that was ushered in by the attacks of September 11, 2001. Paradoxically, in the prior three years, between 3.1 and 4.7 million people had been killed in conflict in the Congo alone. Numerous other wars raged across the globe. Clearly, to say that a time of war has emerged only since 9/11 is, on the one hand, ethnocentric and plain wrong. On the other hand, awareness of war among the general population of the Western world emerged after 9/11; perception rather than reality drives commentators to define the current period as one of conflict and not peace.

It seems almost certain that the current generation of young adults will grow politically mature in a time when the whole world is aware of war. War has been a prevalent occurrence; in the last few decades one can cite Vietnam, the Falklands, Chechnya, Iran and Iraq, Sierra Leone, Nicaragua, and Kashmir, to name only a few. The attacks of 9/11 were, from a global perspective, just one more horrific instance of human carnage. However, geopolitically, targeting the United States on its own homeland has created significant changes. War, the "hot war" on terrorism rather than the Cold War, is dominating global geopolitical imperatives and the national debates of many countries (the United States, the United Kingdom, Iraq, Iran, North and South Korea, and others). As the sole superpower, the United States has set the agenda. The citizens of the West can no longer ignore and avoid war. Despite its associated horrors, this is also an opportunity: we can become knowledgeable about wars beyond our immediate experiences. Geography is a powerful tool to gain and organize such knowledge.

What is war? War takes many forms, from terrorist attacks to interstate conflict. Its form, its scale, its victims, its motives, and its weaponry are varied. But one aspect of war is universal across space and time: war is tyranny.[1] The power of this statement refers to the processes by which people who did not initiate war become cogs in a fighting machine mobilized to defend territory, values, and collective identities from aggression. With no desire to fight, the attacked must adopt the behavior of the attacker to survive. Mobilization takes many forms, including conscription, increased taxation and state authority, and pressure to fulfill defined gender roles. Response to Hitler's aggression meant that my grandfather was called to service in World War II. As a signalman in the Royal Signals, he did not experience the horrors of fighting, unless he declined to say so for the sake of my young, impressionable mind. Yet he was mobilized, and his world outlook and personality were forever altered. The same could be said for my mother. As a child, she had to live through the fear of wondering about her father's predicament, the terror of nightly bombing raids, and the indignities of food rationing. The same torments were suffered by German fathers, mothers, and sons and daughters and by millions across the globe as the world war raged. Today the mobilization of fighters and civilians in response to Charles Taylor's aggressions across West Africa is also a tyranny. Many other examples in different geographic locations could be offered.

The tyranny of war causes experiences, whether in battle or at the home front, that remain important elements of the political mind-set of mobilized generations. Elements of this mind-set are passed on to future generations, so it is no small thing to suggest that across the globe a generation is, yet again, reaching adulthood with war on its mind. It seems that we cannot escape war—even if it is used to define individuals and movements dedicated to peace. There is also a moral imperative to know the horrors of war and disseminate such knowledge. Remaining ignorant of war, and hence being unable to act against it, only benefits the warmongers.

It is, therefore, imperative that we understand war and geography in their many forms. The two are entwined. For example, consider two well-known images of warfare, each with different geographic overtones. The first is the monument to the troops killed in the battle of Iwo Jima in World War II, which shows battle-weary marines who are raising the American flag to claim their control over the island—a territorial victory in a global war. The second image is the picture, widely circulated after the terrorist attacks of September 11, 2001, that depicts Osama bin Laden upon a flying carpet that is being chased, and about to be destroyed, by an American fighter plane; the U.S. combatants are now faceless, and the battle is seemingly detached from territorial claims. The reach of al-Qaeda and the U.S. military is seemingly disconnected from national constraints or goals. Both the warfare and the geography of how and why it is fought are dramatically different in these two images, but consideration of the images suggests that war and geography are closely related, and their dynamism is a product of the relationship.

If there is one single purpose to this book, it is to debunk Nicholas Spykman's belief that "Geography is the most important factor in foreign policy because it is the most permanent."[2] The quote is illuminating because of its inaccuracy. Indeed, geography and foreign policy, particularly issues of war and peace, are connected, but the geography is far from permanent, as is the nature of warfare. The relative permanency of physical geographic features is important for both tactical and strategic military concerns.[3] But this is a limited understanding of geography, one that does not take into consideration the political geographies that shape and are shaped by the many processes of war and peace. In the current academic jargon, war/peace and geography are mutually constituted and socially constructed. In other words, geography and war are the products of human activity; war creates geographies of borders, states, empires, and so on, and in turn these geographic entities are the terrain over which peace is maintained or new wars are justified. Rather than being as permanent and sedate as a mountain range, the geography of war is as fluid and volatile as a lava flow.

Since the 1980s power relations in the world have changed dramatically. The collapse of the Soviet empire, the expansion of NATO at the same time as its relevancy is challenged, U.S.-led military intervention in Afghanistan and Iraq, and violent resistance to America's power have all changed the geopolitical landscape. Attempted genocide in Southeast Europe and central Africa has questioned the notion of progress in human relations. War has become pervasive and part of our taken-for-granted world. For example, the killing of occupying military forces and civilians in "postwar" Iraq, civil wars indistinguishable from turf battles over drugs and other illicit goods, and terrorism and counterterrorism are defined currently as the most pervasive and politically imperative forms of conflict. The nature of war has changed dramatically since the mutually assured destruction philosophies of the Cold War. Moreover, the form of war is as varied as its geographical locations. Carpet bombing and suicide bombers have been interrelated expressions of contemporary conflict during the past decade. It is time for a renewed geographic exploration of the topic.

Geography is an increasingly diverse discipline. The subdiscipline of political geography has blossomed during the past twenty years or so and has created a vibrant, if hard-to-define, body of knowledge. A host of theories and methodologies have been brought to bear upon a wide range of processes deemed political (from patriarchy in the household to global geopolitics). The aim of this book is to take advantage of the diversity of theoretical perspectives in contemporary political geography. To this end, key geographical themes and concepts will be defined to guide the reader to the ways in which geography can provide insight into the causes and consequences of war. The choice of particular theoretical perspectives and methodological tools used to enlighten both the geographic themes and the chapter's particular subject matter has been left to the discretion of the authors.

Before I outline the themes, it should be stated that this book is not another example of critical geopolitics. Critical geopolitics has been an essential, provocative, and informative component of political geography.[4] Its aim and ability to deconstruct the spatial ingredient of political tropes to illustrate the power relations that lie behind the "naturalization" of political spaces have produced some of the most compelling contemporary political geography. In addition, critical geopolitics has spawned a large number of books, book chapters, and journal articles.[5] In this book, analyses of war rely less on deconstruction and more on the explanation of political processes of war and their spatial expression. In other words, this book will provide constructions of theoretically derived geographies that explain war to complement critical geopolitics that deconstruct discourses.

Geographic Themes in the Study of War and Peace

The key geographic themes in this book are territoriality, borders, regionalization, network relationships between places across space, and scale. Territoriality is the social construction of spaces by political processes that act as platforms for the expression of power.[6] Rioters who barricade neighborhoods to prevent police access or the construction of regions within Colombia that are controlled by guerrillas and criminals are both illustrations of how gaining control of territory by conflict is an expression of political power. War, whether interstate or guerrilla, is a political process that has as its purpose the control of territory to enable subsequent projections of power. The recent al-Qaeda terrorist attacks against the United States have as their territorial goal the removal of the American military presence from the Arabian peninsula.

In our interstate system, borders are the geographic features that demarcate the key political institution, the state.[7] Competition over a variety of resources and historically legitimated claims to national homelands has inspired war throughout history. The construction of the sovereign nation-state gave border disputes a political-legal framework in which they were to be resolved peacefully, understood as unfortunate tinkering with the geographic expression of taken-for-granted institutions (Cyprus), or condemned as illegitimate actions of international pariahs (Hitler or Hussein). The changing nature of borders and the continued dynamism of existing ones are examples of the way in which constructing geographies through war is a key component of exercising politics.

Investigating borders should not lead us into a territorial trap of considering sovereign states as the only political territory worthy of investigation.[8] Regions are constructed both within states and across them, NATO, for example. Particular countries may experience zones of peace and zones of conflict. For example, Israel created a zone of war in southern Lebanon to provide peace to its northern border region. On a grander scale, the process of NATO expansion has been justified by the hoped-for zone of European peace that will extend through the Balkans and to the Russian border. Related to this process is the regionalization of zones of intra-European conflict, such as Kosovo or Transylvania. In other words, the attempt to construct regions of peace creates, at the very least, the potential for regions of conflict. In addition, contemporary conflicts, especially those over the control of resources, may transcend political borders, which adds a particular dynamic to both waging war and finding a lasting peace.

On the other hand, current and emerging world political maps are not defined just by territorial political units and biophysical regions.[9] Networks of migrants, arms trading, drug smuggling, terrorists, and security forces define the terrain and practice of war more and more. The world political map is an interaction between territorial political units and legal and illicit networks.[10] Consequently, the reasons for war, the means to wage war, and the way it is fought result from an intersection of networks and territories. Sadly, the residents of New York City, Kabul, and Baghdad have experienced how the geographies of networks and territories have intersected to create and facilitate warfare.

But though war may transcend political spaces by networks, it is actually manifested in particular places. Place is both the outcome and mediator of politics, including warfare.[11] Tensions within places can erupt into armed conflict, and, in turn, war can produce new places. In accordance with the views of Tuan and Taylor,[12] if place is considered as an identity with a range of geographic scales, then we can see how cities such as Sarajevo are constructed by warfare as well as how civil wars stem from competing visions of the national homeland.

The final geographic concept that may be put to use in explaining war is scale.[13] A geohistorical approach to warfare defines the contextual setting for war. The cyclical rise and fall of great powers and the consequent dynamism of geopolitical world orders provide a structural setting in which global wars are initiated and geopolitics is manifested in the form of proxy wars.[14] The local experiences of war create, in aggregate, regions of conflict or peace and historic periods of world war. Furthermore, separatist and civil wars are violent manifestations of the social construction of scale as groups try to create national or subnational entities of governance on a scale that best reflects their identity and ideology. O'Sullivan identifies the interaction of societal and military processes on three scales: the geopolitical global scale, the strategic theater scale, and the tactical local scale.[15] The benefit of such a scalar analysis is that opportunities and constraints for local action are identified, the role of agency in creating broader structures is emphasized, and the interaction of many processes is illuminated.

The authors in this volume were not required to address all of these concepts. Instead, they selected those concepts that were most efficacious in explaining their particular subject. Also, authors were free to choose from the different theoretical frameworks that may be used to address these concepts. Instead, the theme that runs through all the chapters is of the dynamism of war and peace, on the one hand, and political and social geographies, on the other, and the interaction of the two.

War and peace are not easily conceptualized. Contemporary warfare includes the continuing threat of global nuclear holocaust as well as the brutal house-to-house savagery of ethnic cleansing that uses clubs and knives. Peace is understood to be not only the absence of war, but also the possibility of maximizing human potential.[16] For some, peace is diplomatic talks between well-armed and potentially hostile states, while for others, it is the vision of new social relations in harmony with the environment. Again, each author approaches the definition of war and peace in a way that is best suited to his or her topic and argument.

Organization of the Book

It has been more than ten years since the last edited volume on the geography of war and peace.[17] Given the dramatic changes that occurred in the last decade or so in the means and goals of war and global geopolitics,[18] this book aims to update the analysis of the previous books. In a reflection of the growing diversity of political geography and, sadly, the multifaceted nature of contemporary conflict, this volume attempts to expand the content of the political geography of war and peace. No claims are made for a "complete" coverage of the topic, but the book is organized with the following logic. The first section attempts to establish foundations for understanding and utilizing the geographic perspective upon war and peace, including the dynamism of the topic, the tortured history of geography's engagement with conflict, and the overarching patterns of conflict.

The second section concentrates upon geographies of war. The first five chapters are related to issues of identity and warfare. Chapters 11–13 discuss the growing and renewed emphasis upon the relationship between resources and warfare. The final three chapters of the second section discuss geographies of territorial control and their role in legitimizing warfare and either negating or promoting peace.

The book concludes with a section on geographies of peace, with discussion of the role of diplomats and social movements in promoting peaceful relationships, followed by analysis of how military organizations are part of wider political processes that illustrate the power relations behind the construction of peace. Finally, a geographic perspective upon the increasingly important topic of postwar recovery is presented.

Chapter Outlines

Chapter 2, "Geographies of War: The Recent Historical Background" by Jeremy Black, provides a historical overview of the changes in the practice of warfare, with an emphasis upon the modern period and the spatial manifestations of warfare. Much of what we understand as "modern" warfare is much more short term than is frequently appreciated. The modern spatial configuration of global power is just over a century old. Second, a model is required that accepts that there are multiple military capabilities and that different methods may be operating in the same spaces. Furthermore, contemporary spaces of control are increasingly defined by air power and its limitations. A final section looks forward to the spatial characteristics of future warfare.

Chapter 3, "Geography and War, Geographers and Peace" by Virginie Mamadouh, examines the ways in which geographers and other academics and opinion leaders frame war and peace. Geography (i.e., the mapping of the world out there) has traditionally strong connections to rulers and their attempt to control territories and peoples. It has always been connected to the waging of war, a point strongly made by the French geographer Yves Lacoste in 1976. But in the past decades geographers have tended to take a more neutral position to research the occurrence of conflicts empirically or to be involved in the critical deconstruction of discourses that legitimate conflicts.

Chapter 4, "Violence, Development, and Political Order" by Herman van der Wusten, notes that there is an intimate connection between violence and development if one takes them both in a broad sense. Development is the realization of human potential; it needs a material base and consequently translates into levels of prosperity, but also gives rise to more deadly weaponry and accompanying harm. Violence is premature death, or life chances thwarted; it is often caused by the anonymous forces of social inequality and then is referred to as structural violence. Considered in this way, structural violence is the reverse of development, and in this chapter van der Wusten maps their common incidence as a result of poor endowment and core-periphery relations. He focuses upon the relationships between variously organized systems of political order, levels of development, and the use of violence.

Chapter 5, "The Political Geography of Conflict: Civil Wars in the Hegemonic Shadow" by John O'Loughlin, examines the geography of conflict at the beginning of the twenty-first century in light of the renewed emphasis on the switch from interstate war to civil strife, terrorism, and religious-cultural clashes. In the past decade, a new kind of conflict has ensued from the collapse of state regimes in which one side has appealed for international support to reduce the power imbalance and to "maintain human rights." Increasingly, such support is being justified within the pervasive "war on terrorism." The United States has taken upon itself the mantle of international arbiter and decides where and when the force of military dominance should be exerted. The increasingly dominant military power of the United States, and its ability to become involved in conflicts across the globe or, as in the case of the Congo, ignore them are explained by reference to the role of the United States as hegemonic power, or even "hyper-power."

The section on geographies of war begins with a discussion of political identity and warfare. Chapter 6, "Soldiers and Nationalism: The Glory and Transience of a Hard-Won Territorial Identity" by Gertjan Dijkink, notes that by "democratizing" war, nationalism introduced the most dramatic change in warfare in human history. From the moment that masses started to identify themselves with the visions and interests of states, wars became utterly destructive and could even aim at exterminating the "Other." This model also foreboded new rules of the game that shifted the focus from strictly national identification to ideological justification through liberalism, fascism, or Communism. The changing global context has introduced new military dimensions in the shape of foreign interference and strategic misperceptions. Nationalism has helped to overcome some of the most difficult problems in the logistics of war, but it has also given free rein to territorial strategies that diminish a stable solution in the long term.

Chapter 7, "Amazonian Landscapes: Gender, War, and Historical Repetition" by Lorraine Dowler, examines the spatial construction of gender roles in a time of war. During a period of armed conflict there is a predisposition to perceive men as violent and action oriented and women as compassionate and supportive to the male warrior. These gender tropes do not denote the actions of women and men in a time of war, but function instead to re-create and secure women's position as noncombatants and that of men as warriors. Thus women have historically been marginalized in the consciousness of those who have researched the events of war. The construction of a unified national ideology is frequently dependent on powerful gendered identities. Moreover, it creates differential access to real and ideological spaces according to assigned gender roles in which women are relegated to private spaces away from the male-dominated public sphere. It is this power differential that becomes enacted in times of heightened nationalism and war. This chapter exemplifies representations of women in war in two historical-geographic settings, revolutionary Ireland and New York City after 9/11.

Chapter 8, "Religion and the Geographies of War" by Roger W. Stump, addresses the geographical dimensions of religious wars, which are identified here as violent political conflicts whose meanings, motivations, and goals are defined by combatants in explicitly religious terms. Contemporary warfare has often developed between groups that have different religious identities, but only in certain cases has religion played a central role in the conflict. This chapter focuses primarily on such cases and examines how they differ from other types of warfare. The discussion is organized around three themes: place-based processes through which religious warfare develops, the role of territoriality (or the contested use or control of sacred space) in the concerns that motivate religious warfare, and the ways in which religious objectives and ideologies shape the spatial strategies employed in religious warfare.

Chapter 9, "Geographies of Genocide and Ethnic Cleansing: The Lessons of Bosnia-Herzegovina" by Carl Dahlman, begins by briefly outlining the definitions of and proscriptions against genocide under international humanitarian law, the functional presumptions of the international community of states such laws contain, the relationship between ethnic cleansing and genocide, and the explicit and implicit spatial epistemology that is presented by the treaties, namely, the protected territorial identities of populations and the geographic parameters of their destruction or transfer. The second part of the chapter details a case study of the former Yugoslavia, with particular attention to Bosnia-Herzegovina, to more fully explore, through the concepts of genocidal space and genocidal place, the manner in which territory, power, and identity intersect in genocidal campaigns.

Chapter 10, "Dynamic Metageographies of Terrorism: The Spatial Challenges of Religious Terrorism and the 'War on Terrorism'" by Colin Flint, explores the intersecting political geographies of contemporary terrorism, with emphasis upon the United States as terrorist target and main agent of counterterrorism. The overarching context that frames a political geography of terrorism is a metageographic transition from the geopolitics of states versus states to states versus networks. The chapter explores the extent to which contemporary terrorism may be seen as a reaction to the global presence of the United States of America. The growth of religious terrorism is addressed, especially as a reaction to the way of life that is being defined and disseminated by the United States. The implications of the emerging geopolitical situation are examined, in which governments that are used to defining security in terms of interaction with sovereign states have to adapt to the threat posed by terrorist networks.

Chapter 11, "The Geography of 'Resource Wars'" by Philippe Le Billon, is the first of three chapters that focus upon the linkage between warfare and access to resources (oil, timber, gems, and drugs, for example). The chapter describes how so-called resource wars are multifaceted, ranging from fears of civil strife that result from overpopulation and land scarcity to military interventions to secure "strategic" minerals. This chapter specifically examines the changing geography of relations between war and the exploitation of internationally traded commodities. Building upon the idea that war represents not only a breakdown, but also an alternative system in which violence serves key economic functions of appropriation, this chapter presents a framework that articulates the geographical construction and significance of resource dependence, the conflictuality of natural resource exploitation, and relations between violence, territorialization, and resource control.

Chapter 12, "Landscapes of Drugs and War: Intersections of Political Ecology and Global Conflict" by Michael K. Steinberg and Kent Mathewson, begins by outlining the historical connections between warfare and the exploitation of resources that serve as stimulants, including tea, coffee, and spices, as well as those that are more commonly identified as "drugs." Today, and as a continuation of this history, the global drug trade creates problems that not only arise from the use and abuse of substances that circulate through geographic spaces, but also increasingly involve inter- and intrastate conflict and instability. Throughout the twentieth century, governments, especially that of the United States, conducted campaigns that purported to target drug production, the so-called War on Drugs. However, these efforts were complicated and tarnished by other imperatives, especially during the Cold War, that resulted in tacit support of illegal drug production and trafficking. Furthermore, this chapter notes the importance of place specificities by examining who grows drug plants (indigenous groups or ethnic minorities) and why. The answer lies in place-specific combinations of unstable political landscapes, economic necessity, ecological constraints, and cultural tradition.

Chapter 13, "Navigating Uncertain Waters: Geographies of Water and Conflict, Shifting Terms and Debates" by Leila M. Harris, focuses upon an increasingly important natural resource, water. The concept of geographic scale highlights how the focus upon interstate warfare has prevented analysis of the complexity of relationships between the changing geographies of water resources and sociopolitical conflicts. Local scales and watershed dynamics that transcend borders show that conflict over water is manifested in many ways other than war. Moreover, consideration of scale suggests ways in which water conflicts may be resolved, and how concerns over the control of water are integral to other violent conflicts. Water is both the source of conflict and the resource that may provoke peace across and within borders. A case study of the Tigris-Euphrates river system and the ongoing planning and implementation of the extensive state-led Southeastern Anatolia Project (Güneydoğu Anadolu Projesi [GAP]) in Turkey are used to further illustrate these points.

The final three chapters of the second section concentrate upon the linkages between territory and war. Chapter 14, "Territorial Ideology and Interstate Conflict: Comparative Considerations" by Alexander B. Murphy, notes that during the past century, territory has been at the heart of most armed interstate conflicts. The centrality of territory to modern warfare is a product of the norms of the modern state system, which accord primary power and legitimacy to those in control of juridically sovereign territorial states. By extension, understanding the dynamics of conflict requires consideration of the ways in which different states (or state leaders) conceptualize and articulate their territorial domains. State "sense of territory" differs from place to place because it is rooted in different constructions of history, culture, and environment. A comparative analysis of interstate conflict among states with different "national" senses of territory can provide insights into the ways in which territorial ideologies shape the character and evolution of conflict.

Chapter 15, "Peace, Deception, and Justification for Territorial Claims: The Case of Israel" by Ghazi-Walid Falah, observes that part of the strategy of warfare is to "sell" it as morally appropriate under the gaze of global media coverage, diplomatic comment, and public opinion. To be prosecuted, wars must be portrayed as being "just." In other words, territory, an essential ingredient of the nation-state, is claimed and controlled through a variety of political strategies.

Many of these strategies are explicitly or implicitly conflictual, but are portrayed as morally necessary and unavoidable. The Israeli-Palestinian conflict over the land of Palestine provides an excellent case study for examining the political geographic strategies of making a war "just." The strategies by which the territories of Israel and Palestine have been constructed over time constrain the emergent Palestinian Authority in a way that can be used by the Israelis to justify further military action and territorial control.

Chapter 16, "Conflict at the Interface: The Impact of Boundaries and Borders on Contemporary Ethnonational Conflict" by David Newman, discusses the role of borders in ethnonational conflicts. The focus is upon conflicts in which ethnoterritorialism and its associated tensions take place around the boundary, and in which the processes of bordering are key in determining group identities and the respective access to power for majorities and minorities. Conflicts such as those in Cyprus, the Balkans, and Israel-Palestine are drawn upon to illustrate the interaction between conflict and the definition of borderlands. The chapter notes how academic study of borders has moved from the physical presence of the dividing fences and walls to the role of borders in creating identities. However, much of state politics is still driven by issues of precise demarcation that often provoke violent policies. Alternatively, Newman suggests that borderland regimes of interstate interaction are a more sensible route because they promote interaction, of varying degrees, across the border rather than construct barriers to cooperation.

The final section of the book looks at the other side of the coin, politics of peacemaking and war prevention. Chapter 17, "The Geography of Peace Movements" by Guntram H. Herb, reasserts that peace is more than the absence of war. Peace movements strive not only to abolish the overt violence of war, but also to minimize structural violence in human society and its relationship with the environment. The chapter addresses the geography of peace movements in three steps that focus on the key geographic themes of scale, borders, interrelationships between places across space, regionalization, and territoriality. The first section provides a geographic history of modern peace movements that emphasizes the different geographic scales that frame peace activism. The second part of the chapter addresses places, regions, and networks of contemporary peace movements, especially the role of key cities such as Geneva. The chapter's final section examines the territorial practices of peace movements to illustrate how symbolic locations, landscapes, and scale are used in nonviolent strategies to overcome conflicts and the abuse of power.

Chapter 18, "The Geography of Diplomacy" by Alan K. Henrikson, engages the important processes of diplomacy through a geographic lens. He asks whether a logical pattern in "the geography of diplomacy" can be discerned and explicated. The hypothesis here offered is that there is such a logic, and that the siting of diplomatic meetings can be not only explained but, to a degree, even predicted. In total, twelve categories of meeting places are identified and exemplified. For example, cooperative discussions and encounters between adversaries who are engaged in open or latent conflict exhibit different geographical patterns. Some encounters between mutually antagonistic or at least mutually suspicious parties have been carefully arranged at "halfway" places between the capitals of the opposed countries. The chapter concludes that there is a trend toward meetings that facilitate increased cooperation rather than those that attempt to manage conflict.

Chapter 19, "Shifting the Iron Curtain of Kantian Peace: NATO Expansion and the Modern Magyars" by Ian Oas, focuses upon the power politics that are, in their own rhetoric and the perception of some states, designed to create regions of peace. NATO has, since its inception, promoted itself as an institution designed to maintain peace over a particular region. However, since the collapse of the Soviet Union it no longer has an external threat to the maintenance of its territorial control. Instead, it has resorted to a policy of territorial growth with rhetoric that creates a mission of diffusing a European modernity in order to expand a region of peace. The new politics of NATO are exemplified through a case study of Hungary that looks at how Hungarian opinion toward NATO expansion has been forged by two processes: awareness through history that its nation-state of ten million persons is incapable of providing long-term military security, and a 150-year attempt to become accepted as a modern member of Western Europe.

The final chapter, "The Geopolitics of Postwar Recovery" by Brendan Soennecken, breaks new ground by offering a geographic perspective to the emerging field of postwar recovery. A historical review of the academic engagement with postwar recovery illustrates the key themes and questions and, notably, how they have been driven by practitioners rather than intellectual endeavors. Throughout this history geographic concepts have been important, without their explicit incorporation. In particular, territorial sovereignty, international intervention, and the interaction of subnational, national, and global scales are highlighted. To illustrate the practical utility of including geographic concepts in an academic understanding, the author draws upon his own experience in a case study of northern Afghanistan to see how both subnational and transborder regional identities in postwar environments have an impact upon field-level recovery. Soennecken's analysis also illustrates that such geographic engagement with issues of war and peace is cross-cultural, with all the pitfalls that entails.[19]

Conclusion

In the current geopolitical climate, there will be much temptation to continue to utilize geographic knowledge for the purpose of war. My hope is that this book will be a useful addition to the pathway that is being constructed by geographers for peace. The relative brevity of the book's section on geography and peace should not diminish the role of the discipline in understanding peace. Particularly, discussion of the role of geography in conflict resolution would have been beneficial. Perhaps too, analysis of the "quiet successes," everyday settings where humanity nurtures mutual respect and interaction, should become the focus of attention, rather than being obscured by concentration upon warfare. Other important topics omitted from this book include a geographic perspective upon the philosophies of war, the way the usage of geographical information science in modern weaponry changes the geography of war, and the microscale geographies of soldiering. I hope that these sins of omission can be excused.

A volume such as this can offer no conclusion or end. Instead, it presents particular issues that warrant investigation and questioning, as well as perspectives from which to wrestle with humanity's problem of the unequal social and geographic distribution of risk of violent death. It was in the spirit of offering questions rather than answers that I conceived of this book. I hope that it inspires further investigation by the reader.

Notes

1. Clausewitz, *On War*, as discussed in Walzer, *Just and Unjust Wars*, 23–33.
2. Spykman, *Geography of the Peace*, 41.
3. O'Sullivan, *Geography of War in the Post Cold War World*, 149–166.
4. Ó Tuathail, *Critical Geopolitics*.
5. Dodds and Atkinson, *Geopolitical Traditions*; Ó Tuathail and Dalby, *Rethinking Geopolitics*.
6. Sack, *Human Territoriality*.
7. Donnan and Wilson, *Borders*; Newman and Paasi, "Fences and Neighbours in the Postmodern World."
8. Agnew and Corbridge, *Mastering Space*.
9. Ó Tuathail, "Postmodern Geopolitical Condition"; Taylor, "Embedded Statism and the Social Sciences."
10. Murphy, "Emerging Regional Linkages within the European Community."
11. Agnew, *Place and Politics*.
12. Tuan, *Space and Place*; Taylor, "Spaces, Places, and Macy's."
13. Marston, "Social Construction of Scale."
14. Proxy wars are conflicts at or below the regional scale that are supported by superpower states without their actual presence on the battlefield. See Halliday, *Making of the Second Cold War*. For an analysis of global political structures and the timing of war, see Modelski, *Long Cycles of World Politics*.
15. O'Sullivan, *Geography of War in the Post Cold War World*, 3.
16. Galtung, *Peace by Peaceful Means*; Wallensteen, *Understanding Conflict Resolution*.
17. Kliot and Waterman, *Political Geography of Conflict and Peace*; Pepper and Jenkins, *Geography of Peace and War*.
18. O'Sullivan, *Geography of War in the Post Cold War World*; van Creveld, *Transformation of War*.
19. Lederach, *Preparing for Peace*.

References

Agnew, John. *Place and Politics*. Boston: Allen and Unwin, 1987.

Agnew, John, and Stuart Corbridge. *Mastering Space: Hegemony, Territory, and International Political Economy*. London: Routledge, 1995.

Clausewitz, C. von. *On War*. Ed. M. Howard and P. Paret. Princeton, NJ: Princeton University Press, 1976.

Dodds, Klaus, and David Atkinson, eds. *Geopolitical Traditions: A Century of Geopolitical Thought*. London: Routledge, 2000.

Donnan, Hastings, and Thomas M. Wilson. *Borders: Frontiers of Identity, Nation, and State.* Oxford and New York: Berg, 1999.
Galtung, Johan. *Peace by Peaceful Means.* London: Sage, 1996.
Halliday, Fred. *The Making of the Second Cold War.* London: Verso, 1983.
Kliot, Nurit, and Stanley Waterman. *The Political Geography of Conflict and Peace.* London: Belhaven, 1991.
Lederach, John Paul. *Preparing for Peace: Conflict Transformation across Cultures.* Syracuse, NY: Syracuse University Press, 1995.
Marston, Sallie A. "The Social Construction of Scale." *Progress in Human Geography* 24 (2000): 219–242.
Modelski, George. *Long Cycles of World Politics.* Seattle: University of Washington Press, 1987.
Murphy, Alexander B. "Emerging Regional Linkages within the European Community: Challenging the Dominance of the State." *Tijdschrift voor Economische en Sociale Geografie* 84 (1993): 103–118.
Newman, David, and Anssi Paasi. "Fences and Neighbours in the Postmodern World: Boundary Narratives in Political Geography." *Progress in Human Geography* 22 (1998): 186–207.
O'Loughlin, John, and Herman van der Wusten. "Political Geography of War and Peace." In *Political Geography of the Twentieth Century*, ed. Peter J. Taylor, 63–113. London: Belhaven Press, 1993.
O'Sullivan, Patrick M. *The Geography of War in the Post Cold War World.* Lewiston, NY: Edwin Mellen, 2001.
Ó Tuathail, Gearóid. *Critical Geopolitics.* Minneapolis: University of Minnesota Press, 1996.
Ó Tuathail, Gearóid. "The Postmodern Geopolitical Condition." *Annals of the Association of American Geographers* 90 (2000): 166–178.
Ó Tuathail, Gearóid, and Simon Dalby, eds. *Rethinking Geopolitics.* London: Routledge, 2000.
Pepper, David, and Alan Jenkins. *The Geography of Peace and War.* New York: Blackwell, 1985.
Sack, Robert. *Human Territoriality: Its Theory and History.* Cambridge: Cambridge University Press, 1986.
Spykman, Nicholas. *The Geography of the Peace.* New York: Harcourt, Brace, 1944.
Taylor, Peter J. "Spaces, Places, and Macy's: Place-Space Tensions in the Political Geography of Modernities." *Progress in Human Geography* 23 (1999): 7–26.
Taylor, Peter J. "Embedded Statism and the Social Sciences 2: Geographies (and Metageographies) in Globalization." *Environment and Planning* A 32 (2000): 1105–1114.
Tuan, Yi-fu. *Space and Place: The Perspective of Experience.* Minneapolis: University of Minnesota Press, 1977.
Van Creveld, Martin. *The Transformation of War.* New York: Free Press, 1991.
Wallensteen, Peter. *Understanding Conflict Resolution.* London: Sage, 2002.
Walzer, Michael. *Just and Unjust Wars: A Moral Argument with Historical Illustrations.* 3rd ed. New York: Basic Books, 2000.

I

FOUNDATIONS FOR UNDERSTANDING GEOGRAPHIES OF WAR AND PEACE

2

JEREMY BLACK

Geographies of War

The Recent Historical Background

The dominant metanarrative of war is one that is securely located within the Western intellectual tradition. The stress is on the material culture of war, and the explanatory approach focuses on the capabilities of particular weapons and weapons systems and a belief that progress stemmed from their improvement. This approach extends across time. Thus, for example, when the Iron Age replaced the Bronze Age, the emphasis is on how the superior cutting power of iron and the relative ease of making iron weapons led to a change in civilizations.

Mechanization indeed plays a major role in the modern concept of war, and in spatial terms this relates to the collapsing of distance strategically, operationally, and tactically. Thus the entire world is literally under the scrutiny of surveillance satellites, missiles and planes that benefit from midair refueling can deliver warheads continents away, and units can be rapidly transported to and on the battlefield and, once there, can use real-time information to increase their effectiveness. Space no longer appears to be an encumbrance, let alone a friction.

This approach to space essentially dates from major shifts in the nineteenth century, in particular, the ability, thanks to steamships, railroads, and telegraphs, to overcome distance. This was linked to (although far from coterminous with) a more extensive application of European military power, especially in East and central Asia, Oceania, and the interior of Africa. Centers that had not hitherto been brought under European control were captured, both coastal (Algiers in 1830 and Aden in 1839) and internal (Beijing in 1860). This reconfiguration of the spatial dimension of global power was apparently dependent on new technology as applied by Western imperialism. Thus limitations on the projection of power that had been apparent earlier in the period of European expansion in the sixteenth century were overcome. For example, metal-bottomed steamships could penetrate deltas, estuaries, and other inshore waters and sail up great rivers, such as the Irrawaddy, Nile, or Paraná in a way in which the deep-draught wooden warships earlier used by Europeans could not. This transformed the geography of maritime force projection.

The approach to space in which it no longer seems an encumbrance appears to have remained valid since, although the technology and the political parameters have both been transformed. In technology, the most decisive development has been that of air power. This has transformed space by overcoming terrain and ensuring that the straight line on the map becomes the key axis and has also added the vertical dimension. The orthographic projections and aerial perspectives introduced to American journalism by Richard Edes Harrison in the 1930s brought together the United States and distant regions and were part of a worldwide extension of American geopolitical concern and military intervention. The role of air power, dramatized for Americans by the Japanese surprise attack on Pearl Harbor in 1941, led to a new sense of space that reflected both vulnerability and the awareness of new geopolitical relationships. The Mercator projection was unhelpful in the depiction of air routes: great-circle routes and distances were poorly presented in this projection because distances in northern and southern latitudes were exaggerated. Air travel, air power, and assumptions about the need to encompass the aerial perspective all thus encouraged "real-space" mapping of land and sea, because this was the background against which moves in the air could be planned.

The doctrine of air power sought to collapse space by using fighter aircraft to deny opposing powers command of the air over their territory and then employing bombers as a strategic tool in order to hit the fundamentals of their war economy and civilian morale. Air power also altered the parameters of conflict at sea. The vulnerability of capital ships to air attack, even if they were protected by antiaircraft weaponry, was amply demonstrated in World War II, as was that of submarines. As a result, bodies of water within ready reach of aircraft, whether they were based on carriers at sea or on land, were rendered dangerous, if not out of bounds.

These tendencies were given a further twist with the development of missiles. In tactical terms, these accentuated the characteristics of air power by permitting accurate standoff fire from a distance, as they were used by the Argentineans in the Falklands War of 1982. In strategic terms, rockets threatened to give effect to the doctrine of air power that had been advanced in the 1920s and 1930s. The development of intercontinental missiles altered the parameters of vulnerability and ensured that space was even more seen in terms of straight lines between launching site and target. As the major targets were in the United States and the Soviet Union, this led to concern with axes via the North Pole and to the consequent mapping of these short routes.

This process has culminated in interest in "Son of Star Wars" technology, specifically, the combination of satellite surveillance and rocket interceptors designed to destroy incoming missiles in tiny fragments of time. Satellite technology exemplifies the intersection between technological and political power that focuses on information, and also the ability to increase the geographical scope of vision and reach by controlling "inner space." The digitization of the Earth's surface that has resulted from satellite mapping has played a major role in enabling weapons to operate by remote control, following, for example, predetermined flight-height trajectories.

This technologically driven approach to war, however, has serious flaws. In particular, it pays insufficient attention to the diversity of military force structures, methods, goals, and cultures that exist and have existed. The conventional Western approach is an idealistic one that assumes a clear paradigm of excellence, as well as an obvious means by which capability is to be ranked: in terms of the quality and quantity of resources applied in accordance with an effective doctrine and organization. In short, the world is seen as an isotropic surface: the space employed is one that is unvarying, and from that perspective also, space has ceased to exist.

In practice, there is a variety in structures, methods, organizations, goals, and cultures that raises serious questions about the understanding of the spatial dimensions of conflict. The order in which this issue is considered is a tricky one because there is a danger that Western analytical concepts will prevail. At the same time, it is necessary to give due weight to the variety of the "non-West" or "Rest." For example, to suggest that the Western military approach places particular weight on battle, with a corresponding spatial awareness, while the non-West does not, may well be valid with regard to the guerrilla and irregular campaigns of the 1950s–1970s, especially in the wars of decolonization, but is less valid as a general conclusion.

Nevertheless, such a contrast between battle and nonbattle as goals does capture the role of antitactics and antistrategy in warfare. Instead of imagining that two sides in conflict approximate to the same methods and therefore can be understood in the same spatiality, it is more pertinent to note the degree to which the advantages of one power are countered not by emulation, so that the key spatial model is diffusion, but by the choices of weaponry, tactics, operational methods, strategy, and doctrine that nullify the effects of the former—in short, a model that sees contrasts and thus boundaries.[1] This was shown to decisive cinematic effect in the Sergio Leone film *A Fistful of Dollars* (1964), in which the chief villain tells Clint Eastwood that the man with the Winchester (rifle) always beats the man with the revolver, only to be killed in the climactic duel by Eastwood, who nullifies the impact of the Winchester's firepower by outthinking his opponent.

To focus on battle for a moment, there is another problem that stems from the assumption that the "face of battle," the essentials of war, are in some fashion timeless because they involve men's willingness to undergo the trial of combat. In practice, the understanding of loss and suffering, at both the level of ordinary soldiers and that of societies as a whole, is far more culturally conditioned than any emphasis on the sameness of battle might suggest, and the resulting cultural contrasts can be depicted in diagrammatic form to produce a map of bellicosity.

At the bluntest of levels, the willingness to suffer losses varies, and this helps to determine both military success and differences in combat across the world in any one period. To contrast the willingness of the Western powers to suffer heavy losses in the world wars, especially World War I, with their reluctance to do so subsequently, and also the different attitudes toward casualties of the Americans and the North Vietnamese in the Vietnam War, is to be aware of a situation that has a wider historical resonance. It is far from clear that variations and changes in these "cultural" factors and related norms should play a smaller role in the history of war than weaponry.[2] As a linked factor, morale remains the single most important factor in war. Furthermore, war, when it is seen as an attempt to impose will, involves more than victory in battle.

Organizational issues—how troops are organized on the battlefield, the nature of force structures, and the organization of societies for conflict—also vary greatly. Instead of assuming that these are driven by weaponry, specifically, how best to use weapons, and perhaps also how to move and supply them, it is necessary to appreciate the autonomous character of organizational factors and their close linkage with social patterns and developments. A parallel case can be made with the causes of war, which can also be seen as an independent variable and one that does not conform to a chronology determined by technological developments.

Looked at differently, armies and navies are organizations with objectives, and in assessing their capability and effectiveness, it is necessary to consider how these objectives change, and how far such changes create pressures for adaptation. This adaptation can be seen both in terms of changes in organizational character and with regard to responsiveness to opportunities, for example, those offered by advances in military (and related) technologies. In short, a demand-led account has to be set alongside the more familiar supply-side assessment that presents improvements in weaponry or increases in numbers without adequately considering the wider context.

"Tasking," the tasks that the military is set by the government, is very important in terms of force structures and is greatly affected by policies. There is a clear geographical dimension. For example, the extent to which strategic cultures, and resulting geopolitical concerns and commitments, are framed by political moments and controversies draws attention to the fluid character of tasking. Strategic cultures require interpretation in particular conjunctures, and this opens up the "space" of historical memory and the way in which it can be contested. For example, Jeffrey Record shows how historical lessons, particularly those of Munich and Vietnam, were misinterpreted and suggests that "the tendency to regard violent nationalism in the Third World as the product of a centrally directed international Communist conspiracy was a strategic error of the first magnitude."[3] In turn, Andrew Bacevich is scathing about the failure of George Bush senior and his advisors to respond adequately "when confronting events without obvious parallel during the 1940s, 1950s, and 1960s."[4]

In the case of the United States today, tasking in part stems from the relationship between the global imperium the United States seeks to direct and the condition of its civil society. Questions about imperial overreach are also important. The long term is more than a series of short terms, and understandable as it is for conservatives (and others) to frame questions and answers in terms of immediate issues—the September 11th–ization of American policy—or at least to focus on post–Cold War paradigms, it is necessary to consider issues in international relations in the longer term. In part, this involves the contested spaces of political traditions, the geographies of their discourses and commitments.

For example, in the United States, traditional conservative values, such as prudence, have been unduly neglected as internationalism, which involves a very different geography, has become the theme of much of the Right. This also has implications not only for conservative positions on domestic politics, particularly low taxation and restricted public debt, but also for the notion of national sovereignty that has played a central role in conservative thought on international relations. Internationalism challenges this notion at a number of levels. For the imperial power, the United States, it poses the difficulty of responding to the expectations of allies and, more seriously, those whose alliance is sought, as well as the issue of how best to answer calls for decision making, judgment, and arbitration through international bodies that the United States both distrusts and finds it necessary to use. For other powers, there is the problem of how best to protect and further traditional national goals while responding to the demands of the imperial power. The ambivalent American response to conservative Arab regimes is indicative of a more general problem, for it is not only in autocratic regimes that conservatism is challenged by American policies and pretensions.

A related modern debate over interests revolves around globalization. The processes that are summarized by this term can be seen as a cause of both instability and stabilization, while, conversely, the opponents of globalization can be seen as defenders of national interests or as a threat not only to themselves but also to global stability. These debates structure political space in a way that has implications for the potential geography of military commitment.

Fundamental issues of social organization within states are also at stake in tasking, for example, the degree to which internal policing is central to military purpose. This tends to be underrated in conventional military history, and yet it is not only important but also raises important questions about how best to consider the geographies of war.

More specifically, should a different geography be proposed for civil wars, the worst-case scenario in internal policing? This geography would relate to the degree to which they are characterized by clear-cut spatial divides and resulting front lines, and, in contrast, the extent to which the situation is more amorphous. Whatever the case on this spectrum is, there is also the need to consider the consequences of the usual mission in civil wars: the creation of a political system that requires the full defeat of one side or the other. This can also be seen as entailing a particular geography.

As far as tasking is concerned, there has recently been a greater willingness to consider the implications of Nazi ideology for the purposes and conduct of the German military in World War II. There is also need for a much more systematic consideration of how ideological assumptions led to counterinsurrectionary and policing policies that affected other militaries. This was (and is) a dynamic process within countries and also at the level of empires.

In the case of the latter, the willingness to accommodate, and indeed to acculturate to, the more powerful, especially conquerors, has been far from constant across history. In general, the availability of syncretic options, for example, the assimilation of local religious cults by the conqueror's religion, and the co-option of local elites have been the most important means of success.[5] All of these points have important implications for senses of spatiality.

The deliberate search for difference in fighting methods in insurrectionary campaigns ensures that there are two rival spatial ranges and awarenesses. It is difficult to show them together without giving undue weight to one. In irregular warfare, the notion of control over territory is challenged by forces that cannot be readily described in terms of conventional military units. They seek to operate from within the civilian population and do so not only for cover and sustenance, but also in order to deny their opponents any unchallenged control over populated areas. Guerrillas do not generally seek to gain control over regions, because that would provide their opponents with targets for their superior firepower; and indeed when they make such an effort, as in Slovakia and on the Vercors plateau in 1944, they become vulnerable. Although the Taliban was not a guerrilla force, it became vulnerable to American air power when this concentrated its forces.

More generally, there is a system of shared presence when regulars confront irregulars. This is, classically, one in which military or police patrols move unhindered or suffer occasional sniping and ambushes and have to consider mines, but otherwise have no power: they control little beyond the ground they stand on. To conceptualize this is problematic, while to map such a situation is extremely difficult. It can be mapped temporally, with the forces of authority shown as in control during the day, their opponents at nighttime, or spatially. The latter poses problems. Generally, the forces of authority operate along, and seek to control, communication routes, which are used for patrol and supply, while their presence in other areas is less common.

Airpower added a particular dimension to this issue. Aerial supply and operational capabilities were enhanced with the improved specifications of aircraft and the development of helicopters. If these affected spatial awareness of conflict, they were, in turn, challenged by antiaircraft weaponry, especially heat-seeking surface-to-air missiles. The safety of low-level operations was therefore limited, and the vertical space of the aerial battlefield was greatly affected. Since the 1990s, irregular forces in the southern Sudan have used such missiles to challenge the resupply of garrisons by government planes, while the British use of helicopters for the supply of garrisons in Northern Ireland took place against a background of concern that the Irish Republican Army (IRA) would obtain antiaircraft weapons.

These problems become even more difficult to manage and conceptualize when the terrain in question is not (really or, at least, apparently) lightly populated, but, instead, is part of the densely inhabited complexity of modern urban society. The difficulties that face the Israelis in the Gaza Strip and the West Bank of the Jordan are a good instance of this. Here there are "mechanical" problems, such as those outlined earlier, and also conceptual ones. The terminology used toward opponents delegitimates them: instead of "freedom fighters" and "war," we have "terrorists" and "terrorism," but this can make it harder to conceive of how best to confront the challenge, either militarily or politically or both, and, in the case of Israel, may well have made it more difficult to probe the possibilities for an acceptable exit strategy.

It is scarcely surprising that at the beginning of 2003 the mapping of war focused on probable conflict with Iraq—a defined target with regular armed forces—rather than on the more intangible struggle with terrorism. In Western conceptual terms, the latter poses intellectual problems that challenge Western conventions of war making, and after the Iraq issue appears to have been resolved, the same approach will be repeated in other contexts. The need to identify and locate the enemy is important to the conceptualization of struggle.

An examination of the last two centuries, reveals a considerable diversity in Western conventions of war making, including an engagement with a range of non-Western forces from imperial China to acephalous societies in parts of Africa;[6] but the issue of how best to confront terrorism outside and, even more, within the West poses particular problems. The difficulty of conceiving of these spatially is both symptomatic of this wider crisis and an important aspect of it.

Notes

1. "Introduction."
2. See Gertjan Dijkink, this volume.
3. Record, *Making War, Thinking History*, 162.
4. Bacevich, *American Empire*, 77.
5. See Brendan Soennecken, this volume.
6. Black, *Western Warfare, 1775–1882*; Black, *Warfare in the Western World, 1882–1975*.

References

Bacevich, Andrew. *American Empire: The Realities and Consequences of U.S. Diplomacy*. Cambridge, MA: Harvard University Press, 2002.

Black, Jeremy. *Western Warfare, 1775–1882*. Bloomington, IN: Indiana University Press, 2001.

Black, Jeremy. *Warfare in the Western World, 1882–1975*. Bloomington, IN: Indiana University Press, 2002.

Pile, Steve. "Introduction: Opposition, Political Identities, and Spaces of Resistance." In *Geographies of Resistance*, ed. Steve Pile and Michael Keith, 1–32. New York: Routledge, 1997.

Record, Jeffrey. *Making War, Thinking History: Munich, Vietnam, and Presidential Uses of Force from Korea to Kosovo*. Annapolis, MD: Naval Institute Press, 2002.

3

VIRGINIE MAMADOUH

Geography and War, Geographers and Peace

La géographie, ça sert d'abord à faire la guerre—geography serves, first and foremost, to wage war. Yves Lacoste made this bold statement the title of a pamphlet against French academic geography in the mid-1970s.[1] He not only exposed the historical importance of geographical knowledge in the waging of war and, more generally speaking, the controlling of people and territories, he also attacked academic and school geography for concealing its political and strategic importance. Geography (i.e., the mapping of the world out there) indeed has strong connections to rulers and their attempt to control territories and peoples. On the other hand, geographers have in the past two decades been keen to promote geography as peace studies.[2]

This chapter examines the ways in which geographers have dealt with war and peace since the establishment of modern Western academic geography. It addresses both the way in which geographers have conceptualized and studied war and peace processes and the way in which geography has been applied and geographers have been implicated in these very processes. The result is an evaluation of whether geography has been converted from a discipline for war into a discipline for peace, to paraphrase O'Loughlin and Heske.[3] This is done by considering three dimensions for which antagonist positions (war minded versus peace minded) are anticipated: the perception of war (a natural event versus an undesirable collective behavior), the focus of geographical studies that deal with war and peace (functions of war versus causes and consequences of war), and the advocated application of geographical knowledge (to win a war versus to prevent a war and to foster peace).

War and peace do not seem to belong to the vocabulary of geography. The terms have no entries in the *Dictionary of Human Geography*[4] or in the *Dictionary of Geopolitics*.[5] This is mainly because war and peace are rather vague concepts. In this chapter, a limited conception of war has been chosen: political violence between states, that is, armed conflict. Therefore, the review neglects urban riots, social struggles, and related conflicts. Metaphorical uses of the term, such as commercial wars[6] or the academic war that resulted in the ending of geography at Harvard University,[7] were disregarded. Peace is even more difficult to characterize. For a limited definition of peace as nonwar, the absence of military or political violence suffices. This is therefore called negative peace; it does not account for structural violence, a term coined by Johan Galtung in his writings on imperialism and peace research to disclose the damages caused by structural inequalities between rich and poor countries.[8] A positive peace approach would include these structural issues as well as discussions of welfare and justice. An additional limitation of this chapter is that it does not deal with all geographies of societies that are enjoying (negative) peace, but only with geographies of peacemaking, peacekeeping, and war avoidance.

This chapter is based on histories of the discipline[9] and more specifically political geography and geopolitics[10] as well as on a literature study.[11] The period under review is divided into two parts, with August 6, 1945 (the first dropping of a nuclear bomb by the United States on Hiroshima, Japan) as a symbolic demarcation. Prior to 1945, war actions were still very much local or state-versus-state concerns. After 1945, the deterrence of a total nuclear war dominated international relations. For each period, the review begins with a preliminary assessment of the international relations context and the key developments regarding war and peace, followed by a short assessment of the position of academic geography. The main section presents geographic perspectives on war and peace; the many references should be seen as invitations to further readings. The last section deals with the involvement of geographers in war waging and peacemaking. The two periods are compared in the concluding section.

Geography and Geographers in the First Half of the Twentieth Century

Key Developments in War and Peace

The close of the nineteenth century was a period of geopolitical anxiety and great competition between European powers.[12] The Franco-Prussian War of 1870–1871 and the unification of Germany and Italy drastically changed the European political map. Competition between European powers intensified, especially for colonies in the rest of the world and for economic development. Wars that marked that period were colonial wars, national wars, interstate wars, and the Great War (1914–1918), a world war with the involvement of a large number of countries on different continents. Nationalism became a predominant ideology in this period of social struggle and democratization, despite a strong internationalist socialist movement. The new involvement of the United States in European affairs and the emergence of the Soviet Union changed the world political map. Peace arrangements were drastically altered by the establishment of the League of Nations as an international body for peace and security, even if major flaws, such as the withdrawal of the United States and the exclusion of defeated states, easily explain its failure to prevent rearmament and war for the next generation. World War II brought even more casualties than World War I, and the civilian population became a key target of warfare activities, with the systematic bombings of cities and the deportation and assassination of complete groups of population.

Key Developments in Academic Geography

Although modern geographic societies were established earlier,[13] modern academic geography was only institutionalized in the last decades of the nineteenth century. The first chair in geography in Prussia was created in Berlin in 1820 (Carl Ritter), but the second one only after the German unification in 1871 (Oscar Peschel). In France, the institutionalization of geography was directly related to the defeat in the Franco-Prussian War and the loss of Alsace and part of Lorraine to Germany (a territory that became known as Alsace-Lorraine): the displaced chair of history of Strasbourg became a chair of history and geography (Paul Vidal de la Blache) in Nancy in 1872, in the part of Lorraine that remained French.[14] In 1877 two chairs in geography were created, one in Bordeaux and one in Lyon; in the same year the Netherlands got its first chair in Amsterdam (C. M. Kan). Finally in the United Kingdom, it was only in 1887 that a chair was established in Oxford (Sir Halford Mackinder). In the United States, the Swiss Arnold H. Guyot was professor of physical geography and geology at Princeton University from 1854 to 1884 (he was earlier professor of history and physical geography at the short-lived Neuchâtel Academy from 1839 to 1848). William Morris Davis taught geography at Harvard from 1878 onward.

Also, geography became institutionalized as a school subject. This was already the case in Germany in the mid-nineteenth century and in Switzerland, thanks to the popularity of the modern pedagogical principles of the Swiss Johann Heinrich Pestalozzi. France emulated early, after the 1870–1871 Franco-Prussian War. Finally, another dimension of the institutionalization of modern geography was the establishment of professional organizations[15] and the foundation of new professional journals.[16]

Geographers about War and Peace

At the end of the nineteenth century, geography was a unitary discipline that tried to grasp the relations between human and physical factors. Geographers were dealing with questions regarding the nature of geography as a nomothetic science that looked for natural laws (or theories, we would say now) or geography as a synthesis discipline based on monographs that were able to render the idiosyncratic characteristics of unique regions. Either way, the connections between physical and social factors were the main interest of geographers, and they saw their discipline as the bridge between (natural) sciences and humanities. In that debate, how much attention to devote to political factors was a disputed matter. The first issue was whether it was appropriate to sketch grand theories of state formation and relations between states. The second discussion was about the degree to which physical aspects such as climate or terrain determine human activities (determinism versus possibilism). Alternative explanations of the differences in wealth and civilization between the peoples of the world were race (the other biological hypothesis) or social factors (nation, civilization). These debates also informed the writings of geographers who were concerned with war and peace and political matters in general.

The German geographer Friedrich Ratzel is generally seen as the founder of political geography because of his *Politische Geographie*, which was published in 1897.[17] He gave the second edition, published in 1903, the title *Political Geography, or, The Geography of the State, Traffic, and War.*[18] In Anglo-American geography, Ratzel has been perceived and consistently portrayed as a determinist thinker, but this owes more to the interpretation of his work *Anthropo-geographie*[19] by Ellen Churchill Semple.[20] What matters for our purpose is that Ratzel saw war as a category as neutral as traffic. Indeed, in his framework based on the spatial characteristics of the state (*Lage*, position; *Raum*, space; and *Raumsinn*, the sense of space of the group that dominates the state), war is a normal phenomenon that is linked to the expansion of dynamic states and the competition between states. He sees war as a school of space:

> The war represents *from the geographical point of view*, a powerful movement, jerky and violent, during which large human masses from one country enter another country; *from the political point of view* it is the most brutal means to relaunch a compromised growth and to clarify ruffled relations between nations. Boundaries, valid in peacetime, and all the limitations to traffic vanish for the belligerents from the moment war is declared, the two territories merge into one and form the war theater in the largest sense of the term. *From the social point of view*, war brings to a paroxysm the virile features of the social instinct and the will to dominate, while peace favors by contrast family life, with its closed and tranquil relational sphere where the man is enchained to his wife and his offspring, and in which prevail the feminine conservative principle and sexual life.[21]

The Swedish political scientist Rudolf Kjellén shared Ratzel's geographic framework and analyzed the spatial and territorial character of the state as opposed to legalistic approaches. Kjellén was influential with his *States as Living Organisms*, and his neologism *geopolitik* shared similar views: "War is the experimental field of geopolitics, as of all politics."[22]

For another founder of geopolitics,[23] Sir Halford Mackinder, a British geographer, war was also a natural event. In 1904, he disclosed the importance of the repartition of land and sea for power relations in his famous lecture "The Geographical Pivot of History."[24] These power relations naturally involved war, and this is addressed at the end of the lecture when he states:

> I have spoken as a geographer. The actual balance of political power at any given time is, of course, the product, on the one hand, of geographical conditions, both economic and strategic, and, on the other hand, of the relative number, virility, equipment, and organization of the competing peoples.

The French geographer Paul Vidal de la Blache stands as the promoter of regional geography, as opposed to the thematic approaches adopted by political geographers. His most famous work, *Tableau of the Geography of France*,[25] was published in 1903 as the first volume of a history of France from the origins to the Revolution. It was meant to set the stage on which the historical events would take place. Vidal saw France as a person and underlined the *personalité* of its regions: he aimed at dealing with permanent features in the ways of life of people in different places. He was therefore very short on cities—even Paris was treated in a few pages—industrialization, state institutions, and other modern changes. Vidal discussed these changes in the final chapter and deplored them. Wars were left to the historians. He portrayed the regions of Alsace and Lorraine, which had been ruled by Germany since 1871, in a similar manner in *East France*, published in 1917.[26]

After the Great War, geographers paid more attention to international relations and the consequences of the peace.[27] Two French geographers, Jean Brunhes and Camille Vallaux, published *The Geography of History: Geography of Peace and War on Land and on Sea* in 1921. The geography of history was for them a synonym for political geography.[28] The first part, titled "The Relations between Geography and History," dealt systematically with key aspects and fundamental problems of political geography (the state and the territory; the state, the road, and the border; the state and the capital city) and underlined "new solutions": regionalism, federalism, and state federation. The second part of the book, "The Geography of Contemporary Struggles: Races, Nationalities, Nations, States, War, and Peace," presented the lessons of the war and the conditions of the peace and dealt extensively with the League of Nations. All in all, although the authors underlined the importance of collaboration between states, they saw these federal solutions only as improvement, not as solution:

> Stability and relative permanence on the map, the spacing out of the warrior convulsions, this is the future that the organization of federations has in store for political societies. What we see growing is not the dawn of universal and eternal peace, nor the triumph of the moral aspirations of justice and humanity over political realism. (p. 428; my translation)

In his more influential *The New World: Problems in Political Geography*, published in 1922 (and later translated into French by Brunhes), Isaiah Bowman voiced similar views.[29] The "New World" was no more the Western Hemisphere, but the world after the Great War. The introductory chapter discussed the problems of the postwar world, the responsibilities of the great powers, and the prospects for peace and war. Each of the following thirty-three chapters dealt with a specific region, country, or people, most of them in Europe and the Middle East, all treated as potential zones of frictions. There were no political-geographic problems in North America, indeed, the only part of the world not addressed (at least in the first edition).[30] Like Brunhes and Vallaux, Bowman saw "the experimentation in the field of cooperative plans" as very important but remained pessimistic:

> Taking it by and large, this is a *competitive* world, and to the costs of ordinary competition must be added the cost of the supreme competition of war. National and racial ambitions, hatred, and rivalries will continue to the end of time, though they may be reduced in scope and intensity.[31]

Almost twenty years later, Derwent Whittlesey offered a mix of systematic and regional approaches in *The Earth and the State: A Study of Political Geography.*[32] He voiced similar views about international cooperation as a partial solution to avoid war, but was even more pessimistic about the prospects of international arrangements to succeed in that task.

In the interwar period, German geographers took a very different approach. Inspired by Kjellén, Ratzel, and Mackinder, but mostly by resentment about the Diktat at Versailles, they developed the school of *Geopolitik*, with theories to justify German claims to new borders and new colonies. In their many publications and books,[33] but foremost in the widely circulated journal *Zeitschrift für Geopolitik* (1924–1944), they clearly promoted war as a way for Germany to reclaim lost territories in Europe and colonies and to expand further. They accepted war "in the best tradition of Von Clausewitz, as continuation of diplomacy by different means."[34]

Most opposed to the German *Geopolitik* were the French geographers. Vidal de la Blache[35] and Emmanuel de Martonne[36] were against the very idea of a political geography. Albert Demangeon wrote about the decline of Europe (1920), about the British Empire (1925), and, with Lucien Febvre, a historian, about the Rhine as French river and what they called the Rhineland civilization, which had been forcibly incorporated into Prussian Germany (1935).[37] Yves-Marie Goblet wrote about the sunset of treaties.[38] More explicitly political geographic was the work of Jacques Ancel, who reclaimed *Geopolitics* for the title of a small book published in 1936.[39] Ancel deals extensively with boundaries, but attacks the importance given to the soil in German political geography (but also by French geographers such as Brunhes and Vallaux);[40] the last sentence of the book reads, "There are no boundary problems, there are only national problems."[41] In his *Geography of Boundaries* (1938),[42] Ancel presented an alternative analysis of state boundaries as they are, as opposed to the normative prescriptions of the *Geopolitiker* and their *echte Grenze* (genuine borders). The geographer should not judge upon the present borders, but should conclude that there are no natural borders, that borders are not necessarily linear, that borders are always moving, that a border is a "political isobar that fixes for a while the equilibrium between two pressures: equilibrium between masses, equilibrium between forces."[43] Whether the pressures meet in a clash of violence is left undiscussed.

Later, the war raised the interest of American geographers and political scientists in geopolitics[44] and its application to American foreign policies.[45] Spykman, for example, echoed German *Geopolitiker* not only in his preoccupation with the strategic interests of his country in his *America's Strategy*,[46] but also in the use of cartography as argument, that is, the contrast of the maps of the encirclement of the Old World and that of the New World.[47] Likewise, Van Valkenburg edited a geographic analysis of *America at War.*[48] By 1942 even Bowman saw war as an essential element of international relations:

> We never put the sword in the picture. Germany and Japan do. And if it is their way and they are powerful, then it must be included in our way of life. Defense

> is a part of our way no matter through what seas of blood it leads—or we shall lose the way of life we cherish. The soldier on a Greek vase of the fifth century B.C. carries a sword without apology: to the Greeks war was one of the arts.[49]

Geographers in War and Peace

In this period of consolidation of the modern nation-states, geographers were using their insights to inform policies of their own states, but the roles of geographers varied greatly according to national needs and interests. German geographers supported the aggressive expansion of the new state—colonialism for Ratzel, expansion in Europe for the *Geopolitiker.* Kjellén favored the maintenance of the union of Norway with Sweden and the containment of Russia in northern Europe, Mackinder promoted the maintenance of the British Empire through alliances with local actors to prevent the constitution of a strong state that would control the heartland. The French geographers underlined the regional personalities of Alsace-Lorraine and the Rhineland to justify their separation from Prussian Germany (the first was returned to France in 1919, and the second was demilitarized after the war, until the Germans abrogated the treaty in 1936). Bowman lobbied against the isolationism of the United States.

Geographers were directly involved in the Great War as soldiers, often in positions where they could apply their knowledge to advise policy makers and military planners and to do fieldwork.[50] In anticipation of the peace settlement, French geographers like Vidal de la Blache and his son-in-law de Martonne were members of a committee that prepared for the French government the justification of the return of Alsace-Lorraine to France after the war, without a plebiscite or a referendum.[51] In Britain geographers seized on the war as an opportunity to position their discipline favorably in schools and universities,[52] without much success, as Mackinder deplored in 1921:

> This was the position when the war came upon us, and then in a rudimentary sort of way the whole people began to think strategically, or in other words, geographically. We who were growing old in the cause thought that when the war was over our favourite study would be permanently established in its rightful place. But as with other sanguine war hopes and forecasts the realization, although not contrary to what was expected, was not complete.[53]

After the war, geographers were directly involved as experts at the peace conferences. The American Isaiah Bowman represented the American Geographic Society as an advisor to President Woodrow Wilson at the Paris Peace Conference. His book *The New World* was primarily based on facts and insights collected in that position. He was one of the founders of the Council of Foreign Relations.[54] Bowman remained an advisor to the U.S. administration who lobbied against isolationism and was as such very active at the State Department during World War II as well. During the Peace Conference, Emmanuel de Martonne and Albert Demangeon held similar advisory positions on the French side. The Serbian Johan Cvijic provides another example of how geographic writings were influential at these conferences. His ethnic maps of the Balkans (more specific ledgment of the existence of Macedo-Slavs in Macedonia, distinc and the Bulgarians) were crucial in the attribution of that reg formed Kingdom of the Serbs, the Croats, and the Slovenians (It is interesting to note that Bowman, de Martonne, and Cvijic spe in physical geography than in political geography, which suggests that the inpu expected from geography was not related to political issues proper, but pertained to the physical context in which they were embedded.

After the peace settlement, German geographers were more directly involved in foreign policy. *Geopolitik* was seen as applied knowledge, to the extent that it was often labeled "pseudoscience." Geographers' ideas, those of *Geopolitiker* but also Ratzel's concept of *Lebensraum*,[56] were applied by the Nazi regime to justify its policies of expansion and extermination. For example, Walter Christaller's theory of central places was used to plan settlements in Eastern Europe. On the American side, similar geopolitical applications that advised foreign policy makers were found too, as was also true of geopolitical schools in many other countries.[57]

War raised the awareness of the relevance of geographic knowledge. This was true of World War I but also of World War II. "Geography is today much in vogue owing to the circumstances which have made the period in which we live one of war on a global scale."[58] The utility of geography was widely recognized. "Geography has always been vital to the prosecution of war, in three ways: first, *intelligence* is critical; secondly *logistics* [. . .]; thirdly, in *action*."[59] Geographers were recruited as such. In the United States, 670 geographers were involved in some way during World War II, including 129 geographers who worked within the Office for Strategic Services, with Richard Hartshorne as chair of the project committee,[60] while British academics published the Naval Intelligence Handbooks, a series of fifty-eight volumes.[61]

Nevertheless, not all geographers were serving the state. The most illustrious opponents were the French anarchist Élisée Reclus and the Russian anarchist Peter Kropotkin at the end of the nineteenth century and the German Marxist Karl Wittfogel, who wrote against the use of *Geopolitik* for the theoretical justification of fascist tendencies and imperialism.[62] Kropotkin pleaded in 1885 for the importance of geography in education for peace:

> In our time of wars, of national self-conceit, of national jealousies and hatreds ably nourished by people who pursue their own egotism, personal or class interests, geography must be [. . .] a means of dissipating these prejudices and of creating other feelings more worthy of humanity."[63]

Fifty years later, Wallace Atwood discussed "the universal demand of the masses of the people for peace" at the end of his presidential address to the Association of American Geographers (AAG).[64] He saw a huge task for geographers, that "of introducing the people of one nation to the people living in the other nations of the world."

> Ignorance breeds suspicion. International understanding cannot be built on fear, or suspicion or hatred. The damnable practices of war must be stamped out and

placed in our historic background along with the torture chamber, the guillotine and private duelling.[65]

Conclusion for the Period 1897–1945

In the first half of the twentieth century, academic geographers were divided into a war-minded camp that saw war as the legitimate expression of competition between states and a peace-minded camp that promoted international cooperation. Publications rarely dealt explicitly with war waging and peacemaking, which were discussed in the relatively small literature on political geography. Studies of the state and international relations mainly paid attention to resources that a state could mobilize to win a war (for example, the location and size of its territory, population, "sense of space," and resources). Geographic knowledge was generally considered an aid to statecraft in the different national settings and a tool in the education of the masses and the army of the nation, but a small group was promoting its potential to foster international understanding and cooperation. Still, geography was mainly an aid to war-waging states.

Geography and Geographers since World War II

Key Developments in War and Peace since 1945

After World War II, European states were not able anymore to contest the superpower status of the United States and the Soviet Union. The United Nations (UN) system gave a more thorough international overarch to the modern state system that further expanded with decolonization. War-making practices were dramatically altered by the proliferation of nuclear armaments as other states—the Soviet Union, the United Kingdom, France, China, India, and others—emulated the United States. Nuclear deterrence was seen as the main stabilizing force during the Cold War, an armed state of nonwar. In addition, there were local conflicts, especially liberation wars, wars by proxy between the two superpowers in the Third World. Conventional war was supplemented by ABC weapons threats (atomic, biological, and chemical instruments of mass destruction).

After the collapse of the Soviet Union and the end of the Cold War, NATO armies redefined their role as peacemaking and peacekeeping agents outside their territories under a UN umbrella. Local conflicts between states and between groups that challenged weak states proliferated and escalated. Last but not least, global terrorist networks became key challengers of a global collective security, as was powerfully demonstrated by the attacks of September 11, 2001.

Key Developments in Academic Geography since 1945

The postwar period has been one of academic consolidation. Universities grew tremendously, especially from the 1960s onward, and their role as teaching institutions changed with the democratization of academic education. The professional future of geography students diversified beyond teaching geography at a school or university. Academic consolidation also meant larger staffs and larger research programs. With quantity also came tremendous qualitative changes in approaches regarding both theoretical and methodological aspects. In geography this led to fragmentation, with a sharper divide between human and physical geography and further specialization into subfields such as cultural geography, economic geography, and political geography, but also urban studies, area studies, and the like. In addition, several general paradigm shifts brought innovations in geography: the quantitative revolution from the 1960s onward, and later, geographic information systems (GIS) and remote-sensing techniques, Marxism and neo-Marxism in the 1970s and 1980s, postmodernism and critical theory in the 1980s and 1990s, and more engaged forms of geographic practices such as radical geography, feminist geographies, or postcolonial geographies. New subdisciplines and alternative schools were institutionalized in an ever-increasing number of geographic or interdisciplinary journals.[66] In addition, it is important to note that peace studies developed from the 1950s onward as an interdisciplinary field of research, distinct from strategic studies, and it institutionalized with its own institutes and journals, such as *Journal of Conflict Resolution* (1957) and *Journal of Peace Research* (1964).

Geographers about War and Peace since 1945

It is customary to write that political geography almost vanished after the war, which is surely true of geopolitics in Germany,[67] but is overstated for political geography in the United States. Derwent Whittlesey seems to have considered starting a journal of political geography,[68] but it was not until 1982 that such a journal (*Political Geography Quarterly*) was established, as an international journal.

In the meantime, political geography became detached from the emotions of war by functionalist approaches. Jean Gottmann, a French geographer of Russian origin who worked in the United States, analyzed the partition of the world through two main factors that caused instability and stability: movement (all exchanges throughout the world) and iconography (symbols in which people believe).[69] Richard Hartshorne offered a functionalist model of state integration and disintegration by accounting for centripetal and centrifugal forces.[70] His concept of state-idea was developed further into a chain from political idea to political area by Stephen B. Jones,[71] who also discussed global views of the political system.[72]

The state system and power relations were not addressed by geographers. One exception was Saul B. Cohen, a student of Whittlesey, through his publication in 1963 of *Geography and Politics in a World Divided.*[73] The purpose of this book was "to present a geographical view of contemporary international politics." Discussing critically Mackinder's, Haushofer's, and Spykman's world maps, Cohen developed his own. In the bipolar world of the 1960s, he distinguished two geostrategic regions and, within these regions, several geopolitical regions, including shatterbelts at the divide between the two geostrategic regions. The regional groupings of states attracted his utmost interest. He updated his maps several times over the years to take into account the ongoing transformation of the world geopolitical system.[74]

Political scientists, rather than geographers, adopted traditional geographic approaches to study international relations and military issues. Harold and Margaret Sprout explored the role of the environment in international politics by focusing on the perception of environmental factors by policy makers.[75] Physical-geographic factors were also addressed in most contributions to a special issue of the *Journal of Conflict Resolution* in 1960.[76] There is a large literature about geopolitics, geostrategy, and military geography,[77] but it is more the work of military schools and naval colleges, and geographers were rarely engaged in that perspective.[78]

The revival of political geography started in France with Yves Lacoste and the foundation of the journal *Hérodote*.[79] Their project was a subversive geopolitics, with the aim of generating activism informed by geographic knowledge. In the end, the work of Lacoste and his associates, such as the thematic issues of *Hérodote*, was more contemplative than their original agenda suggested and often consisted of the confrontation of different representations of the same conflict and their incompatible territorial claims.[80]

Internationally, the foundation of the journal *Political Geography Quarterly* in 1982 by John O'Loughlin and Peter J. Taylor and the establishment of the Commission on the World Political Map of the International Geographical Union (IGU) marked the revival of political geography.[81] Still, political geographers were hardly involved in peace studies and did not pay much attention to war and peace.[82] This has changed in the past two decades, although only three books have engaged explicitly with the geography of war and peace.[83]

The Geography of Peace and War, edited in 1985 by David Pepper and Alan Jenkins, two Oxford geographers, was dominated by nuclear deterrence in the second Cold War.[84] In his introduction, Pepper announced a contribution of geographers and associated scholars to peace studies that focused on the description and the analysis of geographic (i.e., spatial and environmental) aspects of peace and war studies, a limitation Pepper acknowledged. Part I, about the geography of the Cold War and the arms race, covered the geography of conflict since 1945, the geopolitics of deterrence between the United States and the Soviet Union, the geography of arms production and sales, propaganda cartography, and the geography of arms manufacture in the United States. Part II concentrated upon the geography of nuclear war, including doomsday computer forecasts of thermal radiation, blast, and local fallout for the United Kingdom, the climatological effects of a nuclear exchange, and the geography of civil defense in the United States. Part III dealt with geographies of peace, specifically, nuclear-weapon-free zones, the geography of the peace movement, peace education and the geography curriculum, and a Soviet view of the geography of peace and war. The latter chapter featured an antiwar declaration adopted at the Twenty-first International Geography Congress in Paris in 1984 at the proposal of the National Committee of Soviet Geographers.

Apart from this volume, nuclear war and nuclear deterrence have been addressed by geographers in numerous books and journal articles that deal with education,[85] the consequences of nuclear attacks,[86] geographies of military spending,[87] and the peace movement.[88] The topic seems to have vanished into thin air after the end of the Cold War, although obviously the weaponry is still out there.

The Political Geography of Conflict and Peace, edited by Nurit Kliot and Stanley Waterman, two Israeli political geographers, in 1991, by the end of the Cold War, dealt more with territorial conflicts and discursive aspects than with material manifestations proper.[89] In the introduction Nurit Kliot addressed the rapid changes in the international system at the end of the 1980s. Chapters in the book included Saul Cohen's presentation of an emerging world map of peace with the emergence of new states, especially the category he named gateway states. In addition, there was a reflection on a century of geopolitics,[90] a contrast between geopolitics of dominance and international cooperation in Europe, discussions of incomplete surrenders and dealignment, a survey of diplomatic networks and their meaning for stable peace, an analysis of the European Community as a "civilian power," an examination of territorial ideology and international conflict, and a discussion of the nature and causes of national and military self-images. The remaining chapters addressed the following more localized conflicts: the international borders of Arabia, apartheid as foreign policy, a comparative study of minority control in Israel and Malaysia, and two chapters on the Arab-Israeli conflict.

The third volume is the *The Geography of War in the Post Cold War World*, which was published in 2001 by Patrick O'Sullivan, who is one of the few academic geographers who write on the geographical nature of strategic and tactical problems.[91] In this concise book, O'Sullivan provided an overview of the many facets of the geography of war and dealt with warlike traces in the landscape in a historical perspective, with the geography of war in the 1990s, and with military aspects related to geography at different scales (geopolitics, geostrategy, and battlescapes). He considered both the military impact of geography and the geographic impact of the military. The final chapter addressed the warriors (styles of wars across time and space) and victims.

The present volume considerably expands the agenda to the domain of drugs, terrorism, religion, and feminism. The research published in the past two decades shows a similar diversity of topics and approaches.

A first cluster of publications consists of analyses of the state system: the view from nowhere. These geographers dealt with the distribution of conflicts in space and time and possible explanations for these spatial patterns. However, explanatory factors are not sought anymore among physical-geographic factors such as climates, terrain, or the distribution of land and sea. John O'Loughlin and Herman van der Wusten have worked apart and together with large databases on the occurrence of wars and other conflicts, for example, the distribution of battle deaths in different types of war since 1890 and the relations between war cycles and economic cycles.[92] In a similar vein, Jan Nijman studied patterns of relations between the superpowers in the Cold War, Tom Nierop analyzed patterns of relations between states in terms of diplomatic relations, membership in international organizations, and trade relations, and Nijman and Richard Grant scrutinized patterns of foreign aid.[93] Colin Williams and Stephen Williams explored the security architecture of Europe after the Cold War,[94] and Michael Shin and Michael Ward examined the linkage between military spending and economic growth between 1985 and 1995.[95] Related work by political scientists exists, although it sometimes considers the role of physical-geographic facts—how ironic.[96] A separate cluster consists of studies led by structural approaches, both political economy[97] and world-systems analysis,[98] that have paid more attention to structural inequalities than to active periods of war.

Another perspective has been to make visible the effect of war on people on the ground, that is, the view from below. Yves Lacoste revealed the logic behind American dike bombings in North Vietnam in a widely published article.[99] Kenneth Hewitt wrote about the strategic bombing of urban places during World War II, surveying the German and Japanese cities attacked, the resulting destruction of places, and the problem of witnesses and of urban reconstruction.[100] In a later article, he dealt with the "oral geographies" of these bombings, based on questionnaires administered by the Allied forces at the end of the war among civilians affected by the bombings.[101] Similarly, geographies of the Holocaust have been attempted.[102] Hugh Clout wrote about the restoration of fields, farms, villages, and market towns of northern France in the aftermath of the Great War.[103] Geographers have also addressed the tension between states and cities in *War and the City* (1991) and more specifically with regard to military spending in *The Pentagon and the Cities* (1992).[104]

Older periods and other wars have been scrutinized too.[105] Nuala Johnson has documented Irish enrollment in the Great War (with reproductions of fascinating posters) and the spectacle of remembrance on Peace Day, July 19, 1919, in different Irish cities.[106] She wrote earlier about monuments and nationalism,[107] a topic also addressed by James Mayo in his work on war memorials.[108] Karen Morin and Lawrence Berg have analyzed the gendering of resistance in British colonial narratives of land wars of the 1860s in New Zealand by comparing men's and women's voices among the British supporters of the Maori.[109] Alison Blunt studied the representation of home, empire, and British women during the Indian "mutiny" of 1857–1858.[110] Leaving archives and monuments behind, Lorraine Dowler researched the everyday construction of violence in Northern Ireland, dealing with women and war in Belfast through participant observation.[111] B. Graham and P. Shirlow disclosed connections between historical and contemporary conflicts in their analysis of the Battle of the Somme's (1916) role in Ulster Protestant identity.[112]

During the late 1980s and the 1990s, geographers shifted their attention from material to discursive characteristics of conflicts and analyzed historical justifications in conflicts,[113] as well as geographic arguments,[114] geopolitical discourses of formal geopoliticians,[115] foreign policy makers,[116] or news media.[117] K.-J. Dodds studied both elite narratives and popular geopolitics in the Falklands War.[118] Gertjan Dijkink tackled the relation between national identity and geopolitical vision in several countries and the relation between elite geopolitical codes and popular representation.[119] Anssi Paasi addressed the issues of the connections between scales in his study of the social construction of the Finnish-Soviet border, Finnish nationalism, and changing geopolitical relations between Finland and the Soviet Union.[120] O'Loughlin and V. Kolossov analyzed public opinion in seventeen countries toward the NATO intervention in Kosovo in 1999.[121] M. Sparke explored the limits of critique with an analysis of his own conference paper on the "Gulf War."[122]

The relations of geography and nationalism and imperialism have been scrutinized in contributions to conferences organized by the IGU Commission on the History of Geographical Thought.[123] Furthermore, the work and activities of geographers have been extensively examined, especially for those involved in geopolitics, often under the label of critical geopolitics.[124] In 2000 Klaus Dodds and David Atkinson edited *Geopolitical Traditions: A Century of Geopolitical Thought*, a collection of essays that rethought geopolitical histories, the connection between geopolitics, nation, and spirituality. Dodds and Atkinson also included essays about the reclaiming of geopolitics, the changing discourse of Israeli geopolitics, geopolitics and the media, environmental geopolitics, and two closing essays on futures and possibilities.[125]

Political geography also possesses a strong tradition of local case studies, especially about border conflicts and the related war and peace processes. This is a persistent feature, but the research perspectives have shifted. The Israeli-Palestinian conflict is probably the single most researched conflict, which can be explained by the length of the conflict, its many wars, its many ramifications and connotations for religious groups, and the position of the Middle East during the Cold War, but also by some very active political geographers. This large body of literature features contributions of the Israeli geographer David Newman,[126] and the Palestinian geographer Ghazi Falah,[127] as well as common publications.[128] Collections such as the edited volume *Water in the Middle East: A Geography of Peace*[129] and the forum *Israel at 50* in *Political Geography*[130] have extended the debate.[131] The second most studied conflict is probably that in Northern Ireland.[132] The effect of war and subsequent peace settlements has been studied for the partition of Cyprus and its effects on the political landscape of the island,[133] for divided cities,[134] and for the reconstruction of Beirut after the war.[135]

Last but not least, political geographers have addressed more general issues of territoriality and territorial conflicts that are relevant to war and peace,[136] especially border conflicts,[137] ecological problems,[138] peacekeeping operations,[139] and legal aspects of peace settlements such as international courts and peace conferences.[140] The Internet and its potential to disrupt state sovereignty were also acknowledged in accounts of the hardly metaphorical "war of ink and Internet" in Chiapas in the mid-1990s and in a prospective essay by Stan Brunn that called for a Treaty of Silicon.[141] Brunn was also the guest editor of a special 2003 issue of *Geopolitics* focusing on September 11 (Volume 8, Number 3). Although this overview is far from exhaustive and largely limited to the English language literature, it shows the great diversity of an expanding body of geographic literature. Still, few introductory textbooks of political geography use war and peace as their main topic, *Engaging Geopolitics* being an exception,[142] but John Agnew used the art exhibition *The Great War of the Californias*—a fictive retrospective about a future war between San Francisco and Los Angeles—as an illustration on the cover and in the preface of *Making Political Geography*.[143]

Geographers in War and Peace since 1945

Discussing the role of geographers during World War II, Andrew Kirby stated that in the 1990s "Political geographers of the stature of Bowman, or Hartshorne, no longer exist and are no longer represented within government."[144] He made an exception for George Demko, the director of the Geographer of the U.S. Department of State. This is not to say that geographic knowledge is not widely used to prepare and wage war. Geographic information systems and remote sensing are key technologies for intelligence agencies. The difference from the situation fifty years ago is that academic geographers are largely divorced from these uses.

Academic geographers have involved themselves with war and peace in ways other than waging war. In France, the *Hérodote* school of geopolitics proposed a program for an active geography to oppose state oppression that was inspired by the anti-imperialist struggle in (former) colonies.[145] In the Anglo-American world in the 1980s, academic geographers claimed to contribute to peace, mainly through the diffusion of geographic knowledge, the logic being that "If this viewpoint adds to the evidence of its, [war's] ultimate futility, then we have served a useful purpose."[146] Nevertheless, the idea that "every act of war is always a disaster" has been challenged by Ó Tuathail in a critique of the statist research agenda of van der Wusten and O'Loughlin and the limitation of their approach to negative peace and their neglect of structural violence.[147]

Issues of nuclear war and deterrence have prompted many geographers to take a stand for peace. But the numerous calls for action,[148] petitions at the AAG and at the IGU, and the publications mentioned earlier, targeted their own arenas. Geographers were possibly successful in local education and activist initiatives, but they had poor access to decision makers. Susan Cutter addressed this issue in 1988 in her *Geographers and Nuclear War: Why We Lack Influence on Public Policy*.[149] She imputed this poor record to two factors: the absence of a grand theory and the fragmentation of geography. Stating that "Geographers are more important than they think," Peter Slowe argued that geographers should explore more thoroughly the implication for geography of political thought. He illustrated his points with a demonstration of the centrality of geography to the argument in case studies of the five sources of political power (might, right, nationhood, legality, and legitimacy).[150]

Other examples of statements against nuclear deterrence or more specific, localized conflicts have been published in more radical geography journals, for example, *Antipode* or, more recently, the two forums organized by the *Arab World Geographer* that asked geographers for initial reflections upon the second Intifada and the September 11, 2001, attacks.[151] After September 11, 2001, AAG's geographers prepared a research agenda to contribute to the understanding of and the action against terrorism,[152] and *Philosophy and Geography* published a special section on *Geographies of the 11th*.[153] Some geographers are also personally involved as publicists who promote peace settlements in local conflicts, like, for example, the British/Israeli political geographer David Newman in the Israeli public debate about a peace settlement, with columns, canceled by the paper in 2003, in the *Jerusalem Post* and contributions in the *New York Times*, the *Guardian*, the *World Press Review*, and a variety of Jewish newspapers, including the *Los Angeles Jewish Times*.[154]

Finally, one should mention here the International Charter on Geographical Education adopted in 1992 by the Commission on Geographical Education (CGE) of IGU at its 1992 Congress in Washington, D.C. Peace is a preoccupation of the charter, and it explicitly relates to the Universal Declaration on Human Rights, the Charter of the United Nations, and the Constitution of UNESCO and underscores the importance of education in cross-national understanding and cooperation.[155] "Geographical education is ideally suited to promote a sense of mutual respect between nations and people. Geographical knowledge of other cultures, civilizations and ways of life increases our ability to communicate and is a necessary prerequisite for international co-operation and solidarity."[156] This brings us back to Kropotkin's statement of 1885.[157]

Conclusion for the Period since 1945

In the postwar period, academic geographers have been unanimously peace minded and have promoted international cooperation. In the past two decades, more and more publications have dealt explicitly with war waging and peacemaking. A much larger and growing literature on the political geography of the state and international relations has analyzed various aspects of the state system, ranging from relations between states to discursive practices. Studies of the consequences of war for individuals have been a much needed innovation. Geographic knowledge is generally conceived as detached from political practices (with the noticeable exception of French *géopolitique*) or as critical of statecraft. Geographers are sometimes involved directly in peace movements and other political actions, rarely in an army service. Geography is widely seen as an educational tool to foster international understanding and cooperation, in sum, as a science for peace.

Conclusion

During the last century, there has been an obvious shift from "a war geography" to "a geography for peace." War is now widely seen as a condemnable collective behavior rather than a natural opportunity to demonstrate individual and collective strength. In research, there has been an expansion of the study of the causes and the course of war to its effects and consequences, a shift from environmental factors that influence the relative strength of a specific state to relational factors regarding interstate interactions, from the viewpoint of one state both to a global viewpoint from nowhere and to the personal viewpoint of individuals caught in war situations (elites and civilians alike), and finally, from geophysical facts to the perceptions of actors who are involved. In addition, geographers' contribution has changed; the main objective for applying geographical knowledge has shifted from war winning to war avoidance. These shifts echo more general social changes. The connotations of the word "war" were different one century ago when states used to have a Ministry of War (instead of a Ministry of Defense), but also when the military draft was common and giving one's life for the fatherland was no hollow phrase for citizens of democracies. The general shift of "war as an art" to "war as a taboo" is widely echoed among geographers.[158]

Geographers now advocate peace in a globalizing world, but they still achieve poor visibility in public debate. They are less influential than when they wanted to use their skills to draw lessons about winning war. The ambivalent attitude toward policy applications in the field of war and peace is still fueled by the gloomy example of German *Geopolitik*. The growing body of literature that reflects on that period and more generally on the involvement of geographers in nationalist and colonial projects is therefore a welcome step toward more reflexivity but also more assurance.

Nevertheless, for many military-minded people, geography is still about logistics, tactics at the battlefield, and strategy.[159] In other words, whether geography is a study of war or peace[160] depends in the end only partially on geographers. This is true of all (scientific) knowledge and technological application. The highly visible actions of nuclear scientists in campaigns against nuclear deterrence and the attribution to them of Nobel Prizes for Peace and similar awards have not prevented state machineries from investing in huge nuclear arsenals. The task of geographers is much wider than to warn about the effects of nuclear, chemical, or biological wars—others can and do do it better. The expertise geographers can share with others pertains to their understanding of place and regards mainly the role of territory as a control mechanism and in the shaping of identities and representations that mobilize people to seek violent rather than peaceful settlements to their disagreements.[161]

Notes

1. Lacoste, *Géographie, ça sert, d'abord, à faire la guerre*.

2. Pepper, "Introduction"; van der Wusten and O'Loughlin, "Claiming New Territory for a Stable Peace"; Wisner, "Geography: War or Peace Studies?"; O'Loughlin and Heske, "From 'Geopolitik' to Geopolitique.' "

3. O'Loughlin and Heske, "From 'Geopolitik' to 'Geopolitique.' "

4. Johnston, Gregory, Pratt, and Watts, *Dictionary of Human Geography*.

5. O'Loughlin, *Dictionary of Geopolitics*. There are entries for "Paris Peace Conference," "Peaceful Coexistences," "Conception of Peace," and specific wars.

6. Mitchell, "Politics, Fish, and International Resource Management."

7. Smith, " 'Academic War over the Field of Geography' "; Smith, "For a History of Geography"; commentaries in *Annals of the Association of American Geographers* 78 (1988): 144–158.

8. Galtung, "Violence, Peace, and Peace Research"; Galtung, "A Structural Theory of Imperialism."

9. De Pater and van der Wusten, *Het geografische huis*; Claval, *Histoire de la géographie française de 1870 à nos jours*; Johnston, *Geography and Geographers*; Holt-Jensen, *Geography*.

10. Agnew, *Making Political Geography*; van der Wusten, "Political Geography at the Global Scale"; O'Loughlin, *Dictionary of Geopolitics*; Heffernan, *The Meaning of Europe*; Dodds and Atkinson, *Geopolitical Traditions*; Raffestin, Lapreno, and Pasteur, *Géopolitique et histoire*; Claval, *Géopolitique et géostratégie*; Parker, *Geopolitics*.

11. I am indebted to the outstanding service of the library of the University of Amsterdam, with its extensive physical collections of (old) books and journals, its virtual collection of academic journals, its digital catalogs, and the Dutch interlibrary exchange system. Without these facilities, I would not have been able to access so many old and new materials.

12. Heffernan, *Meaning of Europe*.

13. The Société de géographie de Paris in 1821, Gesellschaft für Erdkunde zu Berlin in 1828, the Royal Geographical Society in London in 1830, and later others in Mexico, Germany, Brazil, and Russia. The American Geographical Society was founded in 1852.

14. A German chair of geography was established in Strasbourg in 1874.

15. The Geographical Association was founded in Britain in 1897, and the Association of American Geographers was founded in 1910. The first International Geography Congress was organized in Antwerp in 1871, the second in Paris in 1875, and an International Geographical Union (IGU-UGI) was established in Brussels in 1922.

16. The *Geographical Journal*, begun in 1835 in Britain, was supplemented by new journals such as *Annales de géographie* (1891), *Geographische Zeitschrift* (1895), the *Journal of Geography* (1902), the *Scottish Geographical Magazine* (1902), the *Annals of the Association of American Geographers* (1991), the *Geographical Review* (1911), *Geography* (1916), the *Transactions of the Institute of British Geographers* (1933) and more specialized journals such as *Tijdschrift voor Economische en Sociale Geografie* (1910), *Economic Geography* (1925), and *Zeitschrift für Geopolitik* (1924–1944).

17. Ratzel, *Politische Geographie*.

18. Ratzel, *Politische Geographie oder die Geographie der Staaten, des Verkehres, und des Krieges*. A third edition, revised and enlarged by Eugen Oberhummer and published posthumously in 1923, did not have the subtitle that referred to war.

19. Ratzel, *Anthropo-geographie, I*, and *Anthropo-geographie, II*. Interesting geographic interpretations of Ratzel include Dijkink, "Ratzel's *Politische Geographie* and Nineteenth-Century German Discourse"; Agnew, *Making Political Geography*; and Claude Raffestin in the afterword of the French translation, Ratzel, *Géographie politique*. Another partial translation, *La géoghraphie politique*, based on the third posthumous edition, was published in 1987, with a foreword by Michel Korinman.

20. Semple, *Influences of the Geographic Environment*. For an interesting account of the misconceptions between German and American geographers, see Kristof, "Origins and Evolution of Geopolitics."

21. Ratzel, *Politische Geographie*, 2nd edition, section 48, pp. 93–95 (my translation, based also on the 1988 French translation of that section, pp. 90–93).

22. Kjellén, *Staten som lifsform*, 62. Translated into German a year later, Kjellén, *Der Staat als Lebensform*. My translation from the German edition.

23. Although the term "geopolitics" covers many different approaches, it can broadly be seen as a synonym for the political geography of international relations. For a discussion of the many perspectives on geopolitics, see Mamadouh, "Geopolitics in the Nineties."

24. Mackinder, "Geographical Pivot of History," 437. See also his books *Britain and the British Seas* and *Democratic Ideals and Reality*.

25. Vidal de la Blache, *Tableau de la géographie de la France*.

26. Vidal de la Blache, *France de l'est (Lorraine-Alsace)*. Lacoste has offered a rereading of Vidal as a geopolitician, for example, in the preface to the reedition of *La France de l'est* in 1994.

27. Articles in, for example, the *Geographical Journal* reported about new states and new borderlands. One such article is L'Estrange Bryce, "Klagenfurt Plebiscite."

28. Brunhes and Vallaux, *Géographie de l'histoire*, 3.

29. Bowman, *New World*. The French edition was published in 1928: Bowman, *Monde nouveau*.

30. Smith, "Bowman's New World and the Council on Foreign Relations."

31. Bowman, *New World*, 11; Bowman's emphasis.

32. Whittlesey, *Earth and the State*.

33. Haushofer, *Geopolitik der Pan-Ideen*; Haushofer, *Wehr-Geopolitik*; Banse, *Raum*

und Volk im Weltkriege; Banse, *Geographie und Wehrwille*. See also the older book by Maull, *Politische Geographie*.

34. Kiss, "Political Geography into Geopolitics," 642.

35. Vidal de la Blache, *Tableau de la géographie de la France*; Vidal de la Blache, *France de l'est (Lorraine-Alsace)*.

36. Vidal de la Blache, *Principes de géographie humaine*.

37. Demangeon, *Déclin de l'Europe*; Demangeon, *Empire britannique*; Demangeon and Febvre, *Rhin*.

38. Yves-Marie Goblet, *Crépuscule des traités*.

39. Ancel, *Géopolitique*.

40. Vallaux, *Sol et l'état*; Brunhes and Vallaux, *Géographie de l'histoire*; Brunhes, *Géographie humaine de la France*.

41. Ancel, *Géopolitique*, 196.

42. Ancel, *Géographie des frontières*.

43. Ibid, 195.

44. Bowman, "Political Geography of Power"; Kiss, "Political Geography into Geopolitics"; Isaiah Bowman, "Geography vs. Geopolitics"; Jean Gottmann, "Background of Geopolitics."

45. For a review of the burgeoning geopolitical literature in the United States at that time, see Clokie, "Geopolitics—New Super-science or Old Art?" For later review, see Kristof, "Origins and Evolution of Geopolitics," and Alexander, "New Geopolitics."

46. Spykman, *America's Strategy in World Politics*.

47. See also the cartographic exercises in Spykman, *Geography of the Peace*.

48. Van Valkenburg, *America at War*.

49. Bowman, "Political Geography of Power," 352 (the last two sentences are also quoted in O'Loughlin and Heske, "From 'Geopolitik' to 'Geopolitique,' " 40).

50. Ancel, for example, was awarded le Croix de chevalier de la Légion d'honneur, Croix de guerre, and Officier de la Légion d'honneur for his distinguished military service (Parker, "Ancel," 10–11). Karl Haushofer was a retired general when he became a professor of geography at the University of Munich. Fifty-one of the 76 AAG members were involved in the war in some way (Kirby, "What Did You Do in the War, Daddy?" 304). See also "War Services of Members of the Association of American Geographers."

51. Heffernan, "History, Geography, and the French National Space."

52. Heffernan, "Geography, Cartography, and Military Intelligence"; Heffernan "Professor Penck's Bluff"; Mayhew, "Halford Mackinder's 'New' Political Geography and the Geographical Tradition"; Stoddart, "Geography and War."

53. Mackinder, "Geography as a Pivotal Subject in Education," 376–384.

54. Smith, "Bowman's New World and the Council on Foreign Relations"; Smith, "Isaiah Bowman." See also Kirby, "What Did You Do in the War, Daddy?"

55. This attribution had far-reaching consequences: the creation in 1946 of a Macedonian republic alongside Serbia in the federal state and eventually an independent state in 1991 as the Former Yugoslavian Republic of Macedonia (FYROM). Wilkinson, *Maps and Politics;* Taylor and Flint, *Political Geography*, 209–211.

56. This concept is not from his *Politische Geographie*. See Bücher, et al. eds., *Festgaben für Albert Schäffle zur siebenzigsten Wiederkehr seines Geburtstages am 24* (1901).

57. See Dodds and Atkinson, *Geopolitical Traditions*, part 1.

58. Gottmann, "Background of Geopolitics."

59. Balchin, "United Kingdom Geographers in the Second World War," 160–180.

60. Kirby, "What Did You Do in the War, Daddy?" 306–309.

61. Clout and Gosme, "Naval Intelligence Handbooks."

62. Agnew, *Making Political Geography*; Ó Tuathail, *Critical Geopolitics*; O'Loughlin, *Dictionary of Geopolitics.*

63. Kropotkin, "What Geography Ought to Be," 7, 942.

64. Atwood, "Increasing Significance of Geographic Conditions in the Growth of Nation-States."

65. Ibid, 15.

66. *Acta Geographica* (Paris, 1947; *La géographie* since 2000), *Soviet Geography* (1960; *Post-Soviet Geography* since 1992; *Post-Soviet Geography and Economics* since 1997), *Geographical Analysis* (1965), *Area* (1969), *Antipode* (1969), *Geoforum* (1970), *L'espace géographique* (1972), *Environment and Planning* (1974), *Journal of Historical Geography* (1975), *Hérodote* (1976), *GeoJournal* (1977), *Progress in Human Geography* (1977), *Journal of Geography in Higher Education* (1977), *Journal of Cultural Geography* (1980), *Urban Geography* (1980), *Applied Geography* (1980), *Political Geography Quarterly* (1982; *Political Geography* since 1992), *Environment and Planning B, C,* and *D* series (1983), *Géographie et cultures* (1992), *Journal of Transport Geography* (1993), *Gender, Place, and Culture* (1994), *Geopolitics and International Boundaries* (1995), *Space and Polity* (1997), *Philosophy and Geography* (1998), and *Social and Cultural Geography* (2000).

67. Although even then some qualification is needed, since the periodical, *Zeitschrift für Geopolitik*, reappeared in 1951 (until 1968).

68. Julian Minghi, " 'Do Not Start a Journal on Political Geography.' "

69. Gottmann, "Geography and International Relations"; Gottmann, *Politique des états et leur géographie*; Gottmann, "Political Partitioning of Our World"; Gottmann, *Significance of Territory*.

70. Hartshorne, "Functional Approach in Political Geography." See also Hartshorne, "Political Geography in the Modern World."

71. Jones, "Unified Field Theory of Political Geography."

72. Jones, "Views of the Political World"; Jones, "Global Strategic Views."

73. Cohen, *Geography and Politics in a World Divided.*

74. A revised edition was published in 1973, Cohen, *Geography and Politics in a World Divided.* See also Cohen, "Geopolitical Realities and United States Foreign Policy" (see also comments in the same issue of *Political Geography*); Cohen, *Geopolitics of the World System*; "Global Geopolitical Change in the Post–Cold War Era"; and the special issue of *Political Geography* dedicated to Cohen, 21(5) (June 2002).

75. Sprout and Sprout, "Geography and International Politics in an Era of Revolutionary Change"; Sprout and Sprout, *Ecological Perspective on Human Affairs.*

76. Singer, "Geography of Conflict."

77. See a review in Mamadouh, "Geopolitics in the Nineties."

78. There is some evidence of revived relations between military geographers and academic geographers, such as special editions of *GeoJournal* in 1993 (31 [2]) and 1994 (34 [2]); and the establishment of a specialty group within the AAG. See also Collins, *Military Geography*; Winters, *Battling the Elements*; and Palka and Galgano, *Scope of Military Geography.*

79. Lacoste, "Enquête sur le bombardement des digues du fleuve rouge"; Lacoste, *Géographie, ça sert, d'abord, à faire la guerre.*

80. Lacoste, *Dictionnaire de Géopolitique.*

81. O'Loughlin and van der Wusten, "Political Geography of War and Peace."

82. House, "War, Peace, and Conflict Resolution"; House, "Political Geography of Contemporary Events."

83. See Kidron and Segal, *War Atlas.*

84. Pepper and Jenkins, *Geography of Peace and War.*

85. Solecki and Cutter, "Living in the Nuclear Age."

86. Bunge, "Geography of Human Survival," was an early warning. See also Bunge, *Nuclear War Atlas*; Bach, "Nuclear War"; M. Curry, "In the Wake of Nuclear War"; Green et al., *London after the Bomb*; and Openshaw, Steadman, and Green, *Doomsday*.

87. Malecki, "Government Funded R&D"; Malecki, "Federal R&D Spending in the United States of America"; Malecki, "Military Spending and the US Defense Industry"; Ó hUallacháin, "Regional and Technological Implications of the Recent Buildup in American Defense Spending." On defense cuts after the Cold War, see Atkinson, "Defense Spending Cuts and Regional Economic Impact," and Warf, "Geopolitics/Geoeconomics of Military Base Closures in the USA."

88. Cutter, Holcomb, and Shatin, "Spatial Patterns of Support for a Nuclear Weapons Freeze"; Cutter et al., "From Grassroots to Partisan Politics"; Cresswell, "Putting Women in Their Place"; Miller, "Political Empowerment."

89. Kliot and Waterman, eds. *Political Geography of Conflict and Peace*.

90. O'Loughlin and Heske, "From 'Geopolitik' to 'Geopolitique.' "

91. O'Sullivan, *Geography of War in the Post Cold War World*; O'Sullivan and Miller, *Geography of Warfare*; O'Sullivan, "Geographical Analysis of Guerilla Warfare"; O'Sullivan, *Terrain and Tactics*. See also his work on geopolitics: O'Sullivan, *Geopolitics*, and O'Sullivan, "Geopolitical Force Fields."

92. O'Loughlin, "Spatial Models of International Conflicts"; Ward and Kirby, "Commentary"; O'Loughlin, "In a Spirit of Cooperation, Not Conflict"; O'Loughlin, Mayer, and Greenberg, *War and Its Consequences*; O'Loughlin et al., "Diffusion of Democracy"; O'Loughlin and van der Wusten, "Political Geography of Pan-regions"; O'Loughin and van der Wusten, "Political Geography of War and Peace"; van der Wusten, "Geography of Conflict since 1945"; van der Wusten and van Kostanje, "Diplomatic Networks and Stable Peace."

93. Nijman, *Geopolitics of Power and Conflict*; Nijman and van der Wusten, "Breaking the Cold War Mould in Europe"; Nierop, *Systems and Regions in Global Politics*; Grant and Nijman, "Historical Changes in U.S. and Japanese Foreign Aid to the Asia-Pacific Region."

94. Williams and Williams, "Issues of Peace and Security in Contemporary Europe."

95. Shin and Ward, "Lost in Space."

96. Most and Starr, "Diffusion, Reinforcement, Geopolitics, and the Spread of War"; Starr and Most, "Contagion and Border Effects on Contemporary African Conflict"; Goertz and Diehl, *Territorial Changes and International Conflict*; Vasquez, "Why Do Neighbors Fight?"; Buhaug and Gates, "Geography of Civil War"; Toset, Gleditsch, and Hegre, "Shared Rivers and Interstate Conflict"; Gleditsch et al., "Armed Conflict, 1946–2001."

97. Agnew and Corbridge, *Mastering Space*.

98. Taylor, *Political Geography*; Taylor, *Modernities*; Taylor and Flint, *Political Geography*.

99. Lacoste, "Enquête sur le bombardement des digues du fleuve rouge"; Lacoste, "Geography of Warfare."

100. Hewitt, *Air War and the Destruction of Urban Places*; Hewitt, "Place Annihilation."

101. Hewitt, " 'When the Great Planes Came and Made Ashes of Our City. . . .' "

102. Clarke, Doehl, and McDonough, "Holocaust Topologies"; Doehl and Clarke, "Figuring the Holocaust."

103. Clout, *After the Ruins*.

104. Ashworth, *War and the City*; Kirby, *Pentagon and the Cities*.

105. Special issue of *Transactions of the Institute of British Geographers* 3(23) in 1978, *Settlement and Conflict in the Mediterranean World*.

106. Johnson, "Spectacle of Memory."

107. Johnson, "Cast in Stone."

108. Mayo, "War Memorials as Political Memory." See also Crampton, "Voortrekker Monument."

109. Morin and Berg, "Gendering Resistance."

110. Blunt, "Embodying War."

111. Dowler, " 'And They Think I'm Just a Nice Old Lady' "; Dowler, "Four Square Laundry."

112. Graham and Shirlow, "Battle of the Somme in Ulster Memory and Identity."

113. Murphy, "Historical Justifications for Territorial Claims."

114. Slowe, *Geography and Political Power.*

115. Ó Tuathail, "Putting Mackinder in His Place"; Ó Tuathail, "Problematizing Geopolitics"; Ó Tuathail, *Critical Geopolitics*; Ó Tuathail and Dalby, *Rethinking Geopolitics*; Ó Tuathail, Dalby, and Routledge, *Geopolitics Reader.*

116. Henrikson, "Geographical 'Mental Maps' of American Foreign Policy Makers"; Dalby, *Creating the Second World War*; Taylor, *Britain and the Cold War*; O'Loughlin and Grant, "Political Geography of Presidential Speeches"; Nijman, "Madeleine Albright and the Geopolitics of Europe"; Ó Tuathail, "Foreign Policy and the Hyperreal"; Ó Tuathail and Agnew, "Geopolitics and Discourse"; Ó Tuathail, "Theorizing Practical Geopolitical Reasoning"; Dodds, "Geopolitics in the Foreign Office"; Sidaway, "Iraq/Yugoslavia."

117. Sharp, *Condensing the Cold War*; Myers, Klak, and Koehl, "Inscription of Difference"; Sidaway, "What Is in a Gulf?"; Der Derian, " 'All but War Is Simulation.' "

118. Dodds, "War Stories"; Dodds, "1982 Falklands War and a Critical Geopolitical Eye." See also Dodds, *Geopolitics in a Changing World*, and Dodds, "Political Geography II."

119. Dijkink, *National Identity and Geopolitical Visions*; Dijkink, "Geopolitical Codes and Popular Representations."

120. Paasi, *Territories, Boundaries, and Consciousness.*

121. O'Loughlin and Kolossov, "Still Not Worth the Bones of a Single Pomeranian Grenadier."

122. Sparke, "Writing on Patriarchal Missiles."

123. Hooson, *Geography and National Identity*; Godlewska and Smith, eds., *Geography and Empire.*

124. Apart from the studies used as sources in the sections "Geographers about War and Peace" and "Geographers in War and Peace," such publications include Geoffrey Parker, *Western Geopolitical Thought in the Twentieth Century*; Geoffrey Parker, *Geopolitics of Domination*; Geoffrey Parker, *Geopolitics: Past, Present, and Future*; W. H. Parker, *Mackinder*; O'Loughlin, *Dictionary of Geopolitics*; Blouet, *Halford Mackinder, a Biography*, Bassin, "Race contra Space"; Bassin, "Imperialism and the Nation State"; Bassin, "Nature, Geopolitics, and Marxism"; Korinman, *Quand l'Allemagne pensait le monde*; Raffestin, Lapreno, and Pasteur, *Géopolitique et histoire*; Muet, *Géographes et l'Europe*; and Nierop, "Clash of Civilisations."

125. Dodds and Atkinson, *Geopolitical Traditions.* See also numerous contributions in *Political Geography (Quarterly)* since 1982. A recent example is Power, "Geo-politics and the Representation of Portugal's African Colonial Wars."

126. Newman, "From National to Post-national Territorial Identities in Israel-Palestine"; Newman, "Geopolitics of Peacemaking in Israel-Palestine"; Newman and Paasi, "Fences and Neighbours in the Postmodern World."

127. Falah, "1948 Israeli-Palestinian War and Its Aftermath"; Falah, "Re-envisioning

Current Discourse"; Falah, "Intifadat Al-Aqsa and the Bloody Road to Palestinian Independence."

128. Newman and Falah, "Small State Behaviour"; Falah and Newman, "Spatial Manifestation of Threat"; Newman and Falah, "Bridging the Gap."

129. Amery and Wolf, *Water in the Middle East.* See also Kliot, *Water Resources and Conflict in the Middle East,* and Feitelson, "Implications of Shifts in the Israeli Water Discourse for Israeli-Palestinian Water Negotiations."

130. *Political Geography* 2:18 (1999).

131. There are many more fascinating contributions, such as Cohen and Kliot, "Place-Names in Israel's Ideological Struggle"; Azaryahu and Golan, "(Re)Naming the Landscape"; Kliot, "Grand Design for Peace"; Katz, "Transfer of Population as a Solution to International Disputes"; and Yiftachel, "Internal Frontier." Also worth mentioning is the exchange between Palestinian and Israeli geographers: Falah, "Israelization of Palestine Human Geography"; Kliot and Waterman, "Political Impact on Writing the Geography of Palestine/Israel"; Falah, "Frontier of Political Criticism in Israeli Geographic Practice"; Kellerman, "Comment on Falah"; Falah, "On Israeli Geographic Practice."

132. For example, a special issue of *Political Geography* in 1998: O'Dowd, "Coercion, Territoriality, and the Prospects of Negotiated Settlement in Ireland"; Shirlow and McGovern, "Language, Discourse, and Dialogue"; Douglas and Shirlow, "People in Conflict in Place."

133. Kliot and Mansfeld, "Political Landscape of Partition."

134. Kliot and Mansfeld, "Case Studies of Conflict and Territorial Organization in Divided Cities."

135. Nagel, "Reconstructing Space, Re-creating Memory."

136. Gottmann, *Significance of Territory*; Sack, "Human Territoriality: A Theory"; Sack, *Human Territoriality: Its Theory and History*; Newman, *Boundaries, Territory, and Postmodernity*; Dijkink and Knippenberg, *Territorial Factor.*

137. Knippenberg and Markusse, *Nationalising and Denationalising European Border Regions.*

138. Le Billon, "Political Ecology of War."

139. Grundy-Warr, "Peacekeeping lessons from Divided Cyprus."

140. van der Wusten, "Viewpoint"; Brunn, Nooruddin, and Sims, "Place, Culture, and Peace."

141. Froehling, "Cyberspace 'War of Ink and Internet' in Chiapas, Mexico"; Brunn, "Treaty of Silicon for the Treaty of Westphalia?"

142. Braden and Shelley, *Engaging Geopolitics.*

143. Agnew, *Making Political Geography.*

144. Kirby, "What Did You Do in the War, Daddy?" 314.

145. See Lacoste, *Géographie, ça sert, d'abord, à faire la guerre,* and the first issue of *Hérodote* (1976).

146. O'Sullivan and Miller, *Geography of Warfare,* 162.

147. van der Wusten and O'Loughlin, "Claiming New Territory for a Stable Peace"; Ó Tuathail, "Beyond Empiricist Political Geography"; van der Wusten and O'Loughlin, "Back to the Future of Political Geography."

148. Morrill, "Responsibility of Geography"; White, "Geographers in a Perilously Changing World"; White, "Notes on Geographers and the Threat of Nuclear War"; Wisner, "Geography: War or Peace Studies?"; O'Loughlin and van der Wusten, "Geography, War, and Peace."

149. Cutter, "Geographers and Nuclear War." See also commentaries and a reply in

Annals 78(4) (1988): 715–727, such as Demko, "On Geography, Geographers, and Things Nuclear."

150. Slowe, *Geography and Political Power.*

151. *Arab World Geographer* 3(3) (2000) and 4(2) (2001).

152. Cutter, Richardson, and Wilbanks, *Geographical Dimensions of Terrorism.* A workshop was organized at the AAG Annual Conference in Los Angeles in 2002. See also Flint, "Terrorism and Counter-Terrorism."

153. *Philosophy and Geography* 5 (2002).

154. The listing originates from an announcement for a lecture scheduled in January 2003 at the Center for Near Eastern Studies of the UCLA International Institute in Los Angeles.

155. Stoltman, "International Charter on Geographical Education"; Haubrig, *International Charter on Geographical Education.*

156. Holt-Jensen, *Geography, History,* 31–32.

157. Kropotkin, "What Geography Ought to Be."

158. At the time of writing, though, U.S. war preparations reached their apex in the case of the UN against Iraq, but the glorification of "war making" for itself, as a masculine activity, has lost much of its glow. Governments in Europe, for example, find it difficult to consider the eventual death of professional recruits and expect that their public opinion will not accept such a price.

159. Murray, "Some Thoughts on War and Geography."

160. "Geography: War or Peace Studies?" to quote the title of Wisner's article.

161. The nature of geography as an "integrating science" that studies humankind, machinekind, and nature was for Bunge an argument to call geography "the queen of peace sciences." See Bunge, *Nuclear War Atlas,* 189–194.

References

Agnew, John. *Making Political Geography: Human Geography in the Making.* London: Arnold, 2002.

Agnew, John, and Stuart Corbridge. *Mastering Space: Hegemony, Territory, and International Political Economy.* London: Routledge, 1995.

Alexander, Lewis. "The New Geopolitics: A Critique." *Journal of Conflict Resolution* 5 (1961): 407–410.

Amery, Hussein A., and Aaron T. Wolf, eds. *Water in the Middle East: A Geography of Peace.* Austin: University of Texas Press, 2000.

Ancel, Jacques. *Géopolitique.* Paris: Delagrave, 1936.

Ancel, Jacques. *Géographie des frontières.* Paris: Gallimard, 1938.

Arab World Geographer. http://gp.fmg.uva.nl/ggct/awg/ (accessed February 2003).

Ashworth, G. J. *War and the City.* London: Routledge, 1991.

Atkinson, Robert D. "Defense Spending Cuts and Regional Economic Impact: An Overview." *Economic Geography* 69 (1993): 107–122.

Atwood, Wallace W. "The Increasing Significance of Geographic Conditions in the Growth of Nation-States." *Annals of the Association of American Geographers* 25 (1935): 1–16.

Azaryahu, Maoz, and Arnon Golan. "(Re)Naming the Landscape: The Formation of the Hebrew Map of Israel, 1949–60." *Journal of Historical Geography* 27 (2001): 178–195.

Bach, W. "Nuclear War: The Effects of Smoke and Dust on Weather and Climate." *Progress in Physical Geography* 10 (1986): 315–363.

Balchin, W. G. V. "United Kingdom Geographers in the Second World War." *Geographical Journal* 153 (1987): 159–180.

Banse, Ewald. *Raum und Volk im Weltkriege: Gedanken über eine nationale Wehrlehre*. Oldenburg: Stalling, 1932.

Banse, Ewald. *Geographie und Wehrwille: Gesammelte Studien zu den Problemen Landschaft und Mensch, Raum und Volk, Krieg und Wehr*. Breslau: Korn, 1934.

Bassin, Mark. "Imperialism and the Nation State in Friedrich Ratzel's Political Geography." *Progress in Human Geography* 11 (1987): 473–495.

Bassin, Mark. "Race contra Space: The Conflict between German 'Geopolitik' and National Socialism." *Political Geography Quarterly* 6 (1987): 115–134.

Bassin, Mark. "Nature, Geopolitics, and Marxism: Ecological Contestations in Weimar Germany." *Transactions of the Institute of British Geographers* 21 (1996): 315–341.

Blouet, Brian W. *Halford Mackinder, a Biography*. College Station: Texas A&M University Press, 1987.

Blunt, Alison. "Embodying War: British Women and Domestic Defilement in the Indian 'Mutiny', 1857–8." *Journal of Historical Geography* 26 (2000): 403–428.

Bowman, Isaiah. *The New World: Problems in Political Geography*. London: Harrap, 1922.

Bowman, Isaiah. *Le monde nouveau: Tableau général de géographie politique universelle*. Translated by Jean Brunhes. Paris: Payot, 1928.

Bowman, Isaiah. "Geography vs. Geopolitics." *Geographical Review* 32 (1942): 646–658.

Bowman, Isaiah. "Political Geography of Power." *Geographical Review* 32 (1942): 349–352.

Braden, Kathleen E., and Fred M. Shelley. *Engaging Geopolitics*. Harlow, UK: Prentice Hall, 2000.

Brunhes, Jean. *Géographie humaine de la France*. Paris: Alcan, 1925.

Brunhes, Jean, and Camille Vallaux. *La géographie de l'histoire: Géographie de la paix et de la guerre sur terre et sur mer*. Paris: Alcan, 1921.

Brunn, Stanley D. "A Treaty of Silicon for the Treaty of Westphalia? New Territorial Dimensions of Modern Statehood." In *Boundaries, Territory, and Postmodernity*, ed. David Newman, 106–31. Portland, OR: Cass, 1999.

Brunn, Stanley D., Vaseema Nooruddin, and Kimberly Sims. "Place, Culture, and Peace: Treaty Cities and National Culture in Mediating Contemporary International Disputes." *GeoJournal* 39 (1996): 331–343.

Buhaug, Halvard, and Scott Gates. "The Geography of Civil War." *Journal of Peace Research* 39 (2002): 417–433.

Bunge, William. "The Geography of Human Survival." *Annals of the Association of American Geographers* 63 (1973): 275–295.

Bunge, William. *Nuclear War Atlas*. Oxford: Blackwell, 1988.

Center for Near Eastern Studies, UCLA International Institute. www.isop.ucla.edu/showevent.asp?eventid=554 (accessed February 2003).

Clarke, D. B., M. A. Doehl, and F. McDonough. "Holocaust Topologies: Singularity, Politics, Space." *Political Geography* 15 (1996): 457–489.

Claval, Paul. *Géopolitique et géostratégie; La pensée politique, l'espace, et le territoire au XXe siècle*. Paris: Nathan, 1994.

Claval, Paul. *Histoire de la géographie française de 1870 à nos jours*. Paris: Nathan, 1998.

Clokie, H. McD. "Geopolitics—New Super-science or Old Art?" *Canadian Journal of Economics and Political Science* 10 (1944): 492–502.

Clout, Hugh Donald. *After the Ruins: Restoring the Countryside of Northern France after the Great War*. Exeter: University of Exeter Press, 1996.

Clout, Hugh, and Cyril Gosme. "The Naval Intelligence Handbooks: A Monument in Geographical Writing." *Progress in Human Geography* 27 (2003): 153–173.

Cohen, Saul B. *Geography and Politics in a World Divided.* New York: Random House, 1963.

Cohen, Saul B. *Geography and Politics in a World Divided.* 2nd ed. New York: Oxford University Press, 1973.

Cohen, Saul B. "Global Geopolitical Change in the Post–Cold War Era." *Annals of the Association of American Geographers* 81 (1991): 551–580.

Cohen, Saul B. *Geopolitics of the World System.* Lanham, MD: Rowman and Littlefield, 2002.

Cohen, Saul B. "Geopolitical Realities and United States Foreign Policy." *Political Geography* 22 (2003): 1–33.

Cohen, Saul B., and Nurit Kliot. "Place-Names in Israel's Ideological Struggle over the Administered Territories." *Annals of the Association of American Geographers* 82 (1992): 653–680.

Collins, John M. *Military Geography: For Professionals and the Public.* Washington, DC: National Defense University Press, 1998.

Crampton, Andrew. "The Voortrekker Monument, the Birth of Apartheid, and Beyond." *Political Geography* 20 (2001): 221–246.

Cresswell, Tim. "Putting Women in Their Place: The Carnival at Greenham Common." *Antipode* 26 (1994): 35–58.

Curry, M. "In the Wake of Nuclear War—Possible Worlds in an Age of Scientific Expertise." *Environment and Planning D* 3 (1985): 309–321.

Cutter, Susan L. "Geographers and Nuclear War: Why We Lack Influence on Public Policy." *Annals of the Association of American Geographers* 78 (1988): 132–143.

Cutter, Susan L., Douglas Richardson, and Thomas Wilbanks, eds. *The Geographical Dimensions of Terrorism: Action Items and Research Priorities.* New York: Routledge, 2002.

Cutter, Susan L., H. Briavel Holcomb, and Dianne Shatin. "Spatial Patterns of Support for a Nuclear Weapons Freeze." *Professional Geographer* 38 (1986): 42–52.

Cutter, S. L., H. B. Holcomb, D. Shatin, F. M. Shelley, and G. T. Murauskas. "From Grassroots to Partisan Politics: Nuclear Freeze Referenda in New Jersey and South Dakota." *Political Geography Quarterly* 6 (1987): 287–300.

Dalby, Simon. *Creating the Second World War: The Discourses of Politics.* London: Pinter; New York: Guilford, 1990.

Demangeon, Albert. *Le déclin de l'Europe.* Paris: Payot, 1920.

Demangeon, Albert. *L'empire britannique: Étude de géographie coloniale.* 2nd ed. Paris: Colin, 1925.

Demangeon, Albert, and Lucien Febvre. *Le Rhin: Problèmes d'histoire et d'économie.* Paris: Colin, 1935.

Demko, George J. "On Geography, Geographers, and Things Nuclear." *Annals of the Association of American Geographers* 78 (1988): 715.

De Pater, Ben, and Herman van der Wusten. *Het geografische huis: De opbouw van een wetenschap.* Muiderberg: Coutinho, 1991.

Der Derian, J. " 'All but War Is Simulation.' " In *Rethinking Geopolitics,* ed. Geraóid Ó Tuathail and Simon Dalby, 261–273. London: Routledge, 1998.

Dijkink, Gertjan. *National Identity and Geopolitical Visions: Maps of Pride and Pain.* London: Routledge, 1996.

Dijkink, Gertjan. "Geopolitical Codes and Popular Representations." *GeoJournal* 46 (1998): 397–403 (wrongly numbered 293–299).

Dijkink, Gertjan. "Ratzel's *Politische Geographie* and Nineteenth-Century German Discourse." In *Europe between Political Geography and Geopolitics,* ed. Marco Antonsich,

Vladimir Kolossov, and M. Paola Pagnini, 115–128. Rome: Società Geografica Italiana, 2001.

Dijkink, Gertjan, and Hans Knippenberg, eds. *The Territorial Factor: Political Geography in a Globalising World.* Amsterdam: Vossiuspers UvA, 2001.

Dodds, K.-J. "War Stories: British Elite Narratives of the 1982 Falklands/Malvinas War." *Environment and Planning D: Society and Space* 11 (1993): 619–640.

Dodds, Klaus. "The 1982 Falklands War and a Critical Geopolitical Eye: Steve Bell and the If . . . Cartoons." *Political Geography* 15 (1996): 571–592.

Dodds, Klaus. *Geopolitics in a Changing World.* Harlow, UK: Prentice Hall, 2000.

Dodds, Klaus. "Political Geography II: Some Thoughts on Banality, New Wars, and the Geopolitical Tradition." *Progress in Human Geography* 24 (2000): 119–129.

Dodds, Klaus, and David Atkinson, eds. *Geopolitical Traditions: A Century of Geopolitical Thought.* London: Routledge, 2000.

Dodds, Klaus-John. "Geopolitics in the Foreign Office: British Representations of Argentina, 1945–1961." *Transactions of the Institute of British Geographers* 19 (1994): 273–290.

Doehl, M. A., and D. B. Clarke. "Figuring the Holocaust: Singularity and the Purification of Space." In *Rethinking Geopolitics*, ed. Geraóid Ó Tuathail and Simon Dalby, 170–197. London: Routledge, 1998.

Douglas, Neville, and Peter Shirlow. "People in Conflict in Place: The Case of Northern Ireland." *Political Geography* 17 (1998): 125–128.

Dowler, Lorraine. " 'And They Think I'm Just a Nice Old Lady': Women and War in Belfast, Northern Ireland." *Gender, Place, and Culture* 5 (1998): 159–176.

Dowler, Lorraine. "The Four Square Laundry: Participant Observation in a War Zone." *Geographical Review* 91 (2001): 414–422.

Falah, Ghazi. "Israelization of Palestine Human Geography." *Progress in Human Geography* 13 (1989): 535–550.

Falah, Ghazi. "The Frontier of Political Criticism in Israeli Geographic Practice." *Area* 26 (1994): 1–12.

Falah, Ghazi. "The 1948 Israeli-Palestinian War and Its Aftermath: The Transformation and De-signification of Palestine's Cultural Landscape." *Annals of the Association of American Geographers* 86 (1996): 256–285.

Falah, Ghazi. "On Israeli Geographic Practice: A Brief Response to Kellerman and Thoughts on Future Prospects." *Area* 28 (1996): 225–228.

Falah, Ghazi. "Re-envisioning Current Discourse: Alternative Territorial Configurations of Palestinian Statehood." *Canadian Geographer* 41 (1997): 307–330.

Falah, Ghazi. "Intifadat Al-Aqsa and the Bloody Road to Palestinian Independence." *Political Geography* 20 (2001): 135–138.

Falah, Ghazi, and David Newman. "The Spatial Manifestation of Threat: Israelis and Palestinians Seek a 'Good' Border." *Political Geography* 14 (1995): 689–706.

Feitelson, E. "Implications of Shifts in the Israeli Water Discourse for Israeli-Palestinian Water Negotiations." *Political Geography* 21 (2002): 293–318.

Flint, Colin. "Terrorism and Counterterrorism: Geographic Research Questions and Agendas." *Professional Geographer* 55 (2003): 161–169.

Froehling, Oliver. "The Cyberspace 'War of Ink and Internet' in Chiapas, Mexico." *Geographical Review* 87 (1997): 291–307.

Galtung, Johan. "Violence, Peace, and Peace Research." *Journal of Peace Research* 6 (1969): 167–91.

Galtung, Johan. "A Structural Theory of Imperialism." *Journal of Peace Research* 8 (1971): 81–117.

Gleditsch, Kristian S., and Michael D. Ward. "Double Take: A Reexamination of Democracy and Autocracy in Modern Polities." *Journal of Conflict Resolution* 41 (1997): 361–383.

Gleditsch, Nils Petter, Peter Wallensteen, Mikael Eriksson, Margareta Sollenberg, and Håvard Strand. "Armed Conflict, 1946–2001: A New Dataset." *Journal of Peace Research* 39 (2002): 615–637.

Goblet, Yves-Marie. *Le crépuscule des traités*. Paris: Beger-Levrault, 1934.

Godlewska, Anne, and Neil Smith, eds. *Geography and Empire*. Oxford: Blackwell, 1994.

Goertz, Gary, and Paul F. Diehl. *Territorial Changes and International Conflict*. Studies in International Conflict vol. 5. London: Routledge, 1992.

Gottmann, Jean. "The Background of Geopolitics." *Military Affairs* 6 (1942): 197–206.

Gottmann, Jean. "Geography and International Relations." *World Politics* 3 (1951): 153–173.

Gottmann, Jean. "The Political Partitioning of Our World: An Attempt at Analysis." *World Politics* 4 (1952): 512–519.

Gottmann, Jean. *La politique des états et leur géographie*. Paris: Arm Colin, 1952.

Gottmann, Jean. *The Significance of Territory*. Charlottesville: University Press of Virginia, 1973.

Graham, B., and P. Shirlow. "The Battle of the Somme in Ulster Memory and Identity." *Political Geography* 21 (2002): 881–904.

Grant, Richard, and Jan Nijman. "Historical Changes in U.S. and Japanese Foreign Aid to the Asia-Pacific Region." *Annals of the Association of American Geographers* 87 (1997): 32–51.

Greene, Owen, Barry Rubin, Neil Turok, Philip Webber and Graeme Wilkinson. *London after the Bomb: What a Nuclear Attack Really Means*. Oxford: Oxford University Press, 1982.

Grundy-Warr, Carl. "Peacekeeping Lessons from divided Cyprus." In *Eurasia, World Boundaries*, Vol. 3, ed. Carl Grundy-Warr, 71–88. London: Routledge, 1994.

Hartshorne, Richard. "The Functional Approach in Political Geography." *Annals of the Association of American Geographers* 40 (1950): 95–130.

Hartshorne, Richard. "Political Geography in the Modern World." *Journal of Conflict Resolution* 4 (1960): 52–66.

Haubrig, Hartwig, ed. *International Charter on Geographical Education, Proclaimed by [the] International Geographical Union Commission on Geographical Education, Washington, 1992*. Nürnberg: Hochschulverband für Geographie und ihre Didaktik, 1994.

Haushofer, Karl. *Geopolitik der Pan-Ideen*. Berlin: Zentral, 1931.

Haushofer, Karl, ed. *Macht und Erde*. Leipzig: Teubner, 1932.

Haushofer Karl. *Wehr-Geopolitik: Geographische Grundlagen einer Wehrkunde*. Berlin: Junker und Dünn Haupt Verlag, 1932.

Heffernan, Michael. "Geography, Cartography, and Military Intelligence: The Royal Geographical Society and the First World War." *Transactions of the Institute of British Geographers* 21 (1996): 504–533.

Heffernan, Michael. *The Meaning of Europe; Geography and Geopolitics*. London: Arnold, 1998.

Heffernan, Michael. "Professor Penck's Bluff: Geography, Espionage, and Hysteria in World War I." *Scottish Geographical Magazine* 116 (2000): 267–282.

Heffernan, Michael. "History, Geography, and the French National Space: The Question of Alsace-Lorraine, 1914–18." *Space and Polity* 5 (2001): 27–48.

Henrikson, Alan K. "The Geographical 'Mental Maps' of American Foreign Policy Makers." *International Political Science Review* 1 (1980): 495–530.

Hewitt, Kenneth. *Air War and the Destruction of Urban Places*. Waterloo: Wilfrid Laurier University, Department of Geography, 1982.

Hewitt, Kenneth. "Place Annihilation: Area Bombing and the Fate of Urban Places." *Annals of the Association of American Geographers* 73 (1983): 257–284.

Hewitt, Kenneth. " 'When the Great Planes Came and Made Ashes of Our City . . .': Towards an Oral Geography of the Disaster of War." *Antipode* 26 (1994): 1–34.

Holt-Jensen, Arild. *Geography: History and Concepts, a Student's Guide*. 3rd ed. London: Sage, 1999.

Hooson, David, ed. *Geography and National Identity*. Oxford: Blackwell, 1994.

House, John. "Political Geography of Contemporary Events: Unfinished Business in the South Atlantic." *Political Geography Quarterly* 2 (1983): 233–246.

House, John. "War, Peace, and Conflict Resolution: Towards an Indian Ocean Model." *Transactions of the Institute of British Geographers* 9 (1984): 3–21.

Johnson, Nuala. "Cast in Stone: Monuments, Geography, and Nationalism." *Environment and Planning D: Society and Space* 13 (1995): 51–65.

Johnson, Nuala. "The Spectacle of Memory: Ireland's Remembrance of the Great War, 1919." *Journal of Historical Geography* 25 (1999): 36–56.

Johnston, Ron J. *Geography and Geographers: Anglo-American Human Geography*. 5th ed. London: Arnold, 1997.

Johnston, Ron J., Derek Gregory, Geraldine Pratt, and Michael Watts, eds. *The Dictionary of Human Geography*. 4th ed. Oxford: Blackwell, 2000.

Jones, Emrys. "Problems of Partition and Segregation in Northern Ireland." *Journal of Conflict Resolution* 4 (1960): 96–105.

Jones, Stephen B. "A Unified Field Theory of Political Geography." *Annals of the Association of American Geographers* 44 (1954): 111–123.

Jones, Stephen B. "Global Strategic Views." *Geographical Review* 45 (1955): 492–508.

Jones, Stephen B. "Views of the Political World." *Geographical Review* 45 (1955): 309–326.

Katz, Yossi. "Transfer of Population as a Solution to International Disputes: Population Exchanges between Greece and Turkey as a Model for Plans to Solve the Jewish-Arab Dispute in Palestine during the 1930s." *Political Geography* 11 (1992): 55–72.

Kellerman, Aharon. "Comment on Falah." *Area* 27 (1995): 76.

Kidron, M., and R. Segal. *The War Atlas: Armed Conflict, Armed Peace*. London: Pan, 1983.

Kirby, Andrew, ed. *The Pentagon and the Cities*. Newbury Park, CA: Sage, 1992.

Kirby, Andrew. "What Did You Do in the War, Daddy?" In *Geography and Empire*, ed. Anne Godlewska and Neil Smith, 300–315. Oxford: Blackwell, 1994.

Kiss, George. "Political Geography into Geopolitics: Recent Trends in Germany." *Geographical Review* 32 (1942): 632–645.

Kjellén, Rudolf. *Staten som lifsform*. Stockholm: Politiska handböcker, 1916.

Kjellén, Rudolf. *Der Staat als Lebensform*. Leipzig: S. Hirzel, 1917.

Kliot, N., and Yoel Mansfeld. "The Political Landscape of Partition: The Case of Cyprus." *Political Geography* 16 (1997): 495–521.

Kliot, Nurit. *Water Resources and Conflict in the Middle East*. London: Routledge, 1994.

Kliot, Nurit. "The Grand Design for Peace: Planning Transborder Cooperation in the Red Sea." *Political Geography* 16 (1997): 581–603.

Kliot, Nurit, and Yoel Mansfeld. "Case Studies of Conflict and Territorial Organization in Divided Cities." *Progress in Planning* 52 (1999): 167–225.

Kliot, Nurit, and Stanley Waterman. "The Political Impact on Writing the Geography of Palestine/Israel." *Progress in Human Geography* 14 (1990): 237–260.

Kliot, Nurit, and Stanley Waterman, eds. *The Political Geography of Conflict and Peace*. London: Belhaven, 1991.

Knippenberg, Hans, and Jan Markusse, eds. *Nationalising and Denationalising European Border Regions, 1800–2000: Views from Geography and History*. Dordrecht: Kluwer Academic, 1999.

Korinman, M. *Quand l'Allemagne pensait le monde: Grandeur et décadence d'une géopolitique*. Paris: Fayard, 1990.

Kristof, Ladis K. D. "The Origins and Evolution of Geopolitics." *Journal of Conflict Resolution* 4 (1960): 15–51.

Kropotkin, Peter. "What Geography Ought to Be." *Nineteenth Century* 18 (December 1885): 940–956. Reprinted in *Antipode* 10 (1979/1980): 6–15.

Lacoste, Yves. "Enquête sur le bombardement des digues du fleuve rouge (Vietnam, été 1972): Méthode d'analyse et réflexions d'ensemble." *Hérodote* 1 (1976): 86–117.

Lacoste, Yves. *La géographie, ça sert, d'abord, à faire la guerre*. Paris: Maspéro, 1976.

Lacoste, Yves. "The Geography of Warfare: An Illustration of Geographical Warfare: Bombing of the Dikes on the Red River, North Vietnam." In *Radical Geography*, ed. R. Peet, 244–262. London: Methuen, 1977.

Lacoste, Yves, ed. *Dictionnaire de géopolitique*. Paris: Flammarion, 1993.

Le Billon, Philippe. "The Political Ecology of War: Natural Resources and Armed Conflicts." *Political Geography* 20 (2001): 561–584.

L'Estrange Bryce, Roland. "The Klagenfurt Plebiscite." *Geographical Journal* 60 (1922): 112–124.

Mackinder, Halford. "Geography as a Pivotal Subject in Education." *Geographical Journal* 57 (1921): 376–384.

Mackinder, Halford J. *Britain and the British Seas*. London: Heinemann, 1902.

Mackinder, Halford J. "The Geographical Pivot of History." *Geographical Journal* 23 (1904): 421–437.

Mackinder, Halford John. *Democratic Ideals and Reality: A Study in the Politics of Reconstruction*. London: Constable, 1919.

Malecki, Edward J. "Government Funded R&D: Some Regional Economic Implications." *Professional Geographer* 33 (1981): 72–82.

Malecki, Edward J. "Federal R&D Spending in the United States of America: Some Impacts on Metropolitan Economies." *Regional Studies* 16 (1982): 19–35.

Malecki, Edward J. "Military Spending and the US Defense Industry: Regional Patterns of Military Contracts and Subcontracts." *Environment and Planning C: Government and Policy* 2 (1986): 31–44.

Mamadouh, Virginie. "Geopolitics in the Nineties: One Flag, Many Meanings." *GeoJournal* 46 (1998): 237–253.

Maull, Otto. *Politische Geographie*. Berlin: Borntraeger, 1925.

Mayhew, R. "Halford Mackinder's 'New' Political Geography and the Geographical Tradition." *Political Geography* 19 (2000): 771–791.

Mayo, James M. "War Memorials as Political Memory." *Geographical Review* 78 (1988): 62–75.

Miller, Byron. "Political Empowerment, Local-Central State Relations, and Geographically Shifting Political Opportunity Structures: Strategies of the Cambridge, Massachusetts, Peace Movement." *Political Geography* 13 (1994): 393–406.

Minghi, Julian. " 'Do Not Start a Journal on Political Geography': Bowman to Whittlesey—1945." *Political Geography* 21 (2002): 731–744.

Mitchell, Bruce. "Politics, Fish, and International Resource Management: The British-Icelandic Cod War." *Geographical Review* 66 (1976): 127–138.

Morin, Karen M., and Lawrence D. Berg. "Gendering Resistance: British Colonial Narratives of Wartime New Zealand." *Journal of Historical Geography* 27 (2001): 196–222.

Morrill, Richard L. "The Responsibility of Geography." *Annals of the Association of American Geographers* 74 (1984): 1–8.

Most, B. A., and H. Starr. "Diffusion, Reinforcement, Geopolitics, and the Spread of War." *American Political Science Review* 74 (1980): 932–946.

Muet, Y. *Les géographes et l'Europe: L'idée européenne dans la pensée géopolitique française de 1919 à 1939*. Geneva: Institut européen de Genève, 1996.

Murphy, Alexander B. "Historical Justifications for Territorial Claims." *Annals of the Association of American Geographers* 80 (1990): 531–548.

Murray, Williamson. "Some Thoughts on War and Geography." In *Geopolitics, Geostrategy, and Strategy*, ed. Colin S. Gray and Geoffrey Sloan, 201–217. London: Cass, 1999.

Myers, Garth, Thomas Klak, and Timothy Koehl. "The Inscription of Difference: News Coverage of the Conflicts in Rwanda and Bosnia." *Political Geography* 15 (1996): 21–46.

Nagel, C. R. "Reconstructing Space, Re-creating Memory: Sectarian Politics and Urban Development in Post-war Beirut." *Political Geography* 21 (2002): 717–725.

Newman, David, ed. *Boundaries, Territory, and Postmodernity*. Portland, OR: Cass, 1999.

Newman, David. "From National to Post-national Territorial Identities in Israel-Palestine." *GeoJournal* 53 (2001): 235–246.

Newman, David. "The Geopolitics of Peacemaking in Israel-Palestine." *Political Geography* 21 (2002): 629–646.

Newman, David, and Ghazi Falah. "Small State Behaviour: On the Formation of a Palestinian State in the West Bank and Gaza Strip." *Canadian Geographer* 39 (1995): 219–234.

Newman, David, and Ghazi Falah. "Bridging the Gap: Palestinian and Israeli Discourses on Autonomy and Statehood." *Transactions of the Institute of British Geographers* 22 (1997): 111–129.

Newman, David, and Anssi Paasi. "Fences and Neighbours in the Postmodern World: Boundary Narratives in Political Geography." *Progress in Human Geography* 22 (1998): 186–207.

Nierop, Tom. *Systems and Regions in Global Politics: An Empirical Study of Diplomacy, International Organization, and Trade, 1950–1991*. Chichester: Wiley, 1994.

Nierop, Tom. "The Clash of Civilisations: Cultural Conflict, the State, and Geographical Scale." In *The Territorial Factor*, ed. Gertjan Dijkink and Hans Knippenberg, 51–76. Amsterdam: Vossiuspers UvA, 2001.

Nijman, Jan. *The Geopolitics of Power and Conflict: Superpowers in the International Systems, 1945–1992*. London: Belhaven, 1993.

Nijman, Jan. "Madeleine Albright and the Geopolitics of Europe." *GeoJournal* 46 (1998): 371–382 (wrongly numbered 267–278).

Nijman, Jan, and Herman van der Wusten. "Breaking the Cold War Mould in Europe: A Geopolitical Tale of Gradual Change and Sharp Snaps." In *The New Political Geography of Eastern Europe*, ed. John O'Loughlin and Herman van der Wusten, 15–30. London: Belhaven, 1993.

O'Dowd, Liam. "Coercion, Territoriality, and the Prospects of Negotiated Settlement in Ireland." *Political Geography* 17 (1998): 239–249.

Ó hUallacháin, Breandán. "Regional and Technological Implications of the Recent Buildup in American Defense Spending." *Annals of the Association of American Geographers* 77 (1987): 208–223.

O'Loughlin, John. "Spatial Models of International Conflicts: Extending Current Theories of War Behavior." *Annals of the Association of American Geographers* 76 (1986): 63–80.

O'Loughlin, John. "In a Spirit of Cooperation, Not Conflict: A Reply to Ward and Kirby." *Annals of the Association of American Geographers* 77 (1987): 284–288.

O'Loughlin, John, ed. *Dictionary of Geopolitics*. Westport, CT: Greenwood, 1994.

O'Loughlin, John, and Richard Grant. "The Political Geography of Presidential Speeches, 1946–87." *Annals of the Association of American Geographers* 80 (1990): 504–530.

O'Loughlin, John, and Henning Heske. "From 'Geopolitik' to 'Geopolitique': Converting a Discipline for War to a Discipline for Peace." In *The Political Geography of Conflict and Peace*, ed. Nurit Kliot and Stanley Waterman, 37–59. London: Belhaven, 1991.

O'Loughlin, J., and V. Kolossov. "Still Not Worth the Bones of a Single Pomeranian Grenadier: The Geopolitics of the Kosovo War, 1999." *Political Geography* 21 (2002): 573–599.

O'Loughlin, John, Tom Mayer, and Edward S. Greenberg, eds. *War and Its Consequences: Lessons from the Persian Gulf Conflict*. New York: HarperCollins, 1994.

O'Loughlin, John, Michael D. Ward, Corey L. Lofdahl, Jordin S. Cohen, David S. Brown, David Reilly, Kristian S. Gleditsch, and Michael Shin. "The Diffusion of Democracy, 1946–1994." *Annals of the Association of American Geographers* 88 (1998): 545–574.

O'Loughlin, John, and Herman van der Wusten. "Geography, War, and Peace: Notes for a Contribution to a Revived Political Geography." *Progress in Human Geography* 10 (1986): 484–510.

O'Loughlin, John, and Herman van der Wusten. "Political Geography of Pan-regions." *Geographical Review* 80 (1990): 1–20.

O'Loughlin, John, and Herman van der Wusten. "Political Geography of War and Peace." In *Political Geography of the Twentieth Century*, ed. Peter J. Taylor, 63–113. London: Belhaven, 1993.

Openshaw, Stan, Philip Steadman, and Owen Green. *Doomsday: Britain after Nuclear Attack*. Oxford: Blackwell, 1983.

O'Sullivan, P. "A Geographical Analysis of Guerilla Warfare." *Political Geography Quarterly* 2 (1983): 139–150.

O'Sullivan, Patrick. *Geopolitics*. London: Croom Helm, 1986.

O'Sullivan, Patrick. *Terrain and Tactics*. Westport, CT: Greenwood, 1991.

O'Sullivan, Patrick. "Geopolitical Force Fields." *Geographical Analysis* 27 (1995): 176–181.

O'Sullivan, Patrick, and Jesse W. Miller Jr. *The Geography of Warfare*. Beckenham: Croom Helm, 1983.

O'Sullivan, Patrick Michael. *The Geography of War in the Post Cold War World*. Lewiston, NY: Edwin Mellen, 2001.

Ó Tuathail, Gearóid. "Beyond Empiricist Political Geography: A Comment on van der Wusten and O'Loughlin." *Professional Geographer* 39 (1987): 196–197.

Ó Tuathail, Gearóid. "Foreign Policy and the Hyperreal: The Reagan Administration and the Framing of South Africa." In *Writing Worlds: Discourse, Text, and Metaphors in the Representation of Landscape*, ed. T. Barnes and J. Duncan, 155–175. New York: Routledge, 1992.

Ó Tuathail, Gearóid. "Putting Mackinder in His Place: Material Transformations and Myth." *Political Geography* 11 (1992): 100–118.

Ó Tuathail, Gearóid. "Problematizing Geopolitics: Survey, Statemanship, and Strategy." *Transactions of the Institute of British Geographers* 19 (1994): 259–272.

Ó Tuathail, Gearóid. *Critical Geopolitics: The Politics of Writing Global Space*. London: Routledge, 1996.

Ó Tuathail, Gearóid. "Theorizing Practical Geopolitical Reasoning: The Case of the United States' Response to the War in Bosnia." *Political Geography* 21 (2002): 601–628.

Ó Tuathail, Geraóid, and John Agnew. "Geopolitics and Discourse: Practical Geopolitical Reasoning in American Foreign Policy." *Political Geography* 11 (1992): 190–204.

Ó Tuathail, Geraóid, and Simon Dalby, eds. *Rethinking Geopolitics*. London: Routledge, 1998.

Ó Tuathail, Gearóid, Simon Dalby, and Paul Routledge, eds. *The Geopolitics Reader*. London: Routledge, 1998.

Paasi, Anssi. *Territories, Boundaries, and Consciousness: The Changing Geographies of the Finnish-Russian Border*. Chichester: Wiley, 1996.

Palka, Eugene J., and Francis A. Galgano Jr., eds. *The Scope of Military Geography: Across the Spectrum from Peacetime to War*. New York: McGraw-Hill, 2000.

Parker, Geoffrey. *Western Geopolitical Thought in the Twentieth Century*. London: Croom Helm, 1985.

Parker, Geoffrey. *The Geopolitics of Domination*. London: Routledge, 1988.

Parker, Geoffrey. "Ancel." In *Dictionary of Geopolitics*, ed. John O'Loughlin, 10–11. Westport, CT: Greenwood, 1994.

Parker, Geoffrey. *Geopolitics: Past, Present, and Future*. London: Pinter, 1998.

Parker, W. H. *Mackinder: Geography as an Aid to Statecraft*. Oxford: Clarendon Press, 1982.

Pepper, David. "Introduction: Geographers in Search of Peace." In *The Geography of Peace and War*, ed. David Pepper and Alan Jenkins, 1–11. Oxford: Blackwell, 1985.

Pepper, David, and Alan Jenkins, eds. *The Geography of Peace and War*. Oxford: Blackwell, 1985.

Power, M. "Geo-politics and the Representation of Portugal's African Colonial Wars: Examining the Limits of 'Vietnam Syndrome.' " *Political Geography* 20 (2001): 461–491.

Raffestin, Claude, Dario Lapreno, and Yvan Pasteur. *Géopolitique et histoire*. Paris: Payot, 1995.

Ratzel, F. *Anthropo-geographie, I: Anthropo-geographie oder Grundzüge der Anwendung der Erdkunde auf die Geschichte*. Stuttgart: Bibliothek geographischer Handbücher, 1882.

Ratzel, F. *Anthropo-geographie, II: Die geographische Verbreitung des Menschen*. Stuttgart: Bibliothek geographischer Handbücher, 1891.

Ratzel, F. *Politische Geographie*. Munich and Leipzig: Oldenbourg, 1897.

Ratzel, F. *Politische Geographie oder die Geographie der Staaten, des Verkehres, und des Krieges*. Munich: Oldenbourg, 1903.

Ratzel, F. *Politische Geographie*. Osnabruck: 2 eller, 1923.

Ratzel, F. *La géographie politique*. Paris: Fayard, 1987.

Ratzel, F. *Géographie politique*. Geneva: Editions Régionales Européennes; Paris: Economica, 1988.

Sack, Robert D. "Human Territoriality: A Theory." *Annals of the Association of American Geographers* 73 (1983): 55–74.

Sack, Robert D. *Human Territoriality: Its Theory and History*. Cambridge: Cambridge University Press, 1986.

Semple, Ellen Churchill. *Influences of the Geographic Environment on the Basis of Ratzel's System of Anthropo-Geography*. New York: Holt, 1911.

Sharp, Joanne P. *Condensing the Cold War: Reader's Digest and American Identity*. Minneapolis: University of Minnesota Press, 2000.

Shin, Michael, and Michael D. Ward. "Lost in Space: Political Geography and the Defense-Growth Trade-off." *Journal of Conflict Resolution* 43 (1999): 793–817.

Shirlow, Peter, and Mark McGovern. "Language, Discourse, and Dialogue: Sinn Fein and the Irish Peace Process." *Political Geography* 17 (1998): 171–186.

Sidaway, James D. "What Is in a Gulf? From the 'Arc of Crisis' to the Gulf War.' " In *Rethinking Geopolitics*, ed. Geraóid Ó Tuathail and Simon Dalby, 224–239. London: Routledge, 1998.

Sidaway, James D. "Iraq/Yugoslavia: Banal Geopolitics." *Antipode* 33 (2001): 601–609.

Singer, J. David. "The Geography of Conflict: Introduction." *Journal of Conflict Resolution* 4 (1960): 1–3.

Slowe, Peter M. *Geography and Political Power*. London: Routledge, 1990.

Smith, Neil. "Isaiah Bowman: Political Geography and Geopolitics." *Political Geography* 3 (1984): 69–76.

Smith, Neil. "Bowman's New World and the Council on Foreign Relations." *Geographical Review* 76 (1986): 438–460.

Smith, Neil. " 'Academic War over the Field of Geography': The Elimination of Geography at Harvard, 1947–1951." *Annals of the Association of American Geographers* 77 (1987): 155–172.

Smith, Neil. "For a History of Geography: Response to Comments." *Annals of the Association of American Geographers* 78 (1988): 159–163.

Solecki, W. D., and S. L. Cutter. "Living in the Nuclear Age: Teaching about Nuclear War and Peace." *Journal of Geography* 86 (1987): 114–120.

Sparke, M. "Writing on Patriarchal Missiles: The Chauvinism of the 'Gulf War' and the Limits of Critique." *Environment and Planning* A 26 (1994): 1061–1090.

Sprout, Harold, and Margaret Sprout. "Geography and International Politics in an Era of Revolutionary Change." *Journal of Conflict Resolution* 4 (1960): 145–161.

Sprout, Harold, and Margaret Sprout. *The Ecological Perspective on Human Affairs, with Special Reference to International Politics*. Princeton, NJ: Princeton University Press, 1965.

Spykman, Nicholas John. *America's Strategy in World Politics: The United States and the Balance of Power*. New York: Harcourt, Brace and World, 1942.

Spykman, Nicholas John. *The Geography of the Peace*. New York: Harcourt, Brace, 1944.

Starr, H., and B. A. Most. "Contagion and Border Effects on Contemporary African Conflict." *Comparative Political Studies* 16 (1983): 92–117.

Stoddart, D. R. "Geography and War: The 'New Geography' and the 'New Army' in England, 1899–1914." *Political Geography* 11 (1992): 87–99.

Stoltman, J. P. "The International Charter on Geographical Education: Setting the Curriculum Standard." *Journal of Geography* 96 (1997): 32.

Taylor, Peter J. *Political Geography: World-Economy, Nation-State, and Locality*. Harlow, UK: Longman, 1985.

Taylor, Peter J. *Britain and the Cold War: 1945 as a Geopolitical Transition*. London: Pinter, 1990.

Taylor, Peter J. *Modernities: A Geohistorical Interpretation*. Cambridge, MA: Polity Press, 1999.

Taylor, Peter J., and Colin Flint. *Political Geography: World-Economy, Nation-State, and Locality*. 4th ed. Harlow, UK: Prentice Hall, 2000.

Toset, Hans Petter Wollebaek, Nils Petter Gleditsch, and Håvard Hegre. "Shared Rivers and Interstate Conflict." *Political Geography* 19 (2000): 971–996.

Vallaux, Camille. *Le sol et l'état*. Paris: Doin, 1911.

van der Wusten, Herman. "The Geography of Conflict since 1945." In *The Geography of Peace and War*, ed. David Pepper and Alan Jenkins, 13–28. Oxford: Blackwell, 1985.

van der Wusten, Herman. "Political Geography at the Global Scale: The World Stage, Regional Arenas, the Search for a Play." In *Hundred Years of Progress in Political Geography*, ed. R. Dikshit. New Delhi: Sage, 1996.

van der Wusten, Herman. "Viewpoint: New Law in Fresh Courts." *Progress in Human Geography* 26 (2002): 151–153.

van der Wusten, Herman, and John O'Loughlin. "Claiming New Territory for a Stable Peace: How Geography Can Contribute." *Professional Geographer* 38 (1986): 18–28.

van der Wusten, Herman, and John O'Loughlin. "Back to the Future of Political Geography: A Rejoinder to Ó Tuathail." *Professional Geographer* 39 (1987): 198–199.

van der Wusten, Herman, and H. van Kostanje. "Diplomatic Networks and Stable Peace." In *The Political Geography of Conflict and Peace*, ed. Nurit Kliot and Stanley Waterman, 93–109. London: Belhaven, 1991.

Van Valkenburg, Samuel, ed. *America at War: A Geographical Analysis*. New York: Prentice-Hall, 1942.

Vasquez, John A. "Why Do Neighbors Fight? Proximity, Interaction, or Territoriality." *Journal of Peace Research* 32 (1995): 277–293.

Vidal de la Blache, Paul. *Tableau de la géographie de la France: Histoire de France depuis les origines jusqu'à la Révolution, Vol. 1*. Paris: Hachette, 1903.

Vidal de la Blache, Paul. *La France de l'est (Lorraine-Alsace)*. Paris: Colin, 1917.

Vidal de la Blache, Paul. *Principes de géographie humaine (publiés d'après les manuscrits de l'auteur par Emmanuel de Martonne)*. Paris: Colin, 1922.

Vidal de la Blache, Paul. *La France de l'est: Lorraine-Alsace*, 1917. Avec une présentation de Yves Lacoste, "Géographie et géopolitique." Paris: La découverte, 1994.

"War Services of Members of the Association of American Geographers." *Annals of the Association of American Geographers* 9 (1919): 53–70.

Ward, Michael Don, and Andrew M. Kirby. "Commentary: Spatial Models of International Conflicts." *Annals of the Association of American Geographers* 77 (1987): 279–288.

Warf, Barney. "The Geopolitics/Geoeconomics of Military Base Closures in the USA." *Political Geography* 16 (1997): 541–563.

White, G. F. "Notes on Geographers and the Threat of Nuclear War." *Transition* 14 (1984): 2–4.

White, G. F. "Geographers in a Perilously Changing World." *Annals of the Association of American Geographers* 75 (1985): 10–16.

Whittlesey, Derwent. *The Earth and the State: A Study of Political Geography*. New York: Holt, [1939] 1972.

Wilkinson, H. R. *Maps and Politics: A Review of the Ethnographic Cartography of Macedonia*. Liverpool: Liverpool University Press, 1951.

Williams, Colin H., and Stephen W. Williams. "Issues of Peace and Security in Contemporary Europe." In *The Political Geography of the New World Order*, ed. Colin H. Williams, 100–131. London: Belhaven, 1993.

Winters, Harold A. *Battling the Elements: Weather and Terrain in the Conduct of War*. Baltimore: Johns Hopkins University Press, 1998.

Wisner, Ben. "Geography: War or Peace Studies?" *Antipode* 18 (1986): 212–217.

Wright, John K. "Training for Research in Political Geography." *Annals of the Association of American Geographers* 34 (1944): 190–201.

Yiftachel, Oren. "The Internal Frontier: Territorial Control and Ethnic Relations in Israel." *Regional Studies* 30 (1996): 493–508.

4

HERMAN VAN DER WUSTEN

Violence, Development, and Political Order

How are "development" and "violence" related? What role does "political order" play as an intermediate modulator? Where is the geography in all this? These are the questions I want to tackle in this chapter. "Development" is by now a colloquial expression that needs some washing, cleaning, and pressing to be put to good use. "Violence" always was in and of the streets, but academic introspection has provided it with additional meaning that makes it a slightly ambiguous concept. "Political order" can use a tiny bit of elaboration at the outset.

"Development" in conjunction with rich and poor countries is a notion mainly popularized after World War II that indicated the belief that state societies may normally pass through stages on their way from poor to rich (as individual humans do in their development from child to adult). They may be early or late, quick or slow, and they can be assisted from the outside or hindered. In hindsight one would perhaps have expected more discussion of the possible conditions of "abnormal" or "retarded" development in the case of countries. Subsequently the development of countries became increasingly encompassing (e.g., political, social), but it soon turned out that the concept was clearly overstretched in this way. In addition, "development" became part of controversies where dependency, essential difference, nonlinearity, and contingency in different packages were marshaled against the protagonists of modernization and the policy field that had been put to work to solve the "development issue."

After more than fifty years of trying, development as a practice and an intellectual field is not in good shape. The overall faith is waning and the funding does not grow, many of the recipes do not work, and the field has lost a clear demarcation though not its focus. At the same time much partial progress has been made (e.g., in the field of health and education and in regions such as East Asia). Basic notions of poverty and wealth and their backgrounds are better understood—there are many more data, better models, and more interpretive knowledge. Development is described in levels. Each level refers to an average and a distribution of certain attributes for the population of a country. Development certainly needs institutional underpinnings, but different institutional provisions may be functional for one level of development. Development is realization of the good life and includes health, education, and a certain income, in short, the negative freedoms plus some positive freedoms that are much more difficult to indicate unambiguously. There is no need to renounce the ground gained, and I will therefore use data like those annually published by the World Bank in the *World Development Report* and by the United Nations Development Program (UNDP) in the *Human Development Report* and the insights that inform them in the remainder of this text. Their use does not imply that all state societies necessarily go through the same sequence of stages at the same rate, but it does imply that there are situations across state societies and through time that differ as regards rough levels of development. Each one of them has an accepted average and distribution of well-being. A general aim of governments (notwithstanding other aims that may contradict this one) is a higher level of development, and this is supported by international organizations.

"Violence" is conventionally understood to mean the infliction of bodily harm with the intent to hurt. Discussing this way of demarcating the concept, some have supported the widening of its scope by relaxing the restriction to bodies in order to include mental harm. There have also been proposals to do away with the directness of the act and its intentional character so that conditions where livelihood supports are withheld (enforced or not) can also count as violence. In this way mental and structural violence and all the different combinations they engender have become part of the discourse on violence. All in all, composite violence results in diminished health and in many cases in premature death. But diminished health and premature death cannot at the same time be outside the realm of human development. This means that development and violence, particularly in its extended version, overlap to some extent apart from the meaningful substantive relations they may otherwise entertain. This will be part of my concern in the following sections.

The debate on the preceding notions of violence and development has also been relevant to the conceptualization of peace. Peace may well be seen as absence of violence. As violence becomes multidimensional, so does peace: not only the absence of direct, physical violence, but possibly also the absence of mental and/or structural violence. Galtung, who has been one of the major contributors to these debates during recent decades, has changed one of his basic distinctions in negative and positive peace over time.[1] Originally he looked at negative peace as the absence of direct violence and at positive peace as the absence of structural violence (which would equal social justice and would become a major part of the development concept). In his recent work Galtung adds cultural violence (as the justification of the other two types of violence) to his earlier categories of direct and structural violence.[2] He now sees (positive) direct, structural, and cultural peace as the opposites of their violent counterparts and uses the notion of negative peaces for the midpoints on these scales. From an intervention point of view, action for any kind of negative peace in a situation of violence is curative, while action for any kind of positive peace is preventive. The negative peace syndromes are generally linked to dissociative approaches, the positive ones to associative approaches. Structural positive peace has Galtung's particular version of development as one of its main ingredients.[3]

"Political order" is the framework in which values are authoritatively allocated. The authorities in charge use the legitimate force at their disposal. The presence of a political order presupposes a certain level of acceptance from insiders as well as outsiders. But political order can, of course, be challenged and then be maintained or overrun. A political order disappears as its institutional framework collapses and allocation is the result of mere chance, ruse, and naked force. Political order implies rules about who makes decisions and rules about how decisions are made. Political orders can still hardly do without locations from which authority emanates, but they are not necessarily territorially demarcated, although a territorial base helps greatly. During recent centuries the interstate system has increasingly become the hegemonic global political order. As during earlier episodes such as the Napoleonic era and the years preceding World War I, there is much doubt, hesitation, and uncertainty about its prolongation. The globalization debate of the last ten years has in any case cast doubt concerning the consequences of the challenges to state authority from the regional level below the state, the regional level beyond the state, the global level, alternative state makers (eventually dressed up in one of the earlier roles), and fragmented sovereignties across sectors. Politics was always performed at different scales and in different sectors simultaneously. The state order instilled a certain rank order of importance that is now in jeopardy at different points in different places.[4]

There are three meaningful relations between development and violence. In the study of each of them geographers may fruitfully join, as they have already done on many occasions. In each of them they will benefit from work in different neighboring disciplines.

First of all, development is, among many other things, the decrease of premature death and a healthier quality of life while people are alive, and therefore less "structural violence." Geographers can map levels of structural violence as one dimension of development, look at changes over time, and look for covariation with other dimensions of development and for explanations that are sensitive to natural and social environmental factors. Development and structural violence as partly overlapping concepts are both supposedly sensitive to policy intervention; thus there is an incentive for the production of applied knowledge on a normative basis. In this field geographers will find the work of demographers and and of persons in the fields of in actuarial accounting and social medicine particularly insightful.

Second, development satisfies basic needs and provides opportunities for self-realization, but also new action repertoires. It may enhance the legitimacy of the political order, but may also unhinge it, and may increase social and political strength as well as strain. It therefore partly conditions levels of criminal and political violence directed at persons. These effects are intra-, inter-, and transnational. The overall sign of the impact is disputed. Geographers may particularly concentrate on levels, rates, and dispersal of development across space (which leads to the construction of regions and to the study of interrelations between places) in conjunction with the systems of territoriality in place (highlighting the borders in the political order). Spatial development distributions and the political order in which they take shape will jointly give rise to various types of violence. Geographers can usefully cooperate with political scientists and criminologists in this respect.

Third, structural violence conditions age pyramids, which have an impact on the nature of social problems such as the collective capacity to work and personal violence that may over a certain limit disrupt social life. Consequently, different types of violence will often have negative consequences for development processes. There is also a view that despite all negative consequences, organized violence may help in setting favorable terms for further development by selection and by providing room for innovation. Geographers could well use their skills to look for the contextual impact of certain types of violence on development processes and on how a violent context sets the terms for the institutional buildup that should undergird development processes. Studies that touch upon these issues will also be available in political sociology and anthropology.

Development and Violence Overlap

In the early 1960s, as the deterrent systems of the Cold War blossomed and the new political economy of the Third World was under construction, the Norwegian Johan Galtung started a new attempt to make room for an applied science of peace. In 1969 Galtung extended the traditional notion of violence as hurting or inflicting harm as a consequence of direct action by suggesting additional dimensions and cutoff points, as he has done for many other concepts that are central to peace studies.[5] This was one of a series of programmatic statements aimed at giving a sense of direction and a certain (wide) demarcation of the subject matter. As a point of departure, violence was said to be "present when human beings are being influenced so that their actual somatic and mental realizations are below their potential realizations."[6] The ensuing typology has been used in his work ever since. One major result has been the distinction between personal/behavioral and structural, or direct and indirect, violence. In the case of structural violence, there is no person who is producing the gap between the potential and the actual by directing the hurt or the harm, no subject of the act of violence. However, the structure in which people are embedded results in unequal exchange of goods and bads. Some are worse off and others better off than they would have been if another structure had been in place. The deprivation of those worse off demonstrates a gap between what was possible and what was realized, and this is violence. If only the structure resulted in an equitable distribution, the gap would disappear for those who are deprived, and structural violence would diminish.

From the outset it was obvious that structural violence overlapped with existing concepts ("In order not to overwork the word violence we shall sometimes refer to the condition of structural violence as social injustice")[7] and that conceptual and measurement difficulties abounded ("The meaning of 'potential realizations' is highly problematic").[8] What should count as "valuable"? Boulding mentioned an unkind commentator who thought that structural violence was anything Galtung disliked.[9] Was it an equitable distribution of resources or the equal distribution of power to decide over the distribution of resources that really mattered?[10] Nonetheless, in the first few years the notion of structural violence was picked up and tossed around.[11] A few studies suggested levels of structural violence in a population and some explanations of the variations.

Galtung and Höivik pursued the difference between a potential life expectancy and the actual life expectancy of an existing population as a promising way forward toward an overarching measurement of structural violence levels.[12] Höivik later introduced the index of structural violence as the difference between potential and actual life expectancy expressed in units of potential life expectancy.[13] It is a measure of the intensity of structural violence, as experienced by an average individual, over a complete lifetime. The annual quantity of structural violence can be derived from the intensity by multiplying it by the quotient of population size and life expectancy.

An error in this whole approach is the fact that all the direct violence that has occurred during the demographic history of the current population is (unavoidably) incorporated into the calculations of structural violence. In the execution of these calculations a major problem is the selection of potential values. It is assumed that a completely even distribution of income provides maximal access to health care for all and results in the highest possible life expectancy in a given population. There are two difficulties here. Some incomes will decline. Therefore there will be a decrease of life expectancies for some groups, but they are relatively very small because at the upper end of the income distribution income changes result in much less change in life expectancies. The other problem is the demarcation of the population in which redistribution takes place: national, macroregional, global? The pool of incomes to be redistributed makes an immense difference for those at the bottom and therefore results in very different gains in life expectancies. Höivik finally calculated that in 1970 the index of global structural violence (that is, the loss of life expectancy that could be avoided if incomes were divided equally worldwide) was 26% (with higher than average figures in Africa, India, and China), and the estimate of the number of deaths was eighteen million, assuming a stationary population. This assumption does not hold, and therefore the actual number of deaths would be higher.[14]

Höivik's further calculations were triggered by an article of Köhler and Alcock that produced a list of per country estimates of structural and behavioral violence in 1965 in terms of people killed.[15] Their measurement of structural violence had two versions: one with Swedish life expectancies as the potential values, the other the egalitarian model that assumed redistribution of intercountry differences in income (but did not take away intracountry variation). Their calculations resulted in fourteen to eighteen million deaths from structural violence in 1965. But again, their numbers include the consequences of direct (behavioral) violence in the cohorts that make up the current population in the potential (even Sweden has some deadly crimes) as well as in the actual life expectancies. In 1965 the number of deaths from behavioral violence was on the order of 1% of the level of structural violence, but those relations can fluctuate wildly in time and space. Well-nigh all violence, structural or behavioral, is in what they call the poor South (with 69% of the world's population at the time).

From their synchronic database regarding 1965, Köhler and Alcock had already learned that for lower and middle-income countries every additional 7.7% of gross national product (GNP) per capita results in a rise in life expectancy by exactly 1.0 year. They called this finding the "Economic Law of Life."[16] In a later article they tested their law diachronically. For a set of twenty-six poor countries it was found that in 1955–1965 every 7.3% increase in wealth (this time calculated in larger energy consumption per capita) resulted in a 1.0-year gain in life expectancy.[17] For higher income countries the diachronic data suggested differences in life expectancy that depended on political regime and not on wealth; in the diachronic data an effect of income rise remained, but it was much less pronounced than in poor countries (one-year gain in life expectancy for every 18% increase in wealth).

Although Köhler and Alcock's table showed an impressive cross-country variation in structural violence and their Economic Law of Life strongly suggested an explanation,[18] their article does not show any interest in the geographical distribution of their data. Johnston, O'Loughlin, and Taylor later mapped these same data on structural and direct violence in a contribution that put these results in a Wallersteinian world systems perspective.[19] They distinguished between various forms of behavioral violence (personal, property related, and politically related) and structural violence and connected these to the core-periphery structures that the political economy produces. They emphasized the different geographical scales at which these core-periphery structures and the different types of violence occur (e.g., intraurban segregation and criminal violence patterns versus interstate war). But a clear-cut explanation of patterns of violence by core-periphery formations was certainly not forthcoming. They suggested eight different versions (with various subtypes) of politically induced violence that involve all kinds of actors differently positioned in the core-periphery structure, and no systematic relation was proposed or found.[20]

Despite this incidental reuse of data, there has not been a sustained effort since the late 1970s to study structural violence empirically. Most of the research in peace studies was aimed at direct violence (if widening of the traditional concept took place, it was primarily in the sense of taking in psychic direct violence or violence directed at other sentients) in international wars, civil wars, and terrorism and its prevention. Development studies was the niche for interest in livelihood, survival strategies, and exploitation. The study of premature death, its quantification, and the ensuing loss of life years got much attention in this context. To the extent that demographic parameters were of concern, attention was primarily directed at fertility and the relation between production and consumption units in the household.

In the 1990s there was a renewed interest in this question, but from a completely different angle. In the framework of assessments of the efficacy and efficiency of health care systems and specific health care policies, the need for an appropriate metric had become obvious. This metric, called the global burden of disease (GBD), should have two components. One is the loss of life years on account of premature death; the other is the reduced well-being, possibly for prolonged periods of life, that results from diseases and injuries. The calculation unit is the disability-adjusted life year (DALY). The GBD refers to loss of DALYs. It can be expressed in numbers of DALYs (e.g., estimated at 1,362 million worldwide in 1990) or as lost DALYs in relation to population size in 1990 (e.g., estimated at 259 per 1,000 worldwide in 1990). It should be emphasized particularly in this last instance that DALYs refer to losses in the future as a result of events in a particular year, while they are related to current populations in the year of the events. Nonetheless, the figures are useful for comparative purposes.

One of the most impressive efforts to provide an overall picture of the state of health of the world population and the progress made in recent decades based on these notions is in the *World Development Report* of 1993.[21] It provides a detailed overview of 1990 and also deals with the period 1950–1990. To obtain values for the loss of DALYs in 1990 as a result of premature death, a life table is used for a low-mortality population ("West" family model) with life expectancy for females at 82.5 years and 80 years for males. This is similar to the choice of a potential population encountered in the earlier attempts. For disability resulting from disease or injury, the incidence of cases was estimated; the number of years of healthy life lost was then obtained by multiplying the expected duration by a severity weight (compared to loss of life).

There is a detailed classification of causes of DALYs lost. These refer to communicable and noncommunicable diseases with roughly equal proportions worldwide but much larger proportions of communicable diseases in the developing countries and noncommunicable diseases in the developed world. Injuries as a cause of DALYs lost are much less prominent (11.9% of the total GBD). Within this category there are estimates for homicides and violence (1.3% of total GBD) and war (1.0% of GBD) in 1990.[22] There are striking differences between males and females. The GBD for males is generally higher. This particularly results from the difference in the categories of injuries, from which males suffer to a much larger extent, and which include homicides and wars. In other words, these data suggest that males are particularly the prime victims from direct violence. This is particularly the case in sub-Saharan Africa and the former socialist countries of Europe, while in India and, less pronouncedly, in China, the disease burden for females is more severe than for men.[23]

Life expectancy during the last decades has risen spectacularly. This applies to all countries but particularly to the poorer ones. The gap in life expectancy between countries has appreciably shrunk. While in 1950 the difference between life expectancies in the developed world (capitalist and socialist) and the developing world was still twenty-four years (forty versus sixty-four), in 1990 the difference had diminished to twelve years (sixty-three versus seventy-five). The curve that resulted in Köhler and Alcock's Economic Law of Life still operates, but it changes over time. In fact, since 1900, for every period of thirty years the function of income versus life expectancy has become steeper for poorer countries, which implies that over time ever smaller rates of income growth have resulted in similar gains in life expectancy.

Although we cannot be sure by exactly how much, it is obvious that overall the difference between the potential and the realized life expectancies has diminished if we follow the earlier prescriptions for the calculation of this gap. Consequently—and taking into account the refinements elaborated in the World Bank report—levels of structural violence have diminished during the last few decades. They remain excessively high in sub-Saharan Africa (far more than twice the world average in DALYs per 1,000 population) and also in India. In the new GBD data direct violence is properly distinguished from structural violence. Direct violence was in 1990, as it was in 1965 and 1970, a small fraction of structural violence in whatever way it was measured.

The series of *Human Development Reports* issued by the UNDP has made further attempts to clarify notions of development and structural violence. The human development index (HDI) takes into account life expectancy, income, and educational achievement, which are backed up by further data on income distribution, population proportions lacking vital services, and trend data. The most recent *Human Development Report* has mixed messages.[24] On the one hand, the HDI is generally improving. For life expectancy this repeats the World Bank data for slightly different years. The results, again, are in fact spectacular. Life expectancy for the world increased from 59.9 to 66.4 years from 1970–1975 to 1995–2000. The increase was generally larger the lower the income. While in high-income countries the increase was 5.8 years, in middle-income countries it was 6.6 years, and in low-income countries it was 9.5 years. This general picture was repeated in most parts of the world, with two exceptions. In the former socialist countries there was a small (and probably temporary) setback of life expectancies during 1990–2000, while in sub-Saharan Africa during the same period the decline was more severe, to a large extent due to the HIV/AIDS epidemic.

From the narrow, but important, perspective of length of life as an indication of structural violence and development levels, according to all reasonable assumptions about what should be considered premature in premature death, development is improving and structural violence is receding, although both remain at unsatisfactory levels. At the same time one has to subscribe to one of the box headings in the *Human Development Report* that states, "Global inequality—grotesque levels, ambiguous trends."[25] While the gap in life expectancies is declining, the income gaps (even if they are measured in purchasing power parities) are extreme. The *Human Development Report* stresses the current gaps more than the trends. Some of the lower income countries have indeed grown faster than the high-income countries (notably China, but also India during more recent years), but others have stayed behind. In fact, the annual gross domestic product (GDP) growth rate per capita (in purchasing power parity in U.S. dollars) during 1975–2000 has been 2.1% for high-income countries, 1.8% for middle-income countries, and 1.5% for low-income countries, and thus in absolute terms the gap in wealth has widened enormously. As we saw earlier, the relation of income and health has become less tight for poorer countries, and thus these different indications of development have become ever more diverse. Finally, cross-country inequalities should not hide internal inequalities from view. In terms of income inequality, the *Human Development Report* now has Gini indexes for 117 countries.[26] A Gini index measures the difference between an equal and an actual distribution of an attribute in a population (i.e., income) with scores varing between 0 (perfect equality) to 100 (maximum inequality). These should obviously be used with even more caution than the other figures presented in this section. If we just average the indexes in the classes of countries with high, medium, and low human development indexes, we get, respectively, 32.4, 43.3, and 43.4. In interpreting these figures we should take into account that for countries with higher human development indexes more of the data are based on income than on consumption, and this results in higher inequality rates for similar cases. It is obvious that variations in intracountry inequality do not at all compensate for the stark differences between countries in terms of the number of people who suffer from completely insufficient development levels.

If anything, structural violence in the restricted sense in which we have encountered it here may be slowly receding. This by no means implies that action, political or otherwise, to speed up the process would be superfluous. More easily than in the past, increases in income can be translated into better, more effective health provisions. Information about large-scale food shortages is now generally and quickly available, and sufficient food can be shipped so that catastrophic famines are unnecessary. It is true that completely new challenges may arise at short notice, the HIV/AIDS epidemic or SARS, for example, that put existing health care systems and societies at large under enormous pressure. Nonetheless, the world political order should be able to universally close much of the gap between the potential and the realized in terms of basic health and survival chances. But major impediments to reaching that goal remain. The political order at the international level fails by allowing agricultural trade structures that constrain agricultural production in some of the areas where it is most needed. It also fails in some cases to respond sufficiently promptly to impending disasters. Some of these disasters are "man made," often by "political man." All kinds of conflicts produce environmental damage and disrupt social life, particularly by bringing refugee situations into being.[27]

Geographers could assist in the continued exploration of the notion of structural violence as it has unfolded in this section. Although Galtung initially tried to avoid the overlap of the concepts of structural violence and development, he changed tack later on, I think rightly. If we restrict structural violence to premature death (possibly extended by limited health), it remains important to follow the evolution of its distribution across the globe and to study the covariation with other development dimensions, as I did to some extent with income. The components of the *Human Development Report* are obviously prime subjects for such an exercise. The report only begins to explore the differences in rankings for individual countries.[28] Geographers should further aim their efforts in this area at two points: the contextual factors that impede putting adequate health care in place and making food available in concrete cases, and the comparative politics of livelihood threat.

The Violence-Development Loop

While both violence and development can be considered as broad concepts that at least partially overlap, there is also room for views that consider these notions as smaller in scope and separate. In that case the question is if and how they are related. It was suggested in the introduction that indeed they can be related, and in both directions at that. The connection of violence and development can therefore be conceptualized as a loop but this loop, is not necessarily straightforward in the sense of a positive or negative feedback dynamic. This is so for two reasons. The multidimensional nature of nonoverlapping violence and development allows for different relations that are not necessarily all in the same direction. Many of these relations are complicated because the political order plays an intermediary role that produces further ramifications. In this section I will first briefly look at the ways in which development may be consequential for direct violence and then indicate the chances for development as a result of structural and direct violence. This will finally allow some conclusions as to the possible nature of the violence-development loops that apparently operate simultaneously.

Development: Consequences for Direct Violence

In modulating the impact that development may have on violence, the political order is of the utmost importance. A political order is to a large extent a regulatory mechanism for the control of direct violence, while direct violence or at least the capacity to use it is at the same time supposedly assisting the maintenance of the political order. In the state system, that is still the centerpiece of the political order. States try to hold onto the monopoly of taxation and violence as the bases of their legitimate authority. To the extent that they are successful, imposed taxes are paid and the category of users of violence is restricted by acceptance of a norm (apart from its lawful use by state authority, violence is outside the accepted action repertory) and/or by deterrence. What happens as development increases or decreases, given that violence is as embedded as it is in the political order? What is the current cross-country variation of development and of violence, and do they correlate? If so, is this correlation stable over time? These questions are further complicated by the impact that the political order simultaneously has on development (this is currently known as the "good governance" issue in World Bank parlance). The geographers' special interest in all this will be in the specifics beyond regularities that case studies will uncover due to the contingencies that occur where space paths and time lines meet, but also in the more general guidance that spatial givens still impose on these processes and in the use of territoriality strategies by different actors.

There is obviously no agreement on these general questions or on their geographical elaborations in the literature. I will therefore briefly outline three descriptions of political order with their backward links to development and forward links to violence. These understandings of political orders have been culled from the literature and made into composite pictures that are tagged as liberal, realist, and state makers' order. In the literature the proponents of these models are most of the time in competition about their respective explanatory powers and prescriptive pros and cons. One may also look at them as ideal types approximated by the respective state systems in different parts of the world. In that light Europe would now (but much less in the past) be the closest in the international state system to a liberal order. Africa and Latin America would in slightly different ways qualify as current state makers' orders, while Pacific Asia would be the approximately realist order. Apart from the problem of how permanent such configurations will be, given their own dynamics, the intriguing question is how the current hyperpower, the United States, the other major powers with lesser but still existing global pretensions, and the emerging global polity will affect these macroregional configurations.

Since the 1980s, before the end of the Cold War, a huge literature on the "democratic peace" has developed.[29] It deals primarily but not exclusively with interstate relations and continues a position in the eternal debate on the possibilities of a peaceful interstate system that has been going on since the seventeenth century. Earlier emanations that also left traces in the academic literature were inspired by Wilson's views after World War I and transatlantic and Western European cooperation after World War II.[30] It puts itself up against the realist tradition that emphasizes the indivisible nature of states and the power distribution among them as the essential features to look at. The liberal (or idealist) tradition, on the other hand, emphasizes popular government and societal (transnational) interdependencies as the most important incentives to peace.

The democratic peace literature starts from the observation that democratic states rarely if ever go to war against each other. The interest in the taming of violence in mutual international relations has on a number of occasions been extended to the taming of internal violence by democracies. There has been a renewed focus on the analysis and prescriptions of Kant as set out in a number of texts, for example, "Perpetual Peace," which was written amid the onslaught of the French Revolution and continued a long-standing literary tradition among the cosmopolitan population of Europe.

Kant formulated three conditions that should jointly result in peaceful intra- and interstate relations. At the state level one needs liberal democracy (this is the contemporary translation of his ideas; Kant put particular stress on a good political constitution that guarantees civil rights). Democratic states will voluntarily join a confederation that will guarantee internal freedom to each partner and stimulate and, if need be, lawfully enforce peaceful mutual relations and collective defense against outside aggression. Citizens of democracies will freely enter into commercial and other relations with citizens of other democracies and thus forge ever-growing interdependencies. This is also the best basis for the creation of social wealth. Kant does not propose that this scheme be put in place in one stretch. In his view there is an evolutionary trend in this direction based on selection and learning behavior. Democracies have more survival chances and superior capacities to learn to follow the rule of law and to educate their citizens to act as supporters of peace. The evolutionary process is not without reversals, but the general trend should be clear in the longer term. War and upheaval (Kant was surrounded by them) act as incentives to give up a lawless state of savagery. The dynamics are important.[31]

For the last two centuries there is considerable evidence that democracies that are at least potentially relevant to each other (not too distant or with at least one major power in the dyad) tend to show less propensity to engage in mutual violent conflict relations, either wars or militarized disputes, than other dyads. This is particularly true for dyads that have been democracies for a long time (the maturity effect). It is possible that dispute probabilities generally, that is, in all types of dyads, go down over time, but these results need further confirmation. The two world wars were major upheavals of the system, and their consequences for the further spread of interstate peace have to be assessed.[32] At the same time intrastate violent conflict and war are also dependent on the nature of the political order. Democracies, but also autocracies, show lower propensities to civil war than regimes between these two polar types. Democracies simultaneously sustain higher levels of serious political conflict than other regime types, but fatalities, though frequently encountered, are rarely high in number. Polity change on the autocracy-democracy scale in whatever direction increases the chances of civil war. Halfway regimes and regime change each result in higher chances of civil war. Democracies diffuse in waves that are followed by partial reversals. On the average, democracies are more lasting political regimes than others.[33]

In the case of interstate conflict and war as well as in the case of serious political internal conflict and civil war, development level plays an important role. It diminishes violent conflict levels.[34] In addition, there is a fairly strong mutual positive relation between development and democracy.[35] There has been much debate about the proper sequencing and the leading factor. In Kant's view there is a virtuous circle in the dynamic relations between both phenomena, but this will not be generally supported. In sum, according to this argument, development through the character of the state and the state system lowers the chances of high-fatality political conflict. Development also makes a significant direct contribution in the same direction. Consequently, it is not impossible that the political world moves slowly, uncertainly, and with setbacks by way of waves of democratization and ongoing development in the direction of generalized democracy and higher development levels accompanied by fairly stable civil peace and a very low probability of interstate warfare and militarized disputes.

But there are still many uncertainties and countermovements that may not all result in positive selection and benign learning processes. The Kantian prescription of a general evolution in the direction of a confederacy still seems far-fetched. It is less than clear if recent democracies will be able to withstand the inevitable strains that they suffer, and it is very uncertain if the distribution of cosmopolitan citizens needed to breathe life into the whole scheme will result in sufficient numbers in the different parts of the state system. In the empirical record of the last two centuries, the uncanny presence of two devastating world wars demonstrates the frailty of the historical trends. For all types of wars taken together, there seems not to be any trend in the severity of war during the last two centuries. While interstate wars may slowly subside and wars conducted by members of the state system outside the system are a thing of the past as long as the state system remains universal in scope, the number of civil wars indeed increases.[36] The trend for civil war risks indicates steep increases from the 1940s to the 1980s. This is partly due to the increased number of states in the system, but there is an extra increase not predicted by the explanatory variables in the model that in themselves already account for rising numbers. A steep fall in this risk to the end of the research period in 1992 should, however, be added.[37] Other data indicate further decreases afterwards, contrary to popular belief and policy assumptions.[38]

Realists ground their argument on the continuing existence of a state system. The state system consists of sovereign powers that have the ultimate say over a piece of territory and the population that lives there. There is no overarching authority in the state system, and every member is ultimately acting alone. A state is a homogeneous unit. The ultimate way of conducting foreign relations is through the threat or the use of armed force, which is the power that really counts. Peaceful international relations are temporary states of the system that come about as a result of power balances (distribution plus links in alliances between system members). Peaceful balances provide a sense of security to supporters of the status quo and block opportunities for challengers to change the status quo to their own advantage.[39]

The realist argument generally had the upper hand during the Cold War and in many earlier periods of history, particularly among practitioners of statecraft. It is attractive to them because it makes a strict distinction between those who guide the state and the remainder of the population. It concentrates all attention on a small group of power holders who may put to use the assets of state power at their disposal. There is much to say to the idea that those in charge of foreign and security policy have long been a select club with internal codes who could do their business largely separate from the population at large. At the same time they were an international club that respected the rules of their own power games; that is, they could quarrel relentlessly and at the same time have a shared ethos to maintain peace as best they could, which occasionally may have run counter to the "objective" facts of power. A challenger, of course, could aim for a separate position, but he might very much look like a person in search of a new, very similar club.[40]

The realist argument is still preponderant as a working philosophy in the policy-making echelons of the armed forces and the diplomatic service in many countries, and the elegance of its few axioms and its logically derived wide-ranging consequences arouses respect. However, some of its most basic assumptions are increasingly undermined. Many states can under most conditions no longer be seen as homogeneous units. For states deeply enmeshed in the international co-operation of different kinds, the centers of command of the different policy sectors are to such an extent intertwined with those of other countries that they find it increasingly difficult to act alone. The recent tensions within the British cabinet have been called a Mozart opera by well intentioned observers,[41] but less friendly metaphors are prominently in use. For those states that lack the infrastructural power to act as a powerful mold to direct social life, potential assets on state territory cannot be mobilized when they are needed. The worst cases are known as failed states. In the first case, state organization fragments into a set of barely coordinated nodes in various networks; in the second case, state organization evaporates and transforms into an unpredictable vampire.[42] In both cases people's allegiances transnationalize and localize. Another realist assumption that has become debatable is the use of violence as the ultimate expression of power. The efficacy of organized violence in imposing states of affairs has become increasingly uncertain (perhaps less in preventing others from reaching their goals). The translation of other assets (loyalty, money) in organized violence has also become more problematic because force requirements can no longer be taken for granted.[43]

In the realist view it is the "wrong" distribution of supportive links (alliances) and military power among states that finally results in violence. This is interstate violence. Realism does not deal with intrastate violence: it is only a sign of weakness, possibly fatal, of an actor. Development may be relevant to the realist argument in two ways. First of all, a certain level of development required for a functioning state system must be maintained. The tax monopoly is an essential ingredient of the state as an institution; it assumes a certain level of commercialization of the economy. As the claims on states by their populations grow, their tax base has to grow. Within certain limits, this is only feasible in a growing economy. There is in a globalizing world a universalization of the norm of what a state minimally is, and the norm has an ever higher threshold value.[44] Many states fail to meet the expectations of their population. This may well result in growing numbers of failed states.[45] Second, to the extent that wealth can be translated into military power, development is part of a state's power base. Therefore, development level is a relevant item in assessing the balance of power that is the best guarantee for interstate peace. The direct positive influence of development on lowering the chances of violent conflict and war inside states and between them has already been mentioned. It cannot be properly incorporated into the realist argument because of its negligence of internal conflict and strongly distributional perspective.

The state makers' order is all about the construction and reconstruction of authority.[46] While the realist perspective draws all attention to cross-country variation, the main line of analysis here is the temporal change in individual countries, with the remainder of the state system at every moment as the context. Macro-historical changes in technology and social organization are taken into account. Political entrepreneurs manipulate, and social differentiation encourages, the emergence of tax and violence monopolies on which authority is ultimately built.[47] To enforce that monopoly in a certain territory, the means of violence are amassed by coercion (initial amounts of organized armed force organize larger installments from within the requested domain), by capital (extra taxation buys military force), or by both. These last states are the most successful ones. In the process, state organizations and their societies get necessarily ever more intimately interwoven.[48] The state collects much infrastructural power in the process, which allows it to become the most prominent societal mold. In the longer run, the state demand for extra tax payments is more easily accepted after popular claims have been met: if that does not happen, more coercion can be brought to bear. In the first case, states get more democratic and possibly more peaceful. In the second case, despotic power in Mann's terms predominates. These two paths do not necessarily diverge in a permanent way. A country's position may shift from despotism to democracy and back (this is in fact Mann's conclusion from the historical record).[49]

In this view the violence issue (its repression and its controlled application) is integral to the evolution of states. The means of violence are amassed in state organizations, and violence may disappear to a large extent from society. This is the civilizing effect of state making. The means of violence can be used either internally or externally by state organs, but it is risky, and there may be strong popular pressure to refrain from its use. However, the civilizing effect may be undermined and violence may be used in an upsurge of criminal behavior, or in collective politicized violence, or in severe repression by state organs, or in unrestrained international warfare. These different instances of decivilization often result from international instability in which the position of the state is considered to be at stake.[50]

This version of the state makers' order has two weak points. In its singular concentration on the internal rivalries that state makers have to sustain in their efforts to construct a viable and successful state, the external context tends to remain static. Although a large part of the function of the violence monopoly is obviously directed at possible external intruders, the dynamic interactions with outsiders get only scant attention. But much of the state makers' initial energy is necessarily directed at staking a claim against outsiders. In addition, in stages of the evolution of a state system when this demarcation is still a major issue within the system as a whole, the distinction between inside and outside is still extremely ambiguous, and a proper exclusion of outsiders cannot even occur. A second weak point is the inability to deal in greater detail with the conditions of civilization and decivilization. A major point should be the success or failure to maintain the monopoly of legitimate violence while simultaneously assessing the level of violence in which the state apparatus is engaged. Galtung is extremely dismissive of all claims of the peacefulness of Western democracies.[51] Lilla has proposed a historical analysis of the abuse (in terms of repression and violence) that polities commit.[52] In his view the abuse of political form should give rise to a typology of tyrannies. His primary attention is directed to states outside the circle of mature democracies, but there is no a priori reason why they should not be included. Instead of the pinpointing of an axis of evil, Lilla encourages the study "of the geography of a new age of tyranny" and laments, "As yet we have no geographers of this new terrain."[53]

Development is related to two aspects of state making: the mechanism of mobilization and the level of infrastructural power. Mobilization is achieved through coercion or through capital. If it is achieved through capital, it presupposes a commercialized and wealthy economy to pay for the soldiers of fortune.[54] In the current world there is in addition the question of financing the armaments. There is one exception to the commercial economy as a necessary condition in the contemporary world: the state maker who controls a valuable resource, for example, oil or diamonds. Their availability allows even quite underdeveloped economies where the distribution of wealth may be extremely uneven to mobilize armed force through capital. The level of infrastructural power is also closely connected to the level of social development. Many of the devices that are the basis of infrastructural power (stocked in an elaborate bureaucracy) are derived from social organizations outside the state and then put to use on behalf of the state.[55] The building of these surveillance equipments is often technologically driven, and they can only be operated in more developed environments. Consequently, as a general rule the level of infrastructural power is related to development levels.

What does this mean for the state makers' order in its dealing with violence in different developmental settings? Other things being equal, highly developed states will be less dependent on their population than on their financial means to engage in all sorts of violent encounters (this results in high levels of mechanization of armed forces, a nonconscript army, and privatization of security services). Higher levels of development result in higher levels of infrastructural power. The capabilities and therefore the dangers for state repression and violence primarily from that side mount accordingly (Mann's extreme type is the totalitarian state that combines a high level of infrastructural power with a high level of despotic power). Whether these dangers will materialize is utterly dependent upon the strength of civil society, the ability to complement state power with its control by the representatives of societal forces, in short, a high-quality democracy that includes the taming of social and political violence.

In conclusion, liberal, realist, and state makers' political orders deal differently with the problem of violence and are differently affected by changing levels of development. This is irrespective of the fact that development has a direct dampening effect on violence. In a liberal order violence disappears as a result of a recurrent learning process of a norm of nonviolence and the preponderance of the enlightened self-interest of those who thrive and let society thrive. In a realist order interstate violence is at best held in check by professional diplomacy that follows the natural givens, while intrastate violence is a sign of fatal failure in the functioning of one of the basic units. In a state makers' order interstate violence is a constant background threat that allows state makers to construct a tax base, while intrastate violence indicates the presence of dangerous rivals who should be outcompeted. Development helps dissolve violence in a liberal order, may benefit some while depriving others in a realist order, and dangerously strengthens the state's hand in a state makers' order by opening up multiple sources for the procurement of an organization of violence.

Geographers may particularly concentrate on matters that challenge their specific expertise as regards the specificities that remain when the general traits of a case have been dealt with, the impact of spatial givens, and the application of territoriality strategies. Let me give an example of each of them in dealing with the various political orders that I have distinguished in their connection with violence and the direct impact of development level on violence.

I start with examples where specificities come to the fore. In assessing the effect of development on violence, the connection of development and ethnicity is a major point of consideration. Development levels and ethnicity may coincide in a country, but they may also crosscut and everything in between. The precise relation and its dynamics are undoubtedly relevant for the chances of violent outbreaks. This has been extensively studied for many secessionary conflicts. These may occur under very different relative levels of development (e.g., Slovenia and Kosovo in the former Yugoslavia), and the question is how the specifics are relevant for the conflict in such cases. In the liberal order the conditions for successful confederal solutions may well differ, for example, depending on the distribution of strengths and weaknesses between the potential partners. This is relevant in the different successes of the European Union and transatlantic cooperation. In the realist order relevant items in the balance of power may well vary from one configuration to the next. Mackinder's initial warnings about changing geopolitical realities during the Great Game between Russia and Britain around 1900 were based on the recent introduction of railway infrastructure in the Asiatic part of Russia.[56] In the state makers' order the psychohistory of key figures is important, each with their idiosyncrasies. In some contexts place of origin plays a considerable role, for example Tikrit in the case of Saddam Hussein.

As regards spatial givens, the relation between development and violence may be clarified by the spatial patterns of development and the terrain conditions set for military campaigns.[57] The success of a liberal order may well be compromised by the spatial concentration of the cosmopolitans needed to civilize the population at large. This would occur by an excessive concentration of central functions such as one finds in the classic cases of primary cities, currently, for example, in Bangkok. Alliances in a realist order may partly be based on connectivities that find their origin in the spatial arrangement of countries, while such alliances may not be favorable for a balance of power, which theoretically should keep the system pacified. In a state makers' order the spatial distribution of economic activity indicates ways in which the all-important tax collection can most profitably be arranged.

Territoriality strategies are also relevant in all these different instances. The secession option that we just encountered is a typical strategy that uses territoriality and that quite possibly disturbs any outcome developmental level may otherwise have on violence. In a liberal order the porosity of borders and incorporation policies regarding new migrants are extremely important. Their nature is supposedly important for the chances of a liberal order to remain peaceful. A realist order would put stress on territoriality strategies from the standpoint of including a desirable resource base and excluding inconvenient assets from the perspective of contributing to an appropriate balance of power. In a state makers' order states manipulate their internal administrative structure with an eye to optimize state unity. Famous contrary cases are the French departmental system that blotted out traditional units of cohabitation (the *pays*) and the Soviet constitution that provided room for ethnic constructions that finally helped destroy the state.

Structural and Direct Violence Complicate the Chances for Development, but. . . .

Structural violence as earlier defined tends to complicate the development process. Paradoxically, its abolition might hurt development as well. As the opportunities for prolonging life open up, infant mortality tends to decrease first. But structural violence remains large as long as infant mortality is still higher than elsewhere and mortality in the higher age brackets is still much higher. This may turn into a demographic catastrophe when mortality in productive age groups goes up disproportionately, for example, as a result of infectious diseases like HIV/AIDS. Consequently, at least initially, the number of consumption units in a population tends to grow much faster than the number of production units. This makes a rapid pace of economic growth more difficult (but straightforward Malthusian links should not be made).[58] As mortality chances decrease over an ever larger part of the whole lifetime, the difference between production and consumption units subsides, but it will again increase as the retirement population grows faster than those in their productive years. In addition, as a population ages (and structural violence thus recedes), the chances for further development are complicated from a different corner. Population growth may turn negative; this tends to produce scarcities on the labor market that hamper growth. In addition, many product markets shrink, which also may diminish per capita growth. Finally, older populations may collectively lack the incentive to weigh the future very heavily and to invest in growth; most spectacularly, the interest in and need of care arrangements will grow, and the interest and drive to invest in education may subside. This does not stimulate the growth of human capital, which is a vital ingredient of economic growth and development more generally.

Direct violence destroys human life and very often damages the material infrastructure of society, including the capital goods that enable economic growth. In this way it hampers development. This is true of all forms of direct violence, from individual criminal acts to large-scale war damage. High-technology war has the promise of limiting the "collateral damage" by precision guidance of weapon systems and superior intelligence to pinpoint the targets, but it has the capacity of unheard of human-caused disaster from physical, chemical, and biological impacts. Direct violence has further, more hidden unfavorable consequences for development. It undermines the trust between people that is necessary for the engagement in market relations and the taking of longtime economic risks that underpin many investment behaviors. Engaging in direct violence also undermines the rule of law. It is a direct infraction by those who should abide by the law. If it is used frequently by the forces of order, it is a sign of weak legitimacy of the political order because this presupposes that the monopoly use of legitimate violence should have to be activated only rarely in order not to be eroded. The rule of law, the presence of a stable, regulatory environment, is a necessary condition for the flourishing of economic life and thus for development.

Two further possible links between violence and development should perhaps be briefly mentioned. There is one further possible connection between the age pyramid and development, but the age pyramid in this case conditions direct, not indirect, violence. It has often been mentioned that the proportion of young, male adults (perhaps, in particular, singles) increases the probability of violence. It is, after all, this category that engages most frequently in this kind of behavior in criminal settings as well as in politicized violence and in the fighting part of the army and policy forces. This demographic feature has been mentioned as an explanatory factor in the subsiding of urban violence in the United States during the 1990s and in the volatility of politicized violence in the Middle East. The other link is that between defense expenditures and development budgets, that is, to what extent there is a choice for governments in the orientation of their budgets that would then result in consequences for the rate of actual development.

Direct violence tends to hamper development, but this, again, is not the entire story. There is a contrary long-standing view that considers war and its concomitant destruction as one of the fairly rare occasions where societies are challenged to the utmost, where the best prevail, and additionally, where destruction opens up opportunities to start anew with well-adapted new versions of equipment and institutions. These peak experiences would thus result in Darwinian selection and adaptation and consequently stimulate development.[59] Such views have always been strongly opposed, for example, by peace researchers in the tradition of Wright, Boulding, and Galtung.[60]

One pressing task for geographers is the assessment of material and environmental damage by large-scale violence that balances the claims of precision versus destructive potential. Material and environmental destruction is a major item in the balance sheet of warfare. In the first instance it is less crucial than the direct fatalities, but it may well result in further losses of life, which brings us back to the other part of the violence-development loop. In the same perspective this balance of destruction is a crucial pillar in the argument about the functionality of large-scale violent conflict for further development. This argument should be empirically countered head on. How well did Germany's and Japan's late war destruction serve their postwar redevelopment? How functional are Angola's thirty-year civil war and Iraq's damage in both Gulf Wars for their reconstruction? One may have moral qualms about such claims. The destruction should certainly not be exclusively assessed in these terms. But a complete discussion of the morality of such destructive acts should also include the assessment of these consequences and they require a hard-nosed calculation.

A Summary Answer

Is there a development-violence loop, a general interconnection that tends to move the levels of development and violence upward or downward or holds dynamics in check by a feedback mechanism? It seems that very generally there is: development tends to press down violence, and low levels of violence tend to stimulate development. But there are many countermovements and confounding consequences. In an evolving liberal order where development grows, violence may further dissolve. But in a realist order the distribution of development is crucial, and it may well disturb the chances of a continuing interstate peace. In a state makers' political order development induces the concentration of increasing power in the hands of a state apparatus that may consequently misuse it in repression and violence. From the other side, the question remains whether under certain conditions diminishing structural violence may not at the same time introduce new handicaps for further development and whether the challenge and the damage of large-scale organized violence may not sometimes remove some of the obstacles for renewed development. Geographers should contribute by considering the balance of the major loop of development and violence versus the potentially disturbing factors in each specific case, by assessing the importance of the spatial givens that are the unavoidable ingredients of the material world, and by concentrating on the territoriality strategies that are a vital part of the politicomilitary sphere.

Conclusion

This effort to explore the intellectual territory of the concepts of violence and development does not end in a few neatly drawn conclusions that unambiguously mark the current state of affairs and point to the highway ahead that is already under construction. I hope to have indicated a small number of credible positions from which to explore these issues and to have probed into the future by putting up some signposts and indicators that refer to what may lie ahead. Let me slightly elaborate on two points made earlier.

Development as welfare and violence as premature death are partially overlapping concepts. This is particularly true for welfare and structural violence, which refers to the harm suffered from inadequate social structures. The notion of structural violence is difficult to operationalize. If measurements as proposed in the 1970s (notably based on the distribution of expectations of life at birth) are accepted as approximations, structural violence has declined since that time. But the relation between income (another vital aspect of welfare) and premature death has become less narrow during the same period. Consequently, even in these simple terms, development has become more multidimensional. While global income differences have remained "grotesquely unequal," global differences in health and structural violence have declined. This is not to say that metrics like the gross burden of disease are roughly invariant across the world; far from it. New communicable diseases like HIV/AIDS and a possible new scare around SARS may rapidly and importantly change the picture.

Although development and violence are separated conceptually, they are related in various ways. Political orders play an important intermediary role. Even before one draws out the various connections in specific cases, it would perhaps be wise to follow Lilla's call for a study of the geography of new tyrannies in an extended version.[61] The years 1989–2001 may be seen as a lull in the evolution of the interstate system that included a series of failed efforts to draw definite new lines and to build a new architecture for the institutionalization of this new stage. More recently the one hyperpower, the United States has put itself up as a new activist in world affairs, and the nature of its approach has induced others to more pronounced points of view. Too many new world orders have been announced in the past without clear result, but this could now be different. What is badly needed under the circumstances, among other things, is a renewed composite mapping of the various ways in which political orders—states and emerging alternatives—deteriorate into violence and decivilize: tyrannies as malformed apparatuses of rule, politicized collective violence and criminal violence as derailed citizenship. These are all signs of bad or failing governance. How do the approximations of liberal orders, realist orders, and state makers' orders fare? How harmful are these signs of bad governance for the various dimensions of development? Contrary to this, where are the systems with the strength to withstand decivilizing impulses? How well do they cope with the requirements of developmental processes? The ensuing atlas is a tall order, but it would be extremely useful as a road map of what to avoid and what to pursue.

Notes

1. One of his earliest substantive contributions is Galtung, "Violence, Peace, and Peace Research."
2. Galtung, *Peace by Peaceful Means*, 196–210.
3. Ibid., 3, 32, 33, 61.
4. Anderson, "Exaggerated Death of the Nation-State"; Held et al., Perraton *Global Transformations*; Van Creveld, *Rise and Decline of the State*.
5. Galtung, "Violence, Peace, and Peace Research."
6. Ibid., 168.
7. Ibid., 169.
8. Ibid.
9. Boulding, "Twelve Friendly Quarrels with Johan Galtung," 84.
10. Galtung, "Violence, Peace, and Peace Research," 171.
11. Galtung and Höivik, "Structural and Direct Violence."
12. Ibid.
13. Höivik, "Demography of Structural Violence."
14. Ibid.
15. Ibid.; Köhler and Alcock, "Empirical Table of Structural Violence."
16. Köhler and Alcock, "Empirical Table of Structural Violence," 354.
17. Alcock and Köhler, "Structural Violence at the World Level," 261.
18. Köhler and Alcock, "Empirical Table of Structural Violence."
19. Johnston, O'Loughlin, and Taylor, "Geography of Violence and Premature Death."
20. Ibid., 249.
21. World Bank, *World Development Report 1993*.
22. Ibid., tables B2 and B3, 216–219.
23. Ibid., 28.
24. United Nations Development Program (UNDP), *Human Development Report 2002*.
25. Ibid., 19.
26. Ibid., table 13, 194–197.
27. Homer-Dixon, *Environment, Scarcity, and Violence*.
28. UNDP, *Human Development Report 2002*, 35.
29. For a first summary, see Russett, *Grasping the Democratic Peace*.
30. Deutsch, *Political Community and the North Atlantic Area*.
31. Cederman, "Back to Kant."
32. Ibid.
33. Hegre et al., "Toward a Democratic Civil Peace?"; Gleditsch, "Special Section on Democracy, War, and Peace."
34. Cederman, "Back to Kant," tables 3 and 4; Hegre et al., tables 2 and 3.
35. Lipset, "Some Social Requisites of Democracy."
36. Sarkees, Wayman, and Singer, "Inter-state, Intra-state, and Extra-state Wars."
37. Hegre et al., "Toward a Democratic Civil Peace?"
38. Wallensteen and Sollenberg, "Armed Conflict, 1989–2000," 635–649.
39. The classic statement is Carr, *Twenty Years' Crisis, 1919–1939*, which was followed

by Morgenthau, *Politics among Nations.* A renewed neoclassic formulation is Waltz, *Theory of International Politics.*

40. For a thorough treatment of the underpinnings of these clubs, see Watson, *Diplomacy.*

41. McGrew, "Power Shift," 145.

42. A classic image is provided by Naipaul, *Bend in the River.*

43. Van Creveld, *Technology and War.*

44. Charles Tilly, *Coercion, Capital, and European States,* AD *990–1992.*

45. A successful explanatory model for state failure is Esty et al., "State Failure Task Force Report."

46. Inspired by Max Weber, the main protagonist used here, are Elias, *Über den Prozess der Zivilisation*; Tilly, *Coercion, Capital, and European States*; and Mann, "Autonomous Power of the State."

47. This is central to Elias's view. See Elias, *Über den Prozess der Zivilisation.*

48. This is the thrust of Tilly, *Coercion, Capital, and European States.*

49. Mann, "Autonomous Power of the State."

50. Zwaan, *Civilisering en decivilisering.*

51. Galtung, *Peace by Peaceful Means.*

52. Lilla, "New Age of Tyranny."

53. Ibid., 29.

54. Tilly, *Coercion, Capital, and European States,* uses the Netherlands during its Golden Century period in the seventeenth century as his prime example.

55. Mann, "Autonomous Power of the State."

56. Mackinder, "Geographical Pivot of History."

57. In Keegan and Wheatcroft, *Zones of Conflict,* these items play a major role.

58. Easterlin, *Population, Laborforce, and Long Swings in Economic Growth.*

59. Steinmetz, *Philosophie des Krieges,* reissued and updated as *Soziologie des Krieges.*

60. Galtung, *Peace By Peaceful Means*; Wright, *A Study of War,* Boulding, *Stable Peace.*

61. Lilla, "New Age of Tyranny."

References

Alcock, Norman, and Gernot Köhler. "Structural Violence at the World Level: Diachronic Findings." *Journal of Peace Research* 16 (1979): 255–262.

Anderson, James. "The Exaggerated Death of the Nation-State." In *A Global World? Re-ordering Political Space,* ed. James Anderson, Chris Brook, and Allan Cochrane, 65–112. Oxford: Oxford University Press, 1995.

Boulding, Kenneth E. "Twelve Friendly Quarrels with Johan Galtung." *Journal of Peace Research* 14 (1977): 75–86.

Boulding, Kenneth E. *Stable Peace.* Austin: University of Texas Press, 1981.

Carr, E. H. *The Twenty Years' Crisis, 1919–1939. An Introduction to the Study of International Relations.* London: Macmillan, 1939.

Cederman, Lars-Erik. "Back to Kant: Reinterpreting the Democratic Peace as a Macro-historical Learning Process." *American Political Science Review* 95 (March 2001): 15–31.

Deutsch, Karl W. *Political Community and the North Atlantic Area.* Princeton, NJ: Princeton University Press, 1957.

Easterlin, Richard. *Population, Laborforce, and Long Swings in Economic Growth: The American Experience.* New York: Columbia University Press, 1968.

Elias, Norbert. *Über den Prozess der Zivilisation: Soziogenetische und psychogenetische Untersuchungen. Teil 2: Wandlungen der Gesellschaft: Entwurf zu einer Theorie der Zivilisation.* Basel: Haus zum Falken, 1939.

Esty, Daniel C., Jack A. Goldstone, Ted Robert Gurr, Barbara Harff, Marc Levy, Geoffrey D. Dabelko, Pamela T. Surko, and Alan N. Unger. "State Failure Task Force Report: Phase II Findings." *Environmental Change and Security Project Report of the Woodrow Wilson Center* (summer 1999): 49–72.

Galtung, Johan. "Violence, Peace, and Peace Research." *Journal of Peace Research* 6 (1969): 167–191.

Galtung, Johan. *Peace by Peaceful Means: Peace and Conflict, Development and Civilization.* Oslo: PRIO; London: Sage, 1996.

Galtung, Johan, and Tord Höivik. "Structural and Direct Violence: A Note on Operationalization." *Journal of Peace Research* 8 (1971): 73–76.

Gleditsch, N. P., ed. "Special Section on Democracy, War, and Peace." *Journal of Peace Research* 29 (1992): 377–434.

Hegre, Håvard, Tanja Ellingsen, Scott Gates, and Nils Petter Gleditsch. "Toward a Democratic Civil Peace? Democracy, Political Change, and Civil War, 1816–1992." *American Political Science Review* 95 (March 2001): 33–48.

Held, David, Anthony McGrew, David Goldblatt, and Jonathan Perraton. *Global Transformations: Politics, Economics, and Culture.* Cambridge, MA: Polity, 1999.

Hibbs, Douglas A. *Mass Political Violence: A Cross-National Causal Analysis.* New York: Wiley, 1973.

Höivik, Tord. "The Demography of Structural Violence." *Journal of Peace Research* 14 (1977): 59–74.

Homer-Dixon, Thomas F. *Environment, Scarcity, and Violence.* Princeton, NJ: Princeton University Press, 1999.

Johnston, R. J., J. O'Loughlin, and P. J. Taylor. "The Geography of Violence and Premature Death: A World-Systems Approach." In *The Quest for Peace: Transcending Collective Violence and War among Societies, Cultures, and States,* ed. R. Väyrynen, D. Senghaas, and Schmidt, 241–259. London: Sage, 1987.

Keegan, John, and Andrew Wheatcroft. *Zones of Conflict—An Atlas of Future Wars.* London: Cape, 1986.

Köhler, Gernot, and Norman Alcock. "An Empirical Table of Structural Violence." *Journal of Peace Research* 13 (1976): 343–356.

Lilla, Mark. "The New Age of Tyranny." *New York Review of Books* 41 (October 24, 2002): 28–29.

Lipset, Seymour Martin. "Some Social Requisites of Democracy: Economic Development and Political Legitimacy." *American Political Science Review* 53 (1991): 69–105.

Mackinder, Halford J. "The Geographical Pivot of History." *Geographical Journal* 23 (1904): 421–437.

Mann, Michael. "The Autonomous Power of the State." *Archives européennes de sociologie* 25 (1984): 185–202.

McGrew, Anthony. "Power Shift: From National Government to Global Governance?" In *A Globalizing World? Culture, Economics, Politics,* ed. David Held, 127–167. London: Routledge, 2000.

Morgenthau, Hans J. *Politics among Nations: The Struggle for Power and Peace.* New York: Knopf, 1978.

Naipaul, V. S. A *Bend in the River*. New York: Knopf, 1979.

O'Loughlin, John, Michael D. Ward, Corey L. Lofdahl, Jordin S. Cohen, David S. Brown, David Reilly, Kristian S. Gleditsch, and Michael Shin. "The Diffusion of Democracy, 1946–1994." *Annals of the Association of American Geographers* 88 (1998): 545–574.

Russett, Bruce M. *Grasping the Democratic Peace: Principles for a Post–Cold War World*. Princeton, NJ: Princeton University Press, 1994.

Sarkees, Meredith Reid, Frank Whelon Wayman, and J. David Singer. "Inter-state, Intra-state, and Extra-state Wars: A Comprehensive Look at Their Distribution over Time, 1816–1997." *International Studies Quarterly* 47 (March 2003): 49–70.

Steinmetz, Sebald Rudolf. *Philosophie des Krieges*. Leipzig: Barth, 1907. Reissued as *Soziologie des Krieges*. Leipzig: Barth, 1929.

Tilly, Charles. *Coercion, Capital, and European States*, AD *1990–1992*. Cambridge, MA: Blackwell, 1992).

United Nations Development Program. *Human Development Report 2002: Deepening Democracy in a Fragmented World*. New York: Oxford University Press, 2002.

Van Creveld, Martin. *Technology and War: From 2000 B.C. to the Present*. Rev. and exp. ed. New York: Free Press, 1991.

Van Creveld, Martin. *The Rise and Decline of the State*. Cambridge: Cambridge University Press, 1999.

Wallensteen, Peter and Margareta Sollenberg. "Armed Conflict, 1989–2000." *Journal of Peace Research* 38 (2001): 635–649.

Waltz, K. *Theory of International Politics*. Reading, MA: Addison-Wesley, 1979.

Watson, Adam. *Diplomacy: The Dialogue between States*. London: Methuen, 1983.

World Bank. *World Development Report 1993: Investing in Health*. New York: Oxford University Press, 1993.

World Bank. *World Development Report 1997: The State in a Changing World*. New York: Oxford University Press, 1997.

Wright, Quincy. A *Study of War*. Chicago: Chicago University Press, 1981.

Zwaan, Ton. *Civilisering en decivilisering: Studies over Staatsvorming en geweld, nationalisme en vervolging*. Amsterdam: Boom, 2000.

5

JOHN O'LOUGHLIN

The Political Geography of Conflict

Civil Wars in the Hegemonic Shadow

The attack by the United States on Iraq in March 2003 was atypical of contemporary conflicts. While the attempt to kill Saddam Hussein on March 19 marked the opening of hostilities and was broadcast worldwide instantaneously, a much more destructive conflict that had raged for five years in the Democratic Republic of the Congo continued to receive hardly any notice. The war to depose the Hussein regime resulted in fewer than 12,000 dead (122 U.S. and U.K. troops, 6,000–7,000 civilians, and about 5,000 Iraqi military casualties).[1] The civil wars in the Congo (formerly Zaire) since 1998 have resulted in 3.1 to 4.7 million dead, with 250,000 killed in the fighting near Bunia (eastern Congo) in 2002–2003.[2] Conflict directly caused 300,000 deaths worldwide in 2000, more than half of them in Africa. Conflict directly accounts for 0.5% of all global deaths; the indirect effects are significantly larger.[3]

These gruesome comparative statistics on casualties illustrate well the main themes of this chapter about post–Cold War conflicts. First, contemporary wars are disproportionately civil conflicts; only a handful of interstate wars have occurred in the last decade. Second, the United States has been disproportionately involved in both interstate and civil wars, either directly by attacking another country (Panama in 1989, Iraq in 1991, Yugoslavia in 1999, Afghanistan in 2001, Iraq in 2003) or indirectly by supporting governments that are under pressure from rebels (e.g., Haiti, Pakistan, Colombia, Israel, Turkey, the Philippines, Macedonia, Indonesia, and Saudi Arabia). Third, civil wars are lasting longer than ever before; the average length is now eight years. Fourth, civil wars are much more destructive of life and property than interstate wars, partly because international structures and rules are either unavailable or ignored. More mechanisms exist to resolve interstate disputes. Fifth, overwhelming U.S. military power and a growing disparity with its opponents have resulted increasingly in asymmetric use of force and "risk-transfer wars."[4] Tiny U.S. casualties stand in sharp contrast to large numbers of civilian and military deaths in the countries under attack. The gap is expected to grow as U.S. military expenditures soon equal those of *all* other countries combined and new high-tech weaponry is rushed into production. In the 1989 world, the superpowers blackmailed each other through the threat of nuclear annihilation; the new world order is completely dominated by an American hegemon that shows little hesitation in pushing its ideological agenda by using military and economic weapons.

In this chapter, I focus on two big developments and one corollary in world politics during the past fifteen years. Despite expectations of a surge in ethnic-based conflict when the standoff of Soviet and U.S. military forces ended, the number of wars has not changed appreciably from the Cold War years. Gurr claims that ethnic-based wars have been on the decline since the early 1990s.[5] Civil wars are still found predominantly in poor Third World countries, though the end of the Soviet Union's domination of its region has allowed ethnic strife in the Caucasus, the Balkans, and central Asia. For every interstate war, there are more than eight civil wars ongoing. In this regard, not much has changed since the pre-1989 world.

The second big development is the growing lead of the United States over any putative challengers. In the last years of the Cold War, American commentators expressed fears about the relative decline of the United States, especially in face of the growth of China and Japan.[6] These concerns seem laughable in hindsight because of the subsequent implosion of the Japanese economy, the sluggish growth of European states, and the dependence of China on a growth model that, in turn, depends on international institutions dominated by the United States. By contrast, the U.S. economy boomed in the 1990s. Military spending skyrocketed after September 11, 2001 (it is now more than $400 billion a year and is projected to rise to $2.7 trillion over the next six years) despite the huge budget deficits to which it contributed. "Hyperpuissance" (hyperpower), a term popularized by Hubert Vedrine, a former French foreign minister in reference to the United States, indeed characterizes the contemporary presence of the United States on the global scene.

The corollary of the second trend is that the United States is not shy about using its power to reshape the world-system to its liking. As Walter Russell Mead notes: "Since the Vietnam War, taken by some as opening a new era of reluctance in the exercise of military power, the United States has deployed combat forces in, or used deadly force over, Cambodia, Iran, Grenada, Panama, Lebanon, Libya, Saudi Arabia, Kuwait, Iraq, Turkey, Somalia, Haiti, Bosnia, Sudan, Afghanistan, the South China Sea, Liberia, Macedonia, Albania and Yugoslavia. This is a record that no other country comes close to matching."[7] At the time of the 1991 Iraq War, I developed ten scenarios for the "new world order," as it was called by then President George H. W. Bush. I ranked the probabilities from lowest to highest and plunked for "unilateralism by the United States" as the most probable scenario for the 1990s.[8] Despite the tentative on-off embrace of the Clinton presidency (1993–2001) of global institutions such as the United Nations, the World Court, and the World Trade Organization, his successor George W. Bush has matched my expectations.

My accurate prediction was based on what I saw (and still see) as the most abiding quality of the United States, called a "garrison state" by Harold Lasswell.[9]

Characterized by enormous military expenditures, a world-ordering vision (democracy and capitalism), and a need of enemies, coupled with a tendency to lash out at enemies supposed and real, the United States is now truly engaged in a unilateralist enterprise to remake the world in its image. McDougall shows that this crusading spirit is not of recent vintage but can be traced back to the founding of the Republic.[10] In this enterprise, there is no room for neutrals, quibblers, naysayers or skeptics. As President Bush said to Congress after the September 11, 2001, terrorist attacks, in the war against terror "either you are with us or with the terrorists." The United States has been unflinching about killing its enemies in the pursuit of its geostrategic goals (900,000 Japanese dead in the last five months of World War II, not counting the victims of the atomic weapons in Hiroshima and Nagasaki; more than 1 million North Koreans killed out of a population of 9.3 million; and about 365,000 Vietnamese civilians killed).[11]

The same certainty, ruthlessness, and directness of purpose have continued in the U.S. global vision during the second Bush presidency. The Bush Doctrine enunciated in the *National Security Strategy of the United States* (September 2002) states, "To forestall or prevent such hostile acts by our adversaries, the United States will, if necessary, act preemptively"; this preemptive action includes invasion and attacks on countries that are supposedly supporting terrorism. The hubris of such a self-designation as judge and executioner violates the spirit of the charter of the United Nations that the Truman administration was instrumental in getting passed in 1945 and stands as a clear indication of the unilateralist stand of the Bush administration.

Civil Wars: Poverty and Geography

Despite Mearsheimer's expectations,[12] the number of wars in the post–Cold War period did not skyrocket in the decade and a half after the collapse of the Soviet Union. Between 1945 and 1999, about 3.33 million battle deaths occurred in twenty-five interstate wars and involved twenty-five countries. In contrast, 127 civil wars in the same period killed 16.2 million (five times more). These occurred in seventy-three countries and lasted on average about six years. Continually, about one in six countries has had a civil war since the end of World War II.[13] If one looks at all years for all countries (the total set of all possible country war years), 127 civil war starts in a sample of 6,610 years produces a rate of 1.92%. In absolute terms, more civil wars began in the 1990s than in any other postwar decade.[14] It is important to note that the 1990s wars were not the result of new post–Cold War developments. Rather, they were the result of cumulative grievances that had aggregated during the years when the United States and the Soviet Union were dominant in their respective world spheres and kept a lid on local conflicts.[15] With the end of the Cold War order, these superpower controls were removed as both countries turned to domestic matters. Of the wars between 1960 and 1999, there were fifty-two major civil wars, with the typical conflict lasting around seven years and leaving a legacy of persistent poverty and disease in its wake.[16] Recent wars have been longer lasting, from two years on average in 1947 to fifteen years in 1999.[17] This lengthening suggests caution about supposed global interest in settling

Third World conflicts through economic boycotts, military intervention, or negotiations.

It is increasingly evident from research into the causes of contemporary conflicts that the simplest and most common account, ethnic rivalries, falls short of complete explanation. In two-thirds of contemporary civil wars, ethnicity is a dominant or influential factor; about half of these countries become "failed states" with resulting government collapse and widespread famine.[18] Comparing civil wars during 1985–1994 with more recent wars, 1995–2000, Scherrer shows that ethnonationalist and interethnic wars accounted for 52.6% of the conflicts in the earlier period, compared to 49.4% in the later years.[19] While most Third World civil wars have a clear ethnic dimension, expressed in savage butchery such as the Hutu massacre of Tutsi in Rwanda in 1994 or Serb massacres of Bosnian Muslim men at Srebrenica in 1995, the main factor that underlies the outbreak of war is economic. As the *Economist* noted, "[P]overty fosters war, and war impoverishes."[20] The analysis of the World Bank Group on Civil Wars on their causes clearly lends support to the argument that "money trumps kinship."[21]

The skepticism about the ethnic factor (noted earlier) needs to be tempered for one special type of case. If a country has a single large minority juxtaposed to an ethnically different majority (such as Tamils and Sinhalese in Sri Lanka, or Tutsi and Hutu in Rwanda and Burundi), the odds of a civil war double.[22] The reason for this specific correlation is that the minority feels that it stands no chance of effecting change through the usual political process of elections and democratic competition; it will always lose in an ethnically divided polity. The more diverse the country (multiple smaller ethnic groups), the lower the chances of war since coalitions between the groups are necessary to form a majority and political bargaining can garner a victorious coalition.

Powerful evidence in support of the economic hypothesis is provided by Fearon and Laitin.[23] Controlling for per capita income in their statistical analysis, they show that ethnically or religiously divided countries have been no more likely to experience significant violence. Another way to look at this conundrum of ethnic wars is to turn the question around. In the 200 or so countries in the world, there are between 6,500 and 10,000 ethnic entities of diverse size.[24] Yet relatively few of these ethnic entities fight with their neighbors. Further, ethnically homogeneous countries like Somalia (1990s) and Ireland (1922–1923) have seen devastating civil violence. How can we reconcile the apparently contradictory (ethnic versus economic) explanations of civil wars?

The ethnic explanation for civil war draws from the "primordialist" model of nationalism. In this view, nations are natural and perennial; they emerged out of the mists of time and are bound together by blood, territorial, historical, language, religious, and emotive ties.[25] If one adopts a pure primordialist perspective, one would expect tensions and competition for state resources from the various ethnic groups that constitute most of the world's states. In a zero-sum calculus, a gain for one group (say, dominating the officer class in the national army) is a loss for the others. As the *Economist* notes, "[R]ebellions always start for political reasons."[26] Political reasons usually involve economic and geographic resources. This is where an alternative economic-Marxist argument enters the picture. In order to alert ethnic groups to their secondary status relative to other groups or the majority, elites point to examples of economic disparity to build the movement. King uses post-Soviet conflicts (South Ossetia, Abkhazia, Trans-Dniester Republic, and Nagorno-Karabakh) to illustrate how this kind of ethnic mobilization occurs in practice.[27]

Tom Nairn developed the "nationalism from above" theory, which describes how the middle class in poor regions could energize and activate ethnically based movements for redress of their subservient status.[28] Especially in poor, peripheral regions far from the core of a state, the combination of feelings of deprivation and ethnic distinctiveness is a powerful force that motivates rebellion. The ethnic factor is a necessary but not always a sufficient condition to bring about action—the sufficiency condition is added by the economic factor, especially poverty.[29] In a statistical analysis, Elbadawi and Sambanis show that ethnic diversity plays a part in promoting the odds of a civil war in a poor and repressive society, but this ethnic factor disappears when countries develop economically and improve their human rights record.[30]

Once civil war begins, both sides need money and must find ways to procure it. If one side is the government, it can switch state spending and develop favorable tax regimes to pay for its war. On the nongovernment side, cash is not as readily available. Two main sources are assistance from neighboring governments (who often have an ongoing dispute with their neighbor) or from an ethnic diaspora overseas. Contemporary examples are the external support for Chechen rebels, for the Irish Republican Army in Northern Ireland, for Congolese rebels (supported by Rwanda), and for Sierra Leone rebels (supported by the Liberian government of Charles Taylor). The fluidity of borders and the nature of global underground financial flows make it almost impossible to stop these kinds of aid.

A second and increasingly common source of funds is gaining control of and selling natural resources within the rebel region or nearby. Natural resources play multiple roles in rebellion. First, rebel leaders can build an argument that they belong to the region, not to the national elite. As Fearon and Laitin say, "[T]he greed of a resource-rich locality can seem ethically less ugly if a corrupt national elite is already hijacking the resources."[31] Second, the presence of valuable natural resources makes rebellion more likely.[32] Third, there is a war dividend in the form of control and sales of the resource to keep the fight ongoing. Well-known examples of the intersection of resources and rebellion are Sierra Leone and Angola (diamonds), Angola, Sudan, Indonesia (Aceh), Chad, and Nigeria (oil), Morocco/Western Sahara (phosphate), and Tajikistan, Afghanistan, the former Yugoslavia, Caucasus, Myanmar, Peru, Colombia, and Kurdistan (drugs).[33] To break the link and to hinder the flows of revenues from the sales of these resources, external actors try to institute embargoes on their flows. The recent global certification of diamonds from known sources, such as South Africa, is one example of these efforts; uncertified diamonds are not supposed to be traded and sold. The breakdown of government control in war-torn regions can be gauged from the World Bank's estimate that 95% of the global production of hard drugs is located in civil war countries.[34]

Collier's work at the World Bank exemplifies a recent interest in the discipline of economics about the impact of poverty on violence and vice versa. Jeffrey Sachs focuses on failed states (failure to provide basic public services to their populations) as "seedbeds of violence, terrorism, international criminality, mass migration and refugee movements, drug trafficking and disease."[35] He accepts the explanation of the Central Intelligent Agency's (CIA) study of 113 cases of state failure: failed states are extremely poor, nondemocratic, and economically closed. Furthermore, they are "tense, deeply conflicted, dangerous, and bitterly contested by warring factions."[36] To these elements, Sachs adds a geographic one: "Physical ecology probably plays a role. Africa is uniquely hampered by extreme conditions of disease and low food productivity that in turn prevent those societies from managing the minimum necessary conditions for growth."[37] The CIA State Failure Task Force reported that almost every case of U.S. military intervention since 1960 had taken place in a developing country that had previously experienced state failure.

There are both expected and unexpected associations between war and political-geographic factors. As might be expected, as a country's income increases, its risk of being a war zone decreases. For a country like the Congo with deep poverty, a collapsing economy, and huge mineral exploitation, the risk of war reaches nearly 80 percent.[38] If per capita income doubles, the risk of war halves; for each percentage point that the economic growth rate increases, the risk of conflict falls by a percentage point.[39] Fearon and Laitin calculate that "every fall in per capita income of $1000 corresponds to a 34% greater annual odds of war outbreak."[40] Economic growth generates more opportunities for youth. "Being a rebel foot soldier is no way to make a fortune but it may be better than the alternative."[41] The average age of the fighters in civil wars continues to fall; children as young as eight years of age are impressed into armies in West and central Africa. War tends to draw in neighboring countries since rebels skip to and fro across borders to sell resources, buy weapons, escape pursuit, and regroup. War in one country tends to depress economic investment and growth in neighboring states. It has long been known that geographic contiguity is significant in determining the diffusion of conflict.[42]

Another expected association of geography with war is that physical geography matters. From Fearon and Laitin's regression model, it is evident that if a country is large, mountainous, and lightly populated, it faces added risks of rebellion.[43] Rebels can hide out and maintain their forces in such environments, particularly if they have support from ethnic kin or neighboring states. Finally, it must be noted that governments kill many more of their citizens than rebels or foreigners. "Democide" (destruction of the people), Rummel's term,[44] is an apt description of the kind of brutality wreaked by Pol Pot in Cambodia, Saddam Hussein in Iraq, Idi Amin in Uganda, Stalin in the Soviet Union, or Emperor Bokassa in the Central African Republic. Overall, more than four times more people are killed by their governments than in wars.

On the unexpected side of the war explanation lie two widely discussed relationships, that democracies are more peaceful and that Islamic states are bloodier. Both suppositions do not hold up to close inspection. The "democratic peace" hypothesis holds that two democratic states will not find themselves on opposite sides in a conflict because of the pressure of their own domestic polities.[45] There is substantial evidence that supports this notion. However, democratic states have been heavily involved in conflicts, as the examples of the United States (discussed later) and the United Kingdom show. Collier and colleagues conclude that democracy fails to reduce the risk of civil war, at least in low-income countries, and Fearon and Laitin concur;[46] civil wars are not less frequent in democracies after controlling for income. The growth of the number of people who live in democratic states and the diffusion of democracy into previously authoritarian regions expected by the globalizers would not predict an overly optimistic outcome in a causal reduction in war.[47] Recent research by Gleditsch and Ward on the transitions between democracy and authoritarianism indicates that uneven transitions (large swings back to authoritarianism and forth to democracy) can increase the probability of war.[48] Taking a long-term perspective since 1816, Hegre and colleagues conclude that intermediate regimes (between democracy and authoritarianism) are most prone to civil war and that becoming a democracy significantly lessens the odds of civil strife.[49] The effects of democracy on conflict are significantly mediated by the regional location of the country of interest. Democracies within democratic regions (e.g., Europe) have much better prospects of peace.

Huntington's book *The Clash of Civilizations* contained the statements that "Islam has bloody borders" and "bloody innards," which he attributed to the nature of the cultural-religious features and demographic characteristics in Islamic societies.[50] Two careful checks of these claims have debunked them. Fearon and Laitin show that adding a variable that measures the percentage of Muslims in each country to the model is not statistically significant (income is still dominant), and Chiozza also dismisses Huntington's hypothesis, using data from 1946 to 1997.[51] In fact, Fearon and Laitin go further to argue that global regional location does not matter; in other words, after controlling for the country characteristics (income, ethnic ratios, and so on), the rate of civil war onset is not significantly different across the globe. However, this conclusion should be accepted with caution since they measured the regional effect by using a crude dummy variable and did not use the more sophisticated geographic methodology that allows careful simultaneous examination of the country and regional factors.[52]

The Geographic Distribution of Conflict

Numerous datasets are now available for the study of conflict. They differ mostly in their definitions of what constitutes war. A minimum number of deaths of 1,000 per year is found in the most widely used dataset, the Correlates of War Project.[53] In this section of this chapter, I will use the Uppsala dataset that has a low threshold of twenty-five deaths per year and is available back to 1946.[54] The Uppsala group counts 225 armed conflicts between 1946 and 2001, with 34 of them active in 2001.[55] Of these 225 wars, 162 were predominantly internal conflicts, 21 were extrastate conflicts (between a state and a nonstate group outside its territory, such as al-Qaeda), and 42 were interstate conflicts. Gleditsch and colleagues, using the Uppsala data, plot the trend over the past fifty-five years and fit a third-degree polynomial trendline to the data.[56] (A third-degree polynomial has two inflexion points. One could fit a fourth degree or higher polynomial, but the additional fit to the data does not compensate for the complexity of the model.) The general pattern is a decline during the early years, followed by a gradual rise in the last two decades of the Cold War, followed by a decline after 1989. I extend their analysis and also examine the specific locations of conflicts. I also replicate the work of Buhaug and Gates who use the Uppsala data and report the exact geographic location of the war zones.[57] For example, they identify the geographic coordinates of the Chechen-Russian war as the republic in the North Caucasus Mountains, rather than all of Russia, which would be identified as the war zone in the traditional method of war analysis.

Given the overwhelming evidence summarized earlier on the impact of wealth on conflict, I examine conflicts since 1946 by presenting them in the context of a country's level of development. Rather than simply using gross domestic product per capita or some other economic measure of development, I prefer to use the broader measure of the United Nations Development Program's (UNDP) human development index. The index is derived from individual scores on a variety of income, educational, literacy, health, and other measures; the goal of the index is to show the extent to which each country's population is able to reach its potential as a full productive citizenry that is following individual needs and interests.[58] The index ranged from .942 (Norway) to .275 (Sierra Leone) in 2000.

An unexpected contrast appears in the long-term trends of conflict when the rich and poor countries are evaluated separately. In Figure 5.1, I replicate the approach of Gleditsch and colleagues, but I calculate the trends separately for Organization for Economic Cooperation and Development (OECD) and non-OECD members.[59] The OECD includes approximately thirty of the richest countries in the world; its numbers have risen from about twenty during the Cold War to include the richest of the post-Communist states in central Europe. Its members are predominantly in Western Europe, but it also includes Australasia, Mexico, Japan, Canada, and the United States. Each graph has two lines. The yearly values show the probability of an OECD (or non-OECD on the bottom graph) country being involved in war, either at home or abroad. It is calculated as the ratio of the states involved in war divided by all states in that group, OECD or non-OECD. Clearly, the yearly values fluctuate greatly, and the index does not measure the severity of the violence or the scale of the involvement. Obvious peaks on the OECD graph correspond to the 1991 Iraq war, Kosovo in 1999, and the post–September 11 attack on the Taliban in Afghanistan. While the United States provided the bulk of the fighting forces in these wars, other OECD members supplied troops, equipment, or support services or otherwise contributed to the war effort. Fitting a third-degree polynomial to the yearly data from 1946 yields a downward-sloping line from the early 1950s but an upward slope for the 1990s. The three peaks of the war years 1991, 1999, and 2001 drive the recent slope, but the trend should give pause to anyone who thinks that rich countries are free from war. With the exception of the terrorist attacks on the United States in September 2001 and the long-established guerrilla wars in Northern Ireland (United Kingdom) and the Basque country (Spain), the OECD wars were conducted offshore.

The trend line for the non-OECD (poor and middle-income) countries is not

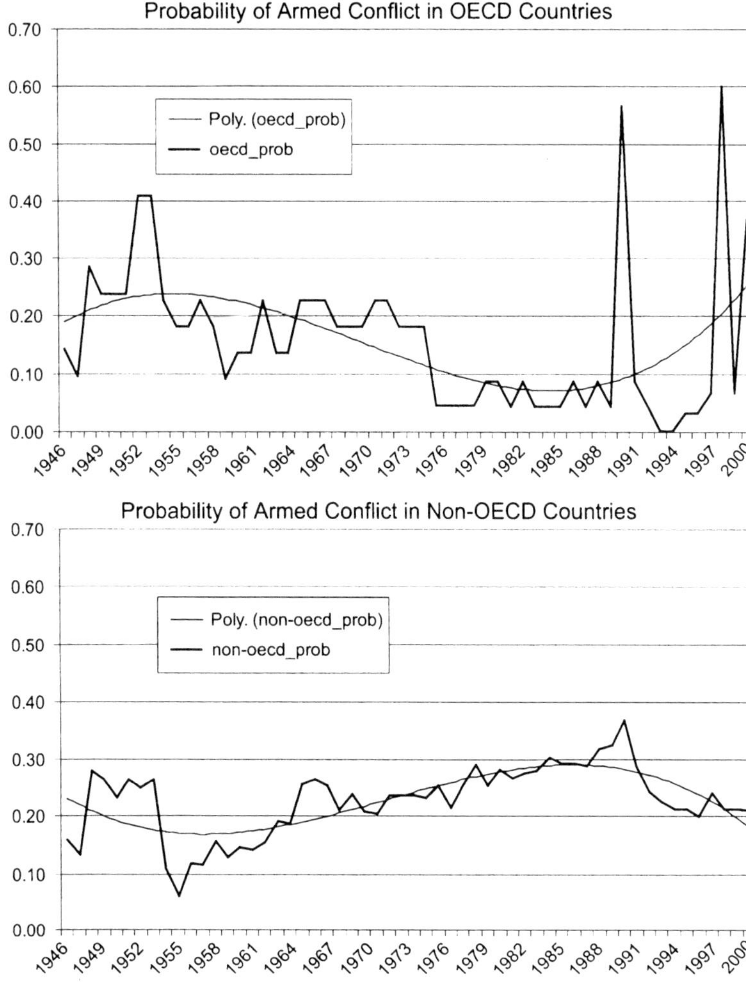

FIGURE 5.1 Probability that a country is involved in armed conflict (all levels and all types) annual figures and third-degree polynomial trend line. *Source:* H. Strand, L. Wilhelmsen, and N. P. Gleditsch, *Armed Conflict Dataset Codebook, Version 1.2* (Oslo: International Peace Research Institute, 2003). *http://www.prio.no/cwp/armedconflict.*

as strongly derived from peaks and troughs. The overall trend matches the line for the world system in Gleditsch and colleagues since about five in six states are not OECD members.[60] From the early 1950s, the trend was gradually upward to a peak at the end of the Cold War in the late 1980s, followed by a decline. The upward trend was promoted by the actions of the superpowers in assisting their proxies in Third World conflicts.[61] Sometimes the proxies were states (e.g., Somalia and Guatemala for the United States; Ethiopia and Nicaragua for the Soviet Union). Sometimes they were rebels (e.g., the Contras in Nicaragua and the mujahideen in Afghanistan for the United States; the Palestine Liberation Organization and the Vietcong for the Soviet Union).

Mearsheimer argued that the probability of conflict was driven by the nature of the international system.[62] In his realist view, bipolar systems are more stable than multipolar ones, and therefore, the end of the dual superpower controls in their respective orbits in 1989 would lead to more war. Additionally, he argued that the growing power inequality between the United States and other states would invite war because it would increase "an aggressor's prospects for victory on the battlefield."[63] The two graphs in Figure 5.1 show that Mearsheimer was both right and wrong. Despite his expectations, there has not been a general upsurge in violence worldwide since the end of the bipolar world-system, as the trend for the non-OECD countries in the 1990s shows. But the trend for the OECD countries, driven by the massive U.S. involvements overseas in the 1990s, supports his expectations about the outcomes of inequality in the world-system. In order to return to the status quo ante, a realist would argue that a reduction in the power disparity is needed. In Mearsheimer's words, "[S]mall gaps foster peace, large gaps promote war . . . deterrence is more likely to hold when the costs and risks of going to war are unambiguously stark."[64]

Robert Kaplan in "The Coming Anarchy" received a great deal of attention with his apocalyptic vision of poor Third World states mired in poverty, racked by civil wars, devastated by AIDS, malaria, tuberculosis, and other diseases, and becoming increasingly remote from the rich world.[65] He started his journey in West Africa: "Disease, overpopulation, unprovoked crime, scarcity of resources, refugee migrations, the increasing erosion of nation-states and international borders, and the empowerment of private armies, security firms, and international drug cartels are now most tellingly demonstrated through a West African prism. . . . To remap the political earth the way it will be a few decades hence . . . I find I must begin with West Africa."[66] Kaplan recognized the dual nature of global conflict, which is concentrated in the poorer parts of the world. "We are entering a bifurcated world. Part of the globe is inhabited by Hegel's and Fukuyama's Last Man, healthy, well fed, and pampered by technology. The other, larger, part is inhabited by Hobbes's First Man, condemned to a life that is 'poor, nasty, brutish, and short.' "[67] This distinction between a Hegelian and a Hobbesian world also garnered a large press because of Robert Kagan's "Power and Weakness" article of 2002.[68] Kagan contrasts the weakness of the European states and the strength of the United States. For Europeans, the world is inexorably evolving into the Hegelian model, a paradise of peace and relative prosperity.[69] Americans, by contrast, remain "mired in history, exercising power in the anarchic Hobbesian world where international laws and rules are unreliable and where true security and the defense and promotion of a liberal order still depend on the possession and use of military might."[70]

The geography of conflict since World War II is mapped in Figure 5.2. The zones of peace and war are clearly demarcated. Against a background of countries shaded according to their UN human development indexes (HDI) in 2000 (high, medium, and low), we can map the exact locations of the war zones. The size of the triangles indicates the scale of the conflict (number of deaths). The visual correlation between the index of human development and war is evident.[71] Almost all wars have occurred in low and medium HDI states.[72] This is not to say that high HDI countries have not been involved in war. The United States (ranked sixth on the HDI in 2000) is the most active, but as an external participant. The three main regional concentrations are in Central America, tropical Africa, and

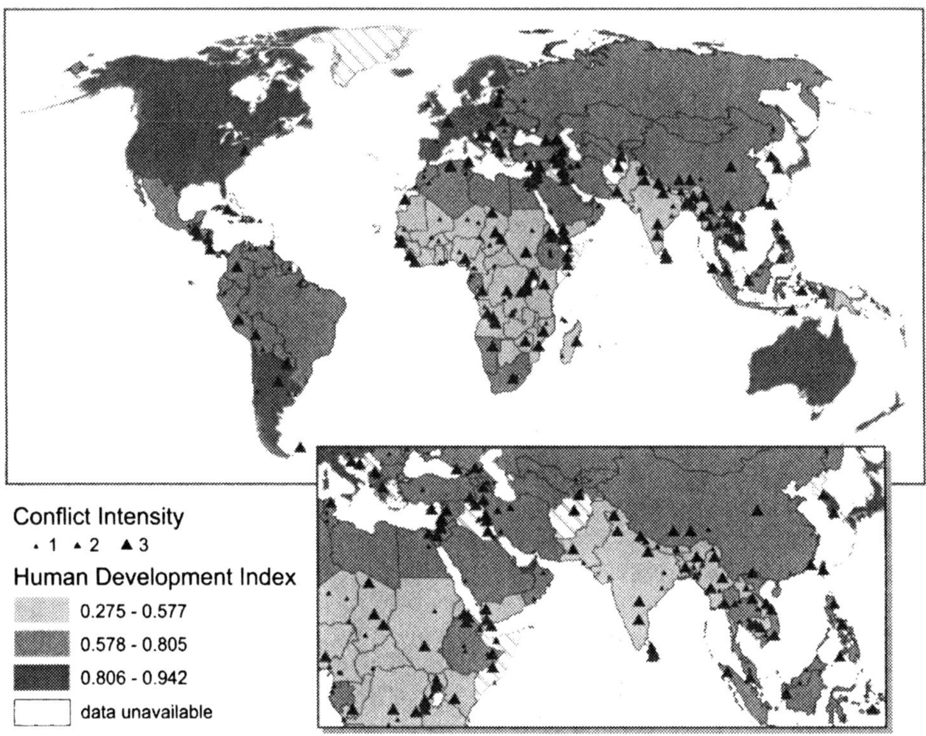

FIGURE 5.2 Geographic distribution of conflict and United Nations Human Development Index scores. Conflict is scaled as (1) between 25 and 1,000 battle deaths over the course of the conflict; (2) over 1,000 battle deaths in the conflict but fewer than 1,000 per year; and (3) at least 1,000 battle deaths a year. *Source: Armed Conflict Dataset Codebook, Version 1.2*; United Nations Development Program, *World Development Report* (New York: United Nations Development Program, 2002).

the "arc of crisis" that stretches from southeastern Europe through the Caucasus and the Middle East into South and Southeast Asia. Within each of these zones, some countries or regions within countries have seen continual endemic violence. Israel/Palestine, the borders between Iraq, Iran, and Turkey, the states of Southeast Asia, the Horn of Africa, and the Congo Basin in central Africa stand out as bloody lands. Most of these triangles represent fairly small conflicts, but some indicate widespread, bloody wars that involve numerous neighboring countries. The current wars in the Congo that have dragged in eight neighboring states (plus UN forces) are only the latest of regional-scale conflicts that include the Korean War of the 1950s, the Vietnam War of the 1950–1970s, Israel/Palestine and other Middle Eastern states, and the West African wars of the 1990s.

A cursory glance at the map in Figure 5.2 or reliance on the images that emerge from Africa, the Caucasus, or most of the Middle East would tend to confirm Kaplan's decade-old projection. Yet these impressions must be tempered by the reality of the data. Conflicts in the Third World and in the former Soviet Union are not of one kind. Many have deep external involvements from rich countries, usually the United States and/or a former colonial power. Some wars have definitely resulted in state failure, especially in the African states of Liberia, Sierra Leone, Côte d'Ivoire, Somalia, and the Congo. Other states, however, such as Mozambique, Angola, and Ethiopia, have returned from the brink of collapse.

With the exception of the short-lived intervention in Somalia in late 1992, U.S. involvement in civil wars has been in pursuit of clear realist goals. President-elect George W. Bush stated in December 2000 that he would not order U.S. troops to any country even to stop another Rwanda-scale genocide. Whether the events of September 11, 2001, will change this strategic vision remains to be seen. The dilemma posed by Kaplan (and by Barnett, discussed later) stands as an ever clearer choice. Should the United States try to bring peace to war zones, either unilaterally or as part of a multilateral force, because war has negative externalities (refugees, disease, starvation, and so on) and the roots of terrorism reach far and deep? Or should the United States retain a respectful distaste for involvement that does not directly contribute to the security of the United States? By choosing the latter, the United States would adhere to an updated version of the Powell Doctrine (named after the current secretary of state) that demands that U.S. forces be used only to promote national strategic interests, be used in overwhelming numbers to ensure a quick victory, and be withdrawn in an expedited manner. Part of the answer might be found in the nature of U.S. foreign relations and military operations in the aftermath of September 11. The indecision in the summer of 2000 over whether to commit U.S. peacekeeping forces to Liberia as part of a multinational effort indicates the tension in American foreign policy between the "Jacksonian" tradition of aggressive self-interest and the "Wilsonian" tradition of internationalism.[73] The debate about the U.S. role in world affairs must be placed against the debate about the strength and sustainability of the hegemonic status of the United States. Despite an appearance of unanimity and clarity in the public posture of the American government in the aftermath of September 11, the questions are not yet resolved.

The Hegemon Acts and Reacts

Since the end of the Cold War, the United States has continued to expand its military lead over all other countries. In 2002, the United States accounted for 43% of global military expenditure, and this figure was expected to rise to more than 50% of the world total within three years. In 2002, the U.S. expenditure equaled that of the next twenty-five countries combined. While there are various ways to measure military strength, military expenditure is the simplest and most generic measure. According to this measure, the United States spends about 3.3% of its GDP on its military, compared to ratios half as large in Western Europe (1.3% in Germany, 2.3% in the United Kingdom and 2.6% in France). Some relatively poor countries spend higher ratios on their military, such as China's 3.5 to 5% estimate, but the absolute amounts are relatively small ($47 billion for China compared to $399.1 billion for the United States in 2002).[74]

More than the increase in U.S. military spending, the collapse of any serious challenge to American military and political supremacy consequent upon the implosion of the Soviet Union widened the gap between the United States and the rest. The balance enforced by nuclear mutual assured destruction (MAD) was erased after 1991. Kagan considers the proliferation of the U.S. exercise of power in a unipolar world a natural consequence of the Soviet Union's collapse.[75] Because of the combination of the removal of the Soviet threat of a countermove with the development of new technologies, especially long-range weapons like cruise missiles, the United States was able to use more force more frequently with less risk of significant casualties. Because of the domestic doubts (which sometimes escalated into opposition) to military actions overseas, U.S. leaders have been careful to build support for war. The Iraq War of the spring of 2003 was undertaken only after a year of massive (and successful) efforts to convince Americans of the dangers of Saddam Hussein's purported possession of weapons of mass destruction (WMD) and the supposed linkage of his regime to al-Qaeda, the September 11 operatives. By the outbreak of war, overwhelming numbers (77%) of Americans supported the Bush administration's actions. A *Washington Post*/ABC poll on April 7, 2003, showed that of the large demographic groups, only African Americans expressed less than majority support for the action (at 49%); by contrast, conservative Republicans gave 99% support to the attack on Iraq.

Why are Americans so willing to support the use of military force abroad? Actually, the gap between Americans and residents of other democratic countries is a recent development. At the time of the Kosovo war in April 1999, citizens of countries like Denmark, Croatia, and the United Kingdom showed higher support for an attack on Yugoslavia than Americans, while the values for Germans, French, Norwegians, and Canadians were not much different from the American ratio.[76] The answer to the question, of course, lies in the attacks of September 11, 2001, which changed the American foreign policy psyche like no event since Pearl Harbor in 1941. But despite the U.S. media hype about the way the world has changed, Saul Cohen, an eminent political geographer, was more sober in answering his own question: "Has September 11, 2001 fundamentally changed the global geopolitical scene? . . . In fact, it is not the world that has changed, but the

American perception of the world. International and domestic terrorism has taken hundreds of thousands of victims over the past half century."[77] However, by changing their perspective on the world, Americans, through their hegemonic power, are thus changing the world.

Kagan and Toal are agreed about the nature of the contemporary U.S. public.[78] For Toal, who draws on Mead,[79] Americans in 2003 are following a Bush presidency that lies squarely in the "Jacksonian tradition" of American foreign policy. Of the four American geopolitical traditions identified by Mead (Hamiltonian, Wilsonian, Jeffersonian, and Jacksonian), it is the Jacksonian one that is most identified with populist aggressive nationalism. The basis for it is an idealized view of Americans as belonging to a community with a strong sense of common values and a common destiny. This view, of course, papers over debates and disputes within the U.S. body politic and uses the argument that "all politics stops at the water's edge" to squelch debate about the nature of American power and the uses to which it is put. Once the Jacksonian ideal was reestablished and widely promoted, it became a "somatic marker" that was used to manipulate public opinion. A somatic marker is, in Connolly's words, "a publicly mobilized, corporeal disposition."[80] The state apparatus through its media access can simplify the process of calculation in foreign policy by emphasizing saturated memory and gut feelings; use of trite expressions by politicians like the title of a country music tune "America Will Always Stand" appeals to the most basic patriotic instincts. The end result is a "public affect" that drives an aggressive foreign policy.[81]

Kagan became famous on the basis of a proposition that Americans have a specific world view that is fundamentally based on the Hobbesian model of world affairs, where anarchy reigns, where laws and rules are flouted or absent, where security is only guaranteed by a strong military deterrent, and where the military can indeed win "the hearts and minds" of foreign opponents.[82] Though the focus of his article is the distinction between Americans as Hobbesians and Europeans as Kantians, and the gulf in understanding that results, the most important conclusion (with which I agree) is that both groups have contrasting views on how to settle difficult international problems. Europeans want to negotiate and pursue multilateral options, while the United States prefers unilateral force to settle matters. Though the United States welcomes assistance from other forces, it is accepted only on the condition that the U.S. leadership and goals remain unchallenged. Recent U.S. military actions in Iraq/Kuwait (1991), Bosnia (1995), Yugoslavia (1999), Afghanistan (2001), and Iraq (2003) have been accompanied by troops from regional allies, but the preponderance of force in numbers and equipment is American. In June 2003, the United States had military forces in 136 countries. Clearly, the term "superpower" is inadequate, and even the term "hegemon" hardly suffices to depict the U.S. lead, by far the greatest of any empire in history.[83]

Why is the United States able to use its military power in such an unrestrained manner? It should be noted that American public opinion for overseas military actions remains highly sensitive to the number of U.S. deaths.[84] We would not expect much opposition from other states, given the size of the gap, and any opposition (from those attacked) has been indirect and evasive, as in Afghanistan and Iraq. Why has the U.S. public not put a brake on military spending and actions? Recall the half-century-old description of Harold Lasswell of the "garrison state" and combine it with the Hobbesian worldview.[85] But as the Vietnam War showed, even the "garrison state" can be undermined through determined and mobilized public opinion that forced a U.S. pullout from Southeast Asia in 1975. The difference now is that U.S. casualties are a fraction of those that occurred in Vietnam because of the asymmetric nature of modern war.

Shaw, in a controversial argument, examines casualty figures for the three wars that the United States initiated (Iraq in 1991, Yugoslavia in 1999, and Afghanistan in 2001); the West has managed to virtually eliminate military casualties on its side, while casualties on the enemy side were high.[86] In Afghanistan, for example, the number of U.S. military deaths from October to December 2001, the time of the greatest amount of fighting, was 1, Afghan civilian deaths reached between 4,200 and 5,000, U.S. allies' deaths ranged in the hundreds, and deaths of enemy combatants (al-Qaeda and the Taliban regime) numbered in the thousands or tens of thousands.[87] Of course, the U.S. military response to these numbers is to claim that they show the success of military strategy, technical skill of the personnel, and the advantages of U.S. weapons and training. While there is little doubt that the United States tries to avoid needless civilian loss of life, the disturbing numbers of civilians killed in "accidents" illustrates another fact of U.S.-style modern war. In order to reduce the risk to U.S. troops, weapons are fired from even greater distances. The advances in the electronic battlefield, combined with the use of global positioning systems, have pushed U.S. military technology far ahead of that of any other country, including its European allies.[88] These distances lead to more "accidents" since they allow the United States to fight wars at little risk to its troops. (How risky is it to drop laser-guided bombs from 29,000 feet against an enemy with weak air defenses?) Shaw concludes that such tactics lead to "errors of targeting in which hundreds or thousands of civilians die in each campaign. So the transfer to civilians of the risks of being directly killed is deliberate and systematic."[89]

"Risk-transfer war" is politically palatable at home in the United States and helps ensure that the "V" word (Vietnam) remains under the covers. What is still unclear is whether it is moral. In Shaw's words, "When one side can minimize the risks to its own soldiers to virtually zero, is it moral to practice industrial killing on a hapless enemy? The image of Iraqi conscripts bulldozed (literally) into the sand at the end of the Gulf War is emblematic of this issue."[90] Political philosopher Michael Walzer goes further in demanding greater attention to the codes implicit in the Geneva Conventions: "[W]hat we look for . . . is some sign of a positive commitment to save civilian lives. Civilians have a right to something more. And if saving civilian lives means risking soldier' lives, that risk must be accepted."[91]

The logical end product of the U.S. "risk-adverse" strategy is the development and production of a new generation of "superweapons" under a program code-named Falcon (Force Application and Launch from the Continental United States). According to the Defense Advanced Research Projects Agency (DARPA), the program is to fulfill the government's vision of an ultimate and prompt global reach capability (up to 2025 and beyond). The weapons program would remove the need to keep U.S. troops overseas, where they could always be attacked. Such weapons would allow the dropping of bombs from space, and the ultimate weapon, a reusable hypersonic cruise vehicle (HCV), is capable of hitting targets 9,000 nautical miles distant in less than two hours.[92] Prototypes of smaller weapons are expected to be tested by 2006.

Since the actions of the United States in Afghanistan as a response to the September 11, 2001, terrorist attacks, there has been much speculation about the nature of the new "empire." From Marxist analyses to world-systems analysis to historical comparison,[93] the United States is viewed as the main cog of the world political and economic system. Empire can be built by conquest and brute force, as the European states showed between 1500 and 1900. But it can also be built by "invitation," where weak regimes invite a major external power to assist them to build up their strength either against domestic opposition or regional enemies.[94] A third way to build an empire is by largesse, that is, by economic aid, favorable trade relations, military hardware and training, and special financial arrangements. The United States with its enormous reserves, including the ability to punish by closing off its market to exports from rival states, has not been reluctant to use its power in this manner in the aftermath of the collapse of the Soviet Union. For the first time ever, the United States had the opportunity to build an empire without the interference of another imperial project, either from the European empires before 1945 or the Soviet Union after that time.

In Figures 5.3 and 5.4, we can see the results of the U.S. efforts of the 1990s. The Integrated Data for Events Analysis (IDEA) database has recently become

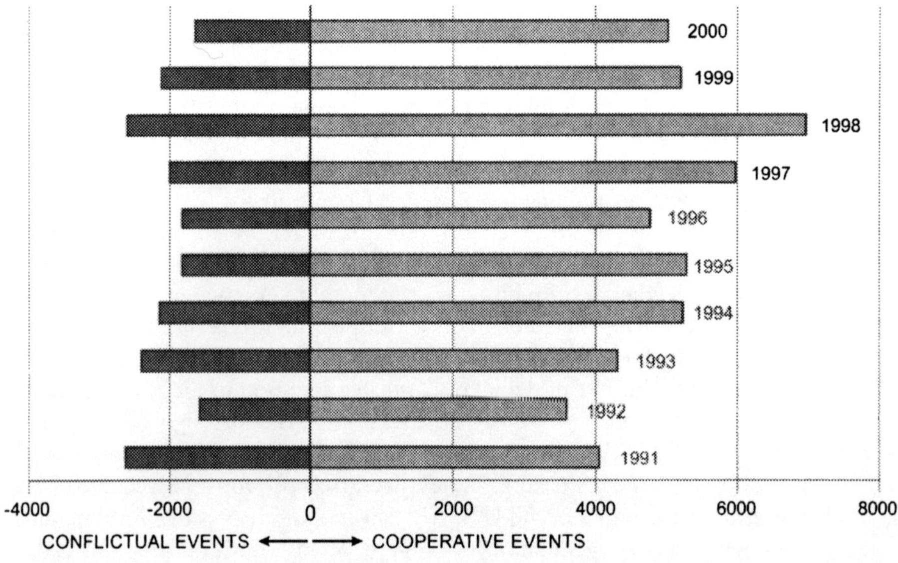

FIGURE 5.3 Yearly distribution of conflict and cooperation from the United States. Yearly totals are the aggregate values of all individual actions by the U.S. government and its agencies. *Source*: D. Bond, J. Bond, C. Oh, J. C. Jenkins, and C. L. Taylor, "Integrated Data for Events Analysis (IDEA): An Event Form Typology for Automated Events Data Development" (Unpublished manuscript, Harvard University, 2001).

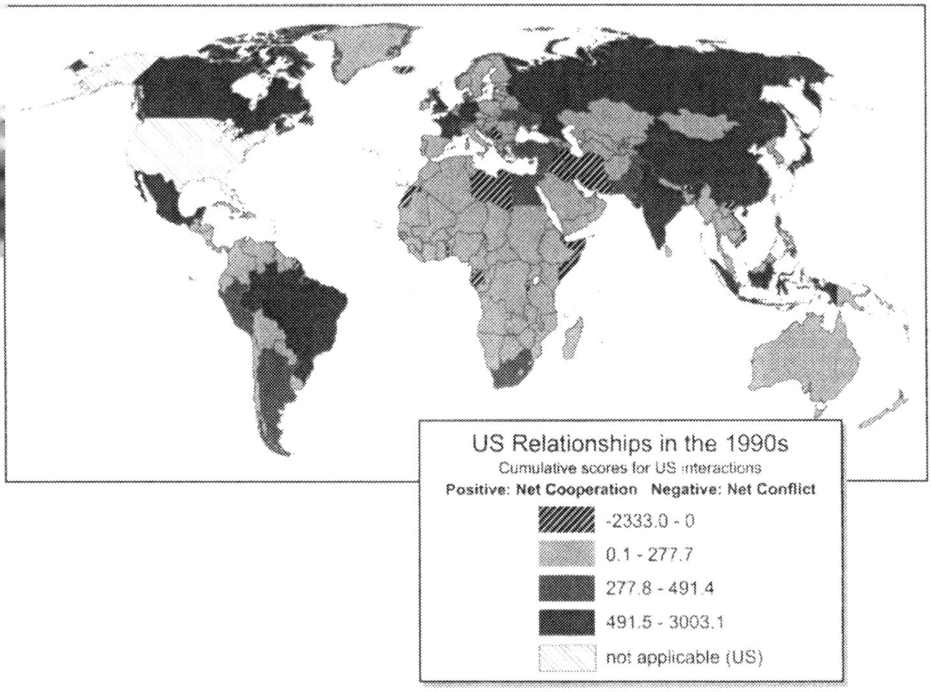

FIGURE 5.4 Geographic distribution of the aggregate of conflict and cooperation from the United States directed to each country, summed for the period 1991–2000. The values are the sum of cooperation minus the sum of conflict scores. *Source*: "Integrated Data for Events Analysis (IDEA): An Event Form Typology for Automated Events Data Development" (Unpublished manuscript, Harvard University, 2001).

available for academic research.[95] Unlike many datasets used in the study of international relations and foreign policy, the IDEA data are designed to be comprehensive. Unlike other data, the IDEA are not coded by humans from newspapers and other sources. Instead, machine-coded data are generated using the VRA Knowledge Manager software.[96] The Knowledge Manager extracts the first sentence or lead from every story in the Reuters Business Briefings as a database record with fields for actor, target, and type of event. These events can be converted into a 157-point scale that is compatible with the widely used international relations conflict-cooperation scale of Goldstein.[97] Other fields give information about such variables as geographic location of the event. More than six million events were extracted for the period 1991–2000. I extracted all events that involved the U.S. government and its agencies as actor, more than 70,000 events in all, and recoded each event using the Goldstein scale. Aggregate values for cooperative and conflictual events (conflict is coded as negative scores and cooperation as positive) are shown separately on Figure 5.3 and mapped for 1991–2000 by country in Figure 5.4. As examples, a military attack is scored as −10, a diplomatic warning as −3, a promise of material support as +3, and military aid as +8.3.

The United States was consistently more cooperative than conflictual with the rest of the world during the 1990s (Figure 5.3). Each year, the United States directed between two and three times more cooperative actions to all other countries combined than conflictual action. The totals and the conflict-cooperation ratios are consistent from year to year, with more of each type in 1998. The geographic distribution of the actions (cumulative from 1991 to 2000) shows that most countries have a positive value (Figure 5.4). Only Belize, French Guiana, Haiti, Western Sahara, Togo, Gabon, Libya, Burundi, Swaziland, Somalia, Iraq, Iran, Vietnam, Bhutan, Serbia, and Iceland have net negative values.[98] Many of these countries (Haiti, Iran, Iraq, Libya, Serbia, Vietnam, and Somalia) were the objects of U.S. diplomatic and military attention during the decade, and these results are not surprising. The other countries are small, and the nature of U.S. relations with them is decidedly hinged on local issues, especially the access of U.S. companies to local resources (phosphate in the Western Sahara, oil in Gabon). Because the size (and geopolitical locations) of these countries does not matter a great deal in the U.S. worldview, the interactions are few, and any single negative action (e.g., a diplomatic protest) can shift the overall score into the negative category.

To isolate hostile states geographically and to have allies in the region that can provide forward bases, the United States cultivates these ties through leverage of its gigantic military and economic arsenal. The United States assists the governments of these countries economically (buying the loyalties of both actual and potential opposition) and militarily (sending trainers and weapons, especially the high-tech missiles and planes that help in suppressing rebels). The United States can thus "shrink the gap" and also pursue the geopolitical aims of having a dominant presence in critical areas of the world. The strategy of empire building by largesse is well engaged. In Barnett's simplistic analysis, the role of the United States is to promote globalization to bring ever more countries into the U.S.-controlled world-economy because globalized countries are not hotbeds of violence and anti-Americanism.[99] But some regions remain mired in the "gap"—the northern part of South America, almost all of Africa, and Southwest, central, Southeast, and South Asia—regions where poverty and civil strife are endemic.[100]

Large or proximate countries (Russia, China, Japan, Germany, the United Kingdom, Brazil, India, France, Mexico, Indonesia, and Canada) dominate the positive side of the U.S. actions. (The data are not standardized by population or some other index of size.) All of these important states have high net positive values. In the 1990s, the United States was concerned with building anti-Iraq (1991) and anti-Serbia (1999) coalitions, both in diplomatic arenas like the United Nations and as military alliances. United States foreign aid and trading advantages were used as key weapons in this effort to sway the policies of large states. Other key regional allies, especially those close to conflict zones like Egypt, Peru, Turkey, the Philippines, Pakistan, Argentina, South Africa, and Ukraine, also show strong positive scores on this measure of international interaction. These regional efforts are in line with the suggestions of Barnett about "shrinking the gap" by using these states as forward bases.[101]

The new push to send troops abroad that has been characteristic of the George W. Bush presidency is not a sudden post–September 11, 2001 development. In 1991–1992, advisors in the Pentagon to the president's father, George H. W. Bush, developed a "Defense Planning Guidance" document. It surfaced a decade later, and its key recommendations made their way into the *National Security Strategy of the United States* published in September 2002.[102] While the main emphasis in the document was the determination to prevent any country from reaching a point of power equality with the United States and the American willingness to use any means necessary (including the military) to prevent that from happening, its regional analysis is also worthy of attention. The Middle East/Caspian Sea region is identified as a key geopolitical zone. After World War II, the United States devoted great efforts to building a zone of containment in the "rimland" that surrounds the Soviet Union and China. While massive numbers of troops were stationed in Europe and Northeast Asia, the Middle East fell between these regions as a zone of great political change, and U.S. attempts to gain stable and strong allies there were partially successful. In the mid-1970s, after the OPEC oil boycott and oil shortages, U.S. troops began to enter the region in large numbers to make sure that this key resource did not fall under the control of rivals. Klare believes that because the Persian Gulf/Caspian Sea area contains 70% of the world's oil resources, the United States is committed to regional domination.[103] Cohen in a classic geopolitical analysis also predicts the continued U.S. strategic interest in this region.[104] Both consider possible competitors for the oil resources and expect future conflicts for them. One can extend the geopolitical analysis to rework the hoary Halford J. Mackinder aphorism "Whoever rules Eastern Europe commands the Heartland: Whoever rules the Heartland commands the World Island: Whoever rules the World Island commands the world"[105] to its contemporary U.S. version "Whoever rules the Persian Gulf/Caspian Sea region commands the world's oil; Whoever rules the world's oil commands the world economy; Whoever rules the world economy commands the world."

Conclusion

The two major themes of this chapter have examined the geographic distribution of war, considering the factors responsible for its concentrations, and have analyzed the recent hyperpower actions of the United States, trying to understand the motivations and strategies behind them. While there is strong evidence of the relationship between poverty and violence, as the careful statistical examinations as well as apologists for U.S. actions such as Barnett both accept,[106] the real question is how to break this connection. The rich world is getting stingier with its aid monies at a time when the demand for help to fight AIDS, famines, and other crises is growing. At the same time, the rich countries cosset their own agricultural and industrial producers as they exclude Third World exports from their markets through tariffs and quotas. The best thing that the West could do to end poverty is to open its markets.[107] Instead, the United States and other Western interests have aimed to control the critical resources of the Third World and, in the process, have produced a massive reaction from Islamists and others.[108]

The word "empire" to summarize the current state of American foreign policy trips easily off many lips, from supporters of the Bush administration to critics at home and abroad. Most accept that the United States is an empire and that its strength is growing relative to its possible competitors. But Wallerstein argues the reverse, that the United States is losing power and that its military actions are those of a weakening state.[109] Ferguson concurs that the American imperial project places too much emphasis on military power and the average American is not vested in its construction.[110] Wallerstein dates the U.S. loss of hegemony from the 1968–1973 period when the indirect power of the hegemon (its economic and military strength and its cultural appeal) was replaced with a "velvet glove hiding the mailed fist." Anti-U.S. challenges were greeted with American military invasion and installation of U.S. puppet regimes (Grenada in 1983, Panama in 1989) or cruise missile strikes (Somalia and Afghanistan in 1998). After a decade of rapid (but artificial) economic growth in the 1990s, the United States is now in a period where the hawks control the administration and the U.S. economy has slowed to a point that is reminiscent of the early 1980s. Economically strong hegemons can use persuasion and emulation as tools for empire building; economically weak (and declining) hegemons assert their faltering power through their military weaponry. The failure of the United States in March 2003 to gain a majority of the UN Security Council in favor of an attack on Iraq is, for Wallerstein, a sign of how far the hegemon has fallen.

Whether one believes that the United States is gaining or losing hegemonic power or is simply maintaining its relative lead depends greatly on one's evidence. What is indisputable is that the United States is willing to use all its weapons to bring about the posture that it wants. There is little doubt that the Bush administration is one of the most unilateralist American presidencies. From rejection of the Kyoto Protocol and sidestepping the UN Security Council on attacking Yugoslavia and Iraq to undermining the International Criminal Court (ICC), the administration has embarked on a course to reassert American power. Using its power nakedly is a hallmark of the strategy. Withdrawing military aid to thirty-five poor countries that have refused to exempt U.S. soldiers and civilians from prosecution in the ICC is just one recent example.[111] Though the number of wars is down slightly from a decade ago, the constellation of U.S. unilateralism, resource greed, local tyrants, and hegemonic competition does not augur a more peaceful world. The Clash sang in "I'm So Bored with the U.S.A." a quarter century ago,

> Yankee dollar talk
> To the dictators of the world
> In fact it's giving orders
> An' they can't afford to miss a word.[112]

Little has changed.

Notes

Thousands of students and a series of superb teaching assistants in Geography 4712 (Political Geography) at the University of Colorado since 1988, either through interest or disdain, have forced me to clarify my ideas about post–Cold War conflicts. Colin Flint's invitation to contribute to this volume enticed me to convert my thoughts from lecture notes into print. Clionadh Raleigh helped in tracking data and bibliographic sources, and Tom Dickinson of the Institute of Behavioral Science prepared the graphics for publication in his customary efficient, timely, and professional manner.

1. See www.iraqbodycount.net (accessed July 1, 2003).
2. "Global Menace of Global Strife," 23–25.
3. Murray et al., "Armed Conflict as a Public Health Problem."
4. Shaw, "Risk-Transfer Militarism."
5. Gurr, "Ethnic Warfare on the Wane."
6. Kennedy, *Rise and Fall of the Great Powers*; Nye, *Bound to Lead*.
7. Mead, "Jacksonian Tradition and American Foreign Policy," 5.
8. O'Loughlin, "Ten Scenarios for a 'New World Order.' "
9. Lasswell, " 'Garrison State' Hypothesis Today."
10. McDougall, *Promised Land, Crusader State*.
11. Mead, "Jacksonian Tradition and American Foreign Polics."
12. Mearsheimer, "Why We Will Soon Miss the Cold War."
13. Data from Fearon and Laitin, "Ethnic Insurgency and Civil War," 75.
14. Ibid., 77.
15. Ibid.
16. Collier, "How to End Civil Wars," 44.
17. Fearon and Laitin, "Ethnic Insurgency and Civil War."
18. Scherrer, *Structural Prevention of Ethnic Violence*.
19. Ibid.
20. "Global Menace of Global Strife," 25.
21. Collier, "How to End Civil Wars"; Collier et al., *Breaking the Conflict Trap*.
22. Collier et al., *Breaking the Conflict Trap*.
23. Fearon and Laitin, "Ethnic Insurgency and Civil War."
24. Scherrer, *Structural Prevention of Ethnic Violence*.
25. Smith, *Ethnic Origins of Nations*; Connor, *Ethnonationalism*.
26. "Global Menace of Global Strife," 24.
27. C. King, "Benefits of Ethnic War."
28. Nairn, *Breakup of Britain*.
29. See Williams, "Question of National Congruence," for an application to Europe of this kind of dual ethnic-primordialist/economic-disparity explanation.
30. Elbadawi and Sambanis, "How Much War Will We See?"
31. Fearon and Laitin, "Ethnic Insurgency and Civil War," 42.
32. Le Billon, "Political Ecology of War," and his contribution to this volume; Collier et al., *Breaking the Conflict Trap*.
33. Le Billon, this volume and "Political Ecology of War."
34. Collier et al., *Breaking the Conflict Trap*, 44.
35. Sachs, "Strategic Significance of Global Inequality," 187.
36. Rotberg, "New Nature of Nation-State Failure," 85.
37. Sachs, "Strategic Significance of Global Inequality," 190.
38. Collier, "How to End Civil Wars."
39. Collier et al., *Breaking the Conflict Trap*.
40. Fearon and Laitin, "Ethnic Insurgency and Civil War," 83.
41. "Global Menace of Global Strife," 25.
42. O'Loughlin, "Spatial Models of International Conflict."
43. Fearon and Laitin, "Ethnic Insurgency and Civil War."
44. Rummel, *Statistics of Democide*.

45. Russett, *Grasping the Democratic Peace.*

46. Collier et al., *Breaking the Conflict Trap*; Fearon and Laitin, "Ethnic Insurgency and War."

47. Elliott, "Radical Thoughts on Our 160th Birthday."

48. Gleditsch and Ward, "War and Peace in Space and Time."

49. Hegre et al., "Toward a Democratic Civil Peace?"

50. Huntington, "*Clash of Civilizations.*"

51. Fearon and Laitin, "Ethnic Insurgency and Civil War"; Chiozza, "Is There a Clash of Civilizations?"

52. For examples of this kind of spatial modeling applied to conflict, see O'Loughlin and Anselin, "Bringing Geography Back to the Study of International Relations," and Gleditsch and Ward, "War and Peace in Space and Time."

53. Singer and Small, "Correlates of War Project."

54. These data are updated yearly and are available from the Department of Peace and Conflict Research, University of Uppsala, Sweden, www.pcr.uu.se (accessed July 1, 2003).

55. Wallensteen and Sollenberg, "Armed Conflict, 1989–2000;" Strand, Wilhelmsen, and Gleditsch, *Armed Conflict Dataset Codebook.*

56. Gleditsch et al., "Armed Conflict, 1946–2001."

57. Buhaug and Gates, "Geography of Civil War."

58. United Nations Development Program, *World Development Report.*

59. Gleditsch et al., "Armed Conflict, 1946–2001."

60. Ibid.

61. O'Loughlin, "World Power Competition and Local Conflicts in the Third World."

62. Mearsheimer, "Why We Will Soon Miss the Cold War."

63. Ibid., 37.

64. Ibid.

65. Kaplan, "Coming Anarchy."

66. Ibid., 46.

67. Ibid., 60.

68. Kagan, "Power and Weakness."

69. This is the vision elaborated by Fukuyama, *The End of History and the Last Man.*

70. Kagan, "Power and Weakness," 3.

71. PIOOM Foundation produces a similar map on world conflicts and human rights; see Jongman, *World Conflict and Human Rights Map 2000.*

72. For more on this theme, see Wusten, this volume.

73. Mead, "Jacksonian Tradition and American Foreign Policy."

74. All figures are from the Stockholm International Peace Research Institute Yearbook 2003 and the CIA's *World Factbook, 2002.*

75. Kagan, *Of Paradise and Power.*

76. O'Loughlin and Kolossov, "Still Not Worth the Bones of a Single Pomeranian Grenadier."

77. Cohen, "Some Afterthoughts," 569.

78. Kagan, "Power and Weakness"; Toal, " 'Just Out Looking for a Fight.' "

79. Mead, "Jacksonian Tradition and American Foreign Policy."

80. Connolly, *Neuropolitics,* 35.

81. Toal, " 'Just Out Looking for a Fight.' "

82. Kagan, "Power and Weakness."

83. Ferguson, *Empire.*

84. Klarevas, " 'Essential Domino' of Military Operations."

85. Lasswell, " 'Garrison State' Hypothesis Today."
86. Shaw, "Risk-Transfer Militarism."
87. Ibid., 347.
88. Ek, "Military Revolution in Military Geopolitics?"; Loeb, "Digitized Battlefield Puts Friend and Foe in Sight."
89. Shaw, "Risk-Transfer Militarism," 349.
90. Ibid., 352.
91. Walzer, *Just and Unjust Wars*, 156. Wheeler, "Protecting Afghan Civilians from the Hell of War," makes a similar argument in respect to U.S. military action in Afghanistan.
92. Borger, "America to Build Super Weapons."
93. Hardt and Negri, *Empire*; Wallerstein, "U.S. Weakness and the Struggle for Hegemony"; Ferguson, "Empire Slinks Back."
94. G. Lundestad, "Empire by Invitation?"
95. Bond et al., "Integrated Data for Events Analysis (IDEA)."
96. For the details on the machine coding, see Virtual Research Associates, www.vranet.com (accessed June 12, 2003). The accuracy of the machine coding is equivalent to that of expert human coders, as King and Lowe showed in an experiment. See G. King and Lowe, "Automated Information Extraction Tool for International Conflict Data."
97. Goldstein, "Conflict-Cooperation Scale for WEIS Event Data."
98. North Korea, with a slight positive score, was the subject of U.S. food aid in the 1990s to try to wean this state from its nuclear program. However, North Korea remained bitterly opposed to the United States.
99. Barnett, "The Pentagon's New Map."
100. For a critique of Barnett's thesis, see Roberts, Secor, and Sparke, "Neoliberal Geographies."
101. Barnett, "Pentagon's New Map."
102. *National Security Strategy of the United States.*
103. Klare, "New Geopolitics."
104. Cohen, "Geopolitical Realities and United States Foreign Policy."
105. Mackinder, *Democratic Ideals and Reality*, 150.
106. Barnett, "Pentagon's New Map."
107. Maskus, "System on the Brink."
108. Achcar, *Clash of Barbarisms*; Flint, "Terrorism and Counterterrorism."
109. Wallerstein, "U.S. Weakness and the Struggle for Hegemony."
110. Ferguson, "Empire Slinks Back."
111. Becker, "U.S. Suspends Aid to 35 Countries over New International Criminal Court."
112. J. Strummer and M. Jones, 1977. "I'm So Bored with the USA." The Clash, Polydor Records, 1977.

References

Achcar, G. *The Clash of Barbarisms: September 11 and the Making of the New World Disorder.* New York: Monthly Review Press, 2003.

Barnett, T. P. M. "The Pentagon's New Map: It Explains Why We're Going to War and Why We Will Keep Going to War." *Esquire* (March 2003): 174–179, 227–228.

Becker, E. "U.S. Suspends Aid to 35 Countries over New International Criminal Court." *New York Times*, July 1, 2003, A12.

Bond, D., J. Bond, C. Oh, J. C. Jenkins, and C. L. Taylor. "Integrated Data for Events Analysis (IDEA): An Event Form Typology for Automated Events Data Development." Unpublished manuscript, Harvard University, 2001.

Borger, J. "U.S. Missiles To Have Global Reach" *Guardian*, July 1, 2003, 3.

Buhaug, H., and S. Gates. "The Geography of Civil War." *Journal of Peace Research* 39 (2002): 417–433.

Central Intelligence Agency World Factbook. Washington, DC; Government Printing Office, 2002. www.cia.gov/cia/publication/factbook.

Chiozza, G. "Is There a Clash of Civilizations? Evidence from Patterns of International Conflict Involvement, 1946–97." *Journal of Peace Research* 39 (2002): 711–734.

Cohen, S. B. "Some Afterthoughts: A Cohen Perspective from Mid-October 2001." *Political Geography* 21 (2002): 569–572.

Cohen, S. B. "Geopolitical Realities and United States Foreign Policy." *Political Geography* 22 (2003): 1–33.

Collier, P. "How to End Civil Wars." *Foreign Policy* 136 (May–June 2003): 38–45.

Collier, P., Elliot, L., Hegre, H., Hoeffler, A, Reynal-Querul, M., Sambanis, N. *Breaking the Conflict Trap: Civil War and Development Policy*. Washington, DC: World Bank, 2003.

Connolly, W. E. *Neuropolitics: Thinking, Culture, Speed*. Minneapolis: University of Minnesota Press, 2002.

Connor, W. *Ethnonationalism: The Quest for Understanding*. Princeton, NJ: Princeton University Press, 1993.

Ek, R. "A Revolution in Military Geopolitics?" *Political Geography* 19 (2000), 841–874.

Elbadawi, I., and N. Sambanis. "How Much War Will We See? Explaining the Prevalence of Civil War." *Journal of Conflict Resolution* 46 (2002): 307–334.

Elliott, B. "Radical Thoughts on Our 160th Birthday: A Survey of Capitalism and Democracy." *Economist* June 28, 2003, Special Report.

Fearon, J., and D. Laitin, "Ethnicity Insurgency and Civil War." *American Political Science Review* 97 (2002): 75–90.

Ferguson, N. "The Empire Slinks Back." *New York Times Magazine*, April 27, 2003, 52–57.

Ferguson, N. *Empire: The Rise and Demise of the British World Order and the Lessons for Global Power*. New York: Basic Books, 2003.

Flint, C. "Terrorism and Counterterrorism: Geographic Research and Questions and Agendas." *Professional Geographer* 55 (2003): 161–69.

Fukuyama, F. *The End of History and the Last Man*. New York: Penguin, 1992.

Gleditsch, K. S., and M. D. Ward. "War and Peace in Space and Time: The Role of Democratization." *International Studies Quarterly* 44 (2000): 1–29.

Gleditsch, N. P., P. Wallensteen, M. Eriksson, M. Sollenberg, and H. Strand. "Armed Conflict, 1946–2001: A New Dataset." *Journal of Peace Research* 30 (2002): 615–637.

"The Global Menace of Global Strife." *Economist*, May 24, 2003, 23–25.

Goldstein, J. S. "A Conflict-Cooperation Scale for WEIS Event Data." *Journal of Conflict Resolution* 36 (1992): 369–385.

Gurr, T. R. "Ethnic Warfare on the Wane." *Foreign Affairs* 79 (May–June 2000): 52–64.

Hardt, M., and A. Negri. *Empire*. Cambridge, MA: Harvard University Press, 2000.

Hegre, H., T. Ellingsen, S. Gates, and N. P. Gleditsch. "Toward a Democratic Civil Peace? Democracy, Political Change and Civil War, 1816–1992." *American Political Science Review* 95 (2001): 33–48.

Huntington, S. P. "The Clash of Civilization" *Foreign Affairs* 72 (Summer 1993): 22–49.

Huntington, S. P. *The Clash of Civilizations and the Remaking of World Order*. New York: Simon and Schuster, 1996.

Jongman, A. J. *The World Conflict and Human Rights Map 2000. "Mapping Dimensions of Contemporary Conflicts and Human Rights Violations."* Leiden: Universiteit Leiden PIOOM Foundation, 2001. www.pcr.uu.se/paperjongman.doc (accessed July 5, 2003).
Kagan, R. "Power and Weakness." *Policy Review* 113 (June–July 2002): 3–28.
Kagan, R. *Of Paradise and Power: America and Europe in the New World Order.* New York: Knopf, 2003.
Kaplan, R. "The Coming Anarchy." *Atlantic Monthly* 273 (February 1994): 44–76.
Kennedy, P. M. *The Rise and Fall of the Great Powers: Economic Change and Military Conflict from 1500 to 2000.* New York: Random House, 1987.
King, C. "The Benefits of Ethnic War: Understanding Eurasia's Unrecognized States." *World Politics* 52 (2001): 524–562.
King, G., and W. Lowe. "An Automated Information Extraction Tool for International Conflict Data with Performance as Good as Human Coders: A Rare Events Evaluation Design." *International Organization* 57 (Summer 2003): 617–642.
Klare, M. "The New Geopolitics." *Monthly Review* 55 (July–August 2003): 51–56.
Klarevas, L. "The 'Essential Domino' of Military Operations: American Public Opinion and the Use of Force." *International Studies Perspectives* 3 (2002): 417–437.
Lasswell, H. "The 'Garrison State' Hypothesis Today." In *The Changing Nature of Military Politics*, ed. S. Huntington, 51–70. New York: Free Press, 1962.
Le Billon, P. "The Political Ecology of War: Natural Resources and Armed Conflict." *Political Geography* 20 (2001): 561–584.
Loeb, V. "Digitized Battlefield Puts Friend and Foe in Sight." *Washington Post*, March 3, 2003: A15.
Lundestad, G. "Empire by Invitation? The United States and Western Europe, 1945–52." *Journal of Peace Research* 23 (1986): 263 77.
Mackinder, H. J. *Democratic Ideals and Reality.* New York: Norton, [1919] 1962.
Maskus, K. E. "A System on the Brink: Pitfalls in International Trade Rules on the Road to Globalization." In *Globalization and Its Outcomes*, ed. J. O'Loughlin, L. Staeheli, and E. Greenberg. New York: Guilford, 2004.
McDougall, W. A. *Promised Land, Crusader State: The American Encounter with the World since 1776.* Boston: Houghton Mifflin, 1997.
Mead, W. R. "The Jacksonian Tradition and American Foreign Policy." *National Interest* 58 (winter 1999/2000): 5–29.
Mead, W. R. *Special Providence: American Foreign Policy and How It Changed the World.* New York: Knopf, 2001.
Mearsheimer, J. J. "Why We Will Soon Miss the Cold War." *Atlantic Monthly* 266 (August 1990): 35–50.
Murray, C. J. L., G. King, A. D. Lopez, N. Tomijima, and E. G. Krug. "Armed Conflict as a Public Health Problem." *BMJ* 324 (February 9, 2002): 346–349.
Nairn, T. *The Breakup of Britain.* London: New Left, 1977.
National Security Strategy of the United States. Washington, DC: Office of the President, September 2002. "The White House." www.whitehouse.gov/nsc/nss.html (accessed July 9, 2003).
Nye, J. S. *Bound to Lead: The Changing Nature of American Power.* New York: Basic Books, 1990.
O'Loughlin, J. "Spatial Models of International Conflict: Extending Current Theories of War Behavior." *Annals of the Association of American Geographers* 76 (1986): 63–80.
O'Loughlin, J. "World Power Competition and Local Conflicts in the Third World." In *A World in Crisis: Geographical Perspectives*, 2nd ed., ed. R. J. Johnston and P. J. Taylor, 289–332. Oxford: Blackwell, 1989.

O'Loughlin, J. "Ten Scenarios for a 'New World Order.'" *Professional Geographer* 44 (1992): 22–28.

O'Loughlin, J., and L. Anselin. "Bringing Geography Back to the Study of International Relations: Spatial Dependence and Regional Context in Africa, 1966–1978." *International Interactions* 17 (1991): 29–61.

O'Loughlin, J., and V. Kolossov. "Still Not Worth the Bones of a Single Pomeranian Grenadier: The Geopolitics of the Kosovo War, 1999." *Political Geography* 21 (2002): 573–599.

Roberts, S., A. Secor, and M. Sparke. "Neoliberal Geographies." *Antipode* 35 no. 4 (2003): 886–897.

Rotberg, R. I. "The New Nature of Nation-State Failure." *Washington Quarterly* 25 (2002): 85–96.

Rummel, R. J. *Statistics of Democide: Genocide and Mass Murder since 1900*. New Brunswick, NJ: Transaction, 1997.

Russett, B. R. *Grasping the Democratic Peace: Principles for a Post–Cold War World*. Princeton, NJ: Princeton University Press, 1994.

Sachs, J. "The Strategic Significance of Global Inequality." *Washington Quarterly* 24 (2001): 187–198.

Scherrer, C. *Structural Prevention of Ethnic Violence*. London: Palgrave Macmillan, 2002.

Shaw, M. "Risk-Transfer Militarism, Small Massacres, and the Historic Legitimacy of War." *International Relations* 16 (2002): 343–359.

Singer, J. D., and M. Small. "Correlates of War Project: International and Civil War Data." no. 9905. Ann Arbor: Inter-University Consortium for Political and Social Research, University of Michigan, 1994.

Smith, A. D. *The Ethnic Origins of Nations*. Oxford: Blackwell, 1986.

Strand, H., L. Wilhelmsen, and N. P. Gleditsch. *Armed Conflict Dataset Codebook*. Version 1.2. Oslo: International Peace Research Institute, 2003. www.prio.no/cwp/armedconflict (accessed June 25, 2003).

Toal, G. "'Just Out Looking for a Fight': American Affect and the Invasion of Iraq." *Antipode* 35 (2003): 856–870.

United Nations Development Program. *World Development Report*. New York: United Nations Development Program, 2002.

Wallensteen, P., and M. Sollenberg. "Armed Conflict, 1989–2000." *Journal of Peace Research* 38 (2001): 635–649.

Wallerstein, I. "U.S. Weakness and the Struggle for Hegemony." *Monthly Review* 55 (July–August 2003): 23–29.

Walzer, M. *Just and Unjust Wars*. New York: Basic Books, 1977.

Wheeler, N. J. "Protecting Afghan Civilians from the Hell of War." New York: Social Science Research Council, 2001. www.ssrc.org/sept11/essays/wheeler.htm (accessed June 26, 2003).

Williams, C. H. "The Question of National Congruence." In A *World in Crisis: Geographical Perspectives*, 2nd ed., ed. R. J. Johnston and P. J. Taylor, 229–265. Oxford: Blackwell, 1989.

II

GEOGRAPHIES OF WAR

6

GERTJAN DIJKINK

Soldiers and Nationalism

The Glory and Transience of a Hard-Won Territorial Identity

Mud, Music, and Blood

Anton von Werner's *Im Etappenquartier vor Paris* (In quarters before Paris) is based on a sketch done by the painter during the German military campaign against France in October 1870 (Figure 6.1). German soldiers amuse themselves with songs at the piano in a requisitioned manor house near Paris (Brunoy). Attracted by the music, the French concierge and child appear in the doorway. Some mundane activities to further enhance the atmosphere are in progress: lamps are lighted and a fire is kindled in the fireplace. We even know the song that is performed: Schubert's "Am Meer" (By the sea), with words by Heinrich Heine.[1] Nothing yet anticipates the disillusioned statement of George Steiner that became characteristic of late-twentieth-century reflection on war and culture: "We know now that a man can read Goethe or Rilke in the evening, that he can play Bach and Schubert, and go to his day's work at Auschwitz in the morning."[2]

In Werner's painting, war still seems to be an innocent affair that first of all produces mud-stained boots. These boots and the sphere of fraternization that even encompasses the French housekeeper were meant to evoke the impression of sincerity in German soldiers, according to a German art historian.[3] Ultimately converted into a painting, the picture became really popular when it was sold on the German market as a small tapestry after 1895. As the German writer and critic Ludwig Pietsch wrote at the time, "[Such pictures show] the good-natured and sentimental nature of the national character [. . .] which even in the rough and wild times of war and in the midst of an irreconcilable enemy cannot be denied."[4] Not surprisingly, the French reading of this picture (once or twice on exhibition in Paris) is somewhat different: "The attitudes of the lumpish soldiers with their blusterous posture, their heavy mud-stained boots, are completely in contrast to the refinement of the furniture. The conquerors behave somewhat like vandals. At the right in the doorway, the maid, on whom an officer seems to have designs,

FIGURE 6.1 Anton von Werner's *Im Etappenquartier vor Paris* (In quarters before Paris). *Source:* Archive for Prussian Art Treasures © Bildarchiv Preussischer Kulturbesitz, Berlin, 2003, Nationgalerie Berlin. Reproduced by permission of Bildarchiv Preussischer Kulturbesitz.

watches the scene accompanied by her daughter, who is hardly able to hide her fear."[5]

The two national commentators are unanimous in accepting the picture as an authentic and honest report of the 1870 events. How wonderful is the way of art! Anyhow, it reveals the penetrating role of the national gaze and the nationalist tendency to link war and culture. The incensed commentary on this painting notwithstanding, the French had led the way seventy years before by presenting their military campaign in Europe as a *mission civilisatrice*, a mission to diffuse French civilization, which according to the revolutionary leader Robespierre was "advanced 2000 years beyond the rest of humankind."[6] The German invasion of 1870 was a sweet revenge conducted in the same vein.

The picture of soldiers outside the battleground, even detached from any type of military activity, offers a wordless account of the way nationalism had changed the meaning of the army in the nineteenth century. It tells that soldiers are not completely at a loss in cultured society, that they are recruited from the higher and lower classes, that they combine mud and civilized music. The pulling together of civil and military affairs changed the face of war by producing soldiers who bring along more "thought." This feature of nationalism is supposed to hav reinforced the morale and strength of armies and, apart from all the other sufferings that war entails, turned war and occupation for civilians into a cultural ordeal that verged on racism. At a period in history that is often described as postnational, we are tempted to interpret such conditions as boosting war and accompanying cruelty, an opinion seemingly substantiated by ethnonationalist outpourings in the post-Communist world or in Africa. But can we equate the historical transformation of nationalism with the perfecting of a war machine? And what does the disappearance of the nationalist sentiment—supposing that this indeed is what happens—mean for postnational (postmodern) warfare? These are questions that will be developed in this chapter, by argumentation rather than by empirical induction.

With some hesitation and compelled by the events of the Napoleonic Wars, the Prussian king and aristocracy after 1813 embraced the idea that education, literacy, and civil rights made an important contribution to the combat power of an army. On the one hand, this was an answer to the new military technology (increased rifle power), which necessitated the spatial dispersal of soldiers on the battlefield and therefore made a strong appeal to individual responsibility and insight, ergo, to education. On the other hand, feelings of national solidarity reinforced the strength of an army by boosting its morale. The Prussians even went a step further by calling in retired soldiers for teaching tasks in regular schools. From the perspective of nationalist aims this was a double-edged sword because it increased discipline and military (geopolitical) thinking in society and because it helped raise the educational level as an important tool in nation building.[7]

Nationalism brought a revolution in warfare by turning the ordinary citizen into an accomplice. It generated an unprecedented material and moral support for war efforts and was able to raise mass armies via conscription or the massive enrollment of volunteers. The small army and ill-paid mercenary of a prenational state or sovereign were no match for such forces, but one would draw a distorted picture of nationalism by focusing only on its quality as a war machine. On the contrary, one of the messages of nationalism was that people should distance themselves from the personal military adventures of kings and autocrats and look at their social and economic interests. The hesitations of the Prussian aristocracy were understandable, but they had little choice if they wished to keep up with the increasing power potential of the state.

At first sight, the national idea seemed to offer the prospect of a fraternity of European nations rather than a struggle for life between peoples.[8] Many nationalist efforts in the nineteenth century were inspired by the idea that they would do away with undemocratic rulers. The longing was for territorial unification that promised status in a quickly internationalizing world and the removal of local rulers who had become museum pieces. If this implied violence, it did not straightaway pit entire people against each other. The qualification "international" war with its terrible connotation of extermination and rate of human loss is more appropriate for the twentieth-century European wars, the American Civil War, or recent ethnonationalism. Yet one must concede that in Europe the process of nationalization also entailed the production of a host of negative stereotypes and even hate among nations, particularly between the French and the English and later the French and the Germans. Where territorial change was not any longer the main objective, nationalism kept reinforcing national unity (identity) by emphasizing national greatness and mission.

Benedict Anderson has greatly helped the diffusion of the idea that nations are first of all products of the imagination.[9] This is also true of war in the life of a nation. Scholars of nationalism and war tend to overlook the fact that imagined wars are perhaps even more important than real wars in nation building. In an exhibition devoted to European national myths as represented in nineteenth-century art and on household goods, 43% of the eighty collected items were myths in which battles played a prominent role.[10] A further 16% were devoted to events that can be interpreted as smaller acts of resistance against an occupying force. But one should emphasize the phrase "can be interpreted" since most of the commemorated battles and violent acts were only "national" from the perspective of the nineteenth century. Wars from the eleventh to the sixteenth centuries, let alone those against the Roman Empire, were obviously never waged with the image of the future nation-state in mind, yet they are with hindsight presented in national myths as important foundational landmarks.

An example is the *Guldensporenslag* (Battle of the Golden Spurs) from 1302 that became a popular topic in Belgian art and graphics after Belgium's independence in 1830.[11] Actually it was a battle between the patricians and commoners (artisans or guilds) in the Flemish cities that got an interterritorial dimension when the "French" king Philip IV ("the Fair") sided with the patricians whereas his vassal, the Flemish count Guy of Dampierre, sided with the commoners. The French king and his army suffered a crushing defeat, and the victors afterwards collected the "golden spurs" of the French knights on the battlefield as trophies that, much later, gave the battle its name. A typical representation from the nineteenth century shows the commoners as a collection of footmen in different uniforms or daily clothes, often without advanced weaponry, in combat with lavishly rigged-out knights. This image enhanced the moral quality of the victory and suggested that a really national force had won it. A late nineteenth century painting by the Belgian artist James Ensor, however, reveals a new perspective by depicting the *Guldensporenslag* as a battle in which both sides are difficult to distinguish (see Figure 6.2). Anyone seems to fight with anyone. It was either a deconstruction of the nationalist myth or a statement about the bloody origins of nations and the irrelevance of the question of who wins.

The latter part of the nineteenth century indeed witnessed the appearance of a new type of war imagination, not about wars from the past but about future wars. In British novels the imagination seemed to thrive on invasion fears that implied a neglect of the defense of the homeland because of imperial preoccupations (The Battle of Dorking)[12] or because the enemy smartly managed to disguise its invasion strategy by exploiting its own geography (*The Riddle of the Sands*).[13] Germans and German legs on precious furniture also stirred the imagination of novelists.[14] As in Werner's painting, war had literally entered the private sphere by showing that the civic culture or the family was at risk or by suggesting that security was a matter of common intelligence rather than heroism. In the course of time national territorial security became even more elusive in war fiction

FIGURE 6.2 James Ensor's depiction of the *Guldensporenslag*. *Source:* © 2004 Artists Rights Society (ARS), New York/SABAM, Brussels; © Museum voor Schone Kunsten Oostende, SABAM, 2003. Reproduced by permission of Museum voor Schone Kunsten Oostende.

since the imagined enemy materialized in the midst of a nation and sucked up its blood (*The War of the Worlds*[15]) or its identity.[16] Fiction writers and artists often seem to have adequately anticipated new vulnerabilities and fears. After 1870 war became more destructive in a material sense, but it also adopted the character of an ordeal in which civic values and identities were at stake. Heroic monuments devoted to generals and landmark battles were substituted by more concrete and mundane witnesses of war: cemeteries and local monuments to the ordinary fallen and—highly significant—the "Unknown Soldier." Here the commemoration included those who died in clashes of which the contribution to the course of war was highly obscure. Nationalism was both experienced and somewhat transcended in this worship of the spilled blood. It appeared as if all soldiers, allied and enemy, had died in a Christian ritual to ban the evil powers from the world. War had engulfed the world of civilians and could be imagined as a struggle in the personal life space.

Readiness to Die

In his voluminous work *The Art of War in the Western World* Archer Jones discusses the battle at Novara (1849), in which the Austrians under the command of

General Joseph Radetzky defeated an army of Italian (Piedmontese) nationalists almost equal in size (about 65,000 soldiers). Jones merely analyzes the outcome as a strategic and tactical game of military commanders.[17] Radetzky had already won his spurs in the Napoleonic Wars, and his tactics and strategies still proved to be sound and better than those of his opponent, King Carlo Alberto. More than half a century before this analysis was published, Antonio Gramsci had made a quite different diagnosis about the disaster of Novara: "At Novara the army did not want to fight, and therefore was defeated," he concludes simply.[18] The point brought up by Gramsci is that "the more numerous an army is . . . the more the importance of political leadership increases in comparison with merely technical-military leadership." The Piedmontese leaders made a mistake by viewing the high level of combativity of the army at the start of the campaign as merely an expression of "abstract military and dynastic spirit." As a consequence, one carelessly allowed infringements on popular freedoms and started toning down expectations of a democratic future. Thereupon the morale of the army fell. Gramsci points to the crucial role of political legitimacy in warfare. Legitimacy and individual dignity (citizenship) assured by the state were central motives of the nationalist movement in the nineteenth century. In Italy these ideals were never fulfilled—the sanctity of national unity put a taboo on discussions of the spatial inequality between the North and the South, says Gramsci—but that is another matter.

Gramsci, in his own way, discusses the change in the history of warfare that is connected with the rise of nationalism. For him, the transcending of mutual differences between people who are uniting in a nation is more perplexing than successful resistance against a "foreign" occupier. This also qualifies the remark made earlier about national states as war machines. Nationalism neither automatically turned states into war machines nor turned human individuals into robots that cry out their wish to die for the *patria*. Readiness to die should at least be seen in the perspective of a future, however illusionary, the belief in a better world for oneself and one's offspring. The established state that feeds a host of civil servants offers its own reasons for people to fight or die because they may lose their job, their sponsor, or simply their footing in the "center" and its rituals. This even extends to such prenational political entities as empires and their elites. We know that the fall of the Chinese Ming dynasty (1644) at the hands of the Mongols who came from the north incited many Chinese to commit suicide.[19] Artists (painters) were for a long period out of balance, as is apparent from the paintings they left behind.[20] However, the fall of the Ming dynasty was itself the result of collapsing political legitimacy because the empire was already stricken by political discord, rebellion, and corruption. The established political and cultural (ritual) order appears to be so important as a source of psychic balance and material well-being for the literate strata that it induces many of them to commit suicide in the case of a foreign takeover. Yet even this undeniable connection between the state and the meaning of life does not necessarily yield armies that wage life-and-death struggles. Would industrializing nation-states, where many more people have a clear stake in the political system and culture, perform any better? One certainly may expect a high level of (manipulated) fear about external dangers in such states, but as Gramsci already intimates in his writings on Italy, nation-states can slip away in embitterment between social classes or regions. Political leaders may go on the warpath to divert attention from such domestic problems, but they may soon lose all credit if they count too much on the readiness to die.

The lack of fighting spirit in the late Ming and the discussion of the failure at Novara provoke another, inverse question: why do soldiers carry on in situations where the outlook seems so unequivocally desperate? The question of why soldiers did not desert en masse has been asked frequently about trench warfare in World War I when time and again waves of attacks by soldiers who left the trenches ended in something like collective death before a firing squad. Officers were expected to hold positions until the last man, without such orders serving any clear purpose in an overall strategy. Yet although they were quite capable of critically distancing themselves from political leaders and national slogans, in the end they kept going as if they were robots. Autobiographical reports and letters from soldiers at the front suggest that they felt an innate drive to behave in a civilized way, to show the composure that seems to belong to the values of the bourgeois or middle class. As a French sergeant who had just gotten the order to attack the enemy across open terrain commented, "You have to behave properly in the presence of death."[21] Such civic values are perhaps specific to the socialization that occurs in the national state, irrespective of the country where soldiers came from. Modris Eksteins suggests, "[The 1914–1918 war] was the civil war of the European middle class above all else."[22]

Another explanation of the disciplined behavior displayed at the front can be found in solidarity with the comrades who face the same desperate situation at the edge of death, but this is remote from national solidarity or patriotism.[23] Instead of what one might have expected, the mood more to the rear of the front could be quite different and sometimes verged on mutiny among French troops.[24] Here the country paid for tensions and divisions within French politics in spite of the nationalist ardor that had been kept burning by remembering the loss of Alsace and Lorraine in 1871. If we connect Gramsci's diagnosis of Novara with zones in the war theater, then we may argue that nationalism's impact on warfare—in either a negative or positive sense—should be more noticeable in the rear, whereas events at the front obey different principles.[25] Here bare survival and comradeship rule human behavior rather than the longing to get immortalized by a national war memorial.

Few systems of thought are so clearly linked with the readiness to die as a religious persuasion. In both Christianity and Islam, martyrdom for the sake of one's belief is a cultural archetype. Nationalism has also been described as a (secular) religion, and certain conflicts that have arisen since the end of the nineteenth century between the state and the church (Germany, Italy) or between the state and religious groups (Netherlands) seem to corroborate this idea. But in comparison to religion or other ideologies (liberalism, socialism), nationalism is notoriously shallow as a system of thought. It mainly corresponds with religion in terms of rituals in which the nation or the "general will" is worshiped.[26] In this respect nationalism may evoke the "religious" experience of being part of a larger whole, but this offers a type of immortality that differs from religion, where the self-sacrificing individual is rewarded in the hereafter. It is no wonder that nation-states painstakingly attempted to preserve some link between national aims and the dominant religion. God is always on one's side. The slogan never was completely convincing in intra-European war, and we may conclude that nationalism is better at selling a war than at consoling people who come face-to-face with death. However uncertain the guidance of nationalism during a war is, its finest moment comes afterward when the nation starts to erect monuments for the fallen.

Since the end of the wars in Korea and Vietnam, Western states have shown extreme restraint in the acceptance of death in combat. The mood in the United States made the term "body bags" proverbial in each discussion on the involvement in military campaigns outside the West, even those under the aegis of the United Nations. This obviously reflects a level of wealth and a feeling of complacency at the end of the twentieth century in the West that did not justify the sacrifice of lives anymore. One of the surprises was the British Falklands/Malvinas expedition in 1982, when the world wondered what the stakes exactly were. Geopolitical arguments or the character of the British prime minister did not completely exhaust the reasons for this war. Public support—whether spontaneous or mobilized—can hardly be explained by the loss of territory; rather, it was indignation over the lack of manners of the adversary. This is the reaction of a nation that is struggling with an evil that touches its principles rather than its boundaries. Terrorist attacks like those of September 2001 have shown a similar ability to skip the balance between accepting and rejecting the risk of deaths in combat. But all this concerns the willingness to send troops and does not say much about the morale of soldiers in an engagement with the enemy. The 1995 events in Srebrenica did not reveal a clear determination to die for the sake of civilization on the part of the (Dutch) UN troops, although we may admit that there was little to recommend such an attitude under the circumstances. For the time being, Western nations, particularly the United States, have repressed reflection about death by taking refuge behind a massive technical supremacy. But even this technical approach cannot eliminate the dependency on people either at home or in the area targeted, which may again make alive Gramsci's statement about political leadership as key to winning a war.

Postmodern War 1: Territorial and Ethnic Stakes

Let us start here from Gellner's definition of nationalism as "a principle which holds that the political and national unit should be congruent."[27] The definition is less straightforward than it looks since it shifts the definitional problem to the questions of what a nation is and what congruent is. We may interpret congruent as territorial coincidence and nation as a group of persons with the same culture. An obvious conclusion is that territorial noncoincidence might be a casus belli. However, since cultural identity is a matter of self-definition and construction, it is not easy to establish objectively when the conditions of noncongruence apply.

Nations have usually adopted "theories" or "geopolitical visions" that explain why a certain territory is a "natural" complement.[28] For the complete nation-state, loss of territory is inevitably something comparable to bodily mutilation. The losses of Alsace and Lorraine for France in 1871 and of large parts of the eastern territories for Germany after the Treaty of Versailles were events with an understa[illegible] impact. A book about the teaching of geography recommended in 1923 [illegible] order to promote "spiritual contact with the violently separated parts of the German territory," each classroom should have a map with the old boundaries of Germany.[29] The 1920s saw the rise of a real *Raum* frenzy in Germany in which the concept of space became a magic wand, a kind of social physics that not only seemed to integrate the most diverse fields of knowledge but also exposed the Allied powers and their "dictate" of Versailles as averse from knowledge about geopolitical laws.[30] The Earth, not Germany, would seek revenge. It was a German formula that mobilized the minds of the people in a direction that pointed to future war. The loss of Alsace and Lorraine had inspired similar but less explicit expectations about "natural" order in France, but these were rather couched in a sociological discourse on the inclination of people to choose for freedom and the kind of "synergy" that only the cultural variety of France could provide. God has often been invoked to bolster the morale of soldiers, but naturalization of the territory is a more modern intellectual device for inspiring faith in the outcome of a war.

In spite of all ambiguities around cultural similarity, there are numerous cases where "ethnic" minorities and the ethnic majority in a neighboring state consider themselves mutually similar: Hungarians in Romania, Russians in Ukraine, Roman Catholics in Northern Ireland, Slavic groups in Greek Macedonia, Armenians in Azerbaijan, Austrians in Italy (Tirol), and so on. Usually the sacred principle of state sovereignty guarded by the international state system is a sufficient guarantee against "irredentism," the outbreak of war motivated by "lost" territories, but guerrilla warfare or terrorist violence can be less easily suppressed (Northern Ireland, South Tirol, Basque country). The greatest opportunity for ethnically motivated war crops up during the emergence of a power vacuum like the rapidly weakening centripetal force of the Ottoman Empire at the beginning of the twentieth century (the Balkan Wars) or the collapse of the Yugoslav Republic and the Soviet Union. The wish to unite all Serbs from Croatia and Bosnia within one Greater Serbia constituted the main motive for the Serb (more properly "Little Yugoslavian") regime to wage war or to support local Serbian military units elsewhere. It is precisely the weakness of the state identities that arise in such cases that promotes the appearance of paramilitary groups (militias) and warlords and causes a high number of atrocities that do not seem to serve any military purpose. Nationalism is often particularly blamed for such atrocities.

Many commentators have been puzzled by the nationalist hate and craving for mutual extermination that emerged in Yugoslavia in the 1990s even between neighbors who only a few years before had still looked at each other as nationally equal. Michael Ignatieff, in talking with a Serbian soldier in a Croatian village that was cut in two by the Serb-Croat war in 1991–1992, tries to discover the nature of the cultural difference and why it is so insurmountable. The soldier first suggests that they smoke different brands of cigarettes over there ("Croatian cigarettes") but soon realizes that this cannot be the essential point. "Look, here's how it is. Those Croats, they think they're better than us. They want to be the gentlemen. Think they're fancy Europeans. I'll tell you something. We're all just Balkan shit."[31] The paradoxical fact is that the argument ends with a statement about similarity: inferior Balkan stock. It echoes the widespread tradition of people in eastern and southeastern Europe to consider their neighbours to the east or south as just located outside the circle of (European) civilization and themselves inside. Croats looked in this way at the Serbs, but the Serbs did the same with the Albanian or Muslim population. But did this start war? The quotation rather suggests that denial of similarity is a cause of war.

Ignatieff assumes that there is a conflict in this soldier between his personal experience of the similarity of all villagers and the civilizational images that the nationalist media and politicians impose on him. This contradiction is unsolvable unless one gives oneself up to the reality of war, which introduces its own simple logic of dividing people into friends and enemies. There is, however, an alternative explanation that suggests that killing and atrocities like rape were intended to deprive the other of his/her identity (or rather "pedestal") and reduce everyone, including oneself, to "Balkan shit."[32] Finally, one may assume that violence, once set in train, provides its own motivation since any death, particularly if it strikes one's own family, demands revenge. Moreover, the treatment of minorities in the newly formed states of the former Yugoslavia understandably added fuel to fears about civil rights.

"Postmodern" ethnic war has called up indignant commentary on the savagery, shallowness and perversity of its "nationalist" arguments and the blindness with which the warriors destroy both the enemy and their own reputation.[33] But didn't we already encounter wild speculations about the enemy (stereotypes) and the most senseless mutual destruction during World War I or the period that preceded it?[34] Have wars attributed to classic nationalism been more benign? The number of war victims in both world wars does not seem to justify such a conclusion. As mentioned earlier, nationalism increasingly involved the entire population and its economic resources in the war effort. Since the power of a state no longer depended on military resources of a sovereign but became a matter of "infrastructural power," hitting factories, transport facilities, or urban agglomerations seemed to have become a rational war aim. Yet at the same time movements tried to civilize war by means of international agreements (or law) that prohibited the targeting of civilians and that provided some leeway for neutral organizations like the Red Cross. This is one of the many paradoxes that fit with Nairn's description of nationalism as a "modern Janus." We already met this double face in nationalism's propensity to propagate a universal civilization and yet to cling to the idea that our nation will always stay the leader in this process.[35] Did the ultimate wish to improve the world disappear in "postmodern" ethnic war?

Writers like Ignatieff and Enzensberger group contemporary ethnic wars in the class of civil wars. "Disintegration of the state comes first, nationalist paranoia comes next. Nationalist sentiment on the ground . . . is . . . a response to the collapse of state order and the interethnic accommodation that it made possible."[36] Since there was no profound tradition of ethnic separation in territories like the former Yugoslavia, so the argument seems to run, nationalist visions are instant and malignant and are intended to stir up hate instead of providing enduring tools for building a community, as "civic" nationalism did. This idea demands a threefold qualification.

First, classic nationalism also divided people who for a long period had shared a common identity. In border regions like the Pyrenees, Spanish and French identities emerged centuries after the boundary had been fixed.[37] Initially, however, people in regions like the Cerdanya started to use their new national affiliation as merely a tactical tool to enforce their claims in traditional quarrels with neighbors about land and rights. Only after local men had been conscripted for the war with Germany in 1870 did feelings of solidarity with the wider French nation evolve.

Second, we already encountered the notion of a "European civil war" as a designation for what happened in 1914–1918.[38] The idea behind this specification is that the war was boosted by similar values on both sides of the dividing line, actually by values of a class—the middle class—that had more to lose than to win in the way the conflict was fought. This class still carried the nationalist conviction that individual economic prospects and the dignity ensuing from acting as good and responsible citizens—the composure of the gently born—were narrowly linked. Now they caught signs of disrespect at the international stage that aroused old sensibilities. But the subsequent war could not end in the same kind of equal rights that nationalism had achieved earlier within the framework of a nation-state. The war destroyed economic assets and human lives and actually stripped Europe of its world power.

Third, ethnic cleansing was already a major objective in the Balkan Wars of 1912–1913. In the first Balkan War Serbia, Greece, and Bulgaria first joined efforts against the Ottoman Empire, which they as good as destroyed in Europe. In the second Balkan War the victors turned toward each other, and now Bulgaria became the loser. It particularly lost its newly acquired Macedonian territory. As historian Stevan Pavlowitch notes: "All participants had behaved in such a way as to show their aim in Macedonia was not only to acquire territory, but to get rid of rival or antagonistic ethnic groups, at least culturally or statistically. All sides had destroyed villages or quarters, killed civilians, practised extortions and forced assimilation, caused violence and bitterness."[39]

Can we now more precisely outline the specificity of "postmodern" ethnic war, or do we have to conclude that there is nothing new under the sun? The shallowness of nationalist ("instant") arguments is nothing new, and the big European wars may be called "civil" wars from a certain point of view. Ethnic cleansing was neither something new in the Balkans nor in the center of European civilization (Auschwitz). The most distinguishing feature of postmodern ethnic war is the absence of an established state with its political order, national tradition, and vision of national progress.[40] This clears the way for a range of obscure combatants—warlords, militias—that exploit the fears of the civilian population without being able to offer the prospect of a viable political future. The nationalism unleashed in these circumstances pivots on the nation as a "chosen people," on cultural and war heroes of the past, and on geopolitical paranoia. In terms of constructing the world, there is no distinction with nationalism in established and powerful states. The only difference is the lack of time and stamina to let these constructions develop in a way that is feasible as well: building trust and boosting cooperation in a territory. This, rather than the nature of the nationalism involved, defines the "savage" war of the late twentieth century.

Postmodern War 2: The Empire and the War Theater

Wars have varied from a single battle to a protracted fight along a spatially moving frontier or against an intangible enemy (guerrilla war). The contiguous "modern" territorial state that emerged from the Middle Ages is most characteristically associated with territorial expansion or loss at the border and later on with extended battle frontiers. Empires—Chinese and Roman as well as European colonial—fought single battles to suppress a mutiny far from the center, but they also waged war against barbarians to expand their territory or to increase security in the empire. During all these operations military strategists had to struggle not only with the logistics of war but also with the attitudes of the local population. Of course, an army has the means of coercion. It can simply confiscate cattle, crops, or means of transport, but this raises the specter of a second war behind the front line and it may also destroy resources that could be useful in the future or even the thing the war actually was about. Moving in friendly territory infinitely simplifies the logistics and informational tasks of a war. In some cases empires have tried to solve the problem by means of population policies at the frontier. From the end of the seventeenth century on, the Hapsburg Empire offered belligerent Serbian fugitives from the Ottoman Empire the possibility to settle in the Krajina or "military frontier" (and this created the ethnic problems that have caused so much human misery in the last decade), and the Chinese Han (221 B.C.–A.D. 220) tried to populate the nomadic frontier with farmer-soldiers, but this plan pitifully failed.[41]

Colonial empires and their successor states have most clearly experienced the limits of coercion in an area that is touched by the virus of nationalism. In Indonesia it facilitated the advance of the Japanese and hastened the fall of Dutch rule. In Vietnam it weakened a regime that had thrown in its lot with the United States in spite of the people's doubts about Communism. Guerrilla war shifted the tactics of war in Vietnam in a way that could not be answered by U.S. troops simply because of their cultural distance from the indigenous population. This is not to say that guerrilla armies do not use coercion or do not violate human rights, but they are better able to apply such methods in a measured way and to involve the people in their own control.

The enormous advance in technical means—the possibility of reconnaissance and destruction from the air with pilotless planes, aircraft carriers, satellite communication, cruise missiles, and cybersoldiers—has not eliminated the reliance on the political and social environment of the war theater. In the Gulf War and in Afghanistan cooperation of local states (Saudi Arabia, Pakistan) was necessary not only to provide an operational base for small military units that execute secret operations in hostile territory but also to close the boundaries of the target state so as to eliminate any help or movement of terrorist units across the boundary. It can now be concluded that the latter failed completely in Afghanistan (2001–2002), particularly because Pakistan's alliance with the United States had no positive meaning for its population or local tribes. There is another problem with an enemy that has become increasingly identified as terrorist. Terrorist retribution does not select a fixed theater for its operations, but hits U.S. or Western representatives or symbols wherever they appear. It is only the assumption that such operations need a central territorial base that feeds the evolving military campaign against "rogue" states. One may seriously doubt if this approach is sufficient to combat terrorism.

Again the historical comparison that urges itself upon us is not the one of battles between national states but of empires with the rest of the world. The term "empire" has been recently used to denote a historical shift in the world order from a system of sovereign states more or less dominated by one hegemonic state to a situation where the entire world is dominated by a global system of exploitation.[42] Contrary to this conception, I will use the term to clarify the experience of the world (the geopolitical vision) in states that have followed a particular course in history with regard to their international relations. Such states have not really incorporated the Westphalian model of multilateral recognition, although they formally endorse international law that originates in this model.

Let me illustrate this point of view with a comparison of the United States and traditional China. Their empires, although keen on drawing sharp demarcation lines, both knew that they could never reconcile security needs with the ideal of a sharp line. The Great Wall never stopped the barbarians (it actually was an expression of the military weakness of the Ming), nor did the Iron Curtain check the extension of Communism. The world order as perceived in empires is rather a number of zones that extend from the center where the emperor is located, to the wilderness outside. The Chinese distinguished the Domain of the Sovereign, the Peace-Securing Domain, the Wild Domain, and several more, each connected with certain strategies and rituals at the center. The United States has used distinctions based on the geographical notions Mainland, Western Hemisphere, the West, and Axis of Evil. In each zone different actions were required, and one always had to be prepared for the moment when some inconspicuous action in the periphery would assume a threatening dimension and could never be sure that the enemy had not already entered the territory. Ritual expressions of loyalty (greeting the flag or paying tribute to the emperor) neutralize barbarian elements that might have entered the core territory. Accommodation with the enemy is always possible but is soon abused by the barbarians to cheat the empire out of extreme tribute. The nomads in China's borderlands needed grain, metal tools, wine, and silk, and their greediness sometimes became unbearable. The United States buys consent with missiles, money, or tolerance of human rights violations but is never sure that such means will not be used against it. In China military campaigns failed when the army entered the plains where horsemen with campsites ruled instead of cities and property rights on land. They pursued the fleeing enemy until their lines of supply failed, and then the enemy turned on them and massacred the Emperor's army. The best of all times had been when an open exchange system carefully balanced the needs for essential goods that both sides could not produce themselves.[43]

Of course, the postnational era does not completely revive the vicissitudes of a Chinese empire. Today ideas about mission and identity abound, newspapers and television have extended war to cultural and psychological spheres, the Internet creates new communities "without propinquity," and holy places have become more rather than less pervasive. This new concoction creates identifications that do not always coincide with the nation-state but that share a number of important features with nationalism: educational zeal, historical myopia, and a degree of selflessness. The willingness to die for the common cause seems even stronger than in the national state. In this situation the empire has put its money on the strong state for suppressing these movements and the security risks they produce. This is the second leg of a strategy that starts with an attack on the dens of terrorism with all the available means of postmodern war, which each time amounts to a new milestone in the separating of (foreign) soldiers and events in the war theater.

A new and stable—not necessarily democratic—state should be the outcome of a procedure that is liable to some serious contradictions. The first is that empires and states do not go together very well. A world of stable states is dependent on symmetric recognition of countries in an international system, but the empire itself is often the greatest spoilsport in this system with its snubbing of the UN or proposals for regulation of the global environment. Second, the operational mode of a postmodern war—distant and safe in terms of soldiers' lives—offers great difficulties in switching to a period of transition in which local forces are not strong enough to safeguard the new political order. As American military interventions after the Karzai regime was set up in Afghanistan have shown, it is not always easy to distinguish friend and foe. Third, the legitimacy of such regimes often depends on paying tribute to (Islamic) values that at the same time strongly deny the authority of the state. The idea of combating terrorism by bolstering the political strength of states as such seems sensible. This requires the stimulation of (civic) nationalism, and we should certainly not overestimate the obstacle posed by fundamentalist Islam to the emulation of this ideal if a new state elite can credibly instill a dose of national pride and produce some economic progress. War fatigue among civilians may in the long run play a role as well but this has also been responsible for the Afghans reconciling themselves with the "stable" Taliban regime.

There is another way in which we can say that the war against terrorism does not rely merely on military aims. On the eve of Iraq's invasion of Kuwait (July 1990), Saddam Hussein made a chilling remark to a visitor, U.S. ambassador April Glaspie: "Yours is a society which cannot accept 10,000 dead in one battle."[44] It was a misjudgment of the chance of American military intervention but a reasonable assessment of the general political constraints in the West on going to war for the sake of a stable world order. One might call this the strength but also the basic weakness of democracies in this world. This assessment, repeated by many non-Western voices, can be seen as a factor that has actually encouraged terrorism and the violation of international law by "rogue" states. An argument like this may underlie the George W. Bush administration's foreign policy as well. The aim is to massively upgrade military interference with the rest of the world if necessary, but foremost to dispel the image of democratic softness. It is a symbolic or psychological war as well. This, rather than the lack of material support, explains irritated American reactions to European aloofness. The symbolic and psychological frame has always been taken care of by nationalism in European history, but European integration after 1945 has eroded the nationalist war reflexes in France and Germany. Moreover, the structure of these reflexes does not fit a war on terrorism. Nationalism was a way to boost the performance of states in a game of mutual emulation and transcendence.[45] The war on terrorism lacks such identifiers and challenging models. The mobilization of support in the United States does not rely on these sentiments but on the fear of intangible enemies that characterizes the postmodern condition, empires, and disintegrating states.

Nationalism and War: A Contingent Relationship

The issue of a link between nationalism and war arises in diverging contexts that depend on the implicit frames activated by authors or discussants. If we see nationalism as a period in European history in which the relations between the classes became redefined in terms of a common national enterprise and culture, the changed role of the soldier is a crucial item to focus on. The soldier became a representative of the nation who identified both with its war aims and with progress on other frontiers. National armies made a deep impression on officials in prenational states by their sheer size but also by the military capability (autonomy and motivation) of the individual soldier. However, those who want to suggest a simple causal relationship between this historical transformation and the incidence of war or its scale of destruction will encounter difficulties in disentangling the complex relationships between the emerging awareness of national identity, the development of military technology, and the increasing infrastructural power of states in history. Both state disintegration and infrastructural power have been facilitated by this (civic) nationalism, but its result was benign modernization and stability as well as war capability. Neither the lingering of a war after its enraptured opening movements, as in World War I, nor the dogged attitude of soldiers in the face of death can be reduced merely to nationalism. Such facts follow the logic of war or the social psychological mechanisms of small groups that are thrown together in a struggle for life. What nationalism certainly has brought is a demand for respect on the international scene and the widespread commitment to decision making about peace and war. I will elaborate on this point in some remarks later.

Another frame for discussing nationalism and war ensues from the conception of nationalism as manipulation by political leaders who are looking for public consent. This may indeed involve the creation of an atmosphere of fear, the construction of external enemies, or even the provocation of war acts by other states. War may easily start unintentionally under these conditions, as events after the seizure of the Falklands/Malvinas illustrate. From the part of the Argentine junta, it was a correct assessment of the public sentiment but a miscalculation of the risk of war. Nationalism in this case means either the process in which an enemy is constructed or the aroused (territorial) sentiments of the public. Apart from that, an unintentional effect of playing the national card is that one not only acquires public consent but also rouses dormant public sentiments in the country of the adversary.

Finally, the term "nationalism" (or ethnonationalism) is applied to situations where an ethnic group in an encounter with other ethnic groups aims at territorial purity by redrawing political boundaries, turning members of other groups into second-class citizens, or executing mass deportations or killings. There is a tendency in the media to equate nationalism, now and in the past, with this pattern. In 1990 *Time* magazine, for example, devoted an issue to the prospects for the new Eastern Europe with the cover title "Old Demon."[46] The cover illustration showed a map of Eastern (or central) Europe with names of capitals and places with an unpleasant historical resonance: Warsaw, Berlin, Munich, Budapest, Trieste, Zagreb, Belgrade, and Bucharest. The designer had curiously overlooked the most ominous name, Sarajevo, perhaps to avoid the accusation of historical determinism. It was clearly a composite map, selective and geometrically unfaithful but also disfigured in such a way that it represented a sad mask with the word "Nationalism" in its mouth. As the leading article explained, Eastern Europe was at the crossroads of democratic liberty and "belligerent nationalism." Notwithstanding the rise of conservative nationalisms,[47] most places and countries shown on the *Time* cover did not experience war after 1990.

Whatever the frame is that is evoked by such discussions, nationalism always implies a personalization of the nation. A nation can be offended or mutilated like a person, but national identity and culture are also part of the individual personality and of private life. In the development of civic nationalism, representations of the collective body are somewhat more obvious than the reverse perspective. The difference is nicely visualized in pictures of war. War is initially represented as a battle between heroes and only later as a violation or expression of dignity in the private sphere. The German soldiers in Werner's painting from the Franco-Prussian War preserve their national culture (songs) "in the rough and wild times of war and in the midst of an irreconcilable enemy," but in the picture the threat significantly comes from refined furniture. Nationalism justifies and defends an order of things, indeed including furniture, which is essential to personal dignity. This involves much that cannot be illustrated easily in a picture: equal rights, freedom of movement in a territory, property, codes for communicating with others or access to institutions and support, and so on. The entire national territory (infrastructure) may become, in a way, the extension of the person, and this explains the personal character of any infringement on this system. Conversely, any breach in a previously shared identity (as in ethnic conflict between neighbors) is experienced as war and may become a war if there is no strong state to reassure a group.

The paradoxical feature of classic nationalism is that it always looks for reassurance by other states. The Other is (ab)used to inflate our self-esteem but is ultimately required as an authoritative institution that recognizes our collective existence. In the international system this mechanism puts a restraint on war, but if war nonetheless breaks out, it evokes a (reluctant) matching of identities, something that, as a manner of speaking, can be represented within the frame of a painting. This relation with the environment is absent in an empire or in a postmodern world without strong states since these do not know the principle of symmetric recognition. External dangers may still (be used to) generate a "nationalistic" mood, and the adversary may deliberately offend basic principles or symbols of an empire or of another culture, but there is no real accommodation in the sphere of the human lifeworld. This will result in an uncontrolled evil hunting that in the end may even destroy the cohesion and solidarity of the offended group.

Nationalism in one or another meaning continues to play a role in wars, but there is no causal relationship that offers the prospect of eliminating war by banning nationalism. Postmodern conditions and increased mobility have in principle offered an incentive for people to mix, to know each other, or to indulge in cultural relativism. Yet at the same time fears have been stirred up because we live in an age in which "big changes are produced by small symbolic multipliers, through action carried by 'active minorities.' "[48] The struggle has become more rather than less cultural, and this sustains nationalism in its classical or in one of its postmodern shapes: imperial or ethnic.

Notes

1. Keisch, "Anton von Werner," 456–457.
2. Steiner, *Language and Silence*, 15.
3. Keisch, "Anton von Werner," 456–457.
4. "[D]as Gutartige und Gemüthvolle des Volkscharakters [. . .], das sich auch in den rauhen wilden Zeit des Krieges und inmitten eines unversöhnlichen Feindes nie ganz verleugnen konnte." Keisch, "Anton von Werner," 457.
5. "Les attitudes des soldats rustauds aux allures bravaches, leurs lourdes bottes crottées, sont en complet contraste avec le raffinement de l'ameublement. Les vainqueurs se comportent un peu comme des vandales. A droite à l'entrée, la bonne, avec laquelle un officier paraît vouloir plaisanter, est accompagnée de sa fille qui a du mal à cacher sa crainte." J. Gauchet, "La guerre de 1870," Histoire de Brunoy (Essonme). The quotation is seemingly from a French exhibition catalog.
6. Tombs, *France, 1814–1914*, 1.
7. Posen, "Nationalism, the Mass Army, and Military Power."
8. Duroselle, *Idée de l'Europe dans l'histoire*.
9. Anderson, *Imagined Communities*. An early version of this point of view can already be found in Renan's famous 1882 lecture "Qu'est ce qu'une nation?" (What is a nation?), of which a translation is included in many readers, for example, Bhabha, *Nation and Narration*, 8–22.
10. Flacke, *Mythen der Nationen*. See also Dijkink, "On the European Tradition of Nationalism and Its National Codes."
11. Kroll, "Belgien."
12. [Chesney], *Battle of Dorking*.
13. Childers, *Riddle of the Sands*.
14. In Chesney, *Battle of Dorking*, German soldiers put their "dirty legs" on English tables. Even in World War II, writers on military affairs still believed that German soldiers used to deposit their excrement on the tables in the houses where they had been billeted.
15. Wells, *War of the Worlds*.
16. Many novels about Communism or Americanism after World War II illustrate this theme.
17. Jones, *Art of War in the Western World*, 387–389.
18. Gramsci, "Notes on Italian History," 87.

19. Struve, *Voices from the Ming-Qing Cataclysm.*

20. Hay, "Suspension of Dynastic Time."

21. Ousby, *Road to Verdun,* 199.

22. Eksteins, *Rites of Spring,* 184–185.

23. In order to denote its special nature, the French soldier Jean Norton Cru invented the label "antipatriotism" in a retrospective from 1929. A more recent source (Antoine Prost) uses the term "patriotic pacifism." See Ousby, *Road to Verdun,* 262. The latter term acknowledges the fact that this attitude did not really lead to soldiers' deserting or protesting. The very isolation of life at the front line is perhaps the most basic explanation of this situation. Protest and even desertion need an audience or receptive community.

24. See Hemingway, *Farewell to Arms,* for an impression of the disorder and disappointment among soldiers in the rear of the front during World War I in Italy.

25. Nationalist feelings may be deemed responsible for support for war efforts in the rear (the logistic field and the home front), but they may in some cases also thwart such efforts when the war is perceived as a betrayal of the people.

26. Mosse, *Nationalization of the Masses,* 13.

27. Gellner, *Nations and Nationalism,* 1.

28. Dijkink, *National Identity and Geopolitical Visions.*

29. Filipp, *Germany Sublime and German Sublimations,* 93.

30. Murphy, " 'A Sum of the Most Wonderful Things.' "

31. Ignatieff, *The Warrior's Honor,* 36.

32. Port, *Gypsies, Wars, and Other Instances of the Wild.*

33. Enzensberger, *Civil Wars.*

34. See note 10.

35. Nairn, *Modern Janus.* In Nairn's book the Janus feature is particularly connected with the fact that nationalism mobilizes people with the prospect of a great future, whereas it searches for arguments by looking deep into the past.

36. Ignatieff, *Warrior's Honor,* 45.

37. Sahlins, *Boundaries.*

38. Eksteins, *Rites of Spring.*

39. Pavlowitch, *History of the Balkans 1804–1945,* 199–200.

40. Kaldor, *New and Old Wars.*

41. Jelavich and Jelavich, *Establishment of the Balkan National States, 1804–1920* Barfield, *Perilous Frontier,* 54, states, "The whole frontier was garrisoned with conscripts, often convicts, who manned the walled defenses and who were expected to be partially self-supporting by establishing farming colonies."

42. Hardt and Negri, *Empire.*

43. For China's territorial order see Barfield, *Perilous Frontier;* Fairbank, *Chinese World Order;* and Waldron, *Great Wall of China.*

44. "The Glaspie Transcript: Saddam meets the U.S. Ambassador (July 25, 1990)" quote p. 125, *The Gulf War Reader.*

45. By "transcendence" I mean the inclination of nations to reformulate the qualities they envy in other nations in such a way that their own qualities (or rather deficiencies) reemerge as a superior form of what the strengths of the Other at first sight seemed to be. The French envied the English their system of popular sovereignty but declared it deficient in terms of culture and spirit, which they considered more important for the unity and strength of a state. For the prerevolutionary role of the French nobility in this process, see Greenfeld, *Nationalism,* 145–172.

46. *Time* International, August 6, 1990.

47. Tismaneanu, *Fantasies of Salvation.*
48. Melucci, *Challenging Codes*, 185.

References

Anderson, Benedict. *Imagined Communities: Reflections on the Origin and Spread of Nationalism*. London: Verso, 1983.

Barfield, Thomas J. *The Perilous Frontier: Nomadic Empires and China*. London: Blackwell, 1989.

Bhabha, Homi K., ed. *Nation and Narration*. London: Routledge, 1990.

Cert, Christopher, ed. *Gulf War Reader: History, Documents, Opinions*. New York: Times Books, 1991.

Chesney, George T. *The Battle of Dorking: Reminiscences of a Volunteer*. Edinburgh: Blackwood, 1871.

Childers, Erskine. *The Riddle of the Sands*. London: Smith/Elder, 1903.

Dijkink, Gertjan. *National Identity and Geopolitical Visions: Maps of Pride and Pain*. London: Routledge, 1996.

Dijkink, Gertjan. "On the European Tradition of Nationalism and Its National Codes." *Geography Research Forum* 19 (1999): 45–59.

Duroselle, Jean-Baptiste. *L'idée de l'Europe dans l'histoire*. Paris: Denoël, 1965.

Eksteins, Modris. *Rites of Spring: The Great War and the Birth of the Modern Age*. New York: Doubleday, 1989.

Enzensberger, Hans M. *Civil Wars: From L.A. to Bosnia*. New York: New Press, 1994.

Fairbank, John K., ed. *The Chinese World Order: Traditional China's Foreign Relations*. Cambridge, MA: Harvard University Press, 1968.

Filipp, Karlheinz. *Germany Sublime and German Sublimations: On Political Education and Its Geography*. Münster: Waxmann, 1993.

Flacke, Monika, ed. *Mythen der Nationen*. Berlin: Deutsches Historisches Museum, 1998.

Gellner, Ernest. *Nations and Nationalism*. Ithaca, NY: Cornell University Press, 1983.

Gramsci, Antonio. "Notes on Italian History." In *Selections from the Prison Notebooks*, ed. Quintin Hoare and Geoffrey N. Smith, 44–120. New York: International Publishers, 1972.

Greenfeld, Liah. *Nationalism: Five Roads to Modernity*. Cambridge, MA: Harvard University Press, 1992.

Hardt, Michael, and Antonio Negri. *Empire*. Cambridge, MA: Harvard University Press, 2000.

Hay, Jonathan. "The Suspension of Dynastic Time." In *Boundaries in China*, ed. John Hay, 171–197. London: Reaktion, 1994.

Hemingway, Ernest M. A *Farewell to Arms*. New York: Scribner's, 1929.

Histoire de Brunoy (L'Essonne). http://sahavy.free.fr/fenetres/p1870.html (accessed January 14, 2003).

Ignatieff, Michael. *The Warrior's Honor: Ethnic War and the Modern Conscience*. London: Chatto and Windus, 1998.

Jelavich, Charles, and Barbara Jelavich. *The Establishment of the Balkan National States, 1804–1920*. Seattle: University of Washington Press, 1977.

Jones, Archer. *The Art of War in the Western World*. London: Harrap, 1988.

Kaldor, Mary. *New and Old Wars: Organized Violence in a Global Era*. Stanford, CA: Stanford University Press, 1999.

Keisch, Claude. "Anton von Werner." In *Nationalgallerie Berlin: Das XIX Jahrhundert: Katalog der ausgestellten Werke*, ed. Angelika Wesenberg and Eve Förschl, 456–457. Berlin: Staatliche Museen zu Berlin—Preussischer Kulturbesitz/Seemann, 2001.

Kroll, Johannes. "Belgien: Geschichtskultur und nationale Identität." In *Mythen der Nationen*, ed. Monika Flacke, 53–77. Berlin: Deutsches Historisches Museum, 1998.

Melucci, Alberto. *Challenging Codes: Collective Action in the Information Age*. London: Routledge, 1996.

Mosse, George. *The Nationalization of the Masses: Political Symbolism and Mass Movements in Germany from the Napoleonic Wars through the Third Reich*. Ithaca, NY: Cornell University Press, 1991.

Murphy, David T. " 'A Sum of the Most Wonderful Things': *Raum*, Geopolitics, and the German Tradition of Environmental Determinism, 1900–1933." *History of European Ideas* 25 (1999): 121–33.

Nairn, Tom. *The Modern Janus: Nationalism and Modernity*. London: Hutchinson Radius, 1990.

Ousby, Ian. *The Road to Verdun: France, Nationalism, and the First World War*. London: Pimlico, 2003.

Pavlowitch, Stevan K. A *History of the Balkans, 1804–1945*. London: Longman, 1999.

Port, Mattijs van de. *Gypsies, Wars, and Other Instances of the Wild: Civilisation and Its Discontents in a Serbian Town*. Amsterdam: Amsterdam University Press, 1998.

Posen, Barry R. "Nationalism, the Mass Army, and Military Power." In *Perspectives on Nationalism and War*, ed. John L. Comaroff and Paul C. Stern, 135–186. Australia: Gordon and Breach, 1995.

Sahlins, Peter. *Boundaries: The Making of France and Spain in the Pyrenees*. Berkeley: University of California Press, 1989.

Steiner, George. *Language and Silence*. Harmondsworth: Penguin, 1967.

Struve, Lynn A. *Voices from the Ming-Qing Cataclysm: China in Tiger's Jaws*. New Haven, CT: Yale University Press, 1993.

Tismaneanu, Vladimir. *Fantasies of Salvation: Democracy, Nationalism, and Myth in Post-Communist Europe*. Princeton, NJ: Princeton University Press, 1998.

Tombs, Robert. *France, 1814–1914*. London: Longman, 1996.

Waldron, Arthur. *The Great Wall of China: From History to Myth*. New York: Cambridge University Press, 1990.

Wells, H. G. *The War of the Worlds*. London: Heinemann, 1898.

Wesenberg, Angelika, and Eve Förschl, eds. *Nationalgallerie Berlin: Das XIX Jahrhundert: Katalog der ausgestellten Werke*. Berlin: Staatliche Museen zu Berlin—Preussischer Kulturbesitz, 2001.

7

LORRAINE DOWLER

Amazonian Landscapes

Gender, War, and Historical Repetition

> The word "Amazon" is thought to be derived from the ancient Greek words *a mazon*—"breastless." According to legend, each Amazon seared off her right breast so it would not interfere with the use of her bow. Over the centuries Amazons came to represent a nation of women warriors. Their home territory moved from place to place depending on the teller, but always Amazons were portrayed as inhabiting a region just beyond the border of the known world, and in this sense their story is a variant of the familiar tale about a distant land where everything is done the wrong way round.
>
> —Cynthia Enloe, *Does Khaki Become You?*

It has been speculated that legends and myths are usually born out of everyday life. Surprisingly, it could be argued that the legend of the Amazons mirrors contemporary life in that women who actively participate in warfare are considered "out of place" with the normative landscape. As Enloe argues, the Amazonian world is a place apart, where gender roles are inverted, or worse, "what is wrong about the Amazons is not only that they are women who fight using military equipment and tactics, but that they live without men."[1] However, unlike the Amazons, Western societies are comforted by men being the soldiers, warriors, and heroes of war, while women are either victims or seraphic icons of war.[2] As a society, we are consoled by nurturing images of women in the role of nurses on the battlefield or, most important, as champions of the home front. Cock contends that when people go to war, they do so specifically as men and women, rather than in nationalist solidarity. She argues that the military, as a masculine power structure, actually magnifies how masculinity and femininity are defined within society.[3]

This seems to hold constant even in the exceptional case of the Amazons. Many feminists argue that throughout history representations of these female warriors have been dichotomous in nature. On the one hand, Amazonian images mark women's emotional and physical strength while simultaneously rendering them erotic, thereby reinforcing men's virility.[4] As Kleinbaum argued, "As surely as no spider's web was built for the glorification of flies, the Amazon idea was not designed to enhance women."[5] In his book *War and Gender* Goldstein details some popular representations of the myth to illustrate this point. In the 1931 play *The Warrior's Husband*, Katharine Hepburn's portrayal of the warrior queen Antiope radically challenged contemporary understandings of gender roles of her time. However, the play's reviews overlooked these questions of identity in favor of essentializing Hepburn's body with such statements as the play where "she first bared her lovely legs."[6] Similarly, a more pop icon, Xena, who was once hailed as "Madeleine Albright's role model," has been described as "the tall, strong, athletic beauty with gloriously blue eyes, who is togged out in boots, leather miniskirt and metal breastplates that do her breathtaking body no harm at all."[7] In this view the Amazon warrior becomes a mix of sex object and power whereby her strength stems from her sensuality. Interestingly, there is little historical evidence that an Amazon society ever existed or of any community in which women were primarily responsible for the violent actions of war. In fact, there is no evidence of any society that was "exclusively populated or controlled by women, nor one in which women were the primary fighters."[8]

Amazonian society does provide interesting material for the analysis of culture and myth. However, it is interesting that although social processes vary across culture, the gendering of war roles remains universally generalized and in opposition to these myths.[9] Across all cultures the fighters are usually male, with the exception of fewer than 1% of all the warriors in history.[10] However, women's roles as noncombatants vary across cultures in such roles as "support troops, psychological war-boosters and peacemakers,"[11] whereas men's war roles are consistently connected with war fighting.

Today twenty-three million soldiers serve in uniformed armies, of whom 97% are male.[12] Only in 11 of 200 nations do women make up more than 5% of the military forces.[13] Most of these women in the military forces worldwide occupy traditional women's roles such as typists and nurses.[14] It is important to state that these statistics do not address the roles of women in revolutionary movements such as those in Nicaragua and El Salvador. However, as Enloe points out, the number of women combatants is significantly larger in revolutionary forces than in uniformed service, but, these women are often relegated to more domestic roles after the revolution. She argues that public images of women in war versus those of men are powerful manufactured symbols of resistance:

> A popular symbol of the many liberation armies in Asia, Latin America, and Africa is the woman with a rifle over one confident shoulder and a baby cuddled in her protective arms. The picture conjures up images of the can-do-everything "super woman." It also seems to imply that the process of revolutionary warfare, on the one hand, can transform women's role and sense of self-worth, while on the other hand, sustain the social order that in the past has ensured the reproduction and nurturing of the next generation.[15]

Uniformed combat forces today almost totally exclude women, and the entire global military system has very few women, which in turn makes many of its most important settings all-male.[16] Most important, these settings are certainly public, which creates a gendered dichotomy of space whereby women are denied access to powerful political spaces such as the battlefield.[17] The creation of all male spaces in the public sphere serves to reinforce difference in terms of the power of men.[18] Goldstein argues that the gendering of warfare is a strategy of war whereby

> killing in war does not come naturally for either gender, yet the potential for war has been universal in human societies. To help overcome soldiers' reluctance to fight, cultures develop gender roles that equate "manhood" with toughness under fire. Across culture and through time the selection of men as potential combatants and of women for feminine war support roles has helped shape the war system. In turn the pervasiveness of war in history has influenced gender profoundly—especially gender norms in child-rearing.[19]

Nature versus Nurture

Goldstein's argument that gender roles are strategic to warfare illustrates what has commonly been referred to as the social constructivist point of view. There has been a long, ongoing debate among feminists about the role of nature versus nurture in the construction of violent identities. However, it is important to state that all feminists stand against the most fundamental principle of the nature argument that male superiority is biologically determined. There are two schools of thought in terms of issues of gender and violence, of which the more prevalent is the social constructivist, which contends that violent behavior is not gender specific, but is the result of environmental forces, such as societal norms. The biological feminist position argues that women are biologically incapable of violence and are the "natural" peacemakers of a society. Illustrative of this would be the "old wives' tale" that if a woman were the president of the United States, there would simply be no more wars, because a woman would never send her son or, more symbolically as the mother to a nation, her nation's sons into battle. Clearly, if we examine the role of other women leaders, such as Margaret Thatcher, this is simply not the case. Biological determinists would also argue that due to science's increasing ability to control genetics, we may someday "end war by getting rid of aggressive genes."[20]

However, these arguments do not take into consideration the influence of human culture on biology. For example, adolescents are now going through puberty younger than a few generations ago—"perhaps as the result of exposure to 'grown-up' influences in teenage culture, or possibly even of higher stress."[21] Interestingly as long as there has been warfare, there have been women who have challenged the biological determinist nature of the system. For example, the first "unofficial" female in the U.S. Marine Corps was Lucy Brewer, who, by taking the name George Baker, served in the Marine Corps on the USS *Constitution* during the War of 1812. Similarly, Loretta Janet Vasques fought for the Confederacy at Bull Run under the name of Lieutenant Harry Buford. Cathay Williams, a former slave, served as Private William Cathay until her sex was discovered due to an illness.[22] Biological determinists would refer to the actions of these brave women as an anomaly. Yet the problem is that not one of the biological explanations is sufficient to explain the conundrum of gendered war roles. Goldstein argues that "biology provides a partial explanation by showing why war would tend to involve mostly men. It does not however provide a sufficient explanation to the puzzle of why war is virtually all-male."[23]

A Case of Historical Repetition

As a point of entry to the gendering of identities in war, I will present two case studies, one historical and one contemporary, that will demonstrate how women's identities are molded and manipulated to serve the needs of war. Most important, I will demonstrate how this political landscape or masculine way of seeing is constructed from antiquated notions of public and private space. In the first case, I will detail how the images of women in the Irish Revolution were constructed as helpmates to the male heroes of the revolution. The Irish Revolution is often heralded as a joint resistance where men and women stood side by side in Irish solidarity. However, despite these images of public cohesion, it is important to examine how the identities of women were relegated to the protection of their immediate environment of the home. Most important, women who challenged the notion of the male warrior by participating in more public roles were simply written out of the political landscape.

The second case study will focus on the gendering of the heroic images of firefighters, police officers, and other rescue workers at the World Trade Center after the attacks of September 11, 2001. Not surprisingly, by juxtaposing this with the historical case of the gendering of women's identities in early twentieth century Ireland, we find that not much has changed in the early-twenty-first-century American political landscape. The case of Ground Zero presents similar discursive issues to those in revolutionary Ireland. First, the definition of warrior is fixed in the public sphere and does not include everyday acts of bravery such as giving aid to the wounded or simply raising a family in the face of the uncertainty of war. Second, society is uneasy with the notion of women being active soldiers and warriors, and although firefighters are not considered uniformed combatants, firefighting has always been considered an act of defending one's community. Since the early 1900s firefighting units have been organized in a parallel fashion to military units, complete with uniforms, ranked officers, battalions, division commanders, and fire commissioners.[24] The role of a firefighter as defender of the hearth and protector of the nation is unpredictable and is a responsibility that, like a war, can erupt any place, any time.[25] Most important, the masculinazation of firefighting is one of the spillovers of the nurture versus nature debate that limits women's participation in more violent or action oriented professions. An examination of women rescue workers at Ground Zero not only details the gendering of roles during violent conflict but points to how these roles can be transferred to other all-male settings such as policing and construction work. For this reason, the thrust of this examination will be on the interdependent relationship between the moral landscape and the appropriate actions of men and women in a time of war.

Warrior Landscapes: Morality as Dictated by Public and Private Space

Till has argued that the reputedly dichotomous relationship between public and private space can shed some light on the processes that have aided in the rendering of landscapes as a masculine way of seeing.[26] Traditionally, private spaces have been associated with the home and designated as feminine, whereas public spaces (or spaces outside the home) have been designated as masculine. Feminist theorists have explored alternative definitions of the public and private by analyzing the public in relation to the private.[27] Rosalyn Deutsche points to an interdependency between public/private distinctions and morality. She argues that definitions of public space are connected to the kind of political community we envision.[28] In a world that values continuity, resistance most likely will be ignored, which will create a distinction between what is recognized in the public realm and what must be hidden out of view. It is this distinction between what is viewed and what is swept away that establishes the fundamental codes in the creation of the moral landscape.[29] Therefore, in order to understand the reactions to the events during the Irish revolution and September 11, 2001, it is critical to understand the ways in which morality is exemplified and acted out in practices associated with landscape, especially the gendering of public and private space.

Hannah Arendt argues that in any discussion of the construction of power, political theorists both left and right agree that violence is nothing more than the most flagrant manifestation of power.[30] For this reason, if nations are invented via gendered identities that (re)inscribe a power imbalance between men and women, it would be beneficial to examine how war reinforces these identities. Despite the burgeoning interest in the intersection of gender with nationalism, we have paid almost no attention to war as a factor for shaping human societies.[31]

Revolutionary Landscapes: Moral Codes of Irish Solidarity

Margaret Ward, a feminist historian, maintains that we need not just rewrite Irish women into history but to understand the motives of why they were left out. Was it just an oversight, or was it a deliberate attempt to keep us in the dark about how history might have otherwise transpired? She contends: "Women have been so marginal in the consciousness of those who have researched events, their significance has remained hidden within historical records, waiting for the understudying of someone who wants to know what women did, what they thought, and how they were affected by the upheavals of the past century."[32]

In this study I will argue that one explanation for the absence of women in the history of the Irish Revolution is that Irish women have never been considered soldiers for the reason that their identities have been erased from the political landscape, which was indeed a masculine way of seeing. Most important, the production of a masculine political landscape is interdependent with the maintenance of the domestic landscape. More specifically, Nash argues that in the historical case of Irish nationalism the exclusion of women from the public arena promoted a gendered relationship to place whereby the political arena was defined as masculine.[33]

In 1914, the formation of Cumann na mBan was the first organized political undertaking by the women of Ireland. The creation of this organization enabled women not only to resist British colonialism but also to write women into the political landscape. Not surprisingly Irish men clearly defined the role of this organization as the gunman's helpmate.[34] The women of Cumann na mBan were relegated to the traditional roles of women in the domestic sphere, ones of support and nurturing such as stretcher bearing, nursing, and fundraising.[35] Although women tried to assert themselves in more "masculine" ways such as acting as couriers and bearing arms, for the most part in the early years, Cumann na mBan remained in the eyes of the male volunteers a shadow organization. However, in 1920 there was a radical displacement when Cumann na mBan took an unprecedented political stand that denounced partition, whereas the Irish Republican Army (IRA) itself as a whole was badly split over the treaty, which would leave the northern counties under British sovereignty.

The treaty was negotiated in 1920 by five Irish delegates, Arthur Griffith, Michael Collins, George Gavan Duffy, Robert Barton, and Eamonn Duggan, who met with British prime minister David Lloyd George in London. These men were appointed by the Dail (the Irish parliament), and many members of Cumann na mBan were outraged by the absence of a woman, in particular, Mary MacSwiney.[36] MacSwiney was a founding member of Cumann na mBan and president of the Cork Branch, for which she was interned after the 1916 Rising. Today historians concur that the course of Irish history might have been drastically altered by the inclusion of this unyielding Republican. The following is an excerpt from a two-hour-and-forty-minute speech MacSwiney made to the Irish Dail:

> You men that talk need not talk to us about war. It is the women who suffer the most of the hardships that war brings. You can go out in the excitement of the fight and it brings its own honor and its own glory. We have to sit home and work in the more humble ways, we have to endure the agony, the torture of misery and the privations which war brings, the horror of nightly visitations to our houses and their consequences. It is easier for you than it is for us, but you will not find in Ireland a woman who has not suffered, who today will talk as the soldiers here today have talked, and I ask the Minister of Defense, if that is the type of soldier he has, in heaven's name send the women as your officers next time.[37]

MacSwiney's words expanded the traditional understanding of a soldier by including acts of warfare that occurred in the private spaces of the home. She argued that the home was not the protected and nurturing place that men have determined it to be. Most important, she obscured the boundary of public and private space within the political landscape when she argued that those very same women who endured the hardships in the home front would make better soldiers than the men who had reaped the glories of the battlefield.

During the weeks of argument and counterargument on this treaty in the

Dail, the six women deputies remained unshakable in their opposition to the treaty. The memories of dead sons, husbands, and brothers were used in justification of their stand.[38] The united front presented by the women of the Dail gave great credence to their claim to represent the views of the majority of Irish women. The sanity of the female Dail members was attacked by some of the male members, who argued that these women had experienced such terrible personal losses that, they claimed, they were incapable of evaluating political issues. These same men asserted that the women were being motivated solely by emotion and stubborn determination to vote the way their dead husbands and sons would have wished. This debate created a political boundary whereby it was deemed that women could not see beyond the borders of their immediate homes. In other words, women were incapable of rationality once they left their homes and entered the public sphere. This was a double-edged sword, for women were not given equal credit for the hardship that war brings, and yet their burden was argued to be so deep that they could not possibly detach themselves from it. The final vote in the Dail was sixty-four to fifty-seven to ratify the treaty. After the ballot count was announced, Mary MacSwiney declared that she "would have neither hand, act nor part in helping the Irish Free State to carry this nation of ours, this glorious nation that has been betrayed here tonight into the British empire."[39]

Although the treaty had been ratified, there was still one last possibility for a rejection of partition. The Dail had been elected by those individuals who resided on the island of Ireland, including citizens of the north, which was no longer part of the Republic. Therefore the existing Dail was not representative only of the provisional government of southern Ireland.[40] Consequently, Eamon de Valera, the current president, called for a new election and the viability of the treaty would now be dependent on whether the new elections would support a pro- or antitreaty Dail.

Ironically, women had been given the right to vote several years earlier, and members of Cumann na mBan felt strongly that women should have the ballot, but it was contrary to their most basic beliefs to seek to elect a British parliament. Tragically, the majority of women were not registered to vote, and in hindsight many now feel that by putting the separatist goal before that of the feminist one, they cut themselves off from the possibility of voting for a richer independence.[41] In order to include those women who were not listed, a motion was made in the Dail by the six women deputies for a new registration, but it was blocked by a majority of the male deputies, which resulted in the severe underrepresentation of women in this election.[42] Ironically, the members of the Dail who were uneasy with a parliament that was inclusive of the northern state were not concerned by the exclusion of a sizable proportion of the voting population: the votes of women. This twist of fate demonstrates the exclusionary nature of the political landscape as a masculine public realm that, to use the ideas of Deutsche, simply swept the dissension of the private realm out of view.[43]

Cumann na mBan decided to register a more active protest when it began a series of raids on the Irish flag whenever it appeared on protreaty platforms. For its members, this flag now symbolized the grossest of betrayals.[44] By a very small margin a protreaty parliament was elected, and a bloody civil war broke out that lasted for six months. When the war ended, four of the six counties of Ulster, once part of the Republic of Ireland, now formed the new province of Northern Ireland.

The benefit of Cumann na mBan's evolution as a separate organization from the male volunteers was that it both allowed many women the space in which they could make a valuable contribution to the military struggle against British rule and also enabled the women to develop their own political strategy and debate the political issues of the day. Interestingly, despite its support to the IRA, Cumann na mBan was not banned by the Free State government as was the IRA in 1936. The reason is obvious: women in this revolution were simply not considered political actors.

However, some women were celebrated in the public sphere for their revolutionary actions. One of the most famous women in the resistance was Countess Constance Markievicz, who was known for her bravery and military might. However, juxtapose the words of Sawyer describing Markievicz's accomplishments with the photograph (see Figure 7.1) that was one of the most celebrated images of women in resistance in Ireland:

> Not content to cook and nurse, Countess Markievicz had been second-in-command of the contingent which occupied Stephen's Green until it had to retreat to the College of Surgeons. She had discharged her pistol frequently, but she was Citizen's Army, and others of that select band who were not of her [social] class also had their moment of glory: ten men and nine women all armed with revolvers were detailed to attack the virtually undefended symbol of British power, Dublin Castle. The women were given arms for self-protection. *Nevertheless*, when it came to launching an assault on the Castle, both women and men took part in charging the gates. But their equality as combatants was short-lived. Having been repulsed, they moved on to the City Hall, where they reverted to the traditional role for women in war; they went to the furthest point from conflict and organized canteen and hospital facilities.[45]

Contrary to the documented actions of Markievicz, the representation of this "heroine" had been skillfully molded to demonstrate to a world theater a proper blend of femininity and status, in contrast to militancy and aggression. This celebrated iconographic image presents her tentatively poised with her pistol and does not reflect the panache of the countess, who kissed her revolver before surrendering it to the British commander.[46] It is also not representative of the woman whose husband, when asked why he ended his marriage to the countess, lamented that the last straw came when she took to hiding guns under the marital bed.[47] It most certainly does not demonstrate the bravery of the woman who cried when her death sentence was commuted to life imprisonment because of her gender.[48] Markievicz's tears were not symptomatic of relief, but rather of disappointment because she was not executed alongside her male comrades from the Easter Rising.

Instead, this photograph provides a model for accepted behavior of women in war. This posed reflection of Markievicz shows a woman of status, by the use of lavish props, and one of femininity, by her feminine posture and plumed headdress. The backdrop of a pastoral landscape that implies a sense of calmness, refinement, and hominess (the garden as an extension of the home) is not compatible with the image of Markievicz storming Dublin Castle. Instead, this image

FIGURE 7.1 Countess Markievicz. *Source:* Courtesy of the National Library of Ireland. Lawrence Collection.

promotes a softer, more palatable image of fighting Irish women. This reproduction is not indicative of the woman who fought side by side with men and women of lesser status. Finally, Markievicz's trigger finger remains extended, as if she is not prepared to fire her beloved pistol. The countess who was quite comfortable with a firearm is portrayed as uneasy, as if she were being forced to be a soldier. This image of Markievicz is one the male-dominated movement found acceptable to promote to a world theater. It exaggerates accepted norms of femininity that are skillfully cultivated, whereby the powerlessness that is associated with this femininity becomes a weapon of solidarity.[49] Jacklyn Cock elaborates on this type of male manipulation of powerlessness when she states, "[P]ower is like the disease of hemophilia. It is transmitted by females but only manifests in males."[50]

Ground Zero

Illustrative of the powerlessness of women that fuels the power of men in a time of war is the media's attention to the wives left behind after the attacks of September 11, 2001, such as Lisa Beamer, whose husband was one of the publicly acclaimed heroes of downed Flight 93. Although she has been lauded in the press as a hero and virtually saintlike, her identity has been relegated to that of a victimized mother and wife. The resulting image of Lisa Beamer has had the same affect as the images of the women in Afghanistan: reasons to go to war.

Therefore, for the purpose of this inquiry I will focus on several points. First, the creation of masculine superheroes is dependent on the domestic landscape. For example, would the words "Let's roll," uttered by Todd Beamer shortly before downing Flight 93, have become such a powerful image of nationalist solidarity without the Madonna-like icon of Lisa Beamer, a pregnant mother who was mourning the courageous act of her husband? Second, the actions of women who take a more active role in warfare, for the purpose of this chapter, women firefighters and police officers, were for the most part ignored in the recording of the events of September 11. Last, the erasure of these women from the landscape creates a public space that is imbued with the characteristics often associated with the domestic landscape, such as nurturing and healing. Therefore, actions such as crying by male firefighters and police officers are considered appropriate. In the absence of women they have created a brotherhood, a public family to mourn. In this specific case the nation was moved to solidarity by an action that was so heinous that pregnant mothers were made widows and superheroes actually cried.[51]

It is important to state that the purpose of this inquiry is not to refute any of the courageous acts that were undertaken by many individuals on September 11, 2001. Instead, the intent is to launch a preliminary inquiry on how after the attacks on the World Trade Center the New York City landscape was rendered masculine as a way of demonstrating how formidable the city was in the face of the attacks. As a point of entry into this discussion, I will analyze the establishment of the moral landscape of New York City by way of popular images released shortly after the tragedy. I will also rely on discussions of the attacks from more feminist viewpoints such as *Firework: The News-letter of Women in the Fire Service, Inc.*[52] These firefighters are concerned that there is a tendency to assume that the heroes of the attacks are all men and ignore the contributions of women firefighters, police officers, and rescue workers who also risked and in some cases lost their lives on September 11. This has led to an even deeper masculinization of the New York City Fire Department, with the revitalization of such designations as firemen rather than firefighters and blood brotherhood. Historically, the challenging of the notion of the male warrior would be deemed unpatriotic. However, in the case of the attacks on New York City, it is important to ask why women's actions are being ignored in the recording of the events of that day and what type of moral codes have been rendered by their absence. Most important, is the historical treatment of the identities of women in war simply being rewritten into the contemporary political landscape?[53]

Towering Heroes

One of the most popular images after the attacks on New York City was a cartoon titled "Our Towering Heroes" that likened the images of the World Trade Center to the bodies of a male firefighter and police officer. The masculinization of the actual landscape is evident. However, how can this image and the images of firefighters hugging and crying work simultaneously in building a national solidarity?[54]

In the case of men who are publicly displaying emotion, it is clear that there is a deep bond that developed in the face of this tragedy, but there is also a sense of power that, as argued earlier, stems from their powerlessness.[55] For example, a *New York Times* article titled "When The Hero Wept" argued: "We've seen brave firemen crying; other men can, too . . . The warm and human responses to the losses of Sept. 11 show us the reality: tears can reveal strength, not weakness; compassion, not fear; maturity, not loss of control. The urge to cry when emotion becomes overwhelming is a part of us and there is nothing noble about denying it."[56] In this case characteristics that are commonly associated with the home, such as compassion and emotion, are brought into the public sphere; however, these traits are translated into strength and maturity as acted out by men in the public realm.

Although there were female heroes at Ground Zero, as mentioned earlier, the acceptable "heroines" of this conflict seem to be white, heterosexual Christian mothers who have been left without a husband. This of course is a tragedy, and nothing justifies the plight of these women; however, it is interesting that they have risen as the moral icons of this conflict, while other women have been ignored.

The point of this argument is not to take away from the courage these women have shown in the face of incomprehensible sorrow, but rather to ask why we have not included other women in this category of iconic hero, such as Moira Smith, a New York Police Department (NYPD) officer who was killed on September 11, 2001. Smith was among the first to respond to the attack at the World Trade Center and was last seen evacuating people out of Tower Two, saving hundreds of lives. She was described by the *Daily News* as having "the face of an angel and the heart of a lion."[57] The angelic packaging of Smith may make it easier for some to accept that she was posthumously awarded the NYPD's Medal of Honor, the department's highest honor. Then there was Yamel Merino, an emergency medical technician, of Dominican ancestry, who while tending to the wounded was killed when Tower Two collapsed. She was a single mother who left behind an eight-year-old son, Kevin, and yet there was very little attention paid to this child who now is going to be raised by his grandmother. Finally, there was Katy Mazza, who was the first female Port Authority officer killed in the line of duty. Mazza was killed while evacuating people from Tower One of the World Trade Center. Her body was recovered exactly five months after the attack.[58]

This raises the question, were there other women who acted bravely, and why are they not proclaimed as heroes of that day? Lieutenant Brenda Berkman had the day off, but like many other firefighters, when she heard of the disaster, she went to the nearest firehouse and jumped on a truck to go to Ground Zero. She worked endless hours at Ground Zero, then returned to her firehouse to grab a meal or a few hours rest, counsel other firefighters, and help plan funerals. In a quote from the *Minneapolis Star Tribune*, "I knew fighters were heroes before 9/11," she said:

> But it hurts that women rescuers who stood shoulder to shoulder with the men at Ground Zero have been so roundly ignored by the media that the term fireman has returned to vogue. Women were down there from the time the first plane hit the first tower, she said. Women were trapped in the rubble. Three women rescue workers were killed that day. I don't think it is patriotic to show just one group of people on the job.[59]

Brenda Berkman showed unprecedented bravery that day. However, she, like many women, has had to go to war to gain access to the political landscape, and certainly she and they are heroes of that war. She was hired by the New York City Fire Department in 1982 as a result of her class-action lawsuit that forced the department to hire her. She became the first woman hired by the department, one of forty to join after the suit. Since then, that number has dwindled to 25 women out of 11,500 firefighters in the department.[60] When she talks about her early days on the job "she explains how oxygen was drained from her air tanks, death threats were left on her answering machine and her few supportive male colleagues had their tires slashed. Most in her firehouse refused to talk, train, or eat with her. Worst of all, she never knew if male colleagues would watch her back in dangerous fires as they did each other."[61] The experience of Brenda Berkman points to how women who seek access to the political landscape engage in combat every day.[62]

Conclusion

When Markievicz learned that she was not to be executed with her male comrades, she berated the British, asserting, "I do wish your lot had the decency to shoot me."[63] Markievicz was questioning the moral codes of this war which denied her the right to make a last nationalist gesture: to publicly die for Ireland. Instead, she argued against the immorality of locking herself and seventy other Irish women away in solitary confinement. In this way, public martyrdom was a place reserved for men, while women's sacrifice was placed out of view and relegated to private spaces, such as the home. Part of the establishment of gender roles in conflict is to dictate what type of sacrifice is morally acceptable in terms of gender. For example, it is permissible for women to suffer in the roles of mothers but not as public warriors. In this way, domestic images of women as powerless empower public images of men as warriors and thereby construct the political landscape as masculine.

The point of juxtaposing the historical case of revolutionary Ireland with the attacks of September 11, 2001, is to demonstrate that the contemporary political landscape remains a masculine way of seeing. For example, images of women as victims, mothers, and widows were liberally utilized to legitimate the bombing of Afghanistan. The heroes of September 11 were the firefighters and police officers and other rescue workers, who were presumed to be men. Ironically the rescue dogs received more media coverage than the women at Ground Zero. As in the case of the Amazons, women who transgress the boundaries of the political landscape are viewed as foreign and out of place. Most important, these two cases demonstrate the effects that war can have on the gendering of societies. For example, how would Ireland's history have been different if the points of view of women had been included in such a momentous political decision as partition? Similarly, would the U.S. invasion of Afghanistan have been different or even encumbered if images of women, whether Lisa Beamer or veiled Afghan women, had not been such a powerful reason to go to war?

Perhaps the words of Markievicz best describe the dual nature of public and private space during war: "*The first road to freedom is to realize ourselves as Irishwomen—not as Irish or merely as women, but as Irishwomen doubly enslaved and with a double battle to fight.*"[64] These words, albeit nation and period specific, ring true to all women regardless of culture, race, or class when they try to rewrite the political landscape as a way of seeing for both men and women. The experience of Brenda Berkman is not unlike that of Mary MacSwiney almost a century earlier. Both Berkman and MacSwiney wanted women to "be counted," whether in a national election and movement or in a response to a national tragedy. Both women risked their lives in acts of service to their respective nations. However, and most important, both women challenged patriarchal systems when they rewrote women into the political landscape during a period of conflict.

Notes

1. Enloe, *Does Khaki Become You?* 117.
2. See Jacobs, Jacobson, and Marchbank, *States of Conflict*; Dowler, " 'And They Think I'm Just a Nice Old Lady' "; Daniels, *White Lies*; Condren, "Work-in-Progress"; Sharoni, "Homefront as Battlefield"; Radcliffe and Westwood, *Viva*; Segal, "Images of Women in Peace and War"; Elshtain and Tobias, *Women, Militarism, and War*; Elshtain, *Women and War*; Ridd, "Powers of the Powerless."
3. Cock, *Women and War in South Africa*.
4. Goldstein, *War and Gender*.
5. Kleinbaum, *War against the Amazons*, as cited in Goldstein, *War and Gender*, 17.
6. Goldstein, *War and Gender*, 17.
7. Ibid., 19.
8. Ibid., 19.
9. Ibid.
10. Ibid., 10.
11. Ibid.
12. Ibid.
13. Australia, 13.4%; Canada, 10.1%; China, 5.5%; Czech Republic, 7.0%; France, 7.2%; New Zealand, 14.3%; Norway, 5.0%; United Kingdom, 7.5%; United States, 14.4%;

South Africa, 24.0%. See Women's Research and Education Institute, *Women in the Military*, 29.

14. Goldstein, *War and Gender*, 59–127.
15. Enloe, *Does Khaki Become You?* 166.
16. Goldstein, *War and Gender*, 59–127.
17. Dowler, " 'And They Think I'm Just a Nice Old Lady.' "
18. McClintock, "Family Feuds."
19. Goldstein, *War and Gender*, 9.
20. Colt and Hollister, "Were You Born That Way?" as cited in Goldstein, *War and Gender*, 129.
21. Goldstein, *War and Gender*, 131.
22. See Women's Research and Education Institute, *Women in the Military*, 1–2.
23. Goldstein, *War and Gender*, 182.
24. Ditzel, *Fire Engines, Firefighters*, as cited in Yarnal and Dowler, "Who Will Answer the Call?" 161–189.
25. Yarnal and Dowler, "Who Will Answer the Call?"; Greenberg, *Cause for Alarm*.
26. Till, "Definition of Landscape."
27. Staeheli, "Publicity, Privacy, and Women's Political Action."
28. Dowler, Carubia, and Szczygiel, *GenderScapes*.
29. Ibid.
30. Arendt, *On Violence*.
31. Ehrenreich, *Blood Rights*.
32. Ward, *Unmanageable Revolutionaries*, 2.
33. Nash, "Remapping the Body/Land."
34. Ward, *Unmanageable Revolutionaries*, 119–155; Sawyer, "*We Are but Women*," 71–99.
35. Ward, *Unmanageable Revolutionaries*, 119–155.
36. Ibid.
37. Ibid., 38.
38. Ibid.
39. Ibid.
40. Ibid., 169.
41. Ibid.
42. Ibid.
43. Dowler, Carubia, and Szczygiel, *GenderScapes*.
44. Ward, *Unmanageable Revolutionaries*.
45. Sawyer, "*We Are but Women*," 90.
46. Ibid, 71–94.
47. Ibid.
48. Ibid.
49. Ridd, "Powers of the Powerless."
50. *Women and War in South Africa*, 27.
51. See Dowler, "Women on the Frontlines."
52. Floren, "Too Far Back for Comfort."
53. See Dowler, "Women on the Frontlines."
54. Ibid.
55. Ridd, "Powers of the Powerless."
56. Boehm, "When the Hero Wept," A27. Frank Boehm is the director of maternal and fetal medicine at Vanderbilt University Medical Center and the author of *Doctors Cry Too*.

57. Marzulli and Hutchinson, "Outpouring for Lost Cops," 47.
58. Dowler, "Women on the Frontlines."
59. Miller, "Invisible Women Firefighters of Ground Zero," 1A.
60. Ibid.
61. Ibid.
62. See Dowler, "Women on the Frontlines."
63. Sawyer, "*We Are but Women*," 9.
64. Ibid., 71.

References

Arendt, Hannah. *On Violence*. New York: Harvest Books, 1970.

Boehm, Frank. *Doctors Cry, Too: Essay from the Heart of a Physician*. Carlsbad, CA: Hay House, 2001.

Boehm, Frank. "When the Hero Wept." *New York Times*, December 5, 2001, A27.

Cock, Jacklyn. *Women and War in South Africa*. Cleveland: Pilgrim, Press, 1993.

Colt, George, and Anne Hollister. "Were You Born That Way?" *Life*, April 1998, 39–50.

Condren, Mary. "Work-in-Progress: Sacrifice and Political Legitimization: The Production of a Gendered Social Order." *Journal of Women's Studies* 6/7 (1995): 160–189.

Daniels, Jessie. *White Lies: Race, Class, Gender, and Sexuality in White Supremacist Discourse*. New York: Routledge, 1996.

Deutsche, Rosalyn. *Evictions: Art and Spatial Politics*. Cambridge, MA: The MIT Press, 1996.

Ditzel, P. *Fire Engines, Firefighters: The Men, Equipment, and Machines from Colonial Days to the Present*. New York: Routledge, 1976.

Dowler, Lorraine. " 'And They Think I'm Just a Nice Old Lady': Women and War in West Belfast, Northern Ireland." *Gender, Place and Culture* 5 (1998): 159–176.

Dowler, Lorraine. "Women on the Frontlines: Rethinking Narratives of Heroism Post 9/11." *GeoJournal* 58 (2002): 157–165.

Dowler, Lorraine. Josephine Carubia, and Bonj Szczygiel, eds. *GenderScapes: Renegotiating the Moral Landscape*. London: Routledge, forthcoming.

Ehrenreich, Barbara. *Blood Rights: Origins and History of War*. New York: Metropolitan Books, 1997.

Elshtain, Jean B. *Women and War*. New York: Basic Books, 1987.

Elshtain, Jean B., and Sheila Tobias. *Women, Militarism, and War*. Savage, MD: Rowman and Littlefield, 1990.

Enloe, Cynthia. *Does Khaki Become You? The Militarisation of Women's Lives*. Boston: South End, 1983.

Floren, Therese. "Too Far Back for Comfort." *Firework: The Newsletter of Women in the Fire Service, Inc.* Women in the Fire Service, October, 2001.

Goldstein, Joshua S. *War and Gender*. Cambridge: Cambridge University Press, 2001.

Greenberg, Amy. *Cause for Alarm: The Volunteer Fire Department in the Nineteenth Century City*. Princeton, NJ: Princeton University Press, 1998.

Jacobs, Susie, Ruth Jacobson, and Jennifer Marchbank, eds. *States of Conflict*. London: Zed Books, 2000.

Kleinbaum, Abby Wettan. *The War against the Amazons*. New York: McGraw-Hill, 1983.

Marzulli, John, and Bill Hutchinson. "Outpouring for Lost Cops: People around the Country Are Offering Their Support." *New York Daily News*, September 18, 2001, 47.

McClintock, Anne. "Family Feuds: Gender, Nationalism, and the Family." *Feminist Review* 44 (1993): 61–79.

Miller, Kay. "The Invisible Women Firefighters of Ground Zero." *Minneapolis Star Tribune*, January 13, 2002, 1A.

Nash, Catherine. "Remapping the Body/Land: New Cartographies of Identity, Gender, and Landscape in Ireland." In *Writing Women and Space: Colonial and Postcolonial Geographies*, ed. A. Blunt and G. Rose, 227–250. New York: Guilford, 1994.

Radcliffe, Sarah A., and Sallie Westwood, eds. *Viva*. London: Routledge, 1993.

Ridd, Rosemary. "Powers of the Powerless." In *Women and Political Conflict: Portraits of Struggle in Times of Crisis*, ed. Rosemary Ridd and Helen Callaway, 1–24. New York: New York University Press, 1987.

Sawyer, Roger. *"We Are but Women": Women in Ireland's History*. New York: Routledge, 1993.

Segal, Mady W. "Images of Women in Peace and War." In *Images of Women in Peace and War*, ed. Sharon MacDonald, Pat Holden, and Shirley Ardener, 23–39. Madison: University of Wisconsin Press, 1993.

Sharoni, Simon. "Homefront as Battlefield: Gender, Military Occupation and Violence against Women." In *Women and the Israeli Occupation*, ed. Tamar Mayer, 212–231. London: Routledge, 1994.

Staeheli, Lynn A. "Publicity, Privacy, and Women's Political Action." *Environment and Planning D: Society and Space* 14 (1996): 600–619.

Till, Karen. "Definition of Landscape." In *Feminist Glossary of Human Geography*, ed. Linda McDowell and Joanne Sharp, 147–148. New York: Arnold, 1999.

Ward, Margaret. *Unmanageable Revolutionaries: Women and Irish Nationalism*. London: Pluto, 1989.

Women's Research and Education Institute. *Women in the Military: Where They Stand*, 3rd ed. Washington, DC: Women's Research and Education Institute, 2000.

Yarnal, Careen, and Lorraine Dowler. "Who Will Answer the Call? Volunteer Firefighting and Serious Leisure." *Leisure/Loisir: Journal of the Canadian Association of Leisure Studies* 27 (3–4): 161–189.

ROGER W. STUMP

Religion and the Geographies of War

Religious meanings and concerns have had a prominent role in a wide variety of political conflicts in recent decades. After the Six-Day War in 1967, for example, religious Zionists interpreted Israel's victory in explicitly religious terms and saw Israeli occupation of the ancient lands of Judea and Samaria in the West Bank and of the Temple Mount in Jerusalem as evidence that the divine redemption of the Jewish people was at hand. Muslims, in contrast, saw Israeli occupation of the Old City of Jerusalem as a threat to al-Haram al-Sharif, the sacred compound atop the Temple Mount and one of Islam's most revered sites. Radical Islamists have cast many other conflicts in religious terms, including the war against the Soviet occupation of Afghanistan during the 1980s, the civil war in Bosnia in the early 1990s, and the conflict between Chechen separatists and Russia that started in the mid-1990s. Interpreting these conflicts as attacks on the global Muslim community, radicals from various Muslim countries took up arms in Afghanistan, Bosnia, and Chechnya in defense of Islam. Out of these contexts, al-Qaeda emerged in the late 1980s and 1990s as a transstate terrorist army that focuses on more dispersed, symbolic targets in its war against Western antagonists.

On a regional scale, tensions between India and Pakistan have contained an overt religious dimension since independence, exacerbated by the rising influence of Hindu and Muslim fundamentalisms in the region. This religious dimension found symbolic expression in the late 1980s and 1990s through military nomenclature, with Pakistani missile systems that bore names linked to the early Muslim conquests of northern India (Ghauri, Ghaznavi), and India's deployment of missile systems named after principal Vedic deities (Agni, Surya) and a Hindu hero in the wars against Muslim conquest (Prithvi). In Africa, political violence has arisen in various states out of postcolonial competition among traditional animists, Muslims, and Christians. In Sudan, for example, conflict between the Muslim majority in the north and animist and Christian minorities in the south has provoked a devastating civil war.

These examples illustrate the persistent complexity of the intersection of religious meanings and war. In recent centuries, the rise of modernist and rationalist worldviews and the spread of secularist and pluralist political structures clearly have not led to the displacement of religion as a potent political force. Interactions between religion and war have taken on new forms in the contemporary world, but such interactions continue to have widespread effects. This chapter examines the nature and consequences of such interactions, particularly as they relate to the geographic dimensions of war. The discussion focuses specifically on two themes: the relationship between geographic context and the religious discourses that have informed the causes or motivations of war, and religion's role in the territorial concerns and spatial strategies of combatants who are pursuing religiously significant objectives. Together, the themes of contextuality and spatiality reveal the complex relationship between religion and the geographies of war and provide a basis for differentiating religiously motivated wars from other forms of conflict. In addition, they illustrate important changes in religious warfare over time and offer insights into why connections between religion and war continue to exist in contemporary settings.

Before I proceed to a detailed examination of these themes, some preliminary words on religions themselves are in order. A religion is interpreted here as a type of cultural system, an integrated assemblage of meanings and behaviors shared by a community of adherents.[1] Religion differs from other types of cultural systems in its concern with beliefs and practices that ultimately relate to superhuman entities, such as deities, natural spirits, venerated ancestors, or perfected individuals, who are believed to possess powers beyond those of ordinary mortals. Beliefs about the superhuman are an essential part of a religion's worldview, its adherents' understanding of reality and the forces that shape it, and of a religion's ethos, the values and emotions that underlie adherents' thoughts and behavior relative to reality and the superhuman. Religions thus resolve basic ontological questions of existence and authority, rendering specific beliefs and practices especially compelling to adherents and often producing concepts of religious obligation. While adherents conceive of their religion as a set of fixed, eternal truths, however, a single religious tradition may take diverse forms as adherents reproduce it in different local circumstances. As cultural systems, religions thus contain inherent tensions between received traditions and the contexts of everyday life in which these traditions are enacted, interpreted, and adapted. The mutability of religions as cultural systems is central, in turn, to the interactions between religion and war, as they are addressed in the remainder of this chapter.

Contextuality

Despite the values of compassion and reconciliation inherent in many of the world's religions, religions as cultural systems have played a significant role in human warfare.[2] At the most basic level, many ancient and tribal religions have identified particular deities with war, and adherents have often taken divine action to be a crucial force in specific conflicts. In the *Iliad*, to cite a notable example, Homer thus describes the gods' participation in the Trojan War: "So did the blessed gods spur on the two hosts and in warfare pitted them, causing to break out among them a furious conflict."[3] Within such contexts, adherents have seen tribal or national deities as essential allies and have construed victory as evidence of the superiority of the victors' gods. The belief that deities, ancestors, or spirits provide support to combatants in wartime has in fact appeared in countless settings up to the present day. Echoes of this view appear in President George W. Bush's declaration to Congress after the attacks of September 11, 2001, that "freedom and fear, justice and cruelty, have always been at war, and we know that God is not neutral between them," and even more overtly in the contemporaneous videotaped assertion by Osama bin Laden that "here is America struck by God Almighty in one of its vital organs, so that its greatest buildings are destroyed."[4] Reference to divine influence in war reflects a totalizing view of religion as a source of meanings relevant to all aspects of human existence. In this sense, any war involving adherents can acquire religious connotations.

In many contexts, however, religious concerns have been more immediately related to the occurrence of war and have served as a primary impetus for conflict. In such cases religious discourses become central to the conduct of war and not merely provide abstract justifications but actually shape the objectives and strategies of combatants. Such conflicts are the principal focus of this chapter. Religiously motivated warfare has taken varied forms, of course, and specific conflicts necessarily reflect concerns related to and articulated in particular settings. The contextuality of such conflicts thus represents one of their essential traits and a principal geographic dimension of the relationship between war and religion. Contextuality, as the term is used here, refers to the intersection in a given place of various processes that are organized at different scales and yield a distinct set of social conditions, relations, and meanings.[5] From this perspective, religion becomes involved in war through the interaction of diverse political and cultural forces, including local reproductions of religious tradition, that acquire concrete form and meaning in specific settings.

Religious motives for war have traditionally developed in contexts where basic issues of religious authority are contested by competing groups. In many cases the rationale for war arose, at least in part, from the role of the state as the agent of the one "true" faith. Along with that role, the state acquired the mandate of advancing the true faith, which in certain contexts led to warfare with others who held different beliefs. The rapid expansion of the Islamic empire in the seventh and eighth centuries C.E. illustrates such a pattern of conquest, justified by religious certainty rooted in an Islamic worldview. The goal of spreading Christianity likewise served to justify colonial wars between European powers and indigenous peoples. The contesting of religious authority has also informed conflicts between Christians and Muslims along the boundary between their traditional spheres of influence, including the Christian expulsion of Muslims from Iberia during the Reconquista and the recurrent wars in southeastern Europe between the Ottoman Empire and various Christian states. The latter reached a climax in the failed Ottoman siege of Vienna in 1683 and the subsequent formation of a Holy League by Poland, Austria, and Venice to turn back the advance of Islam. Combatants on both sides conceived of that conflict in overtly religious terms. Ottoman sultans acted with the title of Warrior of the Faith, and Christian rulers as papally designated Defenders of Christendom.

The spatial intersection of contrary understandings of religious legitimacy has also contributed to internecine warfare within religious traditions. The doctrinal fragmentation of Western Christianity brought about by the Protestant Reformation, for example, contributed to a political context in Europe fraught with both internal and international conflict.[6] The French Wars of Religion during the sixteenth century had diverse social and economic causes, but largely centered on discord between Protestant Huguenots and Roman Catholics. The contemporaneous revolt of the Netherlands against Spanish rule correspondingly pitted Dutch Calvinists against Roman Catholics. England's support for this rebellion and its broader role as a source of Protestant influence in part led to Spain's attempted invasion of England, which was thwarted by the defeat of the Spanish Armada in 1588. In the following century, conflicts between Roman Catholicism and both Calvinist and Lutheran forms of Protestantism played a key role in the Thirty Years' War in central Europe, while discord between Anglicans and Catholics on one side and the predominantly Calvinist Puritans on the other triggered civil war in England.

Similarly, contested notions of religious authenticity in Islam first led to conflict in the seventh century C.E. within the context of the original Islamic state when sectarian strife arose over the proper succession of leadership after Muhammad's death. This conflict ultimately led to the division between Islam's Sunni and Shi'ite branches. In more recent centuries, violent conflicts within Islam that have focused on religious authenticity have continued to develop in specific contexts. Perhaps most significantly, the emergence of the orthodox Wahhabi movement in Arabia during the 1700s and its subsequent association with the Saud dynasty resulted in various conflicts with surrounding Muslim tribes and rulers. To the Wahhabis these conflicts took on the character of a jihad against deviations from orthodox Islam, such as the worship of saints. With the Saudis they occupied Mecca and Medina in the early 1800s, but were driven back into the Arabian interior by Egyptian and Ottoman forces. The Saudis led a second Wahhabi jihad early in the twentieth century, however, and extended Wahhabi dominance throughout the new kingdom of Saudi Arabia.

An important example of this pattern beyond the hearth of Islam was the jihad led by Uthman Don Fodio during the early 1800s in a region that extended across northern portions of present-day Nigeria and Cameroon. As an orthodox Muslim scholar, Uthman led a vigorous campaign against syncretistic forms of Islam and the survival of animistic practices. In response to opposition from local leaders, he ultimately instigated an Islamic rebellion that replaced various tribal states with the orthodox Caliphate of Sokoto. A number of similar jihads that began in the sixteenth century occurred elsewhere in the complex cultural context of West Africa.[7]

While propagation of a "true" faith has historically played a key role in religiously motivated warfare, such violence has in some past contexts focused on other issues. War has emerged, for example, in contexts where minorities have resisted the hegemony of a dominant religious system. Minority resistance in such cases has often focused less on asserting the authority of the group's own religion than on ensuring its survival in hostile surroundings. The Jewish rebellions against the Roman Empire exemplify this pattern. Many Jews saw the Roman conquest of Judea as a threat to their survival as a people. Inspired by belief in the messianic restoration of a Jewish kingdom, the Zealots and similar Jewish sects ultimately rebelled against Roman rule in 66 C.E. This rebellion's failure led to the destruction of the Jerusalem Temple in 70 and to the mass suicide of nearly the entire population of the last Zealot stronghold at Masada. Subsequent Roman suppression of Judaism, for example, by banning Sabbath observances and by erecting a shrine to Jupiter on the site of the Jerusalem Temple, provoked a second rebellion in 132, again motivated by concern for the Jews' survival. Roman victory in this war ended hopes for a Jewish kingdom. As Jews dispersed across the empire, however, Jewish religious traditions did in fact survive in the more decentralized forms of Rabbinic Judaism.

An analogous context developed in South Asia's Punjab region in the seventeenth and eighteenth centuries, where the Sikh population faced intense persecution from Mughal leaders who sought to impose orthodox Islam within their empire. The persecution caused a mass migration during the 1600s from Punjab into the Himalayan foothills, where the Sikh leader Guru Gobind Singh formulated a distinctly martial religious discourse that redefined Sikh identity in terms of the Khalsa, or "pure," a community committed to the realization of divine power and justice symbolized as a double-bladed sword. Under this new identity, Sikhs engaged in a series of wars during the 1700s with the declining Mughal Empire that resulted in the formation of a Sikh empire in Punjab by the early 1800s. In the process, however, the Sikhs did not attempt to impose their religion on others; their primary objectives focused on preservation of the Khalsa.

The control of holy places represents a further source of conflict in contexts where the intersections of political and sacred space have been contested. Concerns over sacred space have obvious links to larger questions of religious authority, but they have also provided a distinct motivation for war. The Crusades, during which Christian princes backed by the pope sought to reclaim the holy land of Christianity, followed this pattern. The Crusades were not solely a religious endeavor; many political and economic factors contributed to the crusader campaigns carried out between the eleventh and fifteenth centuries. In terms of the religious discourses used to justify them, however, the Crusades reflected a specific aspiration to establish Christian rule over key sacred spaces. Control of Islamic sacred sites has similarly been a source of conflict among Muslims. In the campaign led by the Saud dynasty at the turn of the nineteenth century, the Wahhabis saw the control of Mecca and Medina as a crucial religious objective because they denied the religious authority of the Ottoman Empire and thus rejected its right to rule over Islam's holiest sites.[8] Likewise, during the expansion of the Saudi kingdom in the twentieth century, the Wahhabis fought to reclaim control of Mecca and Medina from Sharif Husayn, who with British support had established rule over the surrounding Hijaz region during World War I.[9]

A common motif that runs through historical examples of religious warfare is the idea of war as a religious obligation, for example, to spread the true faith or to defend adherents or sacred places from external threats. This perspective goes beyond the concept of the "just war," broadly defined as a conflict that can be legitimized in moral or religious terms. Instead, it characterizes warfare itself in certain contexts as a religious act, as a direct articulation of the received beliefs that it promotes or defends. Perhaps the most widely recognized expression of this perspective is the Islamic concept of jihad, although it must be recognized that jihad has been interpreted in many different ways, not all of them involving war.[10] In many Islamic traditions, jihad commonly refers to a personal struggle between religious commitment and temptation or doubt. In addition, the representation of war as a religious obligation has clearly not been limited to Islam. Religious and secular leaders in medieval Europe repeatedly characterized the defense of Christendom against the spread of Islam and the reclamation of the Christian holy land from Muslim control in terms of religious duty. This aspect of the medieval Christian ethos also found institutional expression in military religious orders like the Teutonic Knights, who played a crucial role in the conquest of pagan areas in eastern Europe.[11] The development of a martial ethos within Sikhism in response to Mughal persecution and the Zealots' rebellion against Roman rule represent other interpretations of the relationship between religious duty and war.

Despite obvious differences in the specific forms that they have taken, however, premodern conceptions of war as a religious obligation shared certain crucial features. Most important, such conceptions were generally rooted in largely unreflexive understandings of religious absolutism. Accepting the truth of their belief system as indisputable, adherents in diverse contexts also accepted the "naturalized" obligation to preserve or promote that system, even through warfare, as an inherent part of their religious ethos. Within such contexts, religious warfare has typically been understood as an obligation that is defined in broad social terms and engages the resources of entire communities, institutions, or states. Individual leaders often played a central role in this process, but the sense of obligation on which they acted was more communal than personal and was based on widely accepted religious certainties.

In the modern era, and particularly during the past century, the overt contesting of religious legitimacy by competing absolutisms has declined in importance as a factor in religiously motivated wars. This trend in part reflects the influence of secular political discourses across the modern state system and a corresponding secularization of international relations and foreign policy. Saudi Arabia, for example, has established alliances with the United States and other secular states even though it maintains a strict form of Islamic orthodoxy domestically. At the same time, cultural transformations that have arisen within the broader context of modernity have undermined the unreflexive acceptance of religious absolutism characteristic of earlier religious conflicts. Wars waged to assert the absolute authority of a religious system or to enlarge the territorial domain of the "true" faith have thus given way in contemporary settings to conflicts motivated by more complex, and typically more reflexive, religious concerns. Accordingly, the geographic contexts of religious warfare have changed as well. In particular, such warfare has become associated with settings where intersecting cultural and political factors have caused religious issues to acquire compelling symbolic importance, often in connection with other forms of political discourse. In these contexts, religious issues in effect provide a focus for the ideological mobilization of broader political actions, including those that relate to war.

The intersection of religious identity and nationalism has played a major role in the emergence of such contexts of war. Through its strong ties to ethnic identity, religious affiliation has obviously been a key factor in marking the boundaries between warring peoples in the past. Its political role has been transformed in contemporary contexts, however, by the more reflexive character of nationalist ideologies within the modern state system. In such contexts, discourses of religious identity have become central to the legitimization of nationalist aims and the conflicts that arise from them, often by addressing the nature of national identity itself. In Sri Lanka, for example, Sinhalese nationalists have sought to define the modern state's identity in terms of its Buddhist traditions, particularly as expressed in the *Mahavamsa*, a fifth-century epic that includes accounts of miraculous visits made by the Buddha to the island. On the basis of this narrative, Sinhalese nationalists have promoted the centrality of Buddhism as a unifying element within Sri Lankan identity. This ideology has been opposed, however, by ethnic Tamils and other non-Buddhist minorities. Resulting tensions led to the outbreak of civil war in the 1980s, an event that strengthened Sinhalese nationalism as a political force in the years that followed.[12]

A comparable movement emerged on a broader scale among Hindu fundamentalists in India, who have advanced an ideology of national identity grounded in India's indigenous religious heritage. A primary focus of their nationalist discourse is the concept of *Hindutva*, which unifies into a single community those who trace their ancestry, culture, and religion to the Indian subcontinent. *Hindutva*, in other words, represents the common identity of those who recognize this region as both their "fatherland" and their "holy land."[13] This interpretation of Hindu national identity reveals a distinctly modern, reflexive view of national unity in a region that had been highly fragmented historically. At the same time, this concept clearly separates those who share in that identity, including Buddhists, Jains, and Sikhs as well as all varieties of Hindus, from those who do not, including Muslims, Jews, and Christians. The rise of a Hindu nationalist movement based on this concept thus contributed to often violent conflict between Hindus and Muslims both before and after the partition of British India. Within the secularly constituted state of India, moreover, Hindu fundamentalists have continued to advance *Hindutva* as the foundation of Indian nationalism, especially since the rise to power of the fundamentalist Bharatiya Janata Party in the early 1990s. The religious dimensions of this nationalist discourse have in turn played a significant role in the recurring eruptions of communal violence between Hindus and Muslims in India, as well as in ongoing tensions between India and Pakistan.

Discourses of religious identity have been used as well in contexts where a minority seeks to legitimize violence directed against the hegemony of a larger society. Such a pattern appeared in the radical Sikh nationalist movement that emerged in the early 1980s. The primary objective of this group was the creation of a sovereign Sikh state in India's Punjab, where Sikhs represented a majority.

Many Sikhs had supported the goal of greater autonomy within India since the latter achieved independence because they believed that they faced economic, political, and cultural disadvantages within Indian society. The concerns that had motivated this broader support for Sikh autonomy did not focus solely on religious identity, however, and indeed addressed some decidedly secular issues such as water rights and economic development. The radical movement that emerged in the 1980s, on the other hand, adopted an explicitly religious discourse in promoting the cause of Sikh nationalism and used that discourse to validate its terrorist campaign against the Indian government, Hindus, and Sikh moderates. At the heart of the radicals' discourse was a fundamentalist conception of religious identity that drew on the martial traditions of Sikhism but that at the same time recast the unity of the Khalsa in modern, nationalistic terms that focused on the creation of an independent Khalistan.[14] Radical terrorism provoked military action from the Indian government, however, that resulted in 1984 in an assault by the Indian army on the Sikhs' chief temple compound in Amritsar, where many of the radicals had taken refuge. Damage done to that site and the killing of radical leaders provoked a new round of violence, including the assassination of Prime Minister Indira Gandhi by two Sikh bodyguards. That event in turn provoked Hindu riots in which thousands of Sikhs were killed. Escalating violence in the years that followed produced more than 25,000 deaths, but government action against the radical Sikh movement led to its effective suppression by the mid-1990s.

The interactions between religion and nationalism discussed in the preceding examples primarily reflect discourses of group solidarity in which religion provides a coherent foundation for a shared identity. In some instances, however, the association between religion and national identity has been reinforced by equally powerful discourses of opposition to a common enemy. Such a pattern emerged in the 1990s among Orthodox Serbs in Bosnia-Herzegovina following the breakup of Yugoslavia. Militant Bosnian Serbs considered Bosnia-Herzegovina to be part of the territorial domain of the Serbian nation, a position supported by neighboring Serbia. Serbs therefore sought to consolidate their control over territory within Bosnia-Herzegovina to create a distinct Serbian district that could eventually unite with Serbia proper.[15] They faced a major obstacle in the intersecting spatial distributions of Serbs and Muslims in Bosnia, however, and thus adopted a brutal strategy of ethnic cleansing to remove the Muslims who were interspersed among Serb-dominated areas. This caused a civil war that cost 200,000 lives and produced more than 2 million refugees.[16] A key factor in the strategy of ethnic cleansing was the religious discourse asserted by militant Serbs, which focused not only on the role of religion in Serbian nationalism but also on Bosnian Muslims as a wholly "other" religious foe. The nationalist aspect of this discourse was expressed in the ideology of Christoslavism, which asserts that Slavs are intrinsically Christian and that Muslim Slavs have thus forsaken the essence of their heritage. Radical Serbs promoted a parallel discourse, however, based on the martyrdom of Saint Lazar, a Serbian prince who was killed by invading Ottoman forces at the Battle of Kosovo in 1389. For Serbs, Lazar's death symbolized defeat by the Ottoman Empire. Serbian nationalist narratives in turn depicted Lazar as a mythic, Christlike figure and his opponents, including Serbs who betrayed him, as "Christ killers." In the

1990s, radical Serbs defined the Muslims in their midst in the same terms, as Christ killers, and used this discourse to legitimize the atrocities that they committed against Muslims in the areas they sought to control.[17] This militant construction of Serbian nationalism also informed Serbia's actions in Kosovo during the 1990s, as is discussed in the following section.

Like the assertion of national identity, the process of defining the political character of the state has also incorporated religious factors into contemporary contexts of war. Such factors' effects have been most evident in Muslim contexts where the idea of the Islamic state has been contested. The concept of the Islamic state is rooted in early Muslim history and is based on the model of the polity established by Muhammad in 622. Within this original model, religious and secular authority were united and the state itself encompassed a unified Muslim community. With the decline of European imperialism and the dismantling of the Ottoman Empire after World War I, Islamic fundamentalists in various contexts sought to adapt this historical model to the modern state system. Such efforts proved to be problematic, however, for several reasons. Conservative Muslims often rejected discourses that supported the creation of an Islamic state in nationalistic terms and asserted that state-based nationalism was incompatible with and would undermine Muslim unity. Muslim traditionalists in South Asia thus opposed the creation of Pakistan as an Islamic state at the time of partition. In other settings, Muslim modernists opposed the idea of the Islamic state on the basis of the conviction that the separation of secular and religious authority was more appropriate within the context of a modern state. The idea of the Islamic state has also been opposed in various contexts by non-Muslim minorities who are seeking a voice in national affairs.

Because of such opposition, fundamentalist efforts to define modern states in explicitly Islamic terms have in various contexts led to civil war. These state-centered conflicts have taken diverse forms, however, depending on local circumstances. In Egypt a small coalition of radical Islamists who see themselves as a revolutionary vanguard apart from society has in recent decades carried out a sporadic campaign of violence directed at various secular and government targets, including the assassination of Anwar Sadat in 1981.[18] In contrast, broader support for an Islamic state in Algeria has pitted radical Islamists against the Algerian military in a more widespread civil war. This conflict was triggered by the military's cancellation of elections in 1992 because of an expected fundamentalist victory and by most estimates has caused more than 100,000 deaths. Still another type of conflict has emerged in Sudan, where both the military and the ruling political party have supported the creation of an Islamic state. This process began in the early 1980s when the government tried to impose Islamic law, but became more fully realized after a military coup in 1989. The effort to create an Islamic state greatly exacerbated tensions between Sudan's Muslim majority and its Christian and animist minorities, however, and contributed to a civil war that has caused 2 million deaths during the past two decades.

Transstate religious discourses have also been implicated in modern warfare, again most clearly in relation to radical Islamism. Discourses of this type have historical precedents. Papal calls for European cooperation during the Crusades, for example, assumed a common loyalty to the interests of Christendom that transcended traditional political divisions. Within the milieu of Islamic fundamentalism, however, transstate religious discourses in support of political violence have taken distinctly contemporary forms. Most important, such discourses have been articulated primarily by radical groups who have organized outside of the conventional political structures of the state system. Radical Islamists have also used these discourses to focus reflexively on their distinctive identity within the larger Muslim community as holy warriors or revolutionaries. By relating their goals to pan-Islamic concerns, many radical groups have been able to obtain the backing of sympathetic states or Islamic charities. In the process, radical Islamists have directed their religious discourses toward diverse ends, both to mobilize support in specific conflicts and to legitimize broader, symbolic assaults on perceived threats from the non-Muslim world. Nonetheless, despite their significant impacts in various settings, these militants largely remain on the fringes of the Muslim societies in which they have emerged.

An early expression of transstate discourses of religious solidarity arose from the ideology of Islamic renewal articulated by the Muslim Brotherhood, a fundamentalist group organized in Egypt in the late 1920s.[19] The diffusion of the Brotherhood's ideology to other Arab states promoted a sense of common cause among like-minded Islamists who were opposed to European imperialism and Zionism. The discourses of Islamic and Arab solidarity that arose from this process intersected with armed conflict in the Palestinian uprising from 1936 to 1938, during which volunteers from Egypt and Syria joined the local Arab revolt against British rule and Zionist settlement.[20] A decade later, Muslim Brothers from Egypt organized a paramilitary unit to fight alongside Egypt's regular army against the creation of a Jewish state during the Arab-Israeli War. After the war, this paramilitary group brought arms and military experience back to Egypt, where it engaged in domestic terrorism against British imperialism and what it saw as a failed Egyptian regime. Perhaps more important, it reorganized in the early 1950s to join the guerrilla war against British control of the Suez Canal.[21] This action set a significant precedent for future conflicts that involved radical Islamists by mobilizing veterans of one war as an armed force in other contexts.

That pattern became especially pronounced after a resurgence of radical Islamism in the 1970s, as radicals from diverse origins joined the Afghan war against Soviet occupation. The holy warriors or mujahideen who fought in Afghanistan in effect became an informal army that has subsequently taken part in widely dispersed conflicts. In doing so, these fighters have applied a common transstate Islamist discourse to a series of wars in distinct contexts since the early 1990s. In the Algerian civil war, so-called Arab Afghans who had fought in Afghanistan were a key group on the radical Islamist side that dominated the extremist Armed Islamic Group, which has carried out a brutal war against both government and civilian targets.[22] Experienced "Afghans" and other foreign radicals also joined the conflict in Bosnia-Herzegovina and provided the first significant source of external support for the Muslims involved in that conflict. They appear to have played a similar role in the Chechen civil war, often with the backing of Muslim states and charities. Other locations in which they have become involved in political violence during the past decade include Palestine, Kosovo, Kashmir, and Eritrea.

The involvement in these conflicts of radical Islamists from diverse origins has produced among them a common culture of violence that focuses on a martial construction of the concept of jihad. Through their participation in that culture, radicals have constructed a distinct religious identity within the larger Muslim community, which they themselves recognize in their self-characterization as mujahideen or in their narratives of martyrdom. This identity in turn provides the foundation for a politics of authenticity through which they claim to speak and act on behalf of a larger Muslim constituency. Their commitment to war in this sense derives not from unreflexive communal obligation, as in many traditional religious wars, but from a political self-awareness that reflexively draws on religion for its ideological legitmacy. Similar patterns have appeared among religiously motivated combatants in other present-day contexts. Among radical Islamists, however, the authentic identity that they have claimed incorporates an inherent transstate discourse that results in the spread of their activities across conflicts in diverse settings. In addition, this transstate discourse has shifted in emphasis in recent years to focus on a broader assault on the perceived enemies of Islam. The growing influence of al-Qaeda in the 1990s exemplified the latter trend as its leadership sought to cultivate a terrorist network that reached from Southeast and central Asia to the Middle East and North Africa, and into non-Muslim regions as well. The result of that effort has been a war of terror that has been conducted simultaneously on many fronts and has focused both on targets of local significance and on more dispersed targets of largely symbolic importance, as is discussed under the theme of spatiality. These actions reflect a conception of religious warfare oriented toward the expression of fundamental enmity rather than the achievement of immediate, conventional objectives. Such actions represent a form of "prestige" terrorism that serves to aggrandize its perpetrators within the culture of violence in which they participate.

In all of the contexts discussed so far, religious issues have served as a source of motivation or validation for combatants. Contemporary interactions between religion and war have also developed in contexts where conflict is instigated by secular opponents of religious activity. Religion in such cases becomes the target of aggression rather than its inspiration. One notable expression of this pattern has occurred in the conflict between China's secularist government and the Buddhist population of Tibet. Since China's military invasion and annexation of Tibet in 1950, the Chinese government has persistently sought to eliminate Tibetan Buddhism as a source of authority in the region. The destruction of Buddhist monasteries, the imprisonment of monks and nuns, and other assertions of Chinese control provoked sporadic guerrilla warfare during the 1950s and ultimately incited a popular rebellion in 1959, during which the Dalai Lama, Tibetan Buddhism's primary leader, fled to northern India to establish a government in exile. China's violent containment of the 1959 rebellion was followed by a more widespread suppression of Tibetan culture, including all religious activity perceived by Chinese authorities to be linked to political dissent or Tibetan nationalism.

Similar conflicts have emerged in other settings where secular combatants have viewed religious groups as potential threats or obstacles. The Maoist Khmer Rouge waged a massive campaign of violence against Buddhism as it took control of Cambodia in the late 1970s, for example. By the time Vietnam overthrew its regime in 1978, the Khmer Rouge had killed most of the country's Buddhist monks and nuns and destroyed most of its Buddhist temples; by most estimates it had also killed well over half of the country's Muslim population. On a smaller scale, during its insurgency in Peru in the 1980s and early 1990s, the Sendero Luminoso (Shining Path) rebel group frequently targeted evangelical Protestants and Roman Catholic activists, motivated by its Maoist opposition to religion generally and its antagonism toward evangelicals as symbols of U.S. imperialism.

The intersection of religious meanings with acts of war has thus taken place in a great variety of contexts. Some common themes have appeared in both historical and contemporary settings, such as concerns for group survival or the control of sacred space. In contemporary contexts, however, the naturalized, unquestioned absolutism that underlay traditional religious wars has been replaced by more deliberately politicized religious discourses that focus on issues of identity, power, nationalism, and the state. Religious absolutism remains an important part of such discourses, but it has generally been more reflexively integrated with political meanings. In contemporary conflicts, religious absolutism thus provides a foundation not only for faith but also for ideology. The rise of secular ideologies that reject religious absolutism has led to violent conflicts as well. The contemporary transformation of the relationship between religion and war has also recast associated discourses of religious duty in more ideological terms, not as a broad social concern but as a calculated form of political expression. The relationship between religion and war has increasingly taken on compelling symbolic dimensions that have been reflected both in the specific concerns of combatants and in their consequent actions. These symbolic dimensions are of particular interest from a geographical perspective because of their implications for the spatiality of war, the topic to which the discussion now turns.

Spatiality

The preceding analysis of the contextuality of religious warfare reveals that such conflict has involved diverse territorial concerns and spatial strategies. In some ways these concerns and strategies resemble those found in other kinds of war, but ultimately they are distinguished by their relationship to the ontological certainties of religious worldviews, through which adherents ascribe transcendent meanings to human actions. Such certainties cover a great many themes: the nature of reality and divine agency, the transcendent modality of sacred space, the struggle between good and evil, and eternal rewards and punishments for worldly actions. It should be noted that these certainties can find expression as well in opposition to war. Nonetheless, the articulation of religious certainties has had crucial effects, in both traditional and contemporary contexts, not only on the occurrence of war but also on its spatiality. Religious meanings have informed the territorial objectives of combatants with regard to both secular and sacred space and have legitimized the spatial strategies used in pursuing those objectives. In the process, religious discourses have also influenced the scales at which war has been enacted.

Interactions among religious meanings, territoriality, and war have taken varied forms. The historical contesting of territory by religious groups often involved areas that lacked any intrinsic sacred significance. Nonetheless, religious discourses played a role in such conflicts by providing absolute legitimacy for political conquest. Religious discourses have often supported offensive strategies, for example, by expressing a naturalized understanding of the obligation of rulers or states to spread the true faith. The conquests of Spain, Portugal, France, and Britain during the first wave of European colonialism incorporated this idea into the broader discourse of empire, as did the earlier expansion of the Islamic empire out of its Arabian hearth. Offensive strategies have also focused on the reclamation of territory considered to be a rightful part of a religion's traditional domain, as in the efforts of medieval Christian states to push back the boundaries of Islam in Iberia and southeastern Europe. Similar discourses have also supported defensive strategies. The Battle of Tours in 732, in which the Franks halted the Moors' invasion of Christian Europe, acquired significance in European histories as a decisive event in the preservation of Christendom. Medieval Poland, Hungary, and Croatia each acquired similar status at various times as Christian "bulwarks" against the advance of Islam in eastern Europe.

The integration of religion, nationalism, and territorial identity has added a further layer of meaning to the spatial expressions of war. Associations between religious and territorial identities were commonplace and largely unquestioned in traditional settings and arose from the cultural sedimentation of dominant religious systems. As a factor in warfare, however, connections between territory and religious identity have taken on particular significance in modern contexts where they have been linked by combatants to more reflexive and politicized discourses of nationalism. In such cases, territory is not necessarily construed as possessing an intrinsic holiness; rather, it derives its significance at least in part from its role in the fusion of the religious and national identities of a particular group. The territory acquires religious meaning, in other words, because group members understand it in mythic terms, as a place where their national origins and aspirations attained transcendent validation. The control of such territory can thus be represented as both a nationalistic objective and a religious duty.

That pattern has characterized Serbian nationalist attitudes toward Kosovo for more than a century. After Serbia achieved independence from the Ottoman Empire in the 1800s, control of Kosovo became a major concern of Serbian nationalists which led to Serbia's annexation of Kosovo in 1912. Serbian nationalist discourses persistently represented Kosovo in overtly religious terms as the site of the martyrdom of Lazar, as the hearth of the Serbian Orthodox Church, and as a sacred landscape of Orthodox churches and monasteries. Thus in 1939, in commemorating the 550th anniversary of Lazar's death, one Orthodox bishop said of Kosovo that "beside the name of Christ, no other name is more beautiful or more sacred," and another described the region as "our national Golgotha and at the same time our national resurrection."[23] This religious discourse played a major role in the resurgence of Serbian nationalism during the collapse of Yugoslavia, as was seen in the relocation of Lazar's relics from Belgrade to a monastery in Kosovo in 1989 and the circulation of his relics among Serbian villages in the early 1990s. Moreover, this discourse defined the ideological basis for militant Serbs to oppose the efforts of Kosovo's largely Muslim Albanian majority to merge with Albania in the early 1990s. In the late 1990s, that militant opposition escalated into the Milosevic regime's genocidal war against the Albanian Kosovars, which caused the deaths of thousands of ethnic Albanians and the destruction of hundreds of Kosovar mosques before it was halted by NATO intervention.

The territorial concerns that arise from linkages between religious identity and nationalism clearly have a more precise spatial focus than those related to the more traditional goal of expanding a religion's hegemonic domain. At the same time, the integration of religious and nationalist meanings also lends specific territories considerable symbolic value. The complex symbolism of place that emerges in such contexts often has clear political implications, for example, by informing a state's raison d'être. In the previously cited case of Sri Lanka, Sinhalese nationalists have sought to define the modern state not simply as the hearth of Sinhalese identity but as a sacred domain where, according to the *Mahavamsa*, Buddhism will endure in its purest form.[24] By defining the state in this manner, Sinhalese nationalists have addressed the issue of Sri Lanka's postcolonial identity from a fundamentalist perspective rooted in an ideological commitment to a traditional religious worldview. Religious interpretations of national territory have significant repercussions for warfare, then, by rejecting the legitimacy of compromise with regard to territorial control, which becomes a matter of sacred necessity and right. Issues of territoriality thus acquire a strong potential of being triggers for conflict and provoking responses reinforced by religious conviction. In some cases, such responses have in turn involved the characterization of opponents as evil in a religious sense and have led to the use of extreme violence against civilian opponents, as in the ethnic cleansing of Muslims by radical Serbs in Bosnia and Kosovo.

The intersection of religious meanings, nationalism, and territorial objectives reveals the significance of the state as a spatial focus of religiously motivated warfare in contemporary contexts. The importance of the state appears as well in conflicts that arise from the political definition of a state's identity. As discussed earlier, efforts by religious fundamentalists to define modern states as theocracies, ruled according to specific religious principles, have generated conflict in diverse settings. Through such efforts, religious groups have attributed transcendent meaning to the state itself as an expression of religious authority or law. The concept of the Islamic state represents perhaps the most important contemporary manifestation of this pattern, although again this concept has had different implications in different contexts.

In terms of the spatiality of conflict, efforts to impose theocratic rule have taken diverse forms. In states where religious fundamentalists wield significant political power, the territorial focus of their concerns is the state in its entirety. These concerns are expressed in war through strategies aimed at achieving territorial control over the state or, once the group is in control, by suppressing opponents who contest the theocratic definition of the state. Conflicts of this type include the aforementioned civil war in Sudan, the Islamic Revolution in Iran in the late 1970s, and the Taliban's war against various sources of opposition in Afghanistan in the 1990s.[25] Where advocates of theocracy lack the power to rule the state, their strategies have been quite different and have often focused on symbolic violence instead of territorial control. Radical Islamists in Egypt, for example, have attacked secular targets that violate Islamic laws, such as nightclubs and liquor stores. Islamic extremists have also carried out attacks to demonstrate the inability of the government to prevent violence, as in the killing of foreign tourists at Luxor in 1997 or the targeting of civilians and foreigners by the Armed Islamic Group in Algeria in the 1990s. Conflict has developed in some pluralistic societies where religious groups have tried to form theocratic structures at more local scales, as in the communal violence that has resulted from efforts to impose Islamic law in parts of Nigeria in recent years. The civil war waged in the southern Philippines by Islamic separatists reflects a similar concern with local religious territoriality.

The religious potency of territorial meanings in contemporary contexts of war has not been defined solely by discourses of nationalism and state identity, however. Such meanings have also been derived from the sacredness attributed to particular spaces within the worldview of a religious tradition, a central concern in many traditional contexts of war as well. The biblical account of the Israelites' conquest of the promised land of Canaan offers an ancient archetype of this pattern. Within the context of European culture, the Crusades exemplify the traditional power of religious discourses of war that focus on religious authority and sacred space. Although more recent conflicts that have involved sacred space have generally occurred on a more limited scale, they reveal similar concerns with the intersection of religious legitimacy and territorial control. As discussed earlier, the Wahhabi aim of controlling Mecca and Medina emerged not as an overt manifestation of nationalism but as part of a broader discourse of strict Islamic orthodoxy. In asserting control over Islam's holy cities, the Wahhabis sought to bring religious legitimacy to the custody of sacred space. In some conflicts, of course, the significance of contested territory encompasses both nationalistic and religious meanings. The radical Sikh movement of the 1980s, for example, combined the nationalist objective of creating a Sikh state with the more fundamental religious concern of preserving the sacred meaning of the hearth of Sikhism.

The intersection of political conflict and sacred space has found especially complex expression in the Israeli-Palestinian conflict. During the past century, the religious meaning of Zionism and the founding of Israel has been strongly contested by different Jewish groups. Secular Zionists, who dominated the creation of the state, have depicted Israel in nationalist terms as a modern state with the raison d'être of providing a national homeland for the Jewish people. Many ultra-Orthodox Jews have rejected this view, in some cases to the point of denying the legitimacy of Israel itself, on the basis of the belief that a true Jewish state can only be formed through divine action. From this fundamentalist perspective, human efforts to create a Jewish state represent a blasphemous usurpation of divine authority. Religious Zionists, who represent a different branch of Jewish fundamentalism, have adopted a third view that characterizes the formation of Israel as a divinely guided process linked to the prophetic redemption of the Jews.[26] That discourse was strongly reinforced by the Six-Day War, during which Israel gained control of all of Jerusalem and the ancient regions of Judea and Samaria. Religious Zionists interpreted this outcome as a part of a divine plan to reshape the boundaries of Israel to correspond more closely to those of the biblical promised land and heralded these territorial gains as the beginning of the process of redemption. The Yom Kippur War of 1973 heightened the concern of religious Zionists that Jewish control over this sacred space be maintained. In response, religious Zionists led the campaign for Jewish settlement in the West Bank, primarily through the Gush Emunim organization, hoping by their presence to retain control over territory also claimed by the Palestinians. The continued expansion of Jewish settlements in the West Bank has in turn provoked recurring conflict between Israelis and Palestinians since the 1970s.

Palestinian actions in this conflict have focused more on national territorial claims than on sacred space. The emigration of Palestinian Christians after the founding of Israel and the rise of radical Islamist groups in recent decades have contributed, however, to the power of religious discourse on the Palestinian side of the conflict as well. With regard to the issue of sacred space, Palestinian concerns have centered more on local sites than on larger regions. Chief among these sites is al-Haram al-Sharif, the sacred compound that contains the Dome of the Rock, which according to Muslim belief marks the spot from which Muhammad miraculously visited heaven, and al-Aqsa Mosque, one of Islam's earliest communal mosques. Muslim concerns about the site increased sharply after its capture by Israeli forces in 1967, even though the compound itself remains under Muslim supervision. These concerns have been reinforced by the avowed intention of religious Zionists to erect a third Jerusalem Temple in the compound's place atop the Temple Mount. The compound's role as a spatial focus of Palestinian protest has also led to repeated incursions by Israeli security forces. As a result, this site has taken on great symbolic importance for both sides in the Israeli-Palestinian conflict, and concerns over its future remain a significant issue. Similar importance has been attached to the Tomb of the Patriarchs in the West Bank city of Hebron. Jewish and Islamic traditions both identity this site as the tomb of Abraham, the first patriarch in each tradition. The medieval Ibrahimi Mosque that stands on the site had traditionally been used only by Muslims, but after Israel captured Hebron in the Six-Day War, authorities opened the site to Jews as well. Access to the site has subsequently become a contentious issue, especially after a Jewish settler killed twenty-nine Muslims who were praying there in 1994.[27] The establishment of a Jewish settlement in Hebron, in part to preserve access to the site, has contributed as well to the conflict over the Jewish presence in the West Bank.

Again, as the examples in Jerusalem and Hebron suggest, the relationship between war and sacred space has often focused in contemporary settings on local sites rather than on larger territories. In such cases, however, the compelling symbolic importance that combatants have attributed to specific sites has often played a key role in the articulation of broader conflicts. Thus while the territorial discourses of combatants may be highly localized, the resulting symbolism of place can relate to concerns defined at a wider scale. The dispute over the Tomb of the Patriarchs in this sense reflects a nested set of issues that range from access to the immediate site to the issue of Jewish settlement in the West Bank and ultimately to the entire Israeli-Palestinian conflict. This symbolic interaction between local sacred sites and larger conflicts is an important expression of the reflexive integration of religious and political discourses in contemporary settings. Through such processes, combatants represent the meanings of specific sacred sites in overtly ideological terms as a means of legitimizing and mobilizing support for their cause.

A notable example of this pattern has developed around the site of the Babri Mosque in the northern Indian city of Ayodhya.[28] The mosque takes its name from the Mughal ruler Babar who ordered its construction in the early 1500s. Hindu tradition maintains that the mosque was built on the site of a Hindu temple destroyed by the Mughals, a practice that they apparently used elsewhere in northern India to assert their dominance. Hindus nonetheless continued to worship at the site, which they believed to be the birthplace of the god Ram, one of the incarnations of Vishnu. The meaning of the site was thus contested into the colonial period, but mostly at a local scale. After partition, however, the site acquired increased symbolic importance. Attempts by Hindus to reclaim possession of it in 1949 led to widespread violence between Hindus and Muslims that forced the government to close the site to both religious groups. With the rise of a militant Hindu fundamentalist movement in the 1980s, the site became the focus of renewed controversy. Fundamentalists now called for the destruction of the mosque and its replacement with a new temple to Ram, a key figure in their ideological fusion of nationalism and religion. As the goal of building such a temple became increasingly central to the political discourses of militant Hindu fundamentalism, the contesting of the site came to represent tensions between Hindu militants and both the Muslim minority within Indian society and all those who supported India's constitutional secularism as a modern state. The plan for a new temple further came to symbolize the fundamentalists' ultimate goal of establishing Ramrajya, or the rule of Ram, across India as a Hindu nation. The fate of the Babri Mosque thus became a highly contentious national issue during the 1980s and 1990s that provoked repeated episodes of communal violence. The violence reached a peak in the wake of a massive demonstration by Hindu fundamentalists at the site in 1992 during which militants destroyed the mosque, established a makeshift shrine to Ram in its place, and then destroyed a number of other mosques in Ayodhya as well. Thousands died across India in the ensuing violence, which also spread to Pakistan, where Islamic militants attacked or destroyed dozens of Hindu temples in retaliation. Although a decade later the issue of control of the site remains unresolved, the creation of the Ram temple continues to be a key objective in the nationalist discourse advanced by Hindu fundamentalists.

The contesting of the site in Ayodhya illustrates a number of key points about contemporary intersections of sacred space and violent conflict. The attack on the Babri Mosque on one level mirrors traditional strategies, such as those used by the Mughals themselves, that symbolically target specific sacred sites. In contemporary contexts, however, such sites again take on especially compelling meanings through which they become ideologically linked to broader conflicts. Discord over the building of a Ram temple at Ayodhya thus refers not just to the use of that particular site but also to the larger issue of India's national identity. Conflicts over local sacred sites, like those that involve more extensive sacred territories, can therefore serve as triggers for widespread patterns of violence. That violence may contribute to conventional forms of political friction. The situation in Ayodhya significantly increased tensions between Pakistan and India, for example. Pakistan's government strongly denounced the mosque's destruction and declared a day of mourning to commemorate the event, while India accused Pakistan of supporting retaliatory attacks against Indian sites by terrorists. At the same time, in contemporary settings the intense symbolism of sacred sites has also provoked postmodern forms of warfare that are not expressed as traditional military conflict between opposing states.[29] The widespread communal violence that broke out in India following the destruction of the Babri Mosque exemplifies this sort of warfare between nonstate combatants.

Spatial strategies that focus on sacred sites have in fact been adopted by a variety of nonstate combatants. A failed 1979 rebellion carried out by Islamic extremists in Saudi Arabia, for example, involved seizing control of the Great Mosque in Mecca.[30] These extremists adhered to a form of Mahdism, the belief that history will end with the return of a Mahdi or messiah who would reinstate a pure Islamic state. This particular group maintained that the Saudi regime had become tainted by modernization and Western influence and that it therefore lacked the authority to serve as the guardian of Islam's holy cities. The extremists deliberately focused their revolt on the Great Mosque as Islam's most important sacred site and occupied the complex that surrounds the mosque for two weeks as they publicized their demands. Slowed by concerns for hostages and the mosque itself, Saudi security forces eventually overcame the insurgents, whose leaders were later executed.

In the case of Jerusalem, messianic expectations have also been implicated in plans by radical religious Zionists to attack Islamic sacred sites. A number of such plots emerged in the 1980s, the most extreme of which involved radicals who were arrested by Israeli authorities after having stockpiled explosives to be used to destroy the mosques within al-Haram al-Sharif. Violence that focuses on this site has continued as the Temple Mount Faithful, a religious Zionist group, has stated its intention to lay the cornerstone there for a new Jerusalem Temple. Rumors that this action is imminent have led to repeated protests by Palestinian Muslims that often have ended in violence.[31] Through its compelling symbolism, the Temple Mount has thus become an important trigger for hostilities between civilian combatants within the context of the Israeli-Palestinian conflict. The military assault on the temple compound in Amritsar served as a similar trigger for radical Sikh violence. In Sri Lanka, on the other hand, Tamil radicals have used violence against sacred sites in a symbolic strategy of demoralization, particularly in attacks against the Temple of the Tooth, a key Buddhist shrine in Kandy that contains a relic of the Buddha.

The narrow spatial focus of religious concerns expressed in the contesting of sacred sites has an important parallel in the local scale of religiously defined actions used by combatants in contemporary contexts. Along with symbolism of place, such symbolism of action provides a crucial means of introducing religious meanings into political violence. The local spatiality of religious action finds its clearest expression in the concept of martyrdom. This concept of course has a long history in many religious traditions and has often been integrated into discourses of war. Within Christianity, for example, papal guarantees of eternal salvation for those who died in battle while defending the faith appeared as early as the ninth century. In contemporary settings, however, martyrdom has acquired added dimensions of political meaning. The act of martyrdom in such contexts represents not simply an outcome of war but a reflexive strategy adopted to promote specific political ends, such as mobilization of support for the martyr's cause or the demoralization of antagonists through the terrorist violence made possible by suicide attacks. The suicide bomber represents a key expression of contemporary martyrdom, the capability of enacting extreme violence against local targets, but in modern contexts martyrdom has taken quite different forms as well. To cite one contrasting example, the self-immolation of Buddhist monks in Vietnam during the 1960s, first to protest religious discrimination by the regime of Ngo Dinh Diem, a Roman Catholic, and later to protest the Vietnam War, represented an extreme form of political expression that did not involve violence directed at others.

Because of its intense symbolic potential, martyrdom has become a significant strategy in varied expressions of contemporary warfare. The adoption of such a strategy typically draws on a religion's historical tradition of martyrdom for its moral legitimacy. In their conflict with Sri Lanka, radical Tamil separatists have thus constructed a discourse of martyrdom that recasts Hindu and Tamil traditions in the context of Tamil nationalism.[32] Nonetheless, this discourse reflects a political reflexivity not found in more traditional uses of the concept. A similar politicization of martyrdom characterizes its contemporary use by Islamic militants. The Islamic Resistance Movement, or Hamas, a Palestinian outgrowth of the Muslim Brotherhood, has made extensive use of suicide attacks to support its goal of creating an authentic Islamic state in Palestine. This strategy has been used specifically to target the local, routine spaces of daily life in Israel, such as restaurants, nightclubs, and bus stops. A similar strategy has been used by al-Aqsa Martyrs' Brigade, a paramilitary offshoot of the Fatah party, although its primary goal is the creation of an independent Palestinian state, not a strict Islamic polity. Both groups, though, have drawn on religious understandings of martyrdom and its rewards in recruiting Palestinian youth to carry out suicide attacks and in seeking support from other radical Islamists. On a broader scale, Iran's Islamic militants have made extensive use of Shi'ite imagery of martyrdom, particularly in the 1980s during the Iran-Iraq War, when the discourse of martyrdom became essential to the recruitment of volunteers as Iran's casualties rose. As a result of its symbolic power, the concept of martyrdom has also been appropriated by secular regimes, as in Saddam Hussein's call for "martyrdom attacks" against U.S. forces during the war in Iraq early in 2003.[33]

Although it is realized at local scales, symbolism of action, like symbolism of place, derives much of its importance in contemporary contexts from its connections to wider scales of conflict, as the preceding examples suggest. The broader implications of religiously defined actions have developed particular significance within the complex spatialities of the transstate network of radical Islamist movements. These movements have made extensive use of concepts of religious action such as jihad and martyrdom to marshal support and recruit members and have constructed discourses that articulate a close relationship between war and individual matters of religious duty and spiritual reward. In this sense, these movements have supported distinctly postmodern forms of warfare in which irregular forces rather than formal, state-based armies use violence to promote symbolic objectives linked to issues of identity and culture.[34] For radical Islamists, such issues focus specifically on the authenticity of their religious identity. That focus has important implications, in turn, for the spatiality of the violence such groups commit. Much of this violence does not have immediate, clearly defined objectives such as the control of a sacred site or a national homeland. Instead, it primarily serves to express the radicals' discourse of sacred legitimacy. Radical Islamists have sought to demonstrate their religious authenticity, for example, by carrying out terrorist actions against challenging military targets. Such actions include the bombings of U.S. military barracks in Lebanon in 1983 and in Saudi Arabia in 1996, the suicide attack on the USS *Cole* in Yemen in 2000, and the attack on the Pentagon in 2001. By defining their own actions in explicitly religious terms, as those of martyrs and mujahideen, radical Islamists have also sought to legitimize massive attacks against undefended civilian targets, as in the bombing of two U.S. embassies in East Africa in 1998 and the destruction of the World Trade Center in New York City in 2001. Again, as is typical of many expressions of postmodern warfare, these attacks have not focused in an immediate sense on territorial objectives per se, but have used particular targets for their broader symbolic value.

At a different level, however, territoriality continues to play an important role in the discourses of violence espoused by radical Islamists, primarily in reference to the defense of Islam. This concern provides a crucial link, for example, between the symbolic role of the mujahideen and specific conflicts that involve Muslims in dispersed locations, such as Afghanistan, Chechnya, and the Balkans. Although national identity may play a role in such conflicts for local combatants, the transstate force of radicals that joins in these conflicts is motivated by a broader interest in advancing radical Islamism as the foundation of Muslim unity. Indeed, the latter objective has in some places created tensions between local Muslims and outsiders. In Bosnia during the 1990s, for example, many local Muslims resisted the promotion of radical Islamism by foreign mujahideen who had come to fight on their side.[35] The territorial concerns of the transstate mujahideen thus go beyond specific issues of nationalism and focus instead on the relationship between radical Islamism and the global Muslim community.

Terrorism directed at the United States and other Western interests by al-Qaeda follows a similar pattern. Again, the attacks on the World Trade Center and the Pentagon did not reflect territorial objectives of the kind found in conventional warfare. Nonetheless, as symbolic acts they were discursively linked to concerns that have distinct territorial elements. The grievances outlined in al-Qaeda's 1998 manifesto "Jihad against Jews and Crusaders," for example, are explicitly territorial in nature: the U.S. military presence in Saudi Arabia, the impact of the Gulf War and subsequent international sanctions on the people of Iraq, and the existence of a Jewish state in the Middle East.[36] These situations are depicted as aggression not just against Muslims but against Islam itself. An important feature of these grievances is their sharply contrasting interpretation by the different parties involved. Policy decisions in the United States, for example, have presumably not been conceived as an assault on Islam. An asymmetry exists as well in the capabilities of al-Qaeda and its Western antagonists that forces it to wage war at a symbolic level by choosing targets to demoralize its opponents and enhance its own prestige. This strategy has ultimately resulted in a disconnection between the location of symbolic acts of terror and the actual territorial concerns of al-Qaeda, a pattern that is typical of many terrorist groups.

Religiously motivated warfare has, in sum, taken diverse spatial forms in both historical and contemporary contexts. In historical settings, the concerns of combatants have for the most part focused on relatively straightforward issues of religious territoriality that involve the assertion of a particular religious system's hegemony or the control of especially important manifestations of sacred space. Combatants in such instances have understood their territorial concerns and objectives as intrinsically legitimate, based on naturalized assumptions grounded in their worldview. The spatiality of religious warfare in contemporary settings, in contrast, has been made more complex by the reflexive mixing of religious significance with other sorts of meanings. In articulating the importance of controlling certain political regions, for example, combatants have fused religious conceptions with ideological constructions of nationalism or state identity. Similarly, specific sacred sites have played a central role in certain conflicts by providing a symbolic focus for the legitimization of political discourse or the mobilization of political support or by serving as the symbolic object of intended or actual violence. Through the fusion of their religious meanings with ideological objectives, local sacred sites have thus achieved broader significance in discourses of war. The spatiality of contemporary warfare also encompasses politicized forms of religiously defined action, which again forge a symbolic link between localized violence and conflicts that are occurring at wider scales. The rise of religious discourses that embrace the use of terrorism represents an especially devastating expression of this pattern in recent decades, and it is in the context of such discourses that religion and postmodern forms of warfare have become most closely joined.

Conclusion

The preceding discussion has focused on the diverse connections between religion and the geographies of war. Religious belief of course has profound implications as well for opposition to war. The worldviews and ethical teachings of the world's major religious traditions place much emphasis on the values of compassion and reconciliation and have given rise to diverse and very powerful pacifist traditions.[37] Religious motives have thus played a significant role in the political pursuit of peace. The life of Ashoka, an emperor of India's Mauryan dynasty who ruled in the third century B.C.E., provides a well-known early example. As is recorded in one of his so-called rock edicts, narratives carved in stone at various sites throughout his empire, Ashoka had waged a bloody war of conquest to expand his empire in eastern India that had resulted in hundreds of thousands of deaths through battle or famine. His later remorse at the widespread devastation he had caused, according to the traditional account, led to his conversion to Buddhism and his subsequent renunciation of conquest by force in favor of pacifist rule according to Buddhism's moral teachings.[38] In recent times, religious discourses have been central to the development of pacifist ideologies and antiwar movements in response to various conflicts, from the political tensions in Europe before World War I to the nuclear arms race of the Cold War, the Vietnam War, and other postcolonial conflicts.

Nonetheless, religious beliefs remain an important component of many discourses of war. This recurrent association between religion and war in particular contexts essentially reflects the reality of religions as cultural systems. While the basic doctrines of a religion may incorporate principles that are seemingly inconsistent with waging war, religions as cultural systems involve more than a set of theological abstractions. They instead represent a synthesis of beliefs and practices that also derive much of their meaning from the specific contexts in which they are articulated by adherents. In the process, religion, like any system of cultural meanings, can become implicated in diverse aspects of human experience, including political conflict. Thus in settings where war provides an accepted means of achieving political ends, warfare will inevitably interact with patterns of religious belief and practice as contextualized expressions of culture. Religious meanings will take on political importance and, in turn, provide a basis for marshaling support for armed conflict. Moreover, the cataclysmic upheavals of war and, most important, the mortal dangers that it poses for combatants and noncombatants alike motivate those who are involved to construct transcendent explanations of its ultimate meaning. Religious systems provide a source of legitimacy for such explanations by defining the consequences of violence and personal sacrifice in terms of a larger structure of rewards and obligations through which human and superhuman dimensions of existence interact. Religion in essence can offer assurance of supernatural forms of compensation for actions that offer little in the way of immediate personal benefits and that typically involve violence at scales far beyond those of ordinary experience.[39] Religion's various roles in warfare therefore result not only from its cultural inseparability from the concerns and contingencies of specific places and times, but also from its use by adherents as a source of reference in addressing the essential enormity of war.

Notes

1. The primary source for this interpretation is Geertz, "Religion as a Cultural System." Also see Pals, *Seven Theories of Religion*, 233–267.
2. Ferguson, *War and Peace in the World's Religions*; Aho, *Religious Mythology and the Art of War.*
3. Smith and Miller, *Iliad of Homer*, 20, 54–55.
4. "President Bush's Address on Terrorism," B4; "Bin Laden's Statement," B7.

5. Taylor and Flint, *Political Geography*, 336–337; Massey, *Space, Place, and Gender*, 154–155.

6. Dunn, *Age of Religious Wars*; Holt, *French Wars of Religion*.

7. Hiskett, *Development of Islam in West Africa*, 156–171; Lapidus, *History of Islamic Societies*, 508–523.

8. Hourani, *History of the Arab Peoples*, 258.

9. Habib, *Ibn Sa'ud's Warriors of Islam*.

10. On the diverse interpretations of jihad, see Murata and Chittick, *Vision of Islam*, 20–22.

11. Seward, *Monks of War*, 135–193.

12. Stump, *Boundaries of Faith*, 131–133. At the time of this writing, two decades after civil war first broke out, Sri Lanka's government and Tamil separatists have maintained a cease-fire, but they have not yet reached a solution to their conflict.

13. Ibid., 73–77.

14. Ibid., 148–150.

15. White, *Nationalism and Territory*, 234–241.

16. Lopasic, "Muslims of Bosnia."

17. Sells, *Bridge Betrayed*, 29–52.

18. Kepel, *Muslim Extremism in Egypt*.

19. Ruthven, *Islam in the World*, 310–321.

20. Lapidus, *History of Islamic Societies*, 661.

21. Stump, *Boundaries of Faith*, 52–56.

22. Esposito, *Islamic Threat*, 171–191. The term Arab Afghans, or simply Afghans, in this context refers to foreign Muslims who went to Afghanistan to fight in the war against Soviet occupation during the 1980s.

23. Silber and Little, *Death of Yugoslavia*, 72; Emmert, *Serbian Golgotha*, 139.

24. Stump, *Boundaries of Faith*, 198.

25. Ibid., 88–101.

26. For a discussion of both branches of Jewish fundamentalism, see Menachem Friedman, "Jewish Zealots."

27. A detailed analysis of the Tomb of the Patriarchs massacre appears in Mark Juergensmeyer, *Terror in the Mind of God*, 49–52.

28. Stump, *Boundaries of Faith*, 168–172.

29. Van Creveld, *Nuclear Proliferation and the Future of Conflict*, 122–126.

30. Hiro, *Holy Wars*, 128–133.

31. Stump, *Boundaries of Faith*, 159–166.

32. Schalk, "Resistance and Martyrdom in the Process of State Formation of Tamililam."

33. "Saddam Calls for 'Martyrdom' Attacks on US Troops."

34. Munck, "Deconstructing Terror"; Van Creveld, *Nuclear Proliferation and the Future of Conflict*, 126.

35. Sells, *Bridge Betrayed*, 101–102.

36. World Islamic Front, "Jihad against Jews and Crusaders."

37. Ferguson, *War and Peace in the World's Religions*, 156–157.

38. Keay, *India*, 91–92.

39. On religion and the concept of compensators, see Stark and Bainbridge, *Theory of Religion*, 36–42.

References

Aho, James A. *Religious Mythology and the Art of War: Comparative Religious Symbolisms of Military Violence*. Westport, CT: Greenwood, 1981.

"Bin Laden's Statement: 'The Sword Fell.' " *New York Times*, October 8, 2001, 7.

Dunn, Richard S. *The Age of Religious Wars, 1559–1689*. New York: Norton, 1970.

Emmert, Thomas A. *Serbian Golgotha: Kosovo, 1389*. East European Monographs Series, no. 278. New York: Columbia University Press, 1990.

Esposito, John L. *The Islamic Threat: Myth or Reality?* New York: Oxford University Press, 1999.

Ferguson, John. *War and Peace in the World's Religions*. New York: Oxford University Press, 1978.

Friedman, Menachem. "Jewish Zealots: Conservative versus Innovative." In *Jewish Fundamentalism in Comparative Perspective: Religion, Ideology, and the Crisis of Modernity*, ed. Laurence J. Silberstein, 148–163. New York: New York University Press, 1993.

Geertz, Clifford. "Religion as a Cultural System." In *The Interpretation of Cultures: Selected Essays*, by Clifford Geertz, 87–125. New York: Basic Books, 1973.

Habib, John S. *Ibn Sa'ud's Warriors of Islam*. Leiden: Brill, 1978.

Hiro, Dilip. *Holy Wars: The Rise of Islamic Fundamentalism*. New York: Routledge, 1989.

Hiskett, Mervyn. *The Development of Islam in West Africa*. London: Longman, 1984.

Holt, Mack P. *The French Wars of Religion, 1562–1629*. Cambridge: Cambridge University Press, 1995.

Hourani, Albert. *A History of the Arab Peoples*. New York: MJF, 1991.

Juergensmeyer, Mark. *Terror in the Mind of God: The Global Rise of Religious Violence*. Berkeley: University of California Press, 2000.

Keay, John. *India: A History*. New York: Atlantic Monthly Press, 2000.

Kepel, Gilles. *Muslim Extremism in Egypt: The Prophet and Pharaoh*. Berkeley: University of California Press, 1985.

Lapidus, Ira M. *A History of Islamic Societies*. Cambridge: Cambridge University Press, 1988.

Lopasic, Alexander. "The Muslims of Bosnia." In *Muslim Communities in the New Europe*, ed. Gerd Nonneman, Tim Niblock, and Bogdan Szajkowski, 99–114. Reading, UK: Ithaca, 1996.

Massey, Doreen. *Space, Place, and Gender*. Minneapolis: University of Minnesota Press, 1994.

Munck, Ronaldo. "Deconstructing Terror: Insurgency, Repression, and Peace." In *Postmodern Insurgencies: Political Violence, Identity Formation, and Peacemaking in Comparative Perspective*, ed. Ronaldo Munck and Purnaka L. de Silva, 1–13. New York: St. Martin's, 2000.

Murata, Sachiko, and William C. Chittick. *The Vision of Islam*. St. Paul, MN: Paragon, 1994.

Pals, Daniel L. *Seven Theories of Religion*. New York: Oxford University Press, 1996.

"President Bush's Address on Terrorism before a Joint Meeting of Congress." *New York Times*, September 21, 2001, 4.

Ruthven, Malise. *Islam in the World*. New York: Oxford University Press, 1984.

"Saddam Calls for 'Martyrdom' Attacks on US Troops." Asia Africa Intelligence Wire, BBC Monitoring International Reports, April 4, 2003. LexisNexis. http://web.lexis-nexis.com (accessed May 1, 2003).

Schalk, Peter. "Resistance and Martyrdom in the Process of State Formation of Tamililam."

In *Martyrdom and Political Resistance: Essays from Asia and Europe*, ed. Joyce Pettigrew, 61–84. Amsterdam: VU University Press, 1997.

Sells, Michael A. *The Bridge Betrayed: Religion and Genocide in Bosnia*. Berkeley: University of California Press, 1996.

Seward, Desmond. *The Monks of War: The Military Religious Orders*. Hamden, CT: Archon, 1972.

Silber, Laura, and Allan Little. *The Death of Yugoslavia*. New York: Penguin, 1996.

Smith, William Benjamin, and Walter Miller, trans. *The Iliad of Homer*. New York: Macmillan, 1944.

Stark, Rodney, and Williams Sims Bainbridge. *A Theory of Religion*. New Brunswick, NJ: Rutgers University Press, 1996.

Stump, Roger W. *Boundaries of Faith: Geographical Perspectives on Religious Fundamentalism*. Lanham, MD: Rowman and Littlefield, 2000.

Taylor, Peter J, and Colin Flint. *Political Geography: World-Economy, Nation-State, and Locality*. 4th ed. Harlow, UK: Prentice Hall, 2000.

Van Creveld, Martin. *Nuclear Proliferation and the Future of Conflict*. New York: Free Press, 1993.

White, George W. *Nationalism and Territory: Constructing Group Identity in Southeastern Europe*. Lanham, MD: Rowman and Littlefield, 2000.

World Islamic Front. "Jihad against Jews and Crusaders." www.fas.org/irp/world/para/docs/980223-fatwa.htm (February 23, 1998; accessed May 1, 2003).

CARL DAHLMAN

Geographies of Genocide and Ethnic Cleansing

The Lessons of Bosnia-Herzegovina

> During this period Goran Jelisic presented himself as the "Serbian Adolf" and claimed to have gone to Brcko to kill Muslims. [. . .] He allegedly said to the detainees at Luka camp that he held their lives in his hands and that only between 5 to 10% of them would leave there. [. . .] Goran Jelisic remarked to one witness that he hated the Muslims and wanted to kill them all, whilst the surviving Muslims could be slaves for cleaning the toilets but never have a professional job. He reportedly added that he wanted "to cleanse" the Muslims and would enjoy doing so, that the "balijas" had proliferated too much and that he had to rid the world of them. Goran Jelisic also purportedly said that he hated Muslim women, that he found them highly dirty and that he wanted to sterilise them all in order to prevent an increase in the number of Muslims but that before exterminating them he would begin with the men in order [to] prevent any proliferation.
>
> —*Prosecutor v. Jelisic*

The "Serbian Adolf" figures as one of many parallels between the Nazi aggression of World War II and the more recent wars in Bosnia (1992–1995). Though many recognized and drew attention to the atrocities committed against Bosnian civilians, the stories and images of deportation, mass murder, and concentration camps failed to stir an effective response from the international community of states, which had, fifty years before, promised to defend civilians from such abuses. This occurred despite clear signals that the Serb leadership meant not only to run an expansionist campaign to divide Bosnia with Croatia but also to destroy the Bosnian Muslim population.[1] Instead, there were arguments about whether or not the Serb campaign in Bosnia was genocide, and if it was not genocide, whether it required intervention by other governments, especially by the Western powers.[2] This is to say that although the experiences of World War II produced institutions to limit the excesses of war, especially as it affects civilians, this experience does not seem to have significantly changed the narrow political calculus of most states.

In fact, the ideals enshrined in the Charter of the United Nations or the international law that applies to the conduct of modern warfare, such as the Geneva Conventions, are often viewed as outside or antithetical to the "reality" of international politics. It is more productive for the purposes of explanation to recognize that principled institutions, such as the UN or international law, are as much a part of world politics as are the interstate norms of sovereignty or national security. Yet while the institutions that are designed to promote collective security and provide relief from the vagaries of the international state system have gained in the postwar world, they are still beset with the contradictions of those same vagaries, namely, that states must both submit to and enforce the principles that would constrain them. The failure to intervene in Bosnia, at least on behalf of the civilian population if not also for the state of Bosnia itself, is a case in which governments that should have championed principles of international law found it more convenient to demur, despite an international awareness of the war's excesses.[3]

The difficulties of finding champions of principled justice vis-à-vis the territorial ambitions of Serbia and Croatia was compounded in the West by a misconception of the Balkans as characterized by an "atomistic fractiousness and insubordination of the Oriental within"[4] or what Secretary of State Warren Christopher termed a "centuries old" hatred, "a problem from hell."[5] Some who believed that historical patterns of violence in the region reflected primordial and involuntary hatred, discounted the value of intervention and tacitly adopted a model of inexorable regional violence fueled by an apparently telescoping ethnic memory of vengeance. Such a mind-set ignores the fact that the violations of human rights and international law in Croatia, Bosnia, and Kosovo were conducted in a contemporary European society. Further, government officials in the United States and elsewhere were willing to draw equivalence between the Serb program of widespread ethnic cleansing and territorial expansion with the equally horrific but largely uncoordinated and less common abuses committed by Croats and Muslims.[6] That the parties to the conflict might have shown an equal capacity in the extremes of their cruelty is not the same as the conclusion drawn by some that the extent and intention of their crimes somehow cancel each other out or even justify inaction. Far less convincing are the consequences of this equivocation, that the excesses of governments and combatants suspended the need for moral opprobrium and intervention on behalf of civilians trapped by the conflict. Such a conclusion, though it was the tacit platform of the Western governments, could only be maintained with the most impoverished view of humanity, in which imputed ethnicity entails collective guilt and damnation. To cry "A plague o' both their houses," as one might in walking away from a conflict, is to forget that this judgment is Mercutio's, a victim, not an observer, of the conflict in Verona.

The politics of indifference that seem so clear—and so clearly wrong—in hindsight require that greater attention be paid to the confusion that surrounded, some might say enabled, the failure of the international community to stop the wars in the former Yugoslavia. Therefore, this chapter focuses on the concepts of genocide and, by necessity, ethnic cleansing as ideas necessary for comprehending contemporary conflict and, moreover, as ideas that intersect with geographic approaches to explaining conflicts and postconflict society. In considering the war in Bosnia, the problems of identifying genocide and defining ethnic cleansing demonstrate the centrality of sociospatial constructs in geopolitics and international law. Among other fields of social inquiry, geography must address these issues as a contribution to improving their conceptual veracity and the institutions of peace that depend on them for practical action in support of human rights. Genocide and ethnic cleansing elicit extensive and intensive geographic themes: the constitution of spatial identities, the geopolitical imagination of territorial purity, the spatial practice of genocidal campaigns, and the construction of international legal jurisdiction for the relevant protections and the geopolitics of intervention. By necessity, this chapter will address only a portion of these concerns, largely as they relate to the war in Bosnia between 1992 and 1995 and the international effort at prosecuting crimes committed in that war. The next section provides a summary account of the war in Bosnia and describes the process of ethnic cleansing and genocide that accompanied it. In the following section, we review the conceptual and legal basis of genocide and consider the debate over its meaning in explaining ethnic cleansing in Bosnia. The last section examines the prosecution of these crimes in Bosnia, with emphasis on the spatial aspects of international law and its enforcement as itself a geopolitical practice.

The Geopolitics of the Former Yugoslavia

Bosnia was rather unique within the former Federal Republic of Yugoslavia because as it had three constituent peoples, Croat, Muslim, and Serb, none of them a majority, whereas the other republics comprised one constituent group. The constitutional recognition of peoples in the republics of the former Yugoslavia provided for recognition of traditional cultural communities, but it did not, however, mean to legitimize or propel nationalist territorial claims. While ethnic or national identity had been anathema to the Yugoslav Communist movement, nationalist political agitation began to appear after Tito's death in 1980. As Yugoslavia moved toward multiparty elections within the republics, along with much of the rest of Eastern Europe after 1989, nationalist politicians sought to take power away from the Communist Party by appealing to "suppressed" identities and by claiming special rights based on both historical and mythical grievances.[7] More important, the nationalists in the republics began to assert claims to their republics' territories and at times made competing historical claims for land in neighboring republics. This was particularly so in Bosnia, where significant communities of Croats and Serbs were seen by nationalists as members of irredentist communities trapped beyond the Croatian and Serbian republics. As the newly elected nationalist parties made political demands against the Communist regime in Belgrade, political sentiments in some republics began to favor independence. As the dissolution of Yugoslavia became apparent, Serbian nationalists, especially Slobodan Milosevic, sought to "recover" Serb populations and Serb land as part of a "Greater Serbia" project that had broad support from Serb minority enclaves in Croatia and Kosovo as well as from Serbian political and intellectual figures.[8]

After Slovenia and Croatia declared and attained independence from Yugoslavia, the people of Bosnia-Herzegovina voted in a February 29, 1992, referendum to leave Yugoslavia and establish an independent state. However, the leaders of the newly established state of Croatia and the rump Yugoslavia, Franjo Tudjman and Slobodan Milosevic, along with their coethnic allies in Bosnia, had plans to effectively partition the country between them and leave a small area of central Bosnia for the Bosnian Muslims.[9] Complicated by a Serbian boycott of the independence referendum, the declaration of a breakaway Serb Republic within Bosnia-Herzegovina, and Serb attacks on Muslim towns, the political future of a Bosnian state was by no means certain when the European Union and the United States formally recognized the Republic of Bosnia on April 6, 1992. Soon after, the former Yugoslavian National Army, local Serb police, and Serbian paramilitary units backed by Belgrade together conquered territory claimed by the Bosnian Serb leadership, notably Radovan Karadzic. This campaign began in earnest in eastern Bosnia in the cities of Bijeljina and Zvornik before it spread throughout an area that formed an arc from Gorazde in the southeast north through Brcko and included a large portion of western Bosnia. The strategy of the combined Serb forces was to partition by force those areas of Bosnia claimed as Serb land and to remove all non-Serbs who lived there. By the time world attention was trained on the events in Bosnia, the Serb tactics were already known by the name given them by some Serbs themselves, *etničko čišćenje*, or ethnic cleansing.

In Bosnia, ethnic cleansing was primarily a policy of territorial domination by the Serbs, although the Croats followed to a lesser degree a similar policy in southern Bosnia, as did Croatian forces, later, against Serbs in Croatia. The Serb tactics largely remain the focus of explaining what happened in Bosnia since it was the Serb political leadership that is alleged to have directed and organized the campaign that led to territorial gains, massive civilian casualties, and an enormous humanitarian disaster.[10] In a matter of weeks in 1992, Serbs established military domination in large parts of eastern and western Bosnia and emptied the conquered territory of non-Serb inhabitants, many of whom were murdered, raped, deported, or sent to prison camps where many more were tortured and died (Figure 9.1).[11] Moreover, places that had been multicultural or had been home to Muslim or Croat communities were suddenly emptied, and the cultural landscape that bore witness to its former inhabitants was razed. Besides schools, churches, and mosques, individual homes belonging to non-Serbs were systematically destroyed, along with infrastructure, to ensure that they would not return (see Figure 9.2).

The practice of ethnic cleansing was marked by a fairly methodical attack against each town or rural area that was taken by the Serb paramilitary or regular army. Typically, there was a sudden evacuation of Serb civilians from the area, after which non-Serb residential areas were fired upon by artillery and small arms. Serb paramilitaries, including those sent from Serbia, would then enter the area to round up or kill Muslim or Croat community leaders and terrorize the other members of the community through random killings, rapes, and wanton destruction. The Serb combatants forced many to leave or sent them to prison camps, often after they were forced to surrender their property. Finally, control of the area would be transferred to local Serb authorities who would constitute wartime com-

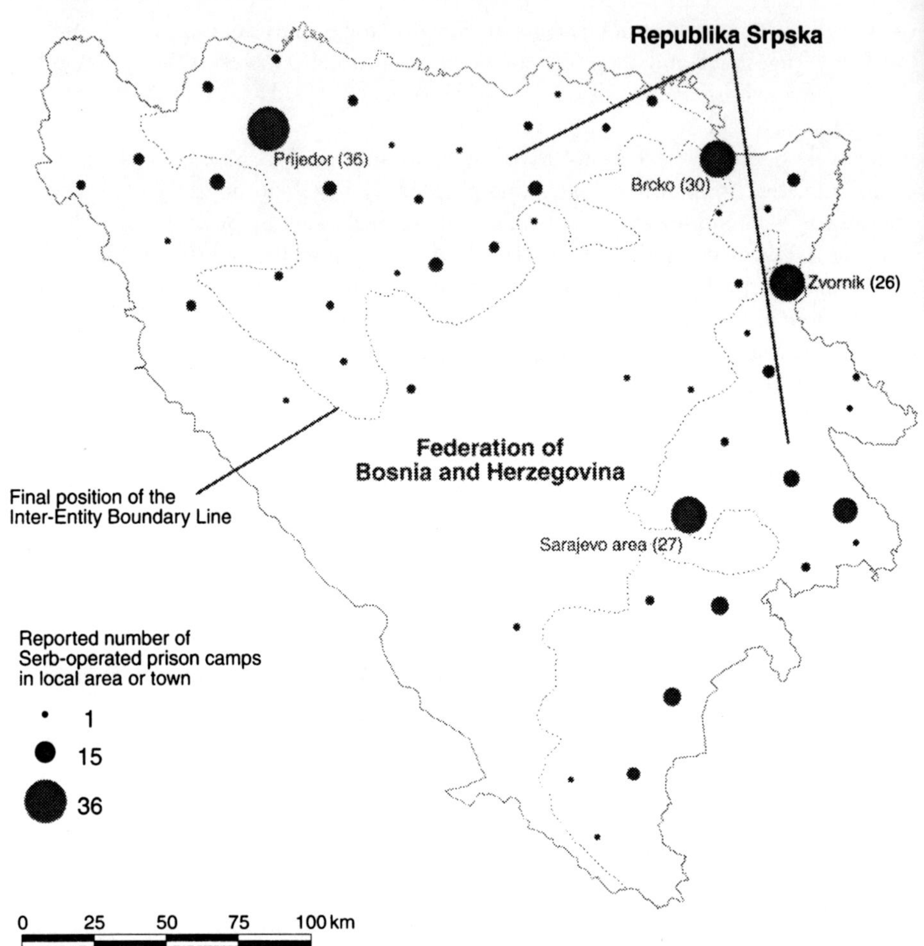

FIGURE 9.1 Serb-operated prison camps in Bosnia and Herzegovina, 1992–1995. *Source:* United Nations, *Final Report of the United Nations Commission of Experts, Established Pursuant to Security Council Resolution* 780 (1992), *Annex VIII*, UN Document S/1994/674, December 28, 1994; Frontline, PBS, 1998.

mittees that would create laws designed to consolidate and formalize the results of ethnic cleansing.[12] Those former residents who were able to flee typically sought refuge in Croatia, especially Croats living near its borders, or in central Bosnia, where large areas of Muslim communities remained and were protected by the Bosnian armed forces. From a prewar population of more than 4.4 million, the war in Bosnia killed more than 200,000 people, mostly civilians, displaced more than 2 million, and rendered uninhabitable more than one-quarter of the homes in the country. Furthermore, torture and rape warfare were routinely practiced as part of ethnic cleansing, especially in the more than 800 prison camps, and affected as many as 20,000 women and 50,000 torture victims.[13] Not only had much

FIGURE 9.2 A newly built and still unconsecrated Orthodox church sits upon the ruins of a mosque in Divic in eastern Bosnia. The town had been almost entirely Muslim before ethnic cleansing by Serb forces in the spring of 1992. *Source:* Carl Dahlman.

of the multiethnic landscape of Bosnia been violently transformed, but many communities' sense of place and memories of home now bore the less visible marks of trauma and fear, as had been intended by the policy of ethnic cleansing.

In Washington, London, and other capitals, however, the debate within governments focused on whether what the world was witnessing was genocide or something else. In the case of genocide, there had always been a presumed moral imperative to intervene and stop the perpetrators, but other crimes, it seemed, did not merit the same concern. Although the UN General Assembly had equated ethnic cleansing with genocide, as had members of the world press and other observers, the United States and other Western powers did not see a role in stopping what they saw as anything but genocide.

Defining Genocide and Ethnic Cleansing

As words in common use, genocide and ethnic cleansing have become important to contemporary world affairs, though their use and meaning are often imprecise or vague. They represent the most serious offenses to humanity and human rights and capture in a phrase our imagination of the unimaginable. Despite being terms invented in the twentieth century that apply to relatively specific acts and events, both terms have diffused through popular and academic writing to the point that critics claim that they have lost any useful rigor, either as concepts that describe human cruelty or even as legal definitions.[14] In popular usage, these terms often paper over the complexities of human experience they denote and replace the messy reality of conflict with relatively neat categories that impart a sense of moral certainty. In some ways, this conceptual diffusion has stretched both concepts to their meaningful limits while, at the same time, they have entered contemporary consciousness as the extreme of cruelty and injustice.[15] But as we shall see in the case of the war in Bosnia, the conflation of the terms went so far as to confound genocide as a category of international law with ethnic cleansing, a less precise description of a violent policy of territorial aggression that nonetheless includes genocide.

Genocide is a term that literally means "race murder" and was coined by the Polish jurist Raphael Lemkin, who is largely responsible for the development of an international legal sanction on the form of systematic killing witnessed in Nazi-occupied Europe, namely, the Holocaust.[16] In addition to the Nazi atrocities against civilians and minority groups in Europe, Lemkin was also troubled by the failure of international bodies to punish mass murder conducted by governments against their own populations, as witnessed in the Turkish massacres of Armenians in 1915. Prevailing international norms on sovereignty at the time meant that governments were not accountable to international bodies for crimes committed against their own citizens in their territory. The postwar emergence of the United Nations provided Lemkin an important organization in which to lobby the world's delegates for an international legal instrument that would present an imperative to states to stop and prosecute regimes that were conducting organized and discriminatory mass murder regardless of where the crime took place or the nationality of the victim. The resulting 1948 Convention on the Prevention and Punishment of the Crime of Genocide was adopted by the United Nations General Assembly and was its first treaty that established human rights protections.[17] Article 2 of the convention defined genocide as

> any of the following acts committed with intent to destroy, in whole or in part, a national, ethnical, racial or religious group, as such:
>
> (a) Killing members of the group;
> (b) Causing serious bodily or mental harm to members of the group;
> (c) Deliberately inflicting on the group conditions of life calculated to bring about its physical destruction;
> (d) Imposing measures intended to prevent births within the group;
> (e) Forcibly transferring children of the group to another group.

Article 3 of the convention enumerated punishable acts as

> (a) Genocide;
> (b) Conspiracy to commit genocide;
> (c) Direct and public incitement to commit genocide;
> (d) Attempt to commit genocide;
> (e) Complicity in genocide.

The convention thus established any of the above acts as a crime, provided that the acts were intended to destroy all or part of a protected group. The requirements to prove intent and to show that the attack targeted a protected group because of the innate characteristics of its members distinguish genocide from other categories of crimes, although there is some overlap between war crimes, crimes against humanity, and genocide.

War crimes, are perhaps best recognized as those enumerated by the 1949 Geneva Conventions and their Additional Protocols, which are often called international humanitarian law. These conventions are intended to provide protections to noncombatants during conflicts and to provide minimal protections to combatants in certain circumstances, such as prisoners of war. Crimes against humanity have been defined in eleven different international legal texts, each time somewhat differently, though they have in common basic proscriptions against mass murder, extermination, enslavement and deportation, and now, in the statute that established the tribunals for the former Yugoslavia and Rwanda, imprisonment, torture, and rape.[18] Unlike the standard of "intent" in the Genocide Convention, for which the perpetrators must have exhibited some coordination in their attempt to destroy one of the protected groups, charges of crimes against humanity have a lower standard that requires only that the perpetrators conducted "widespread and systematic" acts against any identifiable group for whatever purpose. The significant difference is that the charge of genocide only applies when an intentional campaign of destruction was launched against individuals in a protected group because of their membership in that group "as such," for example, because they were Muslims or because they were Armenians. Charges of genocide therefore require prosecutors to show that the perpetrators were trying to destroy some portion of a protected population, while the defense typically argues that the murders were politically motivated or militarily necessary.[19] Another difference is that the persecution of persons because of their political affiliation is not grounds for the charge of genocide but is covered under crimes against humanity. Crimes against humanity and genocide do share an important similarity: both are distinct from war crimes in that prohibitions against them provide specific protection of civilians regardless of whether the victims were nationals or nonnationals of the accused party, which means that states have no implied privilege of sovereignty in committing these acts against their own population.[20]

The crime of genocide is a concept that receives considerable scrutiny as to its provisions and significance because it is a charge that has become frequently leveled but rarely prosecuted. Despite the genocidal campaigns in Cambodia and Iraq in the decades after the convention, some governments, such as the United States, were reluctant to ratify the treaty for fear that its obligation would run counter to their other interests. In fact, after the convention was signed in 1948, it was 50 years before an international conviction for genocide was handed down by the International Criminal Tribunal for Rwanda in 1998. Although meaningful prosecution under the convention was lacking for decades, academic studies have documented genocidal practices by governments and have expanded the concept's ambit well before and after the Holocaust.[21] Others have argued and still argue that genocide is an exceptional case for which the Holocaust remains the only contemporary example. Nevertheless, the Bush and Clinton administrations were well apprised of the nature of ethnic cleansing, and their staffs recognized it as genocide. Yet when Holocaust survivor Elie Wiesel publicly confronted Clinton with the genocide in Bosnia, Clinton duplicitously responded that the Holocaust was "on a whole different level . . . without precedent or peer" and shied away from campaign promises to intervene.[22] Ethnic cleansing, it seemed, was not quite as dire.

The term "ethnic cleansing" was made known during the war in Bosnia and has since become entangled in the debate over genocide and intervention. Like genocide, it has also become a term of moral opprobrium and has been applied, however imprecisely, to times and places beyond the war that first named it.[23] In the former Yugoslavia, the terms *etničko čišćenje*, or ethnic cleansing, and *čišćenje terena*, or cleansing the terrain, had been used by Serbian media to describe the effort of forming a Greater Serbia. Therefore, the emergence of the term in Yugoslavia during the 1980s had militaristic connotations that were expedient for nationalist efforts to claim territory within a society made increasingly paranoid by propaganda that equated ethnic difference with potential violence.[24] Furthermore, the term described a wide array of actions against non-Serbs that ranged from the enforcement of employment quotas, discrimination, limits on mobility, or the suspension of political activities by rival parties to deportation, imprisonment, rape, and murder.[25] While many of these acts violated both Yugoslav national law and international law, by which Yugoslavia was bound, there remains no specific legal definition of "ethnic cleansing" per se. Although the term was an apt description for a policy of territorial conquest by ethnic violence, its very lack of precise definition made it the perfect dodge for governments that were seeking to avoid intervention in Bosnia.

Approaching War Crimes in Bosnia

In trying to understand the chaotic events that unfolded in Bosnia, observers now, as then, are limited to the grounded and institutional perspectives that serve as windows on the conflict. Among the interpretations of the war are media accounts and policy perspectives, which are important for appreciating much of the practical reasoning of geopolitical actors at the time. International print and television journalists reported extensively on the events as they unfolded and drew parallels between the ethnic cleansing in Bosnia and the Holocaust as they made clear that this was a war waged against a civilian population.[26] Meanwhile, interpretation of the conflict by policy makers, at least in Washington, took the form of a debate over whether the conflict was a "Balkan Vietnam," as maintained by the Pentagon, or a "European genocide," the common view in the U.S. State Department.[27] Besides media and policy interpretations, the United Nations established a Commission of Experts charged with investigating war crimes in the former Yugoslavia. Its reports have largely informed both scholarly considerations and legal proceedings aimed at assessing what happened in Bosnia. Toward the end of the war and immediately after, a number of scholarly treatments of the question of genocide raised the question of what constitutes genocide—an important debate since, at that time, there were no convictions for genocide to provide judicial precedent. The remainder of this section describes the emergence of a war crimes tribunal for the former Yugoslavia based on the UN investigations' findings, as well as the scholarly debate on the question of genocide in Bosnia.

Despite the confirmation by Western governments of the media reports from Bosnia, the major powers viewed a limited humanitarian intervention in the Balkans as preferable to what they perceived as a potentially protracted "quagmire." The governments of Britain and France viewed their contribution of troops to the UN humanitarian force (UNPROFOR) as a pretext for remaining neutral on the issue of aggression and genocide and avoiding the question of intervention—to intervene would require taking sides and would put the humanitarian mission at risk. The George H. W. Bush administration was likewise uninterested in getting involved in the conflict and moved from events in Iraq to Somalia. And though candidate Clinton had sounded tough on stopping genocide during the 1992 campaign, he became increasingly reticent once he was in office: the Clinton administration obscured the question of intervention by equivocating on the issue of aggression and blame. In time, the Clinton administration promoted the idea of justice by tribunal and effectively skirted the responsibility of intervention, as one writer puts it, "law became a euphemism for inaction."[28]

In the United Nations, Security Council resolutions from July and August 1992 had affirmed the obligations of the parties in conflict to uphold the Geneva Conventions and other protections under international law and had further stated that these violations required the United Nations to consider action according to Chapter VII of its Charter.[29] Though this opened the door for the legitimate use of force to stop the conflict, the reluctance among the major powers gave momentum to an effort in preparation for a future tribunal. In Resolution 780 in October 1992, the Security Council established the Commission of Experts to collect and analyze evidence related to the violation of international humanitarian law, the international community's first examination of events on the ground in the former Yugoslavia. By February 1993, the Commission of Experts delivered its first report to the secretary-general, which provided evidence of widespread atrocities and concluded that the United Nations was the competent body to establish an ad hoc international tribunal to investigate and prosecute war crimes committed in the former Yugoslavia.[30]

As taken up by the special rapporteur to the United Nations and, later, the Commission of Experts, ethnic cleansing was understood as the elimination of an ethnic group from an area under the control of another group. Interestingly, such an operational definition leaves out the question of home or homeland but rather focuses on the practice of territorial homogenization. In its lengthy report to the United Nations, the Commission of Experts described ethnic cleansing as "rendering an area ethnically homogenous by using force or intimidation to remove persons of given groups from the area" and as comprised of practices "contrary to international law."[31] The report describes the practices of ethnic cleansing as witnessed in the former Yugoslavia, which included "murder, torture, arbitrary arrest and detention, extra-judicial executions, rape and sexual assaults, confinement of civilian population in ghetto areas, forcible removal, displacement and deportation of civilian population, deliberate military attacks or threats of attacks on civilians and civilian areas, and wanton destruction of property."[32] Finally, the report holds that, over and against equivocations of equally guilty parties, ethnic cleansing was primarily a "policy conducted in furtherance of political doctrines relating to 'Greater Serbia.' "[33] The Commissier of Experts found that although Croats in Bosnia and Croatia employed ethnic cleansing practices against Serbs and Muslims, and that Bosnian government forces (representing both Muslims and other ethnic groups) violated the Geneva Conventions, neither had a policy of ethnic cleansing in support of a larger territorial campaign.

Two weeks after the Commission of Experts submitted its interim report, the Security Council adopted Resolution 808, which provided for the establishment of an international tribunal "for the prosecution of persons responsible for serious violations of international humanitarian law committed in the territory of the former Yugoslavia since 1991," which became known as the International Criminal Tribunal for Former Yugoslavia (ICTY).[34] The secretary-general's report of May 3, 1993, provided the framework for the tribunal's legal competency and its jurisdiction over persons, the territory and time period to be considered, and basic investigative and procedural standards, which were formalized in the statute for the tribunal and contained in UN Security Council Resolution 827.[35] By the time the ICTY was established, Serbs had at least 70% of Bosnia under their control; the ethnic cleansing of these areas was largely complete, with only a few remaining "safe area" enclaves that the Serbs would take just before the end of the war in 1995. Frustrated by the limits placed on its powers by Western governments, the ICTY spent its first three years trying to establish its working quarters in The Hague and fighting for the necessary budget while establishing procedural rules and preparing indictments.[36]

After the Srebrenica debacle in 1995, in which UN troops failed to stop Serb atrocities against Muslim civilians, the Western governments, particularly the Clinton administration, changed position on the Bosnia conflict and called for NATO strikes on Serb positions. The end of the war was precipitated by the U.S. shift to an interventionist policy that produced the Dayton Peace Accords, which included provisions for arresting war criminals and transferring them to the ICTY. However, the implementation of the peace by NATO forces conspicuously lacked arrests, which were seen as potentially destabilizing the security situation on the ground. In time, the changing political situation in Bosnia, particularly after the war in Kosovo, brought greater legitimacy to the work of the tribunal, aided, no doubt, by its twin, the Tribunal on Rwanda.[37] By March 2003, the ICTY had brought eighty-three indictees before the court, including Slobodan Milosevic and several high-ranking political and military leaders.

Toward the end of the war, a number of scholarly works took up the question of genocide in Bosnia.[38] This literature represents an important interpretation of the genocide question in Bosnia in the absence of any actually existing case law that applied the Genocide Convention in an international court. Of course, the decisions of the tribunals for the former Yugoslavia and Rwanda are not necessarily the final interpretations of the Genocide Convention, but as the first positive adjudications of the convention, they will set a course for subsequent prosecutions and will necessarily inform a broader consideration of the genocide concept. Among the many contributions on the topic during this period, two are selected here as examples of important interpretations of genocide in Bosnia.

The first is a 1996 article by Robert Hayden in *Slavic Review* that was discussed by Susan Woodward and Paul Wallace and followed by a rejoinder from Hayden. Hayden, a professor of anthropology and of law, develops an exceptionalist argument to ethnic cleansing in Bosnia that draws a distinction between the organized killing of the Holocaust and the historically more frequent violence that accompanied partition: "genocide, after all, was exceptional. Bosnia may not be."[39] Hayden is not alone in defining genocide as both an exceptional crime and one separate from ethnic cleansing.[40] In part, Hayden's position appears to be predicated on a formalized interpretation of ethnic cleansing as population removal of the sort that characterized nation building in central and Eastern Europe after World War II. For him, ethnic cleansing occurs during partition and, though it may involve intercommunal violence, is distinct from plans to exterminate populations, that is, genocide. Of course, to differentiate "ethnic cleansing," which is a description of a policy that encompasses a variety of acts, from other specific criminal categories, such as breaches of the Geneva Convention or genocide, provides the former with a conceptual and legal specificity it does not have. In any case, Hayden's argument that Bosnia is merely another example of partition as witnessed in the Punjab or Cyprus does not necessarily preclude the question of whether there was genocide in Bosnia.

What Hayden appears to be most concerned about is that the prosecutions of genocide presuppose collective guilt: "the defendant is the collective for whom the individual is said to have acted, which cannot be defended."[41] While the collectivization of the victim of genocide is an important aspect for mobilizing genocidal campaigns, Hayden's objection to the charge in Bosnia addresses a concern over the effects of collective guilt of an aggressor as the grounds for future retribution.[42] This is somewhat similar to an argument made by genocide scholar Helen Fein on the intergenerational cycles of collective guilt and retribution in Bosnia.[43] But Fein's argument is based on an appreciation of the construction of collective guilt through transgenerational projection and propaganda, all of which are acts of political interpretation in the present and which can be intermediated. Hayden's argument, however, draws from authors like Franz Kafka and Milan Kundera in predicting that retributive cycles emerge from selective amnesia. In other words, the failure to remember that the last wrongdoing was the act of only a few might compel the next generation of Bosnians to blame the Serbs as a collective. Unlike Fein's argument, Hayden's fails to regard such "forgetting" as always a contemporary political act—the past is always given meaning in the present—and therefore Hayden appears to presume a latent group psychologism that flirts uncomfortably with the primordialist idea of race memory or ancient ethnic hatred.

In sharp contrast to Hayden's interpretation, Norman Cigar's *Genocide in Bosnia: The Policy of "Ethnic Cleansing"* argues that ethnic cleansing is genocide, but that their apparent distinction contributed, in part, to a convenient dodge for governments and observers who wished to maintain either an exceptional interpretation of genocide or who simply did not want to commit to a military intervention.[44] In arguing that the acts carried out under a policy of ethnic cleansing constitute genocide, Cigar, a former Pentagon analyst, maintains that the ideological-political conditions created by Serb nationalists in Yugoslavia provided for the rationalization and mobilization of systematic murder. That the territorial campaign of ethnic cleansing fulfilled a popular vision of a "Greater Serbia" among Serb nationalists only serves to satisfy the legal requirement that genocide is a purposive campaign of killing. For Cigar, genocide is not exceptional; rather, its recognition is exceptional because it depends upon international political processes that allow states to easily evade convention responsibilities. His view has recently been given added credibility in Samantha Power's lengthy historical study of U.S. foreign policy on genocide and its aversion toward an often cited, but rarely acted upon, responsibility to intervene and prosecute genocide.[45]

These perspectives on and interpretations of the conflict are important to understanding both the international failure to respond to the civilian crisis in Bosnia and the limits of international law, especially the Genocide Convention. The debates within Western governments, at the United Nations, and among scholars over the war in Bosnia did not, in and of themselves, answer the question of what ultimately constitutes genocide. The Commission of Experts, the United Nations, and the community of concerned scholars were debating a crime that had not been prosecuted under existing law, which enabled a certain amount of ethical and political turbidity. But neither did these debates lay to rest the problem of stopping ethnic cleansing per se, largely because the policy of ethnic cleansing is a much wider ranging bundle of specific crimes, including genocide, and other less codified acts of cruelty and violence. Certainly the Genocide Convention provides sanctions against the destruction of a people, but international law does not map the entirety of a geopolitical campaign predicated on the erasure of both a people and their cultural landscape, as effected by the policy of ethnic cleansing. The following section examines the work of the International Criminal Tribunal for the Former Yugoslavia to understand how it interprets genocide and ethnic cleansing, and how its interpretation is underwritten by a particular spatial epistemology that is becoming part of the emergent case law on these crimes and which will change our understanding of the terms.

Prosecuting War Crimes in Bosnia

Though we may be dissatisfied with the foregoing interpretations of the atrocities in Bosnia, it is important to examine the manner in which these acts, especially genocide, have been defined by the international legal process that began with the establishment of the ICTY. In so doing, we must remember that criminal categories within international law are also made meaningful through the act of prosecution and adjudication, which thereby establishes a basis in judicial precedent that may change the way we understand and recognize these crimes as they are happening in the future. In fact, our understanding of the crime of genocide has already begun to change in the last few years because of its enforcement through the tribunals for crimes in the former Yugoslavia and Rwanda. The prosecution of genocide in Bosnia is therefore an important geopolitical practice, in and of itself, that is creating interpretations that will shape the subsequent terms that are brought to bear on conflict and the decision to intervene.

Among the contributions of the ICTY to the prosecution of genocide and other war crimes is the development of substantive and procedural rules for an international tribunal. The tribunals for both the former Yugoslavia and Rwanda have had to set precedents on issues that range from the composition of judicial panels to the handling of witnesses and evidence. Importantly, the tribunals have also heard cases and ruled against individuals charged with criminal acts under the courts' jurisdiction. In hearing cases and establishing judicial standards in the process, the justices are reshaping the significance that will be given to various elements of these war crimes in the future. The prosecution of the crimes that constitute ethnic cleansing, especially genocide, also imparts a particular spatial epistemology, one that begins to inform an understanding of how the law both interprets and produces geopolitical space. While several authors address the progress of the tribunals in general, the remainder of this section seeks to identify the spatial epistemology—the geographic categories—brought to bear by the ICTY in adjudicating the crime of genocide in Bosnia.[46] The purpose is twofold: to recognize jurisdiction of the tribunal as geopolitical space and to identify how the crime of genocide is interpreted by the court as part of the geopolitical policy of ethnic cleansing. In doing so, we can identify two primary elements of interest among the rulings of the ICTY thus far. The first concerns the establishment of the court's jurisdiction; the second addresses the jurisprudence on the spatial contingencies of genocide, especially as they relate to the geographic definition of a protected group.

An important part of understanding the geography of genocide and ethnic cleansing is the particular elements of jurisdiction implicit in the treaties and statutes that make prosecution possible.[47] International legal protections and sanctions that relate to atrocities are the jurisdictional responsibility assigned to all states by treaty. Though states are expected to take primary responsibility for the prosecution of such crimes committed within their sovereign territory, many war crimes and atrocities may be poorly prosecuted if prosecution is left to the domestic jurisdiction of the country where they took place. Typically, crimes such as genocide would, at best, be prosecuted as murder under most national legal systems, and this would fail to address the larger legal responsibility of those in command authority for widespread and heinous campaigns against civilians as provided for in the Genocide Convention. Moreover, many national legal systems, especially those in postwar societies, are unprepared and untrained to conduct such prosecutions. In some situations, the officers of the court may lack the political will to put powerful figures in the dock. Therefore, most international law treaties, including the Geneva Conventions that relate to international conflicts, as well as crimes against humanity, provide for the authority of another state's courts or an international tribunal to try those so accused. If a state cannot or will not try an accused individual on its territory, then it must extradite the suspect to a government capable of prosecution, which can try the suspect on the basis of universal jurisdiction. In the case of violations of the Geneva Convention that relates to international conflict, states are further expected to search for and try or extradite the accused, even if this means that a state that does not recognize universal jurisdiction must change its laws to fulfill this requirement.

In the case of genocide, however, universal jurisdiction is not implied in the convention. Instead, the convention provides for prosecution by a "competent tribunal of the State in the territory of which the act was committed, or by such international penal tribunal as may have jurisdiction."[48] The clearest examples of genocide prosecution has been provided by ICTY and the International Criminal Tribunal for Rwanda (ICTR).[49] These two tribunals, located in The Hague, were established by the United Nations Security Council as territorial war crimes courts with territorial and temporal jurisdictions limited to the conflicts in question.[50] In the case of the ICTY, the court has jurisdiction over the territory of the former Socialist Federal Republic of Yugoslavia beginning on January 1, 1991. The subject-matter jurisdiction of the ICTY includes four areas of customary international humanitarian law: grave breaches of the 1949 Geneva Conventions, violations of the laws or customs of war, crimes against humanity, and genocide.[51] The domestic laws of the former Yugoslavia have no hold on the tribunal's subject matter except in sentencing.[52] Instead, by establishing the tribunal's jurisdiction, the Security Council has reorganized geopolitical space and has displaced the jurisdiction of local courts by applying international law to the events of a particular time and space. Consequently, it is the interpretation of the events that led to the dissolution of the former Yugoslavia that often serves as a defendant's challenge to the court's jurisdiction.[53] With its jurisdiction solidly established, the tribunal has considered the prosecution of and challenges to the criminal charges, to which we turn next.

Under the statute that established the ICTY, no provision was made for consideration of ethnic cleansing per se because as it has no separate treaty or customary basis in international law. Instead, ethnic cleansing was discussed as comprising crimes against humanity in the secretary-general's advisory report that provided the rationale and framework of the tribunal's statute. The secretary-general also included under crimes against humanity additional criminal acts that reflected the nature of ethnic cleansing in the former Yugoslavia, namely, rape, sexual assault and enforced prostitution, and torture.[54] Because the proscriptions on crimes against humanity do not meet the full term of ethnic cleansing as witnessed in Bosnia, the ICTY statute is unable to address a considerable aspect of what makes the practices unique, namely, that ethnic cleansing was a policy intended to create an ethnically homogeneous territory as part of a Greater Serbia. Further, in the case against Dusko Tadic, the ICTY ruled that the charge of crimes against humanity only pertains to acts carried out in geographic proximity to an armed conflict as an operational part of that conflict; that is, crimes against humanity do not cover actions outside of combat or crimes conducted by noncombatants.[55] The effect of these judgments, therefore, narrows the legal basis for prosecuting ethnic cleansing by unbundling specific acts from the broader policy and excising those practices that are considered separate from the conflict itself. That nearly all the practices of ethnic cleansing as witnessed in Bosnia could be prosecuted separately under the statute's provisions nevertheless fails to weigh fully the injustice of ethnic cleansing as a geopolitical policy.

With regard to Hayden's objection that the charge of genocide in Bosnia automatically imparts a collective guilt against the Serbs, the actual prosecution of war crimes in the ICTY presents a very different case. Hayden's objection is based on theoretical interpretations of the crime, not least because, at the time of his writing, there existed no jurisprudence or procedural standard for prosecuting genocide, which was developed subsequently in the ICTY and ICTR. When Hayden claims that the charge of genocide already presumes its factuality and instead seeks to lay collective guilt, he is wrong on both counts when we take into consideration the case law that is emerging from the ICTY and the ICTR.[56] In terms of assigning collective guilt, the statute of the ICTY provides jurisdiction over "natural" persons and not "juridical" persons such as organizations or groups.[57] That is, the statute of the ICTY has jurisdiction to put on trial individuals with criminal responsibility for war crimes but cannot try political parties, governments, or an ethnic group. The prosecution must show evidence of both the material acts and the necessary personal intent or willfulness to satisfy the charges against each defendant. Even for charges of genocide, the ICTY prosecution must present a complete case against each person so accused, and, pace Hayden, there is no presumed "fact" of genocide. Several of the charges for which the tribunal has competency, including genocide, provide for the prosecution of those with command responsibility over individuals who commit such crimes on their orders. In fact, the charge of genocide as prosecuted successfully requires that the accused have some command authority so as to prove that the murders were conducted as part of an intentional destruction of a protected group.[58] For the same reasons, political and military commanders attempt to create plausible denial by distancing themselves, at least officially, from the actual perpetrators. Milosevic attempted to provide such an excuse for himself when he released the Jugoslovenstia Narodna

Armija or Yugoslov People's Army (JNA) troops and arms to the Bosnian Serbs at the beginning of the war even though he continued to exercise direct command responsibility over Serb paramilitary units in Bosnia and had influence over and gave material support to Bosnian Serb politicians and their forces.

A second important aspect of the emerging spatial epistemology of the tribunal relates to the interpretation of the Genocide Convention's requirements that the persecution be intentionally aimed at destroying a protected group as such. The matter of intent has typically been understood as requiring a systematic and organized plan to destroy a group. Before the tribunal's work began, the Holocaust represented the exemplar of such a program, and some have argued that more recent genocidal campaigns lacked the premeditated and extensive organization it displayed. Further, the court had to determine the extent, numerically and geographically, of a group's destruction that distinguishes genocide from crimes against humanity. While the convention required that prosecutors show the "intent to destroy, in whole or in part," there was uncertainty as to how much of a population must be destroyed in order to show intent. On the issue of a protected group, the court's interpretation of "national, ethnical, racial or religious" was fairly straightforward: Muslims and Croats in Bosnia were identifiable as separate and distinct communities and therefore constituted protected groups. Nevertheless, genocidal intent is contingent on the geographical and numerical definition of a protected group, as the court ruled in the case of Goran Jelisic and General Radislav Krstic, among others.

In the prosecution of Goran Jelisic and others, the court had to determine whether the accused had intended to destroy a protected group as a separate and distinct community, and not just members who happened to be in a protected group. Further, it had to determine whether his intent to destroy that group extended geographically "to every corner of the globe" or "whether genocide may be committed within a restricted geographical zone."[59] The court faced the same issue in several cases and ruled that the "exterminatory intent" could be limited to a relatively small geographic zone, such as a municipality.[60] The court also had to decide the numerical extent of the intent to destroy; that is, if a defendant intended to destroy only part of a local population of Bosnian Muslims, was this sufficient to prove genocide? The court considered all of these arguments before handing down its first genocide judgment against General Radislav Krstic for his role in the attack on the Srebrenica enclave in 1995. In its decision, the court weighed these issues together in determining that

> a campaign resulting in the killings, in different places spread over a broad geographical area, of a finite number of members of a protected group might not thus qualify as genocide . . . because it would not show an intent by the perpetrators to target the very existence of the group as such. Conversely, the killing of all members of the part of a group located within a small geographical area, although resulting in a lesser number of victims, would qualify as genocide if carried out with the intent to destroy the part of the group as such located in this small geographical area.[61]

In the Krstic case, the court found that the perpetrators had intended to kill all the military-aged male Bosnian Muslims in Srebrenica, which constituted intent to destroy "in part" the Bosnian Muslim group as considered within the context of several related issues. First, the intent to destroy the Bosnian Muslim population in Srebrenica, as a limited geographical zone, meant the intent to destroy "in part" the larger Muslim population of Bosnia, which is the protected group as such. Second, the destruction of a large number of adult men in a "traditionally patriarchal society," including the leadership of the community, was regarded as a deliberate attempt to destroy the conditions of group survival, and therefore the whole group, in that area.[62] Third, the destruction of military-aged Bosnian Muslim males from Srebrenica took place in conjunction with the deportation of the rest of the local Bosnian Muslim population and thereby destroyed the conditions for material existence of the group within that geographic area. Finally, the geographic area in question, Srebrenica, was a target of the Bosnian Serb campaign of ethnic cleansing and a militarily strategic area, which underscored the purposive intent of the perpetrators in destroying the Muslim population there.

With this ruling the tribunal established an important set of precedents that significantly lowers the numerical and geographic elements of intent necessary to prove genocide. The charge of genocide is now understood as contingent on the scale and context of the acts in question in determining the necessary threshold at which murderous intent becomes the intent to destroy in whole or in part a protected group. Further still, the tribunal has provided a precedent for the interpretation of a protected group in the context of a fragmenting polity by ruling that while the protected group in question comprised all Bosnian Muslims, the extermination of a geographically specific portion of that population was genocide. While these judgments represent attempts to apply a deliberative and just sanction on the individuals responsible for heinous crimes, they are, at the same time, judgments with considerable political force in the world's understanding of such acts. As with the tribunal's jurisdiction, its substantive rulings reorder geopolitical space by establishing positive interpretations of acts that constitute genocide while imposing verdicts and sentences that have legitimacy within the international community of states. In the coming years, the tribunals for the former Yugoslavia and Rwanda will provide further interpretations of genocide and war crimes that will not only be key in the work of the International Criminal Court, but will significantly alter the interpretive lens used by governments and institutions in recognizing such crimes.

Conclusion

Though the tribunals for the former Yugoslavia and Rwanda have handed down the world's first convictions for genocide, the international community has yet to fulfill the convention's promise, the prevention of genocide. Although Orentlicher is justified in claiming that the Genocide Convention embodies "the conscience of humanity," the convention has failed to stop recent genocide for a number of reasons.[63] The brutality of the Cambodian Khmer Rouge, Iraq's campaign against the Kurds, the killings in Rwanda, and ethnic cleansing in Bosnia are remarkable not only for their horror, but as evidence of the unremarkable reluctance on the part of other governments to enforce the convention. As Power argues, the decades-long political battle in the United States to ratify the convention is indicative of its cool reception by powerful governments.[64] Even when genocide could be clearly identified in Bosnia and Rwanda, the policy debate in Washington was over whether it was really genocide or "something else," which masked and then displaced the question of humanitarian intervention.[65] But the failure to recognize genocide and do something about it is only half the problem. If genocide, clearly identified, is insufficient to trigger a humanitarian intervention, then all "lesser" wrongs, including crimes against humanity, will never be met with substantive force, and this will signal to those regimes that make a policy of atrocities that no one will stop them. In this condition, neither genocide nor other criminal acts that comprise ethnic cleansing will be prosecuted effectively and be removed as viable geopolitical options.

Along these same lines, the most overlooked aspect of the ICTY is that it has not brought to trial the majority of perpetrators of ethnic cleansing and probably never will. Indeed, many of the local figures involved in ethnic cleansing in Serb-controlled Bosnia remain at large and perhaps even unindicted.[66] Given that a cornerstone of the Dayton Accords and the reconstruction of Bosnia is the return of persons displaced by ethnic cleansing or conflict, the presence of local figures who were personally involved in the brutality has a chilling effect on the peace process. Moreover, many of the individuals involved in local ethnic cleansing campaigns have risen to political and economic power and have effectively consolidated the gains of ethnic cleansing in irreversible ways.[67] Thus while the ICTY has indicted most of the high-profile figures with responsibility for the atrocities in Bosnia, it will probably be left up to a national court to try many lesser officers and perpetrators, if they are tried at all. Besides the sense of insecurity this creates for all returnees in the meantime, some Serbs feel that the crimes committed against Serb civilians will be left untried, which will play into a well-worn and popular sentiment of Serb victimization and slow any reconciliation.[68]

Importantly, however, a geographic sensitivity to the spatial epistemology of scale and context, territorial identity and geopolitics, can serve as an effective interpretive lens on the unfolding prosecution in the tribunal that takes the court's rulings as important maps of how ethnic cleansing can be prosecuted as genocide and crimes against humanity. International law does not exist on the head of a pin, as the prosecution of war crimes in the former Yugoslavia aptly demonstrates. Instead, the protections offered by instruments such as the Genocide Convention are being interpreted within a spatial, geopolitical context that no longer grants prosecutors or states the conceptual flexibility that marked the speculative interpretations of these crimes during the last fifty years. As institutions with the potential to order our world, both through the prosecution of individuals and through the effect prosecution has on international norms, the tribunals may well change the political and moral calculus of both perpetrators and the international community, perhaps for the better. As the outcomes of the tribunals are better understood beyond the courts, these findings may even alter the way in which these acts are popularly understood. Therefore, in appreciating the broader significance of place as a cultural landscape, context of meaning, or modus vivendi, geographic research must bear witness to the devastating effects that such crimes have on the lifeworlds of affected communities, including victims, bystanders, and those caught up in the violence. When scholarship brings together the historical, geopolitical lessons of genocide and ethnic cleansing with an understanding of their legal interpretation and their horrific effect on humanity, it becomes a form of activism that promotes a just and deliberative worldview that may strengthen a resolve to prevent the worst in the human condition.

Notes

1. I follow the conventional terminology for groups in the former Yugoslavia by which Serbs, Croats, and Muslims are "ethnic" groups while state affiliations are designated by adjectival forms: Serbian and Croatian. Likewise, the term "Bosnian" refers to the state itself, so a Bosnian Serb is a Serb from Bosnia. Readers should note that religious and ethnic identity were not necessarily the same in the former Yugoslavia, nor are they today, although the conflict reenergized their overlap. Furthermore, "Muslim" can be used in one of two ways in the former Yugoslavia, as both a religious identity that is a counterpart to the Orthodox and Catholic communities and a national or ethnic identity on equal constitutional terms with Serb and Croat in Bosnia. In this chapter, Muslims refer to the larger ethnic community regardless of religious observance. See Bringa, *Being Muslim the Bosnian Way*, especially 8–11 and 12–36.

2. These include the governments of Western Europe and North America with access to and leverage within major institutions such as the United Nations, the European Union, and NATO.

3. Rieff, *Slaughterhouse*; Owen, *Balkan Odyssey*.

4. Herzfeld, "Foreword," ix–xii.

5. Quoted in Power, *"Problem from Hell,"* xii.

6. The notion of equal guilt in atrocities was a campaign begun by Radovan Karadzic, the Bosnian Serb political leader, and was subsequently echoed by some Western diplomats.

7. Bieber, "Nationalist Mobilization and Stories of Serb Suffering"; Jansen, "Violence of Memories."

8. Silber and Little, *Yugoslavia*, 25–36.

9. Ibid., 131–132, 306–307.

10. For their command responsibility over crimes committed in Bosnia, see the indictments *Prosecutor v. Galic and Milosevic*, Indictment; *Prosecutor v. Milosevic*, Indictment; *Prosecutor v. Karadzic and Mladic*, Indictment.

11. Frontline, "Mapping the Serbian Concentration Camps."

12. United Nations, *Final Report*. Additional testimonials that confirm this pattern of ethnic cleansing are to be found in the transcripts of the International Criminal Tribunal for the Former Yugoslavia, as well as in reports by human rights organizations; see Human Rights Watch, *"Closed, Dark Place."*

13. U.S. Congress, Commission on Security and Cooperation in Europe, *Genocide in Bosnia-Herzegovina*, 7–13.

14. Chorbajian and Shirinian, *Studies in Comparative Genocide*.

15. Orentlicher, "Genocide."

16. Lemkin's campaign to create the convention is well documented by several authors. See Power, *"Problem from Hell,"* 17–65. See also Lemkin, *Axis Rule in Occupied Europe*.

17. United Nations, Convention on the Prevention and Punishment of the Crime of Genocide.

18. United Nations Security Council, Resolution 827, "Statute of the International Tribunal."

19. See Murphy, "Progress and Jurisprudence."

20. Bassiouni, "Crimes against Humanity."

21. See Kuper, *Genocide*.

22. Power, *"Problem from Hell,"* 274–300.

23. See, for example, Martin, "Origins of Soviet Ethnic Cleansing"; Williams, "Hidden Ethnic Cleansing of Muslims in the Soviet Union."

24. For example, Serb propaganda depicted Croats as Ustase fascists and Muslims as mujahideen, while Croat propaganda depicted the Serbs as Chetniks. See Mursic, "Yugoslav Dark Side of Humanity," 58.

25. Power, *"Problem from Hell,"* 250.

26. Ibid., 274–300.

27. Ó Tuathail, "Theorizing Practical Geopolitical Reasoning."

28. Bass, *Stay the Hand of Vengeance*, 215. See also Power, *"Problem from Hell."*

29. United Nations Security Council, Resolution 764, "Bosnia and Herzegovina"; United Nations Security Council, Resolution 771, "Former Yugoslavia."

30. United Nations Secretary-General, *Interim Report*.

31. United Nations, *Final Report*, at 55.

32. Ibid., at 56.

33. Ibid., at 57.

34. United Nations Security Council, Resolution 808, "Tribunal (Former Yugoslavia)," at 1.

35. United Nations Secretary-General, *Report of the Secretary-General*; United Nations Security Council, Resolution 827, "Statute of the International Tribunal."

36. Murphy, "Progress and Jurisprudence," 57–62.

37. Bass, *Stay the Hand of Vengeance*, 206–275; Power, *"Problem from Hell,"* 247–328, 391–474.

38. Hayden, "Schindler's Fate"; Cigar, *Genocide in Bosnia*.

39. Hayden, "Schindler's Fate," 734.

40. See Bell-Fialkoff, *Ethnic Cleansing*, 1–4.

41. Hayden, "Schindler's Fate," 742–743.

42. Kuper, *Genocide*, 55, 87.

43. Fein, "Testing Theories Brutally."

44. Cigar, *Genocide in Bosnia*.

45. Power, *"Problem from Hell."*

46. Bass, *Stay the Hand of Vengeance*, 206–275; Murphy, "Progress and Jurisprudence."

47. Ford, "Law's Territory."

48. United Nations, Convention on the Prevention and Punishment of the Crime of Genocide, at Article 6.

49. Meron, "International Criminalization of Internal Atrocities."

50. United Nations Security Council, Resolution 1411, "Amended Statute of the International Tribunal." See also note 34.

51. See note 34.

52. United Nations Secretary-General, *Report of the Secretary-General*, at 35–36.

53. Murphy, "Progress and Jurisprudence," 65–71.

54. United Nations Secretary-General, *Report of the Secretary-General*, at 47–49; United Nations Security Council, Resolution 1411, "Amended Statute of the International Tribunal," at Article 5.

55. Murphy, "Progress and Jurisprudence," 70–71.

56. Hayden, "Schindler's Fate," 742–743; Ball, *Prosecuting War Crimes and Genocide*, 121. Compare the case brought by the government of Bosnia-Herzegovina against the gov-

ernment of Yugoslavia before the International Court of Justice to cease attacks and provide reparations; see Bello, Bekker, and Szasz, "Application of the Convention."

57. United Nations Secretary-General, *Report of the Secretary-General,* at 50–52; United Nations Security Council, Resolution 1411, "Amended Statutes of the International Tribunal," at Articles 6 and 7.

58. See *Prosecution v. Krstic,* Judgment. Cf. *Prosecution v. Jelisic,* Judgment, at 106–108.

59. *Prosecutor v. Jelisic,* Judgment, at 79–83.

60. Ibid., at 79–83. Municipalities are the local political unit in Bosnia; there were 103 municipalities, not including the Sarajevo area, before the war.

61. *Prosecutor v. Krstic,* Judgment, 590.

62. Ibid., 595.

63. Orentlicher, "Genocide," 153.

64. Power, *"Problem from Hell,"* 511–516.

65. Power, "Bystanders to Genocide."

66. Though the ICTY issues sealed indictments against some individuals, the Tribunal is not expected to exhaust prosecution, but to leave many alleged criminals unindicted and untried.

67. See Human Rights Watch, *"Closed, Dark Place."*

68. Bieber, "Nationalist Mobilization and Stories of Serb Suffering," 106–107.

References

Ball, Howard. *Prosecuting War Crimes and Genocide: The Twentieth-Century Experience.* Lawrence: University Press of Kansas, 1999.

Bass, Gary J. *Stay the Hand of Vengeance: The Politics of War Crimes Tribunals.* Princeton, NJ: Princeton University Press, 2000.

Bassiouni, M. Cherif. "Crimes against Humanity." In *Crimes of War: What the Public Should Know,* ed. Roy Gutman and David Rieff, 107–108. New York: Norton, 1999.

Bell-Fialkoff, Andrew. *Ethnic Cleansing.* New York: St. Martin's, 1999.

Bello, Judith Hippler, Peter H. F. Bekker, and Paul C. Szasz. "Application of the Convention on the Prevention and Punishment of the Crime of Genocide (Bosnia-Herzegovina v. Yugoslavia)." *American Journal of International Law* 91 (January 1997): 121–126.

Bieber, Florian. "Nationalist Mobilization and Stories of Serb Suffering: The Kosovo Myth from 600th Anniversary to the Present." *Rethinking History* 6 (2002): 95–110.

Bringa, Tone. *Being Muslim the Bosnian Way: Identity and Community in a Central Bosnian Village.* Princeton, NJ: Princeton University Press, 1995.

Chorbajian, Levon, and George Shirinian, eds. *Studies in Comparative Genocide.* New York: St. Martin's, 1999.

Cigar, Norman. *Genocide in Bosnia: The Policy of "Ethnic Cleansing."* College Station: Texas A&M University Press, 1995.

Fein, Helen. "Testing Theories Brutally: Armenia (1915), Bosnia (1992), and Rwanda (1994)." In *Studies in Comparative Genocide,* ed. Levon Chorbajian and George Shirinian, 157–164. New York: St. Martin's, 1999.

Ford, Richard. "Law's Territory (A History of Jurisdiction)." In *The Legal Geographies Reader,* ed. Nicholas Blomley, David Delaney, and Richard T. Ford, 200–217. Oxford: Blackwell, 2001.

Frontline. "Mapping the Serbian Concentration Camps." www.pbs.org/wgbh/frontline (February 15, 2003).

GISData, Digital Atlas of Bosnia and Herzegovina 1:200,000 (CD–ROM), GISData d.o.o, 2003.

Hayden, Robert H. "Schindler's Fate: Genocide, Ethnic Cleansing, and Population Transfers." *Slavic Review* 55 (Winter 1996): 727–748.

Herzfeld, Michael. "Foreword." In *Balkan as Metaphor: Between Globalization and Fragmentation*, ed. Dusan I. Bjelic and Obrad Savic, ix–xii. Cambridge, MA.: MIT Press, 2002.

Human Rights Watch. "A *Closed, Dark Place*": *Past and Present Human Rights Abuses in Foca*. New York: Human Rights Watch, 1998.

Jansen, Stef. "The Violence of Memories: Local Narratives of the Past after Ethnic Cleansing in Croatia." *Rethinking History* 6 (2002): 77–94.

Kuper, Leo. *Genocide: Its Political Use in the Twentieth Century*. New Haven, CT: Yale University Press, 1982.

Lemkin, Raphael. *Axis Rule in Occupied Europe: Laws of Occupation, Analysis of Government, Proposals for Redress*. Washington, DC: Carnegie Endowment for International Peace, Division of International Law, 1944.

Martin, Terry. "The Origins of Soviet Ethnic Cleansing." *Journal of Modern History* 70 (December 1998): 813–861.

Meron, Theodor. "International Criminalization of Internal Atrocities." *American Journal of International Law* 89 (July 1995): 554–577.

Murphy, Sean D. "Progress and Jurisprudence of the International Criminal Tribunal for the Former Yugoslavia." *American Journal of International Law* 93 (January 1999): 57–97.

Mursic, Rajko. "The Yugoslav Dark Side of Humanity: A View from a Slovene Blind Spot." In *Neighbors at War: Anthropological Perspectives on Yugoslav Ethnicity, Culture, and History*, ed. Joel M. Halpern and David A. Kideckel, 56–77. University Park: Pennsylvania State University Press, 2000.

Orentlicher, Diane. "Genocide." In *Crimes of War: What the Public Should Know*, ed. Roy Gutman and David Rieff, 153–157. New York: Norton, 1999.

Ó Tuathail, Gearóid. "Theorizing Practical Geopolitical Reasoning: The Case of the United States' Response to the War in Bosnia." *Political Geography* 21 (2002): 601–628.

Owen, David. *Balkan Odyssey*. San Diego: Harvest, 1995.

Power, Samantha. "Bystanders to Genocide: Why the United States Let the Rwandan Tragedy Happen." *Atlantic Monthly* 288 (September 2001): 84–108.

Power, Samantha. "A *Problem from Hell*": *America and the Age of Genocide*. New York: Basic Books, 2002.

Prosecutor v. Galic and Milosevic. Indictment. International Criminal Tribunal for the Former Yugoslavia, IT-98-29-I (March 26, 1999).

Prosecutor v. Jelisic. Trial Judgment. International Criminal Tribunal for the Former Yugoslavia, IT-95-10 (July 5, 2001).

Prosecutor v. Karadzic and Mladic. Indictment. International Criminal Tribunal for the Former Yugoslavia, IT-95-5-I (July 25, 1995).

Prosecution v. Krstic. Judgment. International Criminal Tribunal for the Former Yugoslavia, IT-98-33-I (August 2, 2001).

Prosecutor v. Milosevic. Indictment. International Criminal Tribunal for the Former Yugoslavia, IT-02-54-I (February 1, 2002).

Rieff, David. *Slaughterhouse: Bosnia and the Failure of the West.* New York: Touchstone, 1996.

Silber, Laura, and Allan Little. *Yugoslavia: Death of a Nation.* New York: Penguin, 1997.

United Nations. Convention on the Prevention and Punishment of the Crime of Genocide. December 9, 1948.

United Nations. *Final Report of the United Nations Commission of Experts Established Pursuant to Security Council Resolution 780 (1992), Annex IV.* UN Doc. S/1994/674. December 28, 1994.

United Nations Secretary-General. *Interim Report of the Commission of Experts.* UN Doc. S/25274. February 9, 1993.

United Nations Secretary-General. *Report of the Secretary-General Pursuant to Paragraph 2 of Security Council Resolution 808 (1993).* UN Doc. S/25704. May 3, 1993.

United Nations Security Council. Resolution 764, "Bosnia and Herzegovina." UN Doc. S/RES/764. July 13, 1992.

United Nations Security Council. Resolution 771, "Former Yugoslavia." UN Doc. S/RES/771. August 13, 1992.

United Nations Security Council. Resolution 808, "Tribunal (Former Yugoslavia)." UN Doc. S/RES/808. February 22, 1993.

United Nations Security Council. Resolution 827, "Statute of the International Tribunal." UN Doc. S/RES/827. May 25, 1993.

United Nations Security Council. Resolution 1411, "Amended Statute of the International Tribunal." UN Doc. S/RES/1411. May 17, 2002.

U.S. Congress. Commission on Security and Cooperation in Europe. *Genocide in Bosnia-Herzegovina: Hearing before the Commission on Security and Cooperation in Europe.* 104th Cong., 1st sess., April 14, 1995.

Williams, Brian Glyn. "The Hidden Ethnic Cleansing of Muslims in the Soviet Union: The Exile and Repatriation of the Crimean Tatars." *Journal of Contemporary History* 37 (2002): 323–347.

COLIN FLINT

Dynamic Metageographies of Terrorism

The Spatial Challenges of Religious Terrorism and the "War on Terrorism"

Smoke pluming from the towers of the World Trade Center and a mushroom cloud resulting from a "bunker-buster" bomb dropped on a presidential palace of Saddam Hussein: the two related images suggest that the geopolitics of the twenty-first century will be very much about the "shock and awe" of terrorism. Terrorism and counter-terrorism are both geopolitical in that they utilize and attempt to change geographic structures for political ends. By examining the geographic components in definitions of terrorism, we can understand how changes in the geographic scope of terrorist activity are useful in explaining the changing motivations and implications of terrorism. The rise of terrorism motivated by religious ideologies is especially central to questions of how the geography and goals of terrorism are changing. In addition, states, especially the United States of America, have come to define terrorism as a matter of global geopolitics rather than domestic policing. However, a focus upon the geography of counterterrorism suggests that there is a geographic mismatch between the organization of terrorists and the spatial means and goals of governments. In a word, states still rely upon the control of sovereign territory to counter terrorist networks. This too has implications for future conflict.

Since the attacks of September 11, 2001, there has been a deluge of essays, analysis, and political punditry, often intertwined or disguised, on the topic of terrorism.[1] The justification of another essay must rest on the possibility of further insight. Academic geography is a perspective rather than a defined subject matter, and I hope to use its key concepts to provide new ways of understanding the motivations behind contemporary terrorist acts, the geopolitics of antiterrorism, and its negative political geographic implications.

Geographic Perspectives on Terrorism

Specifically, three geographic concepts are integrated into my argument, and I identify the importance of another that others are more qualified to discuss. First, the concept of geohistorical context is useful in identifying the complexities of the temporal and spatial influences upon, and of, terrorism.[2] For example, the attacks of September 11, 2001, were simultaneously of that hour and of the past and present century. They were also simultaneously local, national, and global events. If we use Wallerstein's ideas of TimeSpace,[3] the immediacy of the event can only be understood by placing it within broader structures and cycles. For the purposes of understanding contemporary terrorism that targets the United States, the relevant structure is the capitalist world-economy and its core-periphery hierarchy, and the key cycle is the rise of the United States to the position of hegemony in the twentieth century and its current disputed status.[4] The United States is the key driving force behind the contemporary economic dynamics of the world-economy. In addition, it is the primary power in terms of economic, political, and cultural influence across the globe. An attack upon the United States at one hour in one place is related to these broader geographic and historic scopes.

The second concept, geographic scale and scope, links the local/immediate to the global/historic. Scales (or the scope of economic, cultural, and political processes) are constructed by terrorist groups and the political entities they are attacking or resisting.[5] For example, tracing the history of the terrorist campaign of the Palestine Liberation Organization (PLO) links its initial local and cross-border tactics to a practice of airline hijackings that established it as an international terrorist group.[6] As the scale of its activity increased, so did the reach or scope of its message. An audience in Europe and the United States was created that became, at the least, aware of its grievances and, in some cases, sympathetic, to varying degrees, to its cause. As another example, the creation of a local al-Qaeda cell is just one component of a global network, though the scope of its finances and organization is a matter of political conjecture.

Furthermore, the optimal geographic scale of governance has been a constant theme for terrorist grievance. This will be discussed in greater detail later, but, briefly, the dominant goal of terrorist acts has been to achieve control of an existing nation-state or create a new one that reflects perceived national connections to a particular piece of territory. It is the geographic scale of the nation-state that has dominated the grievances and goals of terrorist movements.[7] The intriguing question is whether the current wave of religiously motivated terrorism has transcended the agendas contained within the territorial expression of states and the interstate system.[8]

Such a possibility leads us to the third concept I will concentrate upon, metageographies. Since the Treaty of Westphalia (1648), nation-states have been the dominant territorial expressions of political power and the building blocks of the world political map.[9] Most actual politics and academic analysis have been constrained by, and have re-created, this metageography. However, the system of nation-states has never been the exclusive geographic expression of power. Cities and regions have, to varying degrees, resisted central rule.[10] In addition, there have always existed economic flows of trade and investment between states, as well as patterns of migration and networks of political power and resistance.[11]

The fourth concept, one that I will not engage in depth, is the symbolism of place. Cultural, economic, and political meanings are given to sites or whole cities to deem them as targets that will highlight the grievances of the terrorists and illuminate the power structures against which they are fighting.[12] The destruction of the World Trade Center and part of the Pentagon in 2001 as the central nodes of economic globalization and U.S. military power is an example. More generally, police patrols or army barracks are targeted as symbols of occupation or repression, and religious or ethnic buildings and monuments are attacked in ethnonationalist campaigns.[13] At a higher scale, terrorists may attack cities themselves because of their representation of economic or political structures. For example, London and New York as global cities, the hubs of economic networks, are believed to be prime terrorist targets.[14] Also, attacks in the capital cities of colonialist or postcolonialist cities reflect the terrorists' desire to reach the "heart" of imperialist political structures (Algerian terrorist attacks in Paris, for example). There is much potential here for cultural-political geographers to contribute to an analysis of why particular sites become terrorist targets.

Geography and the Conundrum of Defining Terrorism

At the outset, a geographic framework is useful in wrestling with the question, what is terrorism? One of the most respected scholars of terrorism, Walter Laqueur, has professed the impossibility and futility of defining terrorism.[15] The relevance of a definition is specific to its temporal and geographic context, as well as the political needs of institutions. For example, Hoffman shows how the Department of Defense, the FBI, and the State Department all defined terrorism differently to reflect their goals and political terrain.[16] But there is one fundamental litmus test of definitions of terrorism, the decision whether to identify the state as an agent of terrorism. For example, Hoffman's short history of terrorism is replete with the role of the state in creating and practicing terrorism.[17] The "terror" of the French Revolution, which was conducted by the emergent state, is widely accepted as the birth of modern terrorism. Fascism and then Stalinism and, by extension, the oppression of other totalitarian states during the Cold War and into today are also identified as forms of terrorism. Yet in his subsequent definition, Hoffman makes it clear that "a subnational group or non-state entity" commits terrorism.[18]

On the other hand, critics are eager to point out that states have committed and still do commit acts of terrorism. Ahmad defines terrorism as "the illegal use of violence for the purposes of influencing somebody's behavior, inflicting punishment, or taking revenge" and states that it is practiced by both governments and nonstate groups.[19] There are key similarities between Ahmad's definition and Hoffman's view that terrorism is "the deliberate creation and exploitation of fear through violence or the threat of violence in the pursuit of political change."[20] If the political goals of terrorism are emphasized in Ahmad's definition to exclude acts of crime motivated by personal gain, then the two definitions are strikingly similar. Terrorists use force or its threat to change behavior for political ends. Given the ugly history of certain governments, the only logic in excluding them as actors seems to be a geopolitical decision in itself: cleansing states, particularly one's own, from terrorist activities and marginalizing the aims of terrorist groups through the "nonstate entity" label.

As Walzer claims, "The word 'terrorism' is used most often to describe revolutionary violence. That is a small victory for the champions of order, among whom the uses of terror are by no means unknown."[21] Exercises in "shock and awe" are an admission of state-led terrorist activity—violence, its threat, and its psychological implication. The goal is regime change, and the line between targeting combatants and noncombatants (not a feature of Hoffman's definition anyway) is horribly gray. The ferocity and extent of the U.S. bombing campaign in Iraq in 2003, the raw power of the weapons and the number that were dropped, precluded a count of the number killed. The intent was to spread a sense of "awe," which is a polite and self-aggrandizing way of saying fear, through enough of the Iraqi population, including the army, to initiate an uprising against Hussein's regime. In other words, the bombing campaign was the use of violence to spread fear to force political change.

There is reason here for a cautionary note, and not just a critique of U.S. foreign policy. The changing nature of war and terrorism are related. Terrorists expanded their targets from state officials to the general population after the "unmilitary" carpet (and atomic) bombing of cities in World War II.[22] Rather than seeing U.S.-led interventions as just responses to terrorist attacks, one should be aware that they may also catalyze terrorist responses that desire to match the grandeur behind the U.S. military boasting. The possibility that terrorists will use weapons of mass destruction may be created to a certain extent, but it is still a risk we now all live with. Terrorism has evolved from its French Revolution inception as a tool of intranational political control to a global process of geopolitical competition, from assassination with small weapons to the targeting of whole buildings and their occupants. In the process, the targets have expanded from individuals by dint of their political office to whole populations on the basis of their membership in a collective, and usually territorially defined, identity. The geographic processes behind these changes have grave implications for the risks we all face from both terrorism and counterterrorism.

No one definition of terrorism is suitable for all historical or geographic contexts,[23] or institutional or analytic needs, but unpacking definitions does allow for questions regarding what geographic expressions are central to understanding terrorism, and how terrorism is, in part, the real-world contestation of the territorial manifestation of these concepts. I use Hoffman's definition of terrorism, quoted earlier, as my point of departure because of the author's prominence in the analysis of terrorism and his careful consideration of other definitions in the construction of his own. Also, Hoffman's qualification that states do not commit acts of terrorism but crimes against national and international laws provides useful avenues for discussion.

Excluding states from contemporary terrorist acts while acknowledging the history that says otherwise is a finesse that requires an implicit and uncritical usage of geography. First, the argument is developmentalist.[24] Preceding Hoffman's definition is a history of modern terrorism that highlights the "terror" of the French Revolution, or state repression, and the terror of state totalitarianism, especially of the Nazi and Stalinist variety. These historical events are made an important part of the history of terrorism, but not of its contemporary definition, by relegating them to the unfortunate past of state development—something that states have had to do in their growth before they became "good states" of the contemporary liberal democratic variety. In other words, state terror is portrayed as a stage that states may go through in order to "create power where there is none or to consolidate power where there is very little."[25] But this is a convenient fiction that denies the horror that faces citizens of many contemporary states, from North Korea to Zimbabwe and Cuba. Regimes that are consolidating their power under systems of governance that are challenged or illegitimate require acts of terror by the state. It is not something that states have "grown out" of; rather, the political circumstances of some states make it unnecessary, while in others it is integral.

The second geographic finesse is an Orientalist one:[26] "they" are dictatorships or tyrants that foster terrorists, and hence "we" are not. The geographic trickery in this move lies in bordering the "we" both within the past and the "domestic" sphere. Terrorist actions of the United States and European countries are parceled as "regrettable" acts of history—the extermination of the Native Americans, for example. It is easier to see such acts by the state as in the past if the geographic understanding of the world is based upon the axiom of separate and sovereign states.[27] In that way, states are only responsible for acts within their own borders. Yet in the history of the capitalist world-economy the more powerful states have always acted in an extraterritorial fashion by extending their influence and tools of governance into other political spaces.[28] The repression undertaken by British troops across the empire or the numerous covert acts of the CIA in the twentieth century are evidence of this process.[29]

Expunging "our" states from the label of terrorism relies not only upon an understanding of the world political map as the legitimate expression of authority, but each individual state as, at least potentially, a benevolent institution in which its power is somehow hidden. This has occurred by converting the "space" of the state into the "place" of the nation.[30] The apparatus of the state that controls the actions of individuals, sometimes violently, has been hidden behind the notion that we live in nations that nurture our full identity. Thus the nation-state is life giving rather than life threatening.

Hoffman's definition and his related discussion point to the necessary consideration of the role of geography in political marginalization, the distinction between public and private space,[31] and how political change involves the control of territory and/or geographic scales. More generally, definitions of terrorism are trapped within the assumptions imposed by the dominant world political map. As social scientists, our questions follow the assumptions of the "territorial trap" imposed by nation-states that equates the scope of societal processes with the geographic extent of borders.[32] Have terrorists motivated by religion escaped this trap and redefined the scope of politics?

Many definitions agree that terrorism is about spreading fear. Such spread has two geographic aspects. First, it involves the tragic and violent insertion of matters of "state" into the spaces of everyday society. On September 11, 2001, disputes over the military presence of the United States in the Arabian peninsula and its support for Israel were not confined to the arenas of political discussion, but were thrust into the apolitical spaces of commercial airline cockpits and passenger cabins flown into the Pentagon and the World Trade Center. In other cases, a prolonged terrorist campaign will politicize spaces—the shopping district of Omagh was certainly politicized on August 16, 1998, when the Irish Republican Army (IRA) exploded a bomb there that killed 28 people and injured more than 200. But it is more realistic to say that the streets of Northern Ireland had been politicized over time in their identification as "strong" unionist or republican areas, or localities of contestation.[33] To gain an audience, especially when the grievance is that established political channels are deaf to one's claims, requires politicizing the spaces one's target audience frequents. The Irish or Tamil or Basque question becomes a "public" concern if the bars, trains, and markets frequented by the public are part of the battlefield. A political situation that marginalizes some to the point that they resort to terrorism requires the redefinition of the political arena by making noncombatants and the spaces in which they live part of the contest.

Marginalization and betrayal are two common grievances that provoke terrorist movements. They too can be understood geographically, in terms of scale and territory. In a world of sovereign states, political power is ultimately sought at the national scale by controlling the government apparatus.[34] Though politics is conducted at other political scales, frustration may result if representation and action are limited to subregional scales. A voice in the city or local council may be merely token if national policies deny cultural expression in the national curriculum or promote underrepresentation in a national parliament, for example. The nesting of geographic scales is related to the peripheralization of particular regions of a state. Economic inequities that are manifested in spatial uneven development can be compounded by ethnoterritorial affiliations. Cognitive maps of differential life chances in different regions give geographic weight to feelings of social inequity.

Most definitions of terrorism highlight its purpose as political change to distinguish it from the acts of criminals or the insane. Politics and territoriality are inseparable, because politics involves securing control over particular spaces to ensure access to goods.[35] The political change sought by terrorists is, therefore, also a geographic change. This may be the redrawing of existing state borders to create, for example, a Tamil state, a Palestinian state, or a united Ireland. On the other hand, the scale may be broader, the removal of the U.S. presence in the Arabian peninsula, say. To understand the territorial aspect of the grievances of terrorist movements is a means to evaluate the level of injustice they are experiencing and hence the necessity of a negotiated political solution. Moreover, a lasting solution is one that does its best to balance the geographic intricacies of who has power over what in particular regions and at particular scales.

At this stage we should turn to the grievances and geographic visions of some contemporary terrorist movements. On one level, the scale of the political battle has been dramatically altered by the emergence of religiously motivated terrorism. It is important to note, with Juergensmeyer, that this is not solely a phenomenon of the most radical branches of Islam.[36] Terrorism motivated by Christian beliefs in the United States of America and the United Kingdom, Jewish groups in Israel/Palestine, Sikh terrorism in India, and the Buddhist roots of Aum Shrinyiko in Japan suggest that global processes are catalyzing the contemporary surge. The geography behind this terrorism is perhaps truly awesome. These groups, in their own particular ways and with their own contextually specific grievances, are fighting "cosmic wars"—wars over the interpretation of God's will on Earth. A geographic expression of these conflicts is the transcendence of the interstate system into the ultimate battle between good and evil, with millennialist implications.

However, though this rhetoric may be present, the political-geographic reality is often grounded in the existing world political map of nation-states. Terrorism motivated by antiabortion Christian fundamentalists decries the "murder" condoned by the federal government, and Osama bin Laden is critical of the Saudi Arabian government's collaboration with the United States. Though the vision of religious terrorists may transcend the interstate system, their practices are constrained and partially defined by the geography of nation-states.

The comparative advantage political geography has to offer in the analysis of contemporary terrorism is an understanding of how political geographies are multiple, intertwined, and nested.[37] Terrorist movements may construct a network of international linkages, but their goal could remain the control of a national territory. Religious terrorist movements may have visions that "God's politics" cover the world and transcend states, but still have particular state regimes as their targets and allies. Also, practices of the war on terrorism must negotiate understandings of state sovereignty in a global act of military policing.

The Political Geography of Waves of Terrorism

Rapoport's simple but effective typology of the history of modern terrorism is a useful illustration of the changing geography of terrorism.[38] However, Rapoport gives no theoretical insight into the reasons why terrorism has changed over time. A geographic interpretation of Rapoport's typology uses the notion of geohistorical context to explain why the changes have taken place and the concept of the geographic scope to highlight its implications.

The first wave of terrorism began in the 1880s in reaction to political reform in Russia that promised much but supplied relatively little. The practice of terrorism diffused into anarchist movements in Western Europe that were worried about the political impacts of universal suffrage and how it would shore up existing political systems. In addition, nationalist movements in the Balkans resorted to violence in their quest to redraw boundaries as the Ottoman Empire crumbled. These different terrorist movements shared a similar geographic focus: the scope of their activity was the nation-state.

The second wave (approximately 1920–1960) of terrorism shared similar geographic traits. In the wake of Allied victories in the two world wars, terrorist movements acted with the goal of awakening nationalist movements and achieving the successful establishment of independent nation-states. After World War II the collapse of the British Empire, as well as other European and Japanese colonialist projects, was hastened by violent terrorist claims to independence.

Both waves are not merely ones we can relate to; the geographic assumptions that underline their motivation are ones that we actually celebrate. In the United States, July Fourth celebrations and St. Patrick's Day parades are annual cultural practices to instill "heroic" acts of resistance in the name of national self-determination in the public memory. Celebration of "independence days" in, for example, Israel and Kenya are partially the product of the terrorist acts of Irgun and the Mau Mau. These acts of terrorism are blended into an acceptable and dominant latent political geography of the obvious and natural territorialization of states.

Overlapping these two waves was the period of the state terror of totalitarian states, which Rapoport does not identify as a wave.[39] Both the periodization and its geography were driven by the imperatives of the Cold War. Germany had been saved from Nazism through its successful liberation by Allied troops which were increasingly reliant upon the United States. Those parts of Eurasia that were not liberated experienced the repression of the Communist state. I do not mean to deny the horrors of Stalinism or the Cultural Revolution. In fact, along with Nazism, these events are the primary historical exhibits in the prosecution of states as terrorist actors. Rather, the additional point is that by focusing upon these countries, the acts of terror by governments aided by the war's victor, the United States, are conveniently removed from the courtroom. The final important point to remember about this wave is that it again focuses upon a particular geographic scale of political activity, the state.

The third wave of terrorism identified by Rapoport is the ideology-based terrorism that was inspired by America's actions and defeat in the Vietnam War. For example, the Weather Underground in the United States and the Red Army Faction in Germany were motivated by Marxist and anti-imperialist ideologies. In this wave we see a transition as national groups created international connections and fused national political targets with global geopolitical concerns. Thus though all the waves have witnessed different forms of terrorism, they shared a geographic similarity. The actions were framed within the arena of the nation-state—politics that is understood within the state-centric models of social science, the calculations of political leaders, and the cognitive maps of citizens. However, the third wave suggests the transition to the geography of the next wave of terrorism.

The fourth and current wave is somewhat different. The wave of religious terrorism has shattered the geographic assumptions that grounded analysis of the previous waves. Ideologically, at least, the current wave of religious terrorism has increased the scope of the geopolitical conflict to a level that transcends the state. The current conflict is seen as universal; the fate of humanity is at stake because the scale is increased even further in the construction of a cosmic war between good and evil.[40] No longer is the battle over the construction of, or control over, the state apparatus. Terrorism has become "God's will" in the interpretation of a relatively small group of radical religious leaders. In this sense, the political goal of terrorist activity transcends the state because the "charity" of the terrorist leader is aimed not at saving people from a wicked or unjust political situation but at saving their souls. It is this new geography of the political goal of terrorism that has left commentators scrambling to explain it—once political activity, in this case, terrorism, leaves the established framework of the interstate system, it becomes "meaningless" or "unclear."[41] Not at all. For the perpetrators, the motives are quite clear; they are just outside the paradigmatic boundaries of a social science that is still constrained by equating state with society.

Such an analysis must be qualified, however. First, religious terrorists still require the haven of sympathetic states. The sovereignty of states provides territory for terrorists to train and strategize. Also, the diplomatic spaces that are the preserve of recognized states have also been used by terrorists to bypass state security. Collusion between movements motivated by terrorism and sympathetic state authorities is also evident. Second, the recent identification of support from agents of the British government in the 1987 and 1989 assassinations of Brian Lambert and Patrick Finucane by the Protestant and unionist Ulster Freedom Fighters is a clear example that state and religious interests may be intertwined.[42] Indeed, it is controversial to define the conflict in Northern Ireland as religiously motivated, as Juergensmeyer does.[43] For others, this is more clearly an ethnonationalist conflict demarcated, perhaps, by religious signifiers.[44] Third, and despite the religious rhetoric of some terrorist groups, they are targeting change at the state scale. The actions of Jewish terrorist organizations are aimed at expanding the geographic extent of the Israeli state and maximizing its "security" by eliminating Arab enemies both inside and out. Timothy McVeigh and Michael Hill were fixated upon the "godless" actions of the federal state, but it is not hard to imagine that if fundamentalist policies were implemented by state and federal governments, their motivation for terrorist activities would wane. The same argument could be made for Sikh terrorism in India.

Sovereign states are the fundamental political units in today's world. Hence it is not surprising that they frame both the actions and the goals of religious terrorists. But there is something to the idea that there is a political transcendence of the state at the moment and that in the realm of political resistance, religiously motivated terrorism is serving as a vanguard.

Referring back to geohistorical context as a useful geographical concept, we may ask these questions: why is religious terrorism on the rise now, and why is one of its primary targets the United States of America? To answer these questions, we must take a brief detour into a consideration of the United States as a hegemonic power. The theoretical knowledge we gain in this short trip will be useful in explaining not only the motivations behind contemporary terrorism, but also the goals and practice of the "war on terrorism."

The United States as Hegemonic Power

In recent years, and especially since the 2003 war on Iraq, it has become increasingly common to refer to the United States as the creator of an empire.[45] This is a false accusation; it is more accurate to see the actions of the United States as consistent with a period of decline in its power rather than with the apogee of its strength. Such heretical claims require theoretical support.

The twentieth century was "the American century" as the United States rose to be the economic power in the world on the basis of product and production process innovations.[46] Such economic strength allowed the United States to exert its continental and then global political power from the Spanish-American War to its key role in concluding World War II and defining the terms of the subsequent peace.[47] From this position of political strength, the United States established economic (International Monetary Fund, World Bank), political (the United Nations), and military (NATO) institutions to secure its ability to order the world to its liking. Significantly, for the purposes of this chapter, these institutions secured the extraterritorial reach of the United States as hegemonic power.[48] In other words, the United States was able to partially determine the domestic and foreign policy of other sovereign states. Contemporary examples include the pressure brought to bear on certain Arab states to base U.S. troops, as well as the linkage of antiabortion clauses to foreign aid commitments.

Hegemonic power is not a matter of military and political might. It is hard, some say impossible, to maintain power by coercive means alone.[49] It is more cost effective to lead by consensus or integrative power. Hegemonic powers have constructed a prime modernity to fulfill that integrative role. The prime modernity is the form of society defined by the hegemonic power as the epitome of what it means to be "modern."[50] This is a broad term that includes gender and racial roles, cultural landscapes, consumer products, media, and relations of production. For example, through the twentieth century the United States promoted the suburban lifestyle as the most modern with its gendered division of labor and racial exclusion. This lifestyle required the purchase of at least one automobile plus a whole host of other "consumer durables" to fill the house and define the duties of the housewife. Rather than being an industrial modernity (the previous prime modernity of British hegemony in the nineteenth century), the prime modernity of American hegemony centered upon the office worker, usually a male manager with a female assistant or secretary. Finally, and perhaps most significantly, the nature of this prime modernity was disseminated through television and the movies—in many ways the prime modernity was Hollywood.

The prime modernity is a form of integrative power in that it defines the way of life other countries wish to emulate—the ability to become modern.[51] The institutions of the hegemony define the economic and political steps deemed necessary to attain this future—generally speaking, opening borders and markets to the free movement of goods and capital. Through processes of emulation, the hegemonic power is able to assert its extraterritoriality by inserting its influence into the sovereign spaces of other states.

However, and to return to our topic of religious terrorism, the diffusion of the prime modernity is resisted. Resistance may be found both within the borders of the hegemonic power and in foreign countries.[52] In the contemporary case of the United States, extreme Christian fundamentalists are opposed to the worship of consumer materialism and to the redefinition of gender and racial roles that an evolving prime modernity has ushered in. Internationally, the diffusion of American culture—from secular government to the freedom granted to young women—has created resistance movements. It is also worth noting at this point that in his celebration of the triumph of Western consumerism and liberal democracy, Francis Fukuyama was also concerned that it was spiritually vacuous and susceptible to ideologies that professed greater depth to the purpose of life.[53] In a battle over values, it is not surprising that religious motivations come to the fore.

But let us not follow an avenue that is purely a matter of the politics of culture. The extraterritorial reach of the United States is also expressed in the political-military presence of barracks across the globe, notably across Europe, East Asia, and of course central and Southwest Asia. It is the presence of American "infidels" among the holy sites of Islam that has provoked the ire of Osama bin Laden. The growth of American military presence in central and Eastern Europe and central and Southwest Asia may be interpreted through a historical lens as, potentially, another expression of "imperial overstretch."[54]

At the time of its publication, Kennedy's book raised much debate about the dangers of increasing troop presence across the globe, a policy that has, in the past, drawn great powers into more battles and ultimately drained their economic strength.[55] Surprisingly, as America's troops are now stationed in Afghanistan and Iraq, with talk of Syria as the next stop, Kennedy's thesis is conveniently ignored. One possible reason for this is the belief that America's economy is strong enough to support the cost of global troop deployment. That is debatable. An alternative interpretation is that resistance to American hegemony, particularly its model of prime modernity and its political extraterritoriality, has become so strong that the hegemonic world political order must be maintained increasingly by force. This is precisely the historical process that Kennedy identified.

There is another scenario. In the past, hegemonic cycles have begun and ended with a period of global war.[56] Are we in that period now? It is a possibility. Attacks on the World Trade Center in 1993, American embassies in Kenya and Tanzania, U.S. barracks in Saudi Arabia, and the USS *Cole* were, perhaps, opening salvos that were seen as sporadic skirmishes. September 11, 2001, was the first "raid" that set the war machine in full motion. This is, of course and by necessity, conjecture, but it does follow the pattern defined by previous cycles of hegemony and world leadership. If that is the case, it is hard to see any other outcome than the, perhaps eventual, military victory of the United States. The question will be whether it maintains its economic superiority and can define a new prime modernity to reintegrate the world. Another point to consider is that there have been many periods in history where there has been a relative balance of power between a number of strong states rather than the primacy of a hegemonic power. Though such a balance is a possibility, the economic and institutional constraints of Japan and the difficulties of creating unified and coherent policy in the European Union raise questions over whether balance will replace hegemony.

To return to the geohistorical question, why is religious terrorism now targeting the United States? Hegemonic powers are extraterritorial; their power reaches into the sovereign spaces of other states. This power is economic, political, and cultural. Acceptance of and outright desire for the hegemonic influence have been, after the wars that brought it to power, high, though never universal. But people can get tired of military occupation, even if it is benevolent, as demonstrations against the presence of American bases in Japan suggest. Perhaps more significant is the fact that the promises of the prime modernity cannot be diffused to all. The persistent inequalities in the world-economy mean that only a few will gain the trappings of the good life. The majority will be disappointed. In this situation, promises of new ways of life that are seen as superior and more fulfilling and culturally appropriate will become attractive.[57] By fusing economic and political extraterritoriality with an interpretation of the diffusion of prime modernity as "cultural imperialism," religious leaders can portray America's global presence as antagonistic to what are constructed as "traditional" values, and hence as a presence that must be fought violently. The cultural and the military interact to provoke a "holy war." But though the resistors may be confident in their claims to spiritual superiority, they are realistic about the calculation of their military strength. The result is the resort to terrorism, the military strategy of the relatively weak.[58]

But are the goals of religious terrorism as confusing as some say? Not if we break out of the geographic framework of sovereign states and the secularism of developmentalism. People do conceive of the world spiritually and do not act like the "economic man" of social science models;[59] they are motivated by cultural understandings of what is spiritually "good" and not only by rational calculations of gain assigned by economic calculations of secular "goods." But perhaps the greatest leap in our analytical framework must be from the state to the global scale. The conflict over what is good and how it is threatened has become global because of the diffusion of the consumer prime modernity of American hegemony. Given that the flows of "globalization" are part of the process of American hegemony, it is not surprising that religious terrorism utilizes and challenges these flows while at the same time negotiating the existing framework of sovereign states.

The Political Geography of the "War on Terrorism"

In academic writing, it is usually wise to avoid statements such as "the war that is now taking place" because global events unfold at a quicker pace than the publication process and have a shorter shelf life. However, it is a safer bet that the "war on terrorism" will continue for some time. The probable longevity of the U.S. "war on terrorism" stems from both geohistorical and geopolitical reasons. First, geohistorically, and as was discussed earlier, the process of American hegemony suggests that the recent terrorist attacks upon the United States are either a sign of "imperial overstretch," a symptom of hegemonic decline that will usher in a period of global war, or are battles in the war itself. Either way, the U.S. interventions in Afghanistan and Iraq have not resolved anything permanently; they are battles and not the whole war.

In this section I will explore the spatiality of the war on terrorism in terms of the different metageographies used by al-Qaeda and the United States of America. On the one hand, there is a terrorist network, a string of nodes that stems from bin Laden and ends in an unknown number of cells. Along the network, particular nodes will have particular functions—training, finance, or equipment, for example—but the network will branch out so that the final nodes, the cells of people who actually carry out the acts of terrorism—will not be connected to each other. The geographic location of each of these cells will be strategically calculated. The cells of suicide bombers, assassins, and the like will necessarily be located near their targets, while command and control nodes (which may be mobile) will choose places where they are least likely to be disturbed by security forces.[60]

The simple metageographic point to note is that terrorist networks intersect the system of sovereign states. Some nodes must breach the borders of states and remain undetected by domestic security forces, while others choose locations where the state is either sympathetic to their goals or where the power of the state is weak. Though the network structure of contemporary terrorism is often highlighted, such networks both utilize and must negotiate states.

But perhaps the asymmetry in the war on terrorism is more problematic for states than for the terrorists. Immediately after the attacks of September 11 the immediate mission for the war on terrorism was stated clearly: bin Laden was wanted dead or alive. In other words, what was seen as the central node of the al-Qaeda network was to be eliminated. But the geographic strategy of the war soon changed. The target became the Taliban regime that was deemed to be harboring bin Laden. Finally, the focus was on the sovereign state of Afghanistan itself and on the identification of "rogue states."[61] What was initially seen as a deterritorial strategy of eliminating nodes on a network became translated into a more traditional territorial geopolitics of occupying (preferably in a surrogate fashion) sovereign space.

The asymmetry of terrorism and counterterrorism is reflected in their different metageographic forms, networks versus states. To counter networks in its war on terrorism, the United States must impose a territorial presence. In other words, it has been forced to occupy sovereign spaces. The geopolitical dilemma that faces the United States is that part of the motivation behind the terrorist attacks is America's presence in sovereign spaces in the first place, Saudi Arabia being the most important venue. In other words, occupying sovereign spaces to destroy terrorist networks may well be counterproductive counterterrorism.

On the other hand, the United States has been adopting a forceful counterterrorist strategy that is not concerned with occupying territory. The use of an unmanned flying drone to destroy a car in Yemen that contained alleged terrorists and cooperation between national police forces to arrest terrorist suspects are examples of national governments' use of aterritorial methods to counter a network threat. But though such actions may be a prelude, the current geopolitics of counterterrorism is dominated by actual and threatened intervention in sovereign spaces to initiate a "regime change" and create geographies less hospitable to the location of terrorist cells.

War on Terrorism as Just War

The war on terrorism may have been originally scripted as a "new" type of war, but its most recent manifestations have followed the pattern of traditional wars of control of sovereign territory by an occupying force, perhaps temporarily. Like other wars, the war on terrorism must be justified, because "a war called unjust is a war misliked."[62] Wars waged by the hegemonic power possess a particular moral burden because as voice and exemplifier of the prime modernity, the hegemonic power must be seen to be waging war to defend modernity in a just manner. However, the political geography of hegemonic rule complicates the ability of a hegemonic power at war to claim that it is acting justly.

First, the ability to wage a just war is based upon an understanding of a system of sovereign states, each with the ability to make moral claims about state aggression, its own or another state's.[63] The "legalistic paradigm" is the diplomatic manifestation of the territorial trap and denies the extraterritorial capacity of some states, especially the hegemonic power. Merely by exercising its extraterritorial power, the hegemony is violating the geographic axioms of a just war.

Second, wars of defense or "anticipations" are based upon the perceived desire for a balance of power between states, the disruption of which is seen to be detrimental to peace.[64] The existence of a hegemonic power precludes the maintenance of a balance of power. Rather, anticipation becomes another matter—it is the effort of the hegemonic power to prevent challenges to its power. Another way of seeing this conflict is that hegemonic powers fight wars of anticipation against the "heretics," the flies in the ointment of the Kantian universal peace. Preemptive attacks, the contemporary language for anticipations, against rogue nations and the "axis of evil" may be interpreted in this way, as actions against states that deny the authority of the hegemonic power.

Third, sovereign authority becomes hegemonic authority,[65] the ability to decide what is "aggression," "threat," or "evil." The language of war is always another source of contention, including arguments over who has been wronged, who fired the first shot, and so on. As hegemonic power, the United States is currently in the position to identify transgressors of its authority and hence what is justifiable anticipation and intervention.

Most importantly, the hegemonic power is faced with a different geography over the question, what is a threat? In Walzer's seminal work, threat is based upon a territorial understanding of invasion by a contiguous power. If invasion has occurred or is imminent (though what that means is problematic), then a war of defense against such aggression is justified. But for the hegemonic power, there is a different calculation. The hegemon's power is based upon the dissemination of a universal message, a message that is deemed to be equally beneficial to all people everywhere and anywhere. The authority of the hegemonic power is based upon the fiction that this message is not only universally applicable but universally desired. The ideology of the prime modernity allows for the exertion of extraterritoriality that is the foundation of hegemonic power. Any action by a "rogue nation" that denies the universality of the prime modernity or the actual operation of its extraterritorial institutions is a threat to the hegemonic power's global reign and the basis for the construction of a "just" war.

There is another pillar of just war: intervention to prevent violation of human rights.[66] This is a trickier subject because (1) the hegemonic power has the authority to state which rights are being violated by whom, where, and when, (2) usually other reasons for military action exist, such as access to strategic resources, and (3) on the basis of the philosophy of John Stuart Mill,[67] it may be contested whether such intervention does more harm than good. The hegemonic power has the language of prime modernity to define what is and is not a violation and when it is necessary to intervene. Is it merely cynical to suggest that violations of the canons of prime modernity that are also threats to its universality and the hegemonic power's global reach are constructed as justifications for attack?

However, the metapolitical geography of sovereign nation-states, or at least its ideological fiction, is a structure that poses problems for the United States as hegemonic power in creating "just wars." Anticipations,[68] or preemptive attacks, in the name of counterterrorism require the violation of sovereign spaces. However, these spaces are the geographic foundations of the contemporary prime modernity—national self-determination, liberalism, and the equality of states. By fighting a terrorist challenge to its hegemonic power through the invasion of other countries, the United States is in danger of tarnishing the political-geographic ideals that underpin its authority. Finally, despite the weight of other arguments, the political-geographic approach would suggest that the possibility that such "anticipations" and "interventions" are actually moments in a process of imperial overstretch should be not be ignored. It is as likely as the alternative, the triumphal beginnings of a new period of American hegemonic rule.

Conclusion

In this chapter I have suggested ways in which a geographic perspective may add to our understanding of the why and the how of terrorism and counterterrorism and the implications of both. Terrorist acts and the geopolitics of counterterrorism occur within political geographic structures—scalar politics and the mosaic of nation-states, for example. These geographies both facilitate and constrain the geopolitics of terrorism, and their form, both existing and desired, is part of the terrorists' and counterterrorists' goals. An ageographic analysis of terrorism is one that removes actors from their real-world settings. It follows that geographers have much to offer in understanding the motivations and means of terrorists and in contextualizing the geopolitics of counterterrorism within the dynamics of global politics. With this perspective, geographers may suggest ways in which counterterrorism can avoid trampling over other people's geographic understandings in a way that may provoke rather than dampen antagonisms.

Notes

1. Booth and Dunne, *World in Collision*; Carr, *Lessons of Terror*; Cutter, Richardson, and Wilbanks, *Geographical Dimensions of Terrorism*; Halliday, *Two Hours That Shook the World.*
2. Flint, "Terrorism and Counterterrorism"; Flint, "Geographies of Inclusion/Exclusion."
3. Wallerstein, "Time of Space and the Space of Time."
4. Arrighi, *Long Twentieth Century*; Taylor, *Way the Modern World Works*; Wallerstein, *Politics of the World-Economy*, 37–46.
5. Marston, "Social Construction of Scale"; Taylor and Flint, *Political Geography*, 40–46.
6. Bregman and El-Tahri, *Israel and the Arabs*, 182–183.
7. Hoffman, *Inside Terrorism*, 15–28; Rapoport, "Fourth Wave."
8. Juergensmeyer, *Terror in the Mind of God.*
9. Taylor, "Embedded Statism and the Social Sciences"
10. Kirby, *Power/Resistance.*
11. Howitt, "Frontiers, Borders, Edges"; Hugill, *World Trade since 1431.*
12. Cresswell, *In Place/out of Place.*

13. Stump, *Boundaries of Faith*; Stump, this volume.
14. Veness, "Terrorism and Counterterrorism."
15. Laqueur, *Age of Terrorism*, 11.
16. Hoffman, *Inside Terrorism*, 38.
17. Ibid., 15–28.
18. Ibid., 43.
19. Ahmad, *Confronting Empire*, 95.
20. Hoffman, *Inside Terrorism*, 43.
21. Walzer, *Just and Unjust Wars*, 197.
22. Ibid.
23. Crenshaw, "Thoughts on Relating Terrorism to Historical Contexts."
24. Taylor and Flint, *Political Geography*, 9–11.
25. Hoffman, *Inside Terrorism*, 44.
26. Said, *Orientalism*.
27. Agnew, "Territorial Trap."
28. Agnew, "Mapping Political Power beyond State Boundaries."
29. James, *Rise and Fall of the British Empire*; Johnson, *Blowback*.
30. Taylor, "Places, Spaces, and Macy's."
31. Mitchell, *Cultural Geography*, 201–213.
32. Agnew, "Territorial Trap."
33. Dowler, "Preserving the Peace and Maintaining Order."
34. Taylor, "Crisis of the Movements."
35. Sack, "Human Territoriality."
36. Juergensmeyer, *Terror in the Mind of God*.
37. Flint, "Dying for a 'P'?"
38. Rapoport, "Fourth Wave."
39. Hoffman, *Inside Terrorism*, 23–24.
40. Juergensmeyer, *Terror in the Mind of God*, 145–163.
41. Pillar, *Terrorism and U.S. Foreign Policy*.
42. The Guardian Unlimited, "Collusion, Murder and Cover-up," April 18, 2003.
43. Juergensmeyer, *Terror in the Mind of God*, 36–43.
44. McGarry and O'Leary, *Explaining Northern Ireland*.
45. Hardt and Negri, *Empire*.
46. Arrighi, *Long Twentieth Century*, 269–300.
47. Slater and Taylor, *American Century*.
48. Flint, "Geopolitics of Laughter and Forgetting."
49. Boulding, *Three Faces of Power*, Sherman, "Attacks of September 11 in Three Temporalities."
50. Taylor, *Modernities*, 31–34.
51. Ibid., 38–43.
52. Flint, "Right-Wing Resistance to the Process of American Hegemony."
53. Fukuyama, *End of History and the Last Man*.
54. Kennedy, *Rise and Fall of the Great Powers*, 515.
55. Ibid.
56. Arrighi, *Long Twentieth Century*, 58–74.
57. Armstrong, *Battle for God*, xi–xviii; Esposito, *Unholy War*, 26–28.
58. Rekkedal, *Asymmetric Warfare and Terrorism*.
59. Smith, *Why Religion Matters*.
60. Arquilla and Ronfeldt, *Networks and Netwars*; Flint, "Terrorism and Counterterrorism"; Flint, "Geographies of Inclusion/Exclusion."

61. Klare, *Rogue States and Nuclear Outlaws.*
62. Walzer, *Just and Unjust Wars*, 12.
63. Ibid., 10.
64. Ibid., 76–78.
65. Ibid., 10.
66. Ibid., 101–108.
67. Ibid., 87.
68. Ibid., 74–85.

References

Agnew, John. "The Territorial Trap: The Geographical Assumptions of International Relations Theory." *Review of International Political Economy* 1 (1994): 53–80.

Agnew, John. "Mapping Political Power beyond State Boundaries: Territory, Identity, and Movement in World Politics." *Millennium* 28 (1999): 499–521.

Ahmad, Eqbal. *Confronting Empire.* Cambridge, MA: South End, 2000.

Armstrong, Karen. *The Battle for God: A History of Fundamentalism.* New York: Ballantine, 2000.

Arquilla, John, and David Ronfeldt. *Networks and Netwars: The Future of Terror, Crime, and Militancy.* Santa Monica, CA: Rand, 2001.

Arrighi, Giovanni. *The Long Twentieth Century.* New York: Verso, 1994.

Booth, Ken, and Tim Dunne, eds. *World in Collision: Terror and the Future of Global Order.* Basingstoke: Palgrave Macmillan, 2002.

Boulding, Kenneth. *Three Faces of Power.* Newbury Park, CA: Sage, 1990.

Bregman, Ahron, and Jihan El-Tahri. *Israel and the Arabs: An Eyewitness Account of War and Peace in the Middle East.* New York: TV Books, 1998.

Carr, Caleb. *The Lessons of Terror: A History of Warfare against Civilians: Why It Has Always Failed, and Why It Will Fail Again.* New York: Random House, 2002.

Crenshaw, Martha. "Thoughts on Relating Terrorism to Historical Contexts." In *Terrorism in Context*, ed. Martha Crenshaw, 3–24. University Park: Pennsylvania State University Press, 1981.

Cresswell, Tim. *In Place/out of Place: Geography, Ideology, and Transgression.* Minneapolis: University of Minnesota Press, 1996.

Cutter, Susan L., Douglas B. Richardson, and Thomas J. Wilbanks, eds. *The Geographical Dimensions of Terrorism.* New York: Routledge, 2003.

Dowler, Lorraine. "Preserving the Peace and Maintaining Order: Deconstructing the Legal Landscapes of Public Housing in West Belfast, Northern Ireland." *Urban Geography* 22 (2001): 100–105.

Esposito, John L. *Unholy War: Terror in the Name of Islam.* Oxford: Oxford University Press, 2002.

Flint, Colin. "The Geopolitics of Laughter and Forgetting: A World-Systems Interpretation of the Post-modern Geopolitical Condition." *Geopolitics* 6 (2001): 1–16.

Flint, Colin. "Right-Wing Resistance to the Process of American Hegemony: The Changing Political Geography of Nativism in Pennsylvania, 1920–1998." *Political Geography* 20 (2001): 763–786.

Flint, Colin. "Geographies of Inclusion/Exclusion." In *The Geographical Dimensions of Terrorism*, ed. Susan L. Cutter, Douglas B. Richardson, and Thomas J. Wilbanks, 53–58. New York: Routledge, 2003.

Flint, Colin. "Terrorism and Counterterrorism: Geographic Research Questions and Agendas." *Professional Geographer* 55 (2003): 161–169.
Flint, Colin. "Dying for a 'P'? Some Questions Facing Contemporary Political Geography." *Political Geography* 22 (2003): 617–620.
Fukuyama, Francis. *The End of History and the Last Man.* New York: Free Press, 1992.
Guardian Unlimited, "Collusion, Murder and Cover-up," April 18, 2003. www.guardian.co.uk/guardianpolitics/story/0,3605,939100,00.html (accessed April 20, 2003).
Halliday, Fred. *Two Hours That Shook the World: September 11, 2001.* London: Saqi, 2002.
Hardt, Michael, and Antonio Negri. *Empire.* Cambridge, MA: Harvard University Press, 2000.
Hoffman, Bruce. *Inside Terrorism.* New York: Columbia University Press, 1998.
Howitt, R. "Frontiers, Borders, Edges: Liminal Challenges to the Hegemony of Exclusion." *Australian Geographical Studies* 39 (2001): 233–245.
Hugill, Peter J. *World Trade since 1431: Geography, Technology, and Capitalism.* Baltimore: Johns Hopkins University Press, 1993.
James, Lawrence. *The Rise and Fall of the British Empire.* New York: St. Martin's Griffin, 1994.
Johnson, Chalmers. *Blowback: The Costs and Consequences of American Empire.* New York: Holt, 2000.
Juergensmeyer, Mark. *Terror in the Mind of God: The Global Rise of Religious Violence.* Berkeley: University of California Press, 2000.
Kennedy, Paul. *The Rise and Fall of the Great Powers.* New York: Vintage, 1989.
Kirby, Andrew. *Power/Resistance: Local Politics and the Chaotic State.* Bloomington: Indiana University Press, 1993.
Klare, Michael. *Rogue States and Nuclear Outlaws: America's Search for a New Foreign Policy.* New York: Hill and Wang, 1995.
Laqueur, Walter. *The Age of Terrorism.* Boston: Little, Brown, 1987.
Marston, Sallie A. "The Social Construction of Scale." *Progress in Human Geography* 24 (2000): 219–242.
McGarry, John, and Brendan O'Leary. *Explaining Northern Ireland.* Cambridge, MA: Blackwell, 1995.
Mitchell, Don. *Cultural Geography: A Critical Introduction.* Malden, MA: Blackwell, 2000.
Pillar, Paul. *Terrorism and U.S. Foreign Policy.* Washington, DC: Brookings Institution Press, 2001.
Rapoport, David C. "The Fourth Wave: September 11 in the History of Terrorism." *Current History* 100 (2001): 419–424.
Rekkedal, Nils Marius. *Asymmetric Warfare and Terrorism—An Assessment.* Security Policy Library, 5. Oslo: Norwegian Atlantic Committee, 2002.
Sack, Robert. "Human Territoriality: A Theory." *Annals of the Association of American Geographers* 73 (1983): 55–74.
Said, Edward. *Orientalism.* New York: Vintage, 1979.
Sherman, Steven. "The Attacks of September 11 in Three Temporalities." *Journal of World-Systems Research* 9 (2003): 141–169.
Slater, David, and Peter J. Taylor, eds. *The American Century: Consensus and Coercion in the Projection of American Power.* Malden, MA: Blackwell, 1999.
Smith, Huston. *Why Religion Matters: The Fate of the Human Spirit.* San Francisco: Harper, 2001.
Stump, Roger. *Boundaries of Faith: Geographical Perspectives on Religious Fundamentalism.* Lanham, MD: Rowman and Littlefield, 2000.

Taylor, Peter J. "The Crisis of the Movements: The Enabling State as Quisling." *Antipode* 23 (1991): 214–228.

Taylor, Peter J. *The Way the Modern World Works: World Hegemony to World Impasse.* Chichester: Wiley, 1996.

Taylor, Peter J. *Modernities.* Minneapolis: University of Minnesota Press, 1999.

Taylor, Peter J. "Places, Spaces, and Macy's: Place-Space Tensions in the Political Geography of Modernities." *Progress in Human Geography* 23 (1999): 7–26.

Taylor, Peter J. "Embedded Statism and the Social Sciences. Part 2: Geographies (and Metageographies) in Globalization." *Environment and Planning* A 32 (2000): 1105–1114.

Taylor, Peter J., and Colin Flint. *Political Geography: World-Economy, Nation-State, and Locality.* 4th ed. Harlow, UK: Prentice Hall, 2000.

Veness, D. "Terrorism and Counterterrorism: An International Perspective." *Studies in Conflict and Terrorism* 24 (2001): 407–416.

Wallerstein, Immanuel. *The Politics of the World-Economy.* Cambridge: Cambridge University Press, 1984.

Wallerstein, Immanuel. "The Time of Space and the Space of Time: The Future of Social Science." *Political Geography* 19 (1998): 71–82.

Walzer, Michael. *Just and Unjust Wars.* 3rd ed. New York: Basic Books, 2000.

PHILIPPE LE BILLON

The Geography of "Resource Wars"

Competition over natural resources has figured prominently among explanations of armed conflicts, from Malthusian fears of population growth and land scarcity to national security interests over resources defined as "strategic" because of their industrial or military use, such as oil and uranium.[1] Access to natural resources and the transformation of nature into tradable commodities are deeply political processes, in which military force can play a role of domination or resistance. Armed separatism within Indonesia and Nigeria, annexation attempts on Kuwait and the Democratic Republic of the Congo, protracted civil wars in Angola and the Philippines, and coups d'état in Iran and Venezuela have all incorporated important resource dimensions. Arguably, the radical Islamic terrorism that has affected the United States since the early 1990s is to some extent an oil-related "blowback": U.S. military deployment in Saudi Arabia, criticisms against the corruption of the Gulf regimes, and ironically, part of the funding made available to terrorist groups.

This chapter examines relations between resources and armed conflicts, with a focus on commodities legally traded on international markets (thereby excluding drugs, as well as water and land involved, for example, in the Israeli-Palestinian conflict) and on extracted resources such as oil, minerals, and timber, in particular. Beyond a simple reading of so-called resource wars as violent modes of competitive behavior, this chapter argues that resource exploitation and the resource dependence of many producing countries play a role in shaping incentives and opportunities of uneven development, misgovernance, coercive rule, insurrection, and foreign interference. This relationship, however, is not systematic: history, political culture, institutions, and regional neighborhoods, as well as a country's place in the international economy, all play a part these relations. The incorporation of resources into an armed conflict has also specific implications upon its course through their influence on the motivations, strategies, and capabilities of belligerents. Military targets often consist of commercial business opportunities rather than political targets, while the cost of engaging adversaries may be calculated in terms of financial reward. The following sections explore the contending views about resources and conflicts, the role of resource dependence among the causes of intra-state and international conflicts, and the ways in which natural resource exploitation interplays with the course of conflicts.[2]

Resource Wars Hypotheses

As noted by Peter Gleick, natural resources "have been used in the past, and will be used in the future, as tools or targets of war and as strategic goals to be fought for."[3] There is much debate, however, on the links between natural resources, conflicts, and violence.

Strategic thinking about resources has been dominated by an equation that links trade, war, and power, at the core of which are valuable overseas resources and maritime navigation. During the mercantilist period of the fifteenth century, trade and war became intimately linked. Naval powers sought to accumulate "world riches," mostly in the form of precious metals, upon which much of the balance of power was perceived to be based on.[4] Money was the "sinew of war," and for political philosopher Raymond Aron, paraphrasing Carl von Clausewitz, commerce had reciprocally become "the continuation of war by other means."[5] Since sea power itself rested on access to timber, the supply of this resource became a preoccupation for major European powers from the seventeenth century onward that motivated overseas alliances, trade, and indeed empire building. England in particular pursued a policy of open seas at all costs that led to several armed interventions in the Baltic.

With growing industrialization and increasing dependence on imported materials during the nineteenth century, Western powers intensified their control over raw materials. This, along with many other factors such as political ideologies and prestige, eventually led to an imperialist scramble over much of the rest of the world. Late imperial initiatives also influenced the Prussian strategy of consolidating economic self-sufficiency by securing access to resources provided by a "vital space," or *Lebensraum*, while the potential role of railways to allow land-based transcontinental control of resources threatened maritime-based power and motivated the idea of containment of the "Heartland" powers advocated by Halford Mackinder at the turn of the twentieth century.[6] The significance of imported resources, in particular, oil, during World War I reinforced the idea of resource vulnerability, which was again confirmed during World War II. Strategic thinking about resources during the Cold War continued to focus on the vulnerability of rising resource supply dependence and to consider the potential for international conflicts that resulted from competition over access to key resources.[7]

Political scientist Michael Klare notes the growth of mass consumerism and the economization of international affairs in the 1990s and identifies "resource wars" as revolving "to a significant degree, over the pursuit or possession of critical materials," with the combination of population and economic growth leading to a relentless expansion in the demand for raw materials, expected resource shortages, and contested resource ownership.[8] Asia's growing mass consumerism and energy demand are of specific concern with regard to the Persian Gulf, the Caspian region, and the South China Sea. If market forces and technological progress can mitigate some of these problems, Klare remains essentially pessimistic, given the readiness of countries that claim resources or import them, especially the United States, to secure their access to resources through military force, as well as the political instability of many producing regions.

Long ignored by such strategic thinking about resources and security that focuses on the global scale, new hypotheses have focused since the 1970s on the threat of rapid environmental degradation and its effect on local societies and have led to a redefinition of national security.[9] This concept of "environmental security" came about to reflect ideas of global interdependence, illustrated through the debates on global warming, environmental limits to growth, and links to uncontrolled migrations and political instability that could affect both the South and the North.[10] Along with "human security," this concept also emphasized the security interests of individuals rather than states, especially among the poor in developing countries.[11] The "green war" hypothesis associated with the discourse of environmental security argues that a scarcity of mostly renewable resources, such as land, water, or forests, constitutes an underlying stress that contributes to interpersonal or intercommunal violence that possibly escalates into civil wars.[12] As demand grows and depletes environmental resources, resource capture by dominant groups, combined with population pressure, and social frictions increase and lead to weakened institutions, social segmentation, and, ultimately, violent conflicts.[13] In Rwanda, rising domestic and interpersonal violence exacerbated by growing population, pervasive land conflicts, growing inequalities, and the threat of landlessness has been linked to the civil war and genocide in 1994.[14]

Most analyses give particular attention to the history of local environmental conditions and social institutions that allocate resource access while emphasizing the significance of land policy shifts. The long-term crisis of subsistence agriculture in the Peruvian highlands that resulted from the displacement of Indian people to marginal lands during the colonial period, aggravated by population growth and by ineffective land reforms in the 1970s, played a large part in the Sendero Luminoso insurrection.[15] Similarly, in Somalia, tensions over limited riverside agricultural lands that were aggravated by the manipulation of land legislation by Siyad Barre as a strategy to consolidate his regime are identified as being among the major underlying social dynamics in the factional wars that devastated southern Somalia during the 1990s.[16]

While there is convincing evidence about environmental marginalization, grievances, and popular forms of resistance, including violence, some arguments counter the green war hypothesis. Market and solidarity mechanisms can to some extent counterbalance localized scarcities as well as motivate and facilitate innovations and shifts in resources and livelihoods. In this regard, resource scarcity and population pressure can result in socioeconomic innovation, including a diversification of the economy, which often leads to greater food security and a more equitable distribution of power across society.[17] This argues in favor of the role of social institutions over deterministic environmental factors. The argument that an ingenuity gap prevents such mechanisms of adaptation because "scarcities will often make tolerance, generosity, and cooperation less abundant" is relevant, but also dangerous in terms of its cultural and institutional generalization.[18] Critics have frequently denounced the underlying neo-Malthusian assumptions and Western bias of the environmental security agenda and green wars and have stressed the importance of unequal relations of power within local societies and the global political economy, especially through transnational extractive companies, as well as the site specificity of violence "rooted in local histories and social relations yet connected to larger processes of material transformation and power relations."[19]

As the Cold War receded in the late 1980s and more attention was again devoted to the internal mechanisms and outcomes of civil wars, the view that some countries in the South were the victims of environmental degradation gave way to the argument that a new scramble for resources among local warlords and regional powers had become prominent.[20] According to the "greed war" argument, rebellion is not a violent form of protest that results from grievances, but a violent way of generating profits. Rather than being driven by political motives, rebellion would reflect the opportunity of seizing profitable opportunities through large-scale banditry.[21] In this view, wars are driven by greed and the opportunity of looting abundant and internationally tradable natural resources, rather than by grievances over scarce resources mostly associated with subsistence livelihoods.

Oil, diamonds, and timber are some of the resources most frequently listed among the primary commodities that supposedly fuel greed wars.[22] Easily taxable, such resources represent the prize of state or territorial control and would thereby increase the risk of greed-driven conflicts while providing armed groups with the "loot" necessary to purchase military equipment.[23] In Cambodia, Liberia, and the Philippines, insurgent groups have thrived from the logging of valuable tropical hardwoods. In the Democratic Republic of the Congo, the control and exploitation of natural resources such as diamonds, coltan (columbite-tantalite), gold, and timber motivate and finance parties responsible for the continuation of conflict.[24]

Yet given the general absence of foreign state sponsors in most post–Cold War conflicts as well as the frequent lack of popular support for waging war, belligerents have to rely on commercial or predatory sources of funding that often target available natural resources. This does not mean that belligerents are systematically "greedy" and driven by economic agendas, but that they adapt to their new economic environment. Furthermore, a Western-based interpretation of rebellion in peripheral regions of the world as greed driven is somewhat revelatory of the fear of an "anarchic revenge of the poor wanting to get rich," in line with the nationalization of local Western assets by many liberation movements in the 1960s and 1970s. Finally, the notions of greed and grievances are culturally dependent, if generally widespread, and they often coexist as two sides of the same coin: a relation of exploitation in which the greed of some is the grievance of others. Therefore, the border between an aggrieved rebel movement and a greedy one is often blurred as a multiplicity of individual and often fluctuating motivations and constraints gives it shape and direction.

Quantitative examinations of resource availability and armed conflicts confirm that an abundance of primary commodities resources is correlated with a higher risk of war, while environmental scarcity mostly relates to low levels of violence. Economists Paul Collier and Anke Hoeffler find that large primary commodity exporters face a higher risk of outbreak of armed conflict.[25] This risk is maximal when the proportion of primary commodity exports reaches 26% percent of gross domestic product (GDP), with a risk of 23%, compared to 0.5% for a similar country with no primary commodity exports. The risk then drops, which Collier interprets as states being rich enough to defend themselves or deter armed opposition. Many of these states are oil producers in a position to "buy out" social peace from relatively small populations through populist agendas and the co-option of political opponents. In terms of conflict duration, rather than outbreak, Collier finds no correlation with resource dependence, while other scientists and most of the case-study literature argue that continued access to abundant and valuable resources prolongs war.[26] Examining more generally the availability of resources, rather than the level of export dependence on primary commodities, political scientist Indra de Soysa finds that abundant renewable resources in otherwise poor countries and nonrenewable resources in all countries increase the likelihood of armed conflict.[27] With regard to scarce resource wars, low levels of violence (25–1,000 battle-related deaths per year) have a positive relation with environmental degradation.[28] Yet a scarcity of renewable resources is not associated with a higher risk of armed conflict.[29]

Between Resource Curse and Resource Wars

The diversity of cases among resource-rich and resource-poor countries argues against any systematic determinism of "too much" or "too little" resources on the occurrence of armed conflicts. If resource dependence, rather than resource wealth or paucity, links resources to war, Collier's identification of primary commodity dependence as "the most powerful risk factor" of civil war nevertheless requires questioning. The economic and political culture, institutional environment, and individual personalities that create and manage resources, both locally and internationally, are essential factors, but is there a generalized "resource curse" beyond specific contexts? Contemporary resource-linked conflicts are furthermore rooted in the violent history of resource extraction successively marked by mercantilism, colonial capitalism, and state kleptocracy, whether these resources are slaves, rubber, agricultural land, or oil. But are resource sectors specifically more conflictual and violent than others, and if so, in which ways? Moreover, resources present specific contexts and opportunities to belligerents through their different physical characteristics, locations, and modes of production, so how do different resources interplay with conflicts?

An alternative framework of analysis of so-called resource wars should be sensitive to the historical processes and natural resource endowments that create a situation of resource dependence for some countries, and to their associated economic and political vulnerabilities. Resource dependence often reflects a mutual, if unequal, relationship between supply and demand within the world economy. At an international scale, commodity linkages between producers and consumers can reflect a dual dependence, as in the case of petroleum: many oil-export-dependent countries accrue in this way most of their foreign currency earnings, while most other countries are oil import dependent for their energy requirements.[30] The concentration of supply or demand into the hands of a few countries or companies also influences the degree of dependence. For example, the production and marketing of rough diamonds is largely controlled by a cartel of producers and buyers dominated by the South African company De Beers, which was initially founded by the British imperialist Cecil Rhodes. The dependence created by De Beers has long consolidated its controlling power over mining towns, regional politics, or world diamond prices.[31] The flow of resources articulated by such dependence is part and parcel of broader core-periphery exploitative relationships and situations of dependence in peripheral producing countries.[32]

Resource dependence has important political and economic consequences because it creates place-specific politics and influences the development path of producing regions.[33] Overall, the dominance of primary commodity exports in an economy is largely correlated with poor economic growth, low standards of living, corruption, and a dampening of democracy, all factors that are likely to raise grievances and the vulnerability of a country to insurrection or violent political competition.[34] As noted by political economist Michael Moore, many poor and conflict-affected states "live to a high degree on 'unearned income'—mainly mineral resources and development aid—and correspondingly face limited incentives to bargain with their own citizens over resources or to institute or respect democratic processes around public revenue and expenditure."[35] Essentially relying on resource-dependent clientelist networks, these states and their rulers are particularly vulnerable to economic shocks, such as resource price falls, or political shifts, such as democratization.[36] While resource rents occasionally allowed some Third World rulers to maintain a relative political stability—if not through democracy—increasing pressure from declining resource export revenues, as well as terms of trade, structural adjustment, and pressure for democratization from international donors and the frustration of a growing youth population, has led to an aggravation of political instability.[37] In this context, even the "stable autocracies" based on resource export revenues face "politics of failure," that is, a pattern of political instability that results from the failure of successive governments to construct a viable support base for themselves, given the position of the country in the world economy, and leads to systematic disenchantment, opposition, and political turnover through electoral and/or military means.[38] In such contexts, the "politics of failure" that characterized many Third World regimes often turned into "spoils politics" that concentrated on profitable remaining economic sectors, such as valuable minerals and timber that require minimal investments.

A framework that analyzes resource wars should also pay attention to the conditions of resource exploitation and its associated conflicts and forms of violence. Distributional conflicts frequently arise that relate to the ownership of natural resources and the allocation of the revenues and negative externalities they generate among the state, businesses, and local communities. These conflicts can be most easily read within a grid of public versus private control and local communities versus central state. Yet these categories frequently oversimplify, because many public figures control private interests and "local community" leaders defend very narrow interests. An analysis of conflicts must therefore be sensitive to local contexts and histories, as well as cultural values and social practices.

For example, on Bougainville Island in November 1989, a local landowner, Francis Ona, walked out of an environmental assessment meeting at the huge copper and gold Panguna mine that had provided nearly half of Papua New Guinea's export earnings during the preceding twenty years. Mining consultants had just rejected demands for compensation for chemical pollution by his local community on grounds of insufficient scientific evidence. With no other weapons than explosives stolen from the mining company, Ona and other militant landowners blew up within days several electric poles at the mine site and boldly demand $11 billion in environmental compensation payments, the closure of the mine, and secession from Papua New Guinea.[39] Initially dismissed, their actions led to the rapid closure of the mine. Repression and a blockade by the government turned the conflict into a war in which possibly more than 10,000 people died during the next decade.

Besides distributional issues, other potential sources of conflict that directly or indirectly result from resource exploitation include loss of local livelihoods due to land-use changes, pollution, or forced displacement, as well as reallocation of employment opportunities and participation in resource management. The changes of social status, order, and values within communities that result from new economic opportunities and social activities, including ostentatious consumption by privileged groups, exacerbate social fault lines. Migration driven by resource development and rapid urbanization often overstretches local services and economic opportunities and can also lead to tensions among and between newcomers and the native population. Abuses by security forces, including forced displacement and heavy-handed law enforcement, can also be a major source of grievance and violent escalation of conflicts.

Resource exploitation frequently involves specific forms of personal/physical and structural violence, such as resource appropriation, price manipulation, forced labor, or population displacement, as well as a militarization of both legal and illegal exploitation schemes. The production of spaces of power and spaces of resistance in relation to resource exploitation comes to define through material and representational practices geographies of violence within and beyond exploitation sites.[40] Although large-scale armed rebellion is generally the exception in comparison to other social projects, such as accommodation, low-level forms of resistance such as pilfering, or peaceful expressions of grievances such as demonstrations and land occupation, such geographies of violence form the background upon which armed conflict may become a viable and even "justifiable" alternative.[41]

In Chiapas, self-defense groups and the Zapatista movement staged a relatively peaceful armed rebellion to respond to an entrenched local political economy of dispossession and neglect toward indigenous communities, to challenge the "global neoliberal order" that supported it, and to attract the attention of the government and the media as a means of improving their bargaining position.[42] In that case, limited violence was the tool of political leverage and expression rather than a direct mode of reappropriation. The much publicized conflicts over oil exploitation in the Niger Delta embrace such issues as pollution from oil spills and flaring, lack of local employment opportunities and public services, forced displacement, and fire and explosion hazards, as well as brutal repression. Used as a justification for political and armed resistance as well as economically motivated crimes, these environmental or social issues have fed a specific form of "petroviolence" that ranges from the social violence of corruption, repression, and criminality to the ecological violence perpetrated against the environment and its users.[43] The closure of project sites also increases the risk of conflict by, among other factors, raising unemployment and thickening migration flows. A final aspect of the framework, examined in the following section, should consider how the geography of resources and their exploitation comes to influence the course of these wars.[44]

Nature, Resources, and the Geography of War

Belligerents tend to use whatever means are accessible to them to finance or profit from war. Yet the specific characteristics and geography of a resource can provide a context that affects a conflict. During the forty years of conflicts in Angola, the National Union for the Total Independence of Angola (UNITA) armed movement used sources of finance as diverse as foreign support from China and many Western-aligned countries, international investments, gold, timber, wildlife, and diamonds. In the post–Cold War context, however, the geography of oil and diamonds came to dominate the economy of the rebel group and that of the government.[45] While the government in Luanda benefited from quasi-exclusive access to oil fields that were located offshore and thereby protected from rebel attacks, UNITA maintained throughout the war a capacity to access diamond fields spread over a vast territory that proved difficult to fully control by the government. Similarly, trading networks for oil were only accessible to the recognized government in Luanda, while UNITA benefited from access to a myriad of diamond smugglers, traders, and jewelers who channeled diamonds from battlefields to shopping malls. As a result of this territorialization of their respective war economies and networks that linked places of resource extraction to those of consumption, both sides benefited from a constant flow of revenue during the twenty-six-year civil war that devastated Angola and brought about the death of more than half a million people.

Natural resources are particularly prominent in war economies, not only because they are often the only economic resource in poor countries where most wars take place, but also because their fixed location, frequently in remote areas, makes them susceptible to looting or extortion, and the infrastructures often needed to tax, exploit, or trade them are often minimal. Unlike manufacturing and, to some extent, agriculture, extractive activities cannot be relocated. Confronted by war, extractive companies may decide not to invest or to disengage from their current operations, but they generally seek to sustain their access to resources and protect their investments by paying whoever is in power amounts that range from a few dollars to allow a truck past a checkpoint to multimillion-dollar concessions, with signature bonuses or resource-collateralized loans paid in advance of exploitation, to belligerents. Furthermore, resource exploitation can often be sustained throughout a conflict, either through the military protection of infrastructure or because low-investment means prove commercially viable. Investors are unlikely to rush to rebuild a multimillion-dollar mining venture after its destruction, but small-scale entrepreneurs and junior companies are more likely to accept risks to access timber and high-value alluvial minerals that can be extracted with minimal outlays and traded without the need for massive transport capacities.

Although a resource-rich environment is generally propitious for financing rebellion, opportunities for government or rebel groups to access resource revenues will also depend upon several other factors. These include the ability to secure resource sites, which is often jeopardized by underpaid and poorly disciplined government security forces, as well as a high level of armed banditry and criminality associated with marginalization; the specific location and mode of exploitation of resources, which determine the accessibility of resources through production, theft, or extortion; the physical and market characteristics of resources, which help determine the accessibility of markets for belligerents; and the practices and complicity of businesses, which will determine the ease with which belligerents can control resources. The properties and geography of resources are particularly significant (see Table 11.1). Required investment, technological demands for exploitation, and price/weight ratio determine what opportunities are available to rebel forces. Trading facilities, such as trucking and international financial networks, also influence the accessibility of many commodities. In areas like central Africa, the degradation of transport infrastructures has limited economically advantageous exploitation to the most valuable and transportable resources, mainly precious and semiprecious minerals.

Resources can be further distinguished in terms of their proximity to the center of power, in both spatial and political terms. Proximate resources are close to the center of power and are less likely to be captured by rebels than those close to a border inhabited by a group that lacks official political representation. Distant resources are located in remote territories along porous borders or within the territory of social groups that are politically marginalized or in opposition to the extant regime. Oil resources, while usually far from a capital, nevertheless tend to be

TABLE 11.1 Resource accessibility by rebel forces

	Accessibility by rebel forces			
Resource	Exploitation	Theft	Extortion	Price range ($/Kg)[a]
Alluvial gems and minerals	High	High	High	20–500,000
Timber	Medium	Medium	High	0.1
Agricultural commodities	Medium	Medium	Medium	1.5 (*coffee*)
On-shore oil	Low	Medium	High	0.12
Diamonds in volcanic pipes	Low	Medium	Medium	500,000
Deep-shaft industrial metals	Low	Low	Medium	2 (*copper*)
Offshore oil	Low	Low	Low	0.12

[a] Approximate price in producing country during the 1990s.

Source: Adapted from Richard Auty, "Natural Resources and Civil Strife: A Two-Stage Process," *Geopolitics* 9 (2004): 29–49; and interview with Gavin Hayman, *Global Witness*, London, June 2002.

closely safeguarded by the state and difficult to appropriate or loot on a massive scale by opposition forces since companies will only deal with the recognized government. Still, onshore installations, and especially pipelines, remain highly susceptible to extortion schemes. Resources are more accessible to rebel groups if they are highly valuable, easily transported, and spread over a large territory rather than a smaller area that can be more easily defended. Rebel access also depends on the degree of centralization and mechanization of production.

A broad distinction can also be made as to the nature and concentration of the resource in terms of physical characteristics, spatial spread, and socioeconomic linkages between diffuse and point resources.[46] Diffuse resources are more widely spread and include mainly resources exploited over large areas, often by less capital-intensive industries that can employ a large workforce. These include alluvial gems and minerals, timber, agricultural products, and fish. Point resources are concentrated in small areas and include mainly resources that can be exploited by capital-intensive extractive industries, such as deep-shaft mining or oil exploitation, and that generally employ a small workforce.

As sociologist David Keen remarked, economically motivated violence among rebels will be more likely when the potential rewards are great and when "natural resources can be exploited with minimal technology and without the need to control the capital or machinery of the state."[47] Alluvial diamonds perfectly fit this description and it is therefore not a surprise to see that they have been dubbed a "guerrilla's best friend" and that about two-thirds of poor countries that produce alluvial diamonds have been affected by armed conflicts. In Angola, diamond exploitation provided up to $3 billion in revenue to the UNITA rebel movement of Jonas Savimbi during the 1990s.[48] Similarly, the control of the most prolific diamond areas of Sierra Leone may have generated hundreds of millions of dollars for the Revolutionary United Front (RUF) rebel movement during the same period.[49] In eastern Democratic Republic of the Congo, several rebel factions operate as intermediaries for the control of the diamonds by Ugandan interests, while the government has granted the Zimbabwean military some of the best diamond concessions in return for its support. Small, low in weight, and easily concealable, as well as anonymous and internationally tradable, alluvial diamonds are not easily amenable to government control and border-crossing checks. Accordingly, diamonds also represent a "currency of choice" for money laundering and financing of clandestine activities, including those of Islamic terrorist groups such as al-Qaeda.[50] Like gold, diamonds also serve money-laundering purposes for criminal activities, including drug cartels. The low-tech exploitation of alluvial diamonds also facilitates illegal exploitation by networks of diggers, traders, and armed gangs, as well as colluding civilian and military authorities. Unsurprisingly, such a situation erodes the sovereignty and effective rule of states. In response, ruling elites have developed modes of appropriation detached from the legal and institutional apparatus of the state, often by creating parallel mechanisms of involvement and control in the private or informal diamonds sector. The RUF movement argued in its propaganda, "[W]hen a valuable gemstone is found [presidents] jump into a plane and shoot off to Europe to sell the diamonds trusting no one but themselves."[51]

To some extent, the geography of resources can influence the type of armed conflict and its viability. The argument is not that conflicts in oil-producing countries can only be secessions or coups d'état because oil is a point resource, but that resources provide a context for political mobilization as well as the strategy, tactics, and capabilities of belligerents. In other words, because conflicts may need to respond and adapt to the characteristics of available resources presented earlier (point versus diffuse resources and proximate versus distant resources), some types of conflicts are more likely than others (see Table 11.2).

Resources and Coups d'État

Because point resources are generally less lootable than diffuse resources and exploitation and trade often depend on international political recognition for mobilizing investors and accessing markets, they are much more accessible to governments than to rebel movements. In the case of high-investment energy and mineral sectors, only when staff or infrastructures are vulnerable to attacks, as with pipelines or railways, can rebels effectively extort them. In the absence of alternative sources of finance and a political basis for secession, the best option left to an armed opposition movement is to capture the state through a coup d'état in the capital city.

The conflicts between competing politicians in the Republic of the Congo (Brazzaville) in 1993–1994 and 1997, which took place in the context of a botched democratization, were clearly a contest for state power exacerbated by the control of an offshore oil sector that represented 85% of export earnings. The fact that these conflicts took the shape of coup attempts in the capital city was in this respect predictable, and the government of President Pascal Lissouba should have rapidly

TABLE 11.2 Relation between the characteristics of resources and types of conflict

Resource characteristics	Point	Diffuse
Proximate	State Control/coup d'état Algeria (gas) Congo-Brazzaville (oil) Colombia (oil) Iraq-Kuwait (oil) Yemen (oil)	Peasant/mass rebellion El Salvador (coffee) Guatemala (cropland) Mexico-Chiapas (cropland) Senegal-Mauritania (cropland)
Distant	Secession Angola/Cabinda (oil) Chechnya (oil) Indonesia/Aceh–East Timor–West Papua (oil, copper, gold) Morocco/Western Sahara (phosphate) Nigeria/Biafra (oil) Papua New Guinea/Bougainville (copper) Sudan (oil)	Warlordism Afghanistan (gems, timber) Angola (diamonds) Burma (timber) Cambodia (gems, timber) DR of the Congo (diamonds, gold) Liberia (timber, diamonds) Philippines (timber) Sierra Leone (diamonds)

won the war through its control of the oil rent and associated military power. However, the war in 1997 dragged on for five months before being brought to a conclusion in favor of former president Denis Nguesso by a regionalization of the conflict through military intervention of the Angolan government. An ally of Nguesso, the Angolan government was also eager to protect its oil-rich enclave of neighboring Cabinda, where secessionists, have opposed its rule since independence, and to prevent the use of the Congo as a trading platform for UNITA diamonds-for-arms deals. The stalemate in Brazzaville, which destroyed a large part of the capital and left thousands dead, resulted from several factors. First, a large part of the army did not engage in the conflict, while others supported Nguesso, their former patron and ethnic affiliate. Second, both contenders benefited from access to the oil rent, as Nguesso was allegedly favoured over Lissouba by the French oil company that dominated the sector and parallel channels supported Nguesso's arms purchases.[52] Finally, at the street level, the conflict rapidly changed in nature as the different militias supporting politicians benefited from the looting of the capital city. Urban youths on all sides used the political conflict to challenge the legitimacy of a corrupt political elite that had dominated and plundered the country for more than thirty years.[53] Looting became known as "killing the pig" or "taking a share in Nkossa."[54]

Resources and Warlordism

Diffuse resources are more easily exploited and marketed than point resources by illegal groups, especially if they are distant from the center of power. This is typically the case with alluvial diamonds or forests located along so-called porous border areas, hence their association with economically viable forms of warlordism. While rebel movements generally attempt to overthrow the incumbent regime, the existence of accessible (or "lootable") diffuse resources distant from the center of power can provide an economically viable fallback position in case of failure. Rebel groups thereby create areas of de facto sovereignty imposed through violence and defined by criminal and commercial opportunities such as mining areas, forests, or smuggling networks.

In Liberia, Charles Taylor's bid for power in 1989 first targeted the capital, Monrovia. Although he failed to capture the presidential palace because of the intervention of international troops, he nevertheless succeeded in establishing his rule over "Greater Liberia" and took control of lucrative sectors such as timber and rubber, as well as key infrastructure such as the port of Buchanan, which was crucial to iron ore exports.[55] Taylor did not limit his resource grab to Liberia, but extended it to neighboring Sierra Leone, where his support for the RUF provided him with access to diamonds. Similarly, the RUF was able to sustain a guerrilla war that essentially targeted the civilian population during the 1990s thanks to its control of diamond-mining areas as well as gold and cash crops. In the Philippines, the lucrative taxation of logging sustained many insurgent groups and transformed some from political opposition into self-interested groups.[56]

Resources and Secessions

Most secession attempts have a historical basis, but resource wealth offers a strong incentive for secession to local opposition movements. The location of key oil deposits among populations politically and economically marginalized by the central government, as in the case of the Shi'ias and Kurds in southern and northern Iraq, respectively, can be a powerful factor in domestic and regional politics. To access point resources that require large-scale investments, and in the absence of support from the central state, marginalized groups need to acquire sovereign rights over resources for themselves and are therefore more likely to engage in secessionism than warlordism or a coup d'état if they are unable or unwilling to gain control over the existing center of power. Although these valuable resources can prove difficult, if not impossible, to access through direct exploitation, theft, or extortion, their existence (or in some cases the "myth of easy riches" that they would provide to everyone) is a powerful tool for political justification and mobilization, and the prospect of future revenues is an additional source of motivation.

The economic and social changes associated with the development of Western Sahara's important phosphate industry, for example, laid "the basis for the rise of a modern nationalist movement, setting its sights on the creation of an independent nation-state."[57] As Saharawis recognized the prospect of an economically viable or even prosperous country, the simplistic assumption that Morocco aimed to capture their newfound mineral wealth served to mobilize armed resistance. Secessionist armed movements can also emerge around the socioenvironmental impact or wealth redistribution associated with the commercial development of resources. Secessionism in Aceh is historically rooted in the independent sultanate, which prevailed until the Dutch militarily defeated it in the late nineteenth century. Yet the formation of the Aceh Freedom Movement (GAM) coincided with the exploitation of major gas reserves in the early 1970s, and GAM's "Declaration of Independence" in 1976 specifically claimed that $15 billion in annual revenue was exclusively used for the benefit of "Javanese neo-colonialists."[58] Land expropriation and exploitation of other resources such as timber by Javanese-dominated businesses further exacerbated the conflict.

Similarly, the island of Bougainville has a history of separatism based on geographical and identity distinctiveness. Yet local politicians' demands for "special status," including favorable funding allocations during the period of transition to independence, clearly centered on the economic significance of the island's gold and copper mine in Panguna. The secessionist agenda set in 1989 by Francis Ona was related to the impact of copper mining, compensation, and closure of the mine, as well as a "Government of Papua New Guinea [that] is not run to safeguard our lives but rather to safeguard the few rich leaders and white men."[59] Ona, a former mine surveyor, is a local dweller but not a titleholder of the mining lease area. As such, he had little say in the allocation of the new trust fund set up in 1980 by the mine to compensate local communities. Although Ona's agenda "is most reasonably understood as part of his conflict with his own relatives in the kind of land dispute . . . characteristic of [local] Nasioi culture," his analysis nevertheless resonated throughout the local Nasioi community, especially after repression by governmental forces started.[60]

Resources and Peasant/Mass Rebellion

Diffuse resources that involve large numbers of producers are more likely to be associated with rioting in nearby centers of power, such as a provincial or national capital, and with support for peasant or mass rebellions that involve class or ethnicity issues. The displacement or exclusion of peasants by agribusinesses and poor labor conditions on large plantations have prompted political mobilization and the expansion of revolutionary struggles in Latin America and Southeast Asia. In Nicaragua, landlessness as well as neglect by the state and exclusion from or marginalization within local patron-client schemes provided fertile ground for peasant support for the Sandinista revolution. Yet the creation of state farms by the Sandinista regime, rather than the rapid provision of individual plots, reinforced the bonds between some landed patrons and their client peasants and rapidly increased their support for and participation in the U.S.-sponsored Contra movement.[61] In the context of democratization and an economic downturn precipitated by the fall of cacao prices and the liquidation of the commodity Stabilization Fund dictated by the International Monetary Fund (IMF) and the World Bank, the migrant labor issue associated with agriculture was repeatedly used for political gains in Côte D'Ivoire in the late 1990s. Although the media focused on coup attempts in the capital, migrant workers were also the targets of violence, including forced displacement.

Highly coercive forms of warlordism are less likely to be economically viable than participatory forms of rebellions because of the need to sustain a large volume of labor input and the difficulty of controlling workers over large areas. Conditions of slavery and control of labor can be imposed through hostage taking over short periods, but like most predatory economic activities, these cannot be sustained over the long term. Over time, to minimize grassroots challenges, the armed faction is likely to act as a protector toward local populations, even if it does so more in the sense of a Mafia group than a welfare state. The Revolutionary Armed Forces of Colombia (FARC), for instance, provides protection to peasants on land holdings and guarantees minimum prices for both coca and agricultural products.[62] While there has recently been a drift toward more criminal activities, FARC's maintenance of a balance of threats and economic incentives to sustain peasant productiveness has been key to the viability of the revolutionary movement since its inception in the 1950s. Similarly, the expansion of the New People's Army (NPA) in the Philippines in the 1970s and 1980s largely came from a symbiotic relation with a peasant population whose subsistence agriculture was threatened by agribusinesses, logging companies, and hydropower projects. The NPA provided an alternative to the regime of Ferdinand Marcos that had lost all legitimacy and even presence among rural communities. Yet both the FARC and the NPA secured most of their support and funding from taxation and extortion schemes that were related to drug trafficking and cattle ranches, and plantations, logging, and mining, respectively.

Resources and Foreign Interventions

Resources and foreign interventions occur in all types of armed conflicts detailed earlier and often involve indirect control over "strategic resources" such as oil or major mineral deposits and the protection of major commercial and strategic interests. The oil production of countries in the Persian Gulf is crucial to the international economy, and international and regional politics have been heavily influenced by questions of access to and control of this "black gold." This has been especially true of U.S. and British influence in the region, and although the "invasion" or "liberation" of Iraq by these two countries in 2003 should not be read through the simplistic perspective of a war for oil, regional petroleum resources represent a key motivating factor in terms of economic and national security.[63] Iraq contains the second-largest proven oil reserves in the world after Saudi Arabia, and among the cheapest to exploit, while its economic wealth could make it a potentially powerful enemy sheltered from the usual U.S. influence exercised through financial leverage via aid or market access or through international institutions such as the IMF. Similarly, the tacit U.S. support for a short-lived coup by business leaders and military officers against democratically elected President Hugo Chavez of Venezuala on April 12, 2002, demonstrated its distrust of the government regime of a key oil supplier.

Foreign intervention can also reflect vested commercial interests in a regional context, such as the invasion of Kuwait by Iraq, which was in part motivated by a dispute over the ownership of an oil field that straddles the two countries, or the presence and "self-financing" of Zimbabwean, Rwandan, and Ugandan troops in the Democratic Republic of the Congo in the late 1990s. External actors may also intervene in secessionist attempts by manipulating local political identities into providing access to resources. In the late nineteenth century, the discovery of gold and diamonds in the newly created Boer republics in South Africa led to both stronger resistance to annexation by Britain and a massive influx of British prospectors. The refusal of Boer authorities to grant political rights to these British *uitlanders* (outlanders) led British entrepreneurs such as De Beers's founder Cecil Rhodes to arm British settlers' militias and precipitated the Boer War.[64] Despite its political character, the Biafra secession in Nigeria and its repression by the government were largely motivated by local oil reserves. French oil interests supported the Biafra secession attempt, and the Nigerian army started fighting in July 1967 "more than a month after the declaration of independence but only days after Shell . . . agreed to pay its royalties to Biafra rather than Nigeria."[65] Within the turmoil of the Belgian Congo's independence, Anglo-Saxon and Belgian commercial interests eager to secure their hold on copper mines in the province of Katanga supported a secession led by Moise Tshombe that provoked military clashes between corporate-funded foreign mercenaries and UN troops who supported the unity of the country.[66] More recently, the de facto secession of eastern provinces in the Democratic Republic of the Congo since 1998 has been accompanied by a virulent debate over the inclusiveness of Congolese citizenship and the rights of populations from so-called Rwandan origins to access land and mineral resources.[67]

Influencing the Course and Duration of Armed Conflicts

The availability of resources and contests over their control influence conflicts in many ways. Natural resources can support the weaker party and allow it to continue fighting and to maintain access to a source of wealth, thereby prolonging the conflict. Furthermore, as profits take priority over politics, the conflict risks become increasingly commercially driven because the belligerents are correspondingly motivated by economic self-interest. These developments also have a significant impact on the organization and cohesion of armed movements and thereby on the course and duration of the conflict. It does not automatically follow, however, that a war would be shorter or have a more benign impact on populations in the absence of resources. Indeed, desperate belligerents who lack access to resources may well intensify predation and attacks on civilian populations.

As natural resources gain in financial importance for belligerents, the focus of military activities becomes centered on areas of economic significance. This has a critical impact on the location of military deployment and intensity of confrontations. As a complement to guerrilla strategies of high mobility, concentration of forces, and location along international borders, rebel groups seek to establish permanent strongholds or areas of "insecurity" wherever resources and transport routes are located. Government troops generally attempt to prevent this by extending counterinsurgency to these areas, and their efforts occasionally displace and "villagize" populations. In many cases, government troops join in the plunder. The overall effect of natural resources in such contexts is ambiguous, however. On one hand, resources can intensify confrontations over the areas of economic significance. This occurred in Sierra Leone over the best diamond areas and in Cambodia over log yards. On the other hand, armed groups can settle for a "comfortable stalemate" in which opposing parties can secure mutually beneficial deals to produce and market resources. Territorial control by different factions or the crossing of international borders often entails a complicity that is not expected from "enemies" or members of the international community that are implementing economic sanctions. In Cambodia, the Khmer Rouge rebel group indirectly benefited from export authorizations granted by the government to Thai companies that were operating in Khmer Rouge–held territories.[68] The rebel group also collected fees from logging companies licensed and taxed by the government. These fees were crucial to the viability of small Khmer Rouge groups far from their bases.[69] As both the government and the rebels benefited from logging, neither side had an incentive to change the status quo.

Beyond these financial and military effects, resources can also prolong conflicts by providing political networks of support, including "private resource diplomacy." In Angola, UNITA's diamonds not only allowed the rebel movement to buy arms, but also attracted diplomatic and logistical support from regional political leaders.[70] On the other side of that conflict, the Movimento Popular de Liberação de Angola (MPLA) rapidly gained favor with major Western powers and their oil companies once it was established that UNITA had lost the elections and was unable to gain power through military means. In Cambodia, the Khmer Rouge benefited from the support of corrupt Thai military or politicians who used logging revenues to finance their electoral campaigning.

Finally, resource wealth can prolong conflict by weakening the prospects for third-party peace brokerage. Access to resources can act as a divisive factor among international players. Bilateral actors are inclined to accommodate domestic interests in order to secure commercial benefits for their corporations, especially in strategic economic sectors like oil. In addition, the ability of the belligerents to draw on private financial flows decreases the potential leverage of multilateral agencies (e.g., the IMF, the World Bank, and the United Nations) that is exercised through grants and loans. In many contemporary armed conflicts, private capital inflows have assumed greater importance than foreign assistance, especially in comparison to conflicts in the Cold War era.

Although resource wealth tends to prolong wars, it can also shorten them in several ways. Resource wealth can produce an overwhelming concentration of revenues in one party, as oil did in the Angolan government. A government's greater access to resources can also motivate rebel groups to defect to the government, provide an incentive in peace negotiations, or lure rebel leaders to the capital. Agency problems and fragmentation can affect rebel movements as a result of "bottom-up" resource flows.[71] Unless the leadership is able to monopolize the means of exchange (e.g., vehicles, airports, roads, bank accounts, export authorizations, intermediaries, importers) between a resource supplier and its customers, economic space is available for its allies and subordinates to become autonomous through commercial or criminal activities based on local resources. The inherent risk of private appropriation can undermine trust between members of an armed group. More generally, this pattern of resource flow is likely to weaken discipline and chains of command. In contrast, when resources are fed into the conflict from outside—which tended to occur during the Cold War—leaders can maintain the coherence of their armed movements through the tight control of the flow of foreign resources to their allies and subordinates. Complicity in resource trade between "enemies" can also favor local peace agreements and defections. In Cambodia, a Khmer Rouge commander noted, "The big problem with getting our funding from business [rather than China] was to prevent an explosion of the movement because everybody likes to do business and soldiers risked doing more business than fighting."[72] In order to prevent such explosion, or fragmentation, the Khmer Rouge fully supported soldiers and their families and tightly controlled trade and cross-border movements.

Finally, an armed group that exploits natural resources is vulnerable to losing popular support and political legitimacy in the event that its adversary portrays the group as mere bandits or criminals driven more by economic self-interest than by political ideals. Ignoring similar "criminal" practices on the part of government officials or paramilitary groups thus facilitates in turn the sanctioning and political isolation of rebel movements like the RUF, UNITA, and the FARC. Such a policy can, of course, run the risk of marginalizing a political resolution of the conflict in favor of a military solution.

Conclusion

In the absence of strong preexisting institutions and a developed economy, a wealth of resources is likely to result in poor governance, economic crisis, and grievances from a population motivated by the high expectations associated with a resource bonanza. Although the resource curse is not inevitable, the availability of large resource rents tends to structure the choice of rulers and shape powerful coalitions of domestic elites and foreign business interests that dampen political accountability. In their quest for power, rulers often capture and redistribute resource rents at the expense of statecraft and democracy and thus dangerously put their discretionary power and fluctuating rents at the core of the political order. While a resource-rich economy is neither a necessary nor a sufficient condition for politically underdeveloped rule and resultant conflict, it can facilitate it.

The exploitation of resources itself also shapes conditions and motivations—for instance, the exacerbation of competitive politics and corruption, state institutional collapse, the delegitimization of the state monopoly on the use of force, and the rise of sectarianism—that are conducive to localized armed conflicts. In these contexts, violence often becomes the prime means of political action, economic accumulation, or simply survival. In these ways, wars cannot simply be related to the greed of rebels over resource grab opportunities. Yet as political instability escalates into full-scale armed conflict, natural resources often come to play a strategic role in motivating and financing belligerents both before a conflict begins and as it unfolds. Although there is no deterministic relationship, resources can participate in shaping the type of armed conflict that takes place, the territorial objectives of belligerents, their relations with populations, and the duration and the intensity of the conflict. Resources can also affect the internal cohesion of armed movements and occasionally lead to their fragmentation, as well as to instances of collusion between adversaries.

Because of their key role as intermediaries between places of resource extraction and markets, businesses often come to support autocratic regimes and even war criminals. In most cases, businesses seek to maintain a profitable and stable political order rather than to intervene in a democratization process that they are not legitimately or politically qualified to get involved in, even if many businesses would prefer a democratic regime with a strong rule of law. Wary of uncertainty, businesses are often distrustful of fledgling democratic regimes because they fear greater political instability, renegotiation of contracts (and possibly bribe payments), and violence that would threaten their investments. If strongly democratic regimes are more stable than autocratic regimes, the risk of instability and conflict is actually higher for formative democracies that are typical in regime-transition processes.[73] In the context of civil strife that was affecting the Niger Delta oil-producing region and in the wake of the execution of local activists by the Abacha regime, a Shell manager in Nigeria bluntly argued that "for a commercial company trying to make investments, you need a stable environment. Dictatorships can give you that."[74]

The problem, however, is that even autocracies have become increasingly unstable as a result of international and domestic pressure for democracy, transition to market economies that are competing on the world market, declining primary commodity prices, and decreasing international assistance. Since most resource-dependent states tend to be autocratic, it is therefore not surprising that, as a group, they are more susceptible to political instability. In turn, the political economy and territoriality of resource exploitation and trade come to define, in part, the geography of war.

Notes

1. Armed conflicts refer to the deployment of organized physical violence and include coups d'état, terrorism, and intra-or interstate armed conflict. The destructuration of many contemporary armed conflicts also results in a continuum between banditry, organized crime, and armed conflict. In this respect the criteria of annual number of battle deaths (e.g., 25 or 1,000) and of political motivation are not always helpful since the number of violent deaths can be higher in "peacetime" than in "wartime" (e.g., El Salvador, South Africa), and economic motives play a significant role.
2. For a more detailed analysis and examination of initiatives aimed at preventing or ending resource-fueled wars, see Le Billon, *Fuelling War*.
3. Gleick, "Environment and Security," 22.
4. Lesser, *Resources and Strategy*, 9.
5. Aron, *Peace and War*, 244–245.
6. Mackinder, "Geographical Pivot of History"; Ó Tuathail, *Critical Geopolitics*, 314.
7. Westing, *Global Resources and International Conflict*; Cutter, "Exploiting, Conserving, and Preserving Natural Resources."
8. Klare, *Resource Wars*, 10–25.
9. Brown, *Redefining National Security*; Mathews, "Redefining Security."
10. World Commission on Environment and Development, *Our Common Future*; Myers, *Ultimate Security*, 17–30.
11. On the concept of "human security," see Paris, "Human Security."
12. See Bennett, *Greenwar*; Baechler, "Why Environmental Transformation Causes Violence"; Suliman, *Ecology, Politics, and Violent Conflicts*; Homer-Dixon, *Environment, Scarcity, and Violence*.
13. Homer-Dixon, *Environment, Scarcity, and Violence*, 177.
14. André and Platteau, "Land Relations under Unbearable Stress."
15. McClintock, "Why Peasants Rebel."
16. Besteman and Cassanelli, *Struggle for Land in Southern Somalia*.
17. Boserup, *Conditions of Agricultural Growth*; Smith, *Scarcity and Growth Reconsidered*; Tiffen, Mortimore, and Gichuki, *More People, Less Erosion*; Leach and Mearns, *Lie of the Land*.
18. Homer-Dixon, *Environment, Scarcity, and Violence*, 44.
19. Dalby, *Environmental Security*; Jon Barnett, *Meaning of Environmental Security*; Gedicks, *Resource Rebels*; Peluso and Watts, *Violent Environments*, 30.
20. Annan, *Causes of Conflict*; Reno, *Warlord Politics and African States*.

21. Grossman, "General Equilibrium Model of Insurrections"; Keen, *Economic Functions of Violence in Civil Wars.*

22. Le Billon, "Political Ecology of War."

23. Collier, "Economic Causes of Civil Conflict"; Fairhead, "Conflict over Natural and Environmental Resources."

24. Presidential statement dated June 2, 2000 (S/PRST/2000/20), United Nations Security Council Presidential Statement, New York: United Nations Security Council.

25. Collier, "Economic Causes of Civil Conflict," 147. The data set includes fifty-two wars that took place between 1960 and 1999.

26. Collier, Hoeffler, and Söderbom, *On the Duration of Civil War*; Fearon, "Why Do Some Civil Wars Last So Much Longer Than Others?" 34. The data set includes 122 civil wars between 1945 and 1999.

27. Soysa, "Ecoviolence." The dataset includes conflicts with more than twenty-five battle deaths between 1989 and 2000.

28. Hauge and Ellingsen, "Beyond Environmental Scarcity."

29. Soysa, "Ecoviolence," 27.

30. In this chapter, however, "resource dependence" relates to the dependence situation of producing, rather than consuming, countries.

31. Carstens, *In the Company of Diamonds*; Hart, *Diamond.*

32. A discussion of the political-economic concept of "dependency" is beyond the scope of this chapter; for a discussion, see Hout, *Capitalism and the Third World.*

33. Karl, *Paradox of Plenty*; Auty, *Resource Abundance and Economic Development.*

34. Sachs and Warner, *Natural Resource Abundance and Economic Growth*; Leite and Weidmann, *Does Mother Nature Corrupt*; Soysa, "Ecoviolence"; Ross, *Extractive Sectors and the Poor.*

35. Moore, "Political Underdevelopment," 389.

36. Le Billon, "Buying Peace or Fuelling War."

37. On the case of Sierra Leone, see Reno, *Corruption and State Politics in Sierra Leone*; Richards, *Fighting for the Rain Forest.*

38. Taylor and Flint, *Political Geography*, 374.

39. Connell, "Panguna Mine Impact," 43.

40. Pile and Keith, "Introduction."

41. Scott, *Weapons of the Weak*; Cooke, "Vulnerability, Control, and Oil Palm in Sarawak."

42. Harvey, *Chiapas Rebellion.*

43. Watts, "Petro-violence."

44. Le Billon, "Political Ecology of War."

45. Le Billon, "Angola's Political Economy of War," 67.

46. Auty, *Resource Abundance and Economic Development*, 6.

47. Keen, *Economic Functions of Violence in Civil Wars*, 41.

48. Global Witness, *Rough Trade*, 4.

49. Smillie, Gberie, and Hazleton, *Heart of the Matter.*

50. Farah, "Al Qaeda Cash Tied to Diamond Trade," A01.

51. "Footpath to Democracy: Towards a New Sierra Leone." Revolutionary United Front.

52. Pourtier, "1997"; interview with Pascal Lissouba, London, January 2002. Because Nguesso controlled the north of the country, he could also have benefited from logging revenues of timber exports via Gabon and Cameroon (*La lettre du Continent*, January 13, 2000. Cited in "La Forêt Prise en Otage: La nécessité de contrôler les sociétíes forestières transnationales: une étude europééne," Cambridge; Forests Monitor, footnote 31).

53. Pourtier, "1997," 7.

54. Nkossa was the name of an oil field recently awarded to the French oil company Elf Aquitaine. Bazenguissa-Ganga, "Milices politiques dans les affrontements," 52.

55. Ellis, *Mask of Anarchy.*

56. Dañguilan-Vitug, *Politics of Logging.*

57. Hodges, *Western Sahara*, vii.

58. Nazaruddin, "Issues and Politics of Regionalism in Indonesia."

59. Cited in Connell, "Bougainville," 8. See also Boge, "Mining, Environmental Degradation, and War."

60. Claxton, "Bougainville, 1988–98."

61. Horton, *Peasants in Arms*, 155.

62. Labrousse, "Colombie-Pérou," 386.

63. Yergin, *Prize.*

64. Pakenham, *Boer War.*

65. Arbatov, "Oil as a Factor in Strategic Policy and Action," 34.

66. Balancie and La Grange, *Mondes Rebelles*, 446–448.

67. Interview with Professor Séverin Mugangu, Université Catholique de Bukavu, April 2002.

68. Le Billon, "Political Ecology of Transition."

69. Interviews with former Khmer Rouge soldiers and commanders, Pailin and Along Veng, January 2001.

70. United Nations, *Report of the Panel of Experts.*

71. On bottom-up violence, see Keen, *Economic Functions of Violence in Civil Wars.*

72. Interview with the author, Cambodia, January 2001.

73. Hegre et al., "Toward a Democratic Civil Peace?"

74. Hammer, "Nigeria Crude: A Hanged-Man and an Oil-Fouled Landscape," 58–69.

References

André, Catherine, and Jean-Philippe Platteau. "Land Relations under Unbearable Stress: Rwanda Caught in the Malthusian Trap." *Journal of Economic Behavior and Organization* 34 (1998): 69–115.

Annan, Kofi. *The Causes of Conflict and the Promotion of Durable Peace and Sustainable Development in Africa.* New York: United Nations, 1998.

Arbatov, Alexander A. "Oil as a Factor in Strategic Policy and Action: Past and Present." In *Global Resources and International Conflict: The Environmental Factors in Strategic Policy and Action*, ed. Arthur H. Westing, 21–37. Oxford: Oxford University Press, 1986.

Aron, Raymond. *Peace and War.* London: Weidenfeld and Nicolson, 1966.

Auty, Richard. "Natural Resources and Civil Strife: A Two-Stage Process." *Geopolitics*, 9 (2004): 29–49.

Auty, Richard M., ed. *Resource Abundance and Economic Development.* Oxford: Oxford University Press, 2001.

Baechler, Gunther. "Why Environmental Transformation Causes Violence: A Synthesis." *Environmental Change and Security Project Report* 4 (spring 1998). Washington, DC: The Woodrow Wilson Center, 24–44.

Balancie, Jean-Marie, and Arnaud de La Grange. *Mondes rebelles: Guerres civiles et violences politiques.* Paris: Michalon, 1999.

Barnett, Jon. *The Meaning of Environmental Security: Ecological Politics and Policy in the New Security Era.* London: Zed, 2001.

Bazenguissa-Ganga, Rémy. "Les Milices Politiques dans les affrontements." *Afrique Contemporaine* 186 (1998): 46–57.

Bennett, Olivia, ed. *Greenwar: Environment and Conflict.* London: Panos, 1991.

Besteman, Catherine, and Lee V. Cassanelli, eds. *The Struggle for Land in Southern Somalia: The War behind the War.* Boulder, CO: Westview, Press, 1996.

Boge, Volker. "Mining, Environmental Degradation, and War: The Bougainville Case." In *Ecology, Politics, and Violent Conflict*, ed. Mohamed Suliman, 211–228. London: Zed, 1999.

Boserup, Ester. *The Conditions of Agricultural Growth: The Economics of Agrarian Change under Population Pressure.* London: Allen and Unwin, 1965.

Brown, Lester R. *Redefining National Security.* Washington, DC: Worldwatch Institute, 1977.

Carstens, Peter. *In the Company of Diamonds: De Beers, Kleinzee, and the Control of a Town.* Athens: Ohio University Press, 2001.

Claxton, Karl. "Bougainville, 1988–98." *Canberra Papers on Strategy and Defence* 130 (1998).

Collier, Paul. "Economic Causes of Civil Conflict and Their Implications for Policy." In *Turbulent Peace: The Challenges of Managing International Conflict*, ed. Chester A. Crocker, Fen Osler Hampson, and Pamela Aall, 143–162. Washington, DC: United States Institute for Peace Press, 2001.

Collier, Paul, Anke Hoeffler, and Mans Söderbom. *On the Duration of Civil War.* World Bank Policy Working Paper 2861. 2001. Washington, DC: World Bank.

Connell, John. "The Panguna Mine Impact." In Bougainville: *Perspectives on a Crisis*, ed. Peter Polomka, 43–52. *Canberra Papers on Strategy and Defence* 66 (1990).

Cooke, Fadzilah Majid. "Vulnerability, Control, and Oil Palm in Sarawak: Globalization and a New Era?" *Development and Change* 33 (2002): 189–221.

Cutter, Susan L. "Exploiting, Conserving, and Preserving Natural Resources." In *Reordering the World: Geopolitical Perspectives on the Twenty-first Century*, 2nd ed., ed. George J. Demko and William B. Wood, 171–191. Boulder, CO: Westview, 1999.

Dalby, Simon. *Environmental Security.* Minneapolis: University of Minnesota Press, 2002.

Dañguilan-Vitug, Marites. *The Politics of Logging: Power from the Forest.* Manila: Philippine Center for Investigative Journalism, 1993.

Ellis, Stephen. *The Mask of Anarchy: The Destruction of Liberia and the Religious Dimension of an African Civil War.* London: Hurst, 1999.

Fairhead, James. "The Conflict over Natural and Environmental Resources." In *The Origins of Humanitarian Emergencies: War and Displacement in Developing* Countries, ed. E. Wayne Nafziger, Frances Stewart, and Raymo Vayrynen, 147–178. Oxford: Oxford University Press, 2000.

Farah, Douglas. "Al Qaeda Cash Tied to Diamond Trade." *Washington Post*, November 2, 2001, A01.

Fearon, James D. "Why Do Some Civil Wars Last So Much Longer Than Others?" Paper presented to the conference "Civil Wars and Post-conflict Transition," University of California, Irvine, May 18–20, 2001.

Gedicks, Al. *Resource Rebels: Native Challenges to Mining and Oil Corporations.* Cambridge, MA: South End, 2001.

Gleick, Peter H. "Environment and Security: The Clear Connections." *Bulletin of the Atomic Scientists* 47 (1991): 18–22.

Global Witness. A *Rough Trade: The Role of Companies and Governments in the Angolan Conflict.* London: Global Witness, 1998.

Grossman, Hershel I. "A General Equilibrium Model of Insurrections." *American Economic Review* 8 (September 1991): 912–921.

Hammer, Joshua. "Nigeria Crude: A Hanged-Man and an Oil-Fouled Landscape." *Harper's*, Vol. 292, Issue 1753.

Hart, Matthew. *Diamond : A Journey to the Heart of an Obsession*. New York: Walker, 2001.

Harvey, Neil. *The Chiapas Rebellion: The Struggle for Land and Democracy*. Durham, NC: Duke University Press, 1998.

Hauge, Wenge, and Tanya Ellingsen. "Beyond Environmental Scarcity: Causal Pathways to Conflict." *Journal of Peace Research* 35 (1998): 299–317.

Hegre, Håvard, Tanja Ellingsen, Scott G. Gates, and Nils Petter Gleditsch. "Toward a Democratic Civil Peace? Democracy, Political Change, and Civil War, 1816–1992." *American Political Science Review* 95 (2001): 33–48.

Hodges, Tony. *Western Sahara: The Roots of a Desert War*. Westport, CT: Lawrence Hill, 1983.

Homer-Dixon, Thomas. *Environment, Scarcity, and Violence*. Princeton, NJ: Princeton University Press, 1999.

Horton, Lynn. *Peasants in Arms: War and Peace in the Mountains of Nicaragua, 1979–1994*. Athens: Ohio Center for International Studies, 1998.

Hout, Wil. *Capitalism and the Third World: Development, Dependence, and World System*. Aldershot: Elgar, 1993.

Karl, Terry L. *The Paradox of Plenty: Oil Booms, Venezuela, and Other Petro-states*. Berkeley: University of California Press, 1997.

Keen, David. *The Economic Functions of Violence in Civil Wars*. Adelphi Paper 320. Oxford: Oxford University Press for the International Institute for Strategic Studies, 1998.

Klare, Michael T. *Resource Wars: The Changing Landscape of Global Conflict*. New York: Holt, 2001.

Labrousse, Alain. "Colombie-Pérou: Violence politique et logique criminelle." In *Economie des guerres civiles*, ed. François Jean and Jean-Christophe Rufin, 382–421. Paris: Hachette, 1996.

Leach, Melissa, and Robin Mearns, eds. *The Lie of the Land: Challenging Received Wisdom on the African Environment*. Oxford: James Currey, 1996.

Le Billon, Philippe. "The Political Ecology of Transition in Cambodia, 1989–1999: War, Peace, and Forest Exploitation." *Development and Change* 31 (2000): 785–805.

Le Billon, Philippe. "Angola's Political Economy of War: The Role of Oil and Diamonds, 1975–2000." *African Affairs* 100 (2001): 561–584.

Le Billon, Philippe. "The Political Ecology of War: Natural Resources and Armed Conflicts." *Political Geography* 20 (2001): 561–584.

Le Billon, Philippe. "Buying Peace or Fuelling War of Buying Peace: The Role of Corruption in Armed Conflict." *Journal of International Development* 15 (2003): 413–426.

Le Billon, Philippe. *Fuelling War: Natural Resources and Armed Conflicts*. Oxford: Oxford University Press/International Institute of Strategic Studies, 2003.

Leite, Carlos, and Jens Weidmann. *Does Mother Nature Corrupt? Natural Resources, Corruption, and Economic Growth. International Monetary Fund Working Paper WP/99/85*. 1999. Washington, DC: International Monetary Fund.

Lesser, Ian O. *Resources and Strategy: Vital Materials in International Conflicts, 1600–Present Day*. Basingstoke: Macmillan, 1989.

Mackinder, Halford. "The Geographical Pivot of History." *Geographical Journal* 23 (1904): 421–437.

Mathews, Jessica T. "Redefining Security." *Foreign Affairs* 68 (spring 1989): 162–177.

McClintock, Cynthia. "Why Peasants Rebel: The Case of Peru's Sendero Luminoso." *World Politics* 37 (1984): 48–84.

Moore, Michael. "Political Underdevelopment: What Causes Bad Governance?" *Public Management Review* 3 (2001): 385–418.

Myers, Norman. *Ultimate Security: The Environmental Basis of Political Stability*. New York: Norton, 1993.

Nazaruddin, Sjamsuddin. "Issues and Politics of Regionalism in Indonesia: Evaluating the Acehnese Experience." In *Armed Separatism in Southeast Asia*, ed. Joo-Jock Lim and Vani Shanmugaratnam, 111–128. Singapore: Institute of Southeast Asian Studies, 1984.

Ó Tuathail, Gearóid. *Critical Geopolitics: The Politics of Writing Global Space*. Minneapolis: University of Minnesota Press, 1996.

Pakenham, Thomas. *The Boer War*. London: Weidenfeld and Nicolson, [1979] 1997.

Paris, Roland. "Human Security: Paradigm Shift or Hot Air?" *International Security* 26 (2001): 87–102.

Peluso, Nancy L., and Michael Watts, eds. *Violent Environments*. Ithaca, NY: Cornell University Press, 2001.

Pile, Steve. "Introduction." In *Geographies of Resistance*, eds. Steve Pile and Michael Keith, 1–32. London: Routledge, 1997.

Pourtier, Roland. "1997: Les raisons d'une guerre 'Incivile.' " *Afrique Contemporaine* 186 (1998): 7–32.

Reno, William. *Corruption and State Politics in Sierra Leone*. Cambridge: Cambridge University Press, 1995.

Reno, William. *Warlord Politics and African States*. Boulder, CO: Lynne Rienner, 1998.

Revolutionary United Front. www.rufp.org/Documents/footpaths/footpaths.htm (accessed May 22, 2003).

Richards, Paul. *Fighting for the Rain Forest: War, Youth, and Resources in Sierra Leone*. Oxford: James Currey, 1996.

Ross, Michael L. *Extractive Sectors and the Poor*. Oxfam America Report. New York: Oxfam, 2001.

Sachs, Jeffrey D., and Andrew M. Warner. *Natural Resource Abundance and Economic Growth*. National Bureau of Economic Research Working Paper 5398. Cambridge, MA: National Bureau of Economic Research, 1995.

Scott, James C. *Weapons of the Weak: Everyday Forms of Peasant Resistance*. New Haven, CT: Yale University Press, 1985.

Smillie, Ian, Lansana Gberie, and Ralph Hazleton. *The Heart of the Matter: Sierra Leone, Diamonds, and Human Security*. Ottawa: Partnership Africa Canada, 2000.

Smith, V. Kerry, ed. *Scarcity and Growth Reconsidered*. Baltimore: Johns Hopkins University Press for Resources for the Future, 1979.

Soysa, Indra de. "Ecoviolence: Shrinking Pie, or Honey Pot?" *Global Environmental Politics* 2 (November 2002): 1–34.

Suliman, Mohamed, ed., *Ecology, Politics, and Violent Conflicts*. London: Zed, 1998.

Taylor, Peter J., and Colin Flint. *Political Geography: World-Economy, Nation-State, and Locality*. 4th ed. Harlow, UK: Prentice Hall, 2000.

Tiffen, Mary, Michael Mortimore, and Francis Gichuki. *More People, Less Erosion: Environmental Recovery in Kenya*. Chichester: Wiley, 1994.

Ullman, Richard H. "Redefining Security." *International Security* 8 (summer 1983): 129–153.

United Nations. *Report of the Panel of Experts on Violations of Security Council Sanctions against UNITA*. S/2000/203. New York: United Nations Secretariat, 2000.

Watts, Michael. "Petro-violence: Community, Extraction, and Political Ecology of a Mythic Commodity." In *Violent Environments*, ed. Nancy L. Peluso and Michael Watts, 189–212. Ithaca, NY: Cornell University Press, 2001.

Westing, Arthur H., ed. *Global Resources and International Conflict: Environmental Factors in Strategy Policy and Action*. Oxford: Oxford University Press, 1986.

World Commission on Environment and Development. *Our Common Future*. Oxford: Oxford University Press, 1987.

Yergin, Daniel. *The Prize: The Epic Quest for Oil, Money, and Power*. New York: Simon and Schuster, 1992.

MICHAEL K. STEINBERG AND KENT MATHEWSON

Landscapes of Drugs and War

Intersections of Political Ecology and Global Conflict

The maxim of the moment and for the new millennium (at least for now) is that "after 9/11 the world changed." Focused, amplified, and projected by the media, the September 2001 events have echoed with an apparent immensity and a rending of the global geopolitical fabric that merit comparison with Waterloo in June 1815 and Sarajevo in June 1914. In each case, an epoch is said to have ended, the first by conventional battle in concert with peace conventions that ended several decades of global conflict, the latter two with acts of terrorism that precipitated global wars of vastly differing intensities and probable durations. Each of these turning points in global history has, of course, its own character, dynamics, and contexts, which largely transcend the narrower episodes and scenes that constitute the intersections of drugs, war, and peace.

Nevertheless, one of the persistent and little-noticed elements in the history and geography of warfare during the past half millennium has been the role played by psychoactive substances. With the exception of the Sino-British Opium Wars (1830s–1840s), drugs as aids or obstacles, let alone causal factors, of war have been largely overlooked. Yet even a cursory overview, as presented here, should establish the contours of a topic that merits in-depth attention. Here we have only the space to point to some key instances and promising case studies. Future researchers may find these useful points of departure. The three pivotal events noted earlier, plus October 1492 as the antecedent and fourth key moment, mark a fivefold periodization that provides a convenient way of framing the differing historical relations between drugs and warfare.

Prior to Europe's transatlantic expansion and the coeval eruption of capitalism across the globe, the varying articulations between drugs and war were largely local, individual, and particular. With the rise of long-distance trade networks structured by mercantile capitalism, prime commodities such as sugar and tropical spices launched European-based empires and provoked wars from the East Indies to the West Indies, as well as points north and south. At the time of Columbus, tropical spices (mace, nutmeg, cinnamon, and so on) and cane sugars were elite luxuries, consumed conspicuously but also discretely—that is, as mild and solo psychoactive agents rather than admixed as condiments or food additives, as they commonly are today. Mintz and others have argued that sugar and tropical spices in the late Middle Ages and early modern period functioned more as drugs than as food.[1] The diversification and democratization of consumption of these substances came later, toward the end rather than the beginning of this era. In many ways, the half century of nearly continuous war that ended in the Peace of Vienna in 1815 was the culmination of three centuries of imperial conflict fueled at base by territorial rivalries. In turn, the commodities at the center of these battles over land and labor, more often than not, were "soft" psychoactives such as tropical spices, sugar, tobacco, tea, and coffee.

In the century after 1815, a rapidly industrializing Europe and its settler outposts (North America and Australasia) developed new forms of imperial expansion. These forms included using "hard" drugs (mainly opium) to dissolve the walls of sclerotic old empires such as Manchu China[2] and mass-produced alcohol, sugar, and tobacco products to further reduce indigenous populations or incorporate them into commodity exchange networks. At the same time, a number of new psychoactive drugs, both synthetic and derived from natural plant sources, were developed and marketed to colonial as well as metropolitan populations. These included opium derivatives such as morphine (1805) and heroin (1898), the coca derivative cocaine (1860), and synthetics such as barbiturates (1903). In addition, some traditional forms of drug use, long part of the cultural repertoire of particular colonial peoples, diffused through imperial pathways to new lands, including the metropoles. Cannabis and opium are the prime examples here, especially as mediated by the Indian, Arabic, and Chinese labor diasporas during the nineteenth century.[3] Except for local restrictions and censorious rhetoric from some quarters, drug use and commerce in both the imperial centers and their peripheries during the late nineteenth century and the first decade of the twentieth century enjoyed laissez-faire acceptance and even promotion.

The year 1914 not only signaled the start of World War I and the resulting circumstances that led to the emergence of the United States after World War II as the most recent candidate to become world imperial hegemon, but also saw the initiation of phase one of what some fifty years later would be dubbed "the War on Drugs." Although this chapter in the larger history of the rise of the United States of America as the world's solitary superpower has yet be written, it is clear that widening campaigns during the past century to control and suppress illicit drugs will serve as key benchmarks in this process. In 1914 the Harrison Narcotics Act brought cocaine and opiates under U.S. federal control. This act and the Hague Opium Conventions (1912, 1913) that precipitated it ushered in a new era in which psychoactive substances were increasingly prohibited or regulated by national governments rather than by local law or custom.[4] This was an abrupt reversal of attitudes and policies concerning drug use and regulation that had pertained until a few years before. In part it reflected the "progressivist" tendencies in the reform movement to moderate capitalism's unbridled excesses, but it also was a manifestation of deeper "moralistic" currents at work, especially illustrated by American society's willingness to conjoin fundamentalist religious convictions with moves to empower the state's increasing intrusion into private and personal affairs. Viewed at a distance, alcohol prohibition in the United States during the 1920s should not be seen as simply a failed experiment. Rather, it can be seen as phase two in what now seems to be an open-ended "War on Drugs." From the repeal of the Volstead Act in 1933 until the early 1970s (phase three), the "War on Drugs" was expanded to include new prohibited substances, primarily cannabis. However, with the explosion of new drug consumer enthusiasts during the 1960s, the state was largely put on the defensive and waged campaigns of local containment rather than a coordinated global war.

The official "War on Drugs" was decreed by Richard Nixon in 1971. Within three years the United States was mired in a recession that was sparked by price spiking and dependence on petroleum (functionally an addictive substance in current industrial societies) and stalled in a seemingly unwinnable war in Southeast Asia. Indeed, commentators at the time pointed to the escalating use of cannabis and opiates by U.S. troops as one of the obstacles to military success in Vietnam.[5] In this context the War on Drugs offered new opportunities for mobilizing resources and further militarizing domestic (local police) as well as overseas (Drug Enforcement Agency) security forces. At the outset, the War on Drugs may have seemed more rhetorical than real. During the past three decades (phase four) the successes or failures of the drug wars have been hotly debated. More certain, however, have been the gains the state at all levels has made in constructing arguments and infrastructure for a permanent war against drugs and their producers, distributors, and consumers.

The Carter administration of the late 1970s brought a brief respite and even reversed some drug policies and policing, but by the early 1980s the War on Drugs had been fully revived under the Reagan administration. Armed with antidrug slogans ("Just Say No") and pro-drug-enforcement deficit budgets ("Just Say Yes"), the Reaganites carried the battles to new levels and scales of intrigue and intervention. In many ways the antidrug campaigns of the Reagan and George H. W. Bush administrations provided research and development testing grounds and served as dress rehearsals for the coming global war on terrorism. At the scale of individuals, the high-tech tracking and low-tech capture or termination of Colombian drug lords such as Pablo Escobar prefigure the ongoing pursuit of al-Qaeda operatives and their allies. At the scale of sovereign states, the "pre-emptive" invasion of Panama to drug-bust its head, Manuel Noriega, is in many aspects the 2003 invasion of Iraq writ small. At the same time as these backyard maneuvers were being run, the intertwining of the international drug industry and terrorism at different scales was becoming more visible. Solid evidence emerged that linked the Colombian cocaine barons and the Contra terrorist networks. Similar, if somewhat less proven, links were exposed following the Iran-Contra ("arms for hostages") hearings. Hamas heroin and hashish exchanges were allegedly facilitated as part of the complex dealings that involved high-level officials in several governments. Drug policy, both internal and external, under the Clinton administration generally followed the course set by the previous Republican administrations, though in some aspects it was flexed in less muscular ways.

The world George W. Bush inherited has offered new opportunities, or necessities, depending on one's perspective, for merging the War on Drugs with a total war on terrorism. Prior to 9/11 both the Clinton and George W. Bush administrations had orchestrated and escalated U.S. involvement in Colombia's civil war through antidrug intervention to levels reminiscent of the Kennedy-era engagement in Vietnam. The events of 9/11 abruptly halted this momentum and seemingly put direct U.S. military intervention in Colombia on the back burner. The realities of Afghanistan with its own complex equations that combined drug production and commerce, civil war, and terrorist networks have apparently slowed or deflected the momentum of the overseas war on drugs, at least in that theater. Understandably, preserving a fragile peace in Afghanistan has taken precedence over ridding the region of opium production and trade. In the short term, the global war against terrorism has seemingly superseded the global campaign against drugs.

In the "peace" that follows the current Iraq War, one might predict that the two campaigns will become increasingly integrated and perhaps even merge. One can easily envision a united global war on drugs and terrorism. Mild efforts in this direction have already been test-marketed with television commercials that indict illicit drug consumers as active, if unwitting, supporters of terrorist drug networks. To better understand the links between drugs and war, and how the war on drugs and terrorism may be conjoined, the recent history of Afghanistan and Colombia offer prime case studies. Although these are the two places that have been most newsworthy in this regard in the past decade or so, other regions have experienced similar conditions, and still others offer the preconditions for future conjunctions of drug production and commerce, war and terrorism, and superpower interventions.

Drugs, Regional Conflicts, and U.S. Foreign Policy

The recent war in Afghanistan has briefly focused European and American attention on the plight of Afghan farmers, their involvement in the production of opium poppies, and how profits from poppy production have contributed to past and present conflicts in Afghanistan. One of the topics discussed by the media is how and why these farmers immediately returned to poppy farming after the Afghan Taliban government dissolved in the face of U.S. bombing and Northern Alliance territorial gains.[6] The reliance on poppies has not gone unnoticed by Western political leaders. Both British prime minister Tony Blair and U.S. president George W. Bush recently discussed the connection between political instability in Afghanistan and opium poppy production. Both have vowed to make postwar Afghanistan opium free, for it has become clear that opium production has fueled military conflicts in Afghanistan and elsewhere. However, dislodging this agricultural activity and the accompanying political instability it spawns presents many challenges for post-war Afghanistan and in other drug plant production landscapes. In order to understand why people grow drug plants, we must begin to understand the structural forces in place today and in the recent past that often leave farmers few other economic options. We must also recognize the prominent—some would say dominant—role played by the advanced industrial nations in creating these structures.

While opium in Afghanistan and coca in Colombia are now cited as underlying threats to U.S. national security that thereby require direct military action and assistance, in the past these plants have been quietly embraced and/or ignored by the U.S. government when they served the interests of Cold War allies. In some cases, U.S. policies during the past fifty years have directly influenced the creation or expansion of drug plant production landscapes in central and Southeast Asia and have also abetted the narcotics trade in Latin America.[7]

This seemingly contradictory relationship has been particularly evident during recent decades in Afghanistan and Pakistan, two of the focal states in the current U.S. "war on terrorism." There are two main phases of poppy production in recent Afghan history, the first during the war against the Soviet occupation (1978–1989) and the second in the post-Soviet era (1989–present), which has been a time of almost continuous civil war. During the first phase, direct U.S. military aid to the mujahideen was augmented by income from opium and heroin production and trade. This was well known to the U.S. government, but was largely ignored because of Cold War geopolitical goals. Similarly, the role of Pakistan's military and Inter-Service Intelligence (ISI) in facilitating this production and trade was well known.[8] According to former CIA director of Afghan operations Charles Cogan, "Our main mission was to do as much damage as possible to the Soviets. We really didn't have the resources or time to devote to an investigation of the drug trade. I don't think we need to apologize for this. Every situation has fallout . . . there was fallout in terms of drugs, yes. But the main objective was accomplished. The Soviets left Afghanistan."[9]

While opium cultivation has been a significant feature in the culture and cultural landscapes of both Afghanistan and Pakistan for centuries, if not millennia, production exploded during the Afghan-Soviet conflict. For example, in 1971, Pakistan produced ninety tons of opium, while during the next decade production increased tenfold.[10] This dramatic expansion would not have been possible without assistance from the Pakistani military and intelligence communities, which meant complicity by the CIA. By ignoring the rapid expansion of opium poppy production and heroin manufacturing in this region, the U.S. government helped create a landscape where poppies became established and relied upon. As war became endemic to the region, agricultural infrastructure such as irrigation works and orchards, some with centuries-old fixities, were destroyed. Opium poppies proved to be an ideal crop-substitution solution. Preadapted in many ways to the conditions brought on by war, they became further embedded in the rural landscape. In turn, opium commerce was further aided by tapping into the trade networks established by arms traders. As arms flowed into Afghanistan by way of Pakistan, opium and heroin flowed out via the same routes and merchants.

Throughout phase two, opium has remained a major funding source for warfare. During its war against the Northern Alliance, the Taliban collected an opium "tax" from poppy farmers to fill coffers after the rest of the world, with the exception of Pakistan and Saudi Arabia, severed economic and political ties. In early

2001 the Taliban accepted $40 million from the United States in exchange for halting opium poppy cultivation. In the short term this policy change was effective: opium production was reduced as much as 90% according to some estimates. Other observers have suggested that the hiatus simply allowed the Taliban to sell stockpiled opium at much more favorable prices. Moreover, after 9/11 the Taliban abandoned the prohibition, and plantings were again encouraged. In addition to the Taliban's taxing of opium to fund its operations, the Northern Alliance also participated in opium production and exports to fund its war efforts.[11] The defeat of the Taliban has had little effect on Afghan opium production and trade other than that there is no longer taxation and effective regulation by central authorities.

Although the Taliban was in part born of the larger currents that spawned militant Islamic fundamentalisms toward the end of the twentieth century, it was also very much the creation of the Pakistani ISI. With the backing of the CIA, the Taliban was originally designed to fight Communism, but like some designer drug confected in a laboratory, it proved more potent and dangerous than its makers originally intended. One must wonder whether, without the initial aid of the CIA and the financial windfall of opium poppy production, the Taliban would have ever made the U.S. evening newscasts. As the Soviet Union dissolved and the United States lost interest, income generated from opium production in Afghanistan replaced the military funding previously provided by the superpowers during the Cold War. Thus during the past thirty years opium poppies became the most reliable and profitable source of income in war-torn Afghanistan. As a result of the increased interdependence between poppies and war, Afghanistan has become the world's leading producer of opium.[12] The high rate of production has been interrupted because of the Taliban's ouster and the U.S. invasion. However, it appears that farmers have resumed planting opium poppies. This is unlikely to change in the foreseeable future given the unstable political, environmental, and economic atmosphere, which makes conditions right for continued opium production and volatility in Afghanistan.

Parallel Cases

Aspects of the Afghan case can be found in other countries, though none exhibits the complex relationships between governmental entities, war and insurgency, and drug production and trade quite as openly or as deeply rooted.[13] At various times in the past several decades Burma, Vietnam, and Laos in Southeast Asia and Colombia, Peru, and Nicaragua in Latin America have all shared conditions of civil war and insurgency fueled in part by drug production and trade. Among these countries, there are several prominent examples wherein U.S. policies both directly and indirectly aided and abetted drug plant production.

First, after the Chinese Communists defeated the Nationalists in 1949, thousands of Nationalist troops fled to the Shan Plateau in northern Burma. In an effort to destabilize and possibly topple the Communists, President Truman ordered the CIA to arm and train these troops for future incursions into China. As in present-day Afghanistan, these troops soon turned to opium production to financially enhance their operations.[14] The incursions into China failed miserably in 1950 and 1951, which caused the CIA to withdraw support. The Burmese military later expelled the Nationalist troops in 1961. From Burma, the Nationalists moved to Thailand, where they re-created their opium kingdom in collusion with Thai military officials (also U.S. allies). Remnant Nationalist forces controlled the opium trade in this region into the 1980s. This connection between opium, armaments, and warfare in northern Burma and later Thailand laid the foundation for the development of the famed Golden Triangle region. This area, along with Afganistan, has been responsible for a majority of the world's opium and heroin production since the 1960s. For example, opium production increased on the Shan Plateau from 18 tons in 1958 to between 400 and 600 tons in 1970.[15] This region remains a hotbed of violent ethnic, opium-financed conflict today, especially in Myanmar, where various ethnic groups and the Myanmar government have relied almost exclusively on opium production to fuel their military efforts.[16]

Another example of the connection between U.S. policy and opium production was seen in Laos and Vietnam during the Vietnam War years (mainly the 1960s). The CIA enabled local allies such as the Hmong hill tribes to expand their traditional opium cultivation and export it to fund military efforts against the Laotian and North Vietnamese Communist forces.[17] These Hmong paramilitary forces not only fought Communist forces, but also provided intelligence and rescued downed U.S. airmen. In exchange for their assistance, the CIA granted Royal Laotian Army officer Vang Pao (an ethnic Hmong) broad powers over the Hmong ethnic homeland in northern Laos, including control of airspace. Pao controlled everything that entered and left the region, including opium and heroin.[18] This assistance is one of the most explicit examples of ill-conceived policies with regard to the drug trade. In Laos, CIA planes dubbed "Air America" were actually used to carry heroin to outlets in South Vietnam where it was then sold to U.S. troops. Again, the CIA perceived this as collateral damage and did nothing to stop the trade. According to the CIA inspector general, "The past involvement of many of these officers in drugs is well known, yet their goodwill . . . considerably facilitates the military activities of the Agency supported irregulars."[19] As the United States began to withdraw from Indochina, the Hmong suffered extensive casualties at the hands of the victorious Communist forces.[20] As in Afghanistan, the U.S. government helped to create landscapes of drug production and networks of drug distribution in Southeast Asia through its imperial war policies.

Latin America also provides examples of the connection between drugs, war, and U.S. foreign policy. For example, during the Contra War in Nicaragua in the early 1980s, U.S. intelligence officials were aware that certain Contra leaders profited from Colombian drug interests by allowing drug couriers to use their air bases in Central America en route to the United States. Allegations were later made that the CIA knowingly allowed cocaine to enter the United States to be distributed in inner-city neighborhoods via Contra allies and officials who lived in the United States, particularly in Los Angeles. While no "smoking guns" were found that implicated the CIA in such a conspiracy, CIA officials did admit that they knew that some Contra leaders had been helping cocaine reach U.S. territory.[21] Again, as in the aforementioned countries, the CIA simply ignored the fact that groups the United States largely created and supported were breaking U.S. and international law.

In present day Colombia, the Marxist opposition group, Fuerzas Armadas Revolucionarias de Colombia (FARC) largely funds its military operations with profits from coca grown and processed within its territory. As a result, in Colombia today, unlike the previous examples, drug plants have become the enemy of the United States because they fund operations of forces that oppose U.S. allies (the Colombian government). In Colombia, what was once considered "fallout" (drug plants) in other parts of the world has become reason enough to commit billions of dollars of military aid and U.S. military personnel. In addition to FARC, paramilitary groups with ties to the Colombian military have also begun to actively profit from the drug trade that originates in their territory. As a result, the war on drugs is now being co-opted by the military, as is indicated by "Plan Columbia," a multibillion-dollar military aid package that fights both guerrillas and drugs. Because of this co-option, the U.S. military and CIA continue to benefit from drug plant production, albeit indirectly, through increased budgets and greater political influence in Washington. For example, in a *New York Times* story (January 24, 2002), the Pentagon was seeking a $48-billion or more increase in its 2003 budget. Recent events in Afghanistan and Colombia have given the Pentagon confidence that greater support can now be found in the U.S. Congress. Again, these two conflicts have been partially fueled by drug plants.

Competitive Advantages of Drug Plants

The political and military activities described in the preceding sections must be considered at the scale of the farm. In other words, how do the conditions described earlier impact decision making at the farm level? Warfare does not create a secure atmosphere in any setting, but especially not in agrarian landscapes where farmers obviously need time to reap the benefits of their labor. Therefore, in insecure environments, rational farmers will likely choose crops that produce the greatest return in the shortest amount of time, crops that require the fewest inputs, and crops that have consistent demand even in volatile times. Farmers who grow drug plants are not necessarily greedy, for they are rarely the individuals who make great profits from the drug trades commodity chain. For example, a 2001 United Nations report found that Afghan opium farmers earned less than 1% of the profit by the time their commodity reached the streets of Europe.[22] Thus portrayals of Afghan farmers by the media as greedy individuals are largely inaccurate. Instead, in volatile landscapes, drug plants often offer the only manner to make any money in an increasingly cash-dependent global economy.

In Afghanistan, for example, opium poppy farming became the economic mainstay as a result of the unstable social, political, and economic conditions during the past two decades. The same can be said for coca farming in various parts of the foothills in Andean South America. Afghan farmers rushed to sow the seeds of this crop literally days after the Taliban ban on opium production dissolved as a result of its rapidly declining power.

But why have farmers returned to this dangerous harvest? Most drug plants, opium poppies in particular, hold competitive advantages over traditional licit export crops. First, the opium poppy is a hardy plant, able to grow at elevations from tropical lowlands to temperate mountain environments. While the poppy is adaptable, it thrives in temperate montane conditions.[23] Afghanistan's physical terrain is dominated by mountainous landscapes in the northern two-thirds of its territory and provides endless environments suitable for poppy farming. Second, while many crops require specific rainfall and temperature regimes in order to be productive, the opium poppy grows in conditions that range from humid to desert and tropical to subalpine. Given that much of Afghanistan is desert or semiarid, the poppy again finds expanses of suitable habitat. This has been especially important in recent years because Afghanistan is in the midst of a severe, multiyear drought that has left a trail of agricultural destruction in its wake as less tolerant crops, such as wheat, have withered. This adaptability is a key factor in understanding why the opium poppy is now growing in states ranging from Afghanistan to Mexico. Also, unlike other crops such as mangoes, sugar cane, or cut flowers—crops often introduced in drug-replacement development projects—opium produced from poppies is largely nonperishable and concentrated, and is thus relatively easy to store, hide, and export. Unlike typical export crops, many of which are damaged or destroyed en route to the market, opium and heroin are rarely damaged in transit. In other words, unlike licit products produced in the Third World such as bananas, opium and heroin never bruise and rarely spoil.

Another advantage that poppies present is that they can be grown in various soil types (even soils considered poor for other crops) and can be grown continuously for many years. Westermeyer reports that in Laos, poppies have been grown in the same fields for up to twenty years.[24] In this respect, poppies are far superior to typical swidden crops such as maize or dryland rice. Similarly, coca is a shrub whose leaves can be harvested throughout the year and year after year, unlike most other licit crops supported in development efforts. Lastly, many drug plants, such as opium poppies and coca, are well known to local populations because they have been propagated for centuries. This deep ethnobotanical relationship is important for two reasons. First, simply stated, unlike many crops introduced by transient development organizations, local people know how to grow the plant. This is especially important in politically unstable, impoverished areas where individuals likely cannot afford or do not have access to inputs such as pesticides and fertilizers for introduced crops. Also, the margin between life and death is often quite narrow in places such as Afghanistan during times of turmoil; therefore, farmers are unlikely to experiment with a new crop with which they are unfamiliar. Second, the plant is culturally acceptable to local peoples. Opium poppies in much of Asia and coca in Andean South America are not perceived in the same manner as they are portrayed in U.S. antidrug campaigns. While peasant farmers may be aware that these plants are later turned into dangerous substances, the plant itself has such a long cultural and ecological history among local folk that it is considered part of the cultural and ecological core.[25] Thus when drug plants are targeted by interdiction authorities, they often become powerful symbols of resistance or, as Scott described them, "weapons of the weak."[26] This symbol of resistance can be witnessed today in Bolivia, where members of the coca growers' union routinely block highways and clash with police.

Combine these characteristics of the poppy (and similar characteristics of coca) with the unstable political, economic, and environmental conditions in Afghanistan as well as Colombia, Myanmar, and Peru, and an opium- and coca-free future becomes doubtful. This, in turn, likely means a politically unstable future in these states as well.

Marginalized Peasant Farmers

The marginalization of peasant farmers is another reason behind the development and expansion of drug plant producers. For example, economically, Afghanistan has endured decades of "scorched-earth" warfare that has left little in the way of infrastructure for farmers to get licit produce to markets. Again, opium overcomes this problem. Given opium's consistently high demand and price, farmers rarely have to leave their villages to find buyers. International drug cartels send emissaries to villages to buy the crop on site or simply have a standing agreement that all opium produced will be purchased. This relationship is not limited to Afghanistan. Similar arrangements exist between marijuana farmers and market contacts in southern Belize.[27] In this landscape, the powers behind the marijuana economy provided farmers with all necessary inputs (seeds, fertilizer, trucks, and so on) and paid cash directly to the farmer in his village when the crop was harvested, thereby eliminating farmers' potential expenses in getting their crop to a market or buyer.

Second, prices for commodities introduced as replacements for drug plants often fluctuate wildly with the whims of global consumers. Demand for commodities such as coffee and bananas are more elastic than prices for poppies or coca. In other words, while consumers of bananas may find alternative products if price increases dramatically, cocaine addicts are more loyal to their product. Certainly addicts will seek out alternates eventually; however, their addiction makes them more loyal consumers in a pure sense of the definition. While tens of millions of consumers worldwide are habituated to these stimulants, their addictive powers are clearly not as great as opium's or coca's refinements. The current situation in Peru provides an excellent example. With financial assistance from the United States, coffee was expanded as part of a coca crop replacement strategy in the 1990s that was coupled with increased criminalization of coca. Peru's coca crop dropped by two-thirds in the 1990s. However, it now appears that farmers are returning to coca because prices for coffee continue to decline to historic lows.[28] At the same time, prices paid for coca leaves have dramatically increased from $8 per twenty-five pounds in 1997 to $40 in 2002.[29] Expanding coca fields in Peru have corresponded with increased activity by remnants of the Maoist rebel group Sendero Luminoso (Shining Path).

The role of population pressure is another factor that influences decision making in peasant agricultural landscapes. Increasing pressure on available land resources has forced peasant farmers to seek crops that produce greater returns from smaller plots of land. In Guatemala, for instance, the population increased from five million in 1950 to twelve million in 2000. This growth is especially important in the already poverty-stricken western highlands. In 1979, 88% of Guatemala's farms were considered too small to provide for a typical family, while between 1964 and 1979, there was a 60 % increase in the number of farms smaller than 3.5 hectares.[30] Certainly the maldistribution of land resources contributes to this pressure, but population growth has nonetheless dramatically increased pressure on what land is available to smallholders. When land is subdivided as it passes to the next generation, farmers must seek alternative sources of income. In Guatemala, many end up working on distant plantations, but poppies help solve some farmers' dilemma because more money can be earned from small plots of poppies than from any other crop presently grown. Poppy production in Guatemala is presently small, but the potential for increased future production exists. Obviously, population growth alone will not drive farmers to grow drug plants, but in the future it will likely play an important role in certain states.

Next, indigenous and ethnic-minority cultural landscapes, which often overlap with drug plant production hearths, exist on the margins of national economies, with few opportunities beyond semisubsistence agriculture, low-wage labor on commercial agricultural plantations (many of which have laid claim to the most productive agricultural lands), or participation in sporadic boom-and-bust economic opportunities. However, while continuing to exist on the economic margins of national economies, most indigenous groups are increasingly dependent on cash incomes and incorporated into market economies as neoliberal economic policies impact formerly remote subsistence landscapes. Thus drug plant production is well suited to become an increasingly important economic activity. For example, the Golden Triangle is home to many hill tribes long discriminated against by the nationally dominant cultures in Myanmar and Thailand, while in Central America, marijuana and poppy production are found in remote Maya landscapes, the same landscapes in Guatemala where the government carried out genocidal military actions in the 1980s, and where abject poverty dominates.[31] Certainly the fact that these areas are remote facilitates the development of drug production. At the same time, remoteness frustrates other forms of development. Development efforts that are initiated within ethnic-minority and indigenous cultural landscapes are often ephemeral and generally lack consideration of local cultural and ecological traditions. Moreover, many of these development projects are promoted by foreign missionaries whose main objective is the obliteration of local cultural and ecological practices and beliefs.[32]

The Maya landscape in southern Belize, a major marijuana production zone in the 1980s, serves as an important example of how these conditions marginalize peasant farmers and draw them into the drug plant production commodity chain. The Maya landscape is home to many examples of past failed cooperatives and other agricultural modernization efforts.[33] Previous efforts that focused on honey, hogs, maize, rice, and beans failed to find the rare combination (rare in many rural tropical landscapes) of consistently high productivity, high demand, high commodity prices, and easy access to markets. Marijuana contained all of these characteristics and was thus very attractive to farmers who had seen development efforts fail many times in the past due to poor planning, lack of research, or many other factors that help determine success or failure in agricultural development economics.[34]

Marijuana was perceived by Maya farmers as a "get-rich-quick"-type product, unlike any other crop grown in the area. As a result, by the middle of the 1980s, Belize annually produced around 1,300 tons of marijuana, which made it the fifth-largest producer in the world at the time.[35] This is an astounding figure given that the total population of the country at that time was no more than 150,000 people overall. Thus by per capita measures, Belize was the largest producer of marijuana in the world. The amount is significant because the marijuana crop was not grown on large plantation-scale levels or controlled by a few families or commercial interests. Instead, smallholder farmers were growing almost all of this tonnage in rural Belize (regions of the country other than the Maya south contributed significant amounts, with the northern region along the Mexican border leading the way). The small overall population of Belize, coupled with the large amount of marijuana being produced, indicates the importance and popularity of marijuana among Belizean farmers in the 1980s.

This boom economy based on marijuana eventually turned bust when the United States sponsored a campaign of aerial spraying of marijuana that was intercropped with maize, the staple food crop, and a dramatic increase in arrests, fines, and prison terms for producers. However, it continues to be grown on a small scale, and farmers express interest in participating in its resurgence if they are given the opportunity because they again have few opportunities to earn cash incomes within their villages.

Smallholder farmers are rational actors in selecting where they invest labor and other inputs such as fertilizer. Given that few commodities in southern Belize and elsewhere could and can compete with the consistent income earned from marijuana or other drug plants in many Third World landscapes, it is not surprising that many smallholder farmers embrace illegal commodities. Also, many indigenous and ethnic minority groups are politically marginalized as well; thus by growing drug plants they are tapping into the only available economic and political structure present, albeit an illicit one. This conflict strikes at the heart of present-day development policies. On one hand, national governments, international development agencies, and international trade agreements emphasize "global" markets and free trade zones, yet in many Third World indigenous and ethnic minority landscapes, these agreements and policies are postmodern in that present-day farmers have little ability to compete and earn a living wage in the new global economy.

Drugs, Peasant Farmers, and Cultural-Political Ecology

One way to view peasant drug plant production is from a cultural-political ecological perspective. At base, cultural ecology seeks to examine the adaptive processes by which societies adjust through subsistence practices to the local environment.[36] Adaptive change usually occurs under conditions of stress or disequilibrium such as those posed by climatic, demographic, and other disruptions, including conflict, especially warfare. Therefore, farmers who grow drug plants are doing exactly what actors in landscapes that are unstable or present few economic alternatives should do—growing adaptable crops with a consistent demand. These actors are responding to global structures and demands as well as local environmental, political, and economic conditions. Just as opium poppies are the perfect commodity in many ways, poppy farmers are the perfect capitalists, given the current global economic structures and farm-level conditions in states such as Afghanistan and Colombia.

Yet even as the United States and its counterparts promote global neoliberal capitalist development in far-flung corners of the globe, and peasant farmers successfully adapt to these policies, albeit illicitly, the United States targets small-scale actors within this arena even though these individuals are maneuvering within this global system in the only means available. These policies, in turn, further marginalize peasant farmers and deepen poverty, which only expands the conditions that draw farmers into this dangerous harvest. Instead, the advanced industrial nations should ask how they can help peasant farmers adapt to and compete in a mushrooming global marketplace.

Drug Wars without End?

Peasant farmers produce drug plants due to a combination of past and present macrolevel structures and political policies and farm-level adaptive strategies. Will these macro and micro factors continue to draw more farmers to this dangerous harvest in the future? The answer appears to be yes, given current global trends. For example, the world's supply of opium has steadily increased during the past several decades, from 1,200 tons in 1971 to 6,100 tons in 1999.[37] Production has increased for several reasons. First, political instability, a key factor in creating the right microlevel conditions for drug plant production, appears to be increasing around the globe. The end of the Cold War has not brought about global peace, but has instead unleashed or intensified numerous ethnic and culture-based civil wars, especially religious ones, in many regions, including sub-saharan Africa, the Balkans, central Asia, Southeast Asia, and some parts of Latin America. These conflicts create instability, which lends itself to illicit activities such as drug production and commerce. Some actors within these conflicts, such as ones in Afghanistan and Colombia, have turned to drug plants as funding sources for their political and military operations, and this has further embedded them in the local landscape.[38]

United States foreign policy planners have apparently not learned a great deal from past decisions that led to the creation or expansion of drug plant production landscapes. The United States is once again involved militarily in Afghanistan and is arming and aiding groups who presently benefit and in the recent past benefited from opium production. United States involvement in Afghanistan has forced the United States to embrace neighboring central Asian states that are involved in the illegal drug trade, while in Colombia, U.S. attempts to destroy the coca crop essentially drive up coca leaf prices and stimulate the expansion of coca production in other geographic locations such as Peru, where the Shining Path appears to be reorganizing with financial support from increased coca production.[39] Similarly, in Afghanistan, the recent war and its disruption of opium poppy planting have driven global heroin prices up, which has stimulated expanded poppy planting in Thailand and Myanmar's Golden Triangle.[40]

At the same time as coca and opium poppy plantings expand and contract according to market demand and efforts at suppression, the illicit manufacture of cocaine and heroin on massive scales has paved the way for product diversification. With well-established laboratories, workforces, and distribution networks, it is not surprising that new products and markets are being developed. For example, during the past decade or so heroin labs in the Golden Triangle have also been producing methamphetamines derived from wild ephedra gathered in China's Yunan Province. This relatively new product has been embraced by many sectors of Southeast Asian societies, often for utilitarian purposes such as enabling truck drivers or factory workers to labor longer hours. The widespread and surging use of this substance has alarmed many local authorities. Thailand has embarked on a highly controversial campaign of eradicating methamphetamine dealers (and sometimes users as well). Anyone implicated or caught trafficking in *yaa baa* (the local name for methamphetamine) is being summarily executed by local authorities. Despite the outcry from human rights advocates, as of early April 2001, 2,000 alleged dealers had been summarily dispatched.[41] Another 40,000 persons were said to be on the government's surveillance lists. Whether it is anticipating or echoing the U.S. doctrine of "the right of preemptive war" to fight international terrorism, the Thai government is eschewing international norms in its internal war against drugs. One might predict that this kind of behavior will become more widespread, if not generally accepted, as the boundaries between the global war on terrorism and local wars on drugs become ever more blurred.

The intersections of drugs and warfare have a long and complex history. We have focused on just a few of their current manifestations, especially those that involve peasant producers in a few well-documented regions. A more complete accounting of the contemporary picture would include the use of various drugs as battle aids. At one end of this continuum, one finds that many of the child soldiers impressed into West Africa's ongoing serial civil wars are plied with drugs, especially amphetamines or cocaine and alcohol, and are forced to commit their atrocities. At the other end, amphetamines were the apparent cause of the recent U.S. "accidental" high-tech bombing of Canadian peacekeepers in Afghanistan. Various psychoactive substances, including tobacco, caffeine (in coffee, tea, chocolate, and cola drinks), and amphetamines as stimulants and opiates and many related synthetics as painkillers, are indispensable aids to modern warfare. Although alcohol was undoubtedly a common lubricant in premodern warfare, it is also reputed that hallucinogens such as *Amanita muscaria* mushrooms (in Viking berserker maneuvers) or hashish (in certain Islamic assassination corps) were part of the combat tool kit in some warrior traditions. Beyond the generalized use of psychoactive drugs by individual combatants in many, if not all, modern wars, since the 1960s there have been some attempts (in Vietnam and Bosnia most demonstrably) at using drugs such as "BZ" gas (an atropine-like agent) as offensive chemical agents to derange and incapacitate enemy soldiers on the battlefield.

Although the use of "nonlethal" chemical agents as weapons of war runs counter to current proscriptions against chemical warfare in general, this is a wide-open frontier that will no doubt invite future experimentation.

Just as the abolition of war in our times is (unfortunately) a chimera, it is illusionary to believe that drug plants will be completely eradicated. At present, the demand for derivatives such as heroin and cocaine is too strong to eliminate. However, helping create an atmosphere where peasant farming families feel secure about their future can reduce the scale of destructiveness of this commodity on the production end. This will not be accomplished by military action, coercion, or criminalization. Instead, the voices of peasant producers must be heard to learn why they grow the crops, to hear their critiques of existing alternative development projects, and to permit them to articulate their own versions of what alternatives they think would succeed.[42] These insights will help reduce the flow of drugs from current production centers in ways that are less costly in human suffering and environmental degradation than the means currently employed.

Notes

1. Mintz, *Sweetness and Power*; Schivelbusch, *Tastes of Paradise*; Courtwright, *Forces of Habit*.
2. Brook and Wakabayashi, *Opium Regimes*.
3. Rubin, *Cannabis and Culture*.
4. Walker, *Opium and Foreign Policy*.
5. McCoy, *Politics of Heroin*.
6. Baldauf, "Afghan Poppies May Bloom Again," 1.
7. Rupert and Coll, "U.S. Declines to Probe Afghan Drug Trade"; Lintner, *Burma in Revolt*; McCoy, "Mission Myopia"; Goodson, *Afghanistan's Endless War*.
8. McCoy, "Mission Myopia."
9. Ibid., 132.
10. Ibid.
11. Goodson, *Afghanistan's Endless War*.
12. Ibid.
13. McCoy, "Lord of Drug Lords"; Steinberg, "Generals, Guerillas, Drugs, and Third World War-Making."
14. Lintner, *Burma in Revolt*.
15. McCoy, "Lord of Drug Lords"; McCoy, "Mission Myopia."
16. Lintner, *Burma in Revolt*; Renard, *Burmese Connection*; McCoy, *Politics of Heroin*; Meyer and Parssinen, *Webs of Smoke*.
17. Conboy and Morrison, *Shadow War*; McCoy, *Politics of Heroin*.
18. McCoy, "Lord of Drug Lords."
19. McCoy, "Mission Myopia," 123.
20. Hamilton-Merritt, *Tragic Mountains*.
21. G. Webb, *Dark Alliance*.
22. McCoy, "Stimulus of Prohibition."
23. Booth, *Opium*.
24. Westermeyer, "Opium and the People of Laos," 115–132.
25. Gade, *Nature and Culture in the Andes*.
26. Scott, *Weapons of the Weak*.

27. Steinberg, "Marijuana Milpa."
28. Krauss, "Desperate Farmers Imperil Peru's Fight on Coca"; Forero, "Farmers in Peru Are Turning Again to Coca Crop."
29. Forero, "Farmers in Peru Are Turning Again to Coca Crop."
30. Stoll, *Between Two Armies*, 225–226.
31. Lovell, *Beauty That Hurts*.
32. Steinberg, "Political Ecology, Cultural Change, and Their Impact."
33. Wilk, *Household Ecology*.
34. Steinberg, "Marijuana Milpa."
35. Taswell, "Marijuana," 5.
36. Steward, *Theory of Culture Change*,
37. McCoy, "Stimulus of Prohibition," 24.
38. Steinberg, "Generals, Guerillas, Drugs, and Third World War-Making."
39. Forero, "Farmers in Peru Are Turning Again to Coca Crop."
40. Reuters, "Afghan War Hikes Thai, Myanmar Opium Production."
41. Ibid.
42. Hobbs, "Troubling Fields."

References

Baldauf, S. "Afghan Poppies May Bloom Again." *Christian Science Monitor*, November 23, 2001, 1.

Booth, M. *Opium: A History*. New York: St. Martin's Press, 1998.

Brook, T., and B. Tadashi Wakabayashi, eds. *Opium Regimes: China, Britain, and Japan, 1839–1952*. Berkeley: University of California Press, 2000.

Conboy, K., and J. Morrison. *Shadow War: The CIA's Secret War in Laos*. New York: Palidan Press, 1995.

Courtwright, D. T. *Forces of Habit: Drugs and the Making of the Modern World*. Cambridge, MA: Harvard University Press, 2001.

Forero, J. "Farmers in Peru Are Turning Again to Coca Crop." *New York Times*, February 14, 2002, 3.

Gade, D. W. *Nature and Culture in the Andes*. Madison: University of Wisconsin Press, 1999.

Goodson, L. P. *Afghanistan's Endless War: State Failure, Regional Politics, and the Rise of the Taliban*. Seattle: University of Washington Press, 2001.

Hamilton-Merritt, J. *Tragic Mountains: The Hmong, the Americans, and the Secret Wars for Laos, 1942–1992*. Bloomington: Indiana University Press, 1999.

Hobbs, J. J. "Troubling Fields: The Opium Poppy in Egypt." *Geographical Review* 88 (1998): 64–88.

Krauss, C. "Desperate Farmers Imperil Peru's Fight on Coca." *New York Times*, February 23, 2001, 4.

Lintner, B. *Burma in Revolt: Opium and Insurgency since 1948*. Bangkok, Thailand: Silkworm, 1999.

Lovell, W. G. *A Beauty That Hurts: Life and Death in Guatemala*. 2nd ed. Austin: University of Texas Press, 2000.

McCoy, A. W. *The Politics of Heroin: CIA Complicity in the Global Drug Trade*. 2nd ed. New York: Lawrence Hill, 1991.

McCoy, A. W. "Lord of Drug Lords: One Life as Lesson for U.S. Policy." *Crime, Law, and Social Change* 30 (1999): 301–331.

McCoy, A. W. "Mission Myopia: Narcotics as Fallout from the CIA's Covert Wars." In *National Insecurity: US Intelligence after the Cold War*, ed. C. Eisendrath, 118–148. Philadelphia: Temple University Press, 2000.

McCoy, A. W. "The Stimulus of Prohibition: A Critical History of the Global Narcotics Trade." In *Dangerous Harvest: Psychoactive Plants and the Transformation of Indigenous Landscapes*, ed. M. K. Steinberg, J. J. Hobbs, and K. Mathewson. New York: Oxford University Press, 2004: 24–111.

Meyer, K., and T. M. Parssinen. *Webs of Smoke: Smugglers, Warlords, Spies, and the History of the International Drug Trade*. Lanham, MD: Rowman and Littlefield, 1998.

Mintz, S. W. *Sweetness and Power: The Place of Sugar in Modern History*. New York: Viking, 1985.

Renard, R. D. *The Burmese Connection: Illegal Drugs and the Making of the Golden Triangle*. Studies on the Impact of the Illegal Drug Trade, vol. 6. Boulder, CO: Lynne Rienner, 1996.

Reuters. 2002. "Afghan War Hikes Thai, Myanmar Opium Production." www.reuters.com/printerfriendly.jhtml?StoryID=502113 (January 9, 2002; accessed January 12, 2002).

Rubin, V., ed. *Cannabis and Culture*. The Hague: Mouton, 1975.

Rupert, J., and S. Coll. "U.S. Declines to Probe Afghan Drug Trade." *Washington Post*, May 13, 1990.

Schivelbusch, W. *Tastes of Paradise: A Social History of Spices, Stimulants, and Intoxicants*. Translated by David Jacobson. New York: Palidan, 1992.

Scott, J. C. *Weapons of the Weak: Everyday Forms of Peasant Resistance*. New Haven, CT: Yale University Press, 1987.

Steinberg, M. K. "Political Ecology, Cultural Change, and Their Impact on Swidden-Fallow Agroforestry Practices among the Mopan Maya in Southern Belize." *Professional Geographer* 50 (1998): 407–417.

Steinberg, M. K. "Generals, Guerillas, Drugs, and Third World War-Making." *Geographical Review* 90 (2000): 260–267.

Steinberg, M. K. "The Marijuana Milpa: Agricultural Adaptation in a Changing Economic Landscape." In *Dangerous Harvest: Psychoactive Plantso and the Transformation of Indigenous Landscapes*, ed. M. K. Steinberg, J. J. Hobbs, and K. Mathewson. New York: Oxford University Press, 2004, 167–181.

Steward, J. *The Theory of Culture Change*. Urbana: University of Illinois Press, 1995.

Stoll, D. *Between Two Armies in the Ixil Towns of Guatemala*. New York: Columbia University Press, 1993.

Taswell, R. "Marijuana: An Overview." *Cultural Survival Quarterly* 9 (1985): 5.

Walker, W. O., III. *Opium and Foreign Policy: The Anglo-American Search for Order in Asia, 1912–1954*. Chapel Hill: University of North Carolina Press, 1991.

Webb, G. *Dark Alliance: The CIA, the Contras, and the Crack Cocaine Explosion*. New York: Seven Stories Press, 1998.

Westermeyer, J. "Opium and the People of Laos." In *Dangerous Harvest: Psychoactive Plants and the Transformation of Indigenous Landscapes*, ed. M. K. Steinberg, J. J. Hobbs, and K. Mathewson. New York: Oxford University Press, 2004, 115–132.

Wilk, R. R. *Household Ecology: Economic Change and Domestic Life among the Kekchi Maya in Belize*. Tucson: University of Arizona Press, 1991.

LEILA M. HARRIS

Navigating Uncertain Waters

Geographies of Water and Conflict, Shifting Terms and Debates

The debate over whether or not future water scarcities will contribute to heightened conflict and violent war is far from over. In the past decade, there has been a proliferation of books with titles such as *Water Wars: Coming Conflicts in the Middle East, Rivers of Discord: International Water Disputes in the Middle East,* and *Rivers of Fire: The Conflict over Water in the Middle East,* with many more undoubtedly planned or in press.[1] This chapter serves as a critical assessment of some of the major themes of this literature and also contributes several concepts and case study examples in order to shift and reframe some of the common bases and assumptions of ongoing discussions. In particular, the concept of *scale* is used to argue for a broadened notion of "sociopolitical conflict" associated with water resources to overcome weaknesses inherent to dichotomous state-centered understandings of "war" and "peace."

Given the changing nature of contemporary conflicts, "peace" cannot justifiably be understood as the absence of war. Many people, livelihoods, places, and economies are marked by diffuse and persistent conflict. Whether disruptions take the form of gang warfare in cities, the frequency of preventable deaths caused by lack of access to basic needs, or conflict over access to and sharing of critical resources, times of "peace" are notably marked by political instability, death, vulnerability, and other features commonly associated with warfare.[2] Further, given interconnections between environments, people, and places, conflicts at specific sites cannot be abstracted from situations and conditions at other locations and scales. Even if a state is not at "war," situations of resource use or access may still be marked in important ways by sociopolitical conflict, either past conflicts or ongoing conflicts across other sites and scales. In short, narrow attention to state-to-state warfare detracts from the complexity of relationships between the changing geographies of water resources and sociopolitical conflicts. A multiscalar perspective that highlights manifold and interrelated geographies of "water and conflict" across historical and geographical scales and among multiple sites and actors brings this into relief.

The Changing Geography of Water Resources

Because water is a key resource on which all life depends, access to clean and safe freshwater is an issue of grave importance. Each year, as many as ten million people die from preventable health-related effects of unsafe drinking water and improper sanitation, mostly in the developing world.[3] Given the criticality of water for all life forms and interlinked socioeconomic systems (from agriculture to fisheries and industrial activities), it is commonly debated whether future scarcities related to quantity and quality of available freshwater may lead to "resource wars" among states.[4] Some have argued that even without overt violent conflicts, changing uses, conditions, and availability of freshwater may lead to disruptive social instabilities or migrations that may in turn heighten sociopolitical conflict, either within or between states.[5] The common assumption shared by these perspectives is that whatever the particular manifestation, the condition and availability of freshwater is likely to worsen in the future, with devastating outcomes for socioeconomic and biophysical systems.

Indeed, in the absence of technological miracles or wholesale socioeconomic restructuring, the future of freshwater resources does appear to be bleak. Gleick details several disturbing trends with respect to the current situation of the world's freshwater: increasing per capita water demands and declining per capita water availability, accelerating groundwater overdraft, rising incidences of waterborne diseases, and lack of potable drinking water for more than one billion people.[6] In fact, the United Nations estimates that demand for freshwater will exceed supply in more than fifty-two countries by the year 2025.[7] With growing human populations, increasing consumption and pollution of water resources, and future uncertainties with respect to climate change or other factors, all of these trends are likely to be characterized by even more marked severity in the coming decades.

The current and impending situation of freshwater has forced many scholars and politicians to take notice. Notable quotations such as the 1985 declaration by Boutros Boutros-Ghali, formerly Egypt's minister of state for foreign affairs, "The next war in the Middle East will be fought over water,"[8] have been echoed by many political contemporaries, with general agreement that geopolitical futures remain dependent on the ability to manage and maintain scarce freshwater resources. Shared river basins in the Middle East region that are often cited with respect to high potential for future "water wars" include the Jordan River, shared by Israel, Jordan, Syria, and the Palestinians, the Tigris-Euphrates basin, shared by Turkey, Syria, and Iraq, and the Nile River in northern Africa, among others. The list of emerging and potential water and conflict hot spots is not limited to the Middle East, however. Many other potential water-related conflicts have been noted, from the Colorado to the Mekong basin or the Ganges-Brahmaputra Rivers.[9] While I do not ignore the global extent and importance of the potential links between water and conflict, I emphasize examples from the Middle East throughout this chapter.[10]

Water and Conflict/Water for Peace?

As suggested, the link between water resource scarcity and conflict has long been theorized.[11] For freshwater resources in particular, more than 200 of the world's river systems are shared by multiple states, a geography of interdependence that many believe may result in incompatible goals and outcomes among states. To provide just one example of water resource planning of one state that could have important implications for an entire basin, Turkey's continued upstream damming and development of the Tigris and Euphrates Rivers could result in diminished Euphrates flows by as much as 40% to Syria and 80% to Iraq.[12] Ongoing planning and implementation of the extensive state-led Southeastern Anatolia Project (GAP, for Güneydoğu Anadolu Projesi) have continued to alter the rivers largely unimpeded, despite potentially severe consequences for Turkey's downstream neighbors. This example clearly illustrates that the geography of water resources, which are often shared by multiple states, actors, and interests, may lead to contentious outcomes in the future. The situation is further compounded by other geopolitical difficulties and uncertainties, one of the most notable being the contemporary situation in Iraq. With these factors in mind, it becomes easy to imagine that relations between coriparians might worsen in the future and possibly lead to violent conflict.[13]

The water and conflict literature as a whole details similar potential for conflict in a number of other shared river basins. Many of these discussions hinge on the belief that increased scarcities and interdependencies related to the changing geography of water resources will lead to greater political conflict and tension between states, with war as the most drastic possible outcome. In the Tigris-Euphrates case, the fact that Iraq previously amassed troops at the Syrian border in opposition to continued upstream dam building is cited as a reason for concern about the future of this particular basin.[14]

Authors have also underscored linkages between water and conflict by detailing historical conflicts in which water has been implicated. For example, Lonergan and Brooks, and Wolf, have considered the centrality of water resources as an impetus for the 1967 war and Israel's subsequent occupations of southern Lebanon or the West Bank, and have questioned whether such conflicts were in part motivated by Israeli attempts to control critical water resources.[15] Le Billon has noted slightly different elements of the linkages between resources and conflict and has concluded that "armed conflicts and natural resources can be directly related in two main ways: armed conflicts motivated by the control of resources, and resources integrated into the financing of armed conflicts," and that access to resources possibly determines the types of conflicts that are feasible.[16] Through these types of wide-ranging discussions, the combined water and conflict literature as a whole demonstrates the centrality of water resource conditions, needs, and requirements to historic or future interstate wars and geopolitical tensions.

Apart from the focus on the role of water scarcity in past or future conflict, there has also been a parallel focus on the criticality of water as a scarce resource that may prove instrumental to brokering peace and cooperation between states. For example, Kaye, and Kally and Fishelson, explore the role of water negotiations in the Arab-Israeli peace process,[17] and Amery and Wolf have edited a multiperspective collection on water and peace, with a particular focus on the Jordan basin.[18]

As a demonstration of the ways that water might prove instrumental to brokering peace and cooperation, water was recognized as one of five substantive issues of concern to both Arab states and Israel during the peace process of the early 1990s, resulting in the creation of a special working group on water.[19] According to Lowi, the belief that water resources could serve to cement cooperative relations between adversaries echoes the political functionalist movement that emerged after World War II. This movement purported that adversarial states might be able to achieve cooperation on technical issues, with the possibility that such cooperation would then "bind states together so that political differences would recede in importance."[20]

Whether or not there is evidence to support such claims, U.S. diplomacy has relied on similar assumptions in the past and has promoted "water for peace" efforts, especially in the Middle East. Under Dwight Eisenhower, the United States promoted the "Unified Development of the Water Resources in the Jordan Valley Region," and the Carter administration pursued cooperation related to the Maqarin Dam project on the Yarmouk River. Both plans shared the hope that if the hostile states could come to agreement about sharing of water, this technical cooperation might further political rapprochement and greater peaceable interdependence between adversaries.[21] Foundational to this hope was the hope that interchange could build trust and demonstrate the potential benefits of cooperation more generally.

Daniel Hillel explains "water for peace" diplomacy as follows: "[T]he hydrological imperative thus presents a challenge and an opportunity. Water can catalyze and lubricate the peace process, smooth the rough edges, and soften the transition to regional cooperation. The thirst for water may be more pervasive than the impulse towards conflict."[22] In fact, Hillel offers thoughts on a comprehensive plan for a peaceful settlement in the Middle East with water-related cooperation as a cornerstone. Acknowledging that similar efforts have failed in the past, he argues that the criticality of future water issues is now better understood, and that "the cause of Middle Eastern peace is too important to be left to the generals or to the politicians. Now the technical experts—the hydrologists, agronomists, and engineers dedicated to problem solving on a practical level—must be given a role."[23]

This hopeful notion related to an increased role for scientists and engineers resonates with yet another theme of the water and conflict literature. Many studies detail scenarios related to future water requirements and carefully analyze future water balances and requirements in attempts to find technical solutions to the sociopolitical problems that may emerge in coming decades.[24] As such, these works often emphasize hydrological and institutional arrangements that may promote more equitable or need-appropriate water access among actors and offer suggestions for possible sharing arrangements that may serve to avert future conflict.[25] Despite the varying foci of authors with respect to whether changing water resources may prompt conflict, foment peace, or stimulate institutional innovations, all authors agree that water is potentially central to future economies and institutions, political stabilities, and geopolitical outcomes.

Despite the complexity and diversity of approaches and possible outcomes emphasized by different theorists, there remains an inherent pessimism in many assessments, with relatively little empirical evidence to support "water for peace" possibilities. Lowi contends that "water for peace" efforts are unlikely, at least in the context of long-standing conflicts in the Middle East. For instance, she argues that cooperation on the Jordan is unlikely to be reached in the absence of a solution to the Israeli-Arab impasse. Kliot offers similar conclusions on ways that broader conflicts hinder cooperation and draws on the example of the Jordan-Yarmouk system to argue that when states are involved in disputes over issues of "high politics," they are disinclined to cooperate on issues of "low politics" such as the development of water resources in a shared basin.[26]

Precisely the same case studies that Lowi and Kliot examine do give some indication to the contrary. Providing evidence for the suggestion that resource scarcities might foster greater coordination among rivals, Sosland details the long-standing informal arrangements between Israel and Jordan related to the Yarmouk River between 1967 and 1994. After the 1967 war, significant hydropolitical changes accompanied Israel's capture of the Sinai Peninsula, Gaza Strip, West Bank, Golan Heights, and East Jerusalem.[27] Israel took control of the West Bank aquifers that represent one-fourth of Israel's current freshwater sources, while the occupation of the Golan Heights involved Israeli control of the Upper Jordan River and thereby extended Israeli influence over the northern bank of the Yarmouk.[28] From Jordan's perspective, its neighbor across the Yarmouk changed from Syria to Israel, which made the Yarmouk River a contested water resource for all states involved. Sosland documents the emergence of an informal and covert collaboration between Jordan and Israel over division of the Yarmouk waters in response to this new water resource geography. Each year from 1979 to 1994, technical experts from both countries met secretly on the banks of the river to discuss summer water allocations with the purpose of maintaining a 30% water distribution for Israel and 70% for Jordan.[29] Ironically, these informal arrangements occurred at a time when Jordan refused to internationally recognize Israel and thereby refused any formal diplomacy or negotiations. Despite this fragile political situation, formal diplomatic hostilities, and persistent difficulties related to the river system itself, some degree of cooperation was achieved.

This example provides hopeful evidence for "water for peace" possibilities and also supports other work related to common-pool resources that suggests that informal management mechanisms may often be more flexible and successful than formal strategies and institutions.[30] In this case, formal cooperative strategies would have posed difficulties for the coriparians, especially if Jordan's cooperation with Israel had been revealed to other Arab neighbors. The flexibility of the informal arrangements also allowed technicians to adapt to changing seasonal and inter-annual requirements and river conditions. Reinforcing claims that cooperative resource management strategies can bolster trust and cooperation among actors more generally,[31] Sosland also highlights the trust and confidence building that the engineers were able to foster over time. Eventually, army escorts no longer accompanied the participants, and foundational trust was established to maintain secrecy that allowed Jordan's continued participation. In terms of the significance of all of these factors, Sosland implies that the shared trust and cooperation developed through these secret meetings laid the groundwork for the Israeli-Jordanian peace treaty that was eventually signed in 1994 and contained a well-developed water provision. In sum, an examination of the informal Yarmouk management regime validates claims about the effectiveness of self-governing mechanisms and informal resource management institutions and also provides some evidence of the particular types of improved communication, trust building, and sharing of information that may serve to foster more cooperative relations between adversaries.

Despite the hopefulness offered by such examples, focus on broadened notions of security suggests that in "the coming decades the world will probably see a steady increase in the incidence of violent conflict that is caused, at least in part, by environmental scarcity."[32] Consistent with this notion, theorist Homer-Dixon emphasizes linkages between resource-related stress and sociopolitical conflict, though he admits that causality is often very difficult to delineate. His work highlights freshwater as a resource that is particularly prone to conflict, underscores context dependencies of case studies, and suggests an unevenness with respect to how similar issues are likely to play out in different contexts—all factors that underscore the importance of geography. He writes, "developing countries are likely to be affected sooner and more severely than developed countries."[33] His conclusion echoes the possibility of intensified resource-based conflict evident in other water and conflict studies, but notably emphasizes an uneven geography of how this is likely to unfold. Lesser-developed contexts may experience conflict more acutely, given the relative absence of socioeconomic and institutional adaptive capacity to mitigate the effects of resource changes. The changing geography of water resources and the evolving geography of water and conflict are therefore dependent both on changing quality and quantity of water sources and on considerations related to socioeconomic resilience and institutional adaptability. It is clear that these relationships are not only complex, but are also intertwined with a host of historical and contextual factors.

Indeed, one of the reasons for divergent perspectives on whether water scarcities are likely to lead to future conflict or may conversely foster greater peace among actors is the spatial and temporal variability of cases under examination, historical or hypothetical. The context dependency and place-bound complexities of water-related processes and questions are crucial and suggest that such processes are historically and geographically specific and also variable. Further, as is noted by Homer-Dixon, water resources are not likely to be the sole operative factor that critically determines sociopolitical outcomes, but more likely are one of many factors that interact with other social, political, and economic processes.[34] This is suggestive of the ways that water is necessarily embedded in complex webs of social, political, ecological, and biophysical processes. Because water binds all life, it is also integrative in terms of serving as a critical interface between diverse systems and processes.[35]

The complex and integrated nature of freshwater geographies are thus suggestive of the need to move beyond theorizations of water and conflict that maintain artificial separations between notions of war and peace. The very notions and definitions of war and peace need to be retheorized and modified to deal with the changing and fluid nature of increasingly globalized geographies. Peace does not simply mean the absence of war.[36] War is being played on different and less identifiable stages, involves shifting and diffuse state and nonstate actors, and links social, economic, political, or other issues between faraway places.

Furthermore, the vast majority of human mortalities are not necessarily associated with war. In fact, death can be more closely correlated to the geography of poverty and associated disease and to lack of access to resources than to overt conflict or violence (witness the AIDS crisis in Africa, with incalculable deaths expected in coming decades). Our experiences and notions of war or peace are also geographically uneven and even highly variable within proximate geographic locations. For example, even during "warfare," such as the Gulf War of the early 1990s or recent U.S. invasions of Afghanistan and Iraq, war means very different things to each of us depending upon our geographic location and social position. These conflicts have obviously differentiated importance for soldiers coming from impoverished backgrounds, for business executives who profit from military contract or expenditure, or for peace activity in locations far away from war-related dangers. Geographies of peace also can be experienced in ways that are highly differentiated. When other scales of interaction, for example, domestic violence, are added to such an analysis, notions of "peace," "violence," or "war" take an entirely different hue.

Given such changes and such differentiated and simultaneous experiences of war and peace, the effort to ontologically separate the effects of changing water resource geographies in terms of war or peace is highly questionable. Moreover, the question becomes immensely more complicated when we consider that the importance of nonstate actors to geographies of war/peace undermines the state scale as the primary lens through which to evaluate intersections of water and conflict. Rather than attempting to isolate a single endpoint (war or peace), it may be possible to engage analyses that highlight the complex, variable, and interchanging interplay between peaceable and conflictual outcomes. As the following discussion of an explicitly multiscalar approach to these questions further demonstrates, the geography of changing water resources is likely to engage various relations of "conflict." This is especially the case if we understand conflict broadly to include inconsistencies and differences with respect to outcomes, situations, and experiences of changing water uses and conditions. The nature of these conflicts across sites and scales may not be as visible or isolatable as "war," but may still have important consequences for individuals, livelihoods, food security, or landscapes.

Conceptual Tools: Geographies of Water and Conflict

Given these complexities and context dependencies, which are reinforced by the biophysical and geochemical intricacies of aquatic systems themselves, attention to the issue of water and conflict is served by approaches that trace interconnections and linkages between diverse actors and processes. In essence, this is an appeal for geographic and historical approaches to questions of water and conflict that trace complex linkages between conflicts and water-related issues in ecological, biophysical, and sociopolitical senses. Such approaches would move away from linear analyses with unique focus on state scales and actors that attempt to define singular outcomes associated with particular water conditions and uses. Rather than attempting to trace linear causality, illuminating the complexity of issues and interactions involved with respect to water and conflict would provide a basis for much richer understandings of socioeconomic, institutional, and other changes associated with the future conditions and uses of water.

To move toward such a typography of geographies of water and conflict, I draw on the concept of *scale* to enable a shift in the terms of debate from a simplistic notion of "will water scarcity result in conflict?" to a broadened consideration of the multiple, complex, and ambiguous relationships between water resource geographies and sociopolitical conflicts. This approach reveals that conflict is central to water systems and dynamics, though the form, site, or manifestation of conflict may shift and evolve, especially as water resources themselves change. The following discussion draws primarily from my case-study research on changing water uses and conditions of the Tigris and Euphrates Rivers in southeastern Turkey.

Scale

The notion of scale has been the subject of increasing empirical and theoretical attention in geography and elsewhere. Scale is relevant for both physical and human geographic systems and processes and therefore has a variety of definitions and understandings. For purposes of this discussion, I invoke the concept of scale to refer to both "geographic scale," the spatial extent of a phenomenon or process, and "operational scale," or the level at which relevant processes operate.[37] Temporal notions of scale are also relevant for water resources, especially as we consider the ways in which water resources may be affected by past conflicts (e.g., the present water resource geography of the Middle East defined in relation to the 1967 war) or the ways in which water resources may impinge on sociopolitical conflicts in the future (e.g., the potential for "water wars"). However, for this discussion, I primarily emphasize geographic scale, with only tangential consideration of temporal aspects. While definitions and understandings of scale differ, it is important to emphasize that scales are constructed, which means that they are not fixed, but rather change in relation to specific events or processes and may even be actively manipulated, defined, and invoked for certain ends.

There are a few obvious connections between the notion of geographic scale and water resources. For example, much recent work has called attention to the need to consider water-related processes across integrated basins, rather than rely on fragmented or ill-matched geopolitical boundaries that are mapped onto complex and interrelated hydrologic systems.[38] Attention to basinwide scales and processes would include all the catchments and tributaries of interconnected river systems, as well as corollary sociopolitical actors and processes. With respect to a certain river basin, this might involve attention to varied political systems and institutions that operate at village, regional, state (or country), suprastate regional (e.g., the European Union or all countries that share a particular river basin), and even global scales.[39] Consideration of water resources in the western United States, for instance, is importantly affected by institutions and biophysical processes that operate at multiple scales, including effects of El Niño on precipitation and snow melt and various political and institutional jurisdictions that are involved with the integrity and use of particular river systems (from cities to U.S. states and to the United States and Mexico). These processes, institutions, and interactions also serve in part to define and construct relevant scales. In the case of the Tigris-Euphrates basin, many analyses of changes associated with the Turkish state-led GAP emphasize basinwide actors and processes. At times this has been at the expense of careful attention to processes that operate at other scenes and within small geographic areas, for example, within the southeastern region of Turkey itself.

Attention to multiple scales of analysis brings a suite of different issues and possibilities into view. Within the southeastern region of Turkey, finer resolution analysis might include examining effects of irrigation for local economies and ecologies within the southeastern Anatolia region or for upstream and downstream users within the newly established irrigation networks (rather than a focus solely on upstream and downstream effects within the river basin more generally). Alternatively, attention might be paid to state scales, for example, examining effects of river changes for Turkey as a whole. The commonly cited statistics that the Tigris-Euphrates basin represents 28% of Turkey's freshwater potential and that more than a quarter of Turkey's hydroelectricity will be supplied by the rivers,[40] are clear examples that highlight and privilege state scales of analysis. A basin-regional scale of analysis might include consideration of effects for all three coriparians, perhaps with a focus on costs for downstream users, as many analyses have done.[41] Global-scale processes might also impinge heavily on changing uses or conditions of the rivers, such as climate change and associated hydrologic effects, or changing patterns of trade or political negotiations related to Turkey's proposed candidacy to the European Union (EU). As these examples convey, Tigris-Euphrates waters affect, and are affected by, processes, institutions, and actors across multiple scales. In some senses, the changing uses and conditions of the Tigris-Euphrates system might also in turn have implications for redefinitions of and associations with scales themselves. For instance, the Tigris-Euphrates basin as a whole might become more salient and relevant as continued withdrawals upstream affect the entire system and force greater attention to and consideration of the basinwide scale. Alternatively, Turkey's economic development that is associated with the alteration of the river systems might foster redefinition of continent scales as Turkey seeks to gain full admission into the EU.

To some extent, each of these functional scales can be understood in isolation, but must also be understood as being linked to processes, actors, and systems across all other scales of analysis. With respect to the question of geographies of water and conflict, I argue that engaging a multiscalar analysis that considers multiple scales of interaction and their intersection reveals that conflict is nearly always central to water-resource-related uses and changes. As described by Harris,[42] addressing water and conflict across scales of analysis reveals that even without direct implications for violence or war, use of and access to water resources often involve "conflict geographies" of some sort or another.[43] Such conflict geographies can have a variety of manifestations, from overt "war" (past, present, or future) to tensions and conflicts within villages or households around uses of water resources. Consideration of linkages and processes across multiple temporal and spatial scales reveals that "conflict" is critical for water resource use, and conditions though the operative scale, actors, or sites of such conflicts may shift or change with time or with respect to alteration of the water resource itself.

We can further broaden this notion of conflict associated with water resources to also include ecological needs and requirements. In this sense, we might understand conflict in yet another way, to include how human uses or degradation of water can conflict with other needs and requirements, such as sustaining fish populations or maintaining the physical integrity of a river system. In this way, a broadened theorization of water and conflict links directly to notions and critiques of "sustainability," with conflict as a manifestation of or proxy for the incompatibility of diverse sustainability goals and outcomes.[44] In other words, in the absence of holistic sustainability, whereby all aspects of a system are sustained without compromising one another, there will be conflict in one form or another.[45]

Application of the concept of geographies of water and conflict to the Tigris-Euphrates basin reveals multiple sites and instances of conflict with reference to both geographic scale and time scale.[46] Turkey's large-scale alteration of the rivers is intended to serve a variety of needs,[47] including provision of irrigation waters to nearby agricultural areas, with diversions from the rivers eventually to irrigate nearly two million hectares. Among other conflicts that emerge, irrigation is enabling dominance of cotton and other water-intensive crops and squeezing out possibilities for reliance on animal husbandry and other alternative livelihood strategies. Emerging water user groups designed to manage irrigation infrastructure have also created new political tensions around who should manage the water resources, with notable conflicts with respect to corruption associated with these "democratic" water management mechanisms. A scalar conflict is also emerging between immediate irrigation requirements and uses and long-term sustainability of drinking water. As underground water reserves are recharged with irrigation water polluted with pesticides and other agricultural runoff, these changes may threaten long-term drinking water supplies.

Other conflicts can be identified as relevant to village scales in the "beneficiary" communities that have recently received irrigation waters. These might involve gender considerations at household scales or conflicts related to timing and release of irrigation waters for different crops. Current irrigation schedules in the Harran Plain near the border with Syria, for example, revolve around cotton production rather than timing and seasonality suitable for spicy peppers and other crops primarily grown by women.[48] This multiplicity of conflicts between different social, political, and economic uses and conditions of water is only revealed through explicit consideration of multiple scales of analysis. These examples illustrate the utility of engaging a broadened conceptualization of conflict across sites and scales. Doing so also calls attention to the complex web of social, economic, political, and ecological interactions that are relevant for changing water conditions and uses. If we are more effectively able to theorize these interconnections, even in partial senses, we might be better able to understand the complexity and diversity of ways in which water resources are enrolled in conflict—past, present, or future or across sites and scales of analysis.

Consideration of the "state" scale of Turkey reveals still another suite of interrelated conflicts with respect to this changing water resource geography. Benefits of these changes include provision of hydroelectricity, potential economic benefits of irrigated agriculture, and even possibilities of reduced rural-to-urban migration with improved income possibilities in rural areas. These alterations are lived very differently at other sites, however, as whole villages are inundated to make way for the massive infrastructural works. Such differences between places with respect to divergent costs and benefits of water-related transformations illustrate the concept of geographies of water and conflict, in this case by revealing conflicts between interests and actors across sites.

There are also other more violent conflicts that operate across multiple scales that are relevant for the altered water resource geographies of the rivers. The development of the Tigris and Euphrates Rivers is the cornerstone of an "integrated regional development" program that is meant to economically develop the Southeastern Anatolia region to overcome long-standing disparities between this region and the rest of Turkey.[49] Importantly, this region is the only administrative region with a predominantly Kurdish-speaking population and has been the primary focus of ongoing civil strife during the past several decades between Kurdish separatists and state forces.[50] The effort to overcome economic underdevelopment in the southeast is therefore intended, in part, to rectify socioeconomic discrepancies that have fueled Kurdish separatist aspirations during the past several decades. Thus in this case geographies of water and conflict intricately tie current changes to the river system to past histories of violent conflict. The Kurdish question also potentially comes into play at the basin scale because as connections between Kurdish separatists and water uses among the coriparians have been discursively and diplomatically linked. At times, Turkey has refused to negotiate on water issues with downstream Syria absent commitments to discontinue support for Kurdish separatists.

In evaluations of changes to the Tigris-Euphrates to date, much of the analysis has focused on basinwide issues, notably, water budgets for each of the co-riparians and attendant effects of reduced flow for downstream neighbors.[51] The emphasis on state-to-state interactions and diplomatic relations for the Tigris-Euphrates case parallels the general trend in the water and conflict literature to privilege state scales and actors over other possible systems and processes. The narrow and oftentimes singular focus on state scales and processes constrains our ability to understand the complexity and unevenness of geographies of water and conflict and is in part responsible for the excessive focus on state-state warfare that results in an impoverishment of the theoretical salience of water and conflict interconnections.

As the preceding discussion of the ways in which water and conflict might be linked across other scales demonstrates, a multiscalar approach would enrich these discussions. Attention to intrastate processes and violence, historic considerations, and other factors allows us to more fully consider interrelationships between water and conflict. Working along the lines of the notion of geographies of water and conflict to understand multiscalar processes and linkages across contexts and actors, we might consider questions such as "how might changing water uses affect local-scale politics and outcomes within Turkey's southeast?" "how might current or past uses or withdrawals affect future conditions and possibilities with respect to the Kurdish issue?" or "what global-scale processes may impinge on Turkey's planned continued development of the Tigris-Euphrates system?"

Geographers have also examined the idea of "politics of scale," whereby certain scales may be constructed or manipulated by different actors who are seeking certain political ends.[52] An example might be ways that the scale of the state is repeatedly invoked and defended to define state control and legitimacy over a particular territory. There is a clear example of political constructions of scale in the Tigris-Euphrates context. In Turkey's portrayal of the issues related to development of the twin rivers, including assessments of river flows, the two rivers are often joined and considered as a holistic basin. For example, Bilen writes that "the Euphrates and Tigris together have an average annual water potential of about 87.7 billion cubic meters."[53] He continues, "It is misleading to focus on the River Euphrates or the River Tigris in isolation one from the other. These two rivers form one single basin having an annual potential of 87.2 BCM and should be taken as part of the same system. There is no natural barrier between these two rivers and they come very close to each other in the Iraqi territory."[54] He further states at various points that there is "excess water" in the Tigris such that water can be diverted to the Euphrates to meet the needs of the system as a whole (similar to diversions between the rivers already undertaken in Iraq). However, when we consider the breakdown of annual flows and contributions of the riparian states to the river systems,[55] it is clear that to analytically join the two rivers as an integrated basin also has notable political implications.

The idea of "contributions" to river systems is commonly invoked with respect to shared rivers and implies that certain territories contribute to river flows based on the basis of origin sources or tributaries for a particular river. The idea of contributions has become relevant in international legal considerations with respect to shared river sources, though arguments are also made based on "needs," "historical use," and other factors. Considering the rivers separately would reveal that Turkey is the major "contributor" on the Euphrates, but not on the Tigris. Considering the two rivers together as a joint basin, as is argued by Bilen and as often invoked by Turkish planners, instead supports Turkish claims to both rivers as Turkey contributes 52.9% to conjoined river flows. Such scalar constructions therefore bolster Turkey's "rights" to develop both rivers. This is yet another aspect of ways in which scale impinges on how we understand and analyze relationships between water and conflict, and it further clarifies the utility of scalar sensitivity for an appreciation of water and conflict geographies.

Focusing on these types of examples reveals multiple tensions and ambiguities with respect to water and conflict geographies. There is the possibility that provision of irrigation and other water-related changes within Turkey might result in less conflict if it dampens Kurdish separatist aspirations. This may occur concurrently with possibilities for heightened conflict between Turkey and downstream neighbors Syria and Iraq. The relationship between water and conflict in this case therefore may reveal tensions and inconsistencies across sites and scales. Within Turkey, benefits of irrigation provision also proceed in tandem with new emerging conflicts. The delivery of irrigation waters to agricultural areas results in conflicts between different possible livelihood strategies, between irrigation provision and quality of drinking water, or even between members of a household as people attempt to negotiate the new constraints and possibilities associated with the modified waterscape. These types of conflicts are not as visible or explosive as water wars or state-to-state violence, but for certain individuals, the consequences may be of great importance. Conflicts between different possible livelihoods, different uses of and access to resources, and intrastate warfare can all result in long-term instability, degraded resources, and increased illness or mortality. The effort to distinguish certain types of conflicts from others becomes less and less compelling as one begins to understand the complexity of issues and questions that surround the use, degradation, and alteration of water resources.

Just as we cannot wholly understand the changing nature of the water resource geography of the basin without reference to the persistent Kurdish conflict, we also cannot situate current and future alterations of the rivers without attention to other conflicts, notably the Gulf War in the early 1990s, ensuing sanctions against Iraq, and the contemporary U.S.-led invasion and occupation of Iraq. It is clear even to the casual observer that these conflicts have affected geopolitical possibilities for Turkey's continued development and use of the rivers. In the absence of the Iran-Iraq War, the Gulf War, and tensions between Iraq and Turkey's Western allies (all of which compromised Iraq's geopolitical and military position), would Turkey have moved so boldly in an effort to alter the water resources of the basin? Will pressure on Turkey with respect to the uses of the rivers change with increasing U.S. involvement in Iraq's future?

Engaging the concept of scale therefore sheds light on the question of water and conflict in several ways. A multiscalar approach lends support to the notion that instead of a focus on war, a broadened notion of conflict is of particular relevance for an understanding of the ways that water is implicated in changing geographies of war and peace. The possibility that diffuse intrastate or subnational violence may occur even in the absence of overt state-state violence is enlivened by a multiscalar approach that refuses to privilege only state scales of analysis. This suggestion is corroborated by work by Homer-Dixon that similarly suggests that degradation of important resources may not lead to overt violence, but will often foster or maintain important social and political instabilities or intrastate tensions and conflicts.[56] As we see by historical example, ethnic strife or similar intrastate conflicts may often be more protracted and less easily resolved than state-state warfare. The long-standing Kurdish issue or the Israeli-Palestinian situation are just two examples. We also can imagine that just as states are not the only important actors, war is not the only critical outcome that may result from changing conditions and access to water. Other sociopolitical instabilities and water resource conditions and uses may also have crucial importance for certain individuals, livelihoods, or the future of state institutions, structures, and security interests.[57] Explicit attention to multiscalar actors, issues, and processes reveals that conflict is often central to water resource geographies, though the extent, scales, and specific pathways of water and conflict geographies may change.

Ostensibly, our interest in the relationship between water and conflict stems from an interest in curbing the loss of human life and limiting degradation of natural systems, drains on resources, and other effects of warfare. If our interest lies with these aims, then this suggests that we should be concerned with the many interrelated conflicts around water that may have implications for human well-being and resource integrity. As noted in the introduction, the lack of access to clean drinking water already claims more lives annually than warfare, but if we compare our efforts to reduce risks associated with unsafe drinking water with military expenditures or efforts to thwart elusive "terroristic" threats (at least in the case of the United States), the tensions and cost differentials are striking. If unsustainable uses of water resources are likely to lead to sociopolitical tensions or tensions with our ability to maintain freshwater ecosystems,[58] this might also be taken to suggest that a lasting, true "peace" will not be achieved as long as resources critical for human life and well-being, such as water, are not equitably and consistently available. In short, there may not be the possibility of peace without sustainability of water resources.

Other Considerations: Spatiality, Boundaries, and Territory

War is an inherently spatial process. Wars not only are fought with certain spatial tactics and maneuvers, but are often explicitly about control and claims to space and territory, and in fact, wars are often efforts to solidify, draw, or extend the boundaries or claims of a particular sovereign, interest, or actor. As has been noted with respect to the outcomes of the 1967 war in the Middle East, often such renegotiations of territory are either purposely or effectively renegotiations of water resource geographies and boundaries.[59] Many have noted that Israel's capture of key territories in successive wars was very strategic in terms of water resource control. Later, occupations of southern Lebanon further secured access to headwaters of the Jordan. While the issue of whether or not future water resource scarcities will lead to war is being hotly debated, there are many examples of past wars and conflicts that have already been closely tied and connected to interests in water resource control and access. What makes territory appealing to a state may be populations, minerals, or other resources, including water.

Some have noted that persistent crackdowns in Iraq, to maintain control over the Kurdish dominated north or similar militaristic efforts of Turkish forces to maintain control of Turkey's southeast have both in part been motivated by efforts to maintain state control of contested territory and key resources within it (oil and water, respectively). Water has also been used and manipulated as a tool to destabilize adversaries of particular regimes. Again in the case of Iraq, manipulation of river waters to dry up the southern marshes and thus the livelihoods of the ethnically distinct Marsh Arabs is now under investigation by an international committee under the rubric of attempted "genocide." These cases exemplify how water, like other critical resources, is closely bound to spatiality, boundaries, and territory and, by extension, to geographies of war and peace.

These processes are space bound and territorially defined, but there are also ways in which conflict and water and conflict geographies are simultaneously geographically unbound or delinked. Massive infrastructural projects, whether in southeastern Turkey or the southwestern United States, increasingly overcome geographical boundaries or limitations related to water resource uses, with important implications for agriculture, population migration, or other changing socioeconomic and political geographies. War is also becoming less territorially focused because it is increasingly played out in the media, on urban streets, or by global networks who may be pursuing ideological goals rather than any territorial prize. The changing nature of conflict and war poses still other suggestions about the questions of linkages between water and conflict. In bioterrorism and other threats by small-scale actors, minority factions, or global networks, water resources may be prime targets for future attacks. Emerging alliances associated with the "war on terrorism" or NATO similarly have implications for differentiated geographies of water resource access (witness again Turkey's development of the Tigris-Euphrates basin, which is strongly bolstered by its alliance with NATO and the United States).

Geography facilitates a study of these processes not only through a study of space and spatiality, but also by highlighting the linkages and connections between issues, processes, actors, and places. Questions related to water resource use, access, and stability are less about where the river systems appear on the map in a static sense, such as the often cited statistics of the number of river basins that are shared globally. Instead, these questions are increasingly about the dynamic and changing geographies of how freshwater is transformed, used, modified, and linked to complex social, political, and economic systems. Freshwater takes on new meaning and importance with respect to these multiple emerging geographies, whether in relation to globalized terror networks, changing economic geographies of trade and finance, or other processes. These processes increasingly play out in unbounded spaces that at times appear to be territorially delinked, yet that simultaneously maintain distinct spatial expression—often through highly uneven and distinctive geographies. Attention to geography, scale, and the particularities and dissimilarities of "place" with respect to water resources helps underscore these complexities and helps define and highlight complex and changing relationships between water and conflict.

Notes

1. Bulloch Darwish, *Water Wars*; Shapland, *Rivers of Discord*; Sofer, *Rivers of Fire*.
2. See van der Wusten, this volume.
3. Gleick, *World's Water*, 39.
4. For example, see Scheumann and Schiffler, *Water in the Middle East*, or Sofer, *Rivers of Fire*. I do not detail debates related to "environmental security," which are often centered around whether environmental issues should be considered within the realm of "security," including the relationship between environment and security studies, environ-

mental effects of the security and military complex, and debates that mimic the basic question of the water and conflict literature: will environmental changes and coming environmental scarcities result in violent conflict? This literature especially concentrates on state-state scales of interaction and often has a U.S., Eurocentric, and militaristic focus (see Matthews, "Redefining Security"; Matthew, "Environment as a National Security Issue"; Deudney and Matthew, *Contested Grounds*; Dalby, *Environmental Security*; Levy, "Is the Environment a National Security Isssue?"; and Dmitrov, "Water, Conflict, and Security," for discussion of these debates).

5. Homer-Dixon, *Environment, Scarcity, and Violence.*

6. Gleick, *World's Water*, 1–2.

7. Matthew, "Environment as a National Security Issue," 109.

8. Cited in Vesilind, "Middle East Water—Critical Resource," 53.

9. See, for example, Crow and Sultana, "Gender, Class, and Access to Water," for a discussion of the Ganges, and Sneddon, "Water Conflicts and River Basins," and Nguyen, *Mekong River and the Struggle for Indochina*, for discussions of the Mekong.

10. I do so for three primary reasons: the considerable emphasis on this region in the water and conflict literature, the particular geography of the region as predominantly semiarid and characterized by notable histories and intensities of conflict, and my own research interests, which focus on changing water uses and conditions in the Tigris-Euphrates basin.

11. Various authors frame these questions differently. Homer-Dixon, *Environment, Scarcity and Violence*, for example, frames the question in terms of scarcity and looks to demonstrate multiple ways in which scarcity might be experienced or defined (from resource capture by elites to "simple scarcity" associated with degradation of a resource), and how this might link to conflict. Le Billon, "Political Ecology of War," instead emphasizes resource dependence, or the risk of violence associated with specific resources. These framings of the questions are not necessarily oppositional, but represent various aspects of how relationships between resources and conflicts have been theorized. See also Peluso and Watts, *Violent Environments*, for a more general discussion of violence in relation to environmental change and management issues.

12. Hillel, *Rivers of Eden*, 109–110.

13. Beschorner, *Water and Instability in the Middle East*; Lowi, "Rivers of Conflict, Rivers of Peace"; Scheumann and Schiffler, *Water in the Middle East.*

14. McCaffrey, "Water, Politics, and International Law," 93.

15. Lonergan and Brooks, *Watershed*, and A Wolf, *Hydropolitics along the Jordan River.*

16. Le Billon, "Political Ecology of War," 580.

17. Kaye, *Beyond the Handshake*, and Kally and Fishelson. *Water and Peace.*

18. Amery and Wolf, *Water in the Middle East.*

19. Lowi, "Rivers of Conflict, Rivers of Peace"; Wolf, *Hydropolitics along the Jordan River.*

20. Lowi, "Rivers of Conflict, Rivers of Peace," 123.

21. Ibid., and Hillel, *Rivers of Eden*, 168. The U.S. government also established the Regional Cooperation Program in the early 1980s to foster greater peace in the Middle East through technical cooperation, primarily between scientists and engineers from the United States, Israel, and Egypt. The overall goal of the program is to reduce social and political tensions in the region by designing, promoting, and executing cooperative technical projects and services that would demonstrably benefit cooperating countries and organizations. Water resources in particular have been highlighted as crucial to bring countries closer together. Abel, *Influence of Technical Cooperation.*

22. Hillel, *Rivers of Eden*, 283.

23. Ibid., 285.

24. Bilen, *Turkey and Water Issues in the Middle East*; Kolars and Mitchell, *Euphrates River and the Southeast Anatolia Development Project.*

25. Biswas, "Management of International Water Resources"; Kbaroğlu and Ünver, "Institutional Framework"; Kbaroğlu, *Building a Regime for the Tigris-Euphrates River Basin.* In some cases, however, these types of "technical" assessments are used to bolster the case for a particular actor's use of resources (see discussion of Bilen's arguments later in this chapter on scale manipulation in characterizing water resource uses and issues).

26. Kliot, "Building a Legal Regime."

27. Sosland, "Cooperating Rivals." See also Wolf, *Hydropolitics of the Jordan River*, and Amery and Wolf, *Water in the Middle East.*

28. Sosland, "Cooperating Rivals."

29. Ibid. Interestingly enough, during this period of secret agreement between the states, Israel publicly maintained that it was entitled to more than it had agreed to in the secret negotiations, stating that it should get up to 40% of the Yarmouk waters during the summer months.

30. Ostrom, *Governing the Commons.*

31. Brandt, Morgan, and Gerbach, *Conflicts over Natural Resources.*

32. Homer-Dixon, *Environment, Scarcity, and Violence*, 4.

33. Ibid.

34. Ibid.

35. Sneddon et al., "Contested Waters," 664.

36. This overlaps with theorizations of "negative" verses "positive" peace. "Negative peace" refers to the simple absence of war, whereby no organized military violence is taking place. I suggest that given greater interconnections between people and places with increasing globalization, even this notion of peace is difficult to consider, since there has been frequent and persistent violent warring for much of the past century. Even if this violence is seemingly contained within a particular location or confined to a particular set of actors, the implications and interconnections for other locales, economies, or resources make such a notion of peace difficult to imagine. The idea of "positive peace" is also suggestive of some of the arguments I am making in this chapter. The idea of positive peace involves a more holistic notion of peace that extends beyond the absence of overt violence to include the absence of structural violence, such as the denial of rights or the occurrence of preventable diseases. See Barash and Webel, *Peace and Conflict Studies.* I attempt to connect a broadened notion of positive peace to water resource issues through this discussion and also to consider the corollary retheorization of conflict that is implied by these broadened concepts as applied to the water and conflict literature.

37. See Marston, "Social Construction of Scale"; and Delaney and Leitner, "Political Construction of Scale," for discussion.

38. These arguments often state the need to recognize "ecological," "hydrologic," or "ecogeographic" units that are not well served by political and institutional boundaries. In such arguments, the system of "states" is understood to disrupt ecological integrity and cohesiveness (in terms of integrated planning in relation to environmental systems). States are also potentially undermined, because as ecological processes also do not recognize political borders. As is summarized by Dmitrov, "Water, Conflict, and Security," 684, "The indivisible continuum of natural ecosystems is at odds with the territorial compartmentalization of political units" and creates an obstacle to effective management and a potential threat to state integrity.

39. See E. Swyngedouw, "Modernity and Hybridity," for discussion of hydrogeologic and sociopolitical scales that are relevant for water management and conflict questions.

40. Ünver, "Southeastern Anatolia Project (GAP)," 456.

41. For instance, Bulloch and Darwish, *Water Wars*, or Lowi, "Rivers of Conflict, Rivers of Peace."

42. Harris, "Water and Conflict Geographies of the Southeastern Anatolia Project."

43. The term "conflict geographies" is defined in a nondisciplinary sense to refer to a range of interrelated conflicts that are associated with a specific site or place and vary across scales, including the ways in which these conflicts affect other aspects of interrelated geographies. Consideration of the conflict geographies of southeastern Turkey, for example, would include assessments of how the region has been constructed in relation to past conflicts (Turkey's wars of independence after the fall of the Ottoman Empire and periodic regional uprisings that have marked the history of the Turkish republic) and current and ongoing conflicts (such as those related to the Kurdish question and ongoing conflicts with neighboring Iraq). All of these conflicts have marked the geography of the region in compelling ways and have even served to consolidate the scale and notion of the southeast region itself. I invoke water and conflict geographies as an extension of this concept to capture the intersection between water use, access, and integrity and the diverse, interrelated, and multiscalar aspects of conflict that mark and produce particular geographies (and scales). See Harris, "Water and Conflict Geographies of the Southeastern Anatolia Project."

44. See Lélé, "Sustainable Development," or Sneddon, " 'Sustainability' in Ecological Economies, Ecology, and Livelihoods," for critical reviews of sustainability.

45. As I have argued in Harris, "Water and Conflict Geographies of the Southeastern Anatolia Project," we could read shifting water resource conditions and uses worldwide to reveal "conflicts of sustainability"—conflicts between different notions and ideals of sustainability, from livelihoods to ecological integrity. This is consistent with arguments related to "environmental security," whereby the notion of security is extended from a limited focus on violent conflict to broadened conceptions of security that encompass environmental and social instabilities that may be associated with degraded resources and thus link human security and ecosystem health. With respect to water and conflict in particular, Dmitrov, "Water, Conflict, and Security," 683, notes that even without conflict between actors, ecological integrity may be, and often is, compromised when human actors give priority to human needs over other possible interests and uses of water.

46. Harris, "Water and Conflict Geographies of the Southeastern Anatolia Project."

47. See Ünver, "Southeastern Anatolia Project (GAP)," for a review of GAP programs.

48. See also Harris, "Irrigation, Gender, and the Social Geographies of the Changing Landscape."

49. Ünver, "Southeastern Anatolia Project (GAP)."

50. Kirişci and Winrow, *Kurdish Question and Turkey*.

51. For example, Beschorner, *Water and Instability in the Middle East*, and Gleick, *World's Water*.

52. Herod, "Labor as an Agent of Globalization and as a Global Agent"; Herod, "Labor's Spatial Praxis."

53. Bilen, *Turkey and Water Issues in the Middle East*, 56.

54. Ibid., 82.

55. Ibid., 61.

56. Homer-Dixon, *Environment, Scarcity, and Violence*, 179.

57. Ibid., and Harris, "Water and Conflict Geographies of the Southeastern Anatolia Project."

58. Sneddon et al., "Contested Waters." In this article, the authors argue that given the biophysical aspects of water resources, increasing attention must also be directed to ecological, biophysical, and chemical processes to better understand water and conflict. Notably, there is reason to extend the notion more forcefully beyond attention to human-

centered conflict to also include conflicts between different ecosystem uses and requirements.

59. See Wolf, " 'Hydrostrategic' Territory in the Jordan Basin," for a discussion of the connections between water and past conflicts in the Jordan basin. Wolf endeavors to answer the question of whether or not water was the sole factor that resulted in conflict.

References

Abel, R. *The Influence of Technical Cooperation on Reducing Tensions in the Middle East.* Lanham, MD: University Press of America, 1997.

Amery, H., and A. Wolf. *Water in the Middle East: A Geography of Peace.* Austin: University of Texas Press, 2000.

Barash, D., and C. Webel. *Peace and Conflict Studies.* Thousand Oaks, CA: Sage, 2002.

Beschorner, N. *Water and Instability in the Middle East.* London: Brassey's for the International Institute of Strategic Studies, 1992.

Bilen, Ö. *Turkey and Water Issues in the Middle East.* Ankara: Southeastern Anatolia Project (GAP) Regional Development Administration, 1997.

Biswas, A. K. "Management of International Water Resources: Some Recent Developments." In *International Waters of the Middle East: From Euphrates-Tigris to Nile*, ed. A. K. Biswas, 185–203. Bombay: Oxford University Press, 1994.

Brandt, L. K., J. Morgan, and L. Gerlach. *Conflicts over Natural Resources: A Discussion of Positive Outcomes.* Discussion Paper, Strategic Management Research Center. Minneapolis: University of Minnesota, 1991.

Bulloch, J., and A. Darwish. *Water Wars: Coming Conflicts in the Middle East.* London: Gollancz, 1993.

Cox, K. "Spaces of Dependence, Spaces of Engagement, and the Politics of Scale; or, Looking for Local Politics." *Political Geography* 17 (1998): 1–23.

Crow, B., and F. Sultana. "Gender, Class, and Access to Water: Three Cases in a Poor and Crowded Delta." *Society and Natural Resources* 15 (2002): 709–724.

Dalby, S. *Environmental Security.* Minneapolis: University of Minnesota Press, 2002.

Delaney, D., and H. Leitner. "The Political Construction of Scale." *Political Geography* 16 (1997): 93–97.

Deudney, D., and R. Matthew. *Contested Grounds: Security and Conflict in the New Environmental Politics.* Albany: State University of New York Press, 1999.

Dmitrov, R. "Water, Conflict, and Security: A Conceptual Minefield." *Society and Natural Resources* 15 (2002): 677–691.

Gleick, P. H. *The World's Water: The Biennial Report on Freshwater Resources (1998–1999).* Washington, DC: Island, 1998.

Harris, L. "Water and Conflict Geographies of the Southeastern Anatolia Project." *Society and Natural Resources* 15 (2002): 743–759.

Harris, L. "Irrigation, Gender, and the Social Geographies of the Changing Landscape." *Environment and Planning D: Society and Space*, forthcoming.

Herod, A. "Labor as an Agent of Globalization and as a Global Agent." In *Spaces of Globalization: Reasserting the Power of the Local*, ed. K. Cox, 167–200. New York: Guilford, 1997.

Herod, A. "Labor's Spatial Praxis and the Geography of Contract Bargaining in the US East Coast Longshore Industry, 1953–1989." *Political Geography* 16 (1997): 145–170.

Hillel, D. *Rivers of Eden: The Struggle for Water and the Quest for Peace in the Middle East.* New York: Oxford University Press, 1994.

Homer-Dixon, T. *Environment, Scarcity, and Violence.* Princeton, NJ: Princeton University Press, 1999.

Kally, E., and G. Fishelson. *Water and Peace: Water Resources and the Arab-Israeli Peace Process.* Westport, CT: Praeger, 1993.

Kaye, D. *Beyond the Handshake: Multilateral Cooperation in the Arab-Israeli Peace Process, 1991–1996.* New York: Columbia University Press, 2001.

Kıbaroğlu, A. *Building a Regime for the Tigris-Euphrates River Basin.* New York: Kluwer International Law, 2002.

Kıbaroğlu, A., and O. Ünver. "An Institutional Framework for Facilitating Cooperation in the Euphrates-Tigris Basin." *International Negotiation* 5 (2000): 311–330.

Kirişci, K., and G. M. Winrow. *The Kurdish Question and Turkey: An Example of Trans-state Ethnic Conflict.* London: Cass, 1997.

Kliot, N. "Building a Legal Regime for the Jordan-Yarmouk River System: Lessons from Other International Rivers." In *The Peaceful Management of Transboundary Resources,* ed. G. Blake, W. Hildesley, M. Pratt, R. Ridley, and C. Schofield, 187–202. Boston: Graham and Trotman, 1995.

Kolars, J. F., and W. A. Mitchell. *The Euphrates River and the Southeast Anatolia Development Project.* Carbondale: Southern Illinois University Press, 1991.

Le Billon, P. "The Political Ecology of War: Natural Resources and Armed Conflicts." *Political Geography* 20 (2001): 561–584.

Lélé, S. "Sustainable Development: A Critical Review." *World Development* 19 (1991): 607–621.

Levy, M. "Is the Environment a National Security Issue?" *International Security* 20 (1995): 35–62.

Lonergan, S., and D. Brooks. *Watershed: The Role of Fresh Water in the Israeli-Palestinian Conflict.* Ottawa: International Development Research Center, 1994.

Lowi, M. "Rivers of Conflict, Rivers of Peace." *Journal of International Affairs* 49 (1995): 123–144.

Marston, S. A. "The Social Construction of Scale." *Progress in Human Geography* 24 (2000): 219–242.

Matthew, R. A. "The Environment as a National Security Issue." *Journal of Policy History* (2000): 101–122.

Matthews, J. "Redefining Security." *Foreign Affairs* 68 (1989): 162–177.

McCaffrey, S. C. "Water, Politics, and International Law." In *Water in Crisis: A Guide to the World's Freshwater Resources,* ed. P. Gleick, 92–104. New York: Oxford University Press, 1993.

Nguyen, T. *The Mekong River and the Struggle for Indochina: Water, War, and Peace.* Westport, CT: Praeger, 1999.

Ostrom, E. *Governing the Commons: The Evolution of Institutions for Collective Action.* Cambridge: Cambridge University Press, 1990.

Peluso, N., and M. Watts, eds. *Violent Environments.* Ithaca, NY: Cornell University Press, 2001.

Scheumann, W., and M. Schiffler, eds. *Water in the Middle East: Potential for Conflicts and Prospects for Cooperation.* Berlin: Springer, 1998.

Shapland, G. *Rivers of Discord: International Water Disputes in the Middle East.* New York: St. Martin's, 1997.

Sneddon, C. " 'Sustainability' in Ecological Economies, Ecology, and Livelihoods: A Review." *Progress in Human Geography* 24 (2000): 520–549.

Sneddon, C. "Water Conflicts and River Basins: The Contradictions of Comanagement and Scale in Northeast Thailand." *Society and Natural Resources* 15 (2002): 725–742.

Sneddon, C., L. Harris, R. Dmitrov, and U. Ozesmi. "Contested Waters: Conflict, Scale, and Sustainability in Aquatic Socioecological Systems." *Society and Natural Resources* 15 (2002): 663–675.

Sofer, A. *Rivers of Fire: The Conflict over Water in the Middle East.* Lanham, MD: Rowman and Littlefield, 1999.

Sosland, J. "Cooperating Rivals: The Water Scarcity Threat in the Arab-Israeli Arena—The Yarmouk River Case." Paper presented at the International Studies Association, Minneapolis, Minnesota, 1997.

Swyngedouw, E. "Modernity and Hybridity: Nature, Regeneracioismo, and the Production of the Spanish Waterscape." *Annals of the Association of American Geographers* 89 (1999): 443–465.

Ünver, I. H. O. "Southeastern Anatolia Integrated Development Project (GAP), Turkey: An Overview of Issues of Sustainability," *Water Resources Development* 13 (1997a), 187–207.

Ünver, I. H. O. "Southeastern Anatolia Project (GAP)." *Water Resources Development* 13 (1997b): 453–483.

Vesilind, P. "Middle East Water—Critical Resource." *National Geographic* (May 1993): 38–71.

Wolf, A. *Hydropolitics along the Jordan River: Scarce Water and Its Impact on the Arab-Israeli Conflict.* Tokyo and New York: United Nations University Press, 1995.

Wolf, A. " 'Hydrostrategic' Territory in the Jordan Basin: Water, War, and Arab-Israeli Peace Negotiations." In *Water in the Middle East: A Geography of Peace*, ed. H. Amery, and A. Wolf, 63–120. Austin: University of Texas Press, 2000.

ALEXANDER B. MURPHY

Territorial Ideology and Interstate Conflict

Comparative Considerations

We live in profoundly unsettling times. The daily newspapers are filled with stories about terrorist threats, stockpiles of chemical and biological weapons, and the efforts of ever more states to acquire nuclear weapons. At the same time, long-standing interstate and intrastate conflicts continue to dominate the lives of people in such diverse settings as Israel-Palestine, southern Sudan, the India-Pakistan border, and the interior of Colombia. The issues that underlie these conflicts are as diverse as their geographic settings, but they share one commonality: they are all framed by the territorial logic of the modern state system.

The foregoing statement might seem self-evident for intrastate struggles between ethnic groups or for boundary conflicts between states because these conflicts are clearly tied to the territorial reach of the modern state. Yet even the international terrorist activities associated with movements such as al-Qaeda cannot be understood without reference to prevailing international territorial norms. This is because the existing political-geographic order is a fundamental catalyst for such movements and because responses to international terrorism are often channeled in and through states. Consider, for example, the circumstances of the terrorist attacks on the United States of September 11, 2001. Chief among the articulated reasons for the attack was a sense of eroding political and cultural sovereignty in the Islamic world, as symbolized, for example, by the presence of U.S. military bases in Saudi Arabia and by the existence of a number of secular, Western-oriented regimes in the region. On the response side of the equation, a major focus of attention for the U.S. administration in the wake of September 11 was "regime change," first in Afghanistan and then in Iraq.

Against this backdrop, it is clearly important that we seek to understand the territorial logic of the modern state system and its role in different types of conflicts. A great deal of work has been done along these lines in recent decades. Scholars who have focused on the concept of the nation-state have devoted considerable attention to the gap between perception and reality that underlies the concept and have highlighted its pernicious influence in culturally diverse states.[1] Renewed interest in the nature of sovereignty has given rise to a body of literature that traces the social origins and consequences of organizing the earth's surface into a set of nonoverlapping, juridically autonomous spaces.[2] Studies of state territoriality have shed light on the processes by which state boundaries are constructed,[3] as well as prevailing notions of legitimacy that influence how and where territorial claims are pursued.[4] Much has been written about the ways in which the state system itself has co-opted the geographic imagination, which has made the state the privileged unit of analysis while obscuring the nature and significance of extrastate patterns and processes.[5]

Scholarly research along these lines has brought the generalized territorial dynamics of the modern state system into sharper focus, and many commentators have sought to situate their studies of specific conflicts in terms of these dynamics.[6] In so doing, they have demonstrated the importance of looking beyond the scale of the state in studies of war and peace. Because increasing attention is being devoted to the interaction of processes that unfold at the scale of the state and at larger scales, it is important to consider how larger scale processes are conceptualized. To date, the focus of attention has largely been processes that unfold at the global scale (e.g., economic globalization and global geopolitical arrangements), with much analysis of the ways in which these global processes shape state actions. Yet there are also processes that unite multiple states, but are not manifest at the global scale (e.g., processes associated with the effort to forge alliances among certain states based on perceived political, economic, or cultural commonalities). Such processes occur between the global and the state scales and therefore might be termed mesoscale processes.

The importance of focusing on the mesoscale is suggested by the fact that some, but not all, states share territorial understandings that influence how they view their boundaries. Glorified images of an antecedent state or empire play an important role in legitimizing particular territorial claims in a number of states. Modern Greek territorial ideology cannot be understood without reference to the symbolic role accorded to ancient Greece, just as territorial ideologies in Egypt, Iran, and China are framed with reference to the political-territorial precursors to these states. Yet such historical referents are completely lacking in countries such as Sudan, Indonesia, and Chile. This means that territorial claims in the latter cases must be built on different foundations from those in Greece, Egypt, Iran, and China, with clear implications for the types of territorial claims that can or will be pursued.

The foregoing examples suggest that there is something to be learned through investigation of the mesoscale. By definition, mesoscale processes operate within the more generalized logic of the state system, but they are not found everywhere. They are the product of an intersection between the territorial logic of the state system and circumstances that are shared by multiple, but not all, cases. Drawing on a study published in 2002,[7] this chapter identifies a set of mesoscale circumstances that influence the development of what I call "regimes of territorial legitimation" within states. These regimes consist of the institutions, practices, and discourses that are designed to legitimate a particular territorial conception of a state. After examining the character of these mesoscale circumstances, the chapter considers their impacts—first for more conventional boundary conflicts between states and then for conflicts that are challenging the stability of the contemporary international order.

Mesoscale Circumstances that Influence State Territoriality

The evolution of the modern state system is inextricably tied to the emergence of two concepts with clear territorial significance: sovereignty and the nation-state. The former presupposes a world of discrete juridical spaces that are theoretically autonomous with respect to one another. The second assumes a spatial conjunction between the pattern of discrete juridical spaces (states) on the earth's surface and the distribution of peoples that share a sense of common cultural history and a desire to control their own affairs (nations, in the original sense of the term). Although the literature that examines aspects of these two concepts is quite diverse,[8] there is widespread consensus about their foundational significance for the modern state system. In important respects they embody the rules, or at least the goals, that govern the legitimate exercise of power within the system.

The implication of the foregoing is that the concepts of sovereignty and the nation-state frame state efforts to gain and exercise power within the international arena. States may have widely different political systems, internal cultural geographies, and economic possibilities, but their legitimacy as states is tied to the normative territorial ideas associated with these two concepts (i.e., that states should be discrete territories and that the pattern of states should reflect the pattern of nations). By extension, those engaged in state building (sometimes called nation building) seek to sustain the notion that the state's territory is both a discrete unit and one that embodies (or at least can embody) a single nation. This explains why it is commonplace for political elites within states to make reference to the unified nature of their state's territory, no matter how physically, socially, or economically diverse it might be. Similarly, it explains why most political elites purport to speak on behalf of a single nation—referring to all of the people within the state territory—no matter what internal ethnonational divisions might exist.

Focusing on the character of arguments of this sort has clear implications for understanding the construction of regimes of territorial legitimation. Such regimes are a critical component of state building, since they serve to validate and justify the particular territorial foundation that undergirds state nationalism. Indeed, they are integral to the effort to promote state nationalism. The ideology of nationalism presupposes both the distinctiveness of a group and the right of that group to control its own affairs. Territorial understandings are at the heart of these concerns. They play a key symbolic role in the construction and maintenance of group identity and are seen as essential to a group's ability to exercise self-determination. Hence nationalist movements are often built and sustained around particular territorial representations. Repeated emphasis on these representations in the pages of school textbooks, on the walls of government offices, on postage stamps, and in the media continually reinforces notions of national identity.[9]

Since regimes of territorial legitimation must be developed in a normative environment that privileges territorial and ethnocultural unity, they inevitably play off of these norms. Yet state political elites are in very different positions in their efforts to promote notions of territorial or ethnocultural unity because some states evolved in places where certain notions of unity were well established or long-standing, whereas others did not. Understanding the different "positions" of states in this regard provides insights into a key mesoscale circumstance that influences state territoriality.

No two states are in the same position in the construction of regimes of territorial legitimation, of course, but there is a set of specific historical-geographic understandings associated with the development of some (but not all) states that political elites can invoke with particular effectiveness because they articulate well the territorial norms of the modern state system. The types of historical-geographic understandings that fit these criteria are suggested by an examination of the arguments that are repeatedly invoked in the discourse of state nationalism:[10]

1. That the state is the historic homeland of a distinctive ethnocultural group (e.g., France, Poland)
2. That the state is a distinctive physical-environmental unit (e.g., Hungary, Australia)
3. That the state is the modern incarnation of a long-standing political-territorial entity (e.g., Egypt, Mongolia)

It must be stressed that these are ideological arguments, which means that we cannot assume that they necessarily reflect an empirical historical or geographic reality. To put it another way, they are ways in which historical and geographic circumstances are idealized to foster notions of unity. At the same time, political elites cannot make arguments that run completely counter to dominant understandings of historical and geographic circumstance. Governmental leaders in Nigeria, for example, cannot easily contend that their country is the homeland of a single ethnocultural group, just as their counterparts in Mexico cannot easily claim that their country constitutes a physical-environmental unit, and political leaders in Chile cannot easily assert that their country is the modern incarnation of a great historic state or empire.

The point is that regimes of territorial legitimation are influenced by the geographic-cum-ideological context in which they develop. Some states' leaders can (and do) turn to arguments about their country's historic ethnocultural significance, others highlight their country's physical-environmental unity, and yet others draw attention to prior political-territorial formations that arguably gave rise to modern states. In certain states, leaders can even draw on more than one of these discourses (e.g., Japan as both an ethnocultural homeland and a physical-environmental unit). Conversely, many state leaders cannot turn to any of these arguments (e.g., the leaders of many former colonial states in Africa). In effect, then, we can think of situating regimes of territorial legitimation in terms of four mesoscale circumstances: the three listed earlier and a fourth category that represents the unavailability of the three dominant arguments about cultural, natural, or prior political unity.

It cannot be emphasized enough that this is a typology of geographically rooted ideologies, not of any kind of geographic reality. Almost none of the states that invoke an ethnic homeland argument are ethnically homogeneous, and the ethnic groups around which these states are supposedly built are themselves social constructs.[11] Similarly, what constitutes a natural unit is in the mind of the beholder, and the extent to which modern states are lineal descendants of ancient states or empires is an open question. The typology's aim is simply to promote thinking about where particular human or physical-geographic circumstances have been used by political elites to advance regimes of territorial legitimation, for this can provide a starting point for considering how different state-territorial postures can affect the global landscape of war and peace.

Impacts on Interstate Boundary Conflicts

During the past fifty years, disputed boundaries have been at the heart of the majority of conflicts fought between states.[12] Boundary disagreements range from controversies over small pieces of territory along an international boundary (e.g., Chile and Argentina) to cases where states seek a major realignment of the political map (e.g., India and Pakistan). A number of these cases involve territories that have clear economic or strategic value, but many do not. Why do we find India and Pakistan fighting at times over remote, sparsely inhabited areas? Why has Venezuela long pursued a claim over a significant portion of Guyana even though much of the territory in question is uninhabitable and there has been significant international pressure on Venezuela to drop the claim? One cannot answer such questions without considering the regimes of territorial legitimation that frame these conflicts.

Regimes of territorial legitimation are grounded in particular understandings of state entitlement to a certain piece of the Earth's surface, and that sense of entitlement, in turn, is rooted in what the state is imagined to be. This is where the aforementioned mesoscale circumstances that influence state territoriality come into play. A state such as Angola, which emerged out of Portuguese colonial rule in Africa and encompassed a region long thought of as ethnically and physically diverse, could only imagine itself within the context of a geographic unit that had been bequeathed to it by external forces and fate.[13] Under the circumstances, opposition to external control was the prime catalyst for the Angolan independence movement, and the nascent state's regime of territorial legitimation had to be built around the only geographic construct that was in any way present: the territory awarded to Portugal at the 1885 conference in Berlin. Moreover, since the spatial character of that territory has (with one minor exception) not changed since that time, there is little basis for contesting Angola's international boundaries. It is hardly surprising, then, that Angola has not had any boundary conflicts with its neighbors. (Of course, the prevalence of internal conflict within Angola is another matter.)

By contrast, consider the long-standing territorial conflicts between Greece and Turkey. These conflicts have centered both on islands just off the west coast of Turkey and, in a more indirect way, on the island of Cyprus.[14] There are clear strategic and economic dimensions to these conflicts; there is oil, for example, in the continental shelf off Turkey's west coast. But the conflicts are also deeply rooted in the regimes of territorial legitimation that developed in the modern Turkish and Greek states. In the case of Greece, that regime is inextricably tied to the idea that modern Greece is the lineal descendant of a great ancient empire.[15] Under the circumstances, the Greek reaction to the Turkish invasion of Cyprus in 1974 cannot be evaluated simply in economic or strategic terms. As the Greek Ministry of Foreign Affairs unequivocally asserts in a background foreign policy paper on Cyprus:

> The name of Cyprus has always been associated with Greek mythology (mostly famously as the birthplace of the goddess Aphrodite) and history. The Greek Achaeans established themselves on Cyprus around 1400 B.C. The island was an integral part of the Homeric world and, indeed, the word "Cyprus" was used by Homer himself. Ever since, Cyprus has gone through the same major historical phases as the rest of the Greek world (city-states led by rulers like Evagoras who played an important role in Greek history, participation in the campaigns of Alexander the Great, Hellenistic period under his successors, Roman conquest, Byzantine Empire). After the decline of the Byzantine Empire, the island, like the rest of Greece, came under foreign conquerors, notably the [Frankish] Crusaders in 1191 and the Turks in 1571. Throughout history, however, the island's character remained essentially Greek, since neither the disadvantage of its geographical position (distance from mainland Greece), nor the incessant raids and occupations, nor the introduction of foreign languages, religions and civilizations it underwent for centuries on end, were able to alter the religion, the culture, the language and the Greek consciousness of the great majority of its people.[16]

There is clearly something very different at stake here than could possibly be the case along Angola's borders. Because modern Greece is framed with reference to a political-territorial antecedent with different boundaries, questions of the territorial reach of the Greek state are at issue in a way that is inconceivable for Angola.

If the Greek-Turkish case highlights the role of historical-political geographic arrangements in the articulation of territorial claims, the relationship between Northern Ireland and the Republic of Ireland provides insight into the problems that can arise when state boundaries do not conform to a combination of environmental and ethnic conceptions. The Irish who fought for independence from Great Britain in the early twentieth century sought to rid "Ireland" of external domination.[17] If the independence movement had been framed solely in ethnocultural terms, it might have been easier to accept the idea that the portion of northern Ireland dominated by settlers from Great Britain (a smaller area than modern-day Northern Ireland proper) would not become part of an independent Ireland. But the island was also conceptualized as a natural unit, which meant that any solution short of independence for the entire island was seen as less than satisfactory.[18] As a result, a regime of territorial legitimation developed in the Republic of Ireland that was rooted in the idea of insular ethnoreligious unity. In consequence, the Republic of Ireland has never seen Northern Ireland simply as a neighboring state. For a variety of practical reasons, the Republic of Ireland has not aggressively pressed a territorial claim over Northern Ireland, but the Republic's ongoing involvement in the Northern Ireland question only makes sense when one considers the ideological foundations of the Republic's regime of territorial legitimation.

The foregoing examples show that the positioning of a state with respect to the four geographically rooted ideological categories described earlier can profoundly influence interstate boundary questions. Yet focusing on these mesoscale categories (as opposed to describing individual cases) only makes sense if the categories provide insight into commonalities shared by multiple cases. In looking for these commonalities, one should not think about these categories in a deterministic fashion. To have a regime of territorial legitimation rooted in one or another category does not mean that a state will necessarily adopt a particular position on an interstate boundary question; such matters are inevitably meditated by a variety of political, cultural, and economic factors. At the same time, these categories are suggestive of a set of generalized tendencies that can be helpful in understanding patterns of interstate territorial conflict. The most clear-cut of these tendencies are arguably the following:

- An ethnic distribution that crosses state boundaries is most likely to be a source of interstate territorial conflict where the ethnic group in question is the focus of at least one state's regime of territorial legitimation.
- A boundary arrangement is likely to be particularly unstable where it violates a well-established conception of a state's physical-environmental unity.
- States with regimes of territorial legitimation grounded in a preexisting political-territorial formation are likely to have particularly difficult relations with neighboring states that occupy or claim areas that are viewed as core to the prior political-territorial formation.
- States that are not in a position to ground regimes of territorial legitimation in any of the foregoing terms are less likely to have territorial conflicts with their neighbors unless there are strong economic or political motives for pressing a territorial claim and state leaders can point to some preexisting political arrangement or history of discovery and first use that arguably justifies the claim.

The applicability of these tendencies can be assessed by analyzing some of the major boundary conflicts of the last fifty years. In examining these cases, we should not necessarily expect that a given tendency will appear as part of a publicly articulated justification for a territorial claim. As I have argued elsewhere,[19] we live in an era in which claims to territory that are explicitly based on ethnic distributions or physical-environmental conceptions are not widely viewed as legitimate. Instead, prevailing international ideological and legal norms tend to promote historical justifications for territorial claims ("it is rightfully ours, it was wrongfully taken away, and we have the right to recover it"). Yet this does not mean that other factors are not involved. Economic opportunity is the most obvious of these,[20] but economically motivated claims cannot be pursued if there is no basis for justifying them in accordance with prevailing international norms or if they do not conform to dominant territorial ideas as developed through a state's regime of territorial legitimation. Since the latter issue is the crux of this inquiry, my concern is to evaluate whether there is at least indirect evidence that different types of regimes of territorial legitimation are influencing interstate conflict in a manner consistent with the previously identified tendencies.

Some of the most violent interstate conflicts of the modern era appear to bear out the first proposition, that ethnic distributions that cross state boundaries are most likely to be sources of interstate territorial conflict where a given ethnic group is the focus of at least one state's regime of territorial legitimation. Most obviously, at the heart of Nazi Germany's expansionist ideology was the purported "right" of the German state to control areas where ethnic Germans were living.[21] Claims to territory based overtly on ethnic grounds lost their legitimacy in the aftermath of World War II,[22] but the disjunction between political and ethnic boundaries has arguably played a significant role in a variety of territorial conflicts of the last fifty years, including those between India and Pakistan and between Armenia and Azerbaijan.

To understand the links between ethnic patterns and state territoriality, consider the territorial conflict between Armenia and Azerbaijan. The conflict centers on the region of Nagorno-Karabakh, a 4,400-square-kilometer area in the southern Caucasus that is situated inside Azerbaijan. Some three-quarters of the approximately 200,000 residents of Nagorno-Karabakh are ethnic Armenians, many of whom had backed a transfer of the region to Armenia before the collapse of the former Soviet Union.[23] In 1991, as the Soviet Union was being dismantled, the citizens of Nagorno-Karabakh voted overwhelmingly in favor of independence. Azerbaijan's leaders refused to recognize the vote, however, and even abolished the region's autonomous status within Azerbaijan. Conflict soon broke out, and the Armenians quickly came to the aid of the "secessionists" in Nagorno-Karabakh. As a result of this conflict, Azerbaijan lost some 20% of its territory, and relations between Armenia and Azerbaijan have since teetered on the brink of war.[24]

At the heart of this conflict are two states that have regimes of territorial legitimation that are rooted in ethnocultural understandings. Both Armenians and Azerbaijanis claim that their ancestors settled and developed the region, and both states point to the presence of their "peoples" within the territory to justify their claims.[25] As contesters of the status quo, the Armenians see the preindependence border with Azerbaijan as unreflective of the Armenian "nation," which gives them the right, or even the obligation, to intervene on behalf of the inhabitants of Nagorno-Karabakh. These circumstances clearly demonstrate the potential volatility of an ethnic distribution that crosses state boundaries where the ethnic group in question is the focus of a regime of territorial legitimation in one or more interested states. Viewing this conflict in terms of state regimes of territorial legitimation also provides insights into why the conflict has been so intractable.

If we shift attention to the second proposed tendency—that a boundary arrangement is likely to be particularly unstable where it violates a well-established conception of a state's physical-environmental unity—there are multiple cases that arguably lend credence to this proposition. Relations between the United States and Cuba have been complicated by U.S. control over a small part of the island of Cuba (Guantanamo). The United Kingdom's control of the Falkland Islands (off Argentina's southeast coast) has been seen as such an affront by Argentina that it sought (unsuccessfully) to take over the islands by force in 1982. This was not an endeavor to incorporate peoples who identified with Argentina into that country; the small population of the islands is English-speaking and of British descent. Instead, Argentina saw the islands as a natural part of its territory.[26] Yet another example is Spain's effort to gain some control over Gibraltar. This area of just over two square miles was once of great strategic value, but its current importance is largely symbolic.[27] Why should Spain press its case so vigorously? The obvious answer is that a United Kingdom-controlled Gibraltar sits in clear opposition to a regime of territorial legitimation that is rooted in part in a physical-environmental conception of Spain.

In one sense, all countries have regimes of territorial legitimation with some kind of physical-environmental dimension because once territorial constructs are established, they tend to carry with them a sense of naturalness. By extension, arrangements or developments that challenge that sense of naturalness can be foci of conflict even when a state has not developed a regime of territorial legitimation that is tied strongly to natural distinctiveness. Thus even as Spain contests British control of Gibraltar, Morocco contests Spain's control of two small pieces of territory in the Moroccan north (Ceuta and Melilla), as well as some uninhabited islands immediately off Morocco's north coast.[28]

The third mesoscale tendency posits that states with regimes of territorial legitimation that are grounded in preexisting political-territorial formations are likely to have particularly difficult relations with neighboring states that occupy or claim areas that are viewed as core to the antecedent unit. Once again, there is much to suggest that this tendency has some empirical foundation. Perhaps the most obvious case in point is China, which has been embroiled in many territorial disputes with its neighbors, including Vietnam, Japan (the Senkaku Islands), Russia, India, and Bhutan. [29] There are individual issues at play in each of China's boundary disputes, but a unifying theme is a Chinese sense of territory that is rooted in a regime of territorial legitimation that harkens back to the ancient Chinese empire. A similar, historically rooted sense of territory has arguably figured into both Iraq's and Ethiopia's territorial conflicts with neighboring states.

As the four-way typology of territorial ideologies shows, many states around the world did not develop in a historical-geographic context that lent itself to the establishment of regimes of territorial legitimation grounded in a strong sense of ethnic, physical, or historical-political unity. These cases are concentrated in the Western Hemisphere and in Africa. Since these regions have seen many boundary disputes, the absence of an ethnic, physical, or historical-political foundation for a regime of territorial legitimation does not ensure peaceful relations with neighboring states. On the other hand, the geography of interstate territorial conflict is quite uneven throughout this area. Studies by van der Wusten[30] and Chaliand and Rageau[31] clearly show that in the post–World War II era, boundary conflicts have been far more prevalent in Latin America than in sub-Saharan Africa, which even lags behind the Middle East and South/Southeast Asia in interstate border volatility.

The fourth mesoscale tendency identified earlier provides insight into the uneven geography of interstate boundary conflict. Unlike their Latin American counterparts, relatively few sub-Saharan states can point to some preexisting political or settlement arrangement that can justify a territorial claim. The majority of states in the region emerged in spaces that were created by external powers, with boundaries that were fixed from the beginning and did not vary over time.[32] Hence in these cases there was little prospect of forging a regime of territorial legitimation with an embedded sense of territory that differed from inherited colonial boundaries. The relevance of this point is suggested by looking at the places where interstate territorial conflict has occurred in sub-Saharan Africa. Virtually all such cases lie in areas where some kind of boundary adjustment or ambiguity can be traced to the colonial period.

The territorial dispute between Nigeria and Cameroon over the Bakassi Peninsula exemplifies the type of territorial conflict that is most prevalent in sub-Saharan Africa. The conflict focuses on a tiny land mass that juts into the Gulf of Guinea, right along the border between the two countries. The discovery of oil immediately off the coast of the peninsula attracted the interest of both the Nigerian and Cameroon governments, but the conflict has centered on a definition of the boundary in a 1913 treaty that was subject to differing interpretations. The treaty called for the border to be drawn in relation to "navigable waters" in the channel, but in the wake of the discovery of oil, controversies developed over what constitutes "navigability" and what impacts channel dredging might have had. After a series of confrontations between the countries, the dispute was finally sent to the International Court of Justice, which ruled in favor of Cameroon in late 2002.[33] Nigeria was clearly disappointed by the ruling, but the conflict may recede in significance if Nigeria's oil exploitation activities on its side of the border ultimately benefit from stability in the region. The larger question, however, is what conflicts of this sort reveal about states that must ground their regimes of territorial legitimation primarily in terms of externally imposed territorial spaces: ambiguities in the precise configuration of these spaces are what opens the door to competing claims to territory.

Latin America stands in sharp contrast to sub-Saharan Africa in that Latin America has been plagued by comparatively high levels of interstate territorial conflict over the years. Nonetheless, the pattern of interstate conflict in the region is consistent with the fourth tendency identified earlier, for the modern political pattern developed in a very different fashion in Latin America from the way it developed in sub-Saharan Africa. Although there were many large-scale politically organized areas with shifting or flexible boundaries in sub-Saharan Africa prior to extensive European colonization of the continent, few of the present states can trace their origins to these political territories, and most of the colonial borders were established without significant debate and did not change over time. By contrast, the borders of most Spanish administrative units in South America shifted during the long course of Spanish colonialism. Thus the door was open to competing interpretations of state territorial rights.

The long-standing, high-profile conflict between Ecuador and Peru over an area in northwestern Peru that lies to the west of Iquitos provides a classic example of a boundary dispute that emerged out of competing understandings of colonial political-geographic history. In this case, however, the dispute is not simply about the location of administrative boundaries, but also centers on Ecuador's claim that explorers sent out from Quito (Ecuador's capital) first discovered and claimed this area.[34] Ecuador does not rely solely on this argument; it also seeks to base its claim on a sixteenth-century land grant from King Philip II of Spain and on a treaty signed in 1829. But the "discovery argument" introduces an element that goes beyond boundary adjustments or ambiguities. It shows that in parts of the world where a political pattern emerged in the context of "discovery" and settlement, notions of rightful territorial dominion are not tied simply to an inherited political-territorial pattern. The history of exploration and land use can be part of the picture as well (e.g., the United States in its westward expansion).

What seems clear in all of these cases is that state territorial claims cannot be divorced from the regimes of territorial legitimation that frame them. These regimes are based on accepted notions of the nature of the state as a spatial construct, and these notions, in turn, are tied to received understandings of the cultural, physical, or historical foundations of the state. Moreover, as state regimes of territorial legitimation develop, they shape the geographic imaginations of policy makers and citizens and foster territorial ideas and aspirations that underlie all interstate conflicts over territory. The positioning of states in the global political economy will obviously influence whether particular ideas and aspirations lead to overt conflict, but understanding normative influences on particular ideas and aspirations can shed light on the nature and causes of interstate territorial conflict.

Impacts below and above the Scale of the State

Since regimes of territorial legitimation are, by definition, features of individual states, their most direct impact is likely to be on boundary conflicts between states. Yet these regimes also have conflict implications at other scales. For example, they can have a direct bearing on the situation of minority groups within states because they are grounded in a particular vision of what state territory is or should be. It is thus instructive to consider how different mesoscale influences on state territoriality may be implicated in conflicts below and above the scale of the state.

On the substate scale, a 2002 study of intrastate ethnic conflict potential in Asia identified a set of key motivating conditions for intrastate ethnic conflict.[35] The study suggests that ethnic conflict potential is particularly high where a group "is located in a territorial unit controlled by another group that considers the area its sole domain."[36] This type of situation is most likely to occur in a state with a regime of territorial legitimation grounded in the idea that a state is the historic homeland of a distinctive ethnocultural group. Indeed, many of the cases where movements for autonomy or independence have gained momentum among substate minorities are found in states with regimes of territorial legitimation that are focused, at least in part, on the state as an ethnic homeland. Mikesell and Murphy's examination of the evolution of minority group aspirations, for example, analyzes several classic cases where substate nationalist movements have come to be dominated by calls for autonomy and independence: the Tamils in Sri Lanka, the Basques in Spain, the Sikhs in India, and the Kurds in "Kurdistan."[37] In all of these cases, the minority group in question is faced with a state political elite that largely defines the state in terms of a single, dominant ethnic group. The Kurdish case is more complicated because it involves multiple states, but the situation of the Kurds in Turkey certainly conforms to the general pattern.

The foregoing examples suggest that in a wide variety of cases, regimes of territorial legitimation with a strong ethnic component can be catalysts for conflict. By contrast, those regimes that are grounded in physical-environmental or historical-political terms have less clear-cut implications for internal unity. Nonetheless, such regimes can make it more difficult for political elites to acknowledge the territorial claims of substate groups that live in territories that are deemed to be integral to the state. The historical-political element in China's regime of territorial legitimation, for example, is not just an issue for that country's territorial relations with neighboring states; it also has implications for how China views its western territories, particularly Tibet.

This does not mean that states without strong physical or historical foundations to their regimes of territorial legitimation will voluntarily surrender territory; there are few cases where this has happened. Yet a hesitancy to devolve greater power to local areas can be tied to a particularly entrenched state-territorial view. Moreover, in those rare cases where states have ceded territory without attempting to intervene militarily (e.g., Czechoslovakia before the emergence of an independent Slovakia; Yugoslavia with reference to the secession of Slovenia), the territory in question has not been a core element of a regime of territorial legitimation defined in ethnic, physical, or historical-political terms.

The types of regimes of territorial legitimation discussed in this chapter are also implicated in some of the regional and even global geopolitical circumstances that are features of the current landscape of war and peace. Consider, for example, the presence of U.S. military bases in Saudi Arabia. These bases were established in the wake of the 1991 Gulf War; the administration of then U.S. president George H. W. Bush (1989–1993) presumably viewed these bases as essential to U.S. security interests. Yet the presence of these bases has arguably undermined, rather than promoted, U.S. security. Al-Qaeda leaders have focused attention on these bases to reinforce their claims that the United States is seeking domination of the Islamic world,[38] and more generally the bases have served as a catalyst for anti-Americanism in the region.

There are, of course, complex reasons behind the reactions to the U.S. military bases in Saudi Arabia, but it is instructive to consider whether the reactions would have been the same if the bases had been established in Oman or the United Arab Emirates (UAE). It is impossible to know what the implications of alternative base locations might have been, but there is much to suggest that the reaction would have been less intense because Oman and the UAE do not have the same symbolic ethnocultural significance as does Saudi Arabia. The latter presents itself as the Arab-Islamic homeland,[39] and this view has arguably insinuated itself into the country's dominant regime of territorial legitimation. As such, Saudi Arabia has come to occupy a special place in the visions of those who seek to use violence to alter the current geopolitical situation. In keeping with this vision, Osama bin Laden has made clear his ambition to turn Saudi Arabia into a strictly religious Muslim state that will preserve Islam's holiest places (Mecca and Medina) by replacing the secular Saudi royal family with a religious government headed by the Wahhabi sect.[40] The combination of this vision and the failure of the "West" to recognize its power is at the heart of the recent confrontations that have pitted al-Qaeda and its sympathizers against the United States and some of its allies.

In a somewhat more tenuous vein, regimes of territorial legitimation can find expression in the postures states assume in the international arena. Turkey's recent efforts to promote connections with former Ottoman realms and to foster a sense of the country's centrality to a larger "Turkic world" may well reflect the continuing significance of prior political-territorial formations for the modern Turkish state.[41] This is not to suggest that Turkey is pursing an expansionist territorial project. Instead, what it signals is Turkey's effort to define state interests in ways that are consistent with its regime of territorial legitimation.

Particular regimes of territorial legitimation can also lead states to reject initiatives that run counter to the principles that underlie these regimes. The failure of regional integration initiatives in the Middle East and North Africa, for example, can arguably be tied in part to opposing territorial ideologies on the part of participating states.[42] It is even possible that Iranian outrage over U.S. president George W. Bush's 2002 reference to an "axis of evil" (which encompassed Iraq, Iran, and North Korea) reflected not just a sense that the country was being wrongfully maligned, but that it was being lumped together with states that lacked Iran's historical and ethnocultural legitimacy. Such sensibilities are nurtured and channeled through regimes of territorial legitimation.

The foregoing examples suggest that the ideological underpinnings of state regimes of territorial legitimation are not just relevant to an understanding of the particular territorial claims that states make. They can, moreover, insinuate themselves into the geopolitical arena in a variety of ways. It follows that if we are to gain a deeper understanding of the geography of war and peace, consideration must be given to the ideological underpinnings of state territoriality.

Conclusion

The map of states is often treated as a set of defined spaces within which power is exercised.[43] Yet such an approach ignores the territorial ideas and processes that give rise to that map and that shape its character and significance. These ideas and processes can be examined at a variety of scales, and the focus here is only on one of those: the scale at which geographically and historically situated regimes of territorial legitimation develop. The foregoing discussion should not be read as an effort to privilege this scale over others; ultimately, an understanding of state territoriality cannot be divorced from both the large-scale structural forces that frame it and the circumstances of individual cases. By focusing on the mesoscale circumstances and ideologies highlighted in this chapter, however, we arguably gain insight into the complexities of state territorial behavior.

Beyond this general advantage, the mesoscale approach adopted here provides a means of considering commonalities and differences that cut across conventional categorizations of the state system. States are often grouped together on the basis of socioeconomic position or their role in the global political economy, and we learn much from such groupings. Yet these groupings are also likely to place states such as Peru, Gabon, and Myanmar (Burma) all in the same category. A focus on regimes of territorial legitimation, by contrast, provides insights into dynamics within these states that find expression in different approaches to state boundaries and different perspectives on larger scale geopolitical issues. Looking at these dynamics together with more broad-ranging and more localized influences on state territoriality promises to enrich our understanding of the geography of war and peace.

Notes

1. For example, see Eley and Suny, *Becoming National*; Beiner, *Theorizing Nationalism*; B. Parekh, "Defining National Identity in a Multicultural Society"; Appadurai, "Grounds of the Nation-State."
2. Biersteker and Weber, *State Sovereignty as Social Construct*.
3. Paasi, *Territories, Boundaries, and Consciousness*; Sahlins, *Boundaries*.
4. Murphy, "Historical Justifications for Territorial Claims."
5. Taylor, "State as Container"; Taylor, "Beyond Containers."
6. Kliot and Waterman, *Political Geography of Conflict and Peace*.
7. Murphy, "National Claims to Territory in the Modern State System."
8. For example, Murphy, "International Law and the Sovereign State System"; Hooson, *Geography and National Identity*; Krasner, *Sovereignty*.
9. Dijkink, *National Identity and Geopolitical Visions*.
10. This list follows in part Murphy, "National Claims to Territory in the Modern State System," 200–203.
11. For nation as social construct, see Jackson and Penrose, *Constructions of Race, Place, and Nation*; Calhoun, *Nationalism*; Rygiel, "Stabilizing Borders."
12. See the extensive study of territorial conflicts by *Border and Territorial Disputes*.
13. Okuma, *Angola in Ferment*; Birmingham, *Portugal and Africa*.
14. Bahcheli, *Greek-Turkish Relations since 1955*, 190.
15. See Kassimeris, "Greeks, Stop Bearing Grudges."
16. Hellenic Republic Ministry of Foreign Affairs, "Cyprus: Geographical and Historical Background."
17. O'Halloran, *Partition and the Limits of Irish Nationalism*; Oonagh, *Ireland's Independence, 1880–1923*.
18. Kearney, *British Isles*; Keogh, *Twentieth-Century Ireland*.
19. Murphy, "Historical Justifications for Territorial Claims."
20. Goertz and Diehl, *Territorial Changes and International Conflict*, 105–126.
21. Gonen, *Roots of Nazi Psychology*, 99–136.
22. Murphy, "Sovereign State System as Political-Territorial Ideal."
23. Council of Europe, "Report on the Conflict in Magorno-Karabakh."
24. See Human Rights Watch, *Azerbaijan*.
25. See Carley, "Nagorno-Karabakh."
26. House, "Unfinished Business in the South Atlantic."
27. Carlin, "Most Idiotic Quarrel on Earth"; "Spain Seeks Joint Control of Gibraltar."
28. "A Row over Rocks."
29. Day, *Border and Territorial Disputes*, 279–315.

30. van der Wusten, "Geography of Conflict since 1945."

31. Chaliand and Rageau, *Strategic Atlas*, 47–50.

32. Shaw, *Title to Territory in Africa*, 31–51.

33. "Cameroon-Nigeria: Focus on Nigeria's Response to ICJ Ruling on Bakassi Peninsula."

34. Elbow, "Territorial Loss and National Image."

35. Fuller et al., "Potential for Ethnic Conflict in China,"

36. Ibid., 590.

37. Mikesell and Murphy, "Framework for Comparative Study of Minority-Group Aspirations."

38. World Islamic Front, "Jihad against Jews and Crusaders."

39. "Profile of Saudi Arabia."

40. Pfaff, "Strange Alliance with Saudi and Pakistani Foes of Modernity."

41. Evered, "Romancing the Region."

42. Drysdale and Blake, *Middle East and North Africa*, 149–190.

43. Agnew, "Territorial Trap."

References

Agnew, J. "The Territorial Trap: The Geographical Assumptions of International Relations Theory." *Review of International Political Economy* 1 (1994): 53–80.

Appadurai, A. "The Grounds of the Nation-State: Identity, Violence, and Territory." In *Nationalism and Internationalism in the Post–Cold War Era*, ed. K. Goldmann, U. Hannerz, and C. Westin, 129–142. New York: Routledge, 2000.

Bahcheli, T. *Greek-Turkish Relations since 1955*. Boulder, CO: Westview, 1990.

Beiner, R. *Theorizing Nationalism* Albany: State University of New York Press, 1999.

Biersteker, T. J., and C. Weber, eds. *State Sovereignty as Social Construct*. Cambridge: Cambridge University Press, 1996.

Birmingham, D. *Portugal and Africa*. New York: St. Martin's, 1999.

Calhoun, C. J. *Nationalism*. Minneapolis: University of Minnesota Press, 1997.

"Cameroon-Nigeria: Focus on Nigeria's Response to ICJ Ruling on Bakassi Peninsula." IRNNEWS. ORG, UN Office for the Coordination of Humanitarian Affairs, 2002. www.irinnews.org/report.asp?ReportID–30415 (accessed January 28, 2003).

Carley, P. "Nagorno-Karabakh: Searching for a Solution." United States Institute of Peace Roundtable Report, Peaceworks no. 25. www.usip.org/pubs/pworks/pwks25/pwks25.html (December 1998; accessed February 22, 2003).

Carlin, J. "The Most Idiotic Quarrel on Earth—Spain and Britain Go Crazy over Gibraltar." *New Statesman*, April 2, 2001, 32–33.

Chaliand, G., and J.-P. Rageau. *A Strategic Atlas: Comparative Geopolitics of the World's Powers*. 2nd ed. New York: Harper and Row, 1985.

Council of Europe. "Report on the Conflict in Magorno-Karabahl." http://assembly.cue.int/documents/workingdocs/doc94/educ7182.htm (October 17, 1994; accessed February 22, 2003).

"Cyprus: Geographical and Historical Background." Hellenic Republic Ministry of Foreign Affairs. www.mfa.gr/english/foreign_policy/europe_southeastern/cyprus/background.html (accessed April 6, 2004).

Day, A. J., ed. *Border and Territorial Disputes*. 2nd ed., revised and updated. Detroit: Gale, 1987.

Dijkink, G. *National Identity and Geopolitical Visions: Maps of Pride and Pain*. London: Routledge, 1996.

Drysdale, A., and G. H. Blake. *The Middle East and North Africa: A Political Geography*. New York: Oxford University Press, 1985.

Elbow, G. S. "Territorial Loss and National Image: The Case of Ecuador." *Yearbook—Conference of Latin Americanist Geographers* 22 (1996): 93–107.

Eley, G., and R. G. Suny. *Becoming National: A Reader*. New York: Oxford University Press, 1996.

Evered, K. T. "Romancing the Region: Mapping the Discursive Terrains in Turkish Constructs of a 'Türk Dünyasi.' " Ph.D. diss., University of Oregon, 2002.

Fuller, G., R. Morrison, A. B. Murphy, and M. Ridgley. "Potential for Ethnic Conflict in China." *Eurasian Geography and Economics* 43 (2002): 583–609.

Goertz, G., and P. F. Diehl. *Territorial Changes and International Conflict*. New York: Routledge, 1992.

Gonen, J. Y. *The Roots of Nazi Psychology: Hitler's Utopian Barbarism*. Lexington: University Press of Kentucky, 2000.

Hooson, D. J. M., ed. *Geography and National Identity*. Cambridge, MA: Blackwell, 1994.

House, J. W. "The Unfinished Business in the South Atlantic: The Falkland/Malvinas Dispute." *Political Geography Quarterly* 2 (1983): 233–246.

Human Rights Watch. *Azerbaijan: Seven Years of Conflict in Nagorno-Karabakh*. New York: Human Rights Watch, 1994.

Jackson, P., and J. Penrose. *Constructions of Race, Place, and Nation*. Minneapolis: University of Minnesota Press, 1994.

Kassimeris, G. "Greeks, Stop Bearing Grudges; An Arms Race with Turkey Is No Way Forward for Greece; Commentary." *Independent*, January 15, 1997, 13. Retrieved February 7, 2003 through Lexis-Nexis database.

Kearney, H. *The British Isles: A History of Four Nations*. New York: Cambridge University Press, 1989.

Keogh, D. *Twentieth-Century Ireland: Nation and State*. Dublin: Gill and Macmillan, 1994.

Kliot, N., and S. Waterman. *The Political Geography of Conflict and Peace*. London: Belhaven, 1991.

Krasner, S. D. *Sovereignty: Organized Hypocrisy*. Princeton, NJ: Princeton University Press, 1999.

Mikesell, M., and A. B. Murphy. "A Framework for Comparative Study of Minority-Group Aspirations." *Annals of the Association of American Geographers* 81 (1991): 581–604.

Murphy, A. B. "Historical Justifications for Territorial Claims." *Annals of the Association of American Geographers* 80 (1990): 531–548.

Murphy, A. B. "International Law and the Sovereign State System: Challenges to the Status Quo." In *Reordering the World: Geopolitical Perspectives on the Twenty-first Century*, ed. G. J. Demko and W. B. Wood, 209–224. Boulder, CO: Westview, 1994.

Murphy, A. B. "The Sovereign State System as Political-Territorial Ideal: Historical and Contemporary Considerations." In *State Sovereignty as Social Construct*, ed. T. J. Biersteker and C. Weber, 81–120. Cambridge: Cambridge University Press, 1996.

Murphy, A. B. "National Claims to Territory in the Modern State System: Geographical Considerations." *Geopolitics* 7 (2002): 193–214.

O'Halloran, C. *Partition and the Limits of Irish Nationalism: An Ideology under Stress*. Dublin: Gill and Macmillan, 1987.

Okuma, T. M. *Angola in Ferment: The Background and Prospects of Angolan Nationalism*. Boston: Beacon, 1962.

Oonagh, W. *Ireland's Independence, 1880–1923*. New York: Routledge, 2002.

Parekh, B. "Defining National Identity in a Multicultural Society." In *People, Nation, and State: The Meaning of Ethnicity and Nationalism*, ed. E. Mortimer, and R. Fine, 66–74. New York: Tauris, 1999.

Paasi, A. *Territories, Boundaries, and Consciousness: The Changing Geographies of the Finnish-Russian boundary*. New York: Wiley, 1996.

Pfaff, W. "A Strange Alliance with Saudi and Pakistani Foes of Modernity." *International Herald Tribune*. www.iht.com/ihtsearch.php?id=34162&owner=(International%20Herald%20Tribune)&date=20021224074103. (October 1, 2001).

"Profile of Saudi Arabia." Saudi Embassy. www.saudiembassy.net/profile/Saudi-Profileoo.htm (aceessed February 22, 2003).

"A Row over Rocks." *Economist*. www.economist.com/displayStory.cfm?Story_ID=S')H%24(PA7%20%23P!4%0A (July 19, 2002; accessed July 25, 2002).

Rygiel, K. "Stabilizing Borders: The Geopolitics of National Identity Construction in Turkey." In *Rethinking Geopolitics*, ed. S. Dalby and G. Ó Tuathail, 106–129. New York: Routledge, 1998.

Sahlins, P. *Boundaries: The Making of France and Spain in the Pyrenees*. Berkeley: University of California Press, 1989.

Shaw, M. *Title to Territory in Africa: International Legal Issues*. Oxford: Clarendon Press, 1986.

"Spain Seeks Joint Control of Gibraltar." *Commonwealth Law Bulletin* 23 (1997): 590.

Taylor, P. J. "The State as Container: Territoriality in the Modern State." *Progress in Human Geography* 18 (1994): 151–162.

Taylor, P. J. "Beyond Containers: Internationality, Interstateness, Interterritoriality." *Progress in Human Geography* 19 (1995): 1–15.

van der Wusten, H. "The Geography of Conflict since 1945." In *The Geography of Peace and War*, ed. D. Pepper and A. Jenkins, 13–28. Oxford: Blackwell, 1985.

World Islamic Front. "Jihad against Jews and Crusaders." www.fas.org/irp/world/para/docs/980223-fatwa.htm (February 23, 1998; accessed February 22, 2003).

GHAZI-WALID FALAH

Peace, Deception, and Justification for Territorial Claims

The Case of Israel

Television and print news media are replete with images of the Palestinian-Israeli conflict. For most of us, thankfully, that is how we experience war—through media representations and political rhetoric carefully crafted to solicit support and sympathy. Given Walzer's claim that a war deemed unjust is a war misliked,[1] and that conflicts are undertaken within the broader politics of the interstate system, it follows that the geopolitics of conflict includes the battle of projecting war goals, strategy, and tactics to gain the "moral high ground." Mostly, it is the politics rather than the practice of war that we evaluate and respond to.

Though this chapter illuminates the manipulation of the image of the Palestinian-Israeli conflict, it is concerned with the brutal realities "on the ground" that are the manifestations and reasons of the ongoing conflict. Of particular interest is the manner in which an embryonic Palestinian state is represented as failing in the "policing" tasks that are generally understood to be the duty of a sovereign state while, at the same time, it faces political-geographic constraints that deny it the ability to exercise authority. While the Palestinians are denied a functioning state, the establishment of the Palestinian Authority has enabled the embryonic political entity to be labeled a "rogue" that is unwilling to prevent acts of terrorism. The case study shows how intrastate geopolitics, from a Gramscian perspective, is an essential component of exerting power and debilitating opponents. Finally, analysis of this conflict allows us to note how the dynamism of war and peace entails changing political geographies of conflict, especially how the Palestinians have been constrained by abandoning their established geography of resistance and constructing a space of state power amid severe geopolitical constraints.

The Geopolitics of Peace Initiatives

Three territorial suggestions for resolving the Israeli-Palestinian conflict by peaceful means have been envisioned and in the air since the end of the Gulf War in

1991, but despite the involvement of many parties in the process, there has been no meaningful progress on any of them. These suggestions for a lasting peace in the Middle East can be characterized as "land for peace," "comprehensive peace," and "peace for peace." Each of these envisioned formulas entails different territorial components that are differently interpreted by the parties involved.

The land-for-peace concept was and still is the formula that enjoys the highest level of acceptance in the international community, including the United States, the European Union, and the Palestinians. It is also known as the two-state solution for the Israeli-Palestinian conflict. The thrust of this formula is that Israel must comply with UN Security Council Resolutions 242 and 338, which call on it to withdraw from the territories conquered by military force in the June War of 1967, that is, the West Bank and Gaza Strip areas, including East Jerusalem.[2] Significantly, Israel has been in material breach of these resolutions for thirty-five years. Once Israel complies with these resolutions, so goes the narrative, the Palestinians will be given the opportunity to achieve self-determination and assume sovereignty over these territories, which form 23% of their homeland. Needless to say, this solution is viewed by the Palestinian people and their leadership as a historic territorial compromise, one that explicitly recognizes Israel's sovereignty over the remaining 77% of Palestine as defined by the old British Mandate. Significantly, this historic compromise is the substance of President Yasser Arafat's rhetoric in his repeated statement about the "peace of the brave" that he was hoping to conclude with the late Israeli prime minister Yitzhak Rabin within the framework of the Oslo Agreements of 1993 and 1995.

The term "comprehensive peace" suggests that once the Israeli-Palestinian conflict has been resolved on the basis of a land-for-peace formula, Israel is likely to be in a better position to achieve full and comprehensive peaceful relationships with the rest of the Arab countries. Most Arab countries other than Syria and Lebanon do not have any territorial dispute with Israel, and the 2002 Arab League summit held in Beirut reaffirmed Arab readiness to recognize Israel's existence with what was presented as the Saudi peace plan—a plan that was also accepted by most Arab countries.[3]

Unlike the two earlier concepts, the "peace-for-peace" formula has little support in the international community (outside certain conservative circles in the United States) and is totally unacceptable to the Palestinians. This concept sees no need for Israel to withdraw from any territory it has gained by force from the Palestinians and holds that the Palestinians and the Arab world have to accept or acquiesce in Israeli hegemony and territorial control over all of Palestine from the Jordan River to the Mediterranean. Israel will "offer" peace to the Arabs but no land, bypassing Palestinians' quest for self-determination and all UN resolutions altogether. This formula has become almost the tacit blueprint for the current Israeli Likud-led government in dealing with Palestinian issues despite occasional statements made by the prime minister that announce readiness for a certain minimal kind of state under the terms of Israel.[4] Beyond this solution, there are some sectors in the Israeli political class and public who favor an alternative, fundamentally extreme scenario that includes the transfer of Palestinians by force (or choice) from Palestine to areas east of the Jordan River at some point in the future when the political ground for such a drastic move has been prepared and the time appears propitious.[5]

The purpose of this chapter is to spotlight the spatial practices of domination practiced by Israel vis-à-vis the Palestinian people and leadership and on their turf since the Oslo I and II Agreements (1993 and 1995) down to the present. I argue that although the concept of the "land-for-peace" formula was ostensibly adopted by Israel as a geopolitical code when it embarked on peace talks with the Palestine Liberation Organization (PLO) in 1993, Israel's actions on the ground since then have been in striking contradiction to this slogan. It has simultaneously launched and developed a spatial policy for seizing ever more land from the Palestinians, increasing the number of West Bank settlers by more than 100% during the past decade while fragmenting Palestinian space into a territorial patchwork[6]—a policy whose primary aim is to eventually block the establishment of a viable Palestinian state once the stage of negotiation on a final solution is reached. The stress here is on "viable." I further argue that the five successive Israeli governments since 1993 (headed by Rabin, Shimon Peres, Benjamin Netanyahu, Ehud Barak, and now Ariel Sharon) have never made a genuine break with more than a 100-year-old Zionist geopolitical ideological code that calls for the redemption of the entire land in Mandatory Palestine—redemption, a concept laden with theological and millenarian overtones, indeed, a unique and distinctive form of irredentism. In other words, peace talks with the Palestinians were not conceived by these governments as an end but rather as a means, an instrument of discourse designed to further and consolidate Israel's spatial hegemony over Palestinian space (the long lost national-religious irredenta) and implement the overriding aim of the Zionist agenda: redemption of Eretz Israel by wresting it from the control of its "alien" inhabitants.

To be sure, even some Israeli leaders, including the present Prime Minister, Sharon, occasionally announce their readiness to accept the creation of a Palestinian state. Yet an analysis of the politics of deception shows that these pronouncements cannot be taken at face value: crucial here is what is meant by a "state." Will this entity be free to act like any other state in the world with regard to issues of sovereignty and territorial control of its own land? Consider, for example, one version of a Palestinian state envisioned by Sharon after his January 28, 2003, Knesset election, a statement intended as part of more than 100 modifications to the U.S.-backed peace road map: "Palestine would be totally demilitarized; it would only be allowed to maintain a police force and domestic security forces, armed with light weapons; Israel will control all the entrances and exits and the air space above the state; Palestinians would be absolutely forbidden to form alliances with enemies of Israel."[7] It is precisely these diverse Bantustan-like limitations that Israeli leaders and negotiators have systematically attempted to impose on the birth of a viable Palestinian state. The recent tripartite segmentation of occupied Gaza is a further escalation in this turning of the spatial screw.

To illuminate these strategies of deceptive discourse and better understand why progress for peace has been thwarted, it is useful to see this complex within a conceptual framework that can elucidate the practices of hegemonic power and control. In doing so, I intend here to go behind the simple construction much reiterated in the United States and Israel to the effect that Barak made Arafat a generous offer at Camp David but that it was rejected outright, and that then the Palestinians turned to violence and terrorism to achieve their goals. For their part, when the PLO agreed to enter into peace talks with Israel and thereby recognized its existence—a political step with significance for Israel—the PLO agreed in effect to transform the nature of the conflict from violent resistance to temporary domination.[8] Yet after the outbreak of the Intifadat Al-Aqsa in September 2000,[9] the conflict returned to militant "resistance," now with the participation of the Palestinian masses in rebellion against the occupying power.

At this critical juncture, the Oslo Agreements are for all practical purposes dead, nullified by events. At least this is true for the Israeli side after Sharon's repeated declaration that he was no longer bound by these agreements and his orders for Israeli tanks and soldiers to invade Palestinian autonomous areas and ravage homes and households. The emblem of this attack on household space was the siege of Arafat's compound in Ramallah, which penetrated as far as his very bedroom. A military occupation has in effect been reimposed.

The Oslo Agreements and Israel's Strategy for Gaining Control of More Palestinian Land

This section seeks to highlight certain aspects of hegemonic practices employed by Israel during negotiations with the Palestinians. These practices include a strategy that aims to manipulate events to its own benefit and to deny and occasionally discredit the other side for not adhering to the rules of the game. Yet Israel at the same time seeks to portray itself as a peacemaker that supposedly demonstrates great flexibility and is prepared to make "painful" decisions to bring a final peace to the region.

These tactics have a larger geopolitical scope: they are key to preserving the continuing support of the United States (in its self-styled role as international peace broker) while opening windows for eventual peace talks with other Arab countries. On the local level, Israel continues its colonization strategy of incorporating Palestinian land, creating what it calls facts on the ground. Israel's political class does not appear to understand that building confidence measures should also include efforts to make Palestinians feel that they are benefiting from peace.

The reason for these tactics is to enhance the image of Israeli power in Palestinian eyes and to present itself to the Palestinians as a tough negotiating partner—as tough as possible when it comes to territory—that seeks to hold onto as much land as possible before reaching the final stage.[10] Such an approach is predicated on an assessment that the Palestinians are ready to agree to be "temporarily exploited" at this stage of interim talks. Israel has played the game of "take it or leave it." If the Palestinians do not agree, the status quo will remain intact. Meanwhile, Israel has taken control over ever more territory, ostensibly with the hope of using it as a "bargaining chip" in future negotiations.

The Palestinian negotiators, guided by Arafat, adopted a different tack. They sought to gain eventual control over as much territory as possible from which Israel would agree to withdraw once a stage of a "final solution" is reached. That "liberated" territory would also have specific military value should there be a unilateral declaration of a Palestinian state. This notion was clearly stated in a piece posted on the Fateh Online Web site in 1998:

> We in the Fateh movement see May 4, 1999, as the historic day on which we will realize our rights. . . . The declaration of our national state, including Jerusalem, is crucial to the future of the Palestinian people. We are taking the measures that facilitate this historic achievement with the least number of losses. A declaration of statehood, while the PNA controls only 3% of the West Bank, as it does now, would be far weaker than a declaration made with the PNA controlling 17%, in addition to the land in Area B, which amounts to another 25%. The additional land would obviously strengthen our position in any confrontation.[11]

In the international arena, it was very important for Arafat to gain the trust of the White House (as primary broker), and thus he was ready to make certain compromises as long as these compromises were understood to be temporary and did not jeopardize the Palestinian negotiating position later at the final stage. In short, Israeli negotiators have understood Arafat's political vulnerability at two levels: in the eyes of Washington and at home among the Palestinian masses. They have tried to exploit this weak spot. As part of their tactics, they were prepared to dishonor or amend signed agreements to eventually get the Palestinian side to accept less Israeli territorial withdrawal than what had been agreed upon at Oslo.

Kacowicz reminds us that peaceful territorial change is most likely to occur where there is an asymmetrical distribution of power between the parties, but not so asymmetrical as to allow a unilateral solution to the problem.[12] Another perspective on Israel's manner of negotiating with the Palestinians can be contextualized within the dynamic geography of power relations. According to Nietschmann, the state rather than the nation has the power not only to create the agenda but to determine international law.[13] The ability to create the agenda is itself a form of non–decision making by which one side can refuse even to consider proposals made by the other side or even deny their existence.[14] For example, when the Oslo Accords were signed in 1995, the Palestinians tried to address the settlement issue immediately, but the United States insisted that such discussions be delayed.[15] The Palestinians had no other option but to wait.

Israel's first exercise in imposing its hegemony over peace talks was inscribed in the Oslo Agreement itself and managed to postpone negotiations on three so-called thorny issues: Jerusalem, the status of the Jewish settlement in the West Bank, and the fate of the Palestinian refugees.[16] How is this "nondecision" decision being implemented on the ground? One should note that these three issues are linked to a space (i.e., territory) that was slated to be partitioned or shared at some time after the end of the five-year so-called interim period. But that postponement was translated into a strategy of stalling, coupled with a colonizing race for acquiring more and more territory to create an irreversible geographical reality of expanded settlement that would progressively shrink the territory to be shared with the Palestinians.[17] According to Zunes, since the Oslo Accords were signed, Israeli settlers on the West Bank (excluding East Jerusalem) have more than doubled to

200,000, some within thirty new settlements and the rest in expansions of existing settlements. Settlers in greater East Jerusalem have increased by at least one-third.[18] A report released by B'Tselem on May 13, 2002, concerning Israel's settlement policy in the West Bank reveals that while the built-up areas of the Jewish settlements constitute only 1.7% of the land of the West Bank, the municipal boundaries are more than three times as large, 6.8%. Jewish regional councils constitute an additional 35.1%. Thus a total of 41.9% of the area in the West Bank is controlled by Jewish settlement and its authorities.[19] Bear in mind that these settlements are all illegal in the eyes of international law: it is illegal under the Fourth Geneva Convention for any country to transfer its civilian population onto lands seized by military force.[20] The Palestinians view the continuous process of expansion of settlement during extended negotiations with great consternation because it reduces the space over which they can negotiate in the very process of talks. Their protests to the White House changed nothing.

Under the Clinton administration, this settlement policy was simply categorized in diplomatic double-talk as "unhelpful." Under the George W. Bush administration, Israeli settlement expansion was termed "provocative."[21] Probably the most deceptive rhetoric during the peace negotiations is embedded in the language used to describe the areas under Israeli control. The areas in question are "occupied territory" and not "disputed territory," a term introduced by the Israelis as if to claim an Israeli asset (real estate) that Israel was asked to transfer in full or part to the Palestinians. That perception of place is reinforced in the U.S. media, which are heavily influenced by Israeli discourse. As Fisk observed: "The State Department line on the Middle East, always skewed toward Israel, has been followed obsequiously by most American reporters. Only weeks after United States diplomats were instructed to refer to the Israeli-occupied West Bank as 'disputed'—rather than 'occupied'—territory, American journalists began using precisely the same word."[22] Another observation was noted by Nigel Parry: "[The fact] that the 35-year-old Israeli military occupation of the West Bank (including East Jerusalem) and the Gaza Strip is rarely mentioned in reports—as if it were a matter of no real import—is one thing. In the worst cases, the occupation is presented as if it were a matter of perception. CNN has developed this into an art form, talking about 'what Palestinians see as the military occupation.' This obscures the fact that the international community and international law considers Palestinian land as occupied."[23]

Where do these semantics lead? They portray Israel as a beleagured state that is seeking peace and making territorial sacrifices. In practical terms, it wants an array of concessions (i.e., a reward) for a return of what it has taken by force. This deceptive discourse of "disputed territory" was in play when President Arafat was widely blamed for not accepting Barak's so-called generous offer at Camp David II (July 2000). Zunes has commented on this by saying that "[e]ven if Israel had agreed to withdraw from occupied parts of the West Bank and Gaza Strip, including East Jerusalem, and recognized the right of return of Palestinian refugees, it could not be fairly presented as a great act of generosity or even an enormous concession, since Israel is required to do so."[24]

Let me briefly review the scope of Israeli transfer of territory to Palestinian control and authority on the basis of agreements and what was actually implemented on the ground. To this end, three agreements are worth reviewing: The Oslo II (or Taba) Agreement signed on September 28, 1995, the Wye River Memorandum (WRM) signed on October 23, 1998, and the Sharm el-Sheikh Memorandum (SSM) signed on September 4, 1999. The Oslo II Agreement (1995), though accepted by the Palestinians, should not be seen as a genuine compromise on the part of the occupier—it was a clear reflection of the asymmetrical power relation between the two negotiating parties at the time. The set of conditions that were imposed on it reflects the long-standing Israeli ideology of "wanting the land but not the people."[25] The thrust of the agreement is that the entire occupied area is to be divided into three categories for various degrees of Israeli control, along with an *x* percentage of territory to be passed on to Palestinian control within a certain framework of time—but all pending a number of demands the Palestinian authority was requested to fulfill first.

Briefly, the following items in the Oslo II Agreement are of relevance to the present discussion:[26]

- It divided the West Bank into three areas: Area A (Palestinian authority), Area B (Palestinian civil authority and Israeli security control), and Area C (Israeli authority).
- Israeli withdrawal from specific West Bank towns (Bethlehem, Jennin, Nablus, Qalqilya, Ramallah, Tullkarem) was to take place twenty-two days prior to the Palestinian elections (January 1996).
- Additional redeployments from Area C to Area B were to take place in three stages at six-month intervals following the Palestinian elections.
- Permanent status talks were to begin no later than May 4, 1996. Final status issues included Jerusalem, settlements, borders, and refugees.

With regard to the first item, Area A consists of 3% of the territory of the West Bank and 60% in the Gaza Strip. Area B in the West Bank, which is jointly controlled, consists of 27% of the territory, and Area C, where Israel has both civil and security control, totals 70% of the West Bank. Israel maintains full control over East Jerusalem, as well as 40% of the Gaza Strip.[27]

The implementation of this agreement commenced in November 1995 when the Israeli military withdrew from six Palestinian cities. The redeployment from Hebron was scheduled for March 31, 1996, but was delayed. It was not until January 15, 1997, that Israel and the Palestinian Authority signed the Hebron Agreement that guarantees implementation of the Israeli withdrawal from 80% of the city of Hebron. The remaining 20% of the city remains under Israeli control and is home to 400 religious and nationalist Israeli settlers living in the midst of a Palestinian population of some 150,000.[28]

Further redeployments as stated earlier, planned to be completed by October 1997, did not materialize. Not only was there little territorial "gain" for the Palestinians from the Oslo II Agreement, but now they had to face a new challenge from a new Israeli leadership that refused to honor this agreement. This practice was implemented by both prime ministers Netanyahu and Barak, who attempted to distance themselves from the Oslo II Agreement and impose their own conditions for manipulating the Palestinian leadership and extending effective Israeli control of Palestinian lands.

From this impasse came the Wye River Memorandum (October 1998) and the Sharm el-Sheikh Memorandum (September 4, 1999). The WRM was signed on October 23, 1998, to facilitate implementation of the Oslo II Agreement. What specifically concerns us here is the "further redeployment" section. The WRM promised to transfer 13% from Area C to the Palestinian side so as to comply with Phase One and Two Further Redemployment. This 13% was slated to be transferred as follows: 1% to Area A and 12% to Area B (of which 3% would be designated as Green Areas and/or Natural Reserves). In addition, the WRM stated that 14.2% from Area B would become Area A as part of the foregoing implementation of the first and second Further Redeployment. The WRM made no mention of a date or territorial extent for the third redeployment called for in Oslo II that was to have been implemented in October 1997.[29] Yet on the ground, Prime Minister Netanyahu did not implement any of these items in the WRM.

In the spring of 1999, the new government under Barak took office, and there were new expectations among Israelis and Palestinians that Barak would "salvage" the peace process and try to achieve something more advantageous for Israel than the Wye agreement. Barak in effect forced the SSM, also referred to as the Wye II or Wye Plus Agreement, on the Palestinians, but never delivered on it. According to this agreement, Israel made the following commitments with regard to Phase One and Phase Two of the Further Redeployments:[30]

a. On September 5, 1999, to transfer 7% from Area C to Area A and 3% from Area C to Area B
b. On November 15, 1999, to transfer 2% from Area B to Area A and 3% from Area C to B
c. On January 20, 2000, to transfer 1% from Area C to A, and 5% from Area B to Area A

According to Pundak:

> [T]he "Oslo years" under Barak did not see the end of the Israeli occupational mentality, did not enable real Palestinian control over three million citizens of the PA, did not bring an end to building in the settlements or to the expropriation of land, and did not enable economic growth in the territories. In addition, Barak's repeated statements that he was the only Prime Minister who had not transferred land to the Palestinians raised questions for many about his sincerity. The suspicions increased once it became clear to the Palestinians that Barak would not transfer the three villages on the outskirts of Jerusalem (Abu Dis, Al Eyzaria and Arab Sawahra) to PA control after both the Government and Knesset had approved the transfer.[31]

Menachem Klein, who served as advisor to the Israeli delegation to Camp David in July 2000, has noted: "Both Netanyahu and Sharon support a final status agreement that would give the Palestinians a state in only about 40 to 50 percent of the West Bank as a Palestinian state. In private talks in 1999, Barak proposed a similar deal for the Palestinians, and that was his starting point in the subsequent negotiations. So Barak and Netanyahu shared the same concept."[32]

As should be evident, long before the Intifada, which erupted due to popular Palestinian discontent with a process that was delivering virtually nothing, successive Israeli governments engaged in a kind of discursive smoke screen that hinged on (a) specious pretence of negotiating while holding on firmly to land and gaining control over more land through expansion of settlements and (b) perpetuation of the myth of land for peace in the international arena, and Israel as a "reasonable negotiating partner." This is central to the Israeli geopolitical code practiced by all "Zionist parties," as they are termed in Israeli political parlance. In this, there is no distinction between Likud, Labor, the newly successful secular nationalist party Shinui, or the various religious parties on the geopolitical right. The governments exploited the enormous asymmetry in power and in effect imposed a unilateral solution of "no solution." This "nonsolution," drawn out for years, reflects a basic strategy of non–decision making that is most saliently embodied in the postponement of the key "final status" issues—issues of central, even existential, importance to the Palestinian side. Israeli manipulation of public perception on the "international scale" of the conflict, then as now, remains integral to this strategy, as is shown, for example, by equivocation after December 2000 regarding the so-called Clinton parameters, which Israel claimed that it had accepted, but not the Palestinians.[33] This kind of double-talk is integral to Israeli negotiating discourse and the public "spin" that is put on supposed Israeli negotiating positions. As Klein reminds us:

> The Oslo [Agreement] as a model of interim agreements and then gradual movement to a final status agreement was a failure. Today, no Palestinian and very few in Israel would accept another interim process. Now, both Israelis and Palestinians want to know what the endgame is. Israelis, for example, want to know if Palestinian refugees will demand a return to Israel or not? Both sides need to know who will be the sovereign over the Temple Mount and the Old City. Neither side wants to continue playing games by renewing negotiations that leave the future unresolved. Sharon and the settlers, of course, want to leave the future open in order to gain more control over territory, hoping that they can ultimately defeat the Palestinians.[34]

How Israel Envisions a "Palestinian State" for the Palestinians

This section seeks to examine the nature of the Palestinian state that the Israeli leaders had in mind as the eventual product of the Oslo Agreement or any other agreement(s) that they may reach with the Palestinians. In other words, any future Palestinian state that is "allowed" to crystallize has to be consistent territorially, economically, and politically with the grand geopolitical code of the Zionist enterprise of settlement, colonization, land redemption, and aggrandizement of state boundaries and territory, with minor concessions. Otherwise, its leaders and population are decried and demonized as "terrorists," and are delegitimated.[35] Israel wants co-optability on the other side. To date it has not found such Palestinians. This is why it is calling for a new "leadership" to emerge. Israeli strategy is double-pronged here: a war of rhetoric and the war of occupational firepower, both aimed at destroying the current leadership structures.

The Israeli political class, in a situation of radical power asymmetry, is trying to impose its political hegemony—the hegemony of the helicopters—on the contour of the future Palestinian state. Gramsci's analysis of the hegemony of dominant social groups and the way it is implemented can be applied here to help illuminate Israeli government practices in its engagement with the Palestinians. Gramsci suggests three ways by which hegemony is achieved: by coercion, by consent, and by corruption and 'fraud.'[36] Coercion implies the use of force or the credible threat thereof; consent implies moral leadership.[37] In Gramsci's words: "Between consent and force stands corruption/fraud (which is characteristic of certain situations when it is hard to exercise the hegemonic function, and when the use of force is too risky). This consists in procuring the demoralization and paralysis of the antagonist (or antagonists) by buying its leaders—either covertly, or, in case of imminent danger, openly—in order to sow disarray and confusion in its ranks."[38]

Successive Israeli governments that have engaged in peace talks with the Palestinians were in effect acting directly and indirectly to undermine any possible creation of a viable Palestinian state, that is, to nullify the legitimacy of the other side. This has been accompanied by a huge amount of deception by Israel (in the media and many other platforms) against the Palestinian leadership for its supposed inability (or unwillingness) to stop militant attacks against Israeli targets. In a nutshell, how can a leader of a state (and by extension his government) combat terrorism if he is not allowed to have a state and does not have the proper means of control over his population? It is a kind of "catch-22" or what Menachem Klein has called "catch-2002."[39] Indeed, Arafat was not allowed to have any state and viable territorial base for a state, but he was judged by Israel and the U.S. administration as if he indeed was at the head of a fully functioning state that could police its population if it only wanted to. This is a gross deception, one in a catalog of artifices whereby Israel wages discursive war against the Palestinians by making their arguments and proposals appear fraudulent and their leaders "untrustworthy" (which in the Israeli reading means not open to being co-opted).

Consider the basic elements that make a state and how some of these are lacking (or unviable) in the case of Palestine at present. A standard political geography textbook suggests that a state needs five basic elements (land territory, permanent resident population, government, organized economy, and circulation system) in addition to "sovereignty" and "recognition."[40]

My discussion is limited to those elements of the state that relate to the thesis concerning the core deception intrinsic to accusing the Palestinian leadership of not being able to combat and quell terrorism. With regard to territory, not only did the Oslo Agreement and subsequent agreements limit the Palestinian Authority to exercising control over a small percentage of territory (Area A) and sharing control of additional areas in Area B, but these areas are extremely fragmented and resemble enclaves within a much larger space (i.e., Area C) that forms some 70% of the West Bank and is under Israeli control. The extent of such fragmentation is evident from Figure 15.1. While the A areas are estimated to be 15 to 20

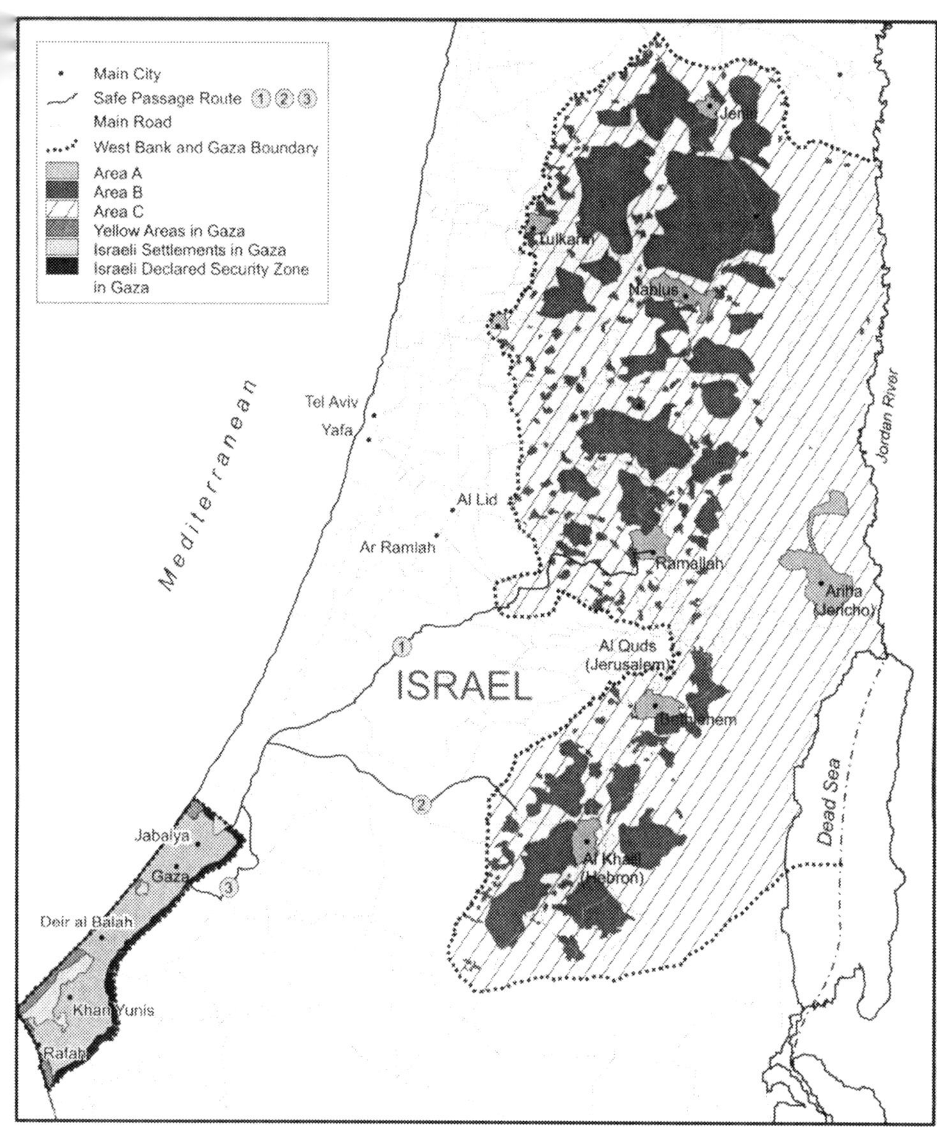

FIGURE 15.1 Territorial division in the West Bank and Gaza Strip as stipulated at the Oslo II Agreement (1995). *Source:* Adapted from "Mid East Maps—Israel and Palestine after Oslo II Agreement." *www.mideastweb.org/palestineisraeloslo.htm* (accessed February 24, 2003).

enclaves, the B Areas number about 190 enclaves. These enclaves are isolated from each other because of the existence of the Jewish settlements and roads (in effect Jewish exclaves) that lead to these settlements that cut through B areas.

To better understand this strategy of fragmentation and segmentation, let us look at the concept of circulation. With regard to social, economic, and political flows, the system of circulation is an important element in the functioning of a state. According to Glassner, "[I]n order for a State to function, there must be some organized means of transmitting goods, people, and ideas from one part of the territory to another. All forms of transportation and communication are included within the term 'circulation,' but a modern State must have more sophisticated forms available to it than runners or the 'bush telegraph.' "[41] If one looks at the fragmentation of Palestinian territory as stipulated by the Oslo Agreement and as produced by later events of Intifada II, it is striking that systematic constraint has been imposed on the movement of people and goods between the Gaza Strip and the West Bank and within these two territories. As the Ramallah-based Law—the Palestinian Society for Protection of Human Rights and Environment—Web site indicates, "[T]ravel restrictions affect everyone. For example, students are also restricted in their movement, those from Gaza in particular are unable to obtain the necessary permits to attend their universities in the West Bank."[42] One strategy for debilitating the power of the Other is to reduce its free movement to a point of absurdity. Thus the Israeli occupational power is well versed in disrupting circulation to paralyze the functioning of the economy, the political system, the system of security, medical care, schools, and other institutions.

In regard to schooling and its disruption, Muna Hamzeh-Muhaisen sketches the following picture:

> Take the Talita School in the town of Beit Jala, for instance. This private Christian school is [situated] at the top of a hill in what is known as Zone C [Area C] and is very close to Road 60—built on confiscated Palestinian land to connect Israeli settlements in southern Hebron with the settlement of Gilo in south Jerusalem. Whenever Israel imposes a closure between Zones A, B and C, Israeli soldiers erect a checkpoint less than one kilometer from the school, sealing other access roads with high piles of dirt. Following such a closure last September 4, teachers and students alike had to sneak past the checkpoint in order to reach the school, while kindergarten children had no classes until the closure was lifted on September 15.[43]

This is proactive fragmentation and blockage of circulation par excellence.

The document "Five Years of Oslo: The Continuing Victimisation of Human Rights—A Summary of Human Rights Violations since the Declaration of Principles" issued by Law and dated September 1998 provides insight on the dysfunctioning of the circulation system at times of closures/blockades:

> The Israeli authorities have been known to impose what could be called blockades, where movement of the Palestinian population is virtually impossible, and humanitarian relief is often impeded. The blockades are usually imposed on Jewish holidays and feasts, after bombings, after clashes with Palestinians or prior to anticipated protest. Closures cause considerable economic hardship, by denying

the possibility of Palestinian workers who earn their living in Israel from getting to their places of employment. Closures often result in the waste of Palestinian agricultural produce as vegetables and the like rot, and in the case of Gaza, the ban on fisherman going to sea denies them the possibility of an income, as they are unable to carry out their livelihood. It has been estimated that closures cost over six million US dollars a day, and in 1997 the total estimated cost of closures for that period was around 230 million US dollars. This has a devastating effect on local industry. Closures also routinely impede the work of the medical emergency services denying individuals urgent care.[44]

Thus closure becomes a tactic that on the surface is imposed for reasons of "security," the grand Israeli watchword, but in effect is a technique of radical proactive fragmentation and stoppage of circulation with an impact that is economic, social, and political. Indeed, at the core of Palestinian economic geography in the West Bank is the growing regime of economic fragmentation, coupled with various modes of land expropriation.

There is a tendency among Israeli commentators and leaders (especially Netanyahu) to obfuscate the geography of fragmentation that was spelled out in the Oslo Agreement and point to the percentage of the Palestinian population that became "autonomous." This is another tactic of deception. A Hebrew University hydrologist, Haim Gvirtzman, as cited by David Makorsky, illustrates this misleading tendency in his examination of the impact of Israel's territorial pullback of 9% to 10% on demography and Jewish settlement during the tenure of Netanyahu:

Approximately 86 percent of the West Bank Palestinian population would live under the Palestinian Authority (PA) and the figure would reach 93 percent if Gaza is included. While Netanyahu likes to boast today that 98 percent of the Palestinians of the West Bank live under autonomy, this figure is very misleading. Netanyahu is referring only to civilian autonomy. In fact, the IDF has overriding control of almost all rural areas, which comprise about 97 percent of the West Bank. According to Gvirtzman's calculations, only 37 percent (588,000 out of 1,561,000) of the Palestinian population in the West Bank live under full PA control today.[45]

If we accept Gvirtzman's statement (quoted in Makovsky) that the Israeli army (IDF) is in control of 97% of the West Bank's territory and has 100% control of the sky and borders of both the West Bank and the Gaza Strip, one could argue that sovereignty as a basic element for the making of a state is absent. The absence of sovereignty alone can be used here to justify that blaming Arafat for not combating terrorism is unfair, and that it would be impossible for him to do so even with a 100% effort. Lack of sovereignty precludes effective control. The Israeli side knows this full well.

Sovereignty is significantly linked to another concept, namely, territoriality and "the control of the means of violence" in Weber's definition of a state. Weber's definition involves three main elements: (1) the existence of a regularized administrative staff that is able (2) to sustain the claim to the legitimate control of the means of violence and (3) to uphold that monopoly within a given territorial area.[46] The scope of the fragmentation of the West Bank and the Gaza Strip into three levels of Israeli control and the overall Israeli military ability to retain control over the means of violence over the entire population constrain Arafat's ability to police space that he has no access to. This situation has been even more evident since the outbreak of the second Intifada when Israeli tanks moved in and placed Palestinian cities and major urban areas under siege and blockade. This military takeover has since prevented Arafat's police from moving from one city to another and has drastically curtailed their ability to perform most of their normal functions. The police have in effect been hamstrung. Gaza has been subjected to a new mode in this imposition of military violence and control that seeks to destroy Hamas in its "spaces of resistance." Figure 15.2 provides cartographic illustration of the siege of Palestinian localities. Nonetheless, Barak was able to tell Madeleine Albright and Jacques Chirac that Arafat "could stop the intifada with just two telephone calls."[47]

Maneuvering an Adversary from a Space of Resistance to a Deformed Space of Power

The form of government that the Oslo Agreement generated and the manner in which this administration has been pressured to comply with endless demands from Israeli leaders were constrained politically by geopolitical imperative. Most significant is the geographic implication behind the change of the title of Yasser Arafat from president of the PLO to chairman of the Palestinian Authority. This change involved structural changes in the body politic of the Palestinian national movement that also transformed the geographies of the Palestinian struggle for self-determination. "Spaces of Palestinian resistance" have been transformed into "spaces of effective power."

As a national liberation movement, the PLO resolved to pursue various methods of struggle against Israel and Israeli targets in Palestinian territory and abroad. It was clear to its leaders that the PLO could not liberate Palestine from outside by military might. Yet the PLO devised a web of counterspatiality, of geographies of resistance. As Pile notes, resistance, among other things, "is about mass mobilization in defence of common interests, where resistance is basically determined by the action: the strike, the march, the formation of community organizations, and so on."[48] The PLO's war ideology was one that followed the Algerian revolutions experience with the French, *thawra shabiyya* (a popular revolt). This could have been applicable if all the Palestinians were inside Palestine as the Algerians were in Algeria. Hence the importance of the two Intifadas in contextualizing the PLO's original idea of popular revolt and the consolidation of geographies of resistance. The PLO created geographies of resistance that were not necessarily a direct confrontation with those in power but were geographies in which "resistance becomes a mode through which the symptoms of different power relations are diagnosed and ways are sought to get round them, or live through them, or to change them."[49] The Oslo Agreement was a strategy by which Arafat (and the PLO, by extension) was forced to distance himself from the practice of a geography of resistance. It channeled him into a new space that would empower him and his structures of control by the promise of recognition and legitimation. In effect,

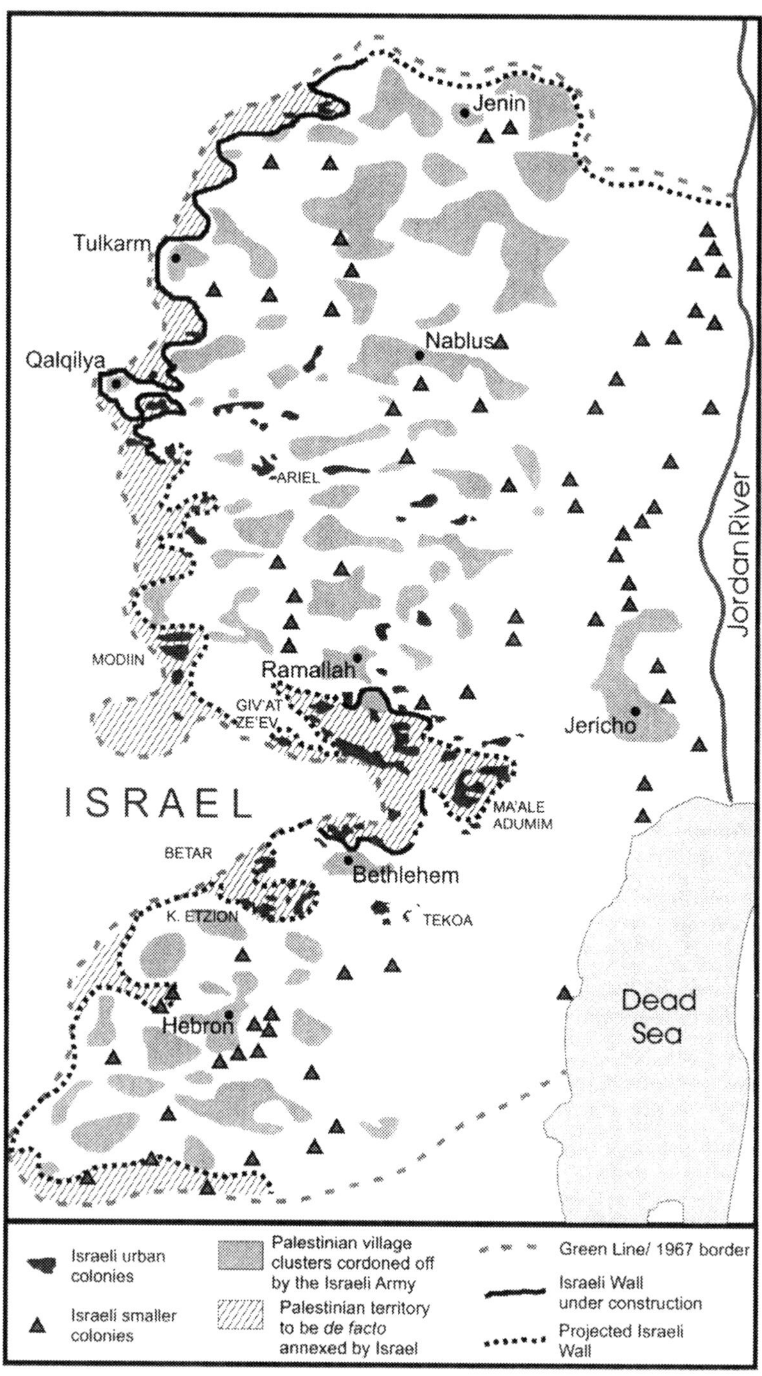

FIGURE 15.2 West Bank: area of Palestinian localities under siege by the Israeli army during Intifada II, 2000–2003. *Source:* Adapted from "Pre-emption of a Compromise on the West Bank and Jerusalem," October 2002. *www.nad-plo .org/maps/pre-emp.htm* (accessed February 24, 2003).

the geography of resistance and its space were nullified by the PLO's transformation. Hence the Palestinian Authority headed by Chairman Arafat and residing in an A Area, which is a form of quasi-autonomous area, is in effect occupying a "space of power," however weak that power is. From this perspective, the Palestinian government that emerged out of the Oslo Agreement was congenitally weak from birth and was conceived as such, a space of debilitated power at best. This is what the Israelis have aimed for in all their discussions and proposals. That debilitated legitimacy emanated by and large from the dominant power, Israel. In order to legitimize this new government, Israel insisted that the PLO had to change its charter and constantly called on the Palestinian leader to condemn terrorism and ensure that he and his associates were "true" partners for peace—a form of political blackmail in a situation where the population in the territories is under a brutal occupation.

That Israel recognized some sort of government for the Palestinians should imply that it will not impose restrictions on its public servants and leadership. Yet according to the Law Web site, "Public servants of the Palestinian National Authority require permission to travel between the West Bank and Gaza Strip. Israel grants VIP status to a number of senior officials and to the Palestinian Legislative Council. However, their movement can still be restricted by delays and harassment at checkpoints. This is a frequent occurrence for PLC members from Gaza traveling to Council's sessions in the West Bank."[50]

The vulnerability of Arafat's government is most evident in the current crises of the Intifada and its paradoxes: on the one hand, Israel insists that Palestinians carry out elections, but at the same time, members of the council are not able to reach Arafat's headquarters in Ramallah. Needless to say the restriction of movement of Arafat outside Ramallah for an extended period of time is in effect a strategy of spatial freezing on movement that rendered his government ineffective in the extreme. It is mistaken to say that Arafat and his associates were tools in the hands of the Israeli leaders and the U.S. administration. On the contrary, Arafat and his negotiating team's performance at Camp David II is instructive: They refused to surrender to Israeli hegemony (backed by the prestige of President Clinton) and were not ready to accept a situation in which Israeli occupation would continue over the territory where the new Palestinian state was envisioned to be born. They grasped the basic contradiction here, that the state they might someday have would be a debilitated space of power, under nearly total manipulation, and they refused to accede.

Palestinian geographies of resistance are segmented and fragmented and their circulation is blocked by the imposition of closures and "spaces of radical control." Palestinian "spaces of power" are shriveled to the point of nonexistence and have become "spaces of powerlessness" or "spaces of immobilization." In effect, one grand strategy of the Israelis in pacifying the Intifada—and in masking the thirty-five-year-old occupation at its root—is to transform Palestinian spaces of resistance into "spaces of nonpower and powerlessness." In other words, a geography of resistance has been transformed into a "geography of immobilization" by choking off circulation, fragmenting territory, carrying violence down to the level of individual households, destroying medical services, and shattering the spatiality of resistance at its most compact level, that of the individual, family, and neighborhood. These are all tactics in an Israeli drive to turn the space of resistance into a space of noncontrol, disempowerment, and an economy that has been withered and literally choked by spatial smothering of its circulation. The weapons are massive firepower on the ground and the power of deception, especially at the scale of the international arena of image manipulation. The most striking deceptive turn is to have branded those who rise up to resist the longest military occupation since World War II, paid for in large part by the U.S. taxpayer, as the victimizers. The rhetorical weaponry is echoed in Washington.

The territorial strategy of political concessions without the necessary territorial control has painted the Palestinian Authority (PA) with the appearance of control and sovereignty without its material reality. The PA has been tainted as being, at best, ineffective in its attempt to control terrorist activity and, at worst, complicit in such acts. However, the PA has been denied control of the territorial interactions that are the geographic foundations of all states, and so its ability to police terrorism has been curtailed. The appearance of a state has allowed the PA to be categorized as a sponsor of terrorism, while the continuing territorial struggle prevents it from policing its territory. Consequently, continued armed struggle activities allow Israel to tighten its territorial control.

To conclude, Israel's attempt to achieve hegemony via means of consent (using Gramsci's terminology) has clearly failed. Nor was Israel able to achieve it by bribing Palestinian leaders (i.e., corruption and fraud). As the second Intifada enters forty-two months and the Israeli electorate has shifted far to the right, it is likely that Sharon is planning to achieve hegemony by intensifying the means of coercion. He told the Israeli newspaper *Ha'aretz* on March 5, 2002, "Don't expect Arafat to act against the terror. We have to cause them heavy casualties and they'll know they can't keep using terror and win political achievements." He was also quoted as saying that the Palestinians must be "hit hard until they beg for mercy."[51] The strategy is twofold: to apply force locally, destroying "spaces of resistance" while assuring that any spaces of effective Palestinian power are rendered "spaces of powerlessness," and at the same time, in the war of discourse, to grind out an imagery and rhetoric of deception at higher scales of the dispute, especially for international consumption in the ongoing propaganda war.

Implications

I have attempted here to outline certain spatiopolitical aspects of the peace agreements between the Israeli government and the Palestinian National Authority during the past decade and highlight its discourse between Israel and the PLO. My prime focus in the first part of the chapter was on territory over which both parties wished to have exclusive control. In the second part, I tried to show the centrality of territory in the establishment of a viable state and how Israeli government practices of creating facts on the ground have effectively rendered that establishment impossible for the Palestinians. While these practices were instrumental in the outbreak of the Intifada II in September 2000, this chapter implicitly acknowledges such consequences but in scope focuses on peace-related issues and agreements.

Discussion here of the Intifada II was meant primarily to underscore the continuity of certain spatial processes down to the present and show that the Intifada in its geography of resistance catalyzed new levels of intensity in these processes.

This chapter calls on scholars to read properly the narrative of the "Oslo years," to look at this period and see what has evolved from it and what is now at a dead end, and to learn the lesson from it. It may sound ridiculous at this time when killing of innocent people is becoming the order of the day to talk of the prospects for peace. Nevertheless, our duty as geographers and scholars is to create a deeper understanding of the events and their distinctive spatiality without being misled by the media's deceptive discourses.

It is useful to put the Oslo years in better perspective. Before the Oslo Agreement, Israel and the PLO were practically in a state of unending war that crested in Intifada I. Israel was able to justify its occupation of the West Bank and Gaza in part by the lack of recognition from the side of the Palestinians. But many other justifications were also trotted out by Israel over the decades to hold onto seized Arab lands before the Oslo period. To name but some, there were justifications that included geographic necessity and self-defense (e.g., Israeli space is narrow or small and therefore vulnerable to external attacks); resources (Israel does not have sufficient water resources); history (restoration of Zion); law of the jungle (lack of a credible and democratic peace partner); Arab "anti-Semitism" (although it should be clear that Israelis are at war with the Arab world because of colonialism, not their Jewish identity); psychology (certain hills and spots adjacent to Israel's pre-1967 border remind Israelis of bad memories because their homes were targeted from these areas); and of course politics (Israel is an enlightened democracy and the Arabs are better off under the rule of Israel, "the only democracy in the Middle East"). This latter justification was put forward largely in association with the Golan Heights Syrian population and argued that the Golan people prefer to stay with Israel rather than to return to Syria in any peace treaty with Syria.

With the signing of the Oslo Agreement between Israel and the PLO, many of these justifications for retaining the Other's territory were no longer valid. So why does the Israeli government still hold onto Palestinian territory if it claims that it is agreeing to a land-for-peace formula, and why does that practice continue even though it has signed an agreement with the Palestinians that explicitly indicates that the Oslo Agreement and all subsequent agreements must lead to the implementation of UN Security Council Resolutions 242 and 338, which in turn will eventually lead to the creation of a Palestinian state next to Israel in territory occupied by war in June 1967?

The answer can be found in the behavior of the Israeli government in its deceptive strategy after signing the agreement: It styles itself as generous and in search of peace, and the other side as not complying with the true interpretation of the agreement. Once Israel signed an agreement, it sought to gain immediate results for itself and at the same time deny the claims of the other side through stalling tactics and inventing a new interpretation for what was agreed upon. This has been Israeli realpolitik, central to its core geopolitical code. Israel gained what it had long desired at Oslo: formal Palestinian recognition of the right to exist on the territory of Palestine, a gain no less important for Israel than the Balfour

Declaration. This was a historic compromise recognized Israel's sovereignty over areas that had been taken from the Palestinians by force in the 1948 war and accounted for 77% of their homeland.

Israel has used the Oslo Agreement as a justification for bypassing international law. The Palestinians for their part were unable to persuade the international community to intervene and stop Israeli violations. In other words, as the Law Web site indicates: "The international community has not been willing to enforce the recognition of basic rights in the Occupied Palestinian Territories. The international community has taken the view that the negotiating process is a two-party process and participation from other states would be regarded as interference."[52] The Oslo Agreement was a diplomatic nightmare for the Palestinians, and this probably can explain in part why Palestinian negotiators were keen to advance to the final stage while, at the same time, they objected to skipping over the implementation of interim agreements that would free Israel from its obligations.

In the Camp David II negotiations, Barak and the U.S. administration under Clinton sought to impose a final solution on the Palestinians that, if successful, was likely to be used in order to supersede relevant UN Security Council resolutions. In fact, throughout the entire peace process, the U.S. administration has supported Israel's position and has attempted to "save" it from the "trap" of the UN Security Council resolutions—a trap that calls on Israel to comply and withdraw completely from the Occupied Territories.[53] Israel's point of departure is that the Occupied Territories are under its effective control. Had the Palestinians not agreed to postpone negotiation over the refugee issue to the final stage and had that issue been raised at the beginning of negotiations, Israel would probably understand that Palestinians have not given up title to pre-1967 territories. From the perspective of the Palestinians, the issue of the Palestinian right of return is non-negotiable and cannot be resolved through a package deal in Camp David, Oslo, or Taba. Indeed, during the two-week meeting in Camp David II (July 2002), the Palestinian refugee voice was raised high everywhere, urging and even "threatening" Palestinian negotiators not to "mess" with the right-of-return question.

Ben-Meir's statement on this issue reflects the official Israeli position at the present time. His "advice" to the Palestinians was as follows:

> The Palestinians must understand and accept the fact that Israel cannot and will not acknowledge the right of return of the Palestinian refugees. Repatriation of Palestinians will effectively obliterate Israel as a Jewish state, a state that was created as the final refuge for the Jews. No Israeli government, whether led by Likud or Labor, will ever accept the right of return. What Israel will probably accept is the return of some 50,000–75,000 refugees in the context of family reunification and also take part in an international effort to compensate the rest.[54]

These words suggest that demography and national identity are being used by Israel as a justification for territorial claims. Yet this claim centered on demography is inherently tinged with racism, the notion of an ethnocracy. The Palestinian citizens of Israel are constantly perceived in some segments of Jewish Israeli society as a threat to the "Jewish identity" of the state.

Paradoxically, consider the present situation and demography of the Jewish settlers in Hebron and elsewhere in the West Bank and Gaza who live surrounded by totally non-Jewish areas. Why don't they want to live in areas densely inhabited by their fellow Jews? Historically, this demographic justification can also be refuted. According to Tikva Honig-Parnass, that claim was not even considered when the Zionist leaders accepted the 1947 UN Partition Plan (UN Special Committee on Palestine [UNSCOP], August 31, 1947). According to this plan, "an almost equal number of Jews and Arabs were supposed to be in the Jewish state. Zionist territorial interests which were supported by the Committee [as 55% of the land was allocated—unfairly—to the Jewish state, when at the time Jewish property in Palestine amounted to no more than 6%] had overridden their aspirations for a state 'clean' of Arabs which thus would inevitably end in a non-Jewish majority."[55]

Parallel to talk on the Palestinian right of return, which has to be dealt with sooner or later in any new initiative for resuming peace talks, certain circles in the Israeli government and public figures are now hinting at a radical "solution" by means of "transfer," relocation of large segments of the Palestinian population across the Jordan River. These voices are growing louder, with disturbing silence on the part of the Israeli government. The timing of these voices (which came with the outbreak of the Intifada) that are calling for transfer of Palestinians from the West Bank and even from Galilee by force suggests that the demographic threat to the Jewishness of space can also be used as a justification for holding onto territory. In other words, Palestinians should accept what Israel is offering now before it becomes too late and they "lose all of Palestine."

What would be the nature of the future Palestinian state, beyond a kind of bifurcated Bantustan? The answer is conjecture. The election of Sharon in a right-wing Israeli government whose constituencies lie in significant part among the settlers bodes ill for a solution. The new Israeli cabinet understands that the Bush Road Map will be whatever Israel stipulates it is willing to accept, that the Israeli political class and a large segment of the Israeli electorate at the moment are in a significant respect Washington's closest ally, and that the strategy of deception, central to the Israeli geopolitical code and its implementation, has reemerged as one of the major weapons in Washington's new geopolitical code to rid the world of "rogue states."

Notes

I thank Colin Flint for his excellent comments and suggestions for revision. I also thank Bill Templer and Virginie Mamadouh for feedback and editorial assistance at the early stages of drafting this chapter. Responsibility for the content of this work, however, is mine alone.

1. Walzer, *Just and Unjust Wars*, 12.

2. Falah, "Re-envisioning Current Discourse"; Newman and Falah, "Bridging the Gap."

3. Arab Gateway, "Arab League"; Global Policy Forum, "Arab Leaders Endorse Mideast Peace Plan;" Guardian Unlimited, "Arab League Summit"; World Press Review, "Saudi Arabia."

4. Among the Israeli political class on the Right, its most enthusiastic advocate is Benjamin Netanyahu, who, as a recent report claims (see The Institute for Advanced Strategic and Political Studies Jerusalem, Washington, "Clean Break), was acting in many ways to implement this strategy from 1996 on while he was Israeli prime minister.

5. See Hass, "Threats of Forced Mass Expulsion."

6. Falah, "Dynamics and Patterns"; Reuveny, "Fundamentalist Colonialism."

7. Benn, "Israel Wants More Than 100 Corrections to Road Map."

8. Further discussion of these terms will be offered later that uses the definition of "geographies of resistance" from Steve Pile and Michael Keith, eds., *Geographies of Resistance* (London: Routledge, 1997).

9. Falah, "Intifadat Al-Aqsa"; Falah, " 'Green Line' Revisited."

10. Shlaim, *Iron Wall.*

11. Fateh Online, "Editorials: From Deception to Joint Control."

12. Kacowicz, *Peaceful Territorial Change*, cited in Newman and Falah, "Bridging the Gap," 114.

13. Nietschmann, "Fourth World."

14. Giddens, *Nation-State and Violence*, 9; Taylor, *Political Geography*, 36.

15. Zunes, "United States and the Breakdown of the Israeli-Palestinian Peace Process," 75.

16. "Declaration of Principles on Interim Self-Government Arrangements," Article V, section 3.

17. Falah, "Dynamics and Patterns."

18. Zunes, "United States and the Breakdown of the Israeli-Palestinian Peace Process," 76.

19. B'Tselem Press Releases, "Settlements Are Built on 1.7% of West Bank Land and Control 41.9%," paragraph 4.

20. Zunes, "United States and the Breakdown of the Israeli-Palestinian Peace Process," 74.

21. Ibid., 75, 76.

22. Fisk, "U.S. Media Mirror Distorts Middle East," paragraph 5.

23. Parry, "Introduction to Media Coverage," paragraph 8.

24. Zunes, "United States and the Breakdown of the Israeli-Palestinian Peace Process," 70.

25. Falah, "Dynamics and Patterns," 183.

26. "Fact Sheet: Peace Process."

27. Ariga, "Summary of Human Rights Violations," paragraph 5.

28. Ibid., paragraph 6.

29. MidEast Web, "Wye River Memorandum."

30. "Sharm el-Sheikh Memorandum 4 September 1999."

31. Pundak, "From Oslo to Taba," 35.

32. Klein, "Origins of Intifada II," paragraph 66.

33. Ibid., paragraph 37.

34. Ibid., paragraph 53.

35. Benvenisti, "Either a Zionist or a Terrorist."

36. Gramsci, *Selections from the Prison Notebooks*,

37. Arrighi, "Three Hegemonies of Historical Capitalism," 149.

38. Gramsci, *Selections from the Prison Notebooks*, 80.

39. Klein, "Origins of Intifada II," paragraph 2.

40. Glassner, *Political Geography*, 35–36.

41. Ibid., 36.

42. Law, "Apartheid, Bantustans, Cantonization," paragraph 11.
43. Hamzeh-Muhaisen, "The ABC's of Oslo," paragraph 5.
44. Law, "Five Years of Oslo," paragraph 19–20.
45. Makovsky, "9 percent? 13 Percent? What Does It All Mean?"
46. Giddens, *Nation-State and Violence*, 18.
47. Klein, "Origins of Intifada II," paragraph 36.
48. Pile, "Introduction," 4.
49. Ibid., 3.
50. Law, "Apartheid, Bantustans, Cantonization," paragraph 11.
51. Cited in Herman, "Wholesale Terrorism Escalates," 120.
52. Law, "Apartheid, Bantustans, Cantonization," paragraph 19.
53. Zunes, "United States and the Breakdown of the Israeli-Palestinian Peace Process," 82.
54. Ben-Meir, "Behind the Palestinian-Israeli Violence and Beyond," 87.
55. Honig-Parnass, "Retreating from Full Recognition of the Right to Return—Now??!"

References

Arab Gateway. "Arab League: Arab Peace Initiative, 2002." www.al-bab.com/arab/docs/league/peace02.htm (last revised March 28, 2002; accessed June 7, 2003).

Ariga. "Summary of Human Rights Violations since the Signing of the Oslo Accords." www.ariga.com/5759/law001.htm (last revised September 1998; accessed June 7, 2003).

Arrighi, Giovanni. "The Three Hegemonies of Historical Capitalism." In *Gramsci, Historical Materialism, and International Relations*, ed. Stephen Gill, 148–185. Cambridge: Cambridge University Press, 1993.

Ben-Meir, Alon. "Behind the Palestinian-Israeli Violence and Beyond." *Middle East Policy* 8 (March 2001): 81–88.

Benn, Aluf. "Israel Wants More than 100 Corrections to Road Map." *Haaretz* (Hebrew daily). www.haaretzdaily.com/hasen/spages/265082.html (last revised February 20, 2003; accessed February 20, 2003).

Benvenisti, Meron. "Either a Zionist or a Terrorist." *Haaretz* (Hebrew daily), January 3, 2002. www.ipc.gov.ps/ipc_e/ipc_e-l/e_Articles/ipc-articles_33.html (accessed March 1, 2003).

B'Tselem Press Releases. "Settlements Are Built on 1.7% of West Bank Land and Control 41.9%." www.btselem.org/English/Press_Releases/2002/020513.asp (last revised May 13, 2002; accessed June 7, 2003).

"Declaration of Principles on Interim Self-Government Arrangements." Jerusalem: Ministry of Foreign Affairs, 1993.

"Fact Sheet: Peace Process. Major Milestones in the Peace Process." Center for Middle East Peace and Economic Cooperation, Washington, DC. www.centerpeace.org/factsheets/fact-sheet-peaceprocess.htm (revised February 28, 2003; accessed June 7, 2003).

Falah, Ghazi. "Re-envisioning Current Discourse: Alternative Territorial Configurations of Palestinian Statehood." *Canadian Geographer* 41 (1997): 307–330.

Falah, Ghazi. "Intifadat Al-Aqsa and the Bloody Road to Palestinian Independence." *Political Geography* 20 (2001): 135–138.

Falah, Ghazi. "The 'Green Line' Revisited: October 2000." In *The Razor's Edge: Interna-*

tional Boundaries and Political Geography, ed. C. Schofield, D. Newman, A. Drysdale, and Janet Allison Brown, 493–511. London: Kluwer Law International, 2002.

Falah, Ghazi. "Dynamics and Patterns of the Shrinking of Arab Lands in Palestine." *Political Geography* 22 (2003): 179–209.

Fateh Online. "Editorials: From Deception to Joint Control." www.fateh.net/e_editor/98/310898.htm (revised 1998; accessed October 9, 2002).

Fisk, Robert. "U.S. Media Mirror Distorts Middle East." www.mideastfacts.com/us_media_fisk.html (revised September 10, 2002; accessed June 7, 2003).

Giddens, Anthony. *The Nation-State and Violence*. Berkeley: University of California Press, 1987.

Glassner, Martin I. *Political Geography*. New York: Wiley, 1993.

Global Policy Forum. "Arab Leaders Endorse Mideast Peace Plan." globalpolicy.org/security/issues/israel-palestine/2002/0328saudi.htm (revised March 28, 2002; accessed June 7, 2003).

Gramsci, Antonio. *Selections from the Prison Notebooks of Antonio Gramsci*. Translated by Q. Hoare and G. Nowell Smith. New York: International Publishers, 1971.

Guardian Unlimited. "The Arab League Summit." www.guardian.co.uk/theissues/article/0,6512,675015,00.html (revised March 28, 2002; accessed June 7, 2003).

Hamzeh-Muhaisen, Muna. "The ABC's Of Oslo." www.jmcc.org/media/report/97/Sep/3.htm#four (revised September 1997; accessed June 8, 2003).

Hass, Amira. "Threats of Forced Mass Expulsion." *Le Monde Diplomatique*, February 19, 2003. www.worldwar3report.com/lmd.html (accessed April 7, 2004).

Herman, Edward S. "Wholesale Terrorism Escalates: The Threat of Genocide." *Arab Studies Quarterly* 24 (spring/summer 2002): 119–128.

Honig-Parnass, Tikva. "Retreating from Full Recognition of the Right of Return—Now??!" between-lines.org/archives/2002/mar/Tikva_Hong-Parnass.htm (revised March 2002; accessed March 2, 2003).

The Institute for Advanced Strategic and Political Studies Jerusalem, Washington. "A Clean Break: A New Strategy for Securing the Realm." www.israeleconomy.org/strat1.htm (revised February 2003; accessed June 7, 2003).

Kacowicz, A. M. *Peaceful Territorial Change*. Columbia: University of South Carolina Press, 1994.

Klein, Menachem. "The Origins of Intifada II and Rescuing Peace for Israelis and Palestinians." middleeastinfo.org/article1705.html (revised December 25, 2002; accessed June 7, 2003).

Law. "Five Years of Oslo: The Continuing Victimisation of Human Rights." www.gush-shalom.org/archives/oslofive.doc (revised September 1998; accessed June 8, 2003).

Law. "Apartheid, Bantustans, Cantonization: The ABC of Oslo." www.lawsociety.org/Reports/reports/1998/abc.html (revised February 28, 2003; accessed June 7, 2003).

Makovsky, David. "9 Percent? 13 Percent? What Does It All Mean?" *Ha'aretz English Edition*, May 21, 1998. www.embajada-isreal.es/political/t-ph-02.html (accessed March 1, 2003).

MidEast Web. "The Oslo Interim Agreement, September 28, 1995." www.mideastweb.org/meosint.htm (accessed June 7, 2003).

MidEast Web. "The Wye River Memorandum, October 13, 1998." www.mideastweb.org/mewye.htm (accessed June 7, 2003).

Newman, David, and Ghazi Falah. "Bridging the Gap: Palestinian and Israeli Discourses on Autonomy and Statehood." *Transactions of the Institute of British Geographers* 22 (1997): 111–129.

Nietschmann, Bernard Q. "The Fourth World: Nations versus States." In *Reordering the*

World: Geopolitical Perspectives on the Twenty-first Century, ed. G. J. Demko and W. B. Wood, 225–242. Boulder, CO: Westview Press, 1994.

Parry, Nigel. "Introduction to Media Coverage." electronicintifada.net/introduction/mediacoverage.html (revised February 17, 2003; accessed June 7, 2003).

Pile, Steve. "Introduction: Opposition, Political Identities, and Spaces of Resistance." In *Geographies of Resistance*, ed. Steve Pile and Michael Keith, 1–32. London: Routledge, 1997.

Pile, Steve, and Michael Keith, eds. *Geographies of Resistance*. London: Routledge, 1997.

Pundak, Ron. "From Oslo to Taba: What Went Wrong?" *Survival* 43 (autumn 2001): 31–45.

Reuveny, R. "Fundamentalist Colonialism: The Geopolitics of Israeli-Palestinian Conflict." *Political Geography* 22 (2003): 347–380.

"Sharm el-Sheikh Memorandum 4 September 1999." *Le Monde diplomatique*. mondediplo.com/focus/mideast/charm99-en (revised February 28, 2003; accessed June 7, 2003).

Shlaim, Avi. *The Iron Wall: Israel and the Arab World*. New York: Norton, 2001.

Taylor, Peter, J. *Political Geography: World-Economy, Nation-State, and Locality*. 3rd ed. London: Longman, 1993.

Walzer, Michael. *Just and Unjust Wars*. 3rd ed. New York: Basic Books, 2000.

World Press Review. "Saudi Arabia: A Prince's Olive Branch." www.worldpress.org/Mideast/505.cfm (revised May 2002; accessed June 7, 2003).

Zunes, Stephen. "The United States and the Breakdown of the Israeli-Palestinian Peace Process." *Middle East Policy* 8 (2001): 66–85.

DAVID NEWMAN

Conflict at the Interface

The Impact of Boundaries and Borders on Contemporary Ethnonational Conflict

Contemporary Ethnoterritorial Conflict and Boundaries

Boundaries may have become more permeable than in the past, but they remain the hard lines that determine the territorial extent of the state and, by definition, the citizenship of those residing therein. Notwithstanding the discourse of deterritorialization and the "end of the state," the hard boundaries that separate states in the international system remain important delimiters of power and partial sovereignty in the contemporary world. The relative impact of these boundaries on the surrounding borderland regimes has changed, in many cases to allow greater movement of people, goods, information, and cultural exchanges.[1] But the impact of these changes remains highly differentiated and affects some areas, such as Western Europe, far more than others, where boundaries retain their traditional role as barriers to movement and interaction.

In attempting to understand these changes, boundary studies have undergone a major renaissance during the past decade.[2] From the study of hard territorial lines and the process of boundary demarcation, contemporary research has taken on a wider range of boundary-related topics, such as territorial identities, borderlands and border regimes, the perception of boundaries, and the nature of boundary management. The analysis of boundaries has also shifted in focus from the preeminence of international boundaries to include a range of spatial and administrative intrastate scales, in which the functional impact of the boundary/border on the daily lives of people is as great as, if not greater than, the line that separates one state from another.

It is the process of bordering, rather than the course of the line per se, that is important to our understanding of how boundaries affect the nature of interaction, cooperation, and/or conflict between peoples.[3] This is part of a dynamic process in which boundaries not only reflect a given formal political or administrative status as determined by the state, but are also reformulated as a result of war, conflict resolution, negotiations, unilateral imposition, and so on. Conflict still takes place in and around boundaries and borderlands, in some cases as a result of traditional issues of demarcation with respect to territorial attributes, such as natural resources, and in others as a result of their incompatibility with the expanding horizons of identity politics. This chapter discusses some contemporary boundary/territory conflicts that have arisen out of past political and colonial legacies, on the one hand, and that reflect identity-territory incompatibilities, on the other. The discussion does not focus only on the traditional analysis of the interstate boundary line, but also examines the way in which these boundary conflicts are expressed at other spatial levels and are, in some cases, as much perceived as they are real and tangible. The discussion shows just how important boundaries remain within our contemporary state system in determining majority-minority power relations and expressing self-determination and independence for ethnic groups.

Some of the major ethnoterritorial conflicts that have occupied a prominent place in the world political map during the past decade have centered around attempts to cleanse territories of minority populations (either through forced expulsion or genocide) and thus create homogeneous ethnic territories. Cases such as the Balkans, Israel-Palestine, Cyprus, and the Kurdish question run counter to the theory that borders are no longer significant, or that shared power and binationalism within a predetermined territory are the new order of the day. Ethnic groups continue to desire their own territories, through which their national identity is expressed and within which their mythical places and spaces are located, and are prepared to fight over their self-perceived right to control and rule the specific "national" territory, which is normally defined as the "homeland." Within the symbolic context of homeland territories, the location, demarcation, and continued preservation of the hard boundaries remain central to our understanding of the spatial and political organization of ethnic groups and their desire to control territories. Homeland spaces constitute a central element in the formation and consolidation of their respective national identities.

The conflicts discussed in this chapter focus on those places where ethnoterritorialism and its associated tensions take place around the boundary, and where the processes of bordering continue to determine the primordial group identity of majorities and minorities and their respective access to power and control over their own destinies. Places such as Cyprus, the Balkans (especially Bosnia and Kosovo), and Israel-Palestine, to name only the most prominent, are places where conflict continues to take place in and around the borderlands. These places were affected by past superimpositions of boundaries that did not take account of ethnonational realities and whose conflictual legacies remain with us in the contemporary reordering of the world political map. The myth of the nation-state had us believe that Westphalian territorial configurations were contiguous with the geographic dispersion of ethnic and national groups. But even in those cases where there was a relatively high contiguity between the two, this has significantly decreased during the past few decades, particularly in those places where mass migration of new groups has taken place and/or where existing ethnic minorities have undergone processes of self-empowerment and are no longer fearful of expressing their own national and territorial aspirations. These boundaries are most often, but not always, territorial; they can be located at the interstate divide or within local municipal, residential, and neighborhood areas. The desire for ethnonational separation and territorial homogeneity remains a major motif for many national groups, especially those that have not experienced independence in the past, and it is this reality that is addressed in this chapter.

But it is not only the hard lines that separate states that give rise to sporadic conflict. Ethnoterritorial boundaries are apparent at a number of other levels, not least the local and micro levels of spatial behavior. The extent to which groups are segregated or mixed in residential neighborhoods, in apartment blocks, and/or in daily economic interactions indicates the presence of boundaries that are more or less permeable to movement and interaction. On the one hand, such boundaries reflect the level of political trust or fear between peoples who are prepared to cross or are fearful of crossing such boundaries. At the same time, the extent to which such transboundary interaction and movement do take place can itself be a factor that determines the formal "opening" and easing of boundary restrictions or, in cases of enhanced ethnic conflict, the "closing" and tightening of the boundary. In many of these cases the boundary is not physically present in terms of a fence, a wall, or boundary guards and formal restrictions. In some cases, these boundaries exist within a single politicoterritorial entity, where the establishment of a physical barrier would give legitimation to the notion of territorial separation that the state opposes. Yet the level of human interaction between ethnic groups and their respective neighborhoods and marketplaces may reflect the presence of a perceived boundary that is far stronger than the simple presence or nonpresence of a physical barrier.

The Ethnic Legacy of Division, Partition, and Superimposition

International boundaries are the legacy of contemporary state formation. Despite the opening of boundaries in Western Europe, the territorial legacy of partition, division, and boundary superimposition remains a prominent component in the world political map. Many of the superimposed partitions and boundaries resulted in conflict, some of which have been resolved peacefully over time, while others remain the source of ongoing conflict and ethnoterritorial tensions, claims, and counterclaims. The legacy of boundary superimposition is still evident in much contemporary territorial conflict, nowhere more so than in Africa,[4] Iraq-Turkey-Iran and the Kurdish homeland,[5] and the Balkans. Problems of partition and division remain critical in Israel-Palestine, Northern Ireland, India and Pakistan, and North and South Korea.[6] The reemergence of states in central and Eastern Europe since the early 1990s has focused around existing boundaries, some of which were state boundaries in the past and were subsumed as internal administrative boundaries during the period of Soviet or Yugoslavian rule.[7] These boundaries have maintained their function as the prior demarcators of ethnic and national groups within the preexisting territorial compartments. In short, the legacy of international boundary formation remains a central component in contemporary ethnoterritorial conflict. These boundaries can be opened, removed, imposed, or functionally changed, but their existence on the ground constitutes a territorial reality and geographic default around which political behavior takes place. Their relative importance may be decreasing, but they are unlikely to disappear altogether, and they will remain an important demarcator of ethnoterritorial groups, many of which will continue to struggle for territorial homogeneity and dominance at the expense of neighboring groups.

Many contemporary boundaries were superimposed upon colonial territories by the colonial powers to create states where none had previously existed, especially in Africa and the Middle East. What were fluid and tribal territories became transformed into fixed state territories with barriers on movement where none had existed in the past. Some tribal and nomadic territories were divided between two or more states, while other tribal groups were enclosed within a single territorial compartment that gave rise to future civil wars, acts of genocide, and a great deal of political and territorial instability. This is ironical given the fact that the legal notion of *uti possidetis* that was at the heart of the Westphalian notion of state sovereignty and was spatially transferred to the areas that later underwent decolonization was intended, first and foremost, to ensure the existing order and stability, regardless of the means through which possession and control were obtained in the first place.[8] Many African states are only now coming to grips with these territorial realities at a time when the Western discourse is telling us that the world has become, or is on its way to becoming, borderless. Territorial fixation remains one of the major legacies of the Westphalian state system, and therefore, the lines drawn in the sand continue to be the focus for conflict, wars, and political tensions.

Boundaries and Ethnic Conflict at the Local Level

Political geography has traditionally made a distinction between the different spatial levels of analysis—the global, the state, and the local. This distinction was common in many of the introductory political geography textbooks of the 1980s and 1990s. As the relevance of the state in the changing world political map decreases, so too the focus of territorial power has shifted in such a way that this distinction, based as it is on space rather than process, is less relevant. Processes of ethnoterritorial conflict become as significant at the local and regional levels as they are at the state level, while in some cases the geographies of fear and threat are reflected through the absence of microspatial interactions and are expressed by residential segregation and separation at the level of neighborhood blocks or monoethnic villages in a way that is not always apparent at the level of the interstate or interregional boundary. The latter is often reflected in formal procedures of separation that are imposed through roadblocks, walls, and customs procedures, while the former is more often than not reflected in the functional patterns that are much more meaningful to most people as they go about their daily activities, crossing the ethnic divide in some places and avoiding it at all costs in others. Ethnonational conflict takes place at the local and the municipal levels and at the perceived line of functional separation as much as, if not more than, at the formal line of interstate separation.

The Israeli-Palestinian conflict is a good example of one where the ethnonational conflict is expressed through the demarcation and imposition of boundaries—real and perceived—at the local level. This has most recently been expressed through the physical construction of a separation fence/wall.[9] Following acts of violence and suicide bombings, there was strong grassroots pressure in Israel to erect a fence that would prevent movement of Palestinians from one side of the boundary to the other and thus, it was argued, would enhance the security of Israeli civilians. The construction of a separation wall was a unilateral decision on the part of the Israeli government, and its course ran parallel to, but not along, the Green Line boundary that separates Israel from the West Bank (Figure 16.1).

The Green Line boundary was superimposed upon the Israeli-Palestinian landscape as a result of Israel's War of Independence and the ensuing armistice talks between Israel and Jordan in 1948–1949. The single functional landscape was divided into two politicoterritorial entities, one that became part of Israel, the other that became known as the West Bank and remained under Jordanian administration until Israel conquered this area in the Six-Day War of 1967. Since 1967, the West Bank has remained an occupied territory, while the Green Line boundary has remained an administrative line of separation. It is generally assumed that any future Palestinian state will have as its border the Green Line, although there are equally strong arguments for making boundary adjustments and territorial exchanges between the two sides as a means of creating a line that reflects the changing geographic realities of both Israeli and Palestinian populations.[10] Not only do Palestinians find themselves on both sides of the boundary, but so do Israeli residents of the settlements. It is assumed that a final territorial resolution of the conflict will necessitate the evacuation of these settlements. For this reason, the settlers feel threatened by the construction of any separation wall or fence, which they see as the first practical stages in the establishment of a political boundary that they oppose.

The recent construction of the separation wall was carried out in such a way as to include some Israeli settlements that were in close proximity to the Green Line, although this also resulted in the inclusion of a small number of Palestinian villages that now found themselves as "spatial hostages," located to the west of the separation wall/fence, but to the east of the Green Line itself. The long-term implications of this wall of separation are unclear. It has enhanced the notion of the border and the fact that conflict resolution, if it is ever to take place in this region, will consist of territorial separation between two territories and their respective peoples. The construction of this wall takes on many of the classic boundary barrier functions, exacerbating and reflecting a situation of extreme conflict, on the one hand, while possibly laying the foundations for territorial demarcation of separate political entities, on the other. The purpose of the wall is to serve as a barrier between two peoples who hate and fear each other, not as a fence between good neighbors.[11] It is erected at the most local of levels and separates some towns and villages across no more than hundreds of meters. The construction of the wall has come at the same time as the construction of the Trans-Israel Highway, a north-south route that runs through the center of the country but that has

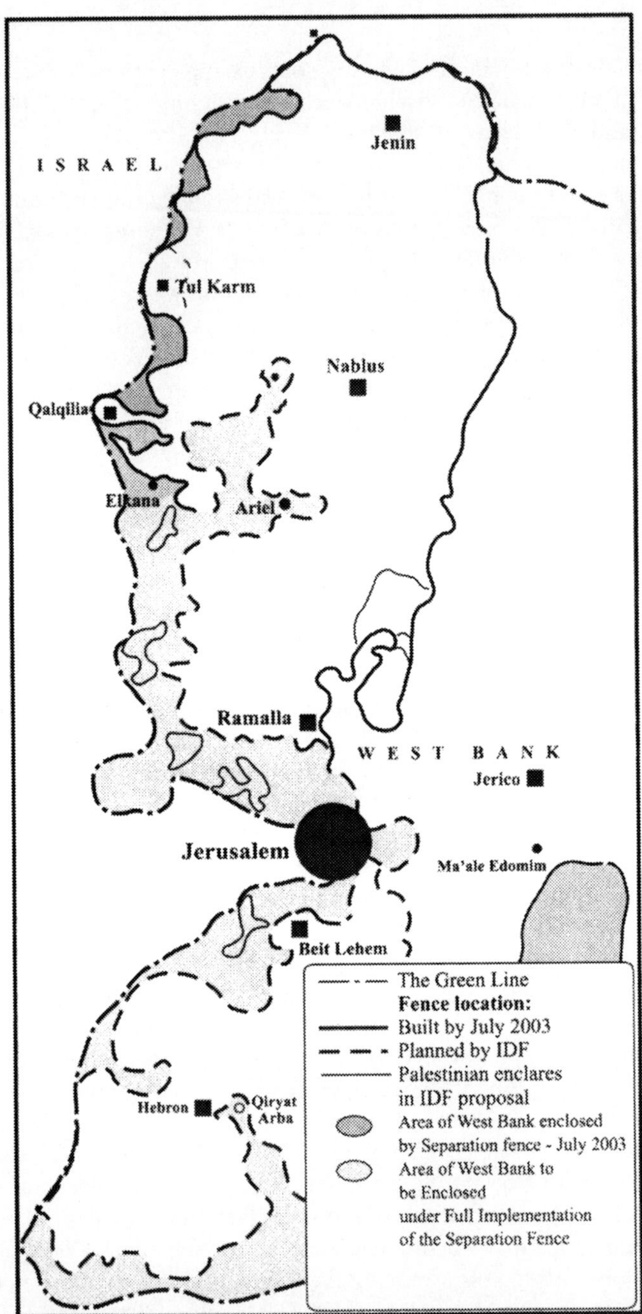

FIGURE 16.1 Competing boundaries: the Green Line and the separation fence between Israel and the West Bank. *Source:* Redrawn from "Anti-Apartheid Wall Campaign Poster Map in Arabic," March 21, 2004, on "Stop the Wall" Web site. *http://stopthewall.org/maps/430.shtml* (accessed May 13, 2004).

been planned so as not to cross the Green Line boundary at any point along its route, a fact that strengthens even further the notion of boundary that separates one developmental region from another.[12]

The division of Nicosia is another example of the presence of a fence/wall that separates two ethnic populations at the microgeographic level. Since the Turkish invasion of the island in 1974 and the forced migration of Greek Cypriots to the south of the island and Turkish Cypriots to the north of the island, Cyprus has consisted of two small, ethnoterritorially homogeneous units. The strongest expression of this physical divide is to be found in Nicosia, the only town that retains both Greek and Turkish Cypriot neighborhoods, but with a clear spatial divide between the Turkish north and the Greek south of the city.[13] Despite its presence in the middle of a bustling city, the wall of separation was as close to a sealed boundary as could be found on the face of the world political map until the first partial opening of the boundary took place in April 2003, a move that signaled a possible rapprochement between the two parts of the island as Cyprus headed full steam into an enlarged European Union (EU). Unlike the case of Israel-Palestine, the forced migration of ethnic populations has made the issue of identity politics less difficult to resolve because it is deemed unlikely that either of the two populations will return to their former homes in the other part of the island if and when conflict resolution and reunification of the island take place. While this does not justify any form of ethnic cleansing, the realities on the ground have created a post factum ethnoterritorial reality that could lend itself to conflict resolution on the basis of a federated state that would consist of two distinct territorial entities. This does not in any way decrease the sense of yearning and attachment for the old landscape, as was clearly indicated by the fact that nearly a third of the island's population crossed the line to see their former homes after the partial opening of the line in 2003.[14]

But for strong ethnoterritorial boundaries to take effect at the local level, the building of a physical fence or wall is not necessarily required. The situation in many of the Balkan regions and towns after the civil wars, ethnic cleansing, and attempted genocides of the 1990s displays patterns of clear territorial separation between the conflicting groups.[15] A mutual geography of fear and/or threat maintains a clear separation between peoples, including those who have been driven from their homes on the "other" side of the boundary. The desire to return to their former homes is mixed with a fear of returning to a situation where an ethnic minority is controlled and dominated by a majority power. While the international forces in such places as Bosnia and Kosovo promote the principle of refugee return, it is not followed through on a practical basis due to the opposition of the dominant ethnic party in each region, the fear that such return will almost immediately ignite renewed violence and conflict, and the understanding that once the international peacekeeping forces leave the region, there will be no umbrella of protection for the returning groups.

Nowhere is the microethnic boundary more prominent than in the town of Mitrovica in northern Kosovo. The river separates the Albanian majority south of the town from the Serbian northern neighborhoods. Serbians used to reside south of the river but were mostly driven out by the Albanian majority, an action that was perceived by the Albanians as being no more than revenge for the violence inflicted upon them by the Serbs. The bridge across the river is a vacant no-man's land that is patrolled by United Nations and other peacekeeping forces, but over which Serbs or Albanians dare cross only with the knowledge that this may endanger their physical safety, despite the claims by the international forces that the city is a single unified unit. Albanians who cross to the northern parts of the city are often identified by Serbian "bridge watchers" who sit in the coffeehouses that overlook the bridge and threaten the lives of transboundary strayers.

A similar nonwall exists in the city of Jerusalem that separates East Jerusalem Palestinian from West Jerusalem Jewish neighborhoods. Prior to the onset of the first Intifada in 1987, Israelis and Palestinians crossed to the other side of the city with relative ease; Palestinians found employment in West Jerusalem, and Israelis found cheaper goods and services in East Jerusalem.[16] One of the main contact points between East and West Jerusalem was the watermelon stalls at the Damascus Gate, where people from both parts of the city would come at night to purchase fruit and drink coffee. The markets of the old city were also frequented by members of both national groups. This is no longer the case. Where there was once a minimal level of economic interaction, these spaces are now almost totally ethnically homogeneous because each population fears crossing the boundary, regardless of the fact that it is not marked in any way. A new internal highway that links the Old City of Jerusalem and the south of the city with the northern neighborhoods has been constructed in close proximity to parts of the old boundary (before 1967, during which period there was a wall and a fence that separated Israeli West Jerusalem from Jordanian controlled East Jerusalem) and thus reinforces notions of separation between Jewish and Palestinian neighborhoods on either side of the road. One of the few spaces of interaction remains the American Colony Hotel, a few hundred yards on the Palestinian side of the road, where foreign journalists hang out and where Israeli and Palestinian peace groups and negotiating teams often undertake meetings.

Perceiving Ethnoterritorial Boundaries

Groups often perceive the lines of separation in places where no physical territorial boundary exists. Perceived boundaries are particularly prevalent in urban neighborhoods where processes of voluntary ethnic segregation create boundaries along streets and other urban landmarks beyond which residents of one part of the city do not cross. These perceived barriers do not necessarily coincide with any form of administrative or municipal boundary. Neighborhood residents create their own internal boundaries; they do not cross certain roads or they shop at specific stores, where the local gossip focuses on their own few residential blocks. These do not always necessarily coincide with the statistical or municipal subdivisions of the city for planning and administrative purposes. Neighborhood groups may often lobby local municipalities for resources and services for their own perceived residential areas, even where this does not fit in with the planning strategies of the city officials. The names given to such neighborhoods tend to self-define the areas in terms of which population groups actually live there, even if they do not appear on the official maps of the city. The construction of new roads, new residential projects, and ethnic food shops and restaurants defines the functional and perceived boundaries, which undergo constant expansion or contraction, regardless of whether or not they fit into the hierarchical system of municipal and statistical lines of administrative separation.

Conflict for resources takes place between and within these neighborhoods, the success or failure to obtain resources constitutes a dynamic factor in the way in which the functional and perceived boundaries continue to be redrawn and redefined. Housing and real estate managers play a major role in the fixation of these perceptual boundaries by opening neighboring streets to "infiltration" by different economic or ethnic groups or maintaining the lines of residential separation through managerial and economic policies aimed at excluding some and including others. Where the urban lines of separation reflect ethnic conflict at the national level (e.g., Jews and Arabs in Israel or Catholics and Protestants in Belfast), the functional and perceptual lines of everyday life can eventually be transformed into formal lines of municipal and administrative separation.

Interstate boundaries are different in that they exist and, as such, do not need to be perceived. There are real barrier functions that operate along the course of these boundaries. They are seen and felt. Nevertheless, the impact of the boundary on the borderland is as much perceived as it is a concrete experience and largely depends on the extent to which the boundary is "open" or "closed" and the degree to which transboundary movement is an accepted norm of borderland life. The manner in which borders are managed to enable greater or lesser interaction at the local level (discussed later) is important in this respect and can bring about the formal "opening" of the boundary, as has occurred across many boundaries in Western Europe during the past fifty years.

In situations of conflict, perceived boundaries can have as great an impact on the nature of interethnic political relations as the hard territorial lines. In many cases, perceived boundaries reflect more accurately the situation on the ground. While Nicosia has a physical barrier that separates Greek and Turkish Cypriots from each other, no such walls exist in either Belfast or Jerusalem, but the geographies of fear that are prevalent among Catholics and Protestants in Belfast or among Jews and Arabs in Jerusalem create a perceptual boundary that no one is prepared to cross.[17] The notions of walls or peace lines in Belfast are a physical manifestation of these perceptions but do not constitute any form of official barrier.

Physical boundaries, such as fences and walls, may be established as a result of a growing awareness among policy makers of the existence of a perceptual boundary, while the perception that a boundary is no longer necessary and that people on both sides can safely interact with each other can, in turn, lead to the removal of formal boundaries such as fences, walls, and customs posts. The fact that French and Spanish residents along the Pyrenees divide crossed the boundary for culinary purposes, or that Dutch and Belgian residents worked in each other's towns and sent their children to schools across the border (to cite but a few examples in Western Europe) was a parallel process to the formal opening of boundaries that took place under the process of EU enlargement and that helped facilitate the relative ease of the boundary-opening process.

Perhaps an arbitrary distinction can be made between the erection of "fences" aimed at creating "good" (stable, orderly) neighbors and relations and the construction of "walls" whose purpose is to function as a hard barrier to prevent all sorts of transboundary communication or movement from taking place. Perceptually, the sight of a wall, a slab of concrete through which the "other" side is invisible (with or without graffiti), is much more menacing and threatening than is a fence that, despite any amount of barbed wire, is open to sight and allows a view, even if it is somewhat distorted by the lines of the wire, of the other side to take place.[18] This may be nothing more than an arbitrary distinction, but given the importance of perception in the eyes of the borderland residents, this can be the whole difference between a desire to retain total separation or to attempt minimal levels of contact, to see the "enemy" on the other side as a human being or simply to block his/her existence out of the psyche altogether. Attempts at conflict resolution along the ethnic conflict interface must take into account the perceptual implications of retaining fences or walls as markers of separation.[19] They must determine whether the function of such separators is as a barrier that excludes or as an interface that allows some levels of transboundary contact to take place. One of the major failures of security experts, to whom states normally turn for advice in the creation of new borders, is their inability to take account of the perceptual and social dimensions of the nature of the boundary. They are only interested in the barrier and control function of the border, whether in peace or conflict. The notion of a border without a physical wall is almost unimaginable in the security discourse.[20]

A wall is a slab of concrete and therefore makes for the complete "othering" of the people on the other side. They become invisible, which makes it easier for people on each side to construct their own separate identities, and the identities of the "other," free from real world views and interactions. The "other" is always a terrorist or a tank commander. Rarely is he/she a parent or employer who is carrying out the same daily practices as the self. The more invisible the other, the less real he/she is, and the greater is the perceived difference and feeling of threat. The physical boundaries strengthen the notion of "difference," especially where ethnic conflict and mutual fear play a role in daily interactions. Thus for conflict resolution to move a step further along the road of a peace process into the world of reconciliation and mutual dialogue, fences and walls—particularly the physical ones—must be removed rather than fortified. If, after the implementation of a peace agreement, residents of neighboring Kefar Sava (in Israel) and Kalkiliya (in the West Bank) continue to wake up to the view of a slab of concrete outside their windows that separates each from the other more than it has ever done in the past, the two peoples will live in close proximity but with little understanding of or interaction with the other. Conflict resolution may take root, but it will be a cold peace where the mutual fears and threats still hang in the air, with little or no reconciliation between the two peoples.

Identity Boundaries as Places of Conflict

In his study of boundary disputes, Daniel Dzurek notes the importance of the identity factors, especially the lethal combination of ethnicity and religion, in making some boundary disputes more important than others.[21] This raises the chicken-and-egg question of boundary studies. Does the demarcation and imposition of a boundary upon a landscape result in the formation of distinct and separate territorial identities as groups establish their residences on each side of the divide, or do existing identities determine the course of the line of separation between their respective territorial ecumenes? There is, of course, no single answer to this question. Power politics has a major role to play in the way in which boundaries are demarcated and the extent to which they coincide with the geographic dispersion of identity groups.[22]

Increasingly, issues of identity lie at the root of boundary conflicts as much as, if not more than, the extent to which the demarcation of the line enables one state to control valuable and scarce natural resources such as water, oil, or minerals. Where boundaries cross both the identity and the resource divide at one and the same time, the potential for boundary conflict is greatest, since minority groups do not necessarily benefit from the potential economic benefits of the natural resources. The Kurdish oil fields in Kirkuk were exploited by the Iraqi government of Saddam Hussein, who also attempted to forcibly change the ethnic balance of this important Kurdish city. The exploitation of offshore oil resources in the North Sea by the government in London only served to strengthen the notion of Scottish identity, which is now reflected in the devolution of some administrative powers to Edinburgh. Where territorial lines cross both the resource and the identity interfaces, governments become most suspicious of their ethnic or national minorities, while these same minorities, in turn, see the resource as belonging to "them." This only serves to exacerbate ethnoterritorial perceptions of difference, coupled with feelings that the "self" group and territory are being unfairly exploited by the "other."

Thus boundaries continue to play an important role in the way in which territorial identities are formed and maintained.[23] The process of territorial socialization, through which national identity is tied in with the mythical spaces and places and through which some territories become more important or "holy" than other territories, will often focus on those territories that lie beyond the state boundary but within the identity ecumene of the particular group. For Israelis, the most important biblical sites are in the West Bank (Judea and Samaria), not inside Israel. Areas beyond the boundary are always perceived as being part of the historic and ancient homeland, while the current boundary demarcation is an aberration that has been brought about by the injustice of history, warfare, colonialism, conquest, and occupation. The sense of territorial "injustice" is a major factor in explaining the continued identity-territory relationship in our world of non–nation-states. As long as there is a minority ethnic group that resides on the "wrong" side of the boundary, there will always be the sense that the boundaries should be redrawn, or that the rights of the minority should be strengthened. The reterritorialization process of the past two decades that has gone a long way toward breaking down the importance of state boundaries has, ironically, strengthened the role of regional and substate territorial identities.

The Israeli-Palestinian boundary may eventually be demarcated along, or in close proximity to, the Green Line that separates Israel from the West Bank. While this may help bring about a resolution of the territorial conflict, it does not resolve the basic ethnoidentity conflict that will straddle whatever line is demarcated. The imposition of this line in 1948–1949 resulted in the division of the Palestinian Arab residents of the area, some of whom became Palestinian inhabitants of the West Bank, while others remained "Israeli Arab" residents of Israel. Despite attempts by Israeli policy makers and academics to maintain this distinction even in the post-1967 period, this is an artificial distinction because it relates to a single ethnonational population group. There are still many Israelis who believe that the artificial boundary superimposed upon the landscape in 1949, the Green Line, which may yet be the boundary of a future Palestinian state, created a division between two distinct groups of Palestinian Arabs. This is a deterministic view of the conflict interface. Short of forced transfer of population, there is no single boundary that can create ethnic homogeneity. The alternative, a single binational or ethnocratic state in which territory and power are shared, with no need for territorial boundaries,[24] is opposed by a majority of both Israelis and Palestinians, neither of whom trusts the other in a framework of power sharing. Moreover, public survey data in Israel show quite clearly that the single most important objective for Israeli Jewish citizens of the state (left- and right-wing alike) is to maintain a clear Jewish demographic majority as the basic cornerstone and raison d'être of the state.

The 2003 war in Iraq brought, yet again, the issue of Kurdish identity boundaries to the fore. The division of the Kurdish territories in the aftermath of World War I and the new geopolitical realities of the region during this period have left one of the most difficult unresolved territory-boundary-identity issues on the face of the globe (Figure 16.2). The importance of the territorial boundary that divides Turkey, Iran, and Iraq has played itself out on numerous occasions during the past fifty years, especially during times of tension between the neighboring states.[25] In the early 1970s, during the first Iran-Iraq conflict, which was ostensibly fought over the control of islands in the Shatt al-Arab, Iran opened its boundaries in the Kurdish areas and thus offered territorial depth for the Iraqi Kurds in their attempt to gain control over the oil fields and towns in Mosul and Kirkuk. The Iraqi regime had to send many of its armed forces to this region, a second front, which diluted its military capabilities elsewhere. After the Algiers Agreement in 1975, in which Iraq relinquished claims to the islands, Iran withdrew its backhanded support from the Kurds and resealed the boundary between the two countries, which resulted in the collapse of the Kurdish revolt and territorial gains inside Iraq. The artificial boundary that split the Kurdish people into separate national minorities was only open for as long as the respective states that controlled the border regime (in this case, Iran) allowed transboundary interaction to take place. Identity boundaries are only as good as the realpolitik situation demands. For the Kurds, these geopolitical realities are no different today than they were in the aftermath of World War I; the superimposition of territorial boundaries in a single ethnonational area perpetuates the situation of territorial fragmentation.

Another case of contemporary territorial conflict around identity boundaries is the Balkans. In comparison to Israel-Palestine and the Kurdish issue, this is by far the most complex mix of territories and ethnonational identities. The boundaries of the Yugoslavian provinces never corresponded to identity boundaries; the

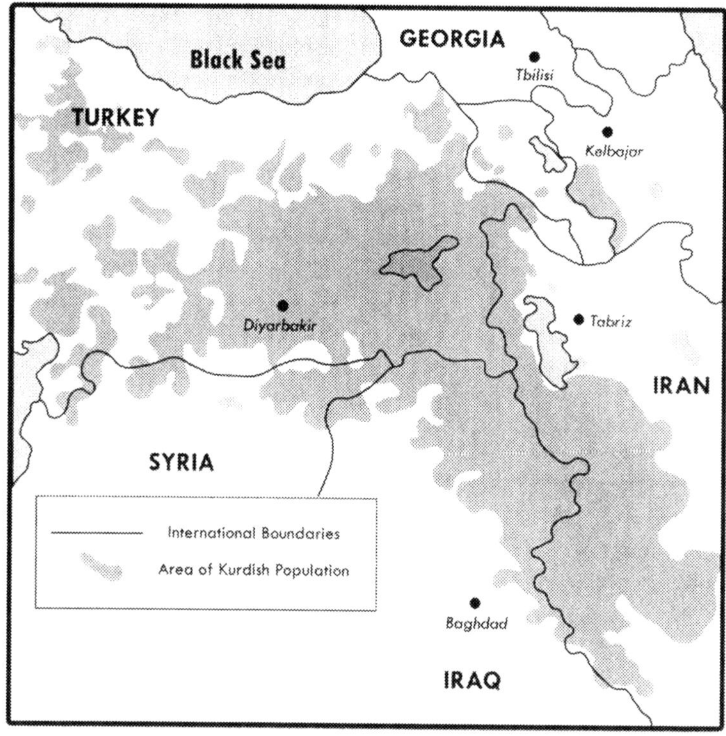

FIGURE 16.2 The cross-boundary distribution of the Kurdish population. *Source:* Thomas Poulsen, *Nations and States: A Geographic Background to World Affairs*, 173 (Upper Saddle River, NJ: Prentice-Hall, 1995).

complex mosaic of ethnonational groups spread throughout each and every region. In the aftermath of the fragmentation of Yugoslavia, pent-up minority frustrations broke out, and civil wars, attempted genocides, and mass ethnic cleansing took place in much of the former country, notably Bosnia and Kosovo. The imposition of international regimes of control brought about a limited level of political stability, although these regimes have so far been unsuccessful in creating a climate whereby expelled minorities can return en masse to their previous places of residence.

The potential territorial configurations for this region are numerous. In Kosovo, the original Serbian minority has been reduced to less than half its original size. The UN and European forces demand that the expelled Serbians be allowed to return to their homes, but the Albanian majority in Kosovo refuses to allow this to take place. It desires eventual independence for Kosovo rather than its remaining a minority province in the new state of Serbia (Yugoslavia), which now incorporates Serbia and Montenegro and in which Serbians are a clear majority (Figure 16.3). The remaining Serbian minority in northern Kosovo opposes Kosovar independence and, at the very least, demands boundary redemarcation in such a way that it can remain part of Serbia. But the international forces are prepared to consider all forms of political solutions as long as the existing boundaries remain in situ. The big powers are in consensus in their refusal to allow even the smallest boundary changes in this region. Territorial change along any single boundary in the Balkans would result in a domino effect for numerous additional potential boundary changes. If the Serbian minority in Kosovo were to remain part of Serbia, this would open the way for the Albanian minority in neighboring Macedonia to demand its own boundary change as a means of being incorporated within Kosovo, and so on.[26] Greater Serbia and Greater Albania are not only slogans of the post–World War I era, but remain relevant ethnonational symbols in our supposedly borderless world and bring, yet again, identity boundaries to the fore of the territorial discourse in these regions.

FIGURE 16.3 Distribution of the ethnic Albanian population in the Balkans. *Source:* Poulsen, *Nations and States*, 124.

From Conflict to Peace: Border Regimes and Boundary Management

While most, if not all, of the world's major territorial boundaries have been demarcated, focus has shifted to an understanding of the way in which boundaries are managed and the border regime is created. Demarcation and redemarcation are only one possible way of resolving ethnoterritorial conflicts, more often than not an unsuccessful one. As borders are becoming increasingly permeable and porous in some regions, the specific course of the territorial and identity lines of separation is more an issue of prestige than one relevant to the daily functioning and management of the boundary regime. It is possible to envisage conflict resolution that takes place through boundary regimes that enable greater transboundary interaction and cooperation between peoples on both sides of the territorial divide without having to undergo the much more problematic and politically sensitive issue of boundary redemarcation.

The classic border regimes run along a functional continuum from the closed or sealed to the open or nonexistent. Most interstate boundaries are located somewhere along this continuum with varying degrees of openness and closedness, depending on the nature of transboundary cooperation and joint management. These are similar in nature to the idealized types of borderlands posited by Oskar Martinez in his study of "the dynamics of border interaction," in which he identifies four borderland ideal types:

1. Alienated borderlands, in which tensions prevail, the border is functionally closed, and cross-border interaction is totally or nearly totally absent
2. Coexistent borderlands, in which stability is an on-and-off proposition, and borders remain slightly open, which allows the development of limited transboundary interaction
3. Interdependent borderlands, in which stability prevails most of the time, and there is increased transboundary interaction, with friendly and cooperative relationships between residents of the borderlands
4. Integrated borderlands, in which stability is strong, the economies of neighboring countries are merged, and there is unrestricted movement of people and goods across the boundary[27]

In situations of conflict, such as those discussed in this chapter, we would expect that the borderland regime—even after the initial implementation of a conflict resolution agreement—will reflect the alienated end of the continuum. But as part of conflict resolution, management of the boundary regime in such a way as to encourage transboundary interaction can potentially bring about greater grassroots cooperation between the peoples on both sides of the territorial divide. Creation of peace parks that straddle both sides of a conflict interface has been attempted in some locations.[28] In such cases, the physical course of the boundary does not necessarily have to undergo change, while the level of transboundary interaction increases. The EU has always invested a great deal of energy and resources into the setting up of transboundary Euro regions, both ones across boundaries within the EU and ones that straddle boundaries between the EU and neighboring countries. This has been successful in creating increased levels of cooperation and mutual understanding between neighboring populations, while the issue of boundary demarcation remains untouched and has become insignificant.

Under conditions of conflict or mutual tensions, the management of the boundary regime would be unilateral, with each side putting into operation those procedures that best fit its own national self-interests (Table 16.1). Under conditions of open and permeable boundaries, the management of the boundary regime would be fully cooperative and even planned jointly in such a way as to maximize transboundary benefits and to minimize the costs of transboundary spillovers and externalities. Most boundary situations will be located somewhere between these polarities, which will give rise to varied levels of coordination in those areas where mutual interests are not threatened (perceptually or actually) by the activities of the "other" side and/or where such coordinated activity is to the mutual benefit of both sides.

The nature of boundary management will change depending on the specific functions in question (Table 16.2). Thus we would expect that countries with a strong defensive or strategic posture (such as Israel) will focus on the barrier function of boundaries or use this discourse as a means of preventing cooperation from taking place in other areas, such as economic cooperation, movement of migrant workers or tourists, joint planning and municipal management, and/or cooperation

TABLE 16.1 Possible types of boundary regime/management

Nature of boundary	Closed/sealed	Open/closed	Open
Type of border regime/ management	Unilateral: No cooperation	Coordination: Functional separation	Joint Planning: Masterplan/blueprint
	The boundary is superimposed by the power-dominant side, which, in turn, determines the course and management of the boundary for its own interests, with little or no regard to the interests of the other side.	Basic agreement exists on the course of the boundary but not on the degree to which it should be open or closed to transboundary movement and cooperation. Defensive considerations tend to the "closed" end of the continuum, while economic interaction and joint environmental concerns tend to more "open" patterns of transboundary activity.	This is a postconflict situation where boundaries are open to maximal interaction and where defensive or security considerations are minimal or nonexistent. Transboundary planning and management of the boundary in all spheres can take place to the benefit of both populations.

TABLE 16.2 Attributes of transboundary activities

Boundary status	Open	Open/closed	Closed/sealed
Functional attributes			
Economic infrastructure (industrial parks / commercial centers)	Jointly owned and planned industrial and commercial areas on either side of the border line.	Jointly managed factories or commercial centers that straddle the border line.	Separate, competing economic activities.
Labor migration (daily commuting)	Daily commuting, no visas required, taxation optional in either state.	Limited daily commuting. Visa system in operation.	No migration. All employment within territory of residence.
Tourism migration (seasonal movement)	Free movement, easy access on daily and seasonal basis.	Limited tourism migration. Visa system in operation.	No tourism movement or entry visas.
Infrastructure coordination (roads, rail, electricity, water, and so on)	Standardization of all infrastructure, sharing of resources, uninterrupted flow of water, electricity, movement, and so on.	Cooperation in standardization of infrastructure and sharing of resources.	Separate electricity, water, road infrastructure. Different gauges.
Environmental management (spillovers, water courses, pollution)	Joint environmental management, joint patrols and enforcement of standards.	Coordination in prevention of noxious and harmful spillover effects.	No environmental management. Ecological damage and heavy cost resulting from spillover effect.
Defensive/security considerations	No defensive or security considerations.	Limited defensive considerations—police checkpoints and passport control.	Militarized and semimilitarized landscapes take precedence over civilian activities.
Municipal administration (garbage disposal, environmental management, social and cultural activities)	Joint transboundary municipalities, joint planning in areas of mutual interest.	Ad hoc municipal coordination between separate municipal authorities.	Separate municipal administration even in areas of common interest.
Law and order (police activities, prevention of smuggling and other transboundary crime)	Coordination of law and order activities, sharing of information, rights to pursue criminals across the border.	Coordination of transboundary law and order activities.	No coordination, with possible exception of smuggling and drugs.

in areas of environmental degradation and spillover. The interplay between these factors is critical in determining the extent to which boundaries retain their existing location and are not subject to politically sensitive redemarcation while, at one and the same time, they become functionally permeable and less relevant as barriers to movement, interaction, and cooperation.

Thus the process through which boundaries are opened cannot come about simply as a result of the signing of an agreement and the imposition of the boundary on the ground. There is likely to be a long transition period after the imposition of the boundary during which each side will gradually build up a new level of trust that, in turn, will bring about increased readiness to create new institutions of transboundary cooperation in a wide variety of fields, including labor migration, tourism, commercial activities, joint industrial parks, environmental management, and so on. This is the process through which conflicts, "highly contingent, communicatively constructed and dynamic phenomenon are transformed from an expected form of connecting operations which is characterized by a *no* to a potential *yes*."[29] The process is dynamic, with the ultimate objective being to create those boundary regimes that will enable the efficient management of the boundary, on the one hand, but will also contribute to a greater level of boundary "opening," on the other.

In cases where new boundaries are demarcated and imposed upon the landscape as part of conflict resolution, as is to be expected in Israel-Palestine, it will be the nature of the border regime that will determine the extent to which some functional normality will be established between the two states that will enable economic, environmental, and planning cooperation or prevent it altogether. The Palestinians will be faced by the classic postcolonialism dilemma—retaining relations through open boundaries for short-term economic benefits or cutting off all relations with the former occupier through closed and sealed boundaries, which will prevent a new neocolonial relationship, but at significant short-term economic costs and dislocation that can, if uncontrolled, bring about even greater political instability. It is never clear whether the short-term political and economic asymmetry that is created in a neocolonial relationship can help bring about longer term economic dependence for the new state. The postcolonial experience has, in most cases, perpetuated economic asymmetry and created long-term structural economic dependence of the new state on its more powerful neighbor. It is for this reason that the decision to seal the borders of a new state is a function of political considerations—the desire to demonstrate political independence and equality among the family of states. The desire for economic and environmental cooperation may be also be offset by an Israeli defensive discourse that demands rigid boundary management and controls and thus creates an atmosphere of tension and potential renewal of conflict even after the implementation of a peace agreement on the basis of clearly defined territorial separation. If the walls remain in situ, the negative perceptions persist despite the conflict resolution. Violence may cease, but little is done to actively promote cooperation between two antagonistic peoples.

The situation in which ethnonational groups remain residents of neighboring countries that are based on existing territorial boundaries (Kurds in Iran, Iraq, and

Turkey; Palestinians in Israel and a newly independent Palestine; Serbians in Serbia and a newly independent Kosovo; Albanians in Macedonia and Kosovo) has a potential, given equality of political rights and a downturn in interstate tensions, for promoting interstate cooperation within homocultural borderland regions, as contrasted with the creation of newly homogeneous ethnoterritorial states that attempt to seal their boundaries from their ethnically different neighbors. Thus conflict resolution in and around boundaries should focus on the nature of interaction within the borderlands, rather than on the almost impossible and highly conflictual task of boundary redemarcation. This is a form of reterritorialization that would create a better fit with territorial and political realities in the current world order, where states continue to vigorously defend their territorial integrity despite the fact that the functional influence of that very same territory and its respective boundaries has changed and has probably become more permeable to movement and vulnerable to challenges to its absolute notion of territorial sovereignty. This has been described by Herbert Dittgen as the "loss of autonomy, the retention of sovereignty" and ties in closely with contemporary functional changes in the role and significance of boundaries in a changing global system.[30]

Interaction and perceptions at the local level may often be at odds with the formal state perceptions of just what the border institution represents. With the exception of heavily sealed and armed boundaries of conflict, residents of the borderland regions are keen to interact with the "other" side, especially where there are benefits (such as economic opportunities or cultural or culinary diversity) to be gained from such transboundary interaction. Boundaries only remain barriers where there is a threat (real or perceived) that emanates from the other side. Where the threat is perceived, it is often the governments that socially construct the threat as a means of emphasizing the cutoff point of the boundary, a last-ditch resort at holding on to traditional notions of territorial absolutism and sovereignty. Within the EU, the physical boundaries may have been removed, but language remains a major barrier, while for some countries the retention of a separate currency from the euro is another form of border that has recently been constructed in new locations and that will remain until all the member states adopt the new single currency.

Where the threat or fear of the other is perceived rather than real, these perceptions can be changed through grassroots interactions between residents of the borderland areas. This is often the case in the immediate aftermath of conflict, where formal agreements have been implemented on the ground, but mutual suspicions remain between respective governments and peoples. The borderland peoples have a major role to play in breaking down the notion of boundaries as barriers through bottom-up transboundary activities that will force governments to change the formal status of the boundary in line with the emerging functional realities rather than the other way round. The geopolitical codes of the people do not always necessarily coincide with the geopolitical codes of governments. As political realities change, as the intensity of conflict diminishes, and as boundaries display the potential for greater permeability, it is often the people who can realize that potential far more quickly than the policy-makers and governments.

Conclusion

This chapter has attempted to refocus the study of boundaries as a component in contemporary ethnoterritorial conflict. The existence of these conflicts demonstrates the importance of territory and boundaries in our so-called deterritorialized and borderless worlds. At the same time, the nature of these conflicts has changed in that it is not the demarcation of the "hard" territorial line of separation that is as important as are the perceptions of the boundary and the interactions around the boundary as part of a borderland regime that reflects the way in which the boundary is managed. Borders and boundaries have to be understood as a dynamic factor in their own right, not just as an output of policy making. Just as the "closing" of boundaries usually signifies conflict and cross-border tensions, the "opening" of borders signifies a transition from conflict and barriers to conflict resolution and contact. Any study of the contemporary role of boundaries in ethnoterritorial conflict should not limit itself only to the analysis of the barrier effect, but should also look at the ways in which borderlands can create transition zones where peoples meet, interact, and cooperate and thus lessen interstate or intergroup tensions.[31] This points to a way forward in the resolution of these conflicts at both the national and local levels in our continued search for a more stable and secure geopolitical environment.

Notes

1. A borderland is an area within which certain practices and activities are influenced by the existence of a proximate boundary. This may be a territorial area or a social ecumene and is not necessarily equal in terms of size or nature of activity on either side of the border. Borderlands may either reflect difference over the boundary or constitute areas of cooperation and interaction between peoples on each side.

2. Newman and Paasi, "Fences and Neighbours in the Postmodern World"; David Newman, "Into the Millennium"; Newman, "Boundaries."

3. Newman, "Theorizing Borders."

4. For various discussions of the contemporary legacy of African boundary superimposition, see Peninou, "Ethiopian-Eritrean Border Conflict"; Daniel, "African Boundaries"; Griggs, "Designing Boundaries for a Continent"; and Lemon, "South Africa's Internal Boundaries."

5. Cizre, "Turkey's Kurdish Problem."

6. For a discussion of partition, see Fraser, *Partition in Ireland, India, and Palestine*; Waterman, "Partitioned States"; and Waterman, "Partition, Secession, and Peace in Our Time."

7. Kolossov, "Political Geography of European Minorities"; Motyl, "Reifying Boundaries—Fetishizing the Nation."

8. Castellino and Allen, *Title to Territory in International Law*.

9. For various discussions of Israeli-Palestinian territorial conflict and boundary demarcation issues, see Newman, "Creating the Fences of Territorial Separation"; Newman, "Geopolitics of Peacemaking in Israel-Palestine"; Falah, "Re-envisioning Current Discourse"; and Falah and Newman, "Spatial Manifestation of Threat"; Newman, "Barriers or Bridges?"

10. Brawer, "Making of an Israeli-Palestinian Boundary"; Falah, "Green Line Revisited"; Newman, *Boundaries in Flux.*

11. Williams, "Territorial Borders, International Ethics, and Geography."

12. For a fascinating account of the interplay between routeways, boundaries, and borderlands, see Ispahani, *Roads and Rivals.*

13. Kliot and Mansfeld, "Political Landscape of Partition."

14. See *New York Times,* May 9, 2003, which describes the cross-border movement of Cypriots in search of their former homes and imagined landscapes.

15. See Dahlman, this volume; Klemencic, "Boundaries, Internal Order, and Identities of Bosnia and Herzegovina"; and Milenkoski and Talevski, "Borders of the Republic of Macedonia."

16. Romann and Weingrod, *Living Together Separately*; Wasserstein, *Divided Jerusalem.*

17. For studies of Jerusalem, see Romann and Weingrod, *Living Together Separately*; Dumper, *Politics of Jerusalem since 1967*; and Wasserstein, *Divided Jerusalem.* For studies of Belfast, see Boal, "Integration and Division"; Bollens, *On Narrow Ground*; and Neill and Schwedler, *Urban Planning and Cultural Inclusion.*

18. The nonphysical line of separation in Jerusalem may be described as constituting a "glass wall" with total cross-border visibility and access, but a perceived wall all the same.

19. Newman, "Theorizing Borders."

20. This has been played up time and time again in the endless negotiations and discussions that have surrounded the nature of a future Israeli-Palestinian boundary.

21. Dzurek, "What Makes Some Boundary Disputes Important?"

22. For varying discussions on the relationships between borders and identity formation see Wilson and Donnan, *Border Identities*; Albert, Jacobson, and Lapid, *Identities, Borders, Orders.*

23. Paasi, *Territories, Boundaries, and Consciousness*; Murphy, "National Claims to Territory in the Modern State System."

24. Yiftachel, "Israeli Society and Jewish-Palestinian Reconciliation."

25. Cizre, "Turkey's Kurdish Problem."

26. Milenkoski and Talevski, "Borders of the Republic of Macedonia."

27. Martinez, "Dynamics of Border Interaction."

28. Duffy, "Peace Parks"; Kliot, "Grand Design for Peace"; Kliot, "Transborder Peace Parks."

29. These ideas have been taken from Luhmann, *Theories of Distinction.* They have been developed as an appropriate analytical framework for the study of Euroborder conflicts as part of an EU-funded research project by Albert, Diez, and Stetter, "European Union and Border Conflicts," and Stetter, "Proposals for a Systems Theoretical Approach"; Stetter, Diez, and Albert, "The European Union and the Transformation of Border Conflicts: Theorizing the Impact of Integration and Association."

30. Dittgen, "The End of the Nation State?"

31. This is different from the notion of a buffer zone, where the object of the "zone" is simply to widen the extent of the barrier rather than to create points of contact.

References

Albert, Mathias, Thomas Diez, and Stephan Stetter. "The European Union and Border Conflicts: Some Conceptual Clarifications." Paper presented at the Twenty-seventh Annual Conference of the British International Studies Association (BISA), London School of Economics, December 2002.

Albert, Mathias, David Jacobson, and Yosef Lapid, eds. *Identities, Borders, Orders: Rethinking International Relations Theory*. Minneapolis: University of Minnesota Press, 2001.

Boal, F. "Integration and Division: Sharing and Segregating in Belfast." *Planning Practice and Research* 11 (1996): 151–158.

Bollens, Scott. *On Narrow Ground: Urban Policy and Ethnic Conflict in Jerusalem and Belfast*. Albany: State University of New York Press, 2000.

Brawer, Moshe. "The Making of an Israeli-Palestinian Boundary." In *The Razor's Edge: International Boundaries and Political Geography*, ed. Clive Schofield, David Newman, Alasdair Drysdale, and Janet Allison-Brown, 473–492. London: Kluwer Law International, 2002.

Castellino, Joshua, and Steve Allen. *Title to Territory in International Law*. Aldershot: Ashgate, 2003.

Cizre, U. "Turkey's Kurdish Problem: Borders, Identity, and Hegemony." In *Right-Sizing the State: The Politics of Moving Borders*, ed. B. O'Leary, I. Lustick, and T. Callaghy, 222–252. Oxford: Oxford University Press, 2001.

Daniel, Tim. "African Boundaries: New Order, Historic Tensions." In *Borderlands under Stress*, ed. Martin Pratt and Janet Allison-Brown, 211–226. London: Kluwer Law International, 2000.

Dittgen, Herbert. "The End of the Nation-State? Borders in the Age of Globalization." In *Borderlands under Stress*, ed. Martin Pratt and Janet Allison-Brown, 49–68. London: Kluwer Law International, 2000.

Duffy, Rosalyn. "Peace Parks: The Paradox of Globalization." *Geopolitics* 6 (2001): 1–26.

Dumper, M. *The Politics of Jerusalem since 1967*. New York: Columbia University Press, 1996.

Dzurek, Daniel. "What Makes Some Boundary Disputes Important?" *Boundary and Security Bulletin* 7 (1999): 83–89.

Falah, Ghazi. "Re-envisioning Current Discourse: Alternative Territorial Configurations of Palestinian Statehood." *Canadian Geographer* 41 (1997): 307–330.

Falah, Ghazi. "The Green Line Revisited: October 2000." In *The Razor's Edge: International Boundaries and Political Geography*, ed. Clive Schofield, David Newman, Alasdair Drysdale, and Janet Allison-Brown, 493–511. London: Kluwer Law International, 2002.

Falah, Ghazi, and David Newman. "The Spatial Manifestation of Threat: Israelis and Palestinians Seek a "Good" Border." *Political Geography* 14 (1995): 689–706.

Fraser, T. *Partition in Ireland, India, and Palestine: Theory and Practice*. London, Macmillan, 1984.

Griggs, Richard. "Designing Boundaries for a Continent: The Geopolitics of an African Renaissance." In *Borderlands under Stress*, ed. Martin Pratt and Janet Allison-Brown, 227–250. London: Kluwer Law International, 2000.

Ispahani, Mahnaz. *Roads and Rivals: The Politics of Access in the Borderlands of Asia*. London: Tauris, 1989.

Klemencic, Mladan. "The Boundaries, Internal Order, and Identities of Bosnia and Herzegovina." *Boundary and Security Bulletin* 8 (2000): 63–71.

Kliot, Nurit. "The Grand Design for Peace: Planning Transborder Cooperation in the Red Sea." *Political Geography* 16 (1997): 581–603.

Kliot, Nurit. "Transborder Peace Parks: The Political Geography of Cooperation (and Conflict) in Borderlands." In *The Razor's Edge: International Boundaries and Political Geography*, ed. Clive Schofield, David Newman, Alasdair Drysdale, and Janet Allison-Brown, 407–437. London: Kluwer Law International, 2002.

Kliot, Nurit, and Yoel Mansfeld. "The Political Landscape of Partition: The Case of Cyprus." *Political Geography* 16 (1997): 495–521.

Kolossov, Vladimir. "The Political Geography of European Minorities: Past and Future." *Political Geography* 17 (1998): 517–534.

Lemon, Anthony. "South Africa's Internal Boundaries: The Spatial Engineering of Land and Power in the Twentieth Century." In *The Razor's Edge: International Boundaries and Political Geography*, ed. Clive Schofield, David Newman, Alasdair Drysdale, and Janet Allison-Brown, 303–322. London: Kluwer Law International, 2002.

Luhmann, N. *Theories of Distinction: Redescribing the Descriptions of Modernity*. Translated and edited by William Rasch. Stanford, CA: Stanford University Press, 2002.

Martinez, Oskar. "The Dynamics of Border Interaction: New Approaches to Border Analysis." In *World Boundaries, vol. 1, Global Boundaries*, ed. Clive Schofield, 1–15. London: Routledge, 1994.

Milenkoski, Mile, and Jove Talevski. "The Borders of the Republic of Macedonia." *Boundary and Security Bulletin* 9 (2001): 79–85.

Motyl, Alexander. "Reifying Boundaries—Fetishizing the Nation: Soviet Legacies and Elite Legitimacy in Post-Soviet States." In *Right-Sizing the State: The Politics of Moving Borders*, ed. B. O'Leary, I. Lustick, and T. Callaghy, 201–221. Oxford: Oxford University Press, 2001.

Murphy, Alexander. "National Claims to Territory in the Modern State System: Geographical Considerations." *Geopolitics* 7 (2002): 193–214.

Neill, William, and Hanns-Uve Schwedler, eds. *Urban Planning and Cultural Inclusion: Lessons from Belfast and Berlin*. Houndmills; UK: Palgrave Macmillan, 2001.

Newman, David. *Boundaries in Flux: The Green Line Boundary between Israel and the West Bank*. Boundary and Territory Briefing, vol. 1. Dunham, UK: International Boundaries Research Unit, University of Durham, 1995.

Newman, David. "Creating the Fences of Territorial Separation: The Discourse of Israeli-Palestinian Conflict Resolution." *Geopolitics and International Boundaries* 2 (1998): 1–35.

Newman, David. "Into the Millennium: The Study of International Boundaries in an Era of Global and Technological Change." *Boundary and Security Bulletin* 7 (1999): 63–71.

Newman, David. "Boundaries." In *A Companion to Political Geography*, ed. John Agnew, Gerard Toal, and Kathryn Mitchell, 123–137. Oxford: Blackwell, 2002.

Newman, David. "The Geopolitics of Peacemaking in Israel-Palestine." *Political Geography* 21 (2002): 629–646.

Newman, David. "Barriers or Bridges? On Borders, Fences and Walls—Israel's Separation Fence." *Tikkun* 18 (2003): 54–58.

Newman, David. "Theorizing Borders." *Journal of Borderland Studies* 18 (2003).

Newman, David, and Anssi Paasi. "Fences and Neighbours in the Postmodern World: Boundary Narratives in Political Geography." *Progress in Human Geography* 22 (1998): 186–207.

Paasi, Anssi. *Territories, Boundaries, and Consciousness*. New York: Wiley, 1996.

Peninou, J. "The Ethiopian-Eritrean Border Conflict." *Boundary and Security Bulletin* 6 (1998): 46–50.

Romann, Michael, and Alex Weingrod. *Living Together Separately: Jews and Arabs in Contemporary Jerusalem*. Princeton, NJ: Princeton University Press, 1991.

Simons, Marlise. "Nicossia Journal; On a Severed Street in Cyprus, the Healing Begins." *New York Times*, May 9, 2003, section A, page 4.

Stetter, Stephan, Thomas Diez, and Mathias Albert. "The European Union and the Transformation of Border Conflicts: Theorizing the Impact of Integration and Association." Paper presented at the International Studies Association Conference, Budapest, June 2003.

Wasserstein, Bernard. *Divided Jerusalem: The Struggle for the Holy City*. London: Profile, 2001.

Waterman, Stanley. "Partitioned States." *Political Geography Quarterly* 6 (1987): 151–170.

Waterman, Stanley. "Partition, Secession, and Peace in Our Time." *GeoJournal* 39 (1996): 345–352.

Williams, John. "Territorial Borders, International Ethics, and Geography: Do Good Fences Still Make Good Neighbours?" *Geopolitics* 8 (2003): 25–46.

Wilson, Thomas, and Hastings Donnan, eds. *Border Identities: Nation and State at International Frontiers*. Cambridge: Cambridge University Press, 1998.

Yiftachel, Oren. "Israeli Society and Jewish-Palestinian Reconciliation: Ethnocracy and Its Territorial Contradictions." *Middle East Journal* 51 (1997): 505–519.

III

GEOGRAPHIES OF PEACE

GUNTRAM H. HERB

The Geography of Peace Movements

Geographers have not been prominent in studying peace movements. This is not surprising, given the strong foundations of the discipline in warfare and imperialism.[1] To date, the only general geographic survey of peace movements appears to be Brunn's 1985 study, a catalog of peace organizations and their activities that covered mainly the United States.[2] Other studies by geographers are few and focus on individual antiwar campaigns or disarmament strategies.[3] However, more recently, geographers have made significant contributions to the analysis of the broader theoretical context of peace movements. These works offer spatial conceptualizations of social movement mobilization.[4] A general appraisal of the geographic dimensions of peace movements is still missing. This chapter represents a tentative step in this direction.

The examination is conducted in four steps. The first section deals with general characteristics of peace movements. It discusses problems of definition and presents the intellectual and philosophical foundations of peace activities. The second section approaches the geography of peace movements from a historical perspective. It examines the development of organized peace groups from their origins in the nineteenth century to the present. Different scales of the changing geopolitical and societal contexts will frame the discussion. Such a geohistory will allow us to identify and interpret changing intensities of activism. The third section addresses the geography of contemporary peace movements from a conceptual viewpoint. Armed with theoretical concepts from the recent literature on social movements, it examines the places and spaces of mobilization. The 1980s peace movement against nuclear armaments will serve as a case study to illustrate the insights that can be gained from a geographic approach. Finally, I will present the major implications that stem from the geohistorical and conceptual discussions in the conclusion.

Characteristics of Peace Movements

Peace is more than the absence of war. Though it is traditionally defined as the opposite of war, peace scholars and activists now embrace a notion of peace that includes the conditions necessary to bring about a nonviolent and just society at all levels of human activity. Contemporary peace movements not only seek to abolish the overt violence of war, but also struggle to transform the social structures responsible for death and human suffering.[5] Such a "positive" view of peace argues that war has the same structural foundations as customary practices of violence, poverty, and environmental degradation. Feminist and radical critiques of patriarchy, capitalism, and imperialism have most heavily influenced this reconceptualization of peace and war, starting in the early 1970s.[6]

The idea of positive peace makes it difficult to distinguish peace movements from the myriad of groups engaged in societal change. Some authors estimate that there are more than 250,000 such organizations in the developing world alone.[7] It is possible to exclude from this list those bureaucratized and apolitical nongovernmental organizations (NGOs) that are only interested in easing the provision of social services, but even groups that work for structural change and consolidate different practices of social protest and social identities defy easy categorization as being primarily dedicated to peace.[8] Moreover, some organizations use the label "peace" to disguise their true intentions. Examples are the pro-Soviet World Peace Council that advocated the policies of a totalitarian regime and pro-NATO organizations that were established to counter nuclear disarmament movements in the 1980s.[9]

Most publications on peace movements do not engage with issues of definition and simply restrict their analyses to organizations and groups that actively oppose wars or war-related activities. Thus the negative peace concept prevails in the literature on peace movements. Treatment of groups that work for positive peace—in particular, the grassroots organizations in the developing world—are generally treated separately in the burgeoning literature on new social movements. Elise Boulding has attempted to bridge this gap and addresses groups that oppose war and arms as well as those engaged in "peacebuilding," that is, activities that are designed to create social justice, but her selection is by necessity eclectic. She uses these examples to underline her central contention that peace cultures have a long tradition and that we can learn from them in designing a world without structural violence.[10]

On a most basic level, there seems to be general agreement in the literature that only those organizations that reject violence in their campaigns and exhibit autonomy from governments should be included under the rubric *peace movements*. Moreover, there is a distinction between movements that work for a fundamental transformation of the existing war system and those that are opposed to a specific war or specific weapons. The complete rejection of militarism, which is often termed absolute pacifism, entails a deep conviction that all wars are wrong and that there is never a justification for killing another human being.[11] True pacifists are deeply committed to these beliefs and are willing to make strong personal sacrifices. They refuse to enlist for the draft, to pay taxes that are spent on the military, and to cooperate with any activity that condones violence and hatred. They will engage in nonviolent resistance even if it means breaking the law and will accept repression by the state, such as serving long prison sentences for being conscientious objectors. Their actions have a long-term focus and are sustained by strong religious or ideological visions. They pursue their goal for a new world with a conviction that could be characterized as a positive form of missionary zeal. As a result of their uncompromising and persistent position, pacifists represent a small minority in peace movements, yet they are the ones who keep the issue of peace alive during times when peace activism experiences a downturn and a loss of general public support.[12]

In contrast to transforming the entire war system, many peace movements focus on a single issue. A clear goal, such as opposition to individual wars or weapon systems, has broader public appeal and helps activists mobilize mass movements. However, such movements generally lack longevity. Once the issue is resolved or a tangible minor success has been achieved, public support wanes quickly and the movement disbands.

While religious traditions have always provided a philosophical inspiration for peace activism—which is attested by the prominent role of Quakers and other religious groups in peace movements to this day—secular peace philosophies became dominant in the late nineteenth century. They were influenced by prevailing intellectual trends and included liberal internationalism, socialism, anarchism, and feminism.

Liberal internationalism, also called idealism, is built on the idea that wars are the result of misunderstandings and that they can be avoided through better international cooperation, arbitration, mediation, and treaties. They work either as elitist projects that appeal to the rational cooperative self-interest of governments or by exerting pressure through popular opinion.[13] Idealism is in direct opposition to realism, which is prevalent in international relations theory. Realism asserts that war and conflict are an inevitable characteristic of the international system and that military power is necessary to ensure national or collective security. According to realism, disarmament would spell disaster.[14]

While liberal internationalism looks to an enlightened middle class to bring about change, socialism and anarchism work toward a radical transformation of society and the end of the capitalist system. The peace advocates in these radical philosophies—both also contain factions that endorse the use of violence—differ markedly in their approaches. Socialists look to the political party as a vehicle for change, and most take the nation-state for granted in this process.[15]

The majority of anarchists are committed to nonviolence and passionately reject the hierarchical power structure of the state, which they consider responsible for war. Their ideas have even influenced peace movements outside of Europe. Gandhi used Tolstoy's writings in developing his civil disobedience campaign in India.[16] Two prominent anarchists, Peter Kropotkin and Élisée Reclus, were geographers who felt that geographic education was key for the creation of peace.[17]

The influence of feminism on peace activism has long been sidelined in scholarship, but works by Betty Reardon and Elise Boulding have shown how gender roles and patriarchal structures are structurally tied to violence and war.

From the beginnings of organized peace groups, feminists were instrumental in helping invent new forms of social activism. For example, Boulding credits social or humanist feminists as the true originators of transboundary networks of groups that work for human welfare and social justice.[18]

Geohistory of Peace Movements

In what follows, I will present a geographic history of peace movements from the nineteenth century to the present to better understand what has influenced mobilizations for peace. By necessity, the picture I show has to be painted with broad strokes, and I will concentrate on four major periods: (1) the early period, which culminated in the first mass peace movement of the late nineteenth century; (2) the impact of World Wars I and II, which marked a turning point in terms of scope and intensity of warfare; (3) the second peak of mass peace mobilization in the 1960s; and (4) the most pronounced peak to date, the 1980s antinuclear campaign. While I recognize that there were often significant regional variations, I am mainly interested in showing the importance of two geographic concepts. First, the geopolitical, social, and intellectual context of mobilization is useful in exploring which forms of action and organizations were dominant. Second, the form of action and organization was facilitated and constrained by its focus upon particular geographic scales that determined the geographic scope of activity. Particularly, the role of the nation-state has been crucial in defining the geographic scope of peace movements and their ability to argue for negative or positive views of peace.

Origins and First Peak

Most histories place the beginnings of organized peace groups in the aftermath of the Napoleonic Wars, but trace the roots of these movements to early faith-based peace activism. Virtually all religions advocate peace and nonviolence, and popular protests by religious orders have been recorded as far back as the dawn of the Common Era. There are early examples of nonviolence by Jews, the Sufi Sect of Islam, and Christians. A striking case from the mid-1200s is a demonstration against a bloody civil war by 400,000 people in Verona. In the mid-1600s, the establishment of William Penn's Quaker colony ensured peaceful relations with Native Americans for seventy years.[19] Yet most religions have an ambivalent attitude toward peace, and history is replete with examples of wars that were given the blessing of religious leaders.[20]

The period after the Napoleonic Wars represents a watershed for peace movements in several ways. In political terms, we see a new concept of government. After the French and American revolutions, on the basis of the contractarian political philosophies of Locke, Montesquieu, and Rousseau, political power was now seen to rest in the people of a given territory.[21] This notion of popular sovereignty encouraged a more active participation of the citizenry in the affairs of the state.

In social terms, the erasure of existing local differences via state-imposed uniform language, education, and iconography engendered resistance and ironically also allowed peace movements to mobilize over larger areas.[22] In economic terms, industrialization brought issues of social justice to the forefront, while urbanization facilitated the assembly of large numbers of people in protests. In military terms, the concept of popular sovereignty introduced a new type of warfare that was based on mass conscript armies. Hence the carnage of the war had a profound impact on the population because the experience of what Clausewitz termed "absolute war" affected vast areas and was brought back home.[23] It was during this time period that the first organized peace groups in the United States and Britain were formed, including the first all-women peace societies.[24] In 1843, the first General Peace Convention was held in London and was attended by 324 delegates from the United States and Europe.[25]

Organized peace movements experienced their first peak of mass popular support in the late nineteenth century. By 1900, more than 400 peace societies existed in Europe and the United States.[26] Their efforts had tangible results. In the last decade of the nineteenth century, international arbitration was successful in preventing war in more than sixty cases, and in 1905 Sweden peacefully separated from Norway with the help of peace movements in both countries.[27] Aided by advances in transportation and communication technologies, such as railroads and telegraphs, transnational mobilization led to the establishment of several international bodies dedicated to peace. The Universal Peace Congress was held annually after 1892, and the Hague Court, the first permanent tribunal for international arbitration, was founded in 1899. As a result of lobbying efforts, national governments became involved and met at the Hague Conferences in 1899 and 1907, which issued declarations that outlawed the use of inhumane weapons, such as poison gas and dumdum bullets, as well as the deliberate killing of civilians.[28]

In the years that led up to World War I, public interest in peace issues grew to such a degree that fifteen bibliographies on the topic of peace were published between 1888 and 1914.[29] The surge in peace activity was clearly in response to heightened international tensions and the arms race among the major European powers. Germany's colonial aspirations that were encapsulated in the vociferous demand for "a place in the sun," Halford Mackinder's warning about the impending challenge to British naval hegemony by landpower, and American territorial ambitions that were in accord with the design of Alfred Thayer Mahan illustrate how geopolitics and militarism were the dominant discourse of the period.[30]

The Impact of World Wars I and II

Destruction and death during World War I reached an unprecedented level. For example, on the first day of the Battle of the Somme in 1916, 60,000 British soldiers died in a matter of hours. By the end of the war, four years of fighting had left 8.5 million soldiers dead.[31] Technological advances in weaponry, transportation, and communication had fundamentally altered the scale and intensity of warfare. War had become a "collective human action" that involved the entire population of a country.[32] In such a total war all resources of a state—human, natural, and technological—became legitimate targets in a battle for national survival. Compromise peace was no longer considered an option.[33]

Yet despite the intensity of the slaughter, the effect on peace activism was mixed because the conflict was framed in nationalist and patriotic terms. During the war, peace activists faced the charge of being traitors and had to contend with government repression. Young claims that the American antiwar movement was virtually destroyed by police raids, arrests, and vigilante actions. Yet thanks to committed pacifists, peace movements did not disappear completely. There were 16,500 conscientious objectors in Britain—about 6,000 of them were court-martialled—and 4,000 in the United States, and several anticonscription movements were founded. The Fellowship of Reconciliation was set up in Britain (1914) and in the United States (1915), and the American Friends Service was created in 1917, the year the United States entered the war.[34]

In addition to these brave efforts by pacifists, feminist agitation became particularly pronounced. In 1914, about 1,500 women marched against war in New York, and a year later, the Women's Peace Party was founded. The renowned socialist Clara Zetkin organized an International Women's Socialist Conference in Switzerland in 1915, and Dutch suffragists held a meeting in The Hague in the same year to issue calls for peace. Both events brought together women from countries that were at war with each other. The meetings in The Hague continued and culminated in the founding of the Women's International League for Peace and Freedom (WILPF) in 1919.[35]

The peace movement also suffered a severe blow because the nationalist dimension of the war split many groups. Some suffrage campaigners abandoned calls for peace and joined the war effort under the banner of patriotism.[36] Most socialist parties succumbed to the nationalist rhetoric at the outbreak of World War I and voted for war credits.[37] The liberally oriented American Peace Society openly supported the American government's decision to join the war against Germany and its allies.[38] Only the anarchists renounced obedience to the national cause.

The breakup of Austria-Hungary and the creation of independent states in the peace treaties that followed the war further promoted nationalism. Combined with the economic turmoil of the 1920s, this tempered public revulsion about the horrific slaughter of trench warfare and hindered transnational peace efforts. Peace activism concentrated on institutions that helped prevent war, such as the League of Nations and the International Court of Justice, on disarmament campaigns, and on anticonscription efforts. Examples are the work of the International Peace Bureau in the League of Nations' Conference on Disarmament in 1932, the creation of the International School in Geneva to infuse the education of children of diplomats with ideas of peace, and the establishment of the Peace Pledge Union and its journal, *Peace News*, in Britain to aid conscientious objectors.[39]

The rise of fascism in Europe in the 1930s had additional negative consequences for peace movements. Prominent pacifists, such as Albert Einstein and Bertrand Russell, became convinced that military means were necessary to stop the dictatorships in Germany, Italy, and Spain. Even the most staunchly antiwar organizations, such as WILPF, partially accepted war in the face of the fascist threat. Just as in the years that had led up to World War I, the peace movement was unable to prevent the arms race.

Young argues that the nationalist tenor of politics in the interwar years supported notions of collective security through force and helped legitimize war as a means of politics. The antifascist fronts aided in this process and laid the groundwork for the just war theory of World War II. The expanding communications network and increased global literacy provided a more effective means of transmission of these ideas and helped drown out the remaining voices of those who advocated a nonviolent approach.[40]

Yet halfway around the globe, Gandhi's movement for social justice and independence flourished in India. Starting in 1917, he led a campaign that was based on the concepts of satyagraha (the power of truth) and ahimsa (nonviolence) that he had developed during his struggle against racism in South Africa in the preceding years.[41] Boulding claims that Gandhi's movement inspired peace activism in Europe, but does not provide much evidence.[42] The gradual transformation of many Western peace groups from a pacifist orientation to one that advocated the use of military power to enforce peace makes this assertion appear questionable. More generally, the widespread assumption that the horrors of total war made people long for peace needs to be reexamined. A more accurate characterization seems to be that people wanted to feel safe and protected.[43]

World War II had even less of a direct impact on peace movement activities than the previous global conflict. While there were almost twice as many battle deaths, and civilian casualties rivaled those of soldiers, a more mobile warfare due to tanks and airplanes replaced the stalemate of the trenches. This revived a sense of excitement and romanticism of battle that has been celebrated in movies and novels for the last fifty years. More significantly, the war was widely considered to be necessary and just. Nazi atrocities that culminated in the Holocaust and Japanese war crimes in the Far East gave the message that appeasement of dictators was fatal. Stalinist terror in the Soviet Union extended this lesson to the early Cold War. The need to rebuild the war-torn economies of Europe further diverted public attention and support from peace movements.[44]

In postwar Asia, decolonization produced a similar nationalist bias in newly independent countries to the one that had hindered transboundary peace activism after World War I in Europe. After the resistance movements had helped throw off the yoke of Japanese occupation, they were not willing to accept the reimposition of Western colonial rule and looked to a national military for security. Only Japan, which had experienced the horrors of the war through the nuclear annihilation of Hiroshima and Nagasaki, boasted a strong peace movement.

Before the mid-1950s, peace activism was a treacherous affair. During the heightened ideological tensions of the early Cold War, which were exemplified by McCarthyism in the United States and staunch anti-Communism in Western Europe, advocates of peace were branded as traitors and blacklisted. Moreover, campaigns by Communist parties in Europe and the Soviet Union disguised official policies of the Soviet bloc as peace. They created the pro-Soviet World Peace Council, which challenged Western peace movements to distinguish their disarmament efforts from this state-sponsored propaganda.

The Second Peak: 1950s to 1960s

About a decade after the end of World War II, peace activism experienced a revival. The main driving force was increasing public concern about the nuclear arms race. First, there was greater awareness of the widespread effects of nuclear tests. The detonation of the first American hydrogen bomb on the Bikini atoll in 1954 had not affected just the indigenous population of the Marshall Islands, which could have been kept secret; the fallout also made several American and Japanese fishermen sick. There was an outcry in Japan when the boat returned home with the crew seriously ill from radiation poisoning, and the news made headlines in the West.

Second, members of the scientific community had become concerned about the dangers of nuclear weapons and the arms race. They engaged in a public debate about the potential dangers of nuclear fallout and founded peace research institutes to help develop alternative policies to war. They voiced their views in meetings such as the Pugwash conferences that brought together scientists from East and West and in publications such as *Bulletin of the Atomic Scientists*.[45]

Third, countries that were not directly a part of the bipolar confrontation between the West and the Soviet sphere worried about being caught in the middle and resented that tests were mainly conducted in less developed areas, in particular, the Sahara and the Pacific Ocean. They called for a moratorium on tests at the 1955 Bandung Conference and held an assembly on disarmament in Accra in 1962. Five years later, in 1967, twenty-four states in Latin America designated themselves as nuclear-weapons-free zones by signing the Treaty of Tlatelolco.[46]

Peace movements acquired an impressive scale of mobilization in response to the nuclear threat. Some organizations, such as the British Campaign for Nuclear Disarmament (CND), which was founded in 1958, had counterpart movements in several countries, including West Germany, Switzerland, Sweden, France, Denmark, Norway, Greece, Canada, New Zealand, and Japan. The demonstrations they organized drew up to 100,000 participants in Britain and West Germany. In the United States, the National Committee for a Sane Nuclear Policy (SANE) had a membership of 25,000 and 130 local chapters by 1958. It carried out public information campaigns, such as an information center in Times Square in New York that drew an estimated 40,000 visitors in four weeks, held mass rallies, and appointed its own lobbyists in Washington.[47]

Two groups in the United States and Canada laid the groundwork for future peace protests and foreshadowed the powerful feminist and environmentalist peace actions of the 1980s. Women Strike for Peace was started by Seattle housewives in 1961 who organized a one-day walkout of thousands of white, middle-class women from their jobs and their kitchens to protest the nuclear arms race. Because it was grounded in everyday material practices and based on a nonhierarchical, grassroots structure, their struggle stood out from more traditional peace organizations.[48]

The Committee for Nonviolent Action (CNVA) gave prominence to civil disobedience actions and nonviolent intervention across borders. It organized protest voyages into U.S. testing zones in the South Pacific, to the Leningrad harbor (today's St. Petersburg), and to the French 1959 test site in the Sahara. While the voyages did not manage to prevent the tests, the actions drew media attention and prefigured the spectacular protests made by Greenpeace in the 1980s.[49] The Sahara protest received hardly any publicity in France or abroad, but was particularly significant since it invigorated peace movements in African countries and led to the establishment of the World Peace Brigade and a training center for nonviolent action in Tanzania in 1961.[50]

Despite the intensity and international scope of the campaign to ban the bomb, the movement's support base dissipated in 1964 after the Limited Test Ban Treaty took effect. Even though the treaty represented only a minor accomplishment since testing continued underground, the major objective had been achieved, and exhausted activists returned to their regular lives or focused their attention on the escalating U.S. war in Vietnam.[51]

The Vietnam War movement was in many respects different from the one on nuclear disarmament. The previous campaign had been mainly supported by middle-class whites and had had a liberal and nonviolent orientation, whereas the resistance to the Vietnam War had a revolutionary rhetoric and also included militant action.[52] Nevertheless, nonviolent pacifists played a critical role, and the movement was further strengthened by the campaign for social justice under the leadership of Martin Luther King Jr.[53] The peace movement against U.S. involvement in Vietnam was influenced and often overshadowed by the protest culture of the late 1960s, including the student movement, the hippy dropout culture, and black power. Thus it lacked the clear agenda and visibly peaceful character of earlier peace movements, but the protests had a decisive effect on U.S. foreign policy.[54] In Vietnam, Buddhist peace movements employed a variety of nonviolent strategies and involved far more people and actions than the few images of monks setting themselves on fire that were picked up by the Western media suggest.[55] However, the Western mass media must be credited for raising awareness about atrocities in Vietnam and were instrumental in broadening the popular base.[56]

The Third Peak: 1980s

In the 1980s, peace activism experienced its most pronounced peak to date. A global movement emerged that involved more transnational and massive protests than any event in the 1960s. Several forces converged that produced a unique set of geopolitical and societal contexts, particularly in Europe, where the movement had its strongest support. In geopolitical terms, this was the period of a renewed Cold War. The 1979 decision by NATO to station medium-range nuclear missiles in Europe to counter the superior conventional forces of the Warsaw Pact destabilized the precarious nuclear weapons equilibrium. The election of Ronald Reagan as U.S. president in 1980 and his espousal of a limited nuclear war as a foreign policy option raised tensions between East and West to new heights. The public response to this new military and ideological situation was expressed in a widespread concern about a new nuclear arms race.

In societal terms, three different agendas came to the forefront during this period. First, there was a strong environmental and anti–nuclear power sentiment that led to the establishment of Green parties, citizens' groups, and organizations, such as Greenpeace. Second, the women's movement started to make inroads into mainstream society. Third, there was a crisis of identity in Western consumer cultures that led to a search for the local roots of communitarian culture.[57] This was exemplified in citizens' groups, the revival of regional folklore and identity in Europe, for example, the Catalans, and a renewed interest in local politics in the United States.

All three of these movements shared concerns with the nuclear disarmament campaign and joined forces. The concern of the environmental movement about the ecological impact of nuclear power could not be separated from nuclear arms since nuclear fuels could be converted to weapons-grade material and the storage of weapons had environmental consequences. Women's empowerment was dependent on a reform of patriarchy, which in turn was recognized as a structural foundation of the military. The expression of local culture and identity was restrained by large-scale power structures, such as national governments or the security interests of NATO vis-à-vis the Warsaw Pact.

The movement had a spectacular inauguration with spontaneous mass demonstrations in twelve European capitals and other major cities against nuclear arms that drew millions of participants between October and December 1981. Public protests continued throughout the 1980s in Europe, Canada, Australia, and the United States, including the assembly of nearly a million people in New York's Central Park in June 1982. Spurred on by the appeal for a nuclear-free Europe issued by British historians E. P. Thompson and Ken Coates, a European Nuclear Disarmament (END) movement emerged, and hundreds of localities all over Europe popularized disarmament by declaring themselves nuclear-weapon-free-zones.[58] Similarly, in the United States, several municipalities passed nuclear freeze referenda that called for a stop to research, testing, production, and deployment of nuclear weapons.[59]

The convergence of nuclear disarmament and other social movements not only created synergy, but also supported innovative methods and organization. Environmental groups, such as Greenpeace were media savvy and staged dramatic civil disobedience actions, such as the scaling of towers and chimneys or boat landings on nuclear vessels. Citizens' and women's groups perfected grassroots organizing to address local community concerns and made protests palpable by connecting them to everyday material practices. Feminist and environmental groups, such as the Green parties, also organized an international grassroots activist network. For example, the Greenham Common protestors invited women from Pacific island states on speaking tours and helped them set up a campaign organization in Britain.[60] As a result of these varied activities, peace activism was no longer mainly a top-down affair, as it had been in the 1950s–1960s campaign, but was based on a nonhierarchical and flexible structure and was truly transnational in scope.

Opponents of the campaign against nuclear weapons tried to present it as a Communist conspiracy and accused it of complicity with the Soviet Union, but the widespread support by respected professionals, such as Physicians for Social Responsibility and the Union of Concerned Scientists, by the entertainment community, by major national organizations in the United States, such as the U.S. Conference of Mayors, by social democratic parties in Europe, and in particular by churches and the mainstream media ensured its credibility. Surveys pegged public support for the movement at between 55% and 81% of the population in NATO countries. Membership in SANE increased from a mere 4,000 in the 1970s to 150,000 in the 1980s. The CND in Britain had 100,000 members in 1984 and 1,000 local chapters in 1981.[61]

In December 1987, nuclear disarmers celebrated victory when Mikhail Gorbachev and Reagan met to sign the Intermediate Nuclear Forces Treaty (INF), which stipulated the removal of all medium and short-range nuclear missiles from Europe. Although conservative groups attributed the agreement more to Reagan's hard-line stance toward the Soviet Union, the peace movement at least has to be credited with opening up defense policy to the democratic process. Moreover, since peace activists had strong links to like groups across the Iron Curtain, they proved to be invaluable for generating a dialogue with opposition groups when the Cold War ended in 1989. However, the movement did not fully succeed in one respect. It was not able to expand the movement to many countries of the global South. Although there were attempts to build alliances, it became clear that the primary agenda for peace movements in developing countries was not nuclear disarmament and the need to overcome the East-West divide, but social justice.[62]

The 1980s anti–nuclear weapons campaign differed from the earlier one in terms of scope and scale, but as before, some of its members became engaged in other struggles for peace. An important motivation behind the 1980s anti–nuclear weapons movement was opposition to the aggressive U.S. foreign policy against the Soviet Union under Reagan. When the United States began to step up its participation in regional wars that involved Communist groups in Central America, such as El Salvador, Nicaragua, and Guatemala, peace activists also shifted their attention to this arena. About 1,000 groups participated in the opposition to war in Latin America, and 70,000 U.S. citizens visited Nicaragua in the 1980s to bring back firsthand observations to counterbalance the information issued by the government and the mass media.[63]

Church organizations were especially prominent in the Latin American campaign. On the one hand, churches had started to pursue a vigorous agenda for peace and had become much more involved in the struggle against nuclear weapons in the 1980s as compared to the 1950s and 1960s. On the other hand, many resistance movements in Latin America had a religious base. Examples are the base community movement in Catholicism and Servicio Paz y Justicia (SERPAJ).[64] American and European activists cooperated closely with these local movements and developed innovative and bold nonviolent methods. Many provided escape routes and sanctuary to El Salvadoran and Guatemalan refugees akin to the Underground Railroad during the period of slavery in the United States, an action punishable by long prison sentences. Four thousand others placed themselves as human shields into combat areas that were threatened by attacks from U.S.-sponsored Contras.[65]

Peace activism declined after the end of the Cold War and the Reagan era, then intensified briefly during the Gulf War. However, since the war against Saddam Hussein was legitimized by a UN Security Council resolution, the protests failed to gain enough popular support to develop into a mass movement. Moreover, the Western military commanders had learned their lessons about the influence of critical media reports on public attitudes during the Vietnam era and held a tight rein over journalists.

In 2003, demonstrations in Europe and the United States against war in Iraq had difficulties in reaching a mass base even though the Bush administration was not able to get support from the UN Security Council for the military action it demanded. It appears that the framing of the war in the aftermath of September 11 as one against terror and in the United States as one of national self-defense once again introduced ideological divisions among people concerned about peace. Moreover, the Western mass media did not adopt a stance that was as critical as during the 1960s and 1980s peaks. In the United States, criticism of the government was denounced as unpatriotic after September 11, and the local media—as well as the Democratic opposition—did not dare to publicly back the peace movement. The independent media and peace groups argued that peace actions were consistently sidelined in the U.S. mass media: reports were short, were buried among other news, and underestimated attendance figures at rallies.

Places and Spaces of Peace Movements: Conceptual Issues

Theoretical approaches to peace movements fall into the large and growing literature on social movements. Sociologists and political scientists have made most of the contributions, but generally neglect spatial dimensions. Even as recently as 2000, Miller lamented the lack of attention to place in the conceptualization of social movement mobilization outside the discipline of geography.[66] In the following pages, I will use the example of the 1980s peak in peace movement activism to discuss how geographers have contributed to our understanding of the places and spaces of peace movements and protests. The most comprehensive and rigorous analysis of the early 1980s peace movements is an edited volume by Bert Klandermans.[67] His study will serve as a backdrop for illustrating geographic concepts applicable to peace movement research. Such an approach will allow me to explain the advantages of a geographic perspective without having to take the reader too far into the linguistic and theoretical thicket of social theory, which underlies the most important conceptualizations by geographers.[68]

Klandermans's conceptual work is based on the findings of case studies of protests in the United States and the five European countries where cruise missiles were to be deployed. His goal is to examine why and how this mass movement mobilized. The question is analyzed in the context of the two dominant conceptual models in social movement research: resource mobilization theory and new social movement theory. After briefly outlining each theory, I will examine his findings in light of insights that are provided by a spatial approach.

Resource mobilization theory posits that social movements form when resources and opportunities are favorable, for example, when political structures facilitate organization and mobilization, when other parties or groups are sympathetic to the cause, or when the general societal situation is opportune for success of the movement. The theory's key point is that grievances are always present in societies. Therefore, they cannot be the decisive factor. Rather, it is the resources available to a movement that trigger mobilization: good organizational resources, political opportunity structures, and a prevalence of protests. The latter argument is based on the belief that protests are more intense during certain periods: they appear in cycles.[69]

By contrast, new social movement theory is premised on the notion that the appearance of new grievances leads to mobilization. The causes of these grievances are sought in broad structural changes in society, in particular, the negative consequences that stem from industrialization and economic growth. Proponents of the theory distinguish these new social movements, such as the women's and environmental movements, from old movements, such as unions, in terms of their rejection of traditional values of capitalist societies, their unconventional forms of organization and tactics of protest, their dissociation from politics, and their constituencies. New social movement participants "seek a different relationship to nature, one's own body, the opposite sex, work, and consumption" and include groups marginalized by industrialization and members of the new middle class.[70]

Klandermans argues that new social movement theory cannot fully explain the peace movement of the early 1980s. While he admits that a "fundamental criticism of modern industrial society was often implicit in peace movement activism," he claims that this criticism was not universally shared by all participants. He posits that in some of the countries there was little overlap among peace activists and other new social movements, such as the women's movement. He also states that its organizational forms and tactics of protest were generally traditional—mainly mass demonstrations and petitions.[71]

Yet Klandermans agrees that the focus of new social movement theory on grievances in triggering mobilization is correct and points to a new sense of urgency about the dangers of nuclear weapons in the late 1970s.[72] He asserts that "peace protest is about *potential* dangers" and that the problems people mobilize against are socially constructed.[73] He identifies the source of the new urgency as a steadily growing concern about nuclear weapons in the public discourse of respected institutions, such as churches, combined with the inflammatory rhetoric of the Reagan administration.

The three major elements of resource mobilization theory help fill in the gaps. Klandermans asserts that the peace movement's mobilization could draw on (1) good organizational resources that the existing new social movements, such as the environmental and women's movements, had developed over the preceding years, (2) favorable political opportunity structures because major traditional political organizations and institutions were eager to form alliances, and criticism of nuclear armaments was seen as a convenient and uncontroversial way for opposition parties to undermine the power of conservative governments in the six countries,[74] and (3) a climate of protest that was formed by the protest cycle of the 1970s. The peace movement, in his view, was an extension of this wave of protests.

Klandermans's explanation does not fully elucidate the processes behind the peace movement mobilization in the 1980s. While he is careful about identifying different social dimensions of the movement, such as its values, membership, and organization, he glosses over regional variations within countries. His analysis is wedded to the national and international levels and ignores geographic context. The geographic concept of place can be used to deepen our understanding of the provenance of the movement.

New social movements are generally recognized as identity based movements, and geographers have argued that all identities are spatially constituted and negotiated through place. Some identities are place based, such as regional identity or national identity, which is premised on the attachment to a specific place. Even identities based on seemingly aspatial, social variables, such as those based on race and gender, are constructed through places of interaction.[75] This place context includes the material realities that are produced by economic and political processes (i.e., the economy and the state) as well as the daily interaction processes that create our existence in and identification with a social community. Moreover, identity, or belonging to a group, is predicated on an opposition to the Other, on being inside as opposed to outside, or in Cresswell's terms, being "in place" versus "out of place."[76]

A focus on place helps us reconcile the fact that the 1980s peace movement had elements of both new and traditional social movements. Rather than viewing the peace movement as a hybrid—which is Klandermans's position—we can posit that in some places, the peace movement took the form of a new social movement while in others it was more traditional.

The Greenham Common protest is a case in point. For several years in the 1980s, a group of women established a peace camp right next to the missile base and modeled the type of world they were seeking to create through their daily lived activities. They practiced "nonviolence, harmony with nature, participatory democracy, and mutual nurturance."[77] Klandermans identifies this action as an aberration in the otherwise squarely traditional types of protests in the 1980s peace movement, such as mass demonstrations. However, Cresswell has shown that the protest was a direct expression of the activists' identity. The daily activities of the women, such as nursing, washing, and singing, were perfectly normal in the home, but did not fit the norm of public places in the upscale English countryside. The activists were viewed as behaving "out of place." The actions initiated two processes. By being confronted with such blatant criticism of traditional norms of modern industrial society, the public was forced to reflect on what was acceptable and what was not. At the same time, the common interaction among the women in this place and the public rejection they faced reinforced their identity as feminists and peace advocates.[78]

In Greenham Common, the peace movement and the new social movement did not just overlap in terms of people and ideas; rather, a "peace identity" (and, to be precise, a gendered peace identity) was constituted in the same place context. The holistic concept of place allows us to see that the location and setting of peace movements matter. Klandermans's stress on the most visible form of protest—mass demonstrations—diverts our attention from the sociospatial processes that underlie mobilization. For Klandermans, the peace movement is evaluated in terms of its appearance rather than its provenance. However, the public location of what are deemed private practices brought issues of nurturing and communality into a public place that stressed military strength and national and ideological differences.

Klandermans's discussion of grievances also could benefit from an attention to the context of place. The sense of urgency about the nuclear arms race, as well as the way this grievance translated into taking action, varied from place to place. It is important to stress again that place is a holistic concept that encompasses not only the social interactions that create a shared framework of interpretation, but also the material realities that directly affect personal experience. For example, during the 1980s nuclear freeze campaign, most of the well-educated and middle class residents of Cambridge, Massachusetts, shared the values that were espoused by the peace movement. Yet in the end, a proposed measure to slow the arms race was voted down in Cambridge because many of its residents worked in the defense industry and feared that it would affect their economic livelihood.[79]

It is important to point out that place is not synonymous with local. Peace mobilization in the 1980s also had place dimensions at regional and national scales. As mentioned earlier, place-based identities define belonging in opposition to the Other. Klandermans's point about grievances in the form of a new sense of urgency about nuclear weapons can be related to place. Perceptions of an outside threat stimulated peace mobilization. For example, when the Thatcher government framed the nuclear missile issue in terms of English national might, peace activism against nuclear armament increased in Wales and Scotland.[80] Nationalist and anti-American sentiments reinforced many of the peace movements in other European countries. Moreover, such regional and national identities helped unite new and old social movement factions.

Finally, Klandermans's discussion of resource mobilization theory could benefit from a geographic approach. While it is important to know that organizational resources of earlier movements as well as a climate of protest were key to successful peace mobilization, we also need to investigate where protests and organizational resources are concentrated. There are cycles of protests as well as places of protests. Protest potential varies from place to place because of the characteristics of the locale as well as its location in larger social networks and economic and political power structures.[81] For example, when military maneuvers are pushed into ecologically sensitive areas, the interests of environmentalists and peace activists converge in one place. However, the mobilization potential of the place will depend on local resources as well as the importance of the place for a regional or national audience. For example, the strong counterculture scene and extraparliamentary New Left in Berlin in the 1980s supported the founding of grassroots peace coalitions among autonomous groups.[82]

In addition to deepening our understanding of why peace movements mobilize, geographers have provided insights into how peace movements carry out their struggle. The key concepts in this regard are space and scale. The effectiveness of peace actions depends on the ability of peace groups to "find and create spaces—metaphorically and materially" in which dominant ideologies can be challenged.[83] Most often, it is in the margins of social power, that is, out of the reach of the government and powerful economic actors, that movements find a space for resistance.[84]

Scale is particularly important in the way space is used. It is important to note that scale is not a fixed entity. Peace movements, as well as the governments and other powerful actors they oppose, can try to determine at which scale the struggle is carried out. For example, the antiapartheid movement in South Africa successfully extended its struggle against the white government from the local to the international scale, while the freeze campaign in the greater Boston area jumped scale too early and failed to repeat the success it had had locally at the much less favorable central state level.[85] Similarly, women's political activism is extremely effective at the local scale, but is generally blocked from being taken to higher scales.[86] Peace movements are most effective when they use local concerns to mobilize at an international scale and transcend the scale of the state with its ties to the ideology of patriotism and its associated military expressions.

Conclusion

Despite temporal disjunctures and setbacks, there are several elements in peace movements that are enduring. First, there is continuity in terms of organization and actions. Committed pacifists can be relied on to carry the torch of peace ideas even during trying times. Striking examples are conscientious objectors and feminists during World War I. Despite the general condemnation of antiwar activists as traitors, war resisters refused to join their national armies, and women joined forces with like-minded activists in enemy countries to call for peace.

As the antinuclear protests have shown, innovations that are spearheaded at one time get picked up and refined in subsequent periods. Grassroots, nonhierarchical organization and media-savvy actions that were pioneered by a few groups in the 1960s became the dominant form of organization and action in the 1980s. Related to this is the collaboration between peace movements and groups that share a concern with some dimension of the war system or weapons. For example, when peace activists and environmentalists joined forces to oppose nuclear fuels, they not only broadened the support base, but also helped diversify protest actions.

Second, a narrow focus on a specific issue is dangerous for the long-term success of peace movements. The mass movements in the 1960s and 1980s dissipated rather quickly after only minor achievements, the signing of international treaties with very limited consequences. Moreover, a single-issue focus makes it easy for governments to dissolve opposition by making only insignificant but visible concessions.

Third, peace mobilization is mainly driven by an impending threat of war, not by the direct experience of war. Despite the horrors of total war in 1914–1918 and 1939–1945, peace activism did not increase in an impressive manner in the period that followed. Rather than trying to abolish the war system, people yearned to feel safe and looked to institutions that were backed by military might, such as collective security arrangements or international organizations, to control the outbreak of hostilities. It appears to be most significant how the threat of war is framed and how it is made credible. Respected institutions, such as churches or scientific organizations, and the mass media play a decisive role in determining the strength of mobilization.

Most of the peace movements discussed in this chapter are from the global North. This might seem puzzling, given that the majority of wars today take place in the global South.[87] Yet apart from a general Western bias in the literature on peace movements that formed the basis of this investigation, there are good reasons for this discrepancy. Most of the current wars are civil conflicts, which means that the population is often sharply divided and peace activism takes on an ideological dimension. Due to the colonial legacy of military rule, there is a lack of civilian institutions and democratic structures in many developing countries. Freedom of expression and public assembly are not universally granted rights. Finally, disarmament is not a prime concern since most of the countries lack the very basic amenities of human existence. As Jeong points out, "[M]uch of the energy of radical activists is dedicated to the struggle for basic rights that the peace movement in the West has taken for granted."[88]

Peace activism in the developing world is focused on injustice caused by the modern economic system. Pursued by tens of thousands of local groups, these hard-to-compartmentalize actions seek to preserve the environment, cultural traditions, and basic freedoms. The struggles are not usually marked by spectacular demonstrations like the ones in the North, but tend to have narrow local or regional relevance. Thus they receive less mass media attention. While new communication technologies, such as the Internet, help link their movements to create networks of peace activism, their mobilization still faces significant challenges, such as access to technology, the danger of becoming technologically dependent on the West, and the need for face-to-face contact to establish a relationship of trust.

Geographers can play an important role in advancing the cause of peace movements in the developing world. Works on the geography of resistance hold important insights for the development of effective strategies and tactics of protests.[89] While some of the case studies, such as the Zapatistas, are outside the scope of peace movements because they include violent actions, concepts such as that of spaces of convergence, which expresses the links between local movements through virtual actions (e.g., the Internet) and material actions (e.g., conferences and demonstrations), are also applicable to nonviolent campaigns.[90] Notably, it is recognition of the way in which the geographic scope of their activity can either hinder or facilitate peace movements that is important in the face of contemporary national conflicts in a context of growing global connectivity. Peace movements of the future will both engage and manipulate this geographical conundrum.

Notes

I would like to thank the students in my course on the Geography of Peace at Middlebury College in the fall of 2002 for their stimulating thoughts on the geographic dimensions of peace. The chapter is dedicated to the Quaker peace activist John Stamm.

1. Stoddart, "Geography and War"; Kirby, "What Did You Do in the War, Daddy?"
2. Brunn, "Geography of Peace Movements."
3. Barnaby, "Nuclear Weapon Free Zones"; Cutter, Holcomb, and Shatin, "Spatial Patterns of Support for a Nuclear Weapons Freeze"; Cutter et al., "From Grassroots to Partisan Politics."
4. See Miller, *Geography and Social Movements*, which includes two of his earlier articles in *Political Geography*.
5. Jeong, *Peace and Conflict Studies*, 23, 337.
6. See, in particular, Boulding, *Cultures of Peace*, and Reardon, *Sexism and the War System*.
7. Price, "Nongovernmental Organizations on the Geopolitical Frontline," 263.
8. See Demirovic, "NGOs and Social Movements," for a well-documented but rather restrictive distinction between NGOs and social movements.
9. Carter, *Peace Movements*, 14.
10. Boulding, *Cultures of Peace*, chapter 3.
11. Jeong, *Peace and Conflict Studies*, 354.
12. Ibid., 354–355; Brock and Young, *Pacifism in the Twentieth Century*, chapter 1.
13. Carter, *Peace Movements*, 20–21; Young, "Peace Movements in History."
14. Carter, *Peace Movements*, 22; O'Loughlin and van der Wusten, "Political Geography of War and Peace."
15. Young, "Peace Movements in History," 144–146.
16. Blunt and Willis, *Dissident Geographies*, 17–18; Ackerman and Duvall, 65.
17. See Breitbart, "Peter Kropotkin, the Anarchist Geographer," and Dunbar, "Élisée Reclus, Geographer and Anarchist." The ideas of Kropotkin and Reclus have been picked up again by Merrett, "Teaching Social Justice," and Marsden, "Geography and Two Centuries of Education for Peace and International Understanding."
18. Boulding, *Cultures of Peace*, especially 108; Reardon, *Sexism and the War System*.
19. Boulding, *Cultures of Peace*, 58–59.
20. Barash, "Religious Inspiration."
21. Herb, "National Identity and Territory," 11.
22. See Dijkink, this volume.
23. Townshend, "Introduction," 6–7.
24. Boulding, *Cultures of Peace*, 60; Carter, *Peace Movements*, 2.
25. Jeong, *Peace and Conflict Studies*, 339.
26. Carter, *Peace Movements*, 6.
27. Boulding, *Cultures of Peace*, 61.
28. Jeong, *Peace and Conflict Studies*, 341; Carter, *Peace Movements*, 6.
29. Boulding, *Cultures of Peace*, 62.
30. Mamadouh, this volume; Parker, *Western Geopolitical Thought in the Twentieth Century*.
31. Van Creveld, "Technology and War I"; O'Loughlin and van der Wusten, "Political Geography of War and Peace," 93.
32. O'Loughlin and van der Wusten, "Political Geography of War and Peace," 101.
33. Townshend, "Introduction," 12–15.

34. Young, "Peace Movements in History," 163; Carter, *Peace Movements*, 7.

35. Boulding, *Cultures of Peace*, 63–64; Carter, *Peace Movements*, 7–8; Jeong, *Peace and Conflict Studies*, 342–343.

36. Carter, *Peace Movements*, 8.

37. Young, "Peace Movements in History," 146; Blunt and Willis, *Dissident Geographies*, 15–17.

38. Jeong, *Peace and Conflict Studies*, 342.

39. Boulding, *Cultures of Peace*, 64; Carter, *Peace Movements*, 10–11.

40. Young, "Peace Movements in History," 149–150.

41. Ackerman and Duvall, *Force More Powerful*, 62–66.

42. Boulding, *Cultures of Peace*, 62.

43. For example, O'Loughlin and van der Wusten, "Political Geography of War and Peace," mention a surge in peace advocacy after World War I. For a discussion of peace movement conversions to collective security ideas, see Hermon, "International Peace Education Movement, 1919–1939," and Josephson, "Search for Lasting Peace."

44. Carter, *Peace Movements*, chapter 2.

45. Ibid., 35–36; Boulding, *Cultures of Peace*, 68–74.

46. Barnaby, "Nuclear Weapon Free Zones." The full text of the Treaty for the Prohibition of Nuclear Weapons in Latin America and the Caribbean (Treaty of Tlatelolco) is available at http://www.unog.ch/frames/disarm/distreat/tlatelol.htm (accessed on June 2, 2003).

47. Carter, *Peace Movements*, 42.

48. Swerdlow, *Women Strike for Peace*.

49. Carter, *Peace Movements*, 44–45.

50. Carter, "Sahara Protest Team"; Jeong, *Peace and Conflict Studies*, 344.

51. Boulding, *Cultures of Peace*, 77.

52. Carter, *Peace Movements*, 85–86.

53. Jeong, *Peace and Conflict Studies*, 344–345.

54. Carter, *Peace Movements*, 86.

55. Boulding, *Cultures of Peace*, 79.

56. Elliot, "Impact of the Media," especially 179.

57. See Ossenbrügge, "Territorial Ideologies in West Germany," 394–396, for a discussion of this societal context in West Germany.

58. Young, "Peace Movements in History," 154–157.

59. Cutter, Holcomb, and Shatin, "Spatial Patterns of Support for a Nuclear Weapons Freeze."

60. Carter, *Peace Movements*, 175.

61. Jeong, *Peace and Conflict Studies*, 348–349, 357; Carter, *Peace Movements*, 148–160.

62. Carter, *Peace Movements*, 149–150, 178–179.

63. Jeong, *Peace and Conflict Studies*, 347.

64. Boulding, *Cultures of Peace*, 83.

65. Jeong, *Peace and Conflict Studies*, 351–352.

66. Miller, *Geography and Social Movements*, 3–7.

67. Klandermans, *Peace Movements in Western Europe and the United States*.

68. For an extensive geographic treatment of social movement theory, see chapters 1 and 2 in Miller's excellent study of antinuclear activism in the Boston area, *Geography and Social Movements*.

69. Klandermans, "Peace Movement and Social Movement Theory," 4.

70. Ibid., 4–5, 27.

71. Ibid., 28–29.

72. Ibid., 30–31.

73. Ibid., 2; Klandermans's emphasis.

74. Klandermans does not offer concrete evidence for this assertion, but the electoral and cartographic analysis of Cutter et al., "From Grassroots to Partisan Politics," confirms his position. Their study revealed that grassroots nuclear freeze actions became part of the agenda for partisan politics.

75. Miller, *Geography and Social Movements*, 34.

76. Cresswell, *In Place/out of Place*.

77. Boulding, *Cultures of Peace*, 119.

78. Cresswell, *In Place/out of Place*, chapter 5.

79. Miller, *Geography and Social Movements*, 170–172.

80. Carter, *Peace Movements*, 258–259.

81. See Agnew, *Place and Politics*, in particular 57, for a discussion of the dimensions of place.

82. Young, "Peace Movements in History," 156. See Miller, *Geography and Social Movements*, for a discussion of the mobilization potential of Cambridge, Massachusetts. The synergy of local groups is also evident in the protest culture at the University of California at Berkeley and other radical university towns, such as Madison, Wisconsin, and Ann Arbor, Michigan.

83. Staeheli, "Empowering Political Struggle," 389.

84. Steinberg, "Territorial Formation on the Margin."

85. Cox, "Spaces of Dependence"; Miller, *Geography and Social Movements*, 169–170.

86. Staeheli and Cope, "Empowering Women's Citizenship."

87. For discussions of the changing geography of war and the new nature of postmodern war, see O'Loughlin, this volume; O'Loughlin and van der Wusten, "Political Geography of War and Peace"; Van Creveld, "Technology and War II."

88. Jeong, *Peace and Conflict Studies*, 360.

89. Pile, "Introduction."

90. See, for example, Routledge, "Our Resistance Will Be as Transnational as Capital," and Slater, "Spatial Politics/Social Movements."

References

Ackerman, Peter, and Jack Duvall. *A Force More Powerful: A Century of Nonviolent Conflict*. New York: Palgrave, 2000.

Agnew, John. *Place and Politics: The Geographical Mediation of State and Society*. Boston: Allen and Unwin, 1987.

Barash, David. "Religious Inspiration." In *Approaches to Peace: A Reader in Peace Studies*, ed. David Barash, 199–202. New York: Oxford University Press, 2000.

Barnaby, Frank. "Nuclear Weapon Free Zones." In *The Geography of Peace and War*, ed. David Pepper and Alan Jenkins, 165–177. New York: Blackwell, 1985.

Blunt, Alison, and Jane Willis. *Dissident Geographies: An Introduction to Radical Ideas and Practice*. New York: Prentice Hall, 2000.

Boulding, Elise. *Cultures of Peace: The Hidden Side of History*. Syracuse, NY: Syracuse University Press, 2000.

Breitbart, Myrna Margulies. "Peter Kropotkin, the Anarchist Geographer." In *Geography, Ideology, and Social Concern*, ed. D. R. Stoddart, 134–153. New York: Barnes and Noble, 1981.

Brock, Peter, and Nigel Young. *Pacifism in the Twentieth Century*. Syracuse, NY: Syracuse University Press, 1999.

Brunn, Stanley. "The Geography of Peace Movements." In *The Geography of Peace and War*, ed. David Pepper and Alan Jenkins, 178–191. New York: Blackwell, 1985.

Carter, April. *Peace Movements: International Protest and World Politics since 1945*. New York: Longman, 1992.

Carter, April. "The Sahara Protest Team." In *Nonviolent Intervention across Borders: A Recurrent Vision*, ed. Yeshua Moser-Puangsuwan and Thomas Weber, 235–254. Honolulu: Spark M. Matsunaga Institute of Peace, University of Hawaii, 2000.

Cooper, Alice Holmes. *Paradoxes of Peace: German Peace Movements since 1945*. Ann Arbor: University of Michigan Press, 1996.

Cox, Kevin. "Spaces of Dependence, Spaces of Engagement and the Politics of Scale; or, Looking for Local Politics." *Political Geography* 17 (1998): 1–23.

Cresswell, Tim. *In Place/out of Place: Geography, Ideology, and Transgression*. Minneapolis: University of Minnesota Press, 1996.

Cutter, Susan, H. Briavel Holcomb, and Dianne Shatin. "Spatial Patterns of Support for a Nuclear Weapons Freeze." *Professional Geographer* 38 (1986): 42–52.

Cutter, Susan, H. B. Holcomb, D. Shatin, F. M. Shelley, and G. T. Marauskas. "From Grassroots to Partisan Politics: Nuclear Freeze Referenda in New Jersey and South Dakota." *Political Geography Quarterly* 6 (1987): 287–300.

Demirovic, Alex. "NGOs and Social Movements: A Study in Contrasts." *Capitalism, Nature, Socialism* 11 (2000): 131–140.

Dunbar, Gary. "Élisée Reclus, Geographer and Anarchist." *Antipode* 10 (1978): 16–21.

Elliot, C. L. "The Impact of the Media on the Prosecution of Contemporary Warfare." In *The Science of War: Back to First Principles*, ed. Brian Holden Reid, 164–191. New York: Routledge, 1993.

Herb, Guntram H. "National Identity and Territory." In *Nested Identities: Nationalism, Territory, and Scale*, ed. Guntram H. Herb and David H. Kaplan, 9–30. Lanham, MD: Rowman and Littlefield, 1999.

Hermon, Elly. "The International Peace Education Movement, 1919–1939." In *Peace Movements and Political Cultures*, ed. Charles Chatfield and Peter van den Dungen, 127–142. Knoxville: University of Tennessee Press, 1988.

Jeong, Hon-Won. *Peace and Conflict Studies: An Introduction*. Burlington, VT: Ashgate, 2000.

Josephson, Harold. "The Search for Lasting Peace: Internationalism and American Foreign Policy, 1920–1950." In *Peace Movements and Political Cultures*, ed. Charles Chatfield and Peter van den Dungen, 204–221. Knoxville: University of Tennessee Press, 1988.

Kirby, Andrew. "What Did You Do in the War, Daddy?" In *Geography and Empire*, ed. Anne Godlewska and Neil Smith, 300–315. Cambridge, MA: Blackwell, 1994.

Klandermans, Bert. "The Peace Movement and Social Movement Theory." In *Peace Movements in Western Europe and the United States*, International Social Movement Research, vol. 3, ed. Bert Klandermans, 1–39. Greenwich, CT: JAI, 1991.

Klandermans, Bert, ed. *Peace Movements in Western Europe and the United States*. International Social Movement Research, vol. 3. Greenwich, CT: JAI, 1991.

Marsden, W. E. "Geography and Two Centuries of Education for Peace and International Understanding." *Geography* 85 (2000): 289–302.

Merrett, Christopher. "Teaching Social Justice: Reviving Geography's Neglected Tradition." *Journal of Geography* 99 (2000): 207–218.

Miller, Byron. *Geography and Social Movements: Comparing Antinuclear Activism in the Boston Area*. Minneapolis: University of Minnesota Press, 2000.

O'Loughlin, John, and Herman van der Wusten. "Political Geography of War and Peace." In *Political Geography of the Twentieth Century: A Global Analysis*, ed. Peter Taylor, 63–113. London: Belhaven, 1993.

Ossenbrügge, Jürgen. "Territorial Ideologies in West Germany, 1945–1985: Between Geopolitics and Regionalist Attitudes." *Political Geography Quarterly* 8 (1989): 387–399.

Parker, Geoffrey. *Western Geopolitical Thought in the Twentieth Century*. New York: St. Martin's, 1985.

Pile, Steve. "Introduction: Opposition, Political Identities, and Spaces of Resistance." In *Geographies of Resistance*, ed. Steve Pile and Michael Keith, 1–32. New York: Routledge, 1997.

Price, Marie D. "Nongovernmental Organizations on the Geopolitical Frontline." In *Reordering the World: Geopolitical Perspectives on the Twenty-first Century*, 2nd ed., ed. George J. Demko and William B. Wood, 260–278. Boulder, CO: Westview, 1999.

Reardon, Betty. *Sexism and the War System*. New York: Teachers College Press, 1985.

Routledge, Paul. "Our Resistance Will Be as Transnational as Capital: Convergence Space and Strategy in Globalising Resistance." *GeoJournal* 52 (2000): 25–33.

Slater, David. "Spatial Politics/Social Movements: Questions of (B)Orders and Resistance in Global Times." In *Geographies of Resistance*, ed. Steve Pile and Michael Keith, 258–276. New York: Routledge, 1997.

Staeheli, Lynn. "Empowering Political Struggle: Spaces and Scales of Resistance." *Political Geography* 13 (1994): 387–391.

Staeheli, Lynn, and Meghan Cope. "Empowering Women's Citizenship." *Political Geography* 13 (1994): 443–460.

Steinberg, Philip. "Territorial Formation on the Margin: Urban Anti-planning in Brooklyn." *Political Geography* 13 (1994): 461–476.

Stoddart, D. R. "Geography and War. The 'New Geography' and the 'New Army' in England, 1899–1914." *Political Geography* 11 (1992): 87–99.

Swerdlow, Amy. *Women Strike for Peace: Traditional Motherhood and Radical Politics in the 1960s*. Chicago: University of Chicago Press, 1993.

Townshend, Charles. "Introduction: The Shape of Modern War." In *The Oxford Illustrated History of Modern War*, ed. Charles Townshend, 3–18. Oxford: Oxford University Press, 1997.

Van Creveld, Martin. "Technology and War I: To 1945." In *The Oxford Illustrated History of Modern War*, ed. Charles Townshend, 175–193. Oxford: Oxford University Press, 1997.

Van Creveld, Martin. "Technology and War II: Postmodern War." In *The Oxford Illustrated History of Modern War*, ed. Charles Townshend, 298–314. Oxford: Oxford University Press, 1997.

Young, Nigel. "Peace Movements in History." In *Towards a Just World Peace*, ed. S. Mendlovitz and R. B. Walker, 137–169. London: Butterworths, 1987.

18

ALAN K. HENRIKSON

The Geography of Diplomacy

Why do diplomatic encounters—international meetings of all kinds, including major international conferences—occur where they do? What are the reasons for and what may be the effects of the selection of one meeting site rather than another for discussions between nations? The focus of attention, for diplomats themselves as well as for scholars of diplomacy, usually has been on the participants, on their instructions and interests, on their tactics and strategies, on the interplay of these in actual negotiation, and on the outcomes of the process in terms of formal agreement and other results. The fascination of diplomacy is thought to lie in the "foreground"—that is, the dynamics of the meeting itself. The physical setting, including the geographic location, of diplomatic encounters tends to be taken for granted. The purpose of this chapter is not to propose that this emphasis be reversed, but rather to suggest that the question of where diplomacy takes place is of much greater significance than is generally appreciated. Moreover, it is to suggest that the selection of a diplomatic venue—the physical location and surrounding environment—is not entirely free or a matter of arbitrary choice. Territorial and other factors, including the history of diplomacy, work to produce a field, or geography, of diplomacy that conditions and can even constrain the choice of site and setting.

On one level, the issues involved in what here is called "the geography of diplomacy" are pragmatic in nature and sometimes can be the primary ones. The "where" question is often the first one to be considered. "Site selection, in fact, is always an important decision in negotiation," as the analysts of negotiation Jeswald Salacuse and Jeffrey Rubin point out. "Parties frequently negotiate long and hard about where they are to meet long before they sit down to discuss *what* they will negotiate. The reason for this concern is that disputants almost always assume—and with good reason—that the particular location in which they negotiate will have consequences for the ensuing process and, ultimately, its results." Colloquially, but with a theoretical comprehensiveness, Salacuse and Rubin observe that the parties to a bilateral negotiation have but four options in selecting a site: "your place, my place, another place, and (as a result of advances in communications technology) 'no place.' "[1] This basic categorization is a useful starting point and will be taken up again later for the purpose of presenting a more fully elaborated and substantiated typology of diplomatic "place" choices.

On another level, the question of diplomatic geography is deeply systemic. It involves not so much the choices that the diplomatic players themselves make, in a highly deliberate fashion or not, as to where they meet, but instead, the structural layout of the international playing field for the diplomatic game—that is, the arena within which diplomacy can take place. This field is not only geophysical, that is, the natural world itself, but also geopolitical. Its pattern is defined by the international distribution of power, by political boundaries, by organizational jurisdictions, and by the record of past diplomatic practice. Traditionally, the geographic sphere of diplomacy has been Eurocentric. Today, many observe, it is centered on the United States of America, the sole surviving superpower of the Cold War. More inclusively, it has been "Western" or "Euro-Atlantic," with Japan sometimes included in it as well. Although the processes of decolonization, depolarization, democratization, deregulation, and digitalization—in a word, globalization—are opening up more of the world to diplomacy, the "center" arguably has not greatly shifted. Meetings do occur elsewhere, of course, not only in the "West" but also among the "Rest." The spatial area of actual diplomacy, however, is still not coextensive with the entire planet.

The need for diplomatic contact has greatly increased. Globalization itself is a powerful force: its various processes have multiplied and compounded the relationships between countries. There are now approximately 200 sovereign entities in the world, many of them small and dependent.[2] Their leaders—ministers, presidents, and even monarchs, as well as the diplomats who represent them—require international connections. These are best established through personal contact and discussion. In order to form and to maintain them, leaders and their representatives must travel and meet. Just as Archimedes, to lift the world, needed "a place to stand," diplomats need "a place to sit together."[3]

Sometimes their meetings are congenial and constructive. Sometimes they are confrontational and competitive, or worse. Are there differences that relate to this basic distinction in where international meetings take place? Is there, with reference to the central theme of this volume, a "war"/"peace" variable in determining the location of diplomatic meetings? Do statesmen choose, or otherwise find themselves negotiating in, one sort of location when conflict ("war") is in the offing and another kind of location when cooperation ("peace") is the issue? Is there even a kind of "map" that could be drawn that would describe the geographic field of diplomatic behavior according to the variable expectations of conflict or cooperation? Might such a map even be used to predict where diplomatic encounters of various kinds are likely to take place?

To embark upon such a cartographic project would require a comprehensiveness of historical knowledge and geographic understanding that certainly is not being claimed or aspired to here. Nonetheless, it might be possible, even within the span of a brief survey of both diplomatic history and diplomatic geography, to identify and make clear certain patterns of diplomatic behavior that show significant connections between the "where" (the locations chosen) and the "what" (the issues negotiated) of diplomacy as it has developed into our time.

In order to exhibit the evolving pattern of the interaction of the history and geography of diplomacy, with a focus on the previously mentioned conflict/co-operation issue, one must both generalize and differentiate. A typology affords a way of separating while grouping. An inclusive outline of distinct types that is illustrated by examples from past as well as present-day diplomacy will be presented in what follows. Like the basic Salacuse-Rubin categorization, which it adapts, extends, and fills in, this conceptual scheme is premised on the proposition that different types of diplomatic representation and communication that concern different subjects and agendas ("conflictual" or "cooperative") can have different geographic bearings.

The hypothesis here offered is that international "borderline" or geographic periphery-focused negotiations tend to be conflictual and that international "cross-roads" or geographic center-focused negotiations tend to be cooperative. This is basically because a borderline is inherently divisive. It tends to produce opposing parties with opposed positions—in short, "sides." A crossroads, being a place of intersection and not direct opposition, is a focal point. Physical convergence facilitates and at times may even seem to force compromise among, not opposite sides, but "points of view." It is further hypothesized that there is a prevailing historical trend from one to the other, from borderline-based diplomacy to crossroads-focused diplomacy. To the extent that there is a gradual displacement of international conflict by international cooperation in the world system, then there should be, in correlation with this, a shift in the venues chosen for important diplomatic meetings from "borderline" locations, that is, border sites themselves and also those that may involve the conscious passing-through or transcending of boundaries or frontier zones, toward "crossroads" sites, that is, internationally central, well-established, and often cosmopolitan sites, where bargaining, settlement, and cooperation are not the exception but the norm.

With this theoretical-analytical contrast in mind, twelve types of diplomatic sites, each of them illustrated by historical and contemporary examples, will be distinguished, beginning with the most basic. The first, following the Salacuse-Rubin nomenclature, is "Your Place." The second, the obverse of the first, is "My Place." The third, which refers to both, is "Our Places." The fourth, which might involve a third party as facilitator, is "Neutral Places." The fifth, which refers to a common border location or other intermediate site, is "Halfway Places." The sixth, which involves a great power in its primary city and possible sponsorship by its national government, is "Metropolitan Places." The seventh, which refers to ancient or classical sites or, especially, headquarters of international organizations that are multilateral and universal, is "Everyone's Places." The eighth, which relates to dramatic events such as military battles or natural disasters or to continuing international disturbances or confrontations, is "Dangerous Places." The ninth, which reflects a desire to find security in remoteness and sometimes also low visibility, is "Safe Places." The tenth, which is partly recreational in purpose but is also possibly aimed at the exploration of new agendas, is "Exotic Places." The eleventh, where the locale chosen is intrinsically related to the thematic issue or policy discussed, is "Demonstration Places." The twelfth and final type is the previously noted "No Place," in which the use of modern telecommunications may seem to make it possible for diplomacy to occur without reference to geography at all.

These will be considered in what follows with, as noted earlier an analytical interest in whether the conflictual or the cooperative aspect of diplomatic meetings that exemplify each type of venue tends to dominate. An important disclaimer should here be made: except through highly detailed historical scholarship, including analysis of private papers and, when possible, personal interviews with relevant officials, it can be difficult to know all of the reasoning that influenced the decision to choose one diplomatic venue rather than another. The "real" reasons for the choice of location may not be the ones publicly stated or even the ones generally accepted as the controlling reasons. Part of the advantage of a geographic field approach to the problem is that it somewhat shifts the burden of explanation from the subjective thinking of the decision makers to the objective physical and political realities of the situation in which they are making a decision. To be sure, some international meetings acquire, over time, a "standard" historical interpretation that includes explanations of why they took place where they did. Though they are always subject to revisionism, these explanations take on a reality of their own and may be incorporated into analyses such as the one presented here.

Your Place

In diplomacy, which takes place across distance, travel is required, and borders as well as territory usually must be crossed. In bilateral relations, as distinct from multilateral diplomacy that might occur at another location, "your place" is, from the point of view of one or the other of the parties, the place where meetings of necessity often must occur. In a sense, the "other's" place is the inevitable and the primary place of diplomacy. As noted, emissaries usually must traverse boundaries. Apart from the inconveniences and costs that are involved in such journeying from one side's home or capital to that of another, there may be symbolic issues involved. At a minimum, a certain deference is shown to the other side by the gesture of journeying all the way to it. The trip can signify acceptance of inequality—inferiority in terms of rank, power, or even moral quality. One-way travel implies supplication. At the same time, going to the other party's place in seeming deference can conceal strategic purposes and result in gains. Nearly always there is anxiety, however, even if the relationship between the parties is not openly a conflictual one.

A legendary example of traveling a distance to meet the other is Emperor Henry IV's journey in 1077 to Canossa, a castle southwest of Reggio nell'Emilia in Italy, where Pope Gregory VII was staying. He hoped thereby to avoid being deposed. Henry approached the castle as a simple penitent and, after waiting for three days, was given absolution. This did not mark a lasting victory for the papacy, yet the name "Canossa" has become associated with the submission of the secular power to the church and, more generally, with the risk to one's prestige in going too far to meet a rival authority. This was remembered by Otto von Bismarck when, during Prussia's *Kulturkampf* against the influence of the Roman Catholic Church in Germany, he said: "Nach Canossa gehen wir nicht" (We are not going to Canossa).

Traditionally, in dealing with China (Zhonghua, or the Middle Kingdom), the establishment of contact meant paying tribute and delivering it at the Chinese imperial court itself. There a ritual act of repeated low bowing, the kowtow, was required. Diplomacy in the sense of relations between sovereign and equal nations did not exist. Surely something of historical China's attitude toward foreign visitors remained when, startlingly, the president of the United States, Richard M. Nixon, secretly indicated to the Chinese leadership that he would be interested in visiting China. His forerunner to Beijing, National Security Adviser Henry A. Kissinger, was well aware of the controversy that might arise over this unprecedented presidential trip to the People's Republic of China—seemingly an act of obeisance, quite apart from its ideological and political meaning. Kissinger therefore requested of his Chinese hosts that his preparatory mission be given no publicity. The announcement that President Nixon himself would visit China was made from Washington, D.C.

When the Nixon trip took place in February 1972, it was as if the American leader had landed on the moon, so far away and unknown was China to most Americans at that time. The inherent fascination of the transpacific trip largely overcame the loss-of-face issue. Various geographic aspects of the president's journey were noted even in the resulting Shanghai Communiqué, which recorded that "President Nixon and his party visited Peking and viewed cultural, industrial and agricultural sites, and they also toured Hangchow and Shanghai where, continuing discussions with Chinese leaders, they viewed similar places of interest." On a metageographic and political plane, the United States "acknowledged" in the Shanghai Communiqué that "all Chinese on either side of the Taiwan Strait maintain there is but one China and that Taiwan is part of China."[4] Although this was a very careful formulation that was not itself a concession, it did help to establish internationally the notion of "one China," and it made eventual formal recognition by the U.S. government of the People's Republic of China almost unavoidable, though this did not come until the presidency of Jimmy Carter at the beginning of 1979. The fact that President Nixon had crossed over a geographic and political line and had gone to "mainland China" made "island China" (Taiwan), though it was still the seat of the Nationalist government of the Republic of China, appear almost a satellite.

Offsetting the negative meaning that can be given to a diplomatic meeting by going to the "other's" place is the positive effect such a gesture can have, especially if it is made from a position of strength, openheartedly, and, in some cases, out of a sense of reciprocation and even of obligation. When President Franklin D. Roosevelt in February 1945 flew by stages all the way to the Crimea to meet with the Soviet leader, Joseph Stalin, and British prime minister Winston Churchill, he did so, despite the physical difficulty for him in his semiparalyzed and infirm state, in order to express his recognition of the importance of future Soviet-American cooperation as well as to plan the final stages of the war against

Germany and also Japan. In order to win Soviet agreement on some points, he made concessions on others, particularly with regard to Poland and to China.[5] Although, overall, the Yalta understandings were realistic and reasonably balanced, Roosevelt's travel to Yalta was later characterized by some conservative critics as "another Munich."[6] The comparison was to British prime minister Neville Chamberlain's surrender of the interests of Czechoslovakia when, three times in succession, he crossed the Channel in September 1938 to meet with Nazi leader Adolf Hitler at various places, including Munich, that were more convenient for the latter, in order to achieve "peace for our time."[7]

A shorter distance but perhaps even more heroic political gesture (for he later was assassinated) was the trip that Egypt's president Anwar Sadat made in November 1977 to Jerusalem. There he placed before the Israeli Knesset a proposal of peace between his country and Israel. This became the first peace agreement between any Arab country and the Jewish state. President Sadat, together with Israel's prime minister Menachem Begin, duly was awarded the Nobel Prize for Peace in 1978. Had the Egyptian leader not made the first move by crossing the Suez Canal and flying all the way to the Israeli religious and political center, this result would not have been possible. The diplomatic gesture he made, however, left him vulnerable.

My Place

There are, as previously noted, asymmetries between meeting at home and meeting abroad. Home base and the other's place are not perfectly interchangeable. Perhaps the greatest advantage that can be gained from meeting at home, particularly in one's own national capital or seat of government, is to be able to control the conditions of the interchange, including the basic organizational arrangements that usually must be made. At the psychological as well as the organizational level, there is a factor of "territorial dominance" in play.[8] In bilateral relations there is a very obvious "pull" factor if one of the parties manages to have most of the discussion between them take place at its center. Tensions are less likely to arise in multilateral diplomacy, where many points of view rather than only two opposite sides are represented. The issues relating to the venue are somewhat different.

Being host and organizer of the grand gathering of crowned heads and statesmen that was the Congress of Vienna (September 1814–June 1815) enabled the Austrian foreign minister, Prince Clemens von Metternich, to exercise a "crossroads" and a peacemaking function. Having this meeting, whose purpose was to restore harmony to Europe after the international struggle against Napoleon, take place in Vienna conferred many advantages, as well as responsibilities, upon Austrian diplomacy. Metternich used the city itself as an ally. He kept the monarchs who were present busy with festivities while he, enjoying the social life as well as monitoring the diplomatic intrigue, concentrated, together with statesmen who represented other great powers, on the territorial and other practical issues that had to be settled.[9] The result was not just peace between France and the countries allied against it but what became, during the next half century or so, the stabilizing

Concert of Europe. At least until the Paris Peace Conference that followed World War I a century later, the Congress of Vienna stood for postwar peacemaking and international reordering, though of a heavily great-power-dominated kind, and the Hapsburg capital was widely recognized as the "home" of diplomacy.

After World War II, there was a shift in international decision-making power from the Old World to the New—from the point of view of the U.S. leadership, to "my" side of the Atlantic, which reached even to the Pacific. The second war in Europe further discredited European diplomacy and even those cities in Europe, including Vienna, where historic diplomatic events had taken place. An oceanic boundary was to be crossed. This diplomatic transition was closely associated with a major shift in power away from Europe toward the United States. Even before the war ended, the United Nations Conference on International Organization was held in San Francisco from April to June 1945. Afterward there was strong sentiment within the United States, against European feelings in favor of one or another European site, to locate the new international organization itself on U.S. soil. The U.S. Congress, with both the Senate and the House of Representatives acting unanimously, formally resolved "that the United Nations be, and hereby are, invited to locate the seat of the United Nations Organization with the United States of America"[10]—in short, at my place.

The planning for what ultimately became the North Atlantic Treaty Organization also marked a transatlantic shift in power and political influence. Although the story of NATO began in the aftermath of the London meeting of the Council of Foreign Ministers in December 1947, it continued in Washington, D.C., where, in secret talks in the recently built Pentagon, discussions advanced until, with the subsequent inclusion of other countries besides the United States and the United Kingdom and also Canada, the North Atlantic Treaty, the Treaty of Washington, was signed on April 4, 1949.[11] The fact that NATO was based on the Treaty of Washington is significant. Being in Washington made it possible for the Department of State and Department of Defense negotiators of this unprecedented commitment to mutual defense with countries in Europe to consult closely with the Republican and Democratic leaders of the U.S. Senate, without whose two-thirds vote there would have been no Atlantic pact.[12]

In time, the relatively small capital city of Washington, D.C., came to have a "crossroads" function, especially in the field of international defense. "All roads lead to Rome," it classically has been said. Transatlantic tension between "my place" or "your place" even in the defense field, however, persists. Some European countries, even though they are NATO members, today wish to establish a European military headquarters separate from the NATO structure in order to give more operational reality to the declared European objective of a European Security and Defense Identity (ESDI). Belgium, France, and Germany, in particular, hold this view. A treaty that was made in Washington may be easier for European leaders to gain political distance from, as essentially an "American" construction, than one that is put together in one of their own homelands. Whether a treaty or organization is considered to be "mine" or "yours" depends partly on where, diplomatically and also geographically, it originated.

Our Places

The usual places for the conduct of diplomacy on a daily basis, especially bilateral diplomacy, are embassies and also the foreign ministries of the countries to which the ambassadors who head those embassies are accredited. These are the "our" places of the diplomatic world, particularly the *corps diplomatiques* who live in national capitals all around the globe today. Their presence represents an institutionalization of the "your place"/"my place" relationship, the essence of which is reciprocity. So systematized has the exchange of ambassadors and other diplomatic personnel between national governments now become that issues of the "face" that may be gained or lost in discussing a matter in one capital or the other scarcely even arise anymore.

The system today is a universal one that was codified in the Vienna Convention on Diplomatic Relations, which was adopted at the United Nations Conference on Diplomatic Intercourse and Immunities that took place in Vienna in 1961. The characteristics of this system, especially those that are noteworthy from a geographic perspective, are the ones that involve extraterritoriality—the legal sanctity and physical safety of embassies and the privileges and immunities of diplomats and their families who are quasi-geographically associated with this protected status. An embassy is considered "foreign territory," which even local firefighters cannot enter without the foreign government's consent. Moreover, as stated in Article 22, paragraph 2, of the Vienna Convention, "The receiving State is under a special duty to take all appropriate steps to protect the premises of the mission against any intrusion or damage and to prevent any disturbance of the peace of the mission or impairment of its dignity." The "territory" of a country inside another is also somewhat mobile. Article 26 of the Vienna Convention obligates the receiving state, subject to its own laws and regulations concerning national security "zones," to "ensure to all members of the mission freedom of movement and travel in its territory." The convention further specifies that the personal baggage and household effects of diplomats and their families normally cannot be inspected when they are entering or leaving the country either by the host state or by third states crossed in transit. Diplomatic couriers and packages constituting the so-called diplomatic bag also are inviolable under the convention. Thus the "our places" of diplomacy are not merely the totality of diplomatic outposts established abroad but also the network of travel and communication that unifies them.

Although the system of establishing national embassies on foreign territory was adopted by nearly universal international agreement, it is not conflict free. During the Iranian Revolution of 1979, for example, the U.S. Embassy in Tehran was seized and its staff held hostage by a mob of Iranian students who demanded the extradition of the shah, who had fled to the United States for personal safety and medical treatment. A flagrant violation of the Vienna Convention on Diplomatic Relations, the seizure of the American Embassy seemed an assault on the diplomatic system itself. The fact that the students' action appeared to be sanctioned by the revolutionary regime of Ayatollah Ruhollah Khomeni heightened the sense of challenge to the long-established diplomatic order. The discovery by the students inside the embassy of secret CIA files enabled them, however, to make an international moral, if not legal, case for what they had done. Article 41, paragraph 3, of the Vienna Convention states that the premises of a diplomatic mission "must not be used in any matter incompatible with the functions of the mission." Among these functions is "ascertaining by all lawful means conditions and developments" in the receiving states and also "reporting thereon" (Article 3, paragraph 1.[d]). Thus some intelligence gathering was legitimate. To the students and other Iranian revolutionaries, however, the U.S. Embassy, with CIA agents in it, seemed to be a veritable nest of spies who were plainly involved in activities in violation of the "duty not to interfere in the internal affairs" of the host country (Article 41, paragraph 1, of the Vienna Convention).

The Tehran embassy takeover in 1979 served to announce, just as the Boxer Rebellion and the siege of the foreign legations in Beijing had done more than three-quarters of a century earlier, in 1900, that states and governments are not the only actors on the international scene and that the political-geographic right of diplomatic extraterritoriality can arouse nationalistic as well as religiously based protests against its exercise. Permanent missions established abroad are themselves becoming sources of conflict, despite the mostly cooperative activity in which the diplomats who serve in them are engaged.

Neutral Places

Some sites for diplomatic meetings are attractive mainly by virtue of the neutrality of the countries within which the meetings take place. In some cases, for example, Switzerland, the country's neutral status is historic and is recognized internationally, as well as being self-chosen and carefully self-maintained. Such "identity" neutrality, as it may be called, is held to firmly in peacetime as well as in wartime. In other instances, the neutrality of a place may derive mainly from a country's physical location or from its relationship to a particular international conflict in which the country happens not to be involved. This might be termed "situation" neutrality. Essential to the idea of a neutral site, of whatever kind, is that there has been, is now, or will be a surrounding conflict—to be avoided or to be resolved.

As for the selection of a neutral site, as Salacuse and Rubin note, the decisive consideration should be that "each side gains no special advantage or disadvantage stemming from location."[13] The example they give is the December 1989 meeting between U.S. president George H. W. Bush and Soviet president Mikhail Gorbachev off the coast of Malta, a country that, though then under a conservative government, under its previous socialist leadership had actively pursued a policy of nonalignment.

Most neutral states, it may be noted, are lesser countries in terms of magnitude that do not purport to be "powers," or poles of international influence or even of high international interest. Their geography in some cases conditions their policy. Switzerland, though central in Europe, is largely isolated by mountain ranges and thus realistically can imagine staying out of conflicts that may arise around it. It is, however, a crossroads. Its physical control of the tunnels that have been built through the mountains is a factor in support of its neutrality. By closing these routes, it could stop much of Europe's rail and highway traffic, which gives it political leverage if needed. Malta, geostrategically in the middle of the Mediterranean, is tiny and exposed. Being exceptionally vulnerable, especially since it lost its British protector with independence in 1964 and the total closure of the British naval base there in 1979, it naturally seeks to deal commercially and nonconfrontationally with everyone. Its main built asset is its dockyard, which is also a neutrality-enhancing factor, for, as an entrepôt or maritime crossroads, it must be open for business to the world without partiality.

Switzerland's diplomacy has been dominated by the neutrality concept and by the country's intermediate relation to the conflicts of Europe since its neutrality was affirmed during the time of the Congress of Vienna. Its international role is illustrated by the "spirit of Geneva" that resulted from meeting of the four powers—France, Great Britain, the Soviet Union, and the United States—in July 1955. The place of this meeting, home of John Calvin, birthplace of the Red Cross, and seat of the former League of Nations, was idealistic by tradition—the "Protestant Rome," it has been called. Its special atmosphere of serenity was conducive to a relaxation of political tension between the two blocs—the Communist East and capitalist West—whose armed opposition along the nearby Iron Curtain defined the Cold War. The leaders of the four powers, Premier Edgar Faure of France, Prime Minister Anthony Eden of Great Britain, Premier Nikolai Bulganin and Premier Nikita Khrushchev of the Soviet Union, and President Dwight D. Eisenhower of the United States, agreed to meet, for the first time since the comparable leaders' meeting of the World War II era, on the invitation of the Swiss government and under the aegis of the United Nations. Although little actual progress was made toward East-West disarmament, apart from President Eisenhower's floating of an innovative "open skies" inspection scheme, the conference did result in a palpable measure of détente for a period. As Premier Faure then declared, "The spirit blowing on Geneva and the Helvetic soil is one of peace, in the strict meaning of the word."[14]

Malta was a much less obvious choice for an East-West summit meeting site. In 1989 President Bush, wishing to test the waters with his Soviet counterpart, wrote President Gorbachev a letter in which he proposed a small "non-agenda" meeting with him—the kind of encounter that would have been more difficult to arrange in one large capital or the other, where bureaucratic involvement would be greater. "So then we kind of went back and forth as to where we might have such a meeting," Bush later recalled. "I made a couple of proposals that couldn't work out from Gorbachev's schedule, and we finally hit upon Malta because it was a nice peaceful harbor, a place that never had bad weather and nobody would get seasick."[15] As things turned out, a major winter storm blew up during their meeting, and President Gorbachev "couldn't even come out to the *Slava*, his cruiser."[16] So they met instead aboard a large Soviet cruise ship, the *Maxim Gorky*, which was tied up in Valletta harbor. This first bilateral summit meeting between these two American and Soviet leaders—to the latter's discomfiture, the "seasick summit"—by itself produced no major gain for either side, but it did enable the American and Soviet presidents to confer directly, at a time when there was widespread international criticism of their not having yet done so. The meeting helped to develop a bilateral relationship that, within several years, helped to overcome the division of Europe and to end the Cold War. For the local hosts, the Bush-Gorbachev meeting was "Malta's opportunity of a lifetime," in the words of one Maltese official. It changed Malta's "profile." No longer "a piece on the international chessboard," it was "a place where one could invest safely, retire peacefully, and enjoy a well earned holiday without a care in the world."[17] Diplomacy can affect geographic imagery as well as be affected by it.

Halfway Places

The most obvious "halfway" place to meet in political-geographic terms is at or near a border that is shared between countries, and also at a point more or less on a straight line between the two countries' capitals. Such a meeting point need not be, in a strict mileage sense, equidistant between their national capital cities. Symbolically, however, a border location is "midway" between the countries. The advantage of meeting at such a place is that, especially when a bilateral relationship is conflictual (as relations between immediately neighboring countries often are), neither side risks losing "face." The leaders of both sides have to move in order to make a meeting possible.

A politically significant recent example of a borderline encounter between adversaries was the February 20, 1999, meeting between the prime minister of India, Atal Behari Vajpayee, and the then prime minister of Pakistan, Nawaz Sharif, at "Line Zero" at Wagah on the Punjab border between their countries, which was followed by discussions at the nearby city of Lahore in Pakistan.[18] This unprecedented encounter initiated a promising, though regrettably short-lived, Lahore "process" of dialogue. In a humble and nonthreatening gesture, Prime Minister Vajpayee traveled to the meeting by bus, nominally to inaugurate a scheduled bus service between New Delhi and Lahore across the previously closed India-Pakistan border. His experiment in "bus diplomacy" highlighted the need for more practical connections between the two nations, which had been somewhat artificially separated by the partition of 1947. Even more recently, in April 2003, Prime Minister Vajpayee again, though more cautiously, extended a "hand of friendship," this time during a visit to Srinagar, the summer capital of the Indian state of Jammu and Kashmir and not far distant from the Pakistani capital, Islamabad.[19] In conjunction with this effort, a number of members of Pakistan's Parliament, in an expression of goodwill, crossed the border at Wagah, there to be showered with petals—a gesture subsequently reciprocated by Indian MPs.

Meeting "halfway" at various border locations can not only initiate dialogues that do not exist but also sustain relationships, formerly hostile, that have turned friendly. The U.S.-Mexico relationship is a case in point. The 1848 Treaty of Guadalupe Hidalgo, as is never forgotten by Mexicans or by Americans, ceded to the United States much of the present-day U.S. Southwest and also California. In such historical and geographic contexts, it can be difficult for border encounters to be much more than "fence mending." Though the juxtaposed countries may be unequal in size, wealth, and power, their leaders, meeting at a border, can be equal in dignity. Typically, a new U.S. president goes to meet his Mexican counterpart at a location on or near the U.S.-Mexican border as his administration is beginning—an example being the *encuentro* between President-elect Ronald Reagan and Mexico's president, then José López Portillo, at Ciudad Juárez in early January 1981. The current U.S. president, George W. Bush, formerly the governor of Texas, went further inward on the other side to meet his Mexican counterpart, President Vicente Fox, at the latter's ranch in San Cristóbal in the state of Guanajuato, where he had served as governor. Sensitive issues, such as Mexican migration to the United States, often can more easily be explored in such informal, non-capital-city settings. Some issues that are geographically especially pertinent to a border—water management, electricity transmission, or drug smuggling—may receive more attention than they would if they were discussed in a capital. Trans-border diplomacy, though it may be fraught with tension, can reconcile and unite. "Geography has made us neighbors," as President Bush stated at his meeting with President Fox; "cooperation and respect will make us partners."[20]

When countries are not contiguous, the "halfway" meeting place must be produced by factors other than the location of an existing political boundary line or zone or, more broadly, a common neighborhood. In battle, generals, and sometimes even political leaders, meet in the field, which can be far from the "home" of either. Famously, Emperor Napoleon of France and Tsar Alexander I of Russia met in the summer of 1807 on a raft in the middle of the Niemen River near Tilsit, then in northern Prussia. There they became allies and divided up Europe between them. This encounter took place "halfway," not at a formal position in between but rather at a point along a kind of geopolitical "equilibrium" line between the centers of French power and Russian power that emanated, respectively, from Paris and from Moscow, far away.

A summit meeting that did take place precisely at a midpoint between two specific centers—one a national capital and the other an international headquarters—was the Glassboro Summit of 1967. The premier of the Soviet Union, Aleksei Kosygin, came to New York to address a special session of the United Nations. The outbreak of the Six-Day War in the Middle East and the escalating conflict in Vietnam heightened Cold War tensions. The idea of Kosygin's meeting, while in the United States, with President Lyndon B. Johnson arose. However, the Soviet premier did not wish to go to Washington, and it was not customary for U.S. presidents to receive foreign visitors in New York. Therefore a compromise, negotiated by the governor of the state of New Jersey, Richard J. Hughes, was worked out: that they would meet halfway in Glassboro. Located in the southwestern part of New Jersey, this small manufacturing and college community—henceforth able to describe itself as the "Summit City"—was easily reached, if not exactly convenient. The precise meeting place was Hollybush, the hastily evacuated and quickly reoutfitted house of the president of Glassboro State College (now Rowan University). Logistical matters were not, of course, the primary considerations. Physically, the two leaders could have met almost anywhere. The political geometry of the halfway position between New York City and Washington, D.C.—and a site other than UN headquarters or the White House—had a compelling diplomatic logic, however.

Metropolitan Places

"World cities," like New York, have a gravitational attraction that even powerful national capitals that in urban terms are small, like Washington, D.C., do not.[21] Diplomacy, like other human activities that are transactional and information based, naturally is drawn to places where contact with wealthy, knowledgeable, culturally heterogeneous, and thus usually interesting as well as simply powerful persons can be maximized. Metropolitan centers, of course, also offer a spectrum of facilities—for accommodation, entertainment, specialized research, business transactions, and transportation and communication—that lesser cities, including smaller national capitals of even very large countries like the United States, may not have.

Historically, conference diplomacy, which involves delegations from many countries and also the nongovernmental organizations (NGOs) of the time, has mostly been held in the major cities, especially in Europe. Notable examples of metropolitan-centered diplomacy are the 1815 Congress of Vienna, the 1884 Berlin Conference, the 1919 Paris Peace Conference, and the 1933 London Economic Conference. It was only logical, therefore, that permanent conferences—that is, international organizations—also would come to be situated in major urban centers. When the decision after World War II was made to locate the new United Nations Organization (UNO) not in Europe but rather in the United States, where a historical fresh start would be possible, attention inevitably was drawn to New York City, the heart of what the geographer Jean Gottmann called "Megalopolis."[22]

Many other possible sites in North America in fact were also considered, including San Francisco, where the conference that produced the UN Charter took place, Philadelphia, and Boston. But in the end, a consensus formed around the idea of situating the new world body in the vicinity of New York. Although consideration was briefly given to establishing the UNO in a "small" rather than a "large" city, lest proximity to a powerful urban center prevent the international organization from forming its own distinct personality, the members of the Preparatory Commission with responsibility for selecting the site for a UN headquarters came to think "a little more kindly of the big cities" for, among other reasons, the "educational and cultural facilities" they offered. A reinforcing reason was that a big-city location would make it easier to recruit and retain a superior staff for the Secretariat for the new organization. Its officials "might become bored with country life." Another point made, which revealed a preoccupation of the time, is that it would be "less dangerous to locate the seat in the centre of a big city than to have it too far away from contact with public opinion."[23] World War II had created a strong presumption in favor of democracy, the wisdom of letting the people have their say about matters of war and peace and be able to see how they were being represented internationally. The United Nations headquarters should be, in a later phrase, a "fishbowl."

The trauma of September 11, 2001, which removed the twin towers of the World Trade Center from the New York skyline and cost many New Yorkers and others their lives, also focused the eyes of the world on the city, and on the United Nations as well. Almost immediately after the al-Qaeda attacks, the United Nations unanimously condemned terrorism and its acts in decisive and also very practical resolutions. "The UN's presence in New York creates an inherent solidarity with New Yorkers in a time of peril from terrorism," a New York Bar Association report noted shrewdly. "The reaction in the General Assembly and the Security Council might not have been quite so overwhelming or so sustained had the violence of September 11 happened at a place distant from the UN."[24] A suggestion was even made that the organization should move its headquarters to the devastated World Trade Center site when it was excavated. "The U.N. is the ideal tenant—its presence would give every country, friend or foe, a stake in keeping New York safe."[25]

Other major cities also have profited, on balance, from being headquarters of international diplomacy. Geneva, "the smallest of the big capitals," as it styles itself, was the home of the League of Nations, as earlier noted, and it continues its active international role as a second headquarters of the United Nations.[26] Some 150 diplomatic missions are accredited to Geneva's many UN-affiliated bodies, for example, the International Labor Organization (ILO), which dates from 1919. As a "congress center," Geneva still is unequaled. It has more than 200 meeting halls, some of them capacious, and it hosts hundreds of conferences and exhibitions every year. As the "City of Peace," Geneva also is the headquarters of many humanitarian institutions, including the International Committee of the Red Cross, which originated there in 1863.[27] In geographic terms, the city views itself as having a "privileged location along the main axes of the West."[28] It surely is the most pacific of all crossroads locations.

Vienna is another major city that has become a permanent international center. One of the oldest diplomatic metropolises—at the time of the Congress of Vienna it was the fourth-largest city in the world—has now reemerged as a major international meeting place. "With the Cold War, Vienna became the western world's chilly eastern extremity, but for those on the other side it was the only chink in the Iron Curtain," as the city of Vienna notes. The "hard-earned diplomatic experience" that the city fathers gained during that bleak period "stood them in good stead, culminating in their deliverance from the Allies in 1955." In part owing to Austria's formal neutrality after that date, and in particular the Socialist leadership of Chancellor Bruno Kreisky, Vienna became "a mediating power."[29] Later, "With Gorbachev's 'perestroika' and the raising of the Iron Curtain, Vienna was no longer the backend of the western world," as the city officially pointed out. It had "reverted to its geographically designated position as the hub of European convergence."[30] It now is a peace-oriented crossroads location too, conducive to diplomacy, particularly along the axes of what formerly was called the "East" of Europe.

Everyone's Places

Some meeting sites have been regarded, by tradition and also as the result of express international agreement, as having universal significance—as being open to and meaningful for everyone. These commonly are associated with shared activities and aspirations, the most important of which is the search for peace, to be achieved through competition and, eventually, cooperation. One such site is Olympia, home of the ancient Olympic Games, near the western coast of the

Peloponnesus in southern Greece. The tradition that has been handed down by history is that during the period of the games at Olympia there should be a cessation of hostilities among nations to allow the safe passage of athletes—a cessation that, it was hoped, would last.

Today, Olympia is a United Nations Educational, Scientific, and Cultural Organization (UNESCO) World Heritage site and also the symbolic seat of an International Olympic Truce Centre. This center's administrative headquarters is in Athens, the site of the first modern Olympic Games in 1896 and also the location of the 2004 Summer Olympics. On the initiative of the Greek government and also the International Olympic Committee, the idea of the Olympic Truce, or "Ekecheiria," is being fostered in order to promote peace beyond the games themselves, particularly in cases of continuing internecine strife. United Nations secretary-general Kofi Annan, who has supported the Olympic Truce concept as one fully consistent with the United Nations' own ideals, has stated supportively: "While limited in duration and scope, the Olympic Truce can offer a neutral point of consensus, a window of time to open a dialogue, a pause to provide relief to a suffering population."[31]

The primary "everyone's place" is, of course, the United Nations itself. Although the signatories of the UN Charter are states, the preamble of the Charter begins, "We the peoples of the United Nations." A Headquarters Agreement concluded between the United Nations and the United States on June 26, 1947, enables the United Nations to operate in a "headquarters district" under the authority and control of the UN itself, according to the agreement's terms. Transit rights to and from the headquarters district were granted for persons who were accredited. At the same time the UN accepted an obligation to "prevent the headquarters from becoming a refuge."[32]

The issue of whether "everyone" with authority would be allowed into the United States to participate in United Nations discussions was sharply posed in 1988 when then U.S. secretary of state George P. Shultz denied a visa to the chairman of the Palestine Liberation Organization (PLO), Yasser Arafat, who had been invited to address the UN General Assembly. The rationale, beyond a basic fear of terrorism, was that the PLO leader had not fully accepted UN Security Council Resolution 242 with its acknowledgment of the right of "every State" in the Middle East, the State of Israel included, to "live in peace."[33] In response, the UN General Assembly took the unprecedented step of voting to hold an extraordinary session in December 1988 in Geneva, where Chairman Arafat would be able to speak before it, the UN's most representative organ. In part because of this international pressure, as well as modifications in the PLO leader's own policy line, the U.S. government soon established official contact with the PLO in Tunisia, and what seemed to many observers an American "violation" at least in spirit of the 1947 Headquarters Agreement was "corrected." The openness of the UN headquarters in New York as a place of diplomacy for nearly "everyone" was restored.

Dangerous Places

Although a former U.S. permanent representative to the United Nations, Daniel Patrick Moynihan, characterized the United Nations as "a dangerous place," that forum has not been, in fact, the perilous venue for diplomatic talks that many other places have been. Most such places have not been regular meeting places at all but, rather, fortuitous locations for unique encounters such as, for example, clandestine negotiations for the rescue of hostages.[34]

A more fixed "dangerous" place for negotiation on an intergovernmental level is the "truce village" of Panmunjom, which straddles the border between North Korea and South Korea in the Demilitarized Zone that was established by the Korean War armistice in 1953. "Think of it as Dangerland, a bizarre theme park to cataclysmic mass death," wrote one touristic visitor.[35] The 125-acre Joint Security Area has itself been a scene of violence. The most flagrant case occured in 1976 when some North Korean soldiers who wielded axes killed two American soldiers and wounded other members of a UN work team. The workers were engaged in cutting the branches of some poplar trees to improve visibility. In response, U.S. troops were placed on combat-ready status (DEFCON 3). Subsequent negotiations produced an agreement on a line that divided the Joint Security Area and even a written apology from the Korean People's Republic's leader, Kim Il Sung.

This "borderline" relationship is inherently conflictual. The contact between the U.S.-led United Nations command and the North Korean regime along the 38th Parallel at Panmunjom is a military-to-military relationship, as such contacts at the periphery tend to be. The Panmunjom talks have frequently been interrupted and subordinated to higher level diplomatic conversations in New York, Geneva, and also Beijing. In view of the North Korean government's possible development of nuclear weapons, the diplomacy of the Korean problem has greatly intensified and has been lifted to the international if not global level. The "dangerous" venue at Panmunjom continues to be important, however, as a channel for easing tensions, and reducing local frictions in particular. A U.S. officer in charge of the military talks with the North Koreans—at the time deputy chief of staff for the United Nations Command—held not only formal talks with his North Korean counterpart but, in a separate building, informal talks, controversially but perhaps less "dangerously," over whiskey and beer.[36]

Safe Places

The opposite of a highly exposed location for international talks is one that is remote, even inaccessible, and secure—both to keep danger away and the press and other inquisitors at bay and to keep the participants in so that they might quickly reach agreement without diversion or distraction. Wright-Patterson Air Force Base (AFB) near Dayton, Ohio, qualified as such a place when it served as the venue for the Balkan Proximity Peace Talks during November 1995. In "proximity" talks, a relatively recent diplomatic innovation, the parties are brought close to one another, as at a borderline, without actually touching until agreement is reached.

Wright-Patterson AFB solved the problem of finding a suitable site for a summit of the key figures involved in the Bosnian war. It was far enough away from New York and Washington and the media to avoid intrusion, yet it was easily reached by air transport. Using a military base also met the political requirement of offering the representatives of the three warring sides separate but identical facilities. President Alija Izetbegovic of the Republic of Bosnia-Herzegovina, President Slobodan Milosevic of the Federal Republic of Yugoslavia, and President Franjo Tudjman of the Republic of Croatia were housed in separate generals' quarters. They were brought closer together in the meeting rooms, including a large officers' dining hall, of the Hope Hotel, also within the base. At one point the principal American mediator, Richard Holbrooke, found himself carrying napkins on which possible solutions to the geographic problem of connecting the eastern enclave of Goradze to Sarajevo had been sketched from and to the Serb and Bosnian sides, which were seated at opposite ends of the vast dining hall—the "napkin shuttle," this was called.[37]

Military technology also assisted the American-led mediation effort. Powerscene, the Pentagon's computerized terrain visualization system, was deployed. It was used partly just to overawe the Balkan negotiators with the impressive demonstration it implicitly gave of the U.S. military's detailed picture of their own country's geography. It also, however, served practically in defining boundary lines and in adjusting territorial portions of territory so that the Bosnian-Croat Federation would get 51% of the land and the Bosnian Serb entity would get 49%. As one of the military supervisors of this digital mapping system put it, "[T]his commitment of resources said: 'This is the best equipment in the world, manned by the best team in the world; it is an instrument of war but we'll use it for peace because you are willing to come to the table.' "[38] Thus not only forceful diplomacy but also power cartography contributed to the General Framework Agreement for Peace in Bosnia and Herzegovina that was initialed at Dayton on November 11, 1995. The place itself—a somewhat artificial, even partly virtual venue—contributed too. "Today, 'Dayton' is now much more than the name of a great city in Ohio's Miami Valley," recalled Ambassador Holbrooke five years later. "Around the world, Dayton is shorthand for peace." It also was a principle of location selection in support of a method of negotiation. "Other 'Dayton's' have been suggested for many of the world's other festering problems—from the Middle East to Northern Ireland to Cyprus to Congo," as Holbrooke noted.[39]

The closeting of negotiators also can be used to encourage agreement among allies and friends. A remote site is more likely to be used for such meetings when there is controversy on the outside, if not inside. Thus conflict is still a factor in the choice of venue. Recent meetings of the Group of Seven/Eight industrialized countries are a case in point. For the 2002 G7/G8 Summit meeting in Canada, Prime Minister Jean Chrétien chose Kananaskis, a village tucked away in the Canadian Rockies. John Kirton, a scholarly observer of the G7/G8 process, commented that "Canada as host has designed a Summit of retreat." In part for that very reason, he commented, it could be a summit "of real results" that would advance the Canadian government's interest in addressing the problems of Africa, several of whose leaders it invited to attend.[40] Pressure from the outside, particularly the clamor and even threats from antiglobalization protestors, also was a consideration, perhaps the dominant one. "While the Kananaskis Summit will cost on estimated $300 million," commented Gordon Smith, a former personal representative of Prime Minister Chrétien for G7/G8 affairs, "most of the money will go into security which, unfortunately, is needed because of those who are determined to prevent the meeting from taking place. You can't blame government for this."[41]

Even large international meetings, such as the November 2001 Ministerial Conference of the World Trade Organization held at Doha in Qatar, were held where they were in part for reasons of safety. Everyone in the organization had in mind the experience of the WTO's demonstrator-disrupted conference in Seattle two years before. Just months before their meeting, in September, the al-Qaeda attacks occurred. The discussions in Doha, once a sleepy pearling and fishing village that had been transformed by oil wealth and a modernizing monarch into a capital with up-to-date facilities, took place in "a compound hermetically sealed by security guards against a feared terrorist attack," as the *New York Times* described the conference venue.[42] Especially noteworthy among the some 1,440 participants in the WTO conclave was the presence of a large Israeli delegation. "Though the ministers have come to Qatar, a conservative Islamic society that borders Saudi Arabia, Israel's delegation is here en masse," the *New York Times* reported, quoting an Israeli official who said that the Doha WTO conference was the first meeting in the region to accept an Israeli delegation in two years.[43] Without the safe site that the Kingdom of Qatar could afford and the auspices of the WTO required, a major Israeli negotiating presence on Arab soil might then not have been possible.

Exotic Places

What is considered "exotic" depends in part, of course, on the experience and the outlook of the beholder. Most diplomats are well schooled and well traveled and are therefore not likely to be overcome, either positively or negatively, by strangeness. Nonetheless, some locales are more "different" than others, and meetings held there gain mystery and hold excitement that familiar places do not have. The purpose of choosing physically and culturally unfamiliar sites, apart from enhancing interest in a meeting, may be to "open" eyes and enable new ways of seeing things.

The summit meeting of the Asia Pacific Economic Cooperation (APEC) that took place in November 1994 in Bogor, Indonesia, had from American and other northern Pacific perspectives a "foreign" quality that most diplomatic meeting places in Europe or the Western Hemisphere could not have had. Americans knew the APEC grouping of nations, unusual in including both the People's Republic of China and Taiwan, mainly from the first APEC summit, hosted by President William J. Clinton, which had been held in Seattle in 1993. Apart from being on the other side of the Pacific Rim, in a sense diametrically opposite Seattle, Bogor is a rare locale. Meaning "without care," Bogor, which the Dutch established in 1745 and used later as the residence of their governor-general (today the occasional residence of Indonesia's president), is itself a mixture of the indigenous and the exotic. The famous Bogor Botanical Gardens have tropical plants from all around the world. It was a perfect place to articulate the message of open regionalism—

in the words of the APEC leaders' declaration, "free and open trade and investment in the Asia-Pacific no later than the year 2020." Given the natural and cultivated beauties surrounding them, it also was appropriate for them to espouse "sustainable development."[44]

An exotic site also can be a place of transition from one historical and cultural sphere to another. To bring its participants from the edge of one traditional region, "Europe," to that of another, the "Middle East," surely was part of the purpose of the journey arranged by the Greek Presidency of the European Union for the twenty-five foreign ministers of the EU member and also EU candidate countries during their Informal General Affairs and External Relations Council meeting in Greece to the islands of Rhodes and Kastellorizo during May 2–4, 2003. The latter island, the site of a ruined castle built by the Knights of Saint John, is the most easterly of all the Greek islands and is a place of which it is said, "Europe ends and Asia begins." Thus it is a borderline location, with conflict being implicit in it. The islet, to which the ministers traveled aboard ship, is only a few hundred yards off the Turkish coast. The location was used for an act of diplomatic outreach. As Greece's foreign minister, George Papandreou, explained in an advance message to his fellow ministers, "On the island of Kastellorizo, our colleagues from Bulgaria, Romania and Turkey will join us for lunch, during which we will have the opportunity to brief them on our discussions."[45] His government also took the significant step of announcing that it would no longer block Turkey's application for membership in the European Union. Island diplomacy, if it may be so called, was a sequel and a supplement to the earlier "earthquake diplomacy,"[46] which was also imaginatively premised on geography and its events in a zone of cultural clash and exchange. A huge quake in Turkey on August 17, 1999, and a smaller tremor in Greece on September 7, 1999, had brought forth unprecedented Greek-Turkish cooperation.

Demonstration Places

The setting of some diplomatic meetings, even global conferences that involve most of the world, can enhance the particular theme of the meeting and even the policies advocated there. Rio de Janeiro was the venue for the 1992 United Nations Conference on Environment and Development (UNCED), more informally known as the Earth Summit. It seemed the perfect place for such a gathering, the largest diplomatic conference ever up to that point, with 179 countries represented and thousands of nongovernmental organizations and other interested groups also present. The physical proximity of Rio de Janeiro, which was the stronghold of Brazil's Green Party, to the grandeur of luxuriant forests, though not to the vast Amazon interior itself, and also the city's own stark economic and social contrasts vividly illustrated the need to broaden concern about the environment and the course of development, which was the Earth Summit's purpose. The Statement of Forest Principles and United Nations Convention on Biological Diversity, as well as other positions that were formulated by UNCED, could hardly have failed to be influenced by the Brazilian city's evident greenery and poverty.

The city of Istanbul was the scene of the second United Nations Conference on Human Settlements (Habitat II) in 1996. The conference's theme was well fitted to its host geography. The then president of Turkey, Süleyman Demirel, declared frankly in welcoming the conference participants that Istanbul, former "capital of empires" and a "city of mesmerizing history," also "offers all the examples of the urbanization process, with its accomplishments as well as shortcomings." One of "the biggest" and most "densely populated megacities," he said, Istanbul was "in many ways the mirror image of the cities of the world." It also had a "unique geography," however. Spanning two continents, it had "served throughout history as a center for trade and cultural interaction between the cardinal points of the globe." It was, therefore, a crossroads, which, as is here noted, is conducive to mutual understanding and common decision. What, then, could be more appropriate, President Demirel asked, than for the nations of the world to meet here "to unite their efforts to address the issues of sustainable human development and providing adequate shelter for all?"[47]

Durban, South Africa, was the location of the World Conference against Racism, Racial Discrimination, Xenophobia, and Related Intolerance in 2001. It also was a logical venue for the conference's particular theme, which was given worldwide resonance by the selection of a South African site known for its complex racial history and prominent part in overcoming the curse of racial bias. The Durban Conference's controversial final Declaration and Programme of Action, which some observers feared might include the identification of Zionism with racism and also might demand reparations payments for the past harm of colonialism, included explicit references to the South African context of the meeting. "Drawing inspiration from the heroic struggle of the people of South Africa against the institutionalized system of apartheid," the conferees at the Durban Conference condemned racism and promised to fight against it in its many forms, particularly with regard to the African continent and the African diaspora elsewhere.[48]

"No Place"

The relative ease of modern electronic communication, combined with the demands of globalization, including the pressure on political leaders and others to frequently travel to distant places in which they have interests, suggests the possibility, indeed, the necessity, of replacing many international encounters with "virtual" diplomacy. This, one might assume, could occur without regard to geography, or "place," at all. Geography, however, is inescapable. Shifting the focus away from the place of international discussion through the use of teleconferencing or other real-time methods of communication raises, when the longitudes are widely separated, the question of the time of the discussion. For political leaders, as distinct from bureaucrats and diplomats who may be expected to be available around the clock, the issue of the hour of an encounter ("your time or mine?") can be an important one, for it raises not merely practical matters but also the question of who is accommodating whom.[49] When one country systematically dominates the time schedule of international conversation and decision making, there can arise what has been called "time imperialism."[50] Thus, even in a world of fiber optics and satellite communications, physical location—the nonvirtual venue—matters.

Logically, it follows that the greatest use of electronic forms of communication for real-time discussion among government leaders and diplomats occurs within particular geographic regions in which time-zone differences are minimal. The leading example of an electronically connected intergovernmental sphere within a particular geographic region is that of the European Union. The EU's COREU (CORrespondance EUropéenne) system, which was developed for the purpose of exchanging information and views as well as working drafts of documents in the context of the Common Foreign and Security Policy (CFSP), has enabled EU member countries and also EU-associated countries (connected through the Associated Countries Network [ACN]) to coordinate their policy decisions and actions. The EU-wide COREU system is analogous to, and is to some extent modeled on, the Intranet systems of individual EU member governments, which are needed for interdepartmental coordination and the development of positions at the national level.

For purposes of actual international negotiation between parties, especially those that do not belong to the same networked system, the potential of virtual or "no place" diplomacy would appear to be more limited. There have been some successful experiences, however. One of these is the negotiation that occurred during 2000 and 2001 between the Republic of Austria and the United States of America over the difficult issue of property restitution and compensation to victims of the Holocaust. The two heads of delegation, Ambassador Ernst Sucharipa for Austria and Ambassador Stuart Eizenstat for the United States, did meet personally. They did so, importantly, to set the parameters of the negotiation and, implicitly, to establish relations of mutual trust. At one point, teleconferencing, in which representatives of the victims organizations also were included, was tried. This experiment proved a failure. As Ambassador Sucharipa recalled, "[I]t just added to the misunderstanding or confusion that we wanted to clear." However, the Internet—e-mail—was used very successfully. Sending messages and exchanging drafts by e-mail made possible "concentration on content and substance," noted Sucharipa, with "no 'emotional noise.'" The use of e-mail and attachments also contributed to the "lucidity of formulation" when they were finally producing the text of an agreement. Even the "time factor," Sucharipa reflected, turned out to be advantageous, as each delegation could work according to its own "rhythm" without being constrained by the six-hour time difference between Vienna and Washington and the limited opportunity this allowed for real-time voice communication.[51] Thus for complicated negotiations over extended periods, virtual diplomacy, detached somewhat though hardly entirely from geography and place-related temporality, may increasingly be a supplement to reaching understanding and agreement at the international level.

Conclusion

In summary and conclusion, it can be seen that diplomacy today can happen almost anywhere and also almost "nowhere." Formerly Eurocentric, the system of diplomatic relations between states has a pattern. This is not only formal and institutional but also political and geographical. Diplomacy can take place in many more places than before, at accommodating venues around the world. Though it is possible for diplomatic meetings to be held anyplace, they are not. There is a causality and also a logic to what has been called "the geography of diplomacy." The question of site selection, as Jeswald Salacuse and Jeffrey Rubin point out, is often the first question asked. The answer given has consequences as well as, often, powerful forces and compelling reasons behind it. The choice of site for a diplomatic meeting rarely is perfectly arbitrary, though, as has been noted, there can be numerous subjective as well as objective factors that account for a conference's being held in one place rather than another. Underlying the free choice of players of the diplomatic game, however, is the geodiplomatic field on which the game is played. The field is not fixed, like the board on which chess pieces are set. Rather, as in chess, the "field" changes as the chess pieces are moved and assume different configurations that, though sometimes idiosyncratic, usually conform to the inherent logic and also the history of the game.

The choice of location is important because the "where" of diplomacy can affect the "what" of diplomatic subject and also of success or failure. Although the physical and political location of a diplomatic meeting is seldom if ever the decisive factor, it nonetheless conditions what happens there. Whether it is "your place" or "my place" or "another place" is not likely to tip the scales between war and peace. However, from the foregoing brief and illustrative analysis—or sketch for a "map"—of twelve different types of diplomatic location, it can be seen that some venues are more likely to be conducive to conflict and others are more likely to be conducive to cooperation. Generally, the "borderline" locations, at the bilateral interfaces between countries and on the peripheries of relations between them, seem to be the more conflict-related ones. However, confrontation between opposite parties and opposing issues can be a necessary prerequisite of the resolution of conflicts between countries. Equally generally, the "crossroads" locations, at metropolitan and other centers, appear to be the more cooperation-related venues. A trend has been suggested: from borderline-based to crossroads-focused diplomacy. This observation is premised on there being a gradual displacement of international conflict by international cooperation within the world system. As we have seen, however, the nature of the issues has changed. Conflict today is occurring not merely at borders but also within societies, for example, governments engaged in negotiating global economic arrangements and movements opposed to globalization. Protests within diplomatic centers may force diplomacy to the periphery or to virtual "centers" where place considerations, though still relevant, are less compelling.

Notes

1. Salacuse and Rubin, "Your Place or Mine?" 5. See also Salacuse, *Making Global Deals*, 10–21.

2. Henrikson, "Coming 'Magnesian' Age?"

3. Salacuse, *Making Global Deals*, 21, where the reference is to the place need of international businessmen.

4. The text of the U.S.-Chinese Joint Communiqué, February 28, 1972, is printed in Kissinger, *White House Years*, 1490–1492.

5. Clemens, *Yalta*. The selection of the location for the three leaders' meetings is discussed on pp. 107–111.

6. Chamberlin, *America's Second Crusade*, 206–231.

7. Gilbert and Gott, *Appeasers*, 144–185.

8. Salacuse and Rubin, "Your Place or Mine?" 5–6.

9. Webster, *Congress of Vienna*; Nicolson, *Congress of Vienna*.

10. United Nations, *Journal of the Preparatory Commission*, 84.

11. Henrikson, "Creation of the North Atlantic Alliance"; Reid, *Time of Fear and Hope*.

12. Henrikson, "Ottawa, Washington, and the Founding of NATO." By speculative analogy with international trade diplomacy, had the conference held in Havana, Cuba, for the purpose of negotiating a treaty to create an International Trade Organization (ITO) been held instead in Washington, the result might have been establishment of a full-fledged ITO, rather than merely the General Agreement on Tariffs and Trade (GATT), which was eventually replaced by the present World Trade Organization (WTO).

13. Salacuse and Rubin, "Your Place or Mine?" 8.

14. City of Geneva. The official Web Site, "The 'Four Great Powers,' Conference."

15. "Interview with President Bush—October 1997."

16. Ibid.

17. "Ten Years On."

18. Bearak, "India Leader Pays Visit to Pakistan," noted and discussed in Henrikson, "Facing across Borders," 142–143.

19. Waldman, "India Announces Steps in Effort to End Its Conflict with Pakistan."

20. Remarks by President George W. Bush and President Vicente Fox of Mexico in Joint Press Conference, Rancho San Cristóbal, San Cristóbal, Mexico, White House Press Release, February 16, 2001.

21. Hall, *World Cities*.

22. Gottmann, *Megalopolis*, 4.

23. United Nations, Preparatory Commission, *Committee 8: General Questions*, 62–63, *Commission Handbooks, Journal, Reports, Summary Reports* (1945).

24. Association of the Bar of the City of New York, "New York City and the United Nations."

25. Bernstein, "United Nations Should Move to World Trade Center Site."

26. *Geneva, Switzerland, Welcome*, 3.

27. Bugnion, *Comité International de la Croix-Rouge*.

28. *Geneva, Switzerland, Welcome*, 3.

29. At the same time, the city used its well-established and modernizing metropolitan base to become an international headquarters—in 1957 of the International Atomic Energy Organization (IAEO), in 1965 of the Organization of Petroleum Exporting Countries (OPEC), and in 1967 of the United Nations Industrial Development Organization (UNIDO). In 1979 the United Nations made Vienna, after New York and Geneva, its third headquarters, "the only one in an EU capital." See *Livin' Vienna*, 11. The Vienna International Centre, commonly referred to as UNO City, is "the landmark of modern-day Vienna," states its mayor, Michael Häupl; see *International Organizations in Vienna*, 3. A great number of international NGOs also are headquartered in Vienna because of its geographic proximities as well as its social amenities.

30. *Livin' Vienna*, 11.

31. International Olympic Truce Center.

32. Agreement between the United Nations and the United States Regarding the Headquarters of the United Nations, signed on June 26, 1947, and approved by the General Assembly, October 31, 1947.

33. UN Security Council Resolution 242, S/RES/242, November 22, 1947.
34. Picco, *Man without a Gun.*
35. Sullivan, "Borderline Absurdity."
36. Kirk, "U.S. General Defends Chats at Panmunjom."
37. "To End a War" Holbrooke, pp. 280–281.
38. Johnson, "Negotiating the Dayton Peace Accords through Digital Maps."
39. Richard Holbrooke, U.S. permanent representative to the United Nations, speech marking the fifth anniversary of the Dayton Peace Accords, Dayton, Ohio, November 17, 2000.
40. John Kirton, "Canada's G7/G8 Diplomacy and Approach to Kananaskis."
41. Smith, "Defence of Summitry."
42. Kahn, "Nations Back Freer Trade."
43. Kahn, "Equality at Trade Talks."
44. APEC Economic Leaders Declaration, Bogor, Indonesia, November 15, 1994.
45. George A. Papandreou, letter by the President of the Council of Ministers to his counterparts on the Informal Council (GYMNICH).
46. Kriner, " 'Earthquake Diplomacy.' "
47. H. E. Süleyman Demirel, president of the Republic of Turkey.
48. Durban Declaration and Programme of Action.
49. Salacuse, *Making Global Deals*, 21–27.
50. Gleditsch, "Time Differences and International Interaction." 47.
51. Sucharipa, "Use of the Internet in Diplomacy and Negotiations."

References

Association of the Bar of the City of New York. "New York City and the United Nations: Towards a Renewed Relationship." A Report by the Special Committee on the United Nations of the Association of the Bar of the City of New York, December 2001. http://abcny.org (accessed May 18, 2003).

Bearak, Barry. "India Leader Pays Visit to Pakistan." *New York Times*, February 21, 1999, section 1, p. 1, column 5, Foreign desk.

Bernstein, Fred A. "United Nations Should Move to World Trade Center Site." *New York Daily News*, November 6, 2001.

Bugnion, François. *Le Comité International de la Croix-Rouge et la protection des victimes de la guerre*. Geneva: Comité International de la Croix-Rouge, 1994.

Chamberlin, William Henry. *America's Second Crusade*. Chicago: Henry Regnery Company, 1950.

City of Geneva—The official Web Site. "The 'Four Great Powers' Conference." www.ville-ge.ch/site99/politique/e_eynard.htm (accessed May 13, 2003).

Clemens, Diane Shaver. *Yalta*. New York: Oxford University Press, 1972.

Demirel, H. E. Süleyman. Address to the United Nations Conference on Human Settlements, Lüftü Kirdar Convention Center, Istanbul, June 3, 1996. www.un.org/Conferences/habitat/eng-stat/3/trkza.text (accessed May 4, 2003).

Durban Declaration and Programme of Action. World Conference Against Racism, Racial Discrimination, Xenophobia and Related Intolerance. Durban, South Africa, August 31–September 8, 2001.

Geneva, Switzerland, Welcome: Where People Meet. Geneva: Geneva Tourism, n.d.

Gilbert, Martin, and Richard Gott. *The Appeasers*. Boston: Houghton Mifflin, 1963.

Gleditsch, Nils Petter. "Time Differences and International Interaction." *Cooperation and Conflict: Nordic Journal of International Politics* 9 (1974): 35–51.

Gottmann, Jean. *Megalopolis: The Urbanized Northeastern Seaboard of the United States.* Cambridge, MA: MIT Press, 1961.

Hall, Peter. *The World Cities.* 2nd ed. New York: McGraw-Hill, 1979.

Henrikson, Alan K. "The Creation of the North Atlantic Alliance." In *American Defense Policy*, 5th ed., ed. John R. Reichart and Steven R. Sturm, 296–323. Baltimore: Johns Hopkins University Press, 1982.

Henrikson, Alan K. "Ottawa, Washington, and the Founding of NATO." In *Fifty Years of Canada-U.S. Defense Cooperation: The Road from Ogdensburg*, ed. Joel L. Sokolsky and Joseph T. Jockel, 82–125. Lewiston, NY: Edwin Mellen, 1992.

Henrikson, Alan K. "Facing across Borders: The Diplomacy of *Bon Voisinage*." *International Political Science Review/Revue Internationale de Science Politique* 21 (April 2000): 121–147.

Henrikson, Alan K. "A Coming 'Magnesian' Age? Small States, the Global System, and the International Community." *Geopolitics* 6 (winter 2001): 49–86.

Holbrooke, Richard. *To End a War.* New York: Random House, 1998.

Holbrooke, Richard, interview. *NewsHour with Jim Lehrer*, PBS, May 19, 1998.

International Olympic Truce Center. www.olympictruce.org/html (accessed May 25, 2003).

International Organizations in Vienna. Vienna: Press and Information Services, City of Vienna, 2002.

Johnson, Richard G. "Negotiating the Dayton Peace Accords through Digital Maps." Seminar on "Virtual Diplomacy—Case Studies," United States Institute of Peace, Washington, DC, February 25, 1999.

"Interview with President Bush—October 1997." The National Security Archive, The George Washington University, Washington, DC, http://gwu.edu/~wnsarchive/coldwar/interviews/episode-23/bush2.html (accessed May 13, 2003).

Kahn, Joseph. "Equality at Trade Talks: No Country Gets a Vote." *New York Times*, November 12, 2001, section A, p. 3, column 1, Foreign desk.

Kahn, Joseph. "Nations Back Freer Trade, Hoping to Aid Global Growth." *New York Times*, November 15, 2001, section A, p. 12, column 3, Foreign desk.

Kirk, Don. "U.S. General Defends Chats at Panmunjom." *International Herald Tribune*, December 18, 1998, 7.

Kirton, John. "Canada's G7/G8 Diplomacy and Approach to Kananaskis." G8online, 2002 Course, University of Toronto, February 21, 2003. www.library.utoronto.ca/g7/g8online/english/2002/11.html (accessed May 25, 2003).

Kissinger, Henry. *White House Years.* Boston: Little, Brown, 1979.

Kriner, Stephanie. " 'Earthquake Diplomacy' Serves to Unite Two Long-Time Mediterranean Rivals." *Disaster Relief*, September 28, 1999. www.disasterrelief.org/Disasters/990915friendship (accessed May 3, 2003).

Livin' Vienna: Einblicke in das Leben einer Metropole. Vienna: Presse- und Informationsdienst der Stadt Wien, 2000.

Nicolson, Harold. *The Congress of Vienna: A Study in Allied Unity, 1812–1822.* London: Constable, 1946.

Pampandreou, George A. Letter by the President of the Council of Ministers to his counterparts on the Informal Council (GYMNICH), Rhodes and Kastellorizo, May 2–4, 2003. www.papandreou.gr (accessed May 1, 2003).

Picco, Giandomenico. *Man without a Gun: One Diplomat's Secret Struggle to Free the Hostages, Fight Terrorism, and End a War.* New York: Times Books, 1999.

Reid, Escott. *Time of Fear and Hope: The Making of the North Atlantic Treaty*. Toronto: McClelland and Stewart, 1977.

Salacuse, Jeswald W. *Making Global Deals: What Every Executive Should Know about Negotiating Abroad*. Cambridge, MA: PON Books, the Program on Negotiation at Harvard Law School, 1991.

Salacuse, Jeswald W., and Jeffrey Z. Rubin. "Your Place or Mine? Site Location and Negotiation." *Negotiation Journal*, January 1990, 5–10.

Smith, Gordon S. "Defence of Summitry: Here's What Will, or Will Not, Happen When the World's Most Powerful Men Gather in the Hills of Alberta." *Ottawa Citizen*, June 25, 2002, A17.

Sucharipa, Ernst. "The Use of the Internet in Diplomacy and Negotiations—The Experience of a Practitioner." In 36. *Jahrbuch 2001/36th Yearbook, Diplomatische Akademie Wien*, 290–294. Vienna: Diplomatische Akademie Wien, 2000.

Sullivan, Kevin. "Borderline Absurdity: A Fun-Filled Tour of the Korean DMZ." *Washington Post*, January 11, 1998, Travel section, E1.

"Ten Years On," *The Malta Independent on Sunday Online*, November 7, 1999. www.archive.independent.com.mt/385/27.html (accessed May 13, 2003).

United Nations. *Journal of the Preparatory Commission, 24 November–24 December 1945* London: Church House, Westminster, 1945.

United Nations, Preparatory Commission. *Committee 8: General Questions, 24 November–24 December 1945*. London: Church House, Westminster, 1945.

Waldman, Amy. "India Announces Steps in Effort to End its Conflict with Pakistan." *New York Times*, May 3, 2003, section A, p. 1, column 5.

Webster, Charles K. *The Congress of Vienna, 1814–1815*. New York: Barnes and Noble, 1963.

IAN OAS

Shifting the Iron Curtain of Kantian Peace

NATO Expansion and the Modern Magyars

For us, this is a new beginning.

—Romanian president Ion Iliescu,
former Communist minister

This day will become history. We are making a decision that will finally put an end to the era of the divisions . . . and the cold war.

—Polish president Aleksander Kwasniewski,
former Communist minister

I hope that this step will be a reminder to those forces in Russia who may still think in terms of the former Soviet empire that those days are gone . . . they are on the dustheap of history.

—Latvian president Vaira Vike-Freiberga

As the head of Latvia's minute military, Colonel Raimanos Graube, notes, the ascension of the Latvian state into NATO is part of a much larger process than military security alone: "This means we are moving to our goal, which is to be a firm and permanent part of the West."[1] Though such a viewpoint is common among the populaces of ascending member states, it helps raise numerous questions as to several inherent contradictions in the reasoning behind NATO expansion. To begin with, why are numerous states that just over ten years ago regained their sovereign independence from the Soviet empire so suddenly willing to join a new, hegemonic-backed Western empire? Furthermore, what are the true reasons that underlie NATO members' interest in expanding their military alliance into nation-states with military forces comprised of only 5,500 members (e.g., Latvia)?[2]

There is more at play in NATO expansion than simple geopolitical security as defined by the international relations (IR) field. Indeed, it will be argued that above and beyond security for central Europe, contemporary NATO expansion is a moment in the cycle of the U.S. rise to world power. Moreover, it will be illustrated that ascension of central and Eastern European states into NATO may represent the final surrender of the socialist modernity as global competitor to the West. In this historical battlefield between Eastern and Western modernities, the socialist modernity that dominated during much of the region's twentieth-century history is now reviled by these civil societies and viewed as the antithesis of modernity. In the meantime, the Western lifestyle of mass consumption and suburbanism, as well as other dominant core processes from Western Europe in general, raised the flag of market capitalism and democratic institutions in these states and filled the power vacuum just as quickly as the Soviet red stars came down.[3] In this way, NATO is becoming increasingly synonymous with a "zone of peace" wherein all members ascribe to democracy, free trade, and interdependent relations. By joining NATO, new member states are making a political effort to shed the yoke of the failed Soviet modernity and join the hegemonic-led "Western" world (i.e., become "part of Europe").[4] By enlisting the holistic framework of the capitalist world-economy as the underlying structure in which NATO expansion takes place, it is possible to cross-analyze why central European states desire to join NATO with what exactly NATO might expect to gain in return from expansion into former enemy states.

The following research is based solely on archival study of both Hungarian reactions to NATO expansion and NATO's official publications during its continuing expansion. That is, the domestic glee and turmoil that resulted from surrendering state sovereignty to the hegemonic institution will be analyzed, as well as what the United States gains through the institution's expansion. Through the use of comparative analysis to highlight the contradiction between NATO expansion (at a time when NATO matters less than ever) and why states such as Hungary overwhelmingly desire to join the organization, several theoretical scenarios will emerge. More than just for security's sake, Hungary desires to be "modern," a member of Western society, and to separate itself from the past Soviet modernity it was shackled to during the past forty-five years. However, with this desire, domestic and international tensions will arise within Hungarian society, particularly as the United States attempts to use Hungary to its own advantage (e.g., in the war on terrorism).

The rest of this chapter will unfold in the following manner. First, the history and structure of NATO will be reviewed, as well as its dynamic role in international geopolitics during the last fifty years. This will segue into analysis of NATO's "success" as defined within its charter and through the concept of Kantian peace—has NATO provided international peace as an organization that connects interdependent economies? Furthermore, whose peace does NATO represent? A review of the U.S. hegemony's role within the organization and its instrumentalist purpose for forging a hegemonic order will be conducted. How and why does the United States use NATO? These questions will lead to defining the purpose of contemporary NATO expansion within the context of the Soviet Union's demise. Finally, analysis of "who gains what" from NATO in the contemporary geopolitical order will be conducted by looking at the Hungarian condition within the NATO expansion process.

NATO: Place and Role in Current History

The North Atlantic Treaty Organization was forged at the beginning of the Cold War between the emerging U.S. hegemony and the USSR, the only formidable resistance faced by the United States after World War II. Under U.S. guidance, and using the United Nations Charter to support their claims that a military alliance treaty was legal, twelve states signed the NATO Charter and gave birth to the North Atlantic Treaty Organization on April 4, 1949: Belgium, Canada, Denmark, France, Iceland, Italy, Luxembourg, the Netherlands, Norway, Portugal, the United Kingdom, and the United States.[5] The reason for the alliance's development was officially to promote a "secure Europe," but due to its quick creation following the Berlin crisis and a Communist coup in Czechoslovakia, NATO was quite overtly an act whereby the United States was guaranteeing the security of free, democratic states that were partaking in the open-market economy. It was not necessarily offering security to all of "Europe," as Hungary discovered during the 1956 uprising.

NATO is a military agreement between all signatory states to aid one another in case of an attack by another, outside force. That is, an attack on one member state is an attack on all member states. This unity of force is achieved through member states' agreement to surrender certain aspects of their individual sovereignties to this transnational organization in order to ensure protection against hostile takeover by other states. Originally NATO was established as a united front against any potential Soviet military incursion into Western Europe with the backing and membership of the U.S. superpower and its Canadian neighbor. Thus throughout the Cold War NATO continued to grow as new states decided to join for the benefits that mutual security could bring. Eventually NATO expanded over the sovereignty of Turkey, Greece, West Germany, and Spain. It coalesced the militaries of Western European states within one overarching structure of control, primarily under U.S. guidance. Not only did this treaty ensure the security of Western Europe from conventional Soviet attack, but it also allowed for the deployment of U.S. short-range missiles in Europe to balance the Soviet nuclear threat to these states. Furthermore, the treaty virtually precluded the attack of member states against one another and offered Western Europe its first real semblance of security from interstate war in more than 100 years, though disagreements between Turkey and Greece often threatened to disrupt the peace. Though the United States created several other containment pacts, including the Southeast Asia Treaty Organization (SEATO) and the Central Treaty Organization in the Middle East (CENTRO), NATO stood out as the primary one due to the geopolitical and geoeconomic importance of Western Europe to the United States.

After the fall of Communism, particularly the disintegration of the Warsaw Pact in 1991, many argued that NATO's central purpose had disappeared and that it would likely thereafter wither. However, during the past decade NATO has held numerous summit meetings to redefine its primary purpose. On the basis of the agreement that the treaty has always been about security, NATO policy after the Cold War has been one of expanding the alliance eastward to include states that have recently gained independence from Communist regimes. States that previously lay in the Soviet sphere of power or did not exist at all are being admitted to the treaty organization as long as they demonstrate a successful transition to open-market economies and democratic governments. The policy of NATO expansion is premised upon an implicit strategy that Ó Tuathail terms "enlargement geopolitics": the diffusion of democracy and free-market principles through the guise of paninstitutions, in which those that are incorporated will not wage war on one another and thus, in the case of NATO, will stabilize Europe from violent conflict that might otherwise erupt and disrupt the world order.[6]

During its history, NATO has been largely successful at maintaining peace between states and nations that traditionally have waged war against one another (e.g., France, Germany, the United Kingdom, Italy, Spain, and the United States). As a buffer against the Warsaw Pact, NATO played a role in preventing Soviet military incursion into Western Europe. Thus, overall, NATO has performed astonishingly well at containing European interstate disagreements within its institution and preventing violent conflict among member states as well as between member and nonmember states. Thus it only makes sense that NATO's recent goal has been to expand the number of states in its jurisdictional framework to further the territory enveloped by this institution of proto-Kantian peace.

Due to its geographic location within and across the historically volatile continent of Europe, NATO more obviously epitomizes Kant's "zones of peace" argument than many other international institutions.. Immanuel Kant argued that a universalist peace is attainable and that societies are inherently striving for such a peace, even if their overt pronouncements would lead one to believe otherwise.[7] He believed that universal peace is an evolutionary process that is not yet attained and is likely to develop in stages—first through specific zones of peace that coexist and, when these zones of peace eventually become interdependent, will envelop all of civil society. The true underpinnings of conflict within global civil society are ideological, not necessarily national. States simply represent a means of social organization that is loosely based around the concept of the nation, but they do not demarcate the boundaries of human identity and interaction. The ideological battles that ensue (e.g., Communism versus democracy; command economy versus capitalism; Islam versus Western atheism; and so on) in the process of universally uniting human society cut through state boundaries. Once states settle into the same ideological camp (e.g., democratization) and garner enough economic interaction and codependence, they will eventually settle into peace with one another and thus establish zones of peace.[8]

Kantian peace is based on three elements: democratization, codependence as established through economic interaction, and joint membership in international institutions.[9] The first two Kantian principles are general prerequisites before a country joins NATO, whereas the third principle is manifest in NATO itself. NATO represents an institution that bonds together the military organizations of states that agree upon the common ideology of democratic government and free trade. It ties these states together above and beyond simple economic and political selfishness at the state level and propels these states to work in unison for the ideological ideal of a "democratic peace."

However, universalism as defined by Kant will result in ideological battles between the universalist camp (in this case, NATO states) and other, nonuniversalist enemies: "The rules that sustain coexistence and social intercourse among states should be ignored if the imperatives of [universalism] require it. Good faith with heretics has no meaning, except in terms of tactical convenience; between the elect and the damned, the liberators and the oppressed, the question of mutual acceptance of rights to sovereignty or independence does not arise."[10] Put in this light, NATO has succeeded as an institution of interdependence for democratic states in defeating the Soviet "heretical" resistance and in opening up new neighboring states to the ideological underpinnings of NATO's zone of peace: democracy, open trade, and international institutions. However, what are missing from this theoretical argument are discussions concerning what institution has the power to continually propel this universalist battle. Furthermore, with such an inordinate amount of power, why would this institution, for example, a superpower state, promote universalism instead of attempting to subjugate the world?

Peace, but Whose and for What Gain?

The actual North Atlantic Treaty is remarkably basic and to the point. It begins with a five-sentence preamble that declares that the states that are signing the treaty are "determined to safeguard the freedom, common heritage and civilization of their peoples, founded on the principles of democracy, individual liberty and the rule of law."[11] Essentially, the treaty can be read as a direct indictment against those who might militarily confront liberal democracies in Europe—liberal democracies that comprise a large part of the core states in the capitalist world-economy. Thus, given Kant's analysis of international conflict as the clash of universalism and other nonuniversalist ideologies, it is no surprise that immediately after NATO's inception, the Soviet Union protested that it was illegal under the UN Charter and, upon losing, formed its own alliance, the Warsaw Pact. The universalist battle had begun. But is NATO really an institution that is used by democracies to maintain and spread liberal universalism, or is it something more insidious? Evidence supports the argument that NATO was created and has since been maneuvered by a powerful actor in the geopolitical order—the world hegemony.

The United States rose to hegemony from the ashes of World War II. World hegemony is defined by a single state's ability to dominate the world economically, which in turn results in technological and political leadership at the global scale. The United States began its rise to hegemony during the United Kingdom's downfall at the end of the nineteenth century. Competition between the United Kingdom and Germany for the global leadership position eventually plunged the world into chaos, which began World War I and culminated with the end of World War II.[12]

In the past, hegemony has gone through a cycle that has lasted approximately 100 years, and during this cycle its primary role has been to ensure and maintain political and economic stability at the global scale. Toward the end of its cycle, competitive states have attempted to usurp the hegemony, which often leads to great instability such as that witnessed in the first half of the twentieth century. The world hegemony is dependent upon stability and order in the international political economy because it maintains the most dominant domestic market in the world, and only through stable and consistent trading can it maintain its position of power. After World War II, with no direct damage to its infrastructure during the conflict, the United States not only dominated in production and trade, but stood in a position to finance the rebuilding of Europe and rise to high hegemony.[13]

However, hegemonic power is not derived simply from a dominant economy alone. Even before World War II had officially ended, the United States had begun setting up institutions of extraterritorial control to help solidify its position within the world-economy at large. These extraterritorial institutions fostered an interdependent community between participating states. The United Nations, the World Bank, and other organizations were established as instrumentalist tools in order to solidify power and forge stability once the war ended.[14] As these organizations took root and gained acceptance by the international community by the war's end, the United States was ready to take the reins of hegemonic leadership. One such institution of hegemonic extraterritoriality was NATO.

Through this military, codependent institution, the United States successfully gained influence over various aspects of fourteen European militaries.[15] Furthermore, it had largely secured the markets of Western Europe from the competing Soviet empire. With stability largely intact over Western Europe, the capitalist markets of the world-economy could interact harmoniously, and the hegemony could feed its need to exploit capital from foreign markets. The United States did the same thing in Japan by building a constitutional military alliance with Japan in order to prevent Soviet incursions. Even today, stability in the core states of Western Europe and Japan remains a cornerstone of U.S. hegemonic power, and NATO continues to help the hegemony ensure that particular European states do not descend into warfare with one another.

Above and beyond economic dominance, the hegemonic power's ability to forge stability at the global scale is dependent upon two types of extraterritorial power over other sovereigns: political and military.[16] Extraterritorial power begins under the imperatives of economic exploitation, because the hegemony needs open markets to successfully use its dominant economic position and extract surplus capital. It can open markets in numerous ways, most obviously through the threat of, and more rarely the actual use of, force, but most successfully through the establishment of international institutions.[17] By establishing transnational institutions that incorporate other states but fall under the hegemony's control, the hegemony is able to exert its sovereignty and wishes over other states while forbidding these same states from infringing on the hegemony's own sovereignty.[18] The United States has done this more substantially and thoroughly than many past hegemonies. It established economic institutions to help it control other states' economic policies (e.g., the IMF and the General Agreement on Tariffs and Trade). It created an international political institution that fronts as a quasi world government (i.e., the United Nations). Finally, in NATO it forged a transatlantic military alliance to stave off the military threat of the main opposition to its hegemonic power, the Soviet Union.

With institutions of extraterritoriality firmly established in the world-economy, there is yet another more inherent facet to hegemonic power—the prime modernity. Taylor defines "prime modernity" as the dominant way of life in the world-economy that is synonymous with the hegemony itself.[19] The hegemony's technological abilities come to be viewed throughout all societies as the epitome of modernity, and the hegemony's lifestyle and methods of socialization become emulated by other societies. Though the prime modernity is enticing, it is an insidious tool that is used by the world hegemony to ideologically undermine resistance against U.S. extraterritoriality.[20] Prime modernity is centered upon an economic innovation that is brought about by the hegemony and leads to a change in lifestyle—under Dutch hegemony, "mercantilism"; under British hegemony, "industrialization"; and under the United States "mass consumerism."[21] These economic innovations induce a new modern way of life and socialization that is exported as the path to the future for other states. In essence, the hegemony cajoles other societies into opening their economies and political structures to the capitalist world-economy and into accepting the hegemonic institutions of extraterritoriality through the propagation of the belief that through emulation of the hegemonic way, states will be propelled into the "modern" world through "development." Unfortunately, the prime modernity is a mirage, an opulent way of life that is impossible for most societies to ever gain.[22] Because the prime modernity is built upon exploitive processes for the benefit of the hegemony, exploitation must remain for the prime modernity to exist. Thus not every society can "develop."[23] Yet, empty promises aside, the exportation of the "American Dream" remains an inherent aspect of U.S. hegemonic power.

With the fall of the Soviet Union, the United States quickly found itself in a strategic conundrum—it was a hegemony without any true competition. This dramatic void in power conflict at the international scale and the ensuing period of adaptation to it affected not only the hegemonic state, but also the extraterritorial institutions it had established during the height of its hegemony. Suddenly these institutions that had helped to push U.S. sovereignty into other states to protect and spread the "Western way of life" had to redefine their roles in order to stay viable parts of global geopolitics. For many of these institutions, particularly the economic ones, such as the IMF, the GATT, the World Trade Organization, and the World Bank, the collapse of communism was a windfall of opportunity and expansion. With expansive new spaces opening up to capitalist processes, the opportunity for exploitation and spreading the capitalist market increased dramatically. Development of the Second World was a top concern, arguably so that east central Europe could eventually join modern Europe.[24] Yet for other hegemonic institutions, primarily the military alliances that had been forged to prevent the militant spread of global socialism, the end of the Cold War was very confounding. As the international consensus behind the Gulf War of 1991 demonstrated, there were no clearly identifiable resistances against U.S. hegemony at the global scale.[25]

As hegemonic institutions went, NATO was one of the most fallible institutions after the bipolar order had ended, standing out as a glaring example of hegemonic influence within Europe. Though it still worked as a tool for securing Europe from falling into war with itself, long-standing skirmishes between Turkey and Greece offered consistent reminders of the fragility of this supposed mission. Though the hegemony desperately desired to keep NATO as a viable political-military institution, European states could question its need and perhaps see reason to attempt to relinquish the yoke of hegemonic oversight, particularly as more states joined the European Union. In fact, the United Kingdom, Germany, and France have continually discussed the possibility of building a Euro Force that would be comprised of soldiers from EU states to be coupled with an EU foreign policy.[26] Thus in order to keep NATO from dissipating completely, the United States has needed to redefine the organization's role beyond defending Europe against imperial conquest from the east—NATO needed to take on a higher meaning.

This was done by revamping NATO, not as an anti-Communist alliance but as a military alliance among all "modern" (i.e., democratic and open-market) European states. The alliance changed its role from a military defense and counter-attack organization to one of facilitator of peaceful coexistence and builder of trust between democratic nation-states. This transition might have been difficult to swallow for many European states had it not been for other interdependent organizations' incompetence in dealing with the Balkan crisis. By the mid-1990s both UN peacekeepers and European Union mandates had failed to stymie the violent civil wars that had broken out in the "powder keg of Europe." The conflicts in the former Yugoslavia, coupled with ethnic tension between numerous nations across central Europe, made a strong case for an overarching military alliance that would secure Europe from itself. When NATO was used in the Bosnian conflict, it became apparent that within and through this institution members of Western Europe could reach consensus and maintain security for themselves while relying on U.S. hegemonic power.

One method of securing modern Europe from conflicts that spilled over from the tensions of central Europe in the mid-1990s was through the expansion of NATO into states that were stable and developing democratically and further integrating into the capitalist world-economy (i.e., the Czech Republic, Hungary, and Poland).[27] Just as with previous NATO expansion, contemporary expansion into these states was as much about defending the markets and cultures of a democratic, capitalist Europe as it was about providing security to states that were threatened by outside nuisances. Yet for different state actors, the expansion of NATO meant different things.

For Western European states, expansion was largely seen as increasing stability by spreading the buffer zone of mutual security to states that had once been part of modern Europe anyway—the Czech Republic, Hungary, and Poland had distinguished histories in European politics and were Catholic as opposed to Orthodox.[28] Russia saw it as an encroachment and semihostile action that harkened back to the Cold War.[29] To Hungary, joining NATO represented less an increase in security—the Bosnian crisis was not really a serious threat—than an opportunity to ascend to the West and join an alliance that represented the prime modernity.[30] For the United States, expansion of NATO represented an opportunity to seize upon the acquiescence of the hegemonic contender, the former Soviet Union, and extend its extraterritorial grip.[31] Moreover, expansion of NATO would concurrently increase stability further inland from the Atlantic, something important now that the bipolar order of the Cold War was past and the state system was slipping into a perceived period of chaos and ethnic conflict.[32]

In 1998, with little debate and after a national referendum placed support at 85%, the Republic of Hungary bought both the modernity and security facets of NATO expansion and opted to join the hegemonic military alliance less than ten years after gaining its independence from the Soviet-backed Warsaw Pact. On April 4, 1999, at a ceremony in the heart of U.S. hegemonic politics, Washington, D.C., Hungary was officially admitted into the Western military organization. Having reviewed why the United States strongly supported NATO expansion into Hungary, we must now look at the opposite perspective: what did Hungarians see themselves gaining in so strongly supporting their state's ascension into this extraterritorial institution of the world hegemony?

Hungary and NATO: Sovereignty versus Interdependence

Hungary was not on perilous ground before it joined NATO. As it already had UN and NATO peacekeeping troops stationed on its territory due to the Balkan crisis, any potential spillovers from militant neighbor states were preempted. Threats from neighbors were largely innocuous—nothing more than the empty rhetoric of right-wing party spokesmen in Slovakia and Romania who had no real power in their countries' parliamentary processes.[33] It could be argued that the desire to join NATO stemmed from the Hungarian states attempt to extend security to the entire Hungarian nation, including the vast diaspora in neighboring states that represented 33% of the Hungarian nation's population. Romania, Slovakia, and Serbia, in particular, were attempting to forcibly assimilate Hungarian ethnic populations, which numbered around five million, into their societies, much to the ire of the Hungarian Republic.[34] It was argued by some at the time of NATO expansion that once Hungary was in the military organization, it might hold more political sway and power over its neighbors in leveraging an end to ethnic tension in less democratic states.[35] However, such an approach on Hungary's relinquishment of its military sovereignty to the West ignores several larger, external processes that influenced the Hungarian decision to join NATO.[36]

From the Magyar point of view, Hungary's ascension into NATO represents far more than just a simple quest for state security. Though the perceived benefits of ascension into NATO varied drastically among vying political groups and social strata, one underlying trait united a majority of Hungarians—a desire to officially switch sides from the former Eastern modernity of the Soviet empire to a Western modernity as represented by the U.S. hegemony. Indeed, joining the Western military alliance may not have been as much about "security" of sovereignty as it was about gaining "stability" through interdependence. By joining Western states in this alliance, Hungary was solidifying its place as a Western ally in the U.S. hegemonic order, it was ascribing to the prime modernity.

In Hungary this desire for interdependence with the West was felt across a broad spectrum of the population that largely transcended people's ideological, class, ethnic, and otherwise divergent backgrounds. In fact, for Hungarians there was little choice but to integrate into the international institution of NATO if continued economic development was desired. Agh believes that in order for small states in central Europe to maintain their sovereignty in the post-Communist era, they must adapt to and accept the international, extraterritorial institutions that were set up in their period of abstinence from the world-economy.[37] If Hungary and other states in central Europe refuse to accept hegemonic and Western institutions (e.g., NATO, the European Union [EU], and these organizations' policies), certain economic and political aspects of these states' sovereignties may be conveniently ignored by the West entirely (e.g., Serbia's sovereignty in Kosovo was ignored and then stripped away by NATO).[38] Yet it should be noted that there is also much for small states to gain from joining such international political structures. With the backing of the U.S. hegemony and other Western states, Hungary "will certainly have much more influence in the [east central European] and Balkan regions from inside NATO than from the outside."[39]

The importance of increasing the new Hungarian Republic's interdependence in the world-economy can be analyzed by looking at what various Magyar subgroups and institutions stood to gain personally by supporting Hungary's ascension into NATO. The rest of this chapter will analyze the dynamics behind three important Hungarian political institutions' desire to join NATO: the two major Hungarian political parties and the Hungarian military. For the Hungarian Socialist Party (HSP), which was attempting to evolve from being the former Hungarian Communist Party, promoting ascension into NATO became its primary political goal in order to completely shed suspicions concerning its former Soviet linkages.[40] To those of the Right, assimilating into NATO provided insurance against future Russian imperialism, as well as a position of leverage in order to protect Hungarian minorities in states that lie adjacent to Hungary but outside of NATO.[41] Perhaps most important, to the Hungarian armed forces, NATO expansion offered a means by which to update and redefine their place in Hungarian civil society.[42]

Domestic Politics and Interdependence

The decision to hold a referendum on joining NATO—Hungary is the only state to have done this—was inherently political since no major party was against ascension. Yet perhaps due to all the hoopla over the referendum's success, remarkably little was made of the incredible 180-degree turnaround for the Hungarian Socialist Party, which was surprisingly willing to surrender Hungary's sovereignty to the U.S. hegemony only six years after the dissolution of the Warsaw Pact.[43] The former Communist Party had spent nearly four years preparing Hungary for ascension and had pushed the policy through with stunning success. The HSP's ability to move Hungary into NATO represented a triumphant shedding of the Communist legacy that had plagued the party.

In the first democratic elections of 1990, the revamped Communists, who had conveniently renamed themselves the Hungarian Socialist Party, had a very difficult time appealing to the electorate, took only 5% of the national vote, and barely gained representation in Parliament. However, by the national elections of 1994, the economic struggles of transition to an open-market economy were weighing heavily on the population. The Socialists had revamped themselves as professionals and technocrats who knew how to best solve the problems of transition that faced Hungary's workforce, yet at the same time could best integrate Hungary into modern Europe.[44] This turnaround in posture was an explicit strategy of the former Communists to save liberal socialism from dissolving entirely. By revamping the party as anti-Communism but prolabor while at the same time appealing to those who aspired to be Western by arguing that Hungary's rightful place was in "modern" Europe, the Socialists came to dominate the elections of 1994.[45]

Through consistent and incessant lobbying during its four years in power (1994–1998), the HSP easily garnered enough national support for NATO expansion and integration into the European Union. This strategy successfully severed the already rusty connection the party maintained to the old Soviet modernity, but in May 1998, six months after the successful NATO referendum, the HSP lost the national elections to FIDESZ (the Young Democrats Party). Though FIDESZ was not opposed to NATO expansion or EU ascension, it played the xenophobic rhetoric card just enough to bump the triumphant Socialists out of the government. Perhaps due to its progressive and pro-West stance, during its reign the HSP had beleaguered the labor market, which felt that its needs were being circumvented for the benefit of foreign firms. The Young Democrats appealed to voters who were suffering from economic transition with xenophobic rhetoric about the HSP selling the country to foreigners. In a twist of irony, the Socialists suddenly became the cosmopolitan, pro-West party that was attempting to guide Hungary to the new modernity, whereas the Right began seizing the labor vote. Thus during their first tenure in power, the Socialists firmly established their party's position as pro-West and admonished many Communist hangovers, but this success came at a heavy cost: the state ascended into a modern Western institution, but the party lost control of the state apparatus to a party that Magyars viewed as more "national."

Upon the Young Democrats Party's successful election to government in 1998, questions concerning loss of national sovereignty and how much of Hungary's resources had been sold to foreign companies under the Socialist regime became increasingly vocalized. Though initially its political policies were definitively pro-West, upon taking power FIDESZ began to become more cognizant of the growing Hungarian constituency that was distrustful of the previous Socialist government's reforms. Thus FIDESZ became more unilateral and started pandering to the Right by displaying occasional dissatisfaction with the West. This gradual but serious political shift may have been induced by the fact that in the same elections that propelled FIDESZ to power, the extremely nationalist, isolationist Hungarian Truth and Light Party (HTLP) also gained a handful of seats in Parliament. The HTLP was elected on a platform of anti-Semitism, anti-NATO policies, anti-Europeanization, and a vocal desire to annex territory from neighboring states that contained ethnic Hungarians (i.e., Transylvania in Romania, the southern quarter of Slovakia, and Vojvodina in Serbia). Thus less than six months after the successful referendum, the internal dynamics of Hungarian politics quickly changed to reflect more public skepticism over NATO expansion than had previously existed.

The Young Democrats Party gained from NATO expansion because immediately thereafter it was able both to play the cosmopolitan, pro-West card (upon which its party platform rested) and concurrently to shift toward the right by expressing concern that the Socialists had sold out to the West. Thus though it initially supported NATO expansion, during the next four years of power, it increasingly found itself caught in the bind of trying to appease Western supporters while at the same time picking up support from the Right. This was done primarily through the increasingly unilateral leadership of Prime Minister Viktor Orban, which eventually began to erode Hungary's partnership with the West. Before long, Orban was condemned by various states and international political institutions. Thus though FIDESZ took over and rode the success of NATO expansion at the beginning of its run at the helm of Parliament, during the next four years it lost international support for its leadership of Hungary.

Interdependence can affect domestic politics, as FIDESZ discovered in the elections of 2002. The displeasure of other NATO member states with Hungary may have been the catalyst in FIDESZ's electoral loss. A month before the elections that ousted FIDESZ from power, Prime Minister Orban visited Washington, D.C., only to be snubbed by President Bush.[46] Only three years earlier, NATO had helped the recently elected party gain recognition from the United States and core European states, yet during the following years NATO played a considerable role in the party's loss of power. Other NATO member states continually lambasted Hungary, under Orban's leadership, for not pulling its weight in the alliance. Due to external pressures, the originally progressive FIDESZ lost its internal legitimacy to govern for four more years and was narrowly defeated by the HSP in the general elections of 2002.[47]

The Magyar Military

If any part of the state apparatus was pro-NATO during the initial ascension proceedings, it was the Hungarian military. The fall of Communism was difficult for the Hungarian armed forces. It was a conscription-based force, its bases were in ill repair, its supplies were antiquated, its machinery largely consisted of aging Soviet technology, and its role in civil society at large lacked definition.[48] Morale became exceedingly low in the army, and whole groups of soldiers deserted due to low pay and squalid living conditions (e.g., four officers per dormitory room).[49] As the HSP began preparing to apply for NATO membership in the mid-1990s, the military was a firm supporter of the measure. Membership in NATO required extensive updating of military infrastructure and weaponry, which the Hungarian military would otherwise never receive through standard budgets and upgrades.[50] Furthermore, collective security would reduce the risk that potential conflict would spill over from neighboring states—something that Hungary was not entirely prepared to defend against on its own.[51]

The Hungarian military was suffering from a crisis of identity after forty-five years of being a pawn in the Soviet empire; its place in Hungarian society was contestable.[52] Though it was officially transferred to civilian control under the leadership of the president,—the military was loathed by much of Hungarian society and found little financial security in Parliament.[53] The ranks were full of corruption and bribery, and serious breaches in security were taking place.[54] The mandatory conscription laws were continuously debated and changed, from a two-year tour down to six months, then up to eighteen months, and back down to a year. Since the military could find little stability as an institution with a function within its own state, it eventually lobbied to promote its envelopment into a larger, pan-European force with the backing of the U.S. hegemony.[55]

By lobbying to join NATO, the Hungarian armed forces were appealing to an aspect of Hungarians' sense of modernity, for the Western military alliance represented high-tech and modern armies capable of swooping in with their machinery and technology to devastate peripheral militaries, as had been well observed in Bosnia. The Hungarian armed forces argued that their ability to defend the state would become obsolete without NATO. In the long run, after an initial major investment to upgrade the numerous realms in which the Hungarian military was behind, expenditures would be considerably lower for Hungary with the mutual security of NATO as opposed to defending the state alone. In this way the military was able both to appeal to the nationalist heartbeat—defending the nation-state—and at the same time to promote the relinquishment of Hungarian sovereignty.

Ironically, having received what it desired, ascension into NATO and increased funding to upgrade to Western standards, the military was then slighted by its own success. Prime Minister Orban enthusiastically embraced increased funding for the military at the beginning of the FIDESZ government in 1998. However, once the country had been accepted into the NATO club, parliamentary excitement over funding the upgrading of Hungary's military—an increasingly expensive task in a state plagued with the financial difficulties of transforming to the open-market economy—began to wane.[56] This waning has continued to occur to the point where Hungary is now known as one of the NATO members least committed to meeting the technology and reform requirements established in the ascension treaty.[57]

As has been shown, different political institutions within the Hungarian political milieu had varying and vying reasons to join NATO, but one concept underlay all of them—an urge to be conceived of as modern. For the Socialists, membership represented a break from their past affiliation with the now defunct Soviet modernity. For FIDESZ, membership offered a chance for recognition from the epitome of world modernity and power, the U.S. hegemony, and an opportunity for FIDESZ to illuminate its nationalist policies as having the implicit backing of the United States and West. For the Hungarian military, membership offered a chance to redefine its role at the national and international scale and raise morale as it became associated with the world hegemony. In the end, though all of these institutions were affected in different ways after NATO ascension, they were all influenced by the prime modernity and a desire to participate in a Kantian peace with the West.

NATO as Process and Hungary as Space of Opportunism

In November 2002, as NATO encroached on the border of Russia by adding seven new states, the same processes were at work as during the first post–Cold War expansion in 1999.[58] The United States as world hegemon continues to expand its institutions of extraterritoriality into new territories.[59] Moreover, states in central Europe that hope to better their position within the world-economy have little choice but to acquiesce to the onslaught of U.S. extraterritoriality or be excluded from modern Europe.[60] Today there is no state-based ideological opposition to U.S. prime modernity for states to turn to; states in transition can join the West or become further peripheralized.

As NATO faces irrelevance, it continues to redefine itself and operate as a tool of the United States, even in the face of opposition from other extraterritorial institutions. The United States used NATO in Kosovo even though the United Nations had voted against force. Today the United States hopes to use NATO for antiterrorist operations and in multilateral campaigns against those who do not conform to open-market and democratic principles—essentially those who resist the hegemony's extraterritorial powers. Though European opposition and angst toward U.S. hegemony occasionally rise within NATO (e.g., European opposition to U.S. policies in the conflict over Palestine), many European member states will continue to pay homage to the U.S. hegemony and its military institution for some time.

Meanwhile, the new member states will be afforded an opportunity to become defenders of the modern world without needing to supply much in the way of military muscle. Instead, new member states are used for "niche" purposes (e.g., poison gas experts or mountain soldiers) and for the general stabilization of Europe as a whole.[61] Also, new member states provide ever-expanding territorial range for military operations and new spaces for U.S. training.[62] A prime example of this is Hungary. Before the Anglo-American incursion into Iraq in 2003, Hungary offered one of its military bases for the United States to train an Iraqi militia.[63] Once again, the implication of such hegemonic extraterritoriality varies in benefit and impact for different Magyars. The Republic of Hungary has gained millions of dollars in aid by allowing the United States and other NATO states to use its military bases during various Balkan crises and in preparation for war with Iraq.[64] However, the local Magyar villagers near the base are continually upset and disgruntled by the foreign presence, particularly recently—"It's not that we're afraid of foreigners coming here—we're used to it. But they're Arabs, it's different."[65]

Nonetheless, the Hungarian government is happy to put Hungary in the hegemony's good graces again. Moreover, the Hungarian military can always use the influx of capital to help revamp its antiquated military. In return, Hungary contributes remarkably little in exchange for what it receives from its membership in NATO: security, military development, capital investment, and the ear of the hegemony.

In recent years a conflict has been growing between an increasingly integrated EU and the United States over the role of NATO. Continued conflicts of interest have begun to chip away at the established foundations of Kantian peace within the military organization. The universalist ideal that had been cemented by the prime modernity during the past half century has begun to erode within this zone of peace, and increasingly the hegemony faces difficulty keeping member states in tow behind its leadership. Contemporary events have made this chasm all the more apparent, with U.S. political rhetoric divisively naming those states that adhere to U.S. policies the "new Europe" and dismissively labeling those states that oppose U.S. agendas as part of the "old Europe." Perhaps not too ironically, "old Europe" primarily consists of the most powerful European Union members, who in the near future very well may attempt to forge an independent foreign policy separate from the one that the U.S. hegemony leads. Such an Atlantic rift could place new NATO members, such as Hungary, in quite a diplomatic predicament. French president Jacques Chirac has threatened central European governments with vetoing their ascension into the EU due to their support of the U.S. position in NATO's rift over the war in Iraq and has called the central European states "poorly brought up."[66]

Such a collision between core interests within NATO may represent an aspect of a larger process—the decline of U.S. hegemony. If NATO as a hegemonic institution of extraterritoriality and a Kantian zone of peace begins to crumble under the stress of interstate competition against the world hegemony, perhaps so too will the stability that the U.S. hegemonic order has traditionally provided to the world. The question for future studies may then become: have central European states hopped on the USS *Interdependence* just in time to watch it sink?

Notes

1. Weir, "Baltics Step from Russia's Shadow into Western Club."
2. Ibid.
3. Agh, "Processes of Democratization."
4. Ibid.; "Europe: Welcome Aboard!"; Farnam, "Seven Nations Hope to Find a Niche in NATO"; Holley, "NATO Grows, Shifts Focus to Terrorism' " Krauthammer, "Bold Road to NATO Expansion' "; Weir, "Baltics Step from Russia's Shadow into Western Club"; Wines, "Eyeing Moscow Warily, Lithuania Clasps NATO."
5. NATO, *NATO Handbook*.
6. Ó Tuathail, "Postmodern Geopolitics?", 20.
7. Bull, *Anarchical Society*.
8. Cederman, "Back to Kant."
9. Ibid.; Bull, *Anarchical Society*, 24; Huntley, "Kant's Third Image"; Oneal and Russett, "Assessing the Liberal Peace with Alternative Specifications"; Oneal and Russett, "Kantian Peace"; Starr, "Democracy and Integration."
10. Bull, *Anarchical Society*, 25.
11. Ibid., 527.
12. Agnew, "United States and American Hegemony"; Arrighi, *Long Twentieth Century*.
13. Ibid.

14. Ibid.; also Arrighi et al., "Geopolitics and High Finance."
15. NATO, *NATO Handbook*.
16. Hudson, "Offshoreness, Globalization, and Sovereignty."
17. Boulding, *Three Faces of Power*.
18. Hudson, "Offshoreness, Globalization, and Sovereignty."
19. Taylor, *Modernities*, 28–43.
20. Flint, "Right-Wing Resistance to the Process of American Hegemony;" Flint, "A Timespace for Electoral Geography;" Taylor, *Modernities*, 28–43.
21. Flint, "Right-Wing Resistance to the Process of American Hegemony", 769–773; Flint, "Timespace for Electoral Geography", 304–306; Taylor, *Modernities*, 31–38; Taylor, *Way the Modern World Works*.
22. Taylor, *Modernities*, 31–38; Taylor, *Way the Modern World Works*.
23. Taylor, *Modernities*, 38–43.
24. Agh, "Processes of Democratization."
25. Taylor, "Tribulations of Transition."
26. BBC, "NATO Warms to Rapid Reaction Force"; BBC, "Summit Backs Euro Force"; BBC, "US Sounds Alarm over Euro Force"; Keegan, "Euro Force Must Stay under Our Control, Says NATO"; Simeone, "Britain, U.S. Discuss Euro Force."
27. Eekelen, "Security Dimensions of European Integration."
28. Agh, "Processes of Democratization," 273–276.
29. Perlmutter and Carpenter, "NATO's Expensive Trip East."
30. Agh, "Processes of Democratization," 275–278; Biegelbauer, *130 Years of Catching Up with the West*; Szenes, "Implications of NATO Expansion for Civil-Military Relations in Hungary."
31. Agh, "Processes of Democratization," 267.
32. Eekelen, "Security Dimensions of European Integration," 8–21; NATO, "Extending Security in the Euro-Atlantic Area."
33. Reuters, "Slovak Far-Right Leader Threatens to Flatten Budapest."
34. Jeszenszky, "More Bosnias?"
35. Agh, "Processes of Democratization," 274; Bartlett, "Democracy, Institutional Change, and Stabilisation Policy in Hungary."
36. Appadurai, "Sovereignty without Territoriality."
37. Agh, "Processes of Democratization," 264–270.
38. Ibid., 267.
39. Ibid., 274.
40. Ibid.; Bigler, "Back in Europe"; Ziblatt, "Adaptation of Ex-Communist Parties to Post-Communist East Central Europe."
41. Eekelen, "Security Dimensions of European Integration"; "Ethnic Pitch"; Kim, "Budapest Seeks to Strengthen Ethnic Ties That Bind"; Szocs, "Tale of the Unexpected."
42. Agocs, "Dispirited Army," 86–92; Bebler, "Corruption among Security Personnel in Central and Eastern Europe."
43. Bigler, "Back in Europe," 9–11; Ziblatt, "Adaptation of Ex-Communist Parties to Post-Communist East Central Europe," 125.
44. Bigler, "Back in Europe," 1; Ziblatt, "Adaptation of Ex-Communist Parties to Post-Communist East Central Europe," 132–135.
45. Bigler, "Back in Europe"; Ziblatt, "Adaptation of Ex-Communist Parties to Post-Communist East Central Europe," 125.
46. Fisher, "Socialist Party Looks Strong in Hungary."
47. Fisher, "Hungarians Choose Socialist as New Leader."

48. Agocs, "Dispirited Army," 86–92; Yaniszewski, "Post-Communist Civil-Military Reform in Poland and Hungary."

49. Agocs, "Dispirited Army," 86–92.

50. Yaniszewski, "Post-Communist Civil-Military Reform in Poland and Hungary."

51. Eekelen, "Security Dimensions of European Integration."

52. Agocs, "Dispirited Army"; Szenes, "Implications of NATO Expansion for Civil-Military Relations in Hungary."

53. Agocs, "Dispirited Army."

54. Bebler, "Corruption among Security Personnel in Central and Eastern Europe."

55. Eekelen, "Security Dimensions of European Integration and the Central-East European States"; Perlmutter and Carpenter, "NATO's Expensive Trip East," 2–6; Szenes, "Implications of NATO Expansion for Civil-Military Relations in Hungary"; Yaniszewski, "Post-Communist Civil-Military Reform in Poland and Hungary."

56. Jordan, "Iraqi Exile Meeting Rattles Hungarian Town"; Perlmutter and Carpenter, "NATO's Expensive Trip East," 2–6.

57. Deutch, Kanter, and Scowcroft, "Saving NATO's Foundation," 65–67; Jordan, "Iraqi Exile Meeting Rattles Hungarian Town"; Wallander, "NATO's Price."

58. The seven new states were Bulgaria, Estonia, Latvia, Lithuania, Romania, Slovakia, and Slovenia.

59. Black, "Threat of War"; DeYoung and Richburg, "NATO Approves New Direction"; Fisher, "Romania, Wooed by U.S., Looks to a Big NATO Role"; Ford, "Expanded NATO Looks for New Role"; Krauthammer, "Bold Road to NATO Expansion."

60. Agh, "Processes of Democratization." in the East Central European and Balkan States," 264–272.

61. Ash, "Comment and Analysis"; DeYoung and Richburg, "NATO Approves New Direction"; Farnam, "Seven Nations Hope to Find a Niche in NATO"; Squitieri, "Useful 'Niche' Skills Sought from New Member Nations."

62. Fisher, "Romania, Wooed by U.S., Looks to a Big NATO Role"; Jordan, "Iraqi Exile Meeting Rattles Hungarian Town"; MacAskill and Traynor, "Threat of War."

63. BBC, "Villagers Fearful of Iraq Training Mission"; Jordan, "Iraqi Exile Meeting Rattles Hungarian Town"; MacAskill and Traynor, "Threat of War."

64. Ibid.

65. Jordan, "Iraqi Exile Meeting Rattles Hungarian Town."

66. BBC, " 'New Europe' Backs EU on Iraq."

References

Agh, Attila. "Processes of Democratization in the East Central European and Balkan States: Sovereignty-Related Conflicts in the Context of Europeanization." *Communist and Post-Communist Studies* 32 (1999): 263–279.

Agnew, John. "The United States and American Hegemony." In *Political Geography of the Twentieth Century: A Global Analysis*, ed. P. J. Taylor, 207–238. New York: Halsted, 1993.

Agocs, Sandor. "A Dispirited Army." In *Civil-Military Relations in Post-Communist States: Central and Eastern Europe in Transition*, ed. Anton Bebler, 86–92. Westport, CT: Praeger, 1997.

Appadurai, Arjun. "Sovereignty without Territoriality: Notes for a Postnational Geography."

In *The Geography of Identity*, ed. P. Yaeger, 40–58. Ann Arbor: University of Michigan Press, 1996.

Arrighi, Giovanni. *The Long Twentieth Century*. New York: Verso, 1994.

Arrighi, Giovanni, Po-keung Hui, Krishnendu Ray, and Thomas Ehrlich Reifer. "Geopolitics and High Finance." In *Chaos and Governance in the Modern World System*, ed. Giovanni Arrighi and Beverly Silver, 37–96. Minneapolis: University of Minnesota Press, 1999.

Ash, Timothy Garton. "Comment and Analysis: Love, Peace, and NATO: I Watched John Lennon Meet George Bush." *Guardian*, November 28, 2002, 23.

Bartlett, David L. "Democracy, Institutional Change, and Stabilisation Policy in Hungary." *Europe Asia Studies* 47 (1996): 1177–1204.

BBC. "Summit Backs Euro Force." BBC News, November 26 1999. http://news.bbc.co.uk/2/hi/uk~news/politics/536638.stm (accessed February 15, 2003).

BBC. "US Sounds Alarm over Euro Force." BBC News, December 5 2000. http://news.bbc.co.uk/2/hi/europe/1055395.stm (accessed February 15, 2003).

BBC. "Nato Warms to Rapid Reaction Force." BBC News, September 25, 2002. http://news.bbc.co.uk/2/hi/europe/2277578.stm (accessed January 21, 2003).

BBC. "Villagers Fearful of Iraq Training Mission." BBC News, January 2003. http://news.bbc.co.uk/2/hi/europe/2664531.stm (accessed January 16, 2003).

BBC. " 'New Europe' Backs EU on Iraq." BBC News, February 19, 2003. http://news.bbc.co.uk/2/hi/europe/2775579.stm (accessed February 18, 2003).

Bebler, Anton. "Corruption among Security Personnel in Central and Eastern Europe." In *Army and State in Post-Communist Europe*, ed. John Lowenhardt and David Betz, 129–145. Portland, OR: Cass Publishers, 2001.

Biegelbauer, Peter S. *130 Years of Catching Up with the West*. Brookfield, VT: Ashgate, 2000.

Bigler, Robert M. "Back in Europe and Adjusting to the New Realities of the 1990s in Hungary." *East European Quarterly* 30 (1996): 205–234.

Black, Ian. "Threat of War: NATO Puts on Heavy Display of Force as Leaders Seek Role in Bush's Plans." *Guardian*, November 21, 2002, 4.

Boulding, Kenneth E. *Three Faces of Power*. Newbury Park, CA: Sage, 1990.

Bull, Hedley. *The Anarchical Society: A Study of Order in World Politics*. 2nd Ed. New York: Columbia University Press, 1995.

Cederman, Lars-Erik. "Back to Kant." *American Political Science Review* 95 (2001): 15–31.

Deutch, John, Arnold Kanter, and Brent Scowcroft. "Saving NATO's Foundation." *Foreign Affairs* 78: 6 (1999): 54–67.

DeYoung, Karen, and Keith B. Richburg. "NATO Approves New Direction; Enlarged Alliance to Reorganize Forces; Leaders Endorse Statement on Iraq." *Washington Post*, November 22, 2002, 1.

Eekelen, Willem van. "The Security Dimensions of European Integration and the Central-East European States." In *Civil-Military Relations in Post-Communist States*, ed. Anton A. Bebler, 8–21. Westport, CT: Praeger, 1997.

"Ethnic Pitch: Status of Ethnic Magyars in and out of Hungary." *Economist*, April 7, 2001, 55.

"Europe: Welcome Aboard! The Balts and the European Union." *Economist*, December 14, 2002, 42–43.

Farnam, Arie. "Seven Nations Hope to Find a Niche in NATO." *Christian Science Monitor*, November 21, 2002, 7.

Fisher, Ian. "Socialist Party Looks Strong in Hungary." *New York Times*, April 9, 2002, 6.

Fisher, Ian. "Hungarians Choose Socialist as New Leader." *New York Times*, April 20, 2002, 8.

Fisher, Ian. "Romania, Wooed by U.S., Looks to a Big NATO Role." *New York Times*, October 23, 2002, 3.

Flint, Colin. "Right-Wing Resistance to the Process of American Hegemony: The Changing Political Geography of Nativism in Pennsylvania, 1920–1998." *Political Geography* 20 (2001): 763–786.

Flint, Colin. "A Timespace for Electoral Geography: Economic Restructuring, Political Agency, and the Rise of the Nazi Party." *Political Geography* 20 (2001): 301–329.

Ford, Peter. "Expanded NATO Looks for New Role; Alliance Approves Seven New Members and Creates a Rapid-Reaction Force." *Christian Science Monitor*, November 22, 2002, 1.

Holley, David. "NATO Grows, Shifts Focus to Terrorism." *Los Angeles Times*, November 22, 2002, 1.

Hudson, Alan. "Offshoreness, Globalization, and Sovereignty: A Postmodern Geo-political Economy?" *Transactions of the Institute of British Geographers* 25 (2000): 269–283.

Huntley, Wade L. "Kant's Third Image: Systematic Sources of the Liberal Peace." *International Studies Quarterly* 40 (1996): 45–76.

Jeszenszky, Gyula. "More Bosnias? National and Ethnic Tensions in the Post-Communist World." Ph.D. diss., University of Michigan, 1996.

Jordan, Michael J. "Iraqi Exile Meeting Rattles Hungarian Town." *Christian Science Monitor*, January 14, 2003, 6.

Keegan, John. "Euro Force Must Stay under Our Control, Says Nato." *Daily Telegraph*, November 28, 2000. www.mvcf.com/news/cache/00195/ (accessed February 15, 2003).

Kim, Lucian. "Budapest Seeks to Strengthen Ethnic Ties That Bind." *Christian Science Monitor*, August 28, 2001, 7.

Krauthammer, Charles. "The Bold Road to NATO Expansion." *Washington Post*, November 22, 2002, 41.

MacAskill, Ewen, and Ian Traynor. "Threat of War: Bush Approves $92m to Train Iraqi Militia to Fight Saddam Hussein." *Guardian*, December 11, 2002, 17.

NATO. "Extending Security in the Euro-Atlantic Area: The Role of NATO and Its Partner Countries." Brussels: NATO Office of Information and Press, 1998.

NATO. *NATO Handbook*. Brussels: NATO Office of Information and Press, 2001.

Oneal, John R., and Bruce Russett. "Assessing the Liberal Peace with Alternative Specifications: Trade Still Reduces Conflict." *Journal of Peace Research* 36 (1999): 423–442.

Oneal, John R., and Bruce Russett. "The Kantian Peace: The Pacific Benefits of Democracy, Interdependence, and International Organizations, 1885–1992." *World Politics* 52 (1999): 1–37.

Ó Tuathail, Gearóid. "Postmodern Geopolitics? The Modern Geopolitical Imagination and Beyond." In *Rethinking Geopolitics*, ed. Gearóid Ó Tuathail and Simon Dalby, 16–38. New York: Routledge, 1998.

Perlmutter, Amos, and Ted G. Carpenter. "NATO's Expensive Trip East." *Foreign Affairs* 77 (1998): 2–6.

Reuters. "Slovak Far-Right Leader Threatens to Flatten Budapest." Reuters News Service, 1999 [cited May 6, 1999)]. No longer available.

Simeone, Nick. "Britain, U.S. Discuss Euro Force." *Journal of Aerospace and Defense Industry News*, 2001. www.aerotechnews.com/starc/2001/020901/Euro_force.html (accessed February 27, 2003).

Squitieri, Tom. "Useful 'Niche' Skills Sought from New Member Nations." *USA Today*, November 22, 2002, A8.

Starr, Harvey. "Democracy and Integration: Why Democracies Don't Fight Each Other." *Journal of Peace Research* 34 (1997): 153–162.

Steele, Jonathan. "NATO Summit: New Era as Alliance Arrives on Soviet Turf: Russia Remains Impassive on Day Baltic States Get Historic Invitation to Join Atlantic Pact." *Guardian*, November 22, 2002, 16.

Szenes, Zoltan. "The Implications of NATO Expansion for Civil-Military Relations in Hungary." In *Army and State in Post-Communist Europe*, ed. John Lowenhardt and David Betz, 78–95. Portland, OR: Cass, 2001.

Szocs, Laszlo. "A Tale of the Unexpected: The Extreme Right vis-à-vis Democracy in Post-Communist Hungary." *Ethnic and Racial Studies* 21 (1998): 1096–1115.

Taylor, P. J. "Tribulations of Transition." *Professional Geographer* 44 (1992): 10–12.

Taylor, P. J. *The Way the Modern World Works: World Hegemony to World Impasse*. Chichester, UK: Wiley, 1996.

Taylor, P. J. *Modernities: A Geohistorical Interpretation*. Minneapolis: University of Minnesota Press, 1999.

Wallander, Celeste A. "NATO's Price: Shape Up or Ship Out." *Foreign Affairs* 82 (2002): 2–8.

Weir, Fred. "Baltics Step from Russia's Shadow into Western Club." *Christian Science Monitor*, November 20, 2002, 1.

Wines, Michael. "Eyeing Moscow Warily, Lithuania Clasps NATO." *New York Times*, November 20, 2002, 8.

Yaniszewski, Mark. "Post-Communist Civil-Military Reform in Poland and Hungary: Progress and Problems." *Armed Forces and Society* 28 (2002): 385–402.

Ziblatt, Daniel F. "The Adaptation of Ex-Communist Parties to Post-Communist East Central Europe: A Comparative Study of the East German and Hungarian Ex-Communist Parties." *Communist and Post-Communist Studies* 31 (1998): 119–137.

BRENDAN SOENNECKEN

The Geopolitics of Postwar Recovery

Postwar recovery is an elusive term. Often it is identified with words like reconstruction or nation and peace building and may be related to historical events such as the American Civil War or the Marshall Plan. Perhaps, however, the term is elusive because its distinct parts offer it a host of meanings. *Post* is a prefix that means after or later, *war* is the exertion of violence or hostility, and *recovery* is a restoration or return. As such, postwar recovery might be read as "after exerting violence, return later and restore hostility." While this may be a word game, the semantics of postwar recovery, at face value, provoke some very difficult questions. At least, what is war, what is peace, and in the absence of both, what is to be recovered? In the past, recovery has encompassed almost every level of society, from institutions and government to economies, industry, infrastructure, and housing. At its best, recovery has embodied aspirations for future peace; at its worst, it has remained the harsh reality of sifting through ashes to find what is left.

As part of the geographic study of war and peace, this introduction to the field of postwar recovery presents a brief history of its modern development by emphasizing the intersections of territorial sovereignty, international intervention, and subnational spaces. The chapter concludes by discussing its application in the field from the perspective of international practitioners. Part of the analysis reflects calls for further study on issues relevant to both geography and postwar recovery such as the impact of Non-Governmental Organizations on the "front lines" of geopolitics[1] or issues of migration, a major propellant of which is violent conflict.[2] Suggesting potentials for synthesis of postwar recovery and geography, the analysis alludes to different scales of recovery and through a case study of northern Afghanistan presents regional elements of postwar environments and their impact on field level recovery.

Postwar Recovery in the Twentieth Century

The history of postwar recovery parallels that of political geography and has seen the task of civilians to restore, with limited assistance, what was lost in war become a multibillion-dollar industry infused with state responsibilities, international intervention, and structured civilian participation.[3]

Recovering Society after World War I: Government Response and Humanitarianism

While the war to end all wars may not have followed through on its name, World War I did mark a significant shift in Western attitudes toward both war and recovery. In Europe, the horrors of trench warfare, artillery bombardments, and civilian suffering prompted significant social action. The battlefields of France served as a testing ground not only for modern warfare but also for modern responses to war and recovery. Even before fighting commenced, the government of France, under pressure from its citizens, made an unprecedented commitment to their future reimbursement for war damages. As conflict spread, surveys of destroyed countryside helped establish the potential not only for reconstruction, but also for significant development.[4] This was particularly beneficial because many rural inhabitants had lived before the war in conditions far below the standards of modernizing urban centers. For France, seeing disaster as opportunity was an important understanding that became enshrined in the government's reconstruction laws and program for recovery and was a catalyst for civilian and government cooperation.[5] Before World War I, a new generation of architects and planners had become influential in Western approaches to design, urban renewal, and community participation. Optimistic about their developmental approach, the government of France enlisted various foreign experts in the field who essentially acted as the first consultants in postwar recovery.[6]

Recovery in Europe also included other types of foreign involvement. Over a number of years, U.S. president Herbert Hoover's American Relief Administration contributed significant financial support to the French recovery. American bankers and politicians also worked together to help fund the revitalization of German industry and established plans such as that of Charles Dawes in 1924 to help finance German reparation payments that had been set at Versailles. In fact, however, the wide system of loans may have fueled the German rearmament during the interwar period and certainly suggested lessons for proper economic policy that would be revisited after World War II. At the same time, American companies were also contracted in both France and Belgium to reconstruct industries and civilian infrastructure. In addition, international organizations such as the YMCA and the American Friends Service Committee (the Quakers) also took part in France's recovery by working to rebuild and operate schools, coordinate relief, and construct temporary housing.[7] The steps taken at the time to provide assistance within the borders of a sovereign state set a precedent for future international action. By the wars end, international organizations were already moving on to other parts of Europe where they would work to sustain populations that were suffering from the wider consequences of war through civilian relief activities or what is today considered humanitarian relief.

The growth of civil-society and state involvement in recovery activities during and after World War I paralleled the significant development of the International

Committee of the Red Cross and associated principles of humanitarianism. Founded in 1863, the ICRC was initially charged with caring for wounded soldiers. By 1864, however, it had led sixteen states from Europe and the Americas to adopt the first Geneva Convention, seen today as the genesis of international humanitarian law. During both world wars the ICRC actively cared for soldiers and civilians while also spearheading efforts to ban chemical warfare, aerial bombardments of urban centers, and the use of weapons of mass destruction.[8] In so doing, the ICRC was not only caring for victims of conflict but was also influencing the way in which war was fought. Growing political and civil support for humanitarianism eventually led to the significant expansion of the Geneva Conventions into a comprehensive body of law. Having been widely adopted by national governments the Geneva Conventions have essentially helped shape state policies around principles developed by a private international movement. Since the ICRC was founded in Geneva in 1863, the small Swiss city has welcomed a steady migration of humanitarians. As the headquarters of the World Health Organization, UNICEF, and other lead agencies of the United Nations as well as hundreds of international NGOs, Geneva has over the years become the undisputed geographic center of all things humanitarian.

The Internationalization of Recovery after World War II

Just as World War II drew states from around the world into conflict, it also inspired a new international approach to postwar recovery. Much of the devastation during the war was influenced by changing geographies of the industrial era that made heavily populated urban centers the direct targets of military strategy. With high levels of damage to civilian infrastructures, approaches to recovery needed to be comprehensive. The resulting breadth of activity set new standards in reconstruction and recovery. Uniquely, in Europe, recovery emerged within a framework of international cooperation that was established to help move its nations toward a lasting peace. In 1947, the proponents of the Marshall Plan presented a strategy for cooperation that went well beyond post–World War I concepts of development and instead envisioned war recovery as the wider transformation of society.[9] This was particularly the case in Germany, where denazification became the rehabilitation not only of political institutions, but also of such social aspects as architecture, education, and cultural resources.[10] However, the agenda for recovery also looked to avoid the types of mistakes that had been made after World War I that had encouraged the further estrangement of Germany. To achieve this, recovery did not focus on the reconstruction of separate states, but rather on developing interstate cooperation in trade and industrial production in order to fuel regional economic growth and, hopefully, more peaceful European relations.

The important role that economy played in recovery was also understood at the local level, where communities were eager to reestablish personal livelihoods. Throughout Europe, many workers returned to their factories as soon as they could, often without the promise of pay. Europeans also worked together within their communities to adapt resources and share the task of reconstruction. During the war many women had spontaneously assumed duties in the workplace that formerly belonged to men. As men returned home, many of these same women became actively involved in recovery. In this way and despite the wider agenda for recovery, much reconstruction commenced in Europe on the initiative of individuals who worked together to recover their communities. After all, with almost 90% of some cities destroyed, the most prevalent issue facing German women was not the postwar strategy of General Marshall, but the immediate need to clear the rubble of their homes.[11]

At the same time, promises of peace through international assistance and cooperation in Europe did bring a certain enthusiasm to recovery which in turn transferred to hopes for similar action in other parts of the world. In 1944, the International Bank for Reconstruction and Development was established at Bretton Woods, New Hampshire. While its initial task was to finance European recovery, it would not be long before it would extend its reach across the globe as the World Bank. In 1945, the United Nations drafted its charter in San Francisco. Rising from the failure of the League of Nations, the UN brought new onus to the pursuit of peace and cooperation not only in Europe or the Pacific, but throughout the world. Yet even as reconstruction moved ahead in Europe, new wars were looming on the horizon. In 1947, the UN Special Committee on Palestine was formed and put forward its proposal for partitioning the territory. Within a year, the State of Israel was declared. This sparked the first Arab/Israeli War as well as the creation of a second UN organism, the UN Truce Supervision Organization (UNTSO), which evolved into the first and longest running peacekeeping mission of the UN. While the UN was establishing its presence in the Middle East, other conflicts began to call its attention and eventually led to subsequent peacekeeping missions on the Asian subcontinent (India/Pakistan, 1949), in Africa (the Congo, 1960), Asia (West New Guinea, 1962) and the Mediterranean (Cyprus, 1964). Such conflicts provided an opportunity for the UN to assert its presence in humanitarian and peacekeeping operations while at the same time encouraging national governments to acclimate to a new global environment that would be characterized by increased outside intervention in sovereign spaces.

Politics, Aid, and Recovery during the Cold War

In the decades after World War II, it became clear that any juvenile concepts of peace through cooperation would be enmeshed in violent conflicts and Cold War politics that muddied the international humanitarian vision that had seemed so clear at the close of war. As bipolar politics drew the superpowers into involvement in the affairs of other countries, humanitarians needed to pursue their own global agendas and focus on the well-being of civilian populations. Numerous nongovernmental organizations were established separate from foreign governments and the United Nations system. The growth of NGOs effectively privatized international assistance and expanded significantly the number of individuals who could channel their expertise and resources to others, but according to their own agendas. With greater frequency, newly established international relief agencies began mobilizing to support populations in what are today termed *humanitarian emergencies* and in the process redefined approaches to postwar recovery.

Throughout the Cold War, many peripheral countries received both relief and development aid. While relief activity maintained a more neutral posture, development aid was frequently accompanied by military support and was often used to leverage political ambitions. Next to the United States and the Soviet Union, other chief players in development were the UN and the World Bank, both of which were increasingly involved in implementation strategies on the ground. At the same time, the flow of aid to peripheral countries and the geography and politics of development remained distinct from those of relief. On one hand, development was focused on long-term goals such as economic growth, governance, and advances in social services at the national scale. Humanitarian relief, on the other hand, sought to alleviate short-term and acute suffering in geographically defined, subnational spaces.

During the 1960s and 1970s, humanitarian emergencies were largely characterized by natural disasters such as floods, earthquakes, and famines. In this period, the concept of disaster as opportunity reemerged among relief practitioners who recognized the disproportionate influence of disasters on socially vulnerable segments of a population, namely, the poor. Perhaps disaffected by aid politics, many humanitarians sought ways to begin implementing their ideology in their relief projects, seizing their opportunity to personally "change the world" while getting otherwise reluctant governments and donors to pay for their activities.[12] Despite this, international donor governments and organizations perceived humanitarian relief as separate from international development.

Over time, however, these perceptions began to shift, in part because of the increased activity of the international community in countries where violent conflict affected practitioners of both relief and development. In Central America in particular, natural disasters and regional political dynamics brought varying degrees of both conflict and international action. Increasing political instability and the development of humanitarian practices during disasters led relief agencies to branch out into emergency environments that were characterized by violent conflict. By the time civil war broke out in El Salvador in 1981, responsibilities that had once been shouldered by the ICRC were being shared by a number of international organizations. The conflict in El Salvador resulted in more than a million and a half people living as refugees or within the country as (internally displaced persons) (IDPs).[13] Some were forcibly removed from their communities, while others chose to leave conflict zones for more secure urban and mountainous areas. Early on, many Salvadorans found shelter in camps operated by relief agencies and patterned after those established during natural disasters. However, with limited experience in conflict environments, agencies were often overwhelmed by the complexities and early conditions in the camps were seen to suffer as a result.

Recovery and the Changing Geographies of Conflict

By the 1980s, aid organizations were beginning to experience firsthand the significant links between civilian suffering attributed to environmental and social conditions and decaying political climates with associated levels of conflict. Humanitarian emergencies like the famine in Ethiopia with its correlating conflict and the 1986 earthquake that devastated San Salvador were placing international organizations in environments that were complicated by a confluence of both natural and human-caused emergencies. Repeated experience in such situations led to the creation of terms like *complex humanitarian emergency* (CHE), which was first used to describe conditions in Mozambique during the 1980s.[14] By the end of the Cold War, the need to consider development and relief and their influence in conflict environments became more than relevant. Between 1985 and 1989, there was an average of five human-caused emergencies per year, and by 1990 that number had jumped to twenty.[15] Unfortunately, many of these conflicts occurred in countries that had received ongoing development assistance from the UN and had witnessed the growth of civil-society organizations. As hard-sought gains were lost to conflict, it became clear that solutions needed to be found to protect the investments that had been made and to prevent further suffering.

The end of the Cold War brought a paradigm shift in postwar recovery. By the time the Soviet Union collapsed, the need to understand how donors and agencies could integrate experiences in relief and development to become more effective in postconflict recovery weighed heavily on the international community. From the Middle East to the Balkans, from Africa to Asia, latent and low-intensity conflicts quickly escalated into larger turf battles until every corner of the world seemed to be affected by war. The nature of these conflicts allowed them to spread in unimaginable and terrifying ways, often with enormous consequences for civilians. Whether during the genocide in Rwanda or the guerrilla wars of Chechnya, the international community was confronted with its inability to respond effectively. At the same time, tragic military interventions in Somalia and Bosnia revealed the weaknesses of international political cooperation. For international nongovernmental organizations, back-to-back humanitarian emergencies demanded far more from professionals in every field of expertise. From the United Nations down to the smallest NGOs, humanitarian activity expanded geometrically with the onset of each new conflict. In the rush to provide relief, media coverage frequently swayed donor and public interests, and this encouraged rapid shifts in the focus of NGOs toward higher profile crises.[16] Concepts of coordination, best practice, and humanitarian neutrality were brought to the foreground through increased public attention that often saw humanitarian action at best as ordered chaos. In the struggle to assist, the actions of the international community often emerged unfinished or, worse, were perceived to have done more harm than good.

Throughout the 1990s, new agendas for participation in efforts to not only relieve but also recover war-torn societies were being realized, perhaps with less debate than zeal. At the same time, the autonomy of NGOs decreased significantly, particularly as international donor governments such as the United States channeled more and more of their budgets through NGOs instead of directly to state governments. By the end of the 1990s, close to one-quarter of all international funding for humanitarian aid was being directed through NGOs.[17] In particular, the new Balkan wars led to an explosion of humanitarian action and reaction. Lessons learned from mistakes and successes there had a considerable impact on international NGOs and helped identify the need for more informed approaches to postwar recovery. In Croatia for example, places of religious worship were frequently targeted during the war. As a result, international NGOs that worked in reconstruction needed to be especially sensitive to ethnic divisions and design projects that would foster commonalities and not differences. Recovery activities in the Balkans also took on wider approaches in which many NGOs worked in the areas of psychosocial counseling or education. The significance of such projects revealed the growing agenda of the international community to influence society and not just aid in reconstruction. In fact, the mix of NGOs, international militaries, and UN agencies on the ground and their involvement in wider areas of reconstruction meant that in places like Bosnia, Kosovo, and East Timor the international community essentially began to assume the role of a transition government that was waiting for geopolitics to catch up with the consequences of war.

Throughout the twentieth century, the field of postwar recovery evolved dramatically. The sense of responsibility felt by governments to pay reparations and even develop communities after World War I had by the end of World War II been incorporated into larger strategies for managing and preventing conflicts through broad-based international assistance in recovery. Since then a growing number of private organizations that work with governments and within the international system to provide relief and development assistance have essentially created a humanitarian industry that serves recovery in conflicts across the globe.

Postwar Recovery Applied

Contemporary wars are frequently characterized by a unique confluence of factors such as ethnic strife, latent conflict, famine, political unrest, resource disparity, and regional instability.[18] Chechnya is just one example of a modern civil war that is also embedded in wider regional dynamics that have essentially created levels of conflict activity. Together with war, a postconflict environment is also subject to local, regional, and international dynamics that impact a transition from war to peace. The following investigation of the applied field of recovery presents some of these levels or, in geographic terms, scales of activity and reveals postwar recovery foremost as a process instead of as a blueprint of expected outcomes. In turn, contemporary themes and concepts of field-level recovery illustrate how the dynamics of recovery environments influence and are shaped by the applied process.

Civilian Needs in Conflict and Recovery

Postwar recovery may commonly begin prior to the cessation of conflict and emerge as a combined civilian, government, and humanitarian effort to move affected populations from war to peace. Both during and after war, civilians may require alternative sources for such things as food, fuel, and shelter. Some individuals may be able to cooperate within a community to meet needs by adapting resources appropriately to sustain lives and livelihoods and recover war losses.

Alternatively, governments and militaries may offer emergency provision of services such as electricity, food, and water or even reconstruction assistance. In addition, international agencies may become involved to assist in meeting needs.

Early recognition of civilian need helps determine the extent to which international action will influence the overall recovery process. For practitioners, this is achieved in part through the distinction of *capacities* and *vulnerabilities*. Both capacity and vulnerability may be recognized in terms of the *social* and *physical* resources available to civilians. For example, if a community's water supply is disrupted, the ability to drill a well is considered a physical capacity, while the ability to coordinate the project is considered a social capacity. Conversely, ongoing drought and ethnic division would both be characterized as vulnerabilities of the same community. If vulnerabilities outweigh capacities, civilians often choose to seek assistance elsewhere, either within their own country as internally displaced persons (IDPs) or as refugees by crossing a political border. While early recovery commonly focuses on the needs of displaced populations, it also attempts to build capacities and reduce vulnerabilities in order to prevent displacement.[19]

Relief as Recovery

When the international community becomes involved in recovery during a conflict, the assistance it provides, together with assistance in natural disasters, is commonly classified as *relief*.[20] In war, as in natural disasters, the timeliness of relief is critical because coping mechanisms of civilians may quickly disintegrate under direct attacks on lives and livelihoods. However, the extent of relief is often subject to the geography and demographics of the conflict/postconflict environment. While one segment of a population may receive relief aid, other segments may experience other types of activity that resemble development. In theory, civilian vulnerabilities should influence the flow of assistance, with the most vulnerable populations receiving priority. Yet vulnerabilities are not always apparent and are often specific to locations. For instance, high-security zones affected by fighting or banditry may exacerbate vulnerability, as would environmental and geographic factors such as a riverbed that is used as a road, but is subject to floods that cut off outside access. Vulnerabilities may also be compounded by conflict-influenced demographics, with imbalances in a community's ethnic, gender, or age composition that create higher levels of vulnerability. In this regard, accurate and ongoing assessments of vulnerability are an important tool for relief and recovery practitioners.

In populations that are adversely affected by conflict, assessed needs will often compel humanitarians to provide a wide range of services. Taking various forms, recovery assistance may be given in medical care, food, water, temporary shelter, or the transportation of affected populations out of war zones. Depending on the conflict, relief assistance could be granted to a wide segment of the population both within and outside of international borders, as would be the case with the provision of services to Rwandan refugees inside the former Zaire. In both conflict and postconflict environments, significant amounts of assistance may constitute what is referred to as a relief "safety net" for civilians. Furthermore, high levels of relief activity may actually help create *humanitarian spaces*, which are recognized, though not always respected, geographic areas where civilians find greater security and assistance. Examples of humanitarian spaces may be an airport that is secured for relief flights or refugee camps along a border where agencies can operate with reduced risk of attack. The creation of humanitarian spaces may also be directly enhanced through outside political pressure or through the stabilizing actions of international militaries, as with UN safe haven cities in Bosnia and the no fly zone of northern Iraq. Both were initially established to allow aid services to be provided within specific geographic regions.

Conversely, the actions of the international community may have a negative impact on a war/postwar environment.[21] With the cessation of conflict, a civilian population's needs may lead humanitarians to extend the relief safety net. Particularly in the absence of a stable government, agencies may expand into wider areas of reconstruction. In theory, proper implementation of reconstruction assistance necessitates the phasing out of relief activities and should be observable as a transition within recovery rather than an expansion of relief. Failure to move appropriately from relief to reconstruction may significantly complicate recovery. For example, if belligerents are aware of an extensive relief safety net, they may be encouraged to continue or resume fighting because civilian suffering has been minimized. In addition, the activities of international relief agencies may become dependent on the support of localized power structures. In Afghanistan, the safe transit and distribution of supplies by NGOs is often granted by local "commanders." Thus while humanitarians may save lives through their protective actions, they have also been accused of helping sustain or even fuel conflict over prolonged periods of time by helping define spaces in which belligerents can continue their activities. The manipulation of humanitarians, along with the conceptual creation of safety nets and humanitarian space, is part of the debate over effective and appropriate ways to negotiate neutral humanitarian action within sovereign states.[22] With or without discussion, however, early humanitarian action continues to develop relief as a tool of both conflict management and recovery.

Reconstruction as Recovery

When conflict subsides, recovery often moves from relief to rehabilitation and reconstruction. Postwar environments may be characterized by damaged homes, weakened infrastructures, war economies, unstable political arrangements, and affected civilian psychologies. At the local level, the rehabilitation of private businesses, education, and health services may take precedence over housing-stock recovery. Particularly crucial is the restoration of civilian livelihoods that help to kick-start local economies while granting a necessary freedom for individuals to engage in more sustained reconstruction. However, in many postwar environments, reconstruction activity can be hindered by a slow return of displaced populations. Damaged roads and bridges, diminished water supplies, and unreliable public services are common deterrents to return. In addition, displaced persons may be reluctant to face the challenges that await them in their communities. Political or economic uncertainty, unresolved ethnic strife, and the continuing threat of land mines can factor strongly into this equation and often constrain return to a greater degree than physical destruction. As a result, wider recovery efforts may remain limited until solutions can be found that set the imperative for a calculated return of displaced populations.

While communities will inevitably provide the drive for reconstruction, international assistance can be substantial, especially when foreign governments and multinational organizations help finance the process. Sometimes assistance comes with a political price for national governments that reflect foreign interests in their economic or political stability. Conditions for aid may be set by major donors such as the United States, the European Union, and the World Bank and are often spelled out in a framework for assistance. Conditions are often economic in scope, for instance, requirements for bank and currency reform in exchange for international loans. Other times they are political, such as demands for free and fair elections or minority participation in governments in exchange for international financing of military and police forces. Oftentimes high-level economic and political consultants may be introduced at the field level to advise and monitor national governments in the implementation of an internationally funded program. In practical terms, the conditioning of aid may mean that *peace dividends* are paid indirectly through civilian projects such as the rehabilitation of an urban water system funded by the World Bank or the donation of housing-construction materials by the EU.

Attracting donor support for reconstruction is not only the task of national governments; it is shared with both national and international NGOs. Here too, funding guidelines follow donor interests and can work either for or against humanitarian agendas. Often NGOs struggle to express and find a balance between their field experience and the agendas of their donors. Donor support is generally attracted by NGOs' submission of project proposals to donor agencies, of which some of the largest are the U.S. Agency for International Development (USAID), the British Department for International Development (DFID), and the Canadian International Development Agency (CIDA). Project proposals generally present outcomes that are designed to meet a specific need and then detail inputs, such as a budget and civilian participation and implementation arrangements. If they are funded, NGOs are usually obligated to report to donors on their successes and failures. Increasingly, the United Nations and other multinational organizations have contributed to the donor/NGO relationship through field-level attempts to mold NGO projects and implementation strategies around their wider agenda. This may be achieved through the inclusion of NGOs in various coordination, security, and strategy meetings. The UN may also enlist NGOs as implementing partners in already funded programs, as would be the case when a relief NGO distributes supplies procured by the World Food Program. By channeling funding through the UN, donors may feel that their investment is better protected. However, by partnering with the UN and other multinational actors, NGOs may be relying on politically motivated sources for assistance that may restrict their agendas and jeopardize their independence that would otherwise allow a more neutral stance within recovery environments.

Development as Recovery

As rehabilitation and reconstruction progress, so does the challenge to place a society beyond the point where it stood at the onset of conflict. In this regard, a postwar environment can actually provide an opportunity for a society to pursue change from a new vantage. The concept of seeing disaster as opportunity is a recurring theme in the applied field of postwar recovery. It does not, however, imply a social tabula rasa.[23] Rather, in the face of serious social and political failures, civilians, governments, and international actors can cooperate to help construct a framework that will lead to improvements in social and physical infrastructure and more stable political institutions.

Different types of opportunity exist on different scales, however. For practitioners of recovery development is one tool through which certain opportunities for sustainable peace are made possible. Development may occur as individuals and communities realize their potential to use physical and social resources in a sustainable way.[24] In this regard, development is not necessarily dependent on external actors. However, international agencies in recovery can facilitate the process by helping civilians reduce their vulnerabilities and increase their capacities. Technical aid is one form of development that, by improving infrastructures, economies, and livelihoods, has the potential to directly impact the life quality of civilians. However, technical assistance has also created numerous problems in the past and has been criticized for practices that have left populations dependent on increasing amounts of aid or subject to the misappropriation of aid by national leaders. Additionally, improvements gained through development may prove over time to be unsustainable. Particularly in environments where such development occurred prior to conflict, postwar development or development as recovery may need to absolve the sins of the previous aid regime before it can move forward. With this understanding, one of the strategies for development in postconflict recovery has been to avoid unsustainable development by focusing on the empowerment of civilian populations.

During a recovery process, civilians may commonly work alongside foreign experts, and this provides an unprecedented opportunity to build local technical and administrative skills. Training and integrating nationals as project staff are applied strategies for both donors and NGOs that hope to foster innovative and effective recovery methods. The presence of international NGOs may also encourage new relations between members of civil society and the government. Often this is done as NGOs seek government participation in community-based projects such as the construction of access roads or the resettlement of refugees. In addition, the formation of indigenous or local NGOs that display their own unique expertise in recovery and development is not uncommon. While many national NGOs may begin operations under the umbrella of international NGOs, eventually they may receive their own support from donors and become a viable force in sustained development. When such growth of civil society is coupled with international pressure for good governance, it may act as a catalyst for changes in the very structures and institutions of the state. To enhance such processes, recovery activities might focus on community-level approaches for participatory planning and implementation of projects. Community building has become an important theme in recovery, and education and training often accompany projects in public health or micro credit lending.

Recovery as Process

Table 20.1 shows that differing areas of activity, themes, and scales of recovery account for a diverse range of approaches in the applied field of recovery. In fact, field-level recovery can easily become compartmentalized so that relief, reconstruction, and development are viewed as separate processes and are therefore implemented by separate agents. For both NGOs and donors, this differentiation may occur for the very practical need to specialize resources and activities. Unfortunately, the division-of-labor mentality may override the need for a more transitional and even holistic approach to the process of recovery.

One example of how recovery might be viewed as a wider process and how failure to implement recovery at transition scales can have lasting implications is the case of Palestinian refugees. In 1950, the United Nations began relief assistance to Palestinian refugee populations through the United Nations Relief Works Agency for Palestinian Refugees (UNRWA). More than fifty years later, UNRWA continues to care for what are now permanent refugee populations that grew from under a million people in 1953 to nearly five million in 2002.[25] While the United Nations and other actors placed concerted emphasis on relief-scale activities to aid Palestinians, the inexperience of the international community and lack of political will may not have allowed them to foresee the ramifications of creating a relief safety net without securing sufficient regional support for macroscale activities that would lead to a lasting political settlement and substantial recovery. Unfortunately, the inability to negotiate scales of activity that would move from relief activities to those of genuine development left permanent solutions increasingly elusive and has resulted in the current status of Palestinians and the associated cycles of dependency that have impacted four generations of refugees and more than half of all Palestinians worldwide.

Themes of Recovery and Geography: Synergy in the Field

Through consideration of current challenges and solutions in the field, it is possible to detect emerging trends in the theory and practice of postwar recovery. In recent years, the need to recognize how and when to incorporate different activities of recovery has fostered the development of principles of what is referred to as *best practice*. Contemporary concepts of best practice are mainly derived from analysis of past field experiences and are used to develop new strategies for recovery. Through this approach, agents of recovery have not only shaped field-level implementation, but have also influenced donors through the way they design and report on projects. Frequently, donors will use feedback from NGOs and even independent consultants to determine what works in the field and what does not. If viable concepts from the field are adopted by donors, they may then reemerge

TABLE 20.1 Activity, fields, and scales of applied postwar recovery field activity

Areas of Activity			
Technical Assistance	Good Governance	Capacity Building	Economic Support
Minimum Standards/Best Practice	Law/Institutions	Education/Civil Society	Livelihood/Commerce
		Vulnerabilities	
Landmines, drought, war damage	High security zones, minimized government	Conscription, social banditry	Extortion, nepotism, sanctions
		Relief	
Food and nonfood assistance, shelter	International security forces, media attention	Return and reintegration, coping mechanisms	Local supply procurement, fuel/water supply
		Reconstruction	
Mine clearance, infrastructure, housing stock	Peacekeeping, peace dividends, coordination	Demobilization, community participation/ownership	Businesses, industry, livestock and seed recovery
		Development	
Equipment/machinery, expert consultants	War crimes, minority rights, free press	Local NGO growth, cultural heritage	Income generation, microfinance
		National Government	
Structures for compensation and assistance, resettlement programs	Human rights, internaional cooperation, political stability	Systems for local governance and social services	Support for business and industry
		International and Regional	
Aid and support for international NGOs	Diplomacy, force, political conditions	Support for public services/local NGOs	Trade/finance packages

Source: Adapted from Sultan Barakat, "Community Enablement," lecture notes from November 28, 2000, Postwar Reconstruction and Development Unit, University of York, 2000.

in literature, program reviews, or the requirements of donor project solicitations. These relationships have brought an increase in institutional learning, but they have also identified the disparity between field-level knowledge and genuine scholarship. In the past, the field of recovery has received input from international relations theory as well as peace, conflict, and development studies. Only in the 1990s did postwar recovery begin to be considered as a separate academic field that could be enhanced by its own frameworks and methodologies that incorporate both theory and practice.[26]

Inevitably, there are also substantial links between postwar recovery and geography that would indicate potential for a synthesis of study. During the last decade of the twentieth century, the world map underwent rapid changes. Political constructions like the Soviet Union, Indonesia, Yugoslavia, and Zaire have been reduced or have ceased to exist. In many cases, the dissolution and reformation of states was initiated by war, but was realized in recovery. Postwar recovery has relevance to geography because it is a process that involves not only the return of individuals, but also the rehabilitation of place, the reconstruction of state, the reintegration of regions, and the restitution of a society within the global framework. In very practical ways, geographic analysis can support postwar recovery. The previous introduction to applied recovery demonstrated how three areas of recovery—relief, reconstruction, and development—interact over time and across space, influencing and being influenced by activities that span geographic scales. Further analysis will evidence the way regional social and political structures impact both the scale and geography of postwar recovery in the field.

The Case of Northern Afghanistan

Few postwar environments exhibit more of the complexities of geography and recovery than Afghanistan.[27] War against the Soviets (1978–1989) and episodes of intense factional fighting has left the country with a legacy of more than two decades of violent conflict. Throughout, Afghanistan has existed as a diverse mix of cultures and ethnic histories and is a virtual quilt of regions and territories with localized power structures. As a distinct region, northern Afghanistan shares four of the country's six borders, those with Turkmenistan, Uzbekistan, and Tajikistan just across the Amu Darya River, and the mountainous border with China. For purposes of analysis, the region of northern Afghanistan to be considered includes the provinces alongside and opposite the central Asian republics that lie in the valley between the geographic border of the Amu Darya and the southern mountain range. These provinces include Faryab, Jowzjan, Balkh, Samangan, Baghlan, Konduz, Takhar, and Badakhshan (see Figure 20.1).

Border Relations and Regional Ties

Northern Afghanistan shares more than just political borders with its three central Asian neighbors. The most obvious regional links are cultural, with the majority of the North's population consisting of ethnic Uzbeks, Turkmen, and Tajiks, as well as Hazaras, who are believed to be of Mongol origin. Before modern political

FIGURE 20.1 Northern Afghanistan. *Source:* "Afghanistan" from Geocommunity Web site. *http://data.geocomm.com/catalog/AF/index.htmlGIS* (accessed April 22, 2004).

borders, these ethnic groups comprised a dynamic region of culture and trade. Throughout the last century, northern Afghanistan continued to build regional ties through cross-border trade and aid relations. During the Cold War, the Soviets frequently sponsored projects in education, industry, and agriculture in the northern provinces. Examples include a fertilizer factory in Balkh that is still in operation and a gas pipeline that linked large northern reserves in Jowzjan Province with Turkmenistan. The USSR also assisted in the design and construction of coal, gas, and hydroelectric power plants, as well as irrigation systems throughout the North. The University of Balkh, founded in 1986 in Mazar-e Sharif, had its origins in the 1970s as a Soviet-sponsored college for "oil and gas." In addition, Afghans frequently pursued degrees at institutes in Tashkent, Almaty, Dushanbe, and even Moscow. At times, Soviet policy provided more favorable conditions in the North compared to other parts of the country. For example the Soviets encouraged agricultural production in the North in order to leverage other areas of Afghanistan where fields were often incinerated and irrigation systems were destroyed.

After the Soviet withdrawal in 1989, the capacity for northern Afghanistan to mobilize its resources within the region almost disappeared along with the Soviet troops. While recovery could have been greatly assisted by cross-border trade and cooperation with the emerging independent central Asian republics, the rise of factional fighting continued to weaken regional relations. Uzbekistan's border controls were particularly strict in reaction to declarations by the Taliban to expand its influence into Uzbekistan to reclaim "historic" territory along the silk route. The threat was perceived as viable due to repeated assassination attempts on President Islom Karimov by Islamic extremists with links to the Taliban. In 1998 Uzbekistan closed its border with Afghanistan completely at the Friendship Bridge that spans the Amu Darya River. At the same time, Turkmenistan also maintained a heavily controlled border. Turkmen officials were particularly unwilling to accept refugees from Afghanistan, but were simultaneously rumored to be supporting the revitalized and growing Afghan trade in illicit narcotics. Relations between northern Afghanistan and Tajikistan were characterized by even higher levels of illicit trade in both narcotics and weapons, which found an easy path through the longer and more permeable border controlled by Russian troops. Overall, regional border relations during the 1990s had a less than positive impact on recovery in northern Afghanistan as tight controls prevented access to goods, trade, and information and at the same time extended the region's vulnerabilities by facilitating the growth of both poppy production and factional fighting.

In the post-Taliban era, regional relations between Afghanistan and its northern neighbors took on a new and more promising dynamic. In February 2002, just two months after the collapse of the Taliban in the North, Uzbekistan, in part through the brokering of independent humanitarians, agreed to open the Friendship Bridge for aid activities under the control of the United Nations Office for the Coordination of Humanitarian Affairs (UNOCHA). With the growing presence of both U.S. and German forces in Afghanistan and Uzbekistan, the Friendship Bridge once again became a major transit point for military resources. Furthermore, as tensions in Pakistan associated with the war on terror escalated into the spring, Pakistani entry points seemed less welcoming than new routes that were opening in central Asia. With the rapid transition of power relations in the North, few NGOs on the ground could immediately appreciate the full potential for a revival of cross-border relations. Agencies that were working in technical assistance in the North were delighted to discover that authorities in Uzbekistan could, for example, help them retrieve blueprints of Afghan irrigation systems from Tashkent basements. Other NGOs welcomed the unprecedented opportunity to enlist skilled civilian experts from the region. Central Asian engineers found new freedom of movement as humanitarians and with their knowledge of Soviet industrial designs began consulting on the reconstruction of Afghan infrastructure.

Recovery and the Conflict of Scales

Throughout the Cold War, the international humanitarian community was active especially in caring for Afghan refugees along the border with Pakistan. With the withdrawal of the Soviets, many more organizations were able to move into Afghanistan to participate in the resettlement of refugees, reconstruction, and recovery. At the same time, however, northern Afghanistan had received other forms of assistance from the international community. For its part, the United States gave, at different times, military backing to incongruent components of the northern power structure, first by supporting the mujahideen in the 1980s and later by partnering with anti-Taliban forces that included factions of former mujahideen enemies. Simultaneously, some northern warlords also shared strong ties with the Soviets and today do so with the central Asian republics. The continuous involvement of foreign actors in the North meant that in the absence of a national state structure, many warlords needed to independently broker regional and international cooperation on aid and natural resource allocation. Inevitably, many NGOs caught in the middle have been manipulated by warlords and foreign government's who have seen international aid as a force for their influence.

Naturally, humanitarians are reluctant to work with factions that may compromise the end goal of lasting stability by reinforcing the status quo. Yet the power structure does not exist without reason. Localized power structures in the North have successfully worked to resist both hostile factions and foreign influence. In more vulnerable rural communities, village “commanders” work to maintain order, protect culture, and advance community agendas. Usually, commanders will share their influence with village elders and mullahs, a relationship similar in scope to that shared by police chiefs and mayors of Western cities that experience conflict, such as New York. Unfortunately, attempts by a community to maintain security may often be unfairly equated with the tyrannical acts of warlords.

The importance of factions in the North presents considerations for both postwar recovery and geography that highlight apparent conflicts between scales. Particularly for those who are seeking a centralization of power in Kabul, the history and strength of the North's regional ties and power structure are serious concerns. The international community is aware that Afghanistan's future development would benefit greatly from the significant natural, regional, and social resources that are in the North, yet even if cooperation with warlords would substantially benefit recovery efforts in areas of technical assistance and economic growth, humanitarians have other agendas for good governance, such as the rule of law and civic participation. The distinctiveness of the North as a region and the interests of elements of its power structure to maintain control of the region's future economic, religious and social development support conjecture that the North may seek autonomy in a future political framework for Afghanistan. At the global scale, the posturing of some northern warlords appears to be completely incongruous with the aspirations of the international community. Yet in any agenda for recovery in Afghanistan, humanitarians and foreign governments need to look at some very difficult issues of sovereignty and self-determination. On the surface, the impetus for intervention in the North, namely, humanitarian indicators of civilian suffering, would suggest an imperative to work around sovereignty and even subdue warlords. The question remains with what authority and how accurately regional interests, politics, capacities, and vulnerabilities have been assessed. For some time the de facto answer to that question has been that while the international community may prefer a central-state structure, regions gravitate toward a more federal structure, while many Afghans necessarily feel safer and better represented within their own communities and compounds. While the international effort to oust the Taliban has given the crippled economic and social structures of Afghanistan the strongest opportunity for recovery in the last twenty-five years, it remains to be seen how much of that recovery will be dictated by the international community and how many principles of humanitarianism will have to be compromised in order to advance recovery.

Conclusion

With each new threat of violence and increasing levels of political instability, the global system is continually adapting international responses to war. Recovery continues to develop as a means by which international actors influence changing geographies. While recovery will always be dependent on state and civilian initiative, the international community is assuming responsibilities that reflect awareness of the interconnectedness of populations across scales. Over time the practice of recovery is evolving into a professional field with associated theories and principles. Yet the level of professionalism achieved may not as yet be fairly said to reflect the importance of the task. What is more, the international community continues to run the risk of repeating mistakes by failing to adequately understand the structural interplay between international, regional, and local scales. In this, geographers have a significant opportunity to present the field of recovery with tools for analysis and frameworks of understanding that reveal the complexities of postwar environments and transitions to peace. With a combined approach, practitioners of recovery can work with geographers to pursue answers to some of the difficult questions that plague both fields and help define postwar recovery while pointing the way to peace.

Notes

A number of concepts and themes presented herein were introduced in study and discussion with my colleagues of the graduate program in postwar recovery studies at the Postwar Reconstruction and Development Unit of the University of York between September 2000 and September 2001.

1. See Price, "Nongovernmental Organizations on the Geopolitical Front Line."

2. See Wood, "International Migration."

3. I follow Colin Flint's four periods of political geography: from about 1890 to the end of World War II; the 1950s; the 1960s and 1970s; and from the late 1970s to the present. For more analysis of these periods, see Flint, "Changing Times, Changing Scales."

4. American George B. Ford detailed the first comprehensive modern survey of war devastation in his book *Out of the Ruins*.

5. For more on the recovery and geography in World War I France, see Clout, *After the Ruins*.

6. For more on the aspirations of this generation of planners and their view of postwar recovery, see Geddes and Slater, *Making of the Future*.

7. Some of the activities of the AFSC during World War I are detailed in R. Weisbord, *Some Form of Peace*.

8. For a range of information on the work of the ICRC, past and present, visit the Web site of the International Committee of the Red Cross, www.ICRC.org.

9. For accounts of the American influence in the reconstruction of Germany, see Diefendorf, Frohn, and Rupieper, eds. *American Policy and the Reconstruction of West Germany, 1945–1955*, and Ellwood, *Rebuilding Europe*.

10. The term "denazification" is taken from the German as used in Beyme, *Wiederaufbau*.

11. Diefendorf, *In the Wake of War*, 11.

12. This ideology was particularly relevant in Central America, as noted in Scott Anderson, *Man Who Tried to Save the World*, 98–99. One of the most respected humanitarians who espoused disaster as opportunity was Fredrick C. Cuny, who began his career in development and emergency relief and saved lives in disasters and conflict environments around the world until he disappeared in Chechnya in 1995. For an excellent biographical introduction to the evolution of disaster response since the Cold War and the impact of Cuny's life work, see Anderson, *Man Who Tried to Save the World*.

13. World Bank Operations Evaluation Department, "Post-conflict Reconstruction."

14. For more on this topic, see Parry, "Pyrrhic Victories and the Collapse of Humanitarian Principles."

15. U.S. Agency for International Development, *Foreign Aid in the National Interest*, 114.

16. For more on the influence of the media in humanitarian crises, see Benthall, *Disasters, Relief, and the Media*.

17. U.S. Agency for International Development, *Foreign Aid in the National Interest*, 115.

18. For more on this topic, see Sandole, *Capturing the Complexity of Conflict*, and Ramsbotham and Woodhouse, *Humanitarian Intervention in Contemporary Conflict*.

19. For more on this topic, see Minear and Weiss, *Humanitarianism across Borders*.

20. For a practical guide to the work of relief agencies, see Minear and Weiss, *Humanitarian Action in Times of War*.

21. For a critical view of humanitarian work, see Mary B. Anderson, *Do No Harm*.

22. For more on this topic, see Moore, *Hard Choices*.

23. Pugh, "Post-conflict Rehabilitation."

24. Barakat, "Community Enablement."

25. See UNRWA.org for more information. UNRWA, Refugee Statistics.

26. While many academic institutions offer graduate studies in development and conflict resolution, the Post-war Reconstruction and Development Unit of the University of

York in England was the first academic program to offer advanced studies in postwar recovery beginning in the late 1990s.

27. Much of the case study comes from personal research and experience gained while working directly on humanitarian relief and development projects in northern Afghanistan between January and June of 2002 and indirectly between June 2002 and January 2003.

References

Anderson, Mary B. *Do No Harm: How Aid Can Support Peace or War.* Boulder, CO: Lynne Rienner, 1999.

Anderson, Scott. *The Man Who Tried to Save the World.* New York: Random House, 1999.

Barakat, Sultan. "*Community Enablement.*" Lecture notes from November 28, 2000. Postwar Reconstruction and Development Unit, University of York, 2000.

Benthall, Jonathan. *Disasters, Relief, and the Media.* London: Tauris, 1993.

Beyme, Klaus von. *Der Wiederaufbau: Architektur und Städtebaupolitik in beiden deutschen Staaten.* Munich: Riper, 1987.

Clout, Hugh. *After the Ruins: Restoring the Countryside of Northern France after the Great War.* Exeter: University of Exeter Press, 1996.

Diefendorf, Jeffry M. *In the Wake of War: The Reconstruction of German Cities after World War Two.* New York: Oxford University Press, 1993.

Diefendorf, Jeffry M., Alex Frohn, and Hermann-Josef Rupieper, eds. *American Policy and the Reconstruction of West Germany, 1945–1955.* New York: Cambridge University Press, 1993.

Ellwood, David W. *Rebuilding Europe: Western Europe, America, and Postwar Reconstruction.* New York: Longman, 1992.

Flint, Colin. "Changing Times, Changing Scales: World Politics and Political Geography since 1890." In *Reordering the World: Geopolitical Perspectives on the Twenty-first Century*, 2nd ed., ed. George Demko and William Wood, 19–39. Boulder, CO: Westview, 1999.

Ford, George B. *Out of the Ruins.* New York: Century Co., 1919.

Geddes, Patrick, and Gilbert Slater. *The Making of the Future: Ideas at War.* London: Williams and Norgate, 1917.

Minear, Larry, and Thomas G. Weiss. *Humanitarian Action in Times of War: A Handbook for Practitioners.* Boulder, CO: Lynne Rienner, 1993.

Minear, Larry, and Thomas G. Weiss. *Humanitarianism across Borders: Sustaining Civilians in Times of Conflict.* Boulder, CO: Lynne Rienner, 1993.

Moore, Jonathan, ed. *Hard Choices: Moral Dilemmas in Humanitarian Intervention.* Lanham, MD: Rowman and Littlefield, 1998.

Parry, Matthew S. "Pyrrhic Victories and the Collapse of Humanitarian Principles." *Journal of Humanitarian Assistance.* www.jha.ac/articles/a094.htm (October 2, 2002; accessed February 8, 2003).

Price, Marie D. "Nongovernmental Organizations on the Geopolitical Front Line." In *Reordering the World: Geopolitical Perspectives on the Twenty-first Century*, 2nd ed., ed. George Demko and William Wood, 260–278. Boulder, CO: Westview, 1999.

Pugh, Michael. "Post-conflict Rehabilitation: Social and Civil Dimensions." *Journal of Humanitarian Assistance.* www.jha.ac/articles/a034.html (June 3, 2000; accessed January 10, 2003).

Ramsbotham, Oliver, and Tom Woodhouse. *Humanitarian Intervention in Contemporary Conflict: A Reconceptualization.* Cambridge, MA: Polity Press, 1996.

Sandole, Dennis J. *Capturing the Complexity of Conflict: Dealing with Violent Ethnic Conflicts of the Post–Cold War Era.* London: Pinter, 1999.

UNRWA. Refugee Statistics. www.un.org/unrwa/pr/pdf/figures.pdf (accessed January 15, 2003).

U.S. Agency for International Development. *Foreign Aid in the National Interest.* Washington: USAID, 2002. www.usaid.gov/fani/ (accessed January 20, 2003).

Weisbord, Marvin R. *Some Form of Peace: True Stories of the American Friends Service Committee at Home and Abroad.* New York: Viking, 1968.

Wood, William B. "International Migration: One Step Forward, Two Steps Back." In *Reordering the World; Geopolitical Perspectives on the Twenty-first Century*, 2nd ed., ed. George J. Demko and William B. Wood, 154–170. Boulder, CO: Westview, 1999.

World Bank Operations Evaluation Department. "Post-conflict Reconstruction: El Salvador Case Study Summary." *OED Précis* no. 172 (summer 1998): 1–3.

Index

Abkhazia, 89
Abu Dis, 304
Accra, 354
Aceh, 89, 227, 229
Aceh Freedom Movement (GAM), 229
Aden, 19
Afghanistan: and drugs, 89, 245–251, 254, 255; and gender, 142, 145; and postwar recovery, 13, 415, 423, 428–432; and religious war, 149, 158, 163, 168, 208–210; and resources, 227; and United States, 5, 85, 86, 92, 94, 98, 99, 104, 124, 126, 265, 280
Africa: and acephalous societies, 25; and AIDS, 265; and borders, 323, 324; Central, 5, 90, 96, 225; and colonialism, 283; Congo, 418; and diplomacy, 385; East, 168; and ethnonationalism, 115; and failed states, 90, 96, 102; Horn of, 96; Interior, 19; and life expectancy, 65; North, 159, 260, 292; and political order, 70; and peace movements, 355; and Portugal, 284; and postwar recovery, 420; and religious war, 149; Sub-Saharan, 67, 68, 254, 288, 289; Tropical, 95; and war casualties, 85; and war, revolutionary, 134; West, 94, 96, 152, 255
Agh, Attila, 404
Agnew, John, 39
Agni, 149
agriculture: and drugs, 245, 246, 249–252, 256; and resource wars, 221, 225, 226, 227, 230; and water conflict, 260, 268, 269
Ahimsa, 353
Ahmad, Eqbal, 200
AIDS, 94, 103, 265
Air America, 248
air power, 20, 24
Al-Aqsa Martyrs' Brigade, 167
Al-Aqsa Mosque, 164
Albania, 86, 162
Albanian Kosovars, 162
Albanians, 122, 327, 328, 333, 334, 339
Alberto, King Carlos, 118
Albright, Madeleine, 134, 310
Alcock, Norman, 65, 66, 67
alcohol, 243, 244, 255
Alexander I (of Russia), 380
Alexander the Great, 285
Al Eyzaria, 304
Algeria, 157, 158, 163, 200, 227, 310
Algiers, 19
Algiers Agreement, 332
al-Haram al-Sharif, 149, 164, 166
alluvial gems, 225, 226
alluvial minerals, 225
Almaty, 430
Al-Qaeda: and diamonds, 226; and drugs, 244; and Saddam Hussein, 97; and networks, 91, 199, 209, 210; and Qatar, 386; and religious war, 149, 159, 168,

Al-Qaeda: and diamonds (*continued*) 169; and Saudi Arabia, 291, 292; and territoriality, 280; and United Nations, 381; and United States, 6, 99
Alsace-Lorraine, 28, 30, 32, 119, 120, 121
Amanita muscaria mushrooms, 255
Amazon, 387
Amazons, 133, 134
American Colony Hotel, 328
American Friends Service, 352
American Friends Service Committee, 416
American Geographic Society, 32
American Peace Society, 352
American Relief Administration, 416
Americas, 417
Amery, Hussein, 262
Amin, Idi, 90
Amritsar, 156, 166
Amsterdam, 28
Amu Darya River, 428, 430
anarchism, 33, 204, 349, 352
Anatolia, 267, 269
Ancel, Jacques, 31
Andean South America, 249
Anderson, Benedict, 116
Anglicans, 152
Angola: and boundaries, 284, 285; and development, 79; and diamonds, 226, 227, 232; as failed state, 96; and oil, 89, 227, 228, 233; and resources, 217
animism, 149, 157
Annan, Kofi, 383
Anthropo-geographie, 29
apartheid, 37, 362
Arab Afghans, 158
Arab countries, 23, 298, 300
Arab diaspora, 243
Arabian peninsula, 6, 37, 152, 161, 202, 203
Arab-Islamic homeland, 291
Arab-Israeli peace process, 262
Arab-Israeli war, 158, 418
Arab League, 298
Arab revolt, 158
Arab Sawahra, 304
Arab states, 206, 207, 262, 263
Arab world, 314
Arabs, 158, 408
Arabs, in Israel, 316, 329
Arafat, Yasser, 298, 300, 301, 302, 306, 309, 310, 312, 313, 383
Arendt, Hannah, 137
Argentina, 20, 102, 127, 284, 288
Armed Islamic Group, 158, 163
Armenia, 180, 181, 287
Armenians, 121
Aron, Raymond, 218
Ashoka, 169, 170, 250
Asia, 19, 86, 134, 290; Central, 102, 159, 254, 428, 430, 431; East, 61, 208; Northeast, 103; Pacific, 71; and peace movements, 353; and postwar recovery, 420; and resources, 218; South, 96, 102, 153, 157, 288; Southeast, 96, 99, 102, 159, 230, 244, 246, 247, 248, 254, 255, 288; Southwest, 102, 208; and West New Guinea, 418
Asia-Pacific, 387
Asia Pacific Economic Cooperation (APEC), 386, 387
Associated Countries Network (CAN), 389
Association of American Geographers, 33, 40
Atkinson, David, 39
Atlantic Ocean, 403
Atwood, Wallace, 33
Aum Shrinyiko, 203
Auschwitz, 113, 123
Australasia, 92, 243, 356
Australia, 283
Austria, 151, 374, 389
Austria-Hungary, 352
Austrians, 121
authoritarianism, 91
Autocracy, 222, 235
Axis of Evil, 292
Ayodhya, 165, 166
Azerbaijan, 121, 287

Babar, 165
Babri Mosque, 165, 166
Bacevich, Andrew, 22
Badakhshan, 428, 429
Baghdad, 6
Baghlan, 428, 429
Bakassi Peninsula, 289
Baker, George, 135
Balfour Declaration, 314
Balkan Proximity Peace Talks, 384

Balkans: and boundaries, 12, 322, 323, 327, 332, 334; and ethnonationalism, 122, 204; and diplomacy, 385; and genocide, 175, 183, 185; and Johan Cvijic, 32; and Kantian peace, 6, 402–404; and NATO, 402–404, 408; and postwar recovery, 420; and religious war, 168; and United States, 86
Balkan wars, 121, 123
Balkh, 428, 429
Baltic sea, 218
Bandung Conference, 354
Bangkok, 77
Bantustan, 299, 316
Barak, Ehud, 299, 300, 302–305, 310, 315
barbiturates, 243
Barnett, T.P.M, 96, 102, 103
Barre, Siyad, 219
Barton, Robert, 138
Basque, 92, 121, 203, 290
Battle of Dorking, 116
Battle of Kosovo, 156
Battle of the Somme, 351
Battle of Tours, 161
Beamer, Lisa, 142, 145
Begin, Menachem, 374
Beijing, 19, 373, 377, 384
Beirut, 39, 298
Beit Jala, 308
Belfast, 329
Belgian Congo, 231
Belgium, 116, 231, 329, 375, 397, 416
Belgrade, 128, 162, 176
Belize, 92, 251–253
Ben-Meir, Alon, 315
Berg, Lawrence, 38
Berkman, Lieutenant Brenda, 144, 145
Berlin, 28, 128, 361, 397
Berlin, Conference of (1885), 284, 381
Bethlehem, 303
Bharatiya Janata Party, 155
Bhutan, 102, 288
Biafra, 227, 231
Bijeljina, 177
Bikini atoll, 354
Bilen, Ö, 270
Bin Laden, Osama, 4, 204, 208, 210, 291
Bismarck, Otto von, 373
Blache, Paul Vidal de la, 28, 29, 30, 31, 32
Black, Jeremy, 8
Blair, Tony, 245
Blunt, Alison, 38
Boer republics, 231
Boer war, 231
Bogor, 386
Bogor Botanical Gardens, 386
Bokassa, Emperor, 90
Bolivia, 251
Bordeaux, 28
borderlands, 12, 321, 322, 329, 330, 335, 339
borders: and academic geography, 5, 6, 30, 31, 37, 38, 39; Angola, 285; and diplomacy, 371, 379, 380, 390; and ethnonationalism, 12, 321–340; and geography, 5, 6; and networks, 89, 209; and political order, 77; and postwar recovery, 13, 422, 428; and resources, 11, 228, 232; and states, 202; and territoriality, 280; and wars, 96
Bosnia: and borders, 322, 327, 333; and BZ gas, 255; and diplomacy, 384; and ethnonationalism, 121; and genocide, 174–192; and NATO, 402; and postwar recovery, 421, 423; and religious war, 149, 168; and United States, 86, 98
Bosnia-Croat Federation, 385
Bosnia-Herzegovina, 156, 158, 177, 178, 385
Bosnian Muslims, 88, 156, 174, 177, 190, 191
Bosnians, 186
Bosnian Serbs, 156, 177, 191, 385
Boston, 362, 381
Bougainville Island, 222, 227, 229
Boulding, Elise, 348, 349, 350, 353
Boulding, Kenneth, 64, 79
boundaries: and academic geography, 31; and diplomacy, 370, 371; and ethnonationalism, 12, 321–340; and religious war, 155; and sovereignty, 398; and territoriality, 280, 281, 284–290, 293; and water conflict, 272
boundary management, 335–339
boundary studies, 321
Boutros-Ghali, Boutros, 260
Bowman, Isaiah, 30, 31, 32, 39
Boxer Rebellion, 377
Brazil, 102, 387
Brazzaville, 227, 228
Brcko, 174
Bretton Woods, NH, 418

Brewer, Lucy, 135
Bronze Age, 19
Brooks, D., 261
Brunhes, Jean, 30, 31
Brunn, Stanley, 39, 347
Brunoy, 113
B'Tselem, 302
Buchanan, 228
Bucharest, 128
Budapest, 128
Buddha, 166
Buddhism, 155, 160, 162, 166, 167, 170, 203, 355
Buford, Lieutenant Harry, 135
Buhaug, H., 92
Bulganin, Nikolai, 378
Bulgaria, 33, 123, 387
Bulletin of the Atomic Scientists, 354
Bull Run, 135
Bunia, 85
Burma, 227, 247, 248, 293
Burundi, 88, 102
Bush, George H. W., 22, 86, 102, 182, 183, 244, 291, 377–379
Bush, George W.: and diplomacy, 380; and empire, 103; and genocide, 96; and Hungary, 406; and Israel-Palestine, 302, 316; and military intervention, 86, 87, 102; and public support, 97; and religious war, 151; and territoriality, 292; and unilateralism, 104; and war on terrorism, 126, 245
Bush Doctrine, 87
Byzantine Empire, 285
"BZ" gas, 255

Cabinda, 227, 228
Cacao, 230
California, 379
Calvin, John, 378
Calvinists, 152
Cambodia, 86, 90, 160, 182, 191, 220, 227, 232, 233
Cambridge, MA, 361
Cameroon, 152, 289
Campaign for Nuclear Disarmament (CND), 354, 357
Camp David, 300, 302, 304, 312, 315
Canaan, 163
Canada, 97, 102, 255, 354, 356, 375, 385, 397
Canadian International Development Agency (CIDA), 424
cannabis, 243, 244
Canossa, 372, 373
Carter, Jimmy, 244, 373
Caspian Sea, 103, 218
Catalans, 356
Cathay, William (Private), 135
Catholicism, 357
Catholics, 329, 402
Caucasus, 86, 89, 92, 96, 287
Central African Republic, 90
Central America, 95, 248, 252, 357, 419
Central Intelligence Agency (CIA), 90, 202, 246–249, 377
Central Treaty Organization (CENTRO), 397
Cerdanya, 123
Ceuta, 288
Chad, 89
Chaliand, G., 288
Chamberlain, Neville, 374
Chavez, Hugo, 231
Chechnya, 3, 89, 92, 149, 158, 168, 227, 420, 421
chemical warfare, 256
Chiapas, 39, 223, 227
Chile, 281, 283, 284
China: and Afghanistan, 428; and Angola, 224; and Cambodia, 233; and Chinese diaspora, 243; and development, 68; and diplomacy, 373, 386; and direct violence, 67; and Empire, 25, 124, 125; and life expectancy, 65; Manchu, 243; and military expenditure, 97; and Ming dynasty, 118, 119; and nuclear weapons, 34; and territoriality, 281, 288, 291; and Tibet, 159; and United States, 86, 102, 103, 373, 374; Yunan Province, 255
Chinese Communists, 247
Chinese Han, 124
Chinese Nationalists, 247, 248, 373
Chiozza, G., 91
Chirac, Jacques, 310, 409
Chrétien, Jean, 385, 386
Christaller, Walter, 33
Christendom, 154, 158, 161

Christianity, 119, 151, 152, 153, 161, 167, 203, 204, 207
Christians, 149, 151, 157
Christopher, Warren, 175
Christoslavism, 156
Churchill, Winston, 373
Cigar, Norman, 186
Citizen's Army, 140
citizenship, 80, 92, 118, 123, 128, 139, 180, 232, 321, 350
Ciudad Juárez, 380
civil society, 76
civil war: and boundaries, 324; and children, 90; and development, 72; and drugs, 245, 247; and ethnonationalism, 327, 333; and historic trend, 85–88, 91; and peace movements, 350, 363; and postwar recovery, 419, 421; and religious war, 157; and resources, 217, 219–221; and space, 23; and Third World, 86; and United States, 96
Clash, The, 104
Clausewitz, Carl von, 31, 218, 351
Clinton, William, 86, 182, 183, 185, 244, 245, 302, 315, 386
Clout, Hugh, 38
CNN, 302
Coates, Ken, 356
coca, 243, 246, 249, 250, 251, 255
cocaine, 243, 244, 248, 255, 256
Cock, Jaclyn, 133, 141
coffee, 227, 251, 255
Cogan, Charles, 246
Cohen, Saul B., 35, 37, 97, 103
Cold War: and academic geography, 34, 36, 37, 39; and democratic peace, 71; and diplomacy, 370, 378, 380, 382; and drugs, 11, 246, 247, 254; and historic trends, 3, 22, 85–87, 92, 94, 97; and Kantian peace, 397, 401–403; and mutually assured destruction, 5; and peace movements, 170, 353, 355, 358; and peace science, 64; and postwar recovery, 415, 419, 420, 429; and realism, 73; and resources, 218, 220, 233; and totalitarianism, 200, 205
College of Surgeons, 140
Collier, Paul, 89, 91, 220, 221
Collins, Michael, 138
Colombia, 6, 85, 89, 227, 244–249, 251, 254, 280
colonialism, 289, 324
Colorado, 260
coltan (columbite-tantalite), 220
Columbus, Christopher, 242
Commission of Experts (UN), 184
Committee for Nonviolent Action (CNVA), 355
Commodity Stabilization Fund, 230
Common Foreign and Security Policy (CFSP), 389
Communism, 9, 22, 124, 125, 205, 247, 357, 397, 398, 404–406
Communist, former states, 115
Communist parties, 353
Communist Party (Yugoslavia), 176
complex humanitarian emergency, 420
Concert of Europe, 375
Conference of Mayors, 357
conflict resolution, 13
Congo, 3, 85, 89, 90, 96, 385, 418
Congo, Democratic Republic, 85, 217, 220, 226, 227, 231, 232
Congo, Republic of, 227
Congo Basin, 96
Congress of Vienna, 374, 375, 378, 381, 382
Connolly, W. E., 98
conscientious objectors, 349, 352, 362
context: and academic geography, 7, 9, 10, 27, 33; and development, 64, 69; and drugs, 242; and ethnonationalism, 322; and genocide, 191, 192; and nationalism, 127; and peace movements, 347, 350, 355, 360, 361; and political order, 75; and religious war, 150–167, 169, 170; and resource war, 221, 222, 224, 230–234; and territoriality, 284, 288, 290; and terrorism, 199, 200, 201, 204, 206, 212; and war trends, 22, 25, 92; and water conflicts, 263–265, 270
Contras, 94, 230, 244, 248, 358
Convention on the Prevention and Punishment of the Crime of Genocide (Genocide Convention), 180, 181, 185, 186, 188, 190, 191, 192
copper, 223, 227, 229, 231
CORespondance EUropéene (COREU), 389

Correlates of War Project, 91
cosmic war, 204
Côte d'Ivoire, 96, 230. *See also* Ivory Coast
Council of Foreign Ministers, 375
Council of Foreign Relations, 32
counter-terrorism, 5, 198–212, 408
coup d'état, 217, 227, 230, 231
Cresswell, Tim, 360
Crimea, 373
critical geopolitics, 5
Croatia, 97, 121, 161, 174–190, 385, 421
Croats, 122
Crusades, the, 153, 157, 163
Cuba, 202, 287
Cultural Revolution, 205
cultural violence, 62
Cumann na mBan, 138, 139, 140
Cutter, Susan, 40
Cvijic, Johan, 32
Cyprus: and academic geography, 39; and borders, 6, 12; and diplomacy, 385; and ethnonationalism, 322, 327, 329; and partition, 185; and peacekeeping forces, 418; and territoriality, 284, 285
Czechoslovakia, 291, 374, 397
Czech Republic, 402

Dahlman, Carl, 10
Dail, 138
Dalai Lama, 159
Damascus Gate, 328
Davis, William Morris, 28
Dawes, Charles, 416
Dayton, OH, 384, 385
Dayton Peace Accords, 185, 192
De Beers, 222, 231
Declaration and Programme of Action, Durban Conference, 388
Defenders of Christendom, 152
Defense, Ministry of, 41
Defense Advanced Research Projects Agency (DARPA), 99
Demangeon, Albert, 31, 32
Demilitarized Zone, 384
Demirel, Süleyman, 388
Demko, George, 40
democide, 90
Democracy, 72, 75, 91, 126, 222, 398, 399
Democrat Party (USA), 358
Democratic peace, 71, 72
democratization, 72, 222, 227, 230, 234, 398
denazification, 417
Denmark, 97, 354, 397
Department for International Development (DFID), 424
deterritorialization, 210, 321, 340
Deutsche, Rosalyn, 137, 139
developing countries, 67
development: and boundaries, 327; and diplomacy, 387, 388; and drugs, 250, 252–254, 256; and modernity, 401, 404; and political order, 8, 61–80; and postwar recovery, 415–417, 419–421, 425–427, 431; and religious war, 156, 209; and resources, 217, 222, 229; and territoriality, 283; and terrorism, 202, 209; and war, 92, 95; and water, 261, 263, 267, 269–271, 273
diamonds, 75, 89, 220, 222, 224–228, 231–232
Dijkink, Gertjan, 9, 38
diplomacy, 7, 12, 31, 37, 73, 262, 269, 302, 369–390, 427
diplomatic bag, 376
direct violence, 62, 65, 70, 78, 79
Disability-Adjusted Life Year (DALYs), 67, 68
Dittgen, Herbert, 339
Divic, 179
Dodds, Klaus, 38
Doha, 386
Dome of the Rock, 164
Dowler, Lorraine, 9, 38, 39
Drug Enforcement Agency (DEA), 244
drugs, 5, 10, 11, 89, 217, 231, 242–256, 337, 380, 430
Dublin Castle, 140
Duffy, George Gavan, 138
Duggan, Eamonn, 138
Durban, 388
Dushanbe, 430
Dzurek, Daniel, 330

Earth Summit, 387
Easter Rising, 140
East Indies, 242
East Jerusalem, 263, 298, 301, 302, 328
East Timor, 421
Eastwood, Clint, 21
Economic Law of Life, 66, 67
Ecuador, 289, 290

Eden, Anthony, 378
Edinburgh, 331
Egypt, 102, 152, 157, 158, 163, 260, 281, 283, 374
Einstein, Albert, 352
Eisenhower, Dwight, 262, 378
Eizenstat, Stuart, 389
Eksteins, Modris, 119
Elbadawi, I., 89
El Niño, 267
El Salvador, 134, 227, 357, 419
embassies, 376, 377
empire, 5, 19, 22, 23, 125, 126, 206
England, 116, 152, 218, 361
enlargement geopolitics, 398
Enloe, Cynthia, 133, 134
Ensor, James, 116, 117
environmental degradation, 219, 250, 252, 256, 268, 271, 272
Environmental security, 220
Enzensberger, Hans M., 122
Eretz Israel, 299
Eritrea, 159
Escobar, Pablo, 244
Ethiopia, 94, 96, 288, 420
ethnic cleansing, 7, 10, 123, 175–193, 322, 327, 333
ethnonationalism: and borders, 321–340; and Hungary, 403, 405; and peace movements, 356; and postwar recovery, 421, 422, 428; and territoriality, 283, 285–287, 290; and troop morale, 115; and war, 128
Euphrates river, 261, 266, 267, 269, 270
Eurasia, 205
Euro Force, 402
Europe: and academic geography, 27, 30; and Afghanistan, 245; and Balkan wars, 123, 175, 183; Central, 128, 152, 323, 377, 396, 402, 404; Christian, 161; and Cold War, 379; colonialism, 287; and Communist parties, 353; Crusades, 163; and decline of, 31; and democracy, 399; and democratic peace, 91; and diplomacy, 375, 381; and drug policy, 249; East central, 404; Eastern, 33, 122, 128, 154, 161, 176, 185, 208, 323, 396; and empires, 100, 124, 242; and ethnonationalism, 356
Europeans: as Kantians, 98
European Community, 37
European Nuclear Disarmament (END), 356
European Security and Defense Identity (ESDI), 375
European Union: and boundaries, 335; and Cyprus, 327; and diplomacy, 387, 389; Enlargement, 329; and ethnonationalism, 177; and NATO, 402, 404, 405, 408, 409; and Palestine, 298; and postwar recovery, 424; and realism, 77; and sovereignty, 39; and United States, 208
European wars, 115, 120; and fascism, 352; and former socialist countries, 67; and Geneva Conventions, 417; and imperialism, 19, 157, 158, 204, 243; and Kantian peace, 6, 13; and Liberalism, 70; Medieval, 154; and mercantalism, 218; and military power, 19; and Napoleonic Wars, 374; and nationalism, 116, 127; and Ottoman Empire, 123; and Palestine Liberation Organization, 199; and peacekeeping forces, 333; and peace movements, 351, 353, 355, 356, 358; and post-Communist states, 92; and postwar recovery, 416–418; powers, 27; and religious wars, 152; and RUF, 226; Southeastern, 5, 96, 122, 151, 161; and Switzerland, 378; and terrorism, 202; and transatlantic expansion, 242; and troops, 103; and United Nations, 381, 418; and United States, 94, 127, 208; Western, 71, 92, 97, 204, 321, 323, 329, 353, 397, 402; and World War I, 119, 123, 170, 418; and World War II, 400
Evagoras, 285

failed states, 73, 74, 88, 90, 96
Falah, Ghazi-Walid, 11, 39
Falkland Islands, 287
Falklands War, 3, 20, 38, 120, 127
FARC, 230, 233, 249
Far East, 353
Faryab, 428, 429
Fascism, 9, 200, 353
Fatah party, 167
Fateh, 301
Faure, Edgar, 378

Fearon, J., 88, 89, 90, 91
Febvre, Lucien, 31
Federal Bureau of Investigation (FBI), 200
federalism, 30, 77
Fein, Helen, 186
Fellowship of Reconciliation, 352
feminism, 133, 135, 137, 348, 349, 352, 354, 356, 362
Ferguson, N., 104
FIDESZ, 405–407
Finland, 38
Finucane, Patrick, 206
Firefighters, 136, 142–145
Fisk, Robert, 302
Flemish, 116
Flight 93, 142
Flint, Colin, 10, 37
Force Application and Launch from the Continental United States (FALCON), 99
Fox, Vicente, 380
France: and academic geography, 28, 29, 30, 32, 33, 36, 40; and Algeria, 310; and Alsace-Lorraine, 120; and Biafra, 231; and Brazzaville, 228; and diplomacy, 374, 375, 378; and empire, 161; and England, 116; and ethnonationalism, 283; and Euro Force, 402; and Germany, 116; and military campaigns, 114; and military expenditure, 97; and Napoleon, 380; and nationalism, 121, 123, 127; and NATO, 397, 398; as nuclear power, 34; and nuclear weapons, 355; oil companies, 228; pays, 77; and peace movements, 354, 355; and postwar recovery, 416; Pyrenees, 329; and troop morale, 119; and United States, 102; and UNPROFOR, 183; and World War I, 38
Franco-Prussian War, 27, 28, 128
Franks, 161, 285
Free State, Irish, 140
French Guiana, 102
French Revolution, 71, 200, 201, 350
French Wars of Religion, 152
Friendship Bridge, 430
Fukuyama, Francis, 94, 207

G7/G8 Summit, 385
Gabon, 102, 293
Galilee, 316
Galtung, Johan, 27, 62, 63, 64, 65, 69, 75, 79
Gandhi, Indira, 156
Gandhi, Mohandas, K., 349, 353
Ganges-Brahmaputra Rivers, 260
gas, natural, 227, 229, 430
Gates, S., 92
Gaza Strip, 24, 263, 298–299, 302, 303, 307–310, 312, 314, 316
Gellner, Ernst, 120
gems, 10, 227
gender: and peace movements, 349, 352, 356, 360, 361; and postwar recovery, 418, 422; and war, 9, 133–145; and water conflict, 268
General Agreement on Tariffs and Trade (GATT), 400, 401
General Framework Agreement for Peace in Bosnia and Herzegovina, 385
General Peace Convention, 351
Geneva, 12, 352, 378, 382, 383, 384, 417
Geneva Conventions, 99, 174–176, 180–193, 302, 417
Genocide, 5, 10, 96, 162, 272, 324, 327, 333, 420
Genocide Convention, 180, 181, 185, 186, 188, 190, 191, 192
geographical information systems, 13, 35, 40
Geography: as academic discipline, 3, 28, 34, 35; and civil war, 23; and diplomacy, 369–390; and education, 41; and foreign policy, 4; and genocide, 176; and peace, 4, 26–42; of peace movements, 347–363; political, 4, 5, 7, 10; and postwar recovery, 415, 422, 428, 432; and poverty, 265; of power, 310; of resistance, 310, 312, 314; and terrorism, 198–212; and war, 4, 5, 7, 26–42, 351; and water conflict, 259–273
Geopolitical codes, 339
Geopolitical world order, 7
Geopolitics: and academic geography, 33, 35, 36, 38, 39; and boundaries, 340; critical geopolitics, 5; and diplomacy, 370; enlargement, 398; and ethnic cleansing, 176; and genocide, 187; intra-state, 297; and Israel, 305; and Israel-Palestine conflict, 299, 300; and

Kurds, 332; and nationalism, 115; of peace movements, 347, 351, 355; and postwar recovery, 415–432; and scale, 281; and security, 395; and territoriality, 291, 293; and terrorism, 201; and water, 261, 263, 266
Geopolitik, 29, 31, 33, 42
Géopolitique, 41
George, David Lloyd, 138
Germany: and academic geography, 27, 28, 30, 31, 32, 33; and Afghanistan, 430; and church and state, 119; and denazification, 417; and diplomacy, 373; and ESDI, 375; and Euro Force, 402; and France, 113, 114, 116; and geopolitics, 35, 42; and nationalism, 123, 127; and NATO, 398, 399; and Nazism, 205, 287; and peace movements, 352; and post-war development, 79; and postwar recovery, 418; and Red Army faction, 205; and Treaty of Versailles, 121; and United States, 97, 102; and World War I, 416, 418; and World War II, 23, 38, 351, 376
Ghauri, 149
Ghaznavi, 149
Gibraltor, 288
Gilo, 308
Glaspie, April, 126
Glassboro State College, 380
Glassboro Summit, 380
Glassner, Martin I, 308
Gleditsch, K. S., 91
Gleditsch, N. P., 91, 92, 94
Gleick, Peter, 218, 260
Global Burden of Disease (GBD), 66, 67, 68
globalization: and academic geography, 41; and development, 63; and diplomacy, 370, 385, 388, 390; and realism, 74; and territoriality, 281; and United States, 102, 209; and war, 23
global warming, 219
Goblet, Yves-Marie, 31
Golan Heights, 263, 314
gold, 220, 223, 224, 226, 227, 229, 231
Golden Triangle, 248, 252, 255
Goldstein, J., 101, 134, 136
Golgotha, 161
Goradze, 385
Gorazde, 177
Gorbachev, Mikhail, 357, 374, 377, 378, 382
Gottmann, Jean, 35, 381
Governance, 7, 199, 217, 425, 427
Graham, B., 38
Gramsci, Antonio, 118, 119, 120, 297, 306, 313
Grant, Richard, 37
Graube, Raimanos, 395
Great Britain. *See* United Kingdom
Great Game, 77
Great Mosque, 166
Great Wall of China, 125
Great War, 27, 30, 32, 38
Greater Albania, 334
Greater Serbia, 121, 176, 182, 184, 186, 189, 334
Greece, 32, 33, 123, 281, 284–285, 354, 383, 387, 397, 401
Greed war, 220
Greek Cypriots, 327, 329
Greek Macedonia, 129
Greenham Common, 356, 360
Green Line, 325–327, 331, 332
Green parties, Europe, 356
Green Party, Brazil, 387
Greenpeace, 355, 356
Green war, 219, 220
Gregory VII (pope), 372
Grenada, 86, 104
Griffith, Arthur, 138
Guanajuato, 380
Guantanamo, 287
Guatemala, 94, 227, 251, 252, 357
guerilla war, 6, 21, 24, 124, 158, 226, 228, 232, 420
Guldensporenslag (Battle of the Golden Spurs), 116, 117
Gulf of Guinea, 289
Gulf War: and academic geography, 38; and development, 79; and Israel-Palestine conflict, 297; and nationalism, 124, 126; and peace movements, 358; and religious war, 169; and United States, 86, 97, 99, 291, 401; and war, 265; and water conflict, 271
Güneydoğu Anadolu Projesi (GAP), 11, 261, 267
Gurr, Ted R., 86

Guru Gobind Singh, 153
Gush Emunim, 164
Guy of Dampierre, 116
Guyana, 284
Guyot, Arnold H., 28
Gvirtzman, Haim, 309

Hague, the, 184, 352
Hague Conference, 351
Hague Court, 351
Hague Opium Conventions, 243
Haiti, 85, 86, 102
Hamas, 167, 244, 310
Hamseh-Muhaisen, Muna, 308
Hangchow, 373
Hapsburg Empire, 124, 375
Harris, Leila, 11, 267
Harrison, Richard Edes, 20
Harrison Narcotics Act, 243
Hartshorne, Richard, 33, 35, 39
Harvard University, 27, 28
Hashish, 244, 255
Haushofer, Karl, 35
Hayden, Robert H., 185, 186, 189
Hazaras, 428
Hebrew University, 309
Hebron, 164, 303, 308, 316
Hegel, 94
hegemonic power, 8, 206–212, 351, 375, 395–409
hegemony, Gramscian, 299, 306, 312, 313
Hegre, H., 91
Heine, Heinrich, 113
Hellenistic period, 285
Henrikson, Alan K., 12
Henry IV, Emperor, 372
Hepburn, Katherine, 134
Herb, Guntram H., 12
Hérodote, 36, 40
heroin, 243, 244, 246, 248, 250, 255, 256
Heske, Henning, 26
Hewitt, Kenneth, 38
Hijaz, 153
Hill, Michael, 206
Hillel, Daniel, 262
Hinduism, 149, 155, 156, 165, 167
Hindutva, 155
Hiroshima, 27, 87, 353
Hitler, Adolph, 4, 6, 374
HIV/AIDS, 68, 69, 77, 80
Hmong, 248
Hobbes, T., 94
Hoeffler, Anke, 220
Hoffman, Bruce, 200, 201, 202
Höivik, Tord, 65
Holbrooke, Richard, 385
Hollywood, 207
Holocaust, 38, 180, 182, 183, 185, 190, 353, 389
Holy League, 151
Homer, 150, 285
Homer-Dixon, Thomas, 264, 271
Honig-Parnass, Tikva, 316
Hoover, Herbert, 416
Hope Hotel, 385
Horran Plain, 268
Hughes, Richard J., 380
Huguenots, 152
Human Development Index, 68, 92, 95
human security, 219
humanitarian emergencies, 419
humanitarian spaces, 423
Hungarian Communist Party, 404
Hungarian military, 404, 406, 407
Hungarian Socialist Party (HSP), 404–407
Hungarian Truth and Light Party (HTLP), 405
Hungarians, 121, 405
Hungary, 13, 161, 283, 395–409
Huntington, Samuel, 91
Husayn, Sharif, 153
Hussein, Saddam, 6, 77, 85, 90, 97, 167, 198, 358
Hutu, 88

Iberia, 151, 161
Iceland, 102, 397
idealism, 71, 349
Ignatieff, Michael, 121, 122
Iliad, 150
Iliescu, Ion, 395
Im Etappenquartier vor Paris, 113, 114
imperialism, 38
Imperial Overstretch, 208, 209
India: and academic geography, 34, 38; and development, 68; diaspora, 243; and diplomacy, 379; and direct violence, 67; and life expectancy, 65; and partition, 323; and peace movements, 349, 353; and religious

war, 149, 155, 156, 165, 166, 169, 170, 203, 206; and territoriality, 280, 284, 287, 288, 290; and terrorism, 203, 206; and United Nations, 418; and United States, 102
Indochina, 248
Indonesia, 85, 89, 102, 124, 217, 227, 281, 386, 428
Informal General Affairs and External Relations Council, 387
Integrated Data for Events Analysis (IDEA), 100, 101
Intermediate Nuclear Forces Treaty (INF), 357
Internally displaced persons (IDPs), 419, 422, 423
International Bank for Reconstruction and Development, 418. *See also* World Bank
International Charter on Geographical Education, 40
International Committee of the Red Cross (ICRC), 122, 378, 382, 417, 419
International Court of Justice, 289, 352
International Criminal Court (ICC), 104, 191
International Criminal Tribunal for Rwanda, 182, 185, 188, 189, 191
International Criminal Tribunal for Yugoslavia, 184, 185, 187, 188, 189, 191, 192
International Geographical Union, 40; Commission on Geographical Education, 40; Commission on the History of Geographical Thought, 39; Commission on the World political map, 36
International Geography Conference, 36
International Labor Organization (ILO), 382
International Monetary Fund (IMF), 207, 230, 231, 233, 400, 401
International Olympic Truce Centre, 383
International Peace Bureau, 352
International relations (IR), 395
International School, Geneva, 352
International Women's Socialist Conference, 352
Internet, 39, 126, 363, 388, 389
Inter-Service Intelligence (ISI), 246, 247
inter-state war, 259
Intifada, 305, 308, 310–314, 316, 328
Intifadat Al-Aqsa, 300
Iquitos, 289
Iran: and boundaries, 323, 332; and diplomacy, 377; and Iraq, 96, 323; and religious war, 163, 167; and resources, 217; and territoriality, 281, 292; and United States, 86, 102; and war on terrorism, 3
Iran-Contra hearings, 244
Iranian Revolution, 376
Iran-Iraq war, 167, 271, 332
Iraq: and borders, 323, 332, 338; and democide, 90; and development, 79; and genocide, 182, 191; and Hungary, 408, 409; and Iran, 3, 96, 167; and Iraq War, 86, 92, 97, 98, 126, 245; and oil, 227, 229, 231; and peace movements, 358; and postwar recovery, 423; and religious war, 169; and resources, 227, 229, 231; and territoriality, 24, 280, 288, 292; and United States, 5, 85, 86, 99, 102, 104, 183; and war on terrorism, 201, 208, 209, 244; and water conflict, 260, 261, 265, 270–272. *See also* Gulf War
Ireland, 38, 88, 138, 144, 145
Ireland, Republic of, 139, 140, 203, 285
Irgun, 205
Irish Free State, 139
Irish Republican Army (IRA), 24, 89, 138, 140
Irish Revolution, 136, 137
Iron Age, 19
Iron Curtain, 13, 125, 357, 378, 382, 395
iron ore, 228
Irrawaddy River, 19
Islam: and nationalism, 119, 126; and religious war, 149, 151, 152, 153, 159, 161, 164, 166, 168, 169; and territoriality, 291; and Western atheism, 398
Islamabad, 379
Islamic assassins, 255
Islamic empire, 151, 161
Islamic law, 163
Islamic militants, 247
Islamic peace movements, 350
Islamic Resistance Movement, 167

Islamic Revolution, 163
Islamic state, 90, 154, 157, 158, 162, 167
Islamic terrorism, 203, 217, 226
Islamic world, 280, 291
Islamists, 103, 149, 157, 163, 164, 165, 166, 168
Israel: and academic geography, 37, 39, 40; and borders, 325, 326, 330; and diplomacy, 374, 383, 386; and ethnonationalism, 332; and Gaza Strip, 24; and just war, 297–316; and Palestine, 12, 163, 164, 297–316, 338; and religious war, 163, 164, 167, 169; and Six-Day War, 149, 325; and terrorism, 205, 206; and United Nations, 418; and United States, 85, 202; and War of independence, 325; and water conflict, 260–264, 272
Israel-Arab war (1967), 261, 263, 266, 272, 298
Israeli-Arab conflict, 263
Israeli Arabs, 332
Israeli-Defense Forces (IDF), 309, 311
Israeli Jews, 332
Israelites, 163
Israel-Palestine conflict: and academic geography, 39; and airpower, 24; and borders, 96, 322, 323, 325, 338; and ethnonationalism, 325–328, 332; and just war, 12, 297–316; as religious war, 163–166, 203; and Separation Fence, 325–327; and territoriality, 280; and terrorism, 203; as water conflict, 217, 271
Istanbul, 387
Italy, 27, 118, 119, 121, 353, 372, 397, 398
Ivory Coast, 96
Iwo Jima, 4
Izetbegovic, Ayija, 385

Jains, 155
Jammu and Kashmir, 379
Japan: and academic geography, 31; and China, 288; and colonialism, 124; and diplomacy, 370; and hegemonic power, 208; and Hiroshima, 27; and imperialism, 204; and nuclear weapons, 354; as OECD country, 92; and peace movements, 353, 354; and Pearl Harbor, 20; and post-war development, 79; and religious terrorism, 203; and territoriality, 283, 288; and United States, 86, 102; and war casualties, 87; and World War II, 38, 374
Jelisic, Goran, 174, 190
Jenkins, Alan, 36
Jennin, 303
Jeong, Hon-Won, 363
Jerusalem, 149, 164, 166, 301, 303–305, 308, 328, 329, 374; Old city, 328
Jerusalem Temple, 153, 164, 166
Jewish people, 149, 153, 163, 164, 165, 168; of Israel, 315, 316, 329; and peace movements, 350; and West Jerusalem, 328
Jewish settlements, 300–311
Jewish terrorism, 203, 206
Jews, Orthodox, 163
Jihad, 152, 154, 168
Johnson, Lyndon B., 380
Johnson, Nuala, 38
Johnston, Ron J., 66
Joint Security Area, 384
Jones, Archer, 117, 118
Jones, Stephen B., 35
Jordan, 260, 263, 264, 307, 311, 325, 328
Jordan River, 24, 260, 262, 263, 264, 298, 316
Jordan-Yarmouk river basin, 263
Jowzjan, 428, 429
Judaism, Rabbinic, 153
Judea, 149, 153, 164, 331
Juergensmeyer, Mark, 203, 206
Jugoslovenstia Narodna Armija (JNA), 189
Jupiter, 153
just war, 210, 211, 297–316, 353

Kabul, 6, 431
Kacowicz, A. M., 301
Kafka, Franz, 186
Kagan, R., 94, 97, 98
Kalkiliya, 330
Kan, C. M., 28
Kananaskis, 385
Kandy, 166
Kant, Immanuel, 71, 72, 398, 399
Kantian Peace, 13, 71, 211, 395, 396, 398, 407, 409
Kaplan, Robert, 94, 96

Karadzic, Radovan, 177
Karimov, Islom, 430
Karzai, Hamid, 126
Kashmir, 3, 159, 379
Kastellorizo, 387
Katanga, 231
Keen, David, 226
Kefar Sava, 330
Kennedy, John F., 245
Kennedy, Paul, 208
Kenya, 205, 208
Khalistan, 156
Khalsa, 153, 156
Khmer Rouge, 160, 191, 232, 233
Khomeni, Ayatollah Rahollah, 376
Khrushchev, Nikita, 378
King, C., 89
King, Martin Luther, Jr., 355
Kingdom of the Serbs, Croats, and Slovenians, 33
Kirby, Andrew, 39
Kirkuk, 331, 332
Kirton, John, 385
Kissinger, Henry A., 373
Kjellén, Rudolf, 29, 31, 32
Klandermans, Bert, 358–361
Klare, Michael, 103, 218, 219
Klein, Menachem, 304–306
Kleinbaum, Abby, 133
kleptocracy, 221
Kliot, Nurit, 37, 263
Knesset, 299, 304, 374
Knights of St. John, 387
Köhler, Gernot, 65, 66, 67
Kolossov, Vladimir, 38
Konduz, 428, 429
Korean War, 96, 120
Kosovo: and academic geography, 38; and borders, 322, 334, 339; and development, 76; and ethnonationalism, 322, 334, 339; and genocide, 175, 176, 185, 333; and NATO, 404, 408; and postwar recovery, 421; and refugees, 327; and regions, 6; and religious war, 157, 159, 161, 162; and sovereignty, 408; and United States, 97, 408; and war trends, 92
Kosygin, Aleksei, 380
Krajina, 124
Kreisky, Bruno, 382
Kropotkin, Peter, 33, 41, 349
Krstic, General Radislav, 190
Kulturkampf, 373
Kundera, Milan, 186
Kurdistan, 89, 290
Kurds: and borders, 322, 323, 332, 333, 338; and ethnonationalism, 322, 332, 333, 338; and genocide, 191; and oil, 229, 272, 331; and territoriality, 290, 291; and water conflict, 269, 271, 272
Kuwait, 86, 98, 126, 217, 227, 231
Kwasniewski, Aleksander, 395
Kyoto Protocal, 104

Labour Party (Israel), 305
Lacoste, Yves, 8, 26, 36, 38
Laden, Osama bin, 151
Lahore, 379
Laitin, D., 88, 89, 90, 91
Lambert, Brian, 206
Laos, 247, 248, 250
Laqueur, Walter, 200
Lasswell, Harold, 86, 99
Latin America, 70, 134, 230, 246, 247, 248, 254, 288, 289, 354
Latvia, 395
law, international humanitarian, 10
Law—Palestinian Society for Protection of Human Rights and Environment, 308, 312, 315
League of Nations, 27, 30, 352, 378, 382, 418; Conference on Disarmament, 352
Lebanon, 6, 86, 168, 261, 272, 298
Lebensraum, 32, 33, 218
Le Billon, Phillipe, 10, 261
Lemkin, Raphael, 180
Leningrad, 355
Leone Sergio, 21
Liberal democracy, 71, 207, 399
Liberal internationalism, 349
Liberalism, 9, 119, 212
Liberia, 86, 89, 96, 220, 227, 228
Libya, 86, 102
Likud Party, 298, 305
Lilla, Mark, 75, 80
Limited Test Ban Treaty, 355
Lissouba, Pascal, 227, 228
Locke, John, 350
London, 180, 200, 331, 375

London Economic Conference, 381
Lonergan, S., 261
Los Angeles, 39, 248
Lowi, M., 262, 263
Luanda, 224
Lutheranism, 152
Luxembourg, 397
Luxor, 163
Lyon, 28

Mau Mau, 205
Macedonia, 33, 85, 86, 123, 339
Macedonia, Former Yugoslav Republic of, 334
Mackinder, Sir Halford, 28, 29, 31, 32, 35, 77, 103, 218, 351
MacSwiney, Mary, 138, 139, 145
Mahan, Alfred Thayer, 351
Mahavamsa, 155, 162
Mahdism, 166
Makorsky, David, 309
Malaysia, 37
Malta, 377–379
Malthus, Thomas, 78, 217
Malvinas, 120, 127
Mamadouh, Virginie, 8
Mann, Michael, 74, 76
Maoism, 160, 251
Maori, 38
Maqarim Dam, 262
marijuana, 251, 252
Markievicz, Countess Constance, 140, 141, 144, 145
Maros, Ferdinand, 230
Marsh Arabs, 272
Marshall Islands, 354
Marshall Plan, 415, 417, 418
Martinez, Oskar, 335
Martonne, Emmanuel de, 31, 32
martyrdom, 161, 167, 168
Marxism, 33, 35, 88, 100
Masada, 153
Mathewson, Kent, 10
Mauritania, 227
Mauryan, 169
Maya, 252, 253
Mayo, James, 38
Mazar-e Sharif, 429
Mazzo, Katy, 143
McCarthyism, 353
McDougall, W. A., 87
McVeigh, Timothy, 206
Mead, Walter Russell, 86, 98
Mearsheimer, J., 87, 94
Mecca, 152, 153, 163, 166, 291
Medina, 152, 153, 163, 292
Mediterranean Sea, 298, 378, 418
Mekong River, 260
Melilla, 288
mercantalism, 218, 221, 242, 401
Mercator projection, 20
Merino, Kevin, 143
Merino, Yamel, 143
mesoscale, 281
meta-geography, 10, 199, 209, 210
metals, industrial, 225
metamphetamines, 255
Metternich, Prince Clemens von, 374
Mexico, 92, 102, 227, 250, 267, 283, 379, 380
Middle Ages, 124, 243
Middle East: and academic geography, 30, 39; and al-Qaeda, 159; and boundaries, 324; and CENTRO, 397; and demography, 78; and diplomacy, 380, 383, 385; and Israel, 314; and Israel-Palestine conflict, 298, 302; and postwar recovery, 418, 420; and religious war, 169; and territoriality, 288, 292; and United States, 103; and war trends, 96; and water conflict, 259, 260, 262, 263, 266, 272
Middle Kingdom, 373
Mikesell, M., 290
military geography, 36, 42
military organization, 22, 134
Mill, John Stuart, 211
Miller, Byron, 358
Milosevic, Slobodan, 162, 176, 177, 185, 189, 385
mineral resources, 217, 231, 272, 331
Ming dynasty, 125
Mintz, S. W., 243
Mitrovica, 327
Modernity, 13, 396, 405. *See also* Prime Modernity
Mongolia, 283
Mongols, 118, 428
Monrovia, 228
Montesquieu, Charles de Secondat, 350

Moore, Michael, 222
Moors, 161
Morin, Karen, 38
Morocco, 89, 227, 229, 288
Morphine, 243
Moscow, 430
Mosul, 332
Movimento Popular de Liberaçâo de Angola (MPLA), 233
Moynihan, Daniel Patrick, 383
Mozambique, 96, 420
Mughals, 153, 154, 165
Muhammad, 152, 157, 164
Mujahideen, 94, 158, 159, 168, 246
Munich, 22
municipality, 190, 302, 323, 324, 328, 329, 336, 337, 356
Murphy, Alexander B., 11, 290
Muslim Brotherhood, 158, 167
Muslim state, 291
Muslims, 91, 122, 149, 151, 153, 157, 159, 162, 166, 168–169; Bosnian, 174–181, 185, 190
Mutually Assured Destruction (MAD), 5, 97
Myanmar, 89, 248, 251–253, 254, 293

Nablus, 303
Nagasaki, 87, 353
Nagorno-Karabakh, 89, 287
Nairn, Tom, 89, 122
Nancy, 28
Napoleon, Emperor, 380
Napoleonic Era, 63
Napoleonic Wars, 115, 118, 350
Nash, Catherine, 137
Nasioi culture, 230
National Committee for a Sane Nuclear policy (SANE), 354
National Committee of Soviet Geographers, 36
nationalism, 9, 12, 27, 38, 88, 89, 282; and academic geography, 27, 38; and borders, 12; and civil war, 88, 89; and peace movements, 353; and religious identity, 155, 156, 159, 161, 162; and sovereignty, 282; and territoriality, 9; and war, 113–129
National Security Strategy of the United States, 87, 103
nation-state, 6, 11, 32, 282
National Union for the Total Independence of Angola (UNITA), 224, 226, 228, 232, 233
Native American, 202, 350
Nazism, 23, 33, 174, 201, 205, 287, 353, 374
neighborhood, 6, 248, 313, 323, 324, 327, 328, 329
Neo-Liberalism, 254
Neo-Malthusianism, 220
Netherlands, 28, 119–120, 124, 152, 229, 329, 352, 386, 397, 401
networks: and academic geography, 6, 34; and peace movements, 350, 353; and radical Islamist movements, 168; and resources, 228, 232; and terrorism, 10, 159, 198, 199, 209, 210; and war, 273
Netanyahu, Benjamin, 299, 303–305, 309
Neuchâtel Academy, 28
neutrality, 378
New Delhi, 379
New Jersey, 380
New Left, 361
Newman, David, 12, 39, 40
New People's Army (NPA), 230
new social movement theory, 358–360
New York Bar Association, 382
New York City, 6, 142, 143, 168, 200, 352, 354, 356, 380–384, 431; Fire Department, 142, 144; Police Department, 143
New Zealand, 38, 354
Ngo Dinh Diem, 167
Nguesso, Denis, 228
Nicaragua, 3, 94, 134, 230, 247, 248, 357
Nicosia, 327, 329
Niemen River, 380
Nierop, Tom, 37
Nietschmann, Bernard, 301
Niger Delta, 223, 234
Nigeria, 89, 152, 163, 217, 227, 231, 234, 283, 289
Nijman, Jan, 37
Nile River, 19, 260
Nixon, Richard, 244, 373
Nobel Prize for Peace, 42, 374
Non-Governmental Organizations (NGOs), 348, 381; and postwar recovery, 415, 417–427, 430, 431
Noriega, Manuel, 244

North America, 30, 243, 381
North Atlantic Treaty Organization (NATO): and academic geography, 6, 34, 38; and diplomacy, 375; and former Yugoslavia, 162, 185; and Hungary, 395–409; and Kantian peace, 13, 395–409; and peace movements, 348, 355–357; and Turkey, 273; and United States, 207
Northern Alliance, 245–247
Northern Ireland: and academic geography, 39; and boundaries, 323; and civil war, 89; and diplomacy, 385; and ethnonationalism, 121, 323; and gender, 140; and guerilla war, 92; and territoriality, 285; and terrorism, 24, 203, 206
North Korea, 3, 87, 202, 292, 323, 384
North Pole, 20
North Sea, 331
North Vietnam, 21, 38, 248
Norway, 92, 97, 351, 354, 397
Novara, 117, 118, 119
nuclear disarmament, 350, 354–356, 358
nuclear weapons, 34, 36, 42, 170, 354, 355, 357, 359, 361, 384
nuclear war, 7, 27, 40

Oas, Ian, 13
Occupied Territories, 315
Oceania, 19
Office for Strategic Services, 33
Ohio, 385
oil: and Afghanistan, 430; and development, 75; and ethnonationalism, 331; and resource war, 10, 89, 102, 217, 218, 220, 221, 223, 225, 227, 229, 231, 233; and territoriality, 272, 284, 289; and United States, 102, 103
Organization of the Petroleum Exporting Countries (OPEC), 103
O'Loughlin, John, 8, 26, 36, 37, 38, 40, 66
Olympic Games, 382, 383
Omagh, 203
Oman, 291
Ona, Francis, 223, 229
opiates, 243, 244
opium, 243, 245–255
O'Sullivan, Patrick, 7, 37
Orban, Viktor, 406, 407
Orentlicher, Diane, 191
Organization for Economic Cooperation and Development (OECD), 92, 94
Orientalism, 175, 202
Oslo Agreements, 298–301, 303–310, 312, 314, 315
Ottoman Empire, 121, 123, 124, 151, 152, 156, 157, 161, 204, 292
Ó Tuathail, Gearoid, 40, 398
Oxford University, 28

Paasi, Anssi, 38
Pacific island states, 356
Pacificism, 170, 348, 352
Pacific Ocean, 354, 355
Pacific Region, 418
Pacific Rim, 386
Pakistan: and diplomacy, 379; and drugs, 246; and Gulf war, 124; and India, 165, 166, 280; and partition, 323; and religious war, 149, 157, 165, 166; and territoriality, 284, 287; and United Nations, 418; and United States, 85, 102, 125; and war on terrorism, 430
Palestine; and Arab Afghans, 159; and Arab revolt, 158; and boundaries, 325, 332, 339; and ethnonationalism, 332, 339; and Israel, 12, 297–316; and refugees, 426; and religious war, 164, 167; and terrorism, 203; and United States, 408
Palestine-Israel Conflict, 297–316
Palestine Liberation Organization, 94, 199, 299, 310, 312, 314, 383
Palestine Mandate, 299
Palestinian Arabs, 332
Palestinian Authority, 12, 297, 301, 304, 306, 309, 310, 312, 313
Palestinian Christians, 164
Palestinian Legislative Council, 312
Palestinian Muslims, 166
Palestinian Society for Protection of Human Rights and Environment (Law), 308, 312, 315
Palestinian state, 297–316
Palestinians, 260, 332, 338, 339; and East Jerusalem, 328
Panama, 85, 86, 104, 244
Panguna, 223, 229
Panmunjom, 384

papacy, 157
Papandreou, George, 387
Papua New Guinea, 223, 227, 229
Paraná River, 19
Paris, 30, 113, 200; Peace Conference, 32, 375, 381
Parry, Nigel, 302
partition: and British India, 155, 157, 165; and Cyprus, 39; and diplomacy, 379; and former Yugoslavia, 177, 185; and Ireland, 138, 139, 145; and Israel-Palestine, 301, 418; and territoriality, 323, 324; and UN Partition Plan, 316
patriachy, 5, 348, 349
Pavlowitch, Stevan, 123
Peace: and diplomacy, 370, 371; and geography, 4, 7; and imperialism, 27; interstate, 74; negative and positive, 7, 62, 348; and postwar recovery, 432; and states, 352; and territoriality, 7, 11
peacekeeping, 34, 39, 96, 255, 327, 328, 402, 403, 418, 427
peace movements, 12
Peace News, 352
Peace of Vienna, 243
Peace Pledge Union, 352
peace science, 64
peace studies, 35, 64
Pearl Harbor, 20, 97
Peking, 373
Peloponneus, 383
Penn, William, 350
Pentagon, 168, 183, 186, 200, 203, 249, 375, 385
Pepper, David, 36
Peres, Shimon, 299
Persian Gulf, 103, 217, 218, 231
Peru, 89, 102, 160, 219, 247, 251, 254, 289, 293
Peruvian Indians, 219
Peschel, Oscar, 28
Pestalozzi, Johann Heinrich, 28
petroleum, 221, 244
petroviolence, 224
Philadelphia, 381
Philip II (King of Spain), 290
Philip IV, ("the Fair" King), 116
Philippines, 85, 102, 163, 217, 220, 227, 228, 230
phosphate, 89, 102, 227, 229
physical geography, 90
Physicians for Social Responsibility, 357
Piedmontese, 118
Pietsch, Ludwig, 113
Pile, Steve, 310
place: and academic geography, 6, 12, 42; and diplomacy, 369–390; and ethnonationalism, 322; and peace movements, 12, 358, 360, 361; and political order, 63; and religious war, 164, 167; and territoriality, 331; and terrorism, 199, 202; and water conflict, 259, 264, 273
Plan Colombia, 249
Poland, 151, 161, 283, 374, 395, 402
Pol Pot, 90
political ecology, 10, 253
political geography: and academic geography, 27, 30, 31, 33, 35, 39, 41; and boundaries, 324; and critical geopolitics, 5; and diplomacy, 379; and Palestine, 297; and peace, 7; and territoriality, 280; and terrorism, 10, 210; and war, 4, 7; and water conflict, 273
political order, 8, 61, 63, 70, 72, 80; Liberal, 76, 79; Realist, 76, 77, 79; State-makers' order, 75, 76, 79
Politische Geographie, 29
population growth, 260
Portillo, José López, 380
Portugal, 161, 284, 397
postcolonialism, 35
postmodernism, 35
postwar recovery, 13, 415–432
Poulsen, Thomas, 333
poverty, 265
Powell Doctrine, 96
Power, Samantha, 186, 191
powerscene, 385
Prime Modernity, 207, 208, 211, 212, 396, 401, 403, 407, 408
Princeton University, 28
Prithvi, 149
Protestantism, 152, 206
Protestants, 38, 160, 329
proxy war, 94
Prussia, 28, 31, 32, 115, 218, 373, 380
psychoactive agents, 242–256
Pugwash conference, 354

Pundak, Ron, 304
Punjab, 153, 155, 185, 379
Puritans, 152
Pyrenees, 123, 329

Qalqilya, 303
Qatar, 386
Quakers, 349, 350, 416
Quito, 290

Rabin, Yitzhak, 298, 299
Radetzky, General Joseph, 118
Rageau, J. P., 288
Ram, 165, 166
Ramallah, 300, 303, 308, 312
Ramrajya, 165
Rapoport, David, 204, 205
Ratzel, Friedrich, 29, 31, 32
Reagan, Ronald, 244, 355, 357–359, 380
Real IRA, 203
realism, 71, 73, 74, 94, 349
Reardon, Betty, 349
rebellion, 230, 300
Reclus, Élisée, 33, 349
Reconquista, 151
Record, Jeffrey, 22
Red Army Faction (RAF), 205
Reformation, 152
refugees: and Bosnia, 156, 327; and El Salvador, 419; and failed states, 90, 94, 96; and Kosovo, 327; Palestinian, 301–303, 305, 315; and postwar recovery, 422, 425, 426, 431; and structural violence, 69; and West Africa, 94
Reggio nell'Emilia, 372
region, 6, 12, 63
religion, 9, 23, 150; and peace movements, 349, 357; and war, 149–170
religious terrorism, 203–208
remote sensing, 35, 40
resource dependence, 221
resource exploitation, 223
resource mobilization theory, 358, 359, 361
resources: and academic geography, 6; and boundaries, 322, 329, 331; and development, 64, 65, 75; and rebellion, 89; and resource war, 10, 217–235; and United States companies, 102
resource war, 217–235, 261
reterritorialization, 331, 339
Revolutionary Armed Forces of Colombia (FARC), 230, 233
Revolutionary United Front (RUF), 226, 228, 233
Rhineland, 31, 32
Rhodes, 387
Rhodes, Cecil, 222, 231
Riddle of the Sands, 116
right-wing politics, 22
Rio de Janeiro, 387
risk-transfer war, 99
Ritter, Carl, 28
Robespierre, 114
Roman Catholics, 121, 152, 160, 167; church, 373
Roman Empire, 116, 124, 153, 285
Romania, 121, 387, 395, 403, 405
Roosevelt, Franklin D., 373, 374
Rousseau, Jean Jacques, 350
Rowan University, 380
Royal Laotian Army, 248
Royal Signals, 4
rubber, 221, 228
Rubin, Jeffrey, 369, 371, 377, 390
Rummel, R. J., 90
Russel, Bertrand, 352
Russia: and academic geography, 33; and Afghanistan, 430; and Chechnya, 92, 149; and China, 288; and the Great Game, 77; and NATO, 6, 404, 408; and terrorism, 204; and United States, 102
Russians, 121
Rwanda: and civil war, 88, 89; and genocide, 96, 181, 187, 191, 192; and postwar recovery, 420, 422; and resource war, 219, 231, 232

Sachs, Jeffrey, 90
Sadat, Anwar, 157, 374
safe havens, 423
Sahara Desert, 354, 355
Saharawis, 229
Saint Lazar, 156, 161, 162
Salacruse, Jeswald, 369, 371, 377, 390
Samangan, 428, 429
Samaria, 149, 164, 331
Sambanis, N., 89
San Cristóbal, 380

Sandinistas, 230
San Francisco, 39, 375, 381, 418
San Salvador, 420
SANE, 357
Sarajevo, 7, 128, 242, 385
SARS, 69, 80
satellite technology, 20
Satyagraha, 353
Saud dynasty, 152, 153, 292
Saudi Arabia: and diplomacy, 386; and oil, 231; and religious war, 166, 168, 169; and Taliban, 246; and territoriality, 280, 281, 283, 291; and terrorism, 208, 210; and United States, 85, 86, 124, 154, 204, 217, 291
Saudi peace plan, 298
Savimbi, Jonas, 226
Sawyer, Roger, 140
scale: and academic geography, 6, 7, 12, 13; and borders, 322; and drugs, 249; and genocide, 192; and hegemonic power, 401; intrastate, 321, 323; mesoscale, 286; and peace movements, 347, 350, 357, 362, 363; and political geography, 324; and political order, 63; and postwar recovery, 421, 425, 426, 428, 431, 432; and religious war, 165–167; and states, 281; and structural violence, 66; and territoriality, 292; and terrorism, 199, 203; and water conflict, 259–273
Scherrer, C., 88
Scotland, 331, 361
Scott, J. C., 250
Seattle, WA, 354, 386
secession, 228, 229, 231
Second World, 401
Semple, Ellen Churchill, 29
Sendero Luminoso (Shining Path), 160, 219, 251, 254
Senegal, 227
Senkaku Islands, 288
Separation Fence, 325, 326
September 11, 2001: and academic geography, 34, 40; and al-Qaeda, 97; and gender, 136, 137, 142–145; and geography, 3, 4; and peace movements, 358; and religious war, 151, 168; and territoriality, 280; and terrorism, 120, 198–200, 202; and United Nations, 381, 382; and United States foreign policy, 22, 96, 102, 245; and United States as hegemonic power, 208; and United States military spending, 86; and war on terrorism, 87, 100, 210, 247; and war trends, 92, 242
Serb-Croat war, 121
Serbia: and academic geography, 32; and borders, 333, 334; and ethnic cleansing, 123, 333; and genocide, 88, 174–176; and Hungary, 404, 405; and nationalism, 121, 124, 161, 162, 339; and religious war, 156, 161, 162; and United States, 102
Serbia and Montenegro, 333
Serbian Orthodox Church, 161
Serbs: and borders, 334, 339; and genocide, 176, 177, 184–186, 189, 192; and nationalism, 121, 122, 327, 328, 334, 339; and religious war, 156, 157
Servicio Paz y Justicia (SERPAJ), 357
Shanghai Communiqué, 373
Shan Plateau, 247, 248
Sharif, Nawaz, 379
Sharm el-Sheikh Memorandum, 303, 304
Sharon, Ariel, 299, 300, 304, 305, 313, 316
Shatt al-Arab, 332
Shaw, M., 99
Shell Oil Company, 231, 234
Shi'ite Islam, 152, 167, 229
Shin, Michael, 37
Shinui Party, 305
Shirlow, P., 38
Shultz, George P., 383
Sierra Leone, 3, 89, 92, 96, 226, 227, 228, 232
Sikh terrorism, 206
Sikhism, 153–156, 163, 166, 203, 290
Sinai Peninsula, 263
Sinhalese, 88, 155, 162
Sino-British Opium Wars, 242
Six-Day War, 149, 164, 380
slaves, 221
Slavs, 121, 156
Slovakia, 24, 291, 403, 405
Slovenia, 76, 176, 291
Slowe, Peter, 40
Smith, Gordon, 385
Smith, Moria, 143
socialism, 119, 349

social movements, 7
Soennecken, Brendan, 13
Sokoto, 152
Somalia, 86, 88, 94, 96, 102, 104, 183, 219, 420
Somme, Battle of, 38
Sosland, J., 263, 264
South Africa, 89, 102, 222, 231, 353, 362, 388
South America, 102, 249, 250, 289
South China Sea, 86, 218
Southeast Asia Treaty Organization (SEATO), 397
Southeastern Anatolia Project (GAP), 11, 261, 267
sovereignty: and academic geography, 39; and borders, 6, 321, 339; and drugs, 244; and genocide, 175, 180, 182, 188; and globalization, 63; and Ireland, 138; and Israel-Palestine, 298; and nationalism, 115, 121, 122, 125; and NATO, 395, 397, 407; and Palestine, 396, 308, 309; and peace movements, 351; and postwar recovery, 13, 415, 418, 423, 432; and realism, 73; and religious war, 155; and resources, 226, 228, 229; and territoriality, 11, 280–282; and terrorism, 10, 198, 202–212; and United States, 23; and water conflict, 272
South Korea, 3, 323, 384
South Ossetia, 89
South Pacific Ocean, 355
South Vietnam, 248
Soviet Union: and academic geography, 36, 38; and Afghanistan, 149, 158, 246, 247, 428, 429, 430, 431; and Cold War, 86, 87, 419; collapse of, 13, 100, 121, 397, 401, 420, 428; Communist party, 353, 398; and Crimea, 373, 374; and diplomacy, 378; and ethnonationalism, 323; former, 96; and Hungary, 395, 407; and modernity, 396; and Nagorno-Karabakh, 287; and NATO, 395, 397, 399, 401, 402; and peace movements, 357; and post-Soviet Union, 89; and proxy war, 94; and rimland, 103; Stalinism, 90, 353; as superpower, 34, 87; and territoriality, 77; and United States, 20, 377, 380, 397, 400; and Warsaw Pact, 403
Soysa, Indra de, 221
space: and academic geography, 29; and boundaries, 324, 328; and development, 63, 70, 77; and drugs, 243; and gender, 135; and genocide, 190; and ethnonationalism, 322; and Israel-Palestine Conflict, 299; and nation-state, 282; and peace movements, 12; and postwar recovery, 415, 418, 419, 423; of power, 223, 310, 312; private, 135, 136, 137, 138, 139; public, 135, 136, 137, 138, 139; and religious war, 150; of resistance, 223, 310, 312; and resources, 222, 225, 226, 234; sacred, 153, 160, 164; and sovereignty, 281, 282; spatial epistemology, 187, 192; and territoriality, 331; and terrorism, 202; and war trends, 19–21, 23, 24, 25; and water conflict, 272, 273
Spain, 92, 123, 152, 161, 288–290, 329, 353, 397, 398
Spanish-American War, 206
Spanish Armada, 152
Sparke, Matthew, 38
spatial epistemology, 187, 192
spices, 242
Sprout, Harold, 36
Sprout, Margaret, 36
Spykman, Nicholas, 4, 31, 35
Srebrenica, 120, 184, 190, 191
Sri Lanka, 88, 155, 162, 166, 167, 290
Srinagar, 379
Stalinism, 200, 201, 205, 353
Stalin, Joseph, 90, 373
state: and academic geography, 5, 6, 28, 30, 32, 38, 39, 41; and boundaries, 280, 281, 330; Christian, 161; and conflict, 301; and development, 61, 63, 70, 202; failed, 73, 74, 88, 90, 96; and genocide, 188; and inter-state system, 126, 175, 281, 297, 324, 329; and intra-state boundaries, 322; and Israel-Palestine conflict, 297–316; Jewish, 316; and nationalism, 122; and networks, 209; and peace, 352; and peace movements, 350; and political order, 73–75; and postwar recovery, 423, 425;

and religious war, 154; and sovereignty, 308, 309; and state building, 282; and territoriality, 11, 283, 301, 321; and terrorism, 10, 206; and war, 352; and water conflict, 260; and Weber, 309
Statement of Forest Principles, 387
States as Living Organisms, 29
Steinberg, Michael, 10
Steiner, George, 113
Stephen's Green, 140
St. Petersburg, 355
Strasbourg, 28
structural violence, 8, 12, 27, 40, 62–70, 77, 79, 80, 223, 348
Stump, Roger W., 9
Sucharipa, Ernst, 389
Sudan, 24, 86, 89, 149, 157, 163, 227, 280, 281
Suez Canal, 158
Sufism, 350
sugar, 242, 243
suicide bombing, 167, 209, 325
Sung, Kim Il, 384
Sunni Islam, 152
Surya, 149
Swaziland, 102
Sweden, 29, 65, 351, 354
Switzerland, 28, 352, 354, 377, 378, 417
Syria, 158, 208, 260, 261, 263, 268, 269, 271, 298, 314

Taba Agreement, 303, 315
Tableau of the Geography of France, 29
Tadic, Dusko, 189
Taiwan, 373, 386; Taiwan Strait, 373
Tajikistan, 89, 428
Tajiks, 428
Takhar, 428, 429
Taliban, 24, 92, 99, 126, 163, 210, 245–249, 430–432
Talita School, 308
Tamils, 88, 155, 166, 167, 203, 290
Tanzania, 208, 355
Tashkent, 430
tasking, 22, 23
Taylor, Charles, 89, 228
Taylor, Peter J., 6, 36, 66, 401
tea, 255
Tehran, 376, 377
Temple Mount, 149, 164, 166, 305
Temple Mount Faithful, 166
Temple of the Tooth, 166
territoriality: and academic geography, 30, 39, 42; and borders, 322, 323; and conflict, 280–293; and development, 63, 70; and diplomacy, 369; and drugs, 243, 249; and ethnic cleansing, 177, 184; and genocide, 176, 188; and identity, 192; and Israel-Palestine conflict, 297–316; and NATO, 13; and peace movements, 12; and political order, 77; and religious war, 10, 150, 160, 161–164, 168, 169; and resource wars, 224; and states, 11, 280–293, 301 306, 321; and terrorism, 4, 203; and war trends, 24; and water conflict, 272, 273
terrorism: and academic geography, 34; as direct violence, 66; Islamic, 217; and metageography, 10, 198–212; and nationalism, 120, 125, 126; and Palestine, 306, 312; and religious war, 156, 159, 168, 203–208; and territoriality, 280; and war trends, 3, 5, 9, 87, 90
Teutonic Knights, 154
Texas, 380
Thailand, 232, 233, 248, 252, 255
Thatcher, Margaret, 135, 361
Thawra shabiyya, 310
Third World: and academic geography, 34; and civil war, 86, 88; and development, 64, 65; and drugs, 250, 253; and peace movements, 357; and proxy wars, 94; and resource war, 222; and war trends, 22, 96; and world economy, 103
Thirty Years War, 152
Thompson, E. P., 356
Tibet, 159, 291
Tigris-Euphrates river basin, 11, 260, 261, 266–270, 273
Tikrit, 77
Till, Karen, 137
Tilsit, 380
timber, 10, 217, 218, 220, 224–228, 230, 231, 232
Tirol, 121
Tito, 176
Toal, Gerard, 98

tobacco, 255
Togo, 102
Tolstoy, Leo, 349
Tomb of the Patriachs, 164, 165
Trans-Dneister Republic, 89
Trans-Israel Highway, 325
Transylvania, 6, 405
Treaty of Guadalupe Hidalgo, 379
Treaty of Tlatelolco, 354
Treaty of Versailles, 121, 416
Treaty of Washington, 375
Treaty of Westphalia, 199
Trieste, 128
Trojan War, 150
Truman, Harold, 87, 247
Tshombe, Moise, 231
Tuan, Yi-fu, 6
Tudjman, Franjo, 177, 385
Tullkarem, 303
Tunisia, 383
Turkey: and boundaries, 323; and diplomacy, 387, 388; and genocide, 180; and Kurds, 327, 332, 339; and NATO, 397, 401; and territoriality, 284, 285, 291, 292; and United States, 85, 86, 102; and war trends, 96; and water conflict, 11, 259–273
Turkish Cypriots, 327, 329
Turkmen, 428
Turkmenistan, 428, 429, 430
Tutsi, 88

Uganda, 90, 226, 231
Ukraine, 102, 121
Ulster, 38, 140
Ulster Freedom Fighters, 206
Underground Railway, 357
UNESCO, 41
UNICEF, 417
unionism, 206
Union of Concerned Scientists, 357
UNITA, 224, 226, 228, 232, 233
United Arab Emirates (UAE), 291
United Kingdom: and academic geography, 28, 29, 32; and Arab revolt, 158; and British Empire, 31, 32, 139, 204, 222; and British India, 155; cabinet, 73; and Campaign for Nuclear Disarmament D, 354; and Christianity, 203; and conscientious objectors, 352; and Crimea, 373; and democratic peace, 91; and diplomacy, 378; and Euro Force, 402; and Falklands War, 120, 287, 288; and foreign policy, 3; and Great Game, 77; as hegemonic power, 351, 399, 401; and imperialism, 158, 161; and Ireland, 92, 138, 140, 285; and Malta, 378; and military expenditure, 97; and NATO, 397, 398; and North Sea Oil, 331; and Northern Ireland, 24; novels, 116; as nuclear power, 34; and nuclear war, 36; and Palestine Mandate, 298; Parliament, 139; and peace movements, 351; and Persian Gulf, 231; and prime modernity, 207; and public opinion, 97; and Sharif Husayn, 153; and terrorism, 206; and United Nations, 375; and United States, 102; and UNPROFOR, 183
United Nations: and academic geography, 34, 41; and Balkans, 185
Charter, 175, 381, 397, 399, 418; Commission of Experts, 183, 186; and diplomacy, 378, 380, 381, 383; General Assembly, 180, 181; and Geneva, 382; and Korea, 384; and Kosovo, 408; and New York City, 381, 382; and opium, 249; and Palestine Liberation Organization, 383; Partition Plan, 316; and peacekeeping force, 96, 120, 184, 231, 328, 333, 402, 403, 418; and postwar recovery, 417–421, 424, 426; Resolutions, 242, 338, 298, 314, 315; and resource wars, 233; and safe havens, 423; Security Council, 104, 183, 184, 358; Secretary General, 383; Special Committee on Palestine (UNSCOP), 316; and United States, 102, 126, 207, 400; and war trends, 86, 87
United Nations Conference on Diplomatic Intercourse and Immunities, 376
United Nations Conference on Environment and Development (UNCED), 387
United Nations Conference on Human Settlements, 388
United Nations Conference on International Organization, 375

United Nations Convention on Biological Diversity, 387
United Nations Development Program (UNDP), 62, 68; and human development index, 68, 92, 95
United Nations Educational, Scientific, and Cultural Organization (UNESCO), 383
United Nations Office for the Coordination of Humanitarian Affairs (UNOCHA), 430
United Nations Relief Works Agency for Palestinian Refugees (UNRWA), 426
United Nations Special Committee on Palestine, 418
United Nations Truce Supervision Organization (UNTSO), 418
United States Agency for International Development (USAID), 424
United States of America: and academic geography, 28, 31, 33, 35; and Afghanistan, 5, 126, 145, 209, 245, 246, 247, 265, 430, 431; and airpower, 24; and al-Qaeda, 6, 292; and Arab regimes, 23, 202, 203, 207; and Austria, 389; and Balkans, 175, 385; and Bosnia, 177; and Canada, 97, 102, 255; and Christianity, 203, 207; and Civil War, 85, 96, 115, 415; and Cold War, 415, 419; and Colombia, 249; Confederacy, 135; Conference of mayors, 357; Congress, 151, 249, 375; and Contras, 230, 358; and counter-terrorism, 210; and Cuba, 287; and decline of, 86; and democratic peace, 91; Department of Defense, 200, 375; Department of State, 375; and diplomacy, 262, 370, 378; and drug policy, 248–251, 253, 254; and economy, 86; and embassies in East Africa, 168, 208; and empire, 22, 23, 100, 103, 104, 125, 206; and ethnonationalism, 356; and Europe, 27, 94, 127; as garrison state, 86, 99; and gender, 135; and genocide, 180; and Genocide Convention, 182, 191; and geopolitics, 20; and globalization, 102; as hegemonic power, 86, 96, 97, 98, 104, 206, 207, 208, 209, 211, 212, 243, 351, 355, 375, 395–409; and Hiroshima, 27; as Hobbesians, 98; and Hungary, 395–409; as hyperpower, 71, 80, 86, 103; and imperial overstretch, 208; and imperialism, 160; independence, 204; and intercontinental missiles, 20; and inter-state war, 85; and Iran, 376; and Iraq, 5, 85, 201, 209, 265, 271; and Islam, 169; and isolationism, 32; and Israel-Palestine Conflict, 298–302, 313; and Japan, 208; and Korea, 374; and League of Nations, 27; and Lebanon, 168; Marine Corps, 135; and McCarthyism, 353; and Mexico, 379, 380; and military casualties, 99, 120, 126; and military expenditure, 97; and military force, 86, 167; and military intervention, 4, 5, 90, 94, 95, 96, 98, 100, 101, 102, 103, 201, 208, 217, 219, 245; and military power, 85, 86; and national security, 246; and NATO, 395–409; and neo-liberalism, 254; and Richard M. Nixon, 373; and nuclear disarmament, 356; and nuclear war, 36, 354, 355; and opium production; and OECD, 92; and Pakistan, 125; and Palestine Liberation Organization, 199; and peace movements, 347, 351, 352, 354, 356, 358; and Persian Gulf, 231; and postwar recovery, 416, 420, 424; and Prime Modernity, 207, 208, 212, 401; and prohibition, 244; and proxy war, 94; and resources, 219; Revolution, 350; and risk-transfer, 99; and right-wing politics, 22; and Saudi Arabia, 154, 169, 204, 208, 217, 280, 291; Southwest, 379; and Soviet Union, 377, 380, 397, 400, 401; State Department, 32, 40, 183, 200, 302; as superpower, 34, 87; and Taliban, 247; and terrorism, 168, 199, 202, 206, 272; and Thailand, 248, 255; and trade, 103; and troop casualties, 85; and troops and drugs, 244; and Turkey, 273; and Underground Railway, 357; and unilateralism, 86, 87; and United Nations, 207, 375, 381; and urban violence, 78; and Vietnam War, 21, 38, 99, 124; War of 1812, 135; and war

United States of America: and academic geography (*continued*)
on drugs, 11, 244; and war on terrorism, 5, 10, 127, 198, 209; and war trends, 3; and water conflict, 260, 267, 273; and Weather Underground, 205; and westward expansion, 290; and World War II, 205
Universal Declaration of Human Rights, 41
Universal Peace Congress, 351
University of Balkh, 429
UNPROFOR, 183
Uppsala, University of, Department of Peace and Conflict Research, 91, 92
uranium, 217
USS Cole, 168, 208
USS Constitution, 135
Uthman Don Fodio, 152
Uti possidetis, 324
Uzbekistan, 428, 430
Uzbeks, 428

Vajpayee, Atal Behari, 379
Valera, Eamonn de, 139
Valkenburg, Samuel Van, 31
Vallaux, Camille, 30, 31
Valletta, 378
Vang Pao, 248
Vasques, Loretta Janet, 135
Vedic, 149
Vedrine, Hubert, 86
Venezuala, 217, 231, 284
Venice, 151
Vercors plateau, 24
Verona, 350
Versailles, Treaty of, 31
Vienna, 151, 374, 382, 389
Vienna Convention on Diplomatic Relations, 376, 377
Vietcong, 94
Vietnam, 87, 102, 124, 160, 167, 245, 247, 248, 255, 288
Vietnam War: and diplomacy, 380; and drugs, 244, 248; and nationalism, 21, 22, 120; and peace movements, 355, 358; and religious war, 167, 170; and risk-transfer war, 99; and terrorism, 205; and war trends, 86, 96
Vike-Freiberga, Vaira, 395
Vikings, 255
violence: behavioral, 65, 66; direct, 62, 64, 65, 66, 67, 68, 70, 78, 79; structural, 62, 63, 64, 65, 66, 68, 69, 70, 77, 79, 80
Vishnu, 165
Vojvodina, 405
Volstead Act, 244
VRA Knowledge Manager Software, 101

Wagah, 379
Wahhabism, 152, 153, 163, 292
Wales, 361
Wallace, Paul, 185
Wallerstein, Immanuel, 66, 104, 199
Walzer, Michael, 99, 201, 211, 297
war: civil, 5, 7, 8, 66, 72, 85, 86, 87, 88, 90, 91, 157, 217, 219, 220, 221, 245, 247, 324, 327, 333, 350, 363, 419, 421; chemical, 256; cosmic, 204; and democratic peace, 71; and development, 72; and diplomacy, 370, 371; and drugs, 11; ethnic-based, 86, 88; and gender, 9, 133–145; and geography, 4, 5, 7, 8; and geopolitics, 7; guerilla, 226, 228, 232, 420; and identity, 7, 9; inter-state, 9, 66, 72, 85, 86, 87, 91, 259; just, 11, 154; and Kant, 71; Ministry of, 41; and nationalism, 9, 113–129; and peace movements, 348, 362; proxy, 7, 94; and religion, 9, 149–170; and resources, 7, 217–235; revolutionary, 134; risk-transfer war, 99; and territoriality, 7, 161; as tyranny, 3, 4; and weaponry, 19
Ward, Margaret, 137
Ward, Michael, 37, 91
warlordism, 228, 230, 432
War of the Worlds, 117
war on drugs, 11, 243–245
war on terrorism, 5, 9, 10, 87, 127, 198, 209–210, 244–246, 396, 430
Warrior of the Faith, 152
Warrior's Husband, 134
Warsaw, 128
Warsaw Pact, 355, 356, 398, 399, 403, 404
Washington, D.C., 41, 180, 183, 192, 354, 373, 380, 381, 384, 389, 403, 406; and diplomacy, 373, 380, 381, 384, 389, 403, 406; and Hungary, 403, 406; and International Geographical Union, 41;

and peace movements, 354; and U.S. policy on genocide, 180, 183, 192
water, 331, 337, 380, 427; and conflict, 11, 217, 259–273
Waterloo, 242
Waterman, Stanley, 37
weaponry, 19, 22; and peace movements, 349, 351
Weapons of Mass Destruction (WMD), 34, 78, 97, 280, 417
Weather Underground, 205
Weber, Max, 309
Werner, Anton von, 113, 114, 116, 128
West Bank; and borders, 325, 326, 330, 331, 332; and ethnonationalism, 325, 326, 330, 331, 332; and Palestinian state, 298, 299, 301–304, 307–309, 311–316; and religious war, 149, 164, 165; and war trends, 24; and water conflict, 261–263
Westermeyer, J., 250
Western atheism, 398
Western diplomacy, 370
Western discourse, states, 324
Western hemisphere, 288
Western peace movements, 353
Western philosophy, 21, 24
Western powers, 218, 220
Western societies, 133
Western Sahara, 89, 102, 227, 229
West Germany, 354, 397
West Indies, 242
West Jerusalem, 328
West New Guinea, 418
Westphalian system, 125, 322, 324
Whittlesey, Derwent, 31, 35
Wiesel, Elie, 182
Williams, Cathay, 135
Williams, Colin, 37
Williams, Stephen, 37
Wilson, Woodrow, 32, 71
Winchester rifle, 21
Wittfogel, Karl, 33
Wolf, A., 261
Women Strike for Peace, 354
Women's International League for Peace and Freedom (WILPF), 352, 353
Women's Peace Party, 352
Woodward, Susan, 185
World Bank, 62, 68, 70, 89, 207, 230, 233, 400–401, 418–419, 424; Group on Civil Wars, 88
World Conference against Racism, Racial Discrimination, Xenophobia, and Related Intolerance, 388
World Court, 86
World Food Program, 424
World Health Organization, 417
World Peace Brigade, 355
World Peace Council, 348, 354
world-systems analysis, 38, 66, 100
World Trade Center, 136, 142, 143, 168, 198, 200, 203, 208, 381–382, 386
World Trade Organization, 86, 401
World War I: and academic geography, 28, 33; and Arab revolt, 153; and Balkans, 334; and democratic peace, 71, 72; and diplomacy, 375; as Great War, 27, 30, 32, 38; and Kurds, 332; and nationalism, 119, 122, 127; and Ottoman Empire, 157; and peace movements, 170, 350–353, 362; and political order, 63; and postwar recovery, 416, 417, 418, 421; and resource war, 218; and United States, 399; and war on drugs, 243; and war trends, 21
World War II: and academic geography, 27, 32–34, 38, 39; and democratic peace, 71, 72; and development, 61; and diplomacy, 374, 375, 378, 381; and genocide, 174, 185; and Japan, 87; and NATO, 397; and peace movements, 350, 353, 354; and postwar recovery, 416, 417, 418, 421; and resource war, 218; and territoriality, 287, 288; and terrorism, 201, 204–206; and United States, 87, 103, 399, 400; and war trends, 4, 20, 23, 95; and war on drugs, 243
Wright, Quincy, 79
Wright-Patterson Air Force Base, 384
Wusten, Herman van der, 8, 37, 40, 288
Wye Plus Agreement, 304
Wye River Memorandum, 303, 304

Xena, 134

Yaa baa, 255
Yalta, 374

Yarmouk River, 262, 263, 264
Yemen, 168, 210, 227
YMCA, 416
Yom Kippur War, 164
Young, Nigel, 353
Young Democrats Party (FIDESZ), 405–407
Yugoslav National Army, 177
Yugoslav People's Army, 190
Yugoslavia: and academic geography, 33; and borders, 332, 333; and development, 76; and drugs, 89; and ethnonationalism, 323, 332, 333; and nationalism, 121, 122, 156, 162; and NATO, 402; and postwar recovery, 428; and religious war, 156, 162; Socialist Federal Republic, 174–192, 385; and territoriality, 291; and United States, 98, 99, 104; and war trends, 85, 86; and Western public opinion, 97
Yunan Province, 255

Zagreb, 128
Zaire, 85, 422, 428
Zapatista movement, 223, 363
Zealots, 153, 154
Zeitschrift für Geopolitik, 31
Zetkin, Clara, 352
Zhonghua, 373
Zimbabwe, 202, 226, 231
Zionism, 158, 163, 299, 305, 316, 388
Zionists, 149, 166
Zunes, Stephen, 301, 302
Zvornik, 177

Printed in the United States
220896BV00002B/2/A

9 780195 162097